D1491529

THE HIDDEN EVIDENCE

For further information, contact:

S.P.I. Books
99 Spring Street, 3rd Floor
New York, NY 10012
Tel: (212) 431-5011
Fax: (212) 431-8646
E-mail: publicity@spibooks.com

10 9 8 7 6 5 4 3 2 1
First Edition

Library of Congress Cataloging-in-Publication Date available.

S.P.I. Books World Wide Web address: spibooks.com

ISBN: 1-56171-922-6

Also By Jon King

COSMIC TOP SECRET: The Unseen Agenda

THE ASCENSION CONSPIRACY: 2013

PRINCESS DIANA
The Hidden Evidence

How MI6 And The CIA Were Involved In The Death Of Princess Diana

Jon King
&
John Beveridge

S.P.I. Books • New York

Dedication

In memory of Diana, Princess of Wales

CONTENTS

ACKNOWLEDGEMENTS

In researching and compiling evidence for this book we are indebted to all those, both named and unnamed, who were courageous enough to come forward with their information. Plus all those who kindly granted us access to their work and research, and all those who agreed to talk to us in whatever capacity. We should state that we have made every conceivable effort to contact the publishers/authors of all works quoted herein (all of which are fully credited and listed in the *Bibliography*) and we are sincerely grateful for their permissions in this regard. Our sincere apologies to anyone we have been unable to track down, as well as to anyone who feels they should have been included in the *Acknowledgements* and who, for reasons which are entirely innocent, might have been omitted.

In addition to the above we also wish to include the following - a list of those individuals and organizations who, either knowingly or otherwise (and in no preferential order) have contributed to the writing of this book.

Mark Zepezauer; Michael Baigent; Richard Leigh; Henry Lincoln; Ted Harrison; Jeffery Steinberg; Sir Peter Horsley; Sir Ranulph Fiennes; Gary Murray; Sir Laurence Gardner; Morton Mintz; Jerry Cohen; Rodney Atkinson; Anthony Sampson; Mark Aarons; John Loftus; Norman Cohn; Patrick SJ Carmack; Andy Palmer; Professor Murray MacKay; Nicholas Owen; Gary Hunter; Brenda Wells; Francois Levistre; Eric Lee; David Laurent; Trevor Rees-Jones; Alexander 'Kes' Wingfield; Piers Morgan; Thomas Sancton; Scott McLeod; Nic North; David Shayler; Brian Anderson; Thierry H; Dr Martin Skinner; Dr Alastair Hay; Dr Frederic Mailliez; Dr Wolf Ullrich; James Whitaker; John Alderson; Hilda Murrell; William McRae; Jonathan Holborow; John Wadham; Cyril Reenan; James Hewitt; AN Wilson; Andrew Golden; Chris Blackhurst; Dr John Coleman; Claude Garrec; US Special Forces Command Sgt Major, Robert O. Dean; Ivan Fraser; Linda Perham MP; John Swinton; Frank Cook MP; John Keegan; Germaine Greer; Andrew Morton; Leo van de Pas; Nicholas Redfern; our thanks to all.

Also to: the *Mirror*; the *Sunday Mirror*; *Bild Zeitung*; *The Guardian*; *The Scotsman*; *Executive Intelligence Review*; the *Express*; the *Mail On Sunday*; *The Independent*; *The Independent On Sunday*; *Le Monde*; the *Times*; the *New York Times*; *The Daily Telegraph* and *The Spectator*.

A special thanks to those few who must remain anonymous, in particular our SAS source(s), our several British Intelligence/Security sources, our Foreign Office (MI6) source, and one or two other 'silent voices'. Also to Ian Shapolsky and SPI Books for having the courage to publish this work where so many turned tail and ran.

Plus ... a very special thanks to HRH Prince Michael of Albany, a true king; to Stealth, wherever you are; to Mike Grey and Richard Tomlinson, for your courage in speaking out.

And most of all to Pia and Casey for your love, tolerance and support in our darkest moments - of which, during the writing of this book, there were many. Thank you.

FOREWORD

by HRH Prince Michael of Albany

Some believe it was an accident, others that it was murder. Still others remain shocked and confused by the whole affair, desperately wanting to believe in the 'accident' theory yet, in truth, unable to discount the possibility of assassination. Others, of course, simply wish to forget the incident, as though it never happened.

But whatever one's own personal standpoint regarding the death of Princess Diana, one thing remains clear: in life she was sheer mystique. Not only did she become a threat to the very heritage she represented, she possessed a charisma beyond definitions, as well. She was both constrained and wild, compassionate and sexy, a saint to the underprivileged yet at the same time an icon to the world of fashion, glamour and glitz -- the world inhabited by the rich and the famous alike, many of whom she befriended, all of whom she outshone, at one time or another. And because of this unrivalled star quality, her much-publicized campaigns on behalf of AIDS sufferers and victims of anti-personnel landmines drew more attention, and gained more success, than perhaps any other humanitarian campaigns of the twentieth century.

Simply put, enough was never enough to satisfy the immense public appetite for Diana. But even though she used her unprecedented fame to the benefit of others, perhaps in the end it proved her own fatal attraction, too.

But that said, what of the woman behind the mask? What of her blood, her history, her heritage? Is there any possible reason why the British Royal Establishment should have wanted her out of the way?

Genealogically, of course, Diana was a Stuart; in her veins flowed the blood of Britain's ancient Royal Family, and this in itself was a problem. Indeed, for this reason alone Diana was always perceived as a threat by the Establishment, as well as by Britain's current Royal Family, the Windsor Dynasty (otherwise known as 'The Firm'). While her marriage to Prince Charles Windsor was of course a political marriage, serving to reintroduce the Stuart strain into the Windsor bloodline -- and thus, in an historical context at least, further justify the Windsor reign -- her marriage into The Firm was virtually unique in British history. In fact Diana was only the second truly British-born 'outsider' to marry into the German Hanover-Windsor Dynasty in all of its 300-year reign. And she paid a very dear price for the privilege. Her close relationship with her two boys, William and Harry, of course, and the fact that she actively protected them from the stifling, predictable future The Firm had in store for them, only added to the tensions that always existed between the upstart Stuart Princess and the uptight Windsor Household. In short, so far as the Windsors were concerned, Diana was a necessary bane.

To make matters worse, less than a year after her divorce from Prince Charles, Diana flew in the face of British convention and fell in love with an Egyptian Muslim, Dodi Fayed, the son of billionaire businessman and long-term adversary of the British Royal Establishment, Mohamed Al Fayed. The fact is that Diana's proposed marriage to Mohamed Al Fayed's playboy son would have proved more than simply another thorn in the side of the British Royal Establishment: it would have rocked the Establishment to its foundations. The reactionary dinosaur that is the British Royal Establishment simply could not have tolerated the future King William of Britain boasting a Muslim stepfather, much less a Muslim mother. And neither could it have tolerated the future Queen Mother, Diana, bearing Dodi's Muslim children.

But as we all now know, before her proposed marriage to Dodi Fayed could take place Diana somewhat conveniently and tragically died. And when she did the British Royal Establishment breathed an almighty sigh of relief.

But now, more than three years after the tragedy, should we still be pursuing evidence of her assassination? Should we not simply allow Diana to rest in peace?

Moreover, do we really need yet another book about Diana -- the girl who freed herself from the shackles of royal convention, and paid the ultimate price?

Well the authors certainly think so, and as this book is a genuine and respectful attempt to get to the bottom of the mystery surrounding Diana's death, I must admit that I agree with them. Even I am not altogether happy with what we have been told about Diana's death, the 'official story'. Even I am not altogether happy with the 'accident' theory. For one thing, the so-called 'accident' was far too convenient. And for another, there are simply too many unanswered questions regarding the actual circumstances in which Diana died. At the same time too many very real motives for her death have yet to be explored, and too many prime suspects have yet to be interrogated.

We know, for example, that Mohammed Al Fayed is convinced his son and future daughter-in-law were murdered by a conspiracy involving the CIA, MI6 and various members of the Royal Family. He explicitly reiterated this belief in court during a libel case brought against him by ex-MP Neil Hamilton in December 1999, a case that Mr Al Fayed won. While the involvement of the CIA and MI6 is yet to be proven, we do know that the CIA are in possession of an extensive facts file on Diana, and that these files were passed on to British Intelligence (MI6) at some time prior to the 'accident' (it should be noted that, at the time of this writing, Mr Al Fayed is pursuing the release of these CIA files via the Freedom Of Information Act). We also know that, as you will discover in the pages of this book, it was a CIA contract agent assigned to MI6 who -- one week prior to the Paris car crash -- forewarned the authors of the princess's imminent demise. So far as I am concerned, the possible involvement of the CIA and MI6 in Diana's death should be investigated at the highest level.

The precise circumstances surrounding Diana's death, of course, like that of President John F Kennedy, will probably never be known. Certainly the doubts surrounding the manner in which she died will never go away. But the fact that Diana died in a way that was seen by many as highly suspicious, and no less convenient, simply cannot be ignored. And neither can the fact that the last few minutes of her life remain shrouded in complete mystery and controversy. To my mind, far too many questions remain unanswered.

In this uncompromising and ground-breaking book, authors Jon King and John Beveridge endeavour with some vigour to find answers to those questions, and many will no doubt be challenged by the disclosure of their findings. The idea that our intelligence services can plot, organize and execute assassination operations right under the noses of democratically elected governments is not something most people would want even to consider, much less accept. But the simple fact is that certain people, and certain institutions, possess more power even than our elected governments, and they enjoy more freedom to achieve their own sordid agendas than most of us would ever believe. This situation exists today because, as the authors rightly point out, 'democracy' has been effectively hijacked by big business.

In the final analysis this book challenges not only the official theory that Diana's death was an accident, but the very concept of democracy itself, however defined, by whatever government. To my mind, challenging this concept of democracy -- wherein elected governments are effectively underwritten by the wealth and power of a relative few -- is something Diana herself would have supported. And if only for the sake of Liberty and Justice, the pillars of true Democracy, it is certainly something that I support, too.

Indeed, for these same reasons I also support the courageous investigation undertaken by the authors in researching and compiling the 'hidden evidence' revealed in this book. Even if the authorities remain intent on covering up the truth behind Diana's death, the reader, I feel certain, will support the authors in their endeavour to expose that cover-up and force an independent inquiry into the incident. I for one will do all I can to support this endeavour. Indeed, anything less would surely be to disregard Democracy altogether, and that would not only undermine my own integrity. It would undermine everything Diana ever stood for, as well.

As the authors themselves state, if we truly want Diana to rest in peace, then surely we must first uncover the truth regarding the highly suspicious circumstances in which she died. And the only way to successfully achieve that is by open and independent inquiry -- something that, as yet, the British and US intelligence agencies indicted in this case have so deplorably managed to avoid.

INTRODUCTION

by Jon King

Being by profession an investigative journalist, invariably my work has involved rooting out sources of information unavailable to the general public. Over the course of the past five years in particular, my investigations have been specifically targeted on illegally funded 'black projects' undertaken by both the British- and US-based military-industrial complex. Thus during this period my sources have tended to derive from either the military or the intelligence community - or indeed from some other governmental or quasi-governmental department or agency. Many of these sources are named and quoted in my previous book, *COSMIC TOP SECRET: The Unseen Agenda*. In this respect one source in particular stands out.

It was November, 1996. I had just broken a story involving six British soldiers who claimed to have experienced a close encounter with a 'UFO' whilst on night manoeuvres on Salisbury Plain in England. In the event, however, it turned out that the soldiers had been used as unwitting guinea pigs in some highly classified secret-technology experiment conducted by the military (in many respects even more an outrage than the less likely possibility that the British Army had been conducting night manoeuvres with aliens!). Nonetheless my ongoing investigations into this incident led me to suspect that an undisclosed deep-underground military-industrial facility existed beneath Salisbury Plain. And moreover, that it was being used for unlawful purposes.

It was at this point that I was contacted by someone who was to become my most informative - indeed, my most penetrative - intelligence source. For purposes of identification I named this source 'Stealth'.

Over the course of several meetings, Stealth furnished me with information regarding the British government's top-secret deep-underground programme. Indeed, he confirmed to me the existence of numerous deep-underground facilities dotted around Britain, and the unsavoury nature of some of the activities performed in them. Here is not the place to either delve or divulge this information; it is contained in full in my previous book. The point here is to convey the information which is *not* contained in any of my previous works - information directly relating to the tragic and untimely death of Diana, Princess of Wales.

Before I do that, however, perhaps I should say a little - as much as I am able - about Stealth and his mysterious employers.

I should state from the outset that I no longer have access to this source. Our several meetings were always at his convenience (an expected procedure under the circumstances, and certainly in my experience a normal one). He would telephone my office, and we would agree a time and place. We would meet. He would pass relevant information my way and we would part company. This was the extent of our brief acquaintanceship. We have not met and neither have I heard from him since Saturday, August 23rd, 1997, one week prior to the death of the Princess of Wales. I do not know whether he will ever contact me again.

American by accent, quiet, unassuming, approaching sixty years of age, Stealth always maintained that he was first and foremost a US Special Forces veteran and CIA contract agent, but that recently he had been assigned to some covert CIA/MI6 cell stationed in Britain. His reasons for passing information my way, he said, were "personal", though he said this with some bitterness, as though by betraying his employers he might achieve some amount of personal revenge. I should stress, however, that this is my own interpretation.

At any rate, during our final meeting (we met four times in all) Stealth told me that it was becoming increasingly difficult for him to continue our communications, and that in any case he had told me just about everything he could regarding the deep-underground programme and its attendant horrors. At least for the time being. Indeed, he intimated that this would probably be our last meeting - although nothing was written in stone, one way or the other.

That being the case, he said he wanted to leave me with "one last pearl" of information, intended both to prove his credentials (to substantiate the information he had already given me; or at least to demonstrate that the information derived from sources unavailable in the public domain), and also to offer "an angle on which to build your story". (In this regard, of course, he pre-empted my own decision to write it.) Other than this, he said, he did not know of what use the information might be; it was unlikely ever to be effective in bringing those responsible to justice, he said, and I was unlikely to believe it anyway. He was right, on both counts.

He added: "At least until it happens. At least until what I'm telling you actually happens. Then you'll believe it."

Once again, he was right.

It was in this regard, then, that the following information concerning the death of Princess Diana came my way.

Seating himself on a fallen 'standing stone' at one of Britain's best-known megalithic sites, staring thoughtfully ahead, Stealth told me that he had been made aware of a plot "to eliminate one of the most prominent figures on the world stage". And further, that "the hit" would "take place within days from now". Though he did not actually name either Princess Diana or Dodi Fayed at this time, he hinted at Diana's identity clearly enough. And in any case, it soon became patently clear to me that he was indeed referring to the late Princess of Wales.

He also said that the assassination had been planned for a "good many months"; that his own "sources" were "extremely nervous about this one"; that this particular "hit" could turn out to be "bigger than Kennedy"; that the target "has to go ... because they have become carcinogenic to the system"; and further, that behind the plot sat an extremely powerful cabal of "financial, industrial and political godfathers" who wanted this "loose cannon" out of the way, once and for all.

"SIS [MI6] and CIA do the bidding of these people", I was plainly told. "We always do the bidding of these people."

One week later, it seemed to me (Sunday, 31st August, 1997) the bidding was done; on this day both Princess Diana and Dodi Fayed were mysteriously killed in a car crash in Paris. It is a mystery that remains unsolved to this day.

Before parting company for what I sensed would be the final time, Stealth reiterated that, in his opinion, the information he had imparted would make "a compelling read". It was as though he wished to affirm an ulterior reason for letting the information pass my way. He knew I was a journalist; he had already pre-empted my decision to write the information down and present it to the public. But then, he also knew that I could be trusted, and that I would be more likely than most to follow up on the information and publish as much as I was able to corroborate. Indeed, this much I had already done with the previous information he had given me. There was no reason for him to assume that I would not do the same again.

But I should also state that, in this instance, I sensed that *somebody other than Stealth* wanted this information in the public domain. Indeed, from what I learned of the man during our brief acquaintanceship, and from what I have since gleaned from other sources, I now suspect that Stealth was simply a 'go-between' or 'mouthpiece': that he was perhaps part of a more liberal faction within British/US intelligence - a faction who evidently opposed the assassination, but who were powerless to prevent it. And who thus decided to spotlight it instead.

Given Stealth's distrust of the major media and press networks, it is my belief that he passed this information my way precisely for this reason.

Despite having been forewarned of the event one week prior to its occurrence (or perhaps even because of this) the tragic death of Princess Diana came as no less a very profound shock. Indeed, I shared wholly in the nation's deep outpouring of grief and utter, genuine dismay. Like many I was simply devastated at what I saw as such a senseless and brutal waste of this beautiful, vibrant, compassionate young life, the effect being all the more incisive, I believe, for the fact that Diana represented something of such deep and lasting significance to us all. Something to do with hope. It was thus some weeks thereafter before I found the courage - or indeed the inclination - to explore my information further. When I did, however, it paid dividends.

I decided to seek out the only person I knew whom I figured might be able to help, someone with - I must be careful here - 'sources of his own'.

In any event, it was through the help of this contact that, quite independently, the bulk of what Stealth had imparted was confirmed. Indeed, this source seemed as astonished as I on our mutual exchange of information - astonished not so much for its sensation as its corroborative accuracy. The most I am permitted to say here is that the source of this information derives from a department within British Military Intelligence.

This contact told me quite categorically that he had learned of the plot to assassinate Princess Diana "several months" prior to the event. He was further able to confirm that, in this instance, Diana had indeed been named specifically as the target. He also confirmed the joint involvement of SIS (MI6) and the CIA, and went on to identify a number of uncanny similarities in the wording used by our respective sources. The terms "loose cannon", "a cancer in the system" and "bigger than the Kennedys" were cited. It was as though British and US intelligence had provided a script for their informants, we commented - a fact which only served to confirm my belief that Stealth had not been alone in wanting this information in the public domain.

Armed with these staggering corollaries, then, I now became more than ever determined to commit their story to print, even though I was acutely aware of the possible dangers involved, both to myself and my family. I nevertheless resolved to get this information out into the public domain, as much for the sake of everything Diana had stood for as anything else. She had never been one to balk in the face of danger, I told myself. Nor even to surrender for fear of consequence. Indeed, she had flown in the face of such concern, as she had flown in the face of traditions and protocols alike. And more. She had dared to challenge the stuffy conventions of the British Royal Establishment, and she had done so for the sake of others less fortunate than herself. She had championed the cause of justice and compassion no matter the cost. I reminded myself that this was the one quality above all others I had always admired in her. If I was to champion her cause, as she had championed so many, it was a quality I should endeavour to emulate. No matter the cost. I resolved to put pen to paper, then.

It was at this point that our investigation took a most unexpected turn. It was at this point that the final piece of the jigsaw emerged. And it did so as if from nowhere.

Whilst endeavouring to sift through all the relevant nuggets of information (keen to resolve the many glaring anomalies evident in the official investigation, keen to find answers; still unable to piece our information together into a coherent picture, at least sufficiently so to set that picture in print), we were introduced to another, somewhat enigmatic figure - someone, we were told, whose former position as a 'special remit' Foreign Office (MI6) historian had afforded him access to both MI6 and Royal archives, and who thus might be able to shed new light on Diana's death. Indeed, we were assured by the man who brokered our meeting that this person had once worked in a Foreign Office (MI6) department that dealt specifically with the "counter-monarchy problem", and that in the main his task had been to sift and evaluate classified records and documents up for classification review. Some of the information contained in these archives, we were told, might just be of interest to our own investigation.

This person already knew that we wished to interview him; we had sent word to him some weeks earlier, via another source (our broker), telling him of our own information regarding the matter and that we were keen to corroborate and build on that information in order to tell its tale. Owing to this person's somewhat elevated social station we did not necessarily expect a reply. But we received one. Following a series of coded messages, sent back and forth via our broker, we finally arranged to meet him in a London hotel.

Perhaps to be expected, this source offered no concrete conclusions regarding Diana's death. But he did set us on a fresh line of investigation, one that, should its evidence ever be properly extrapolated and presented to the public, he contested, would bear far greater implications even than proving that Princess Diana had been assassinated. He did not believe that would ever be achieved in any case. Not conclusively. So far as he was concerned that was not the point. I should give fair warning that what this source told us, as contained in *Chapter 11*, may at first seem shocking, unbelievable even. But as our investigation progressed it proved chillingly verifiable, just the same.

Naturally we are aware that this story sounds fantastic in the extreme. Indeed, if it were not for the fact that the initial information came our way *when* it did (one week prior to the death of Diana) we would probably not have taken it at all so seriously. We would certainly not have chosen to place our own and our families' lives in such implicit danger in order to tell its grisly detail if we were not certain of our own conviction and the official cover-up now in place. As it is we feel that we have little choice. We cannot deny that a week before it happened our most trusted intelligence source warned us of a plot to "eliminate" a "world stage" figure "within days from now". We cannot deny that he was alluding to Diana, Princess of Wales. And neither can we deny that we have since had this information confirmed and corroborated by a second very reliable source, who also told us that certain factions within Britain's intelligence and security services are keen that the truth should come out. Someone, it seems to us, wants this information in the public domain.

With these things in mind, then, we have endeavoured throughout the course of this book to assume the position of 'prosecuting counsels', so to speak - to present evidence of both the motives and the agencies which we believe were responsible for the princess's death. In the main this process has been a detective one, based as much on information gleaned from our Foreign Office source as anything else. That said, it is not so much our conclusions as the direction of our investigation which resulted from the information gleaned from this source. He gave us a few bricks to work with, true. But the wall is entirely our own.

In the final analysis, our investigation concluded that Princess Diana was indeed assassinated. We make no bones about that. But what we also discovered was that the motive behind her assassination could not be summed up in one simple and concise paragraph. On the contrary, as our investigation progressed it became ever more apparent that said motive was concealed in a veritable knot of political, historical and constitutional intrigue - a knot which, when unraveled, revealed the most scandalous and far-reaching conspiracy of our time. Of this there can be little doubt.

BOOK ONE

THE CRASH

"...No more powerful deed can trigger a legend than young death or martyrdom. Prince Charles, it is said, has often accused her [Diana] of feigning 'martyrdom'. Her dramatic suicide attempts have been reported and one can only speculate on the powerful potential of a Diana cult if the Princess should by any ill chance meet an early end. She would no doubt become a figure as powerful as Evita, President Kennedy and Elvis combined."

Ted Harrison, *DEFENDER OF THE FAITH: The Church And The Crisis In The Monarchy,* 1996.

CHAPTER 1

PARIS
The Princess And The Playboy

"Prince Philip has let rip several times recently about the Fayeds - at a dinner party, during a country shoot and while on a visit to close friends in Germany. He's been banging on about his contempt for Dodi and how he is undesirable as a future stepfather to William and Harry. Diana has been told in no uncertain terms about the consequences should she continue the relationship with the Fayed boy ... *now the royal family may have decided it is time to settle up* **[italics in original copy].".**

Sunday Mirror, **31st August, 1997.**

[Note: the newspaper in which the above quote appeared was already on its way to the news-stands when news of Diana's death reached Britain.]

The Rats

For once she was happy. For once she was in control. For once she was independent of the ominous dark shadow cast by the House of Windsor, a shadow that had made her life such misery for so long. For once she was tasting true freedom. And it showed.

Though several reports claim that Princess Diana and Dodi Fayed had been lovers for some time prior to their last night together in Paris in August 1997 (one report claimed that as far back as November 1996 the couple had been 'together') most reports are happy to agree that, at least for the summer of 1997, Diana, Princess of Wales, had found love.

At the invitation of Dodi's billionaire father, Mohamed al Fayed, Diana had spent much of the summer of 1997 enjoying the Mediterranean sun - at the al Fayeds' secluded and heavily guarded holiday residence at St Tropez with Princes William and Harry; and also on board the family's recently purchased yacht, *Jonikal*, elsewhere in the Mediterranean. Indeed, it was on the $20,000,000 yacht that Diana and Dodi would spend the last week of their lives together, cruising and swimming in the warm, sun-spangled waters off Sardinia's Emerald Coast. But they would not spend it alone. Even though secluded and patrolled by Dodi's personal bodyguards, the beach at Cala di Volpe offered little privacy for the world's most high-profile couple. Paparazzi were on their tail. Having slipped the al Fayed security screen the ever present entourage of 'paparazzi' press photographers staked themselves out under cover of nearby bush and scrub. And like a swarm of stealthy mantis stalking their prey, they waited, telephoto lenses cocked and primed.

Even in the middle of a large ocean, it seemed, there was no privacy to be had for the world's most famous princess. And that went for her partner, too.

At 1.24 pm local time (Saturday, 30th August, 1997) seven days of sun and virtual sanity behind them, Diana and Dodi departed Olbia Airport in Sardinia, bound for Paris. Word of their arrival would precede them. Indeed, as the al Fayeds' Gulfstream-IV jet touched down at Le Bourget Airport some two hours later the couple were once again greeted by the familiar hail of flash-bulbs and jostle. The usual high levels of security at France's busiest airport, it seemed, had failed. And miserably so. Ordinarily the electronically wired gates and high security fences would have been sufficient to repel the attentions of the paparazzi - otherwise known as 'the rats', or 'the rat pack'. Not so this time. The rats had swarmed. And Le Bourget's VIP lounge was bearing the full burden of this twentieth-century plague.

In an attempt to regain control of the situation, airport staff advised that Diana and Dodi should remain on the aircraft. A police escort had been requested, the couple were told. It would be there soon. But neither Dodi nor Diana wished to wait around for a police escort to arrive. Time was pressing: Dodi wanted to get to the Ritz as soon as possible and with the least possible fuss; Diana, too. As it was, only one night of their holiday remained. They wished to spend it in Paris, quietly, privately, intimately. They wished to be alone. This was, after all, the day of their official engagement - the sole specific reason they had decided to stop off in Paris was to collect the ring that Dodi had ordered some three weeks earlier. It was now ready for Dodi to collect. And - much to the disdain of the British Royal Establishment - for the princess to wear.

Instead of accepting the offer from the airport staff, then (and waiting for *Pest Control* to come and remove the 'rats') Dodi called on his personal staff - already waiting at the airport - to bring the cars out on to the tarmac, to the plane, so that he and Diana could be driven directly from the aircraft and out through customs without having to be exposed to the waiting press and cameramen. In the melee that followed, Dodi's bodyguard, Trevor Rees-Jones, attempted without success to persuade the paparazzi to follow him in a decoy car. (In the days and weeks to follow, of course, as details of the tragedy were to make their way eerily back across the English Channel, the words 'decoy car' were to become a haunting melody in the minds of a shocked and disbelieving British public.) At the same time Dodi's driver, Philippe Dourneau, drove the official car - a Mercedes 600 - to the aeroplane steps.

At this point Dodi and Diana were forced to make a dash for it. Hurriedly disembarking they crossed the short stretch of tarmac at the foot of the aeroplane's steps and made their way over to the black Mercedes which had just pulled up at the edge of the runway. Airport staff described the couple as "courteous" but "anxious" at this point; though eager to escape the promise of yet another photo call, Diana was said to have taken the time to greet the staff personally before climbing in the back of the Mercedes with Dodi. As she did so, she would have noticed a second car waiting there, parked immediately behind the Mercedes - a dark-green Range Rover deployed both as back-up vehicle and baggage hold. Behind the wheel was the Assistant Director and Acting Head of Security for the Ritz Hotel, Paris. His name was Henri Paul.

Conscientiously Henri Paul followed the Mercedes out of Le Bourget Airport and on to the highway that would take them back towards the centre of Paris. But they would not travel there directly. At Dodi's personal request they would first stop off at Windsor Villa, the former residence of the Duke and Duchess of Windsor in Rue du Champ d'Entrainment, Paris. There, Dodi would proudly show off to Diana what he hoped would soon be their new home, as husband and wife. Indeed, later that afternoon he would ask his father for the keys.

Purchased on a lease of Fr900,000 a year by Mohamed al Fayed in 1986, this impressive mansion in the exclusive Bois de Boulogne district of Paris boasted good pedigree for housing royal outcasts. It was, after all, the former home of King Edward VIII (abdicated Dec 10th, 1936) and Wallis Simpson. It was where the dishonoured king had come to live in exile with his American wife. Herself a divorcee and social refugee in Britain, Mrs Simpson had been considered wholly unsuitable as queen by the British Royal Establishment. Indeed, in this instance by the British public, too. Considering Edward's overt sympathies towards the burgeoning Third Reich in Germany at the time of his abdication, and his unashamed friendship with its megalomaniac leader, Adolf Hitler (which continued apace even during the war) it is fair to say that the Royal Establishment had good reason to ostracize its most famous member in 1936. The deed had to be done. But surely the same could not be said of its most popular member some sixty years on (at any rate, not with any measure of public support).

Having spent around thirty minutes viewing the property, the ill-fated couple then continued their journey to the Ritz.

Unidentified Faces

If the newspaper reports are to be believed, the journey from Le Bourget Airport that afternoon was aught but a dress rehearsal for what was to happen later that evening. Indeed, the Mercedes in which the couple were travelling was badgered and hounded virtually all the way to the steps of the Ritz Hotel by the hungry 'rats' - on their motorbikes and in their cars. At one point, prior to stopping off at the couple's proposed new home in Bois de Boulogne, a press vehicle, reported to have been a black Peugeot 205 sedan, deliberately swerved in front of the Mercedes while the latter was driving at some speed. It was an act that forced the Mercedes to brake sharply. At which point a motorbike pulled alongside and its pillion passenger, camera and flash-gun in hand, fired off a volley of high-powered *flashes* through the passenger-side window, temporarily blinding both driver and passengers alike. In some respects the couple were fortunate not to have been driven off the road there and then.

But then again, perhaps that wasn't part of the plan.

By now word had spread to just about every paparazzo in town. Plus some. Soon after 4 pm, anticipating the couple's arrival, the cameras and the flash-bulbs and the tripods plus their owners had already begun to assemble outside the exclusive Ritz Hotel in Place Vendome, Paris. Most had arrived on motorbikes and scooters, though some smaller number had arrived in cars. Each had arrived in time to stake out their place for the evening's entertainment: the arrival of a princess and her playboy lover. They did not have to wait long. According to the time signal on the Ritz security cameras it was 4.35 pm when the couple's black Mercedes finally pulled up outside the front entrance. As though the symptom of some strange and morbid custom, the paparazzi were once again there to greet them. But not only paparazzi. Indeed, security footage shows that, by this time, the waiting cameramen had been joined by several *unidentified faces*. According to eyewitness reports, together with video footage retrieved from the Ritz's own security cameras, these still-*unidentified faces* (seven in number) would remain posted in and around the Ritz for the entire evening. They would make their presence known soon after midnight.

For the next couple of hours Diana and Dodi enjoyed some private time in the hotel's most exclusive (and most expensive) apartment - the $10,000-a-night Imperial Suite. Complete with eighteenth-century antique furniture, oak and marble bathroom and private balcony overlooking the fashionable Place Vendome, this palatial apartment was not an unfamiliar sanctuary. Diana knew it from a weekend spent there secretly with Dodi one month earlier; Dodi, of course, knew it like home. When in Paris, but not staying at his luxury apartment on the Champs Elysees, he would stay at the Ritz. And when at the family-owned Ritz he would of course occupy the Imperial Suite. On this occasion, it was from here that Dodi telephoned his father back in England and informed him of his intentions to marry Diana in the near future. Here it was also that Dodi asked his father for the Duke and Duchess of Windsor's former mansion in Bois de Boulogne as a home for himself and Diana once they were married. Although he readily agreed to the request, Mohamed al Fayed is reported to have advised his son not to rush into anything. As is now known, however, Dodi had already ordered Diana's $200,000 engagement ring, which he and Diana had chosen from one of Europe's most exclusive jewellers, *Alberto Repossi*, while in Monte Carlo some few weeks earlier. Dodi had arranged to collect it from the Paris branch of *Alberto Repossi* following their Mediterranean trip.

Indeed, he would collect it personally later that afternoon. And present it to Diana later that evening.

But not before the couple had first returned to Dodi's apartment on the Champs Elysees, where they were scheduled to spend the night. They had not intended to return to the Ritz at all that evening. Instead they were to eat out at Paris's exclusive Chez Benoit restaurant on Rue Saint Martin, where a reservation had been made earlier by Ritz manager, Claude Roulet. Following a romantic 'engagement dinner' the plan was to return to Dodi's ten-room apartment for the night before flying out of Paris the next day. But it was not to be. The traffic was too dense, the city too busy, and too many paparazzi were already staked out outside Dodi's front door for the couple to cross from the apartment unnoticed, unmolested. In consequence, and with some reluctance, they decided to drive back to the Ritz and dine there instead. At least there, they figured, they could dine in peace.

According to the Ritz security cameras the couple's Mercedes arrived back at the hotel at 9.53 pm. If Diana, Dodi and the entire Ritz workforce were surprised at their unscheduled return, strangely, the paparazzi were not. As the couple left the car and entered the hotel it is estimated that well over fifty 'rats' and their cameras were milling outside - some at the front, some to the rear, all seemingly a little uneasy with the mounting tension now evident.

And for some reason the tension was even more aggressive than usual. Insults flew. Scuffles broke out. Shouts went up as bodies jostled for position. The video footage of the couple entering the hotel certainly betrays a sense of tension about them, too. But then again, who could blame them for that? By anyone's standards they had suffered a gruelling day. The long haul from Sardinia to Paris, dodging paparazzi. The almost military operation necessary to escape the paparazzi on arrival at Le Bourget Airport on the outskirts of Paris. Paparazzi *en route* from Le Bourget to central Paris, in particular the incident when their car was almost driven off the highway. More paparazzi on arrival at the Ritz. More on their departure. Yet more paparazzi on arrival at Dodi's apartment, forcing the couple to make last-minute changes to their preferred schedule and drive back across town to the Ritz for dinner. Even more paparazzi waiting for them there. Indeed, one might be forgiven for wondering who in truth was organizing this almost military-precise press operation: *for wondering who was tipping these guys off*. Considering the sheer endeavour involved in obtaining such informed, on-the-spot intelligence of the couple's minute-by-minute movements; the organization necessary to circulate that information throughout the paparazzi network, and with such efficiency - and thereby, of course, the means to orchestrate the movements of the paparazzi themselves - one cannot help but wonder just who might have been overseeing this operation. The paparazzi? Or perhaps someone assisting the paparazzi? Someone with an ulterior motive for wishing to exhaust the couple's inner reserves, perhaps - cause them tension, fear, anxiety. Could these tactics have been part of the operation that would, later that same evening, claim their lives? As a result of this action, for example, would Dodi be tempted to encourage Henri Paul to drive just that little bit faster, take just a little less care than perhaps he normally would? The possibility cannot be ruled out. After all, the couple were anxious. They were hungry. They were tired. All they wanted was to find somewhere quiet to eat. And sleep. In military terms they were, quite simply, sitting targets.

Finally, at around 10 pm, thoroughly wearied, the couple entered the Ritz for dinner. And even then they were forced to retire to the Imperial Suite in order to avoid the scrutiny of other diners in the Ritz's own L'Espadon restaurant. Perhaps if they had simply given in to their own exhaustion at this point, and decided to remain at the hotel until morning, they would have survived to tell their own story of this fraught, frenetic, frightening day. They did not, of course. They did not stay and they did not survive. It is doubtful they were meant to do either.

By the time the couple were ready to leave for Dodi's apartment once more it was 12.15 am. They had been at the hotel for a little under two and a half hours. As Henri Paul prepared to make his getaway from the rear of the building, down Rue Cambon via Place de la Concorde and along the Champs Elysees, two Ritz decoy cars screeched away from the front of the hotel in a bid to lure paparazzi off the chase. They circled the square at the front of the hotel, once, and straight away returned to the hotel's front entrance. To some extent the ploy worked. But not entirely. Perhaps on a hunch, perhaps on a tip-off, it is now known that a small number of *unidentified faces* - posing as paparazzi - were already waiting at the rear of the building. There they watched from the shadows as Diana and Dodi left by the back door and climbed in a spare car - a black Mercedes S280 VIP limousine. They then sped off in pursuit of that spare car, those *unidentified faces*.

It was now 12.20 am.

Precisely what happened during the four minutes following Henri Paul's departure from the rear of the Ritz cannot be so clearly defined - for some bizarre and still-unexplained reason, the dozen or more CCTV cameras lining the route, plus those situated in the Place de l'Alma underpass itself (together with all radar-activated speed cameras in the vicinity) were switched off. Curiously, they would remain 'out of action' for the duration of the princess's fatal journey.

At 12.21 am Diana's car was forced to stop at traffic lights in Place de la Concorde. It is reported to have jumped those traffic lights in order to escape the close attentions of paparazzi and other, as yet *unidentified pursuers*. At 12.22 am, still being pursued by paparazzi - but also by a second Mercedes, a silver 4x4 Jeep, a white Citroen AX and, more significantly, a high-powered motorbike complete with driver and pillion rider - the car was forced to take an unscheduled detour. Instead of taking the more direct route - turning right off Place de la Concorde and heading up the Champs Elysees - Henri Paul was forced to take an alternative route along the right bank of the River Seine and through an underpass, which he negotiated safely.

But there was another underpass ahead.

At 12.24 am Diana's Mercedes entered the Place de l'Alma underpass, later to be identified as Diana's 'crash tunnel'. It was at this point that the operation truly kicked in. As the Mercedes approached the tunnel's entrance, the high-powered motorbike which had tailed them all the way from the Ritz was seen to suddenly pull alongside, and then sweep ahead. As it sped past Diana's Mercedes its pillion rider was seen to aim an anti-personnel flashlight at the Mercedes' front windscreen and fire off a massive and blinding flash of light (many times the intensity of even the most high-powered camera flash). Indeed, the directional intensity of this flash of light - fired from an anti-personnel device developed as a weapon for use by British and US Special Forces - was easily sufficient to debilitate and blind Henri Paul for at least the next 60 seconds (in fact the device was designed to both stun and blind a person for up to three minutes). In this instance, of course, 60 seconds was time enough. Less than 10 seconds later Henri Paul was dead.

The motorbike then screeched to a halt some way further into the tunnel.

Here a second operation vehicle - most likely the Mercedes seen speeding away from the scene moments later - was already waiting to ferry operatives from the scene in the event of injury. So far as we know, none of the operatives were injured in the operation. The Mercedes was ready and waiting just the same. Just in case.

Meanwhile, a third operation vehicle - almost certainly a white, custom-weighted Fiat Uno, as described in some detail by a number of eyewitnesses - was waiting at the tunnel's entrance. As the motorbike sped past, the Fiat Uno - having already slowed sufficiently to force Henri Paul into the far-side lane - edged over and nudged the Mercedes as it pulled alongside. The Mercedes careered out of control. With Henri Paul unable to stop the car due to the presence of a royal passenger, and still blinded by the intensity of the anti-personnel flash of light (and thus unable to regain control of the wheel) the Mercedes clipped the Uno's rear brake light and grazed its wing (fragments of a rear light-casing and traces of white paint belonging to a Fiat Uno, together with a Fiat Uno wing mirror, were later found by investigators at the scene of the crash). In consequence, the Mercedes was propelled, first to the left, then to the right, then back towards the row of reinforced concrete pillars lining the tunnel's central reservation.

Then, *impact*.

As the Mercedes slammed into the thirteenth concrete pillar lining the tunnel's central reservation, it was hurled round a violent 180 degrees, plus a little more. When it finally came to rest its mangled front end faced back towards the Ritz.

But that was not the end of it. According to Britain's foremost crash expert, Professor Murray MacKay of Birmingham University (whom we interviewed), and contrary to initial reports, Diana's Mercedes was travelling no faster than 60/63 mph at the moment of impact. And what is more, Diana herself was seated directly behind the passenger-side front seat - which, according to Professor MacKay, should have been the safest seat in the car. The "most survivable" seat. Even so there was only one survivor, and it was *not* Princess Diana. Operatives at the scene were on hand to make sure of that.

But they had only seconds in which to complete the operation.

Having satisfied themselves that Diana's condition was fatal - having *ensured* that Diana's condition *would be* fatal - they injected Henri Paul with a cocktail-concentrate of drugs and alcohol. They then evacuated the scene at high speed (as reported by at least two eyewitnesses). Mission accomplished. It should be added that, even though involved in a major road traffic accident in the centre of one of Europe's largest and busiest cities - and moreover, an accident which involved the death of a British Royal - none of the persons involved, nor their vehicles, have ever been traced by the French authorities. Curious, to say the least.

Indeed, the assumption must now be that these vehicles will never be traced. And that, in consequence, their occupants (and those for whom they were working) will never be brought to justice.

Fait accompli.

Though deliberately speculative in its conclusion, this report is otherwise based on the facts as known regarding the final few hours of Princess Diana's life. Perhaps details of the final few minutes will never be known. We cannot say. What we can say, however, is that the above conclusion is not necessarily so far-fetched that one should automatically dismiss it out of hand. For one thing it is based on information gleaned from several intelligence and security sources (as presented in the ensuing chapters) and from eyewitnesses to events immediately prior to and following the crash in Paris. As we shall see, eyewitness testimonies that do not support the 'drink-drive' explanation have been virtually ignored by the French investigation team. Other eyewitness testimonies - which include detailed descriptions of the high-powered motorbike and the Fiat Uno observed at the scene of the crash - have simply not been acted upon with any degree of vigour. Certainly not with any degree of success. To add to this, British security forces are known to have employed the 'road traffic accident' in other assassination operations (as we shall see) in particular in Northern Ireland. But in England and other European countries, too. In point of fact, some few months after the crash former MI6 officer Richard Tomlinson divulged to the British press - indeed, testified to the magistrate in charge of the official investigation, Judge Herve Stephan - that the so-called 'road traffic accident' which killed Princess Diana was almost certainly an MI6 operation. And further, that it was virtually identical to an existing MI6 plot to assassinate Serbian President, Slobodan Milosevic - see *Addendum (iii)*. In light of this leak, of course, one must presume that the attempt on President Milosevic's life was put on hold. Or perhaps aborted altogether.

And that, as a result, the Balkans once again erupted into bloody warfare.

In any event, when the full body of available evidence is considered, the conclusion posited above tends to apply itself more readily to open-minded logic than does the official - some say downright contrived - 'drink-drive' explanation so vigorously promulgated by the authorities. Indeed, in our opinion no one in an official capacity has yet proposed anything like a satisfactory explanation regarding the true cause of this horrific and unnecessary tragedy. And what concerns us even more is that, unless we stand up and demand it - at the very least an open and public inquiry presided over by a democratically appointed committee and decided by a jury of randomly selected people - it is unlikely that anyone in an official capacity ever will. And until we achieve this much, of course, the memory of Diana, Princess of Wales, will remain forever fraught with suspicion, speculation and unrest.

If we truly want the People's Princess to rest in peace, it is our belief that we must first uncover the truth regarding the highly suspicious circumstances in which she died. We have a right to know what really happened. And so does Diana.

CHAPTER 2

THE EVIDENCE (Part 1)
Drunk At The Wheel

"The officer [senior French police officer, David Laurent] was
driving towards the Alma tunnel when a white car overtook him and
raced past. As the officer approached the tunnel he again saw the
car, which he recognized as a Fiat Uno. But this time, the Uno
appeared to be creeping along very, very slowly a few metres from
the mouth of the tunnel. It had no reason to slow down or stop, but
it had come to a virtual standstill just before the tunnel entrance ...
The officer drove past, leaving the Uno at the tunnel entrance ...
Later that night he heard about what had happened on the news ...
He now believes the Uno was waiting for ... the Mercedes carrying
Princess Diana."

Mirror, Thursday, 4th June, 1998.

―――――――――――――――――

Case For The Prosecution

Although this book was never intended as an investigation into the
crash itself (but rather into the 'political and historical motives'
behind Diana's death), we nevertheless felt it pertinent to include
here a concise overview of the crash facts as known. In so doing we believe
we will strengthen the case made later in this book. It is worth reiterating that
our own stance as 'advocates *for* assassination' is based on information
received from several very well-placed sources within the intelligence and
security community. How we first came upon this information will be
elucidated fully later in the book.

However, it should also be stated that, subsequent to receiving this
information, our conviction was further strengthened by the fact that - as we
were to discover - so many anomalies and still-unanswered questions abound
with regard to the crash itself. There are just too many problems with this
case - too many facts unresolved, too many avenues unexplored. And too
many loose ends left flailing in the wind for this case ever to reach a satisfactory
conclusion. This situation can only serve to bolster the case presented by the
defence, of course. And at the same time undermine that presented by the
prosecution. In our system of law, remember, the defendant remains innocent

until proven guilty - *beyond all reasonable doubt.* While so many contradictions predominate, and so many flaws and inconsistencies prevail, 'reasonable doubt' must of necessity continue to shadow the proceedings. Thus the defence is able to maintain its somewhat ambiguous posture behind the smug and arrogant cloak of unaccountability.

In order to mitigate this situation, then - also to lay the foundation for our later 'bloodline inquiry' - we have elected to highlight these 'anomalies' and 'still-unanswered questions' here. We have elected to present the facts to you, the jury, from our standpoint as 'prosecuting counsels'. In so doing it is our clear and unambiguous intention to challenge what we believe to be a wholly contrived and unsubstantial official defence of the 'drink-drive accident' theory. We believe the case facts, presented faithfully and stripped of their ambiguity, will show that the 'drink-drive' theory is sham - at best spurious, at worst a pre-planned propaganda sell designed to distract from the true events of that fateful and tragic night in Paris. We also believe that a bold and incisive cross-examination of the facts as presented by the defence will help us to achieve our intended goal.

And in the final analysis, of course, our intended goal - our clear and unambiguous intention - is to influence your own deliberations towards a verdict of 'guilty'. Let us make no bones about that. And in order to achieve this we must begin here, at the beginning, where the mystery first unfolds.

The Witnesses

The official explanation, then, attributes Diana's death to injuries she sustained in what has been described as "an horrific road-traffic accident". The "accident" occurred following a night out in Paris with her new love, Dodi Fayed. As we now know, the couple had just returned from a brief holiday in the Mediterranean, and Diana was due to return to England the following day in order to see her two sons, William and Harry, whom she had not seen for some time. In this respect Paris was to be a routine - though as it turned out, tragic, indeed fatal - stopover. Sadly, the princess would not see her sons again.

According to some reports the Mercedes S280 VIP limousine in which the couple died was doing in excess of 90 mph at the time of the crash - an attempt on behalf of driver Henri Paul, they say, to escape the attentions of that all-too-familiar posse of pursuant paparazzi: *click, click.* The evidence, however, suggests an altogether different explanation.

Somewhat conveniently, many have since commented, the "accident" occurred as the princess and Dodi were driven through the Place de l'Alma underpass on the right bank of the River Seine. If the reports are to be believed, Henri Paul was already worse for a cocktail of drink and drugs by the time he was summoned to drive the couple from the Ritz Hotel to Dodi's exclusive apartment on the Champs Elysees. Indeed, if the reports are to be believed, Henri Paul was in no fit state to be driving *any* car at *any* speed, much less an unarmoured, unchaperoned Mercedes S280 limo plus royal passenger at almost 100 mph. This coupled with the claim that the pack of out-of-control paparazzi was still snapping at the Mercedes' heels as it entered the Place de l'Alma underpass is the official reason given for the cause of the crash. But as we discovered, eyewitness reports tend to seriously challenge this explanation.

More than one witness, for example, recalls seeing a second Mercedes on the royal tail. It is said to have pursued Diana's Mercedes as driver Henri Paul was forced to accelerate through a set of red traffic lights on exiting Place de la Concorde. Initial reports claimed that this mysterious 'second Mercedes' contained "American tourists". However, the Mercedes seen speeding away from the scene of the crash moments after impact was not being driven in a manner consistent with how one might expect tourists to drive - in particular in a foreign country's capital city at half past midnight. At the least it would seem that these so-called "tourists" were on something of a whistlestop tour. Either that, or they were on a rather more official 'tour of duty' altogether.

Other reports speak of a high-powered motorbike swerving in front of Diana's Mercedes as it entered the Place de l'Alma underpass, only seconds before the crash. This vehicle was seen and described in some detail by several witnesses. But to no avail; it has never been traced. Confirmation that Diana's Mercedes was indeed followed by this high-powered motorbike came in an exclusive interview with Dodi's personal bodyguard, Trevor Rees-Jones (the *Mirror,* Monday, 2nd March, 1998). In the interview Mr Rees-Jones stated quite unequivocally that he recalled being followed into the tunnel by a high-powered motorbike. He also recalled being pursued by two other vehicles -cars - one of which he described as a white hatch-back, similar to a Fiat Uno. Not one of these vehicles has ever been traced by the French authorities. Curious, to say the least.

Another witness - London lawyer, Gary Hunter, staying at an hotel a short distance from Pont de l'Alma on the night in question, the Royal Alma Hotel - claims that he heard two explosions inside the underpass. Moments later, he says, he saw a Fiat Uno or Renault Clio together with a larger vehicle - 'probably a Mercedes' - speeding away from the underpass. Mr Hunter described these two vehicles as travelling "bumper to bumper" at high speed. Though we were unable to interview Mr Hunter ourselves, we *were* able to interview someone who had spoken to him on two separate occasions - Jeff Steinberg, noted US investigative journalist, counter-intelligence expert and senior editor of the Washington DC-based international journal, *Executive Intelligence Review* (*EIR*). Mr Steinberg, who has been investigating the crash since September 1997, told us:

"Yes, I've interviewed Gary Hunter, twice. He is one of a number of witnesses who basically got to see snapshots of the event - in other words, to take his case as a good case, Gary Hunter was not an eyewitness to the crash. He and his wife were celebrating their anniversary. They were staying at an hotel just a few blocks away from the tunnel ... Gary heard the crash, the exploding sound from inside the tunnel, raced to his hotel window and a moment or so later he saw two cars go speeding - he estimates 60 to 70 miles an hour - down a fairly narrow street. The two cars were right on each other's tail. One car was a larger vehicle which he thought might have been a Mercedes, and the second was a much smaller car...

"...So basically his mind equated the loud crash noise in the tunnel with these two cars speeding by his hotel window. He went to the French authorities. They expressed absolutely zero interest in even interviewing him, and in fact he was treated rather shabbily by the French when he volunteered to provide them with an account of what he had seen. He then went to the people at the Ritz Hotel. He obviously knew that the al Fayed family were very much interested in finding out what had happened in that crash, and ultimately it was only through the intervention of the al Fayed people with the police and the judge in Paris that a statement was ever even taken from him."

In an exclusive interview with *EIR*, Mr Hunter said:

"There was an almighty crash followed by the sound of skidding, then another crash. My initial thought was that there had been a head-on collision. I went to the window and saw people running towards the tunnel. I heard a screeching of tyres. I saw a small dark car turning the corner at the top of the road. I would say it was racing at 60 to 70 mph. My own feeling is that these were people in a hurry not to be there. I am confident that car was getting off the scene. It was obvious they were getting away from something and that they were in a hurry. It looked quite sinister. I can't recall the type of car, but it was a small dark vehicle. It could have been a Fiat Uno or a Renault. The dark smaller car was followed, on its tail, by a white Mercedes."

[Note: as explained in *EIR*, forensic experts later told *Time* magazine's Paris bureau chief, Thomas Sancton, and its Middle East correspondent, Scott McLeod, that the lighting in the tunnel and along the Paris streets makes it virtually impossible to differentiate colours at night. The lighting, the experts affirmed, can make a white or light-coloured car appear dark-coloured to the naked eye. The fact that Mr Hunter described the Fiat Uno as "dark", then, when in fact it is now known to have been white, is not altogether surprising.]

In any event, Mr Hunter's concerns regarding the cause of the crash have since been shared by several other witnesses. Indeed, many people have come forward with similar statements. Even so, the French authorities seem to have simply brushed them aside. Or at best failed dismally in acting upon them. But then, perhaps this is all we might expect of an authority who had to be coerced into taking Mr Hunter's statement in the first place.

Similar concerns arise with regard to the mysterious white Fiat Uno, of course - with which (it is now known) Diana's Mercedes collided as it entered the tunnel. Though some of the world's most sophisticated technology has been employed in the search, along with substantial resources and manpower - and despite having been seen and described by so many witnesses - the Uno and its occupant(s) are still to be found.

One witness who saw the Fiat Uno is senior French police officer, David Laurent. Back in June 1998 we were told that the French investigators had been given new evidence by Monsieur Laurent, who was off-duty on the night the Uno sped past him on approach to the tunnel. As reported in the *Mirror* (4th June, 1998):

"The officer was driving towards the Alma tunnel when a white car overtook him and raced past. As the officer approached the tunnel he again saw the car, which he recognized as a Fiat Uno. But this time, the Uno appeared to be creeping along very, very slowly a few metres from the mouth of the tunnel. It had no reason to slow down or stop, but it had come to a virtual standstill just before the tunnel entrance. At that stage there was no Mercedes in sight and no evidence that there had been an accident ahead. The officer drove past, leaving the Uno at the tunnel entrance ... Later that night he heard about what had happened on the news."

Mirror reporter Nic North, who wrote the article, went on to affirm that the police officer in question - David Laurent - was indeed a "senior officer". The report concluded: "... He [Monsieur Laurent] now believes the Uno was waiting for another car, quite possibly the Mercedes carrying Princess Diana."

An astonishing conclusion, to be sure. Indeed, it is surely inconceivable that a senior police officer and trained observer should, on learning of the crash, reach such a conclusion - unless, of course, the Uno was being driven in a manner that prompted such a conclusion. And if it was indeed being driven in such a manner, and at the very entrance to the tunnel in which, moments later, Diana was killed, then surely it is reasonable to conclude that it might just have played a part in her death. The only other explanation is 'sheer uncanny coincidence' - instances of which, we soon discovered, riddle this case. And at every juncture.

Another witness who saw the Fiat Uno is British-born secretary, Brenda Wells. Indeed, Ms Wells claims she was almost run off the road by the Uno as it sped past her, and then slowed to a virtual halt as it approached the tunnel entrance ahead of her. We referred the Brenda Wells testimony to *EIR* editor, Jeff Steinberg.

"Brenda Wells was, I believe, English", he affirmed. "She lived and worked in Paris, was married. She just happened to be going into the tunnel at the point that the Mercedes and the Fiat and these other vehicles were driving in, and she was kind of run off the road. She did see the Fiat basically first speeding and then jamming on its brakes, and she saw again kind of snapshots of what happened, literally in the seconds before the crash. She also was not exactly treated with a lot of respect and compassion by the French police, and for a period of time it was thought that she was missing, and may have been a victim of foul play. It later turned out that she just got spooked by the whole situation and spent a couple of weeks in the country with her husband ... Her story holds up with a lot of the other eyewitness accounts, and paints a picture of vehicle attack, as opposed to merely a traffic accident."

Indeed, the fact that the Uno has never been traced only adds weight to the "vehicle attack" hypothesis. The added fact that it has not shown up on any official registration documents, of course, suggests that its driver/owner was/is not a regular French citizen. One's suspicions thus start to run high. And understandably so. Indeed, according to a report published by *The People's* 'Special Investigation' team (Sunday, November 23rd, 1997) the French authorities even considered declaring the case a "murder inquiry" as they searched in vain for the Uno and its driver. In the event, however, it seems they backed down, most likely under pressure from British and US agencies with vested political interests. In this regard Judge Herve Stephan - in charge of the official French investigation - must surely have found his task a tad difficult with his hands tied so firmly behind his back.

Yet another witness said that he heard a "terrific explosion" the instant Diana's car disappeared into the underpass ahead of him. A second witness claimed - as did London lawyer, Gary Hunter - that she heard not one but *two* explosions inside the tunnel. The second "explosion" could of course have been the sound of the Mercedes slamming into the reinforced concrete pillar with which it finally collided. But this still does not account for the first "explosion". In an endeavour to shed some light on this seeming discrepancy, we spoke to a former SAS sergeant, who informed us that the 'first explosion' could have been due to a Special Forces device known as a "blockbuster" bomb - a small remote-controlled, non-detectable explosive concealed beneath the bonnet (hood) and designed to incapacitate, say, the steering column and/ or the brakes. Employed by Britain's intelligence and security forces, it is a device capable of causing precisely the kind of "accident" which killed Dodi and Diana. Indeed, according to our source, it is a device which has been employed against suspected terrorists in Northern Ireland for some years. "We used the blockbuster so many times in Northern Ireland, we got it down to a fine art," he told us. It is certainly interesting to note in this regard that, as reported by the official French investigation team, Diana's Mercedes had been stolen at gunpoint some few weeks prior to the crash. During its week-long absence the "blockbuster" could easily have been planted, our source said.

"That's exactly how they would've done it," he told us. "Borrow the car for a couple of days, fix it, and send it back looking good as new." And further: "It's how they've always done this kind of job. People think: 'How did they know they would use that particular car on that particular night? How did they know Dodi and Diana would stop off in Paris that night?' But, you know, your average man on the street hasn't got a clue. These people can work bloody magic if necessary."

Also of note is the fact that, during this same time-frame, the car's EMS (Electronic Management System) - essentially a microchip which controls the power steering and ABS brakes, among other functions - had been ripped out by the thief(s) and was later replaced. This is particularly interesting for the fact that the EMS had no substantial re-sale value - it is highly unlikely, therefore, that it was stolen for financial gain. One wonders: if not for financial gain, for what reason *would* a VIP limousine be stolen, at gunpoint, and then conveniently 'found' minus its original EMS? Could it have been to replace the system with one that had been tampered with, we wondered?

Our SAS source certainly thought that this could have been the case.

"The new system would have been programmed to override the steering and brakes. Like the blockbuster, it would've been triggered [remotely] from the tail car when it got close in. There would've been absolutely nothing the driver could have done to regain manual control. Absolutely nothing."

This source also told us that the "accident" bore all the hallmarks of a calculated intelligence ("probably MI6") operation, though he said that the "hit" itself would have been ordered from "beyond the normal channels" and carried out by a 'private security firm' - a quasi-official, mercenary-style security firm - "hired by the agency" (see *The Clinic* below). It should be added that this is precisely what we were told by another security source, too - that, in the event that the "accident" *had* been arranged by British Intelligence, it would most certainly have been executed by a 'private security firm' hired specifically for the task. It should be noted in this regard that some of Britain's so-called 'private security firms' are far from the sleazy, backstreet operations their image might suggest. On the contrary, they are multimillion-dollar corporations whose *modus operandi* includes the supply of arms, mercenaries and other 'equipment' to countries worldwide on behalf of the British Crown and British Government, as we shall see.

And what is more, according to one mercenary we interviewed, political assassination is their speciality.

Our SAS source concluded: "There'd been word of something like this happening for quite some time. But I never thought they'd actually do it ... From the minute the decoy car left the Ritz to the moment the tail car closed in ... it was obvious what was going down. Anyone who knows what they're talking about'll tell you the same."

And further: "It wouldn't be the first time this method has been used in a deniable op."

Evidently not - see *The Clinic* below.

Perhaps the most intriguing statement comes from eyewitness, Francois Levistre, who was already halfway into the tunnel when Diana's Mercedes entered. Monsieur Levistre claims that he saw the headlights of a motorbike and a car tailing Diana's Mercedes in his rear-view mirror. (The motorbike had already been witnessed by a number of motorists, including American businessman Brian Anderson, 49-year-old Parisian engineer Thierry H, and French chauffeur, Eric Lee, as it had pursued Diana's Mercedes at some speed - about "80 mph ... aggressively and dangerously" - towards the crash tunnel.) Monsieur Levistre also stated that, a second or two before the crash, he saw the motorbike accelerate past Diana's Mercedes (a statement confirmed by American witness, Brian Anderson, as well as by French witness, Thierry H). In the same instant he saw what he described as a blinding flash of light, much brighter and far more intense than any camera flash he had ever seen. His statement, though since discredited by the relevant authorities (like those of Gary Hunter and Brenda Wells), nevertheless prompted ITN's royal correspondent, Nicholas Owen, to believe that a Special Forces anti-personnel device might have been the cause of the flash - that such a device might have been used to temporarily blind driver Henri Paul as he entered the tunnel. We put this idea to our own Special Forces source, the former SAS sergeant quoted above.

"It's possible. I know the device. I've never used one but I know it, and it's deadly. It's very frightening and very painful on the eyes, much worse than you'd think. It would definitely be the way to do it. The flash would've been rigged as a remote [control] as well ... that set off the blockbuster at the same time ... So what you've got is *flash!* - the driver's blinded for up to two to three minutes and the blockbuster takes care of the brakes and the steering."

Wryly he added: "You'll never prove it, though."

Perhaps not. But it sounds a foolproof method, just the same.

The Clinic

In our efforts to corroborate the claims made by our SAS source, quite by chance we came upon the following story of what appears to have been an assassination operation carried out by a 'private security firm' similar to that referred to by our SAS source above. The incident involved a former Special Forces officer, one Major Michael Marman of the Sultan of Oman's Armed Forces, and a former Equerry to the Queen, Air Marshall Sir Peter Horsley. Only one of the two men survived to tell its tale...

In his autobiography, *Sounds From Another Room*, Air Marshall Sir Peter Horsley describes in chilling detail what happened to him on Tuesday, 11th November, 1986, while driving from his home in Wiltshire to a business meeting, due to take place in Plymouth.

Sir Peter recounts that, on the day in question, he was driving his BMW along the westbound carriageway of the A303, at approximately 60 mph, when he was involved in a very serious 'accident'. As he approached the megalithic monument of Stonehenge, he says, he saw a grey Volvo closing on him "at high speed" in his rear-view mirror. He then saw the Volvo take up position "immediately behind" him.

But what is most intriguing so far as we are concerned is that, just as Sir Peter was about to wave the Volvo past, quite suddenly and inexplicably, he says, he lost control of his BMW.

"...With alarming suddenness," he explains in his book, "my BMW spun sharply to the left, and then, with tyres now screeching, equally sharply to the right and then back again." (Precisely what happened to Diana's Mercedes moments before it crashed.) Sir Peter's BMW then careered across the central reservation and ploughed broadside into an oncoming Citroen 2CV - driven by one Major Michael Marman.

Sir Peter wrote: "Out of the corner of my eye, I saw the grey Volvo accelerating past me at high speed. My car had now developed a mind of its own as it swung broadside and skidded down the road. With a lurch it hit the central reservation, mounted the grass verge separating the two lanes of the highway and crossed over into the opposite carriageway. I just had time to see a small car approaching from the opposite direction. I hit it sideways on with tremendous force. In a split second the driver's horror-stricken face was visible and I clearly heard his hoarse scream above the tearing metal of the two cars momentarily locked together; then came silence as the small car [the 2CV] disappeared, catapulted off the road by the sheer force of the impact..."

Though Sir Peter survived the 'accident', the driver of the "small car", Major Michael Marman, was killed instantly. The question is, of course, was Major Marman the victim of a tragic though innocent 'road traffic accident'? Or was there something more to it?

According to world famous explorer, personal friend of Prince Charles and former SAS officer, Sir Ranulph Fiennes, Major Marman's death was in fact the handiwork of a European 'private security firm' - a firm of professional assassins known as The Clinic. In his book, *The Feather Men*, Fiennes reveals that, due to his tour of duty with the Sultan of Oman's Armed Forces, Major Marman had for some time been the target of a Yemeni assassination plot. He further reveals that The Clinic had been hired to carry out that plot; indeed, that The Clinic's speciality is carrying out assassinations which to all intents and purposes look like accidents. The 'road traffic accident' in particular, he says, was developed in the US by a Clinic member named Meier; it had become known as the 'Boston brakes' method. By employing the 'Boston brakes' method, Fiennes says, Major Marman's death was made to *appear* like an accident - much like Diana's - when in reality it was the result of a pre-planned and well-rehearsed assassination operation.

Fiennes writes: "On the night of Monday, 10 November [the night before the 'accident'], five members of the gang [The Clinic] assembled outside Sir Peter's secluded Victorian house ... Three remained on watch while Jake and Meier began the work of fixing the apparatus to the BMW's braking system ... Meier knew from experience that once he had taken over the control of Horsley's car, he could steer it as he pleased."

In other words, due to the Special Forces device planted on Sir Peter's car the night before the incident, at precisely the intended moment, Clinic member 'Meier' was able to take 'remote control' of Sir Peter's BMW and "steer it as he pleased" - which in this instance was into the 'target vehicle', the oncoming Citroen 2CV driven by assassination target, Major Michael Marman. According to Sir Ranulph Fiennes, this method of assassination is known as the 'Boston brakes' method. It was developed and perfected in America, Fiennes said.

Similarly, then, might also the driver of the Fiat Uno have "taken over the control" of Diana's Mercedes as it entered the tunnel? And having done so, might he then have been able to "steer it as he pleased", as described by Sir Ranulph Fiennes? Once inside the tunnel, Diana's Mercedes certainly acted in a very similar manner to Sir Peter Horsley's BMW, in that it too lurched "sharply to the left, and then, with tyres ... screeching, equally sharply to the right and then back again." And then into the thirteenth concrete pillar lining the tunnel's central reservation.

As Fiennes explains: "[From inside the chasing Volvo] Meier took over Horsley's car and ... he steered the BMW across the centre of the reservation into the path of Marman's approaching car...". And further, in order to cover their tracks: "That night two members of The Clinic broke into the garage and quickly removed all the apparatus from Horsley's car." In other words, they removed all evidence of the device which had enabled them to remotely control Sir Peter's car. Fiennes concluded: "The police arrived the following morning and ... did not have the slightest suspicion that they had been duped."

One wonders who might have been the first to 'examine' the wreckage of Diana's crashed Mercedes, then. The highly organized assassination team who caused the crash in the first place, perhaps? The agency for whom they were working? One thing we know for certain is that it was not the fully qualified Daimler-Benz engineers - the very engineers who *should* have been called upon to analyze the wreckage. In fact the Daimler-Benz engineers - who indeed offered their expert assistance to the French authorities - were refused permission to go anywhere near the wreckage. Very strange.

Or perhaps not. After all, who knows what they might have found? The remains of a blockbuster device, perhaps? Or some other device - a remote-control receiver/transmitter? As outrageous as it may sound, the possibility cannot be ruled out - certainly not according to Prince Charles's personal friend and former SAS officer, Sir Ranulph Fiennes, at any rate.

And there is further evidence to be considered. According to independent eyewitness, Aubrey Allen, who was driving some short distance behind Sir Peter's BMW when it crashed, what appears to have been a small explosion occurred moments before Sir Peter lost control of his BMW. As Mr Allen testified to the inquest into Major Marman's death: "The BMW was travelling normally down the centre of the road in front of me when a large puff of smoke came out of the left rear side of the car." As a result, Mr Allen concluded, Sir Peter's BMW spun out of control.

The question, then, must surely be asked: what *was* the "large puff of smoke" seen by Mr Allen to emerge from Sir Peter Horsley's car moments before he lost control? A blown tyre? No. No evidence of a blown tyre was found. A blown engine, then, a piston ring, a gasket?

No.

Might, then, the smoke have been the result of a small explosion, perhaps the result of a 'blockbuster' bomb triggered from the passing Volvo? The Volvo, remember, was the vehicle in which the assassins - The Clinic - were travelling.

The fact is that this question has quite simply never been answered. Much like the many questions which frankly still remain with regard to the crash which killed Princess Diana. Indeed, the patent similarities in the deaths of Major Marman and Diana, Princess of Wales, simply cannot be ignored.

And other than the 'blockbuster' and 'Boston brakes' methods described by our SAS source and Sir Ranulph Fiennes, neither can they be explained.

A Spurious Blood Test

Most reports certainly now agree that the pack of pursuing paparazzi had been left some two, three or even four hundred metres behind Diana's car by the time it crashed, suggesting that neither camera nor flash-bulb - nor even dangerous driving on the part of the paparazzi - could have substantially contributed to the tragedy. To add to this, prominent sources now claim that driver Henri Paul may neither have been drunk nor under the influence of drugs at the time of the crash. But that consistent with this kind of operation he was either infused with some kind of time-release capsule prior to the journey or, perhaps more likely, simply injected with a concentrate of the appropriate concoction by operatives at the scene of the crash - possibly by the mysterious and still-missing Uno driver and/or one of his accomplices. While this hypothesis may sound overly speculative to some, it should be stated that it is based not on pure conjecture. But on information gleaned from several very well-placed security and intelligence sources, all of whom have agreed that this type of operation, while infrequent, is nevertheless employed in extreme cases.

In any event, subsequent blood tests claiming Paul was three times over the legal limit certainly seem spurious. Or at least highly contestable. For one thing, Paul's blood was found to contain 23+ per cent carbon monoxide trace. According to medical experts - including carbon monoxide expert, Dr Alastair Hay - this is an inexplicably high level sufficient to cause nausea and disorientation in most people, in particular when combined with alcohol and drugs. And yet security footage of Paul's behaviour at the Ritz up to two hours prior to the ill-fated journey suggests that Paul was not even drunk, much less that he was suffering from 23+ per cent carbon monoxide poisoning to boot. As behavioural psychologist, Dr Martin Skinner, told ITN's investigative documentary, *Diana: Secrets Of The Crash*: "I don't think there's evidence from the video that can suggest he looks drunk. You wouldn't look at that not knowing what has happened, and say 'goodness me, that's a drunk person we're looking at'. The pictures of him walking up and down the corridor are straight and smooth - he's standing very still. There's nothing in his demeanour, from these videos, to suggest that there were any problems with his competence."

In the same programme, carbon monoxide expert Dr Alastair Hay was even more forthcoming: "If you've got a level of about 30 per cent [estimated carbon monoxide level in Henri Paul's blood two hours prior to the crash] someone would have a decided headache. You would have real throbbing in the temples; the headache would be unmistakable. There would be certainly a lack of coordination." And further: "It doesn't strike me when you look at the [video] pictures of Henri Paul [that] the man is really suffering. It doesn't look as if he's got a headache; he's not massaging his temples to try and reduce the pain in any way. He seems to be someone who is quite relaxed in his environment, in control - he's talking to people, giving orders; he's affable with the people he comes into contact with, smiles at what I assume were guests and so on."

And in conclusion: "I find it difficult to rationalize everything. I certainly think with a blood carbon monoxide level of 20 per cent ... and a blood alcohol level of about 180 milligrams per hundred mil, that this would be someone who would have a much slower reaction time. [It] would certainly be someone who would be slowed up in the way they did things. It would probably also be somebody who was in some pain. But none of those [things] seem to be evident from the pictures that we see of him [Henri Paul]. So it is a bit of an enigma."

Indeed it is. In particular when you consider that neither Diana nor Dodi - nor indeed Trevor Rees-Jones - suffered any carbon monoxide poisoning whatever. Which of course means that Paul could not have been poisoned by, say, exhaust fumes that might have leaked into the car. Nor by inhaled smoke from cigarettes or cigars. Although Henri Paul did indeed smoke cigars, medical experts say that 10 per cent carbon monoxide trace is high even for the heaviest of smokers. Any higher than this and the symptoms as described above start to kick in, and with some vengeance. And in any event, Paul was not a heavy smoker; according to friends he smoked only a few cigars a day. So where, why, when and how was he poisoned? Just how did this amount of carbon monoxide find its way into Henri Paul's blood? And moreover, when and how? It simply could not have been during the two hours prior to the crash because carbon monoxide trace decreases by roughly half every four to five hours. This means that, if the carbon monoxide level in Paul's blood was around 23 per cent soon after the crash, then two hours prior to the crash it would have been somewhere in the region of 30 or even 35 per cent. According to the experts, these kinds of levels cause severe difficulties, and in some cases can be lethal. And yet the Ritz security footage shows Paul calm, congenial and coherent throughout the two hours prior to the crash. Very curious indeed.

As is the claim that Paul's blood contained very high levels of alcohol, and yet he was able to act and function as though completely sober. Contrary to many press reports, of course, Henri Paul was not a heavy drinker. True, were he an alcoholic - or even someone who drank alcohol more than most - then his alcohol tolerance would have been higher than that of the normal person. Thus he would perhaps have been able to disguise his alleged inebriated condition. But Paul's post mortem showed clearly enough that his liver was in good condition - there was no sign whatever that Paul was a heavy or even a regular drinker. This being the case, then, what are we to make of a blood test that claims a very high alcohol level mixed with a potent concoction of drugs, and a level of carbon monoxide poisoning that should have seen the man reeling, pained and out of control? When in fact he was none of these things. It simply does not add up.

And there are other anomalies in this regard. For one, it seems beyond all reason to even consider the possibility that trained VIP bodyguards such as Trevor Rees-Jones and Alexander 'Kes' Wingfield, both of whom spent two hours with Henri Paul immediately prior to the fateful journey, would have allowed him anywhere near the wheel of a car - even more so *that* car - if they thought for one minute that he had consumed the equivalent of one and a half bottles of wine, the amount he is alleged to have consumed. Indeed, Trevor Rees-Jones said as much himself.

In his much-publicized interview with *Mirror* editor Piers Morgan (the *Mirror*, Monday, 2nd March, 1998) the former al Fayed bodyguard stated quite categorically that, in his professional opinion (and his opinion is indeed a professional one) Henri Paul was not drunk. It should be remembered that Trevor Rees-Jones has run undercover operations with the British Army's elite Parachute Regiment/Special Forces, and is a fully trained VIP bodyguard. He is a professional observer, trained to react to irregular situations and behaviours. He saw nothing irregular in Henri Paul's behaviour that night.

The same can be said of his colleague, Alexander 'Kes' Wingfield, who said that he was within feet of Henri Paul on several occasions during the two hours prior to the departure from the Ritz. Not once did he detect alcohol on Henri Paul's breath. Not once did he suspect that Henri Paul might have been drinking heavily. Not once did he doubt Henri Paul's ability to drive the Mercedes, even though it contained the Princess of Wales and Dodi Fayed. Indeed, in the professional opinion of both these highly trained men, Henri Paul was not drunk. If we are expected to accept the experts' opinion when it supports the 'drink-drive accident' theory, then equally we should consider it when it does not.

And there is one further point worthy of clarification here. Though the post mortem shows beyond question that Paul was not a heavy drinker, the media - in their ruthless attempts to assassinate the character of this man

- persist in claiming the contrary. And because they do, we decided to follow up this line of inquiry to our own conclusion, which is this.

For someone alleged by the press to have been an "habitual drinker", to have registered three times the legal limit when tested is practically impossible. The reason for this is simple: the more regularly a person drinks alcohol the less it tends to register in the blood and the less effect it is likely to have on the consumer. For a so-called "habitual drinker" to register three times the legal limit, as is claimed in Henri Paul's case, he would have had to consume more like one and a half bottles of highly potent whisky, never mind wine. "Habitual drinker" or not, anyone with that amount of alcohol in their system would have found difficulty remaining upright, never mind driving a car. In particular when mixed with a concoction of prescription drugs and excessive levels of carbon monoxide. As one medical expert commented: "For an habitual drinker to be so intoxicated that he registers three times the legal limit ... in my opinion he would have to be so steeped in alcohol that he would be staggering all over the place. And he would be *seen* to be staggering all over the place ... I find it inconceivable that the bodyguards should have remained unaware of this man's state."

And yet, according to every substantial eyewitness bar none - including, of course, the security footage of Paul in the hotel lobby - Henri Paul did not stagger that night. He did not stagger at all. On the contrary, he remained composed, clear-headed and coherent throughout the entire evening. For someone alleged to have been three times over the legal limit this is quite simply not possible.

As Jeff Steinberg observed:

"First of all let's look at the confirmed evidence from the forensic tests on Henri Paul's blood. I am going on the basis of a statement that was released by the Paris Prosecutor's Office on behalf of Judge Stephan about a week before the first anniversary - so towards the middle to the end [27th] of August 1998. I mean, presumably the judge is giving reliable information.

"Anyway, the fact is that Henri Paul - the blood tests that are purported to have been [carried out] on Henri Paul's blood - showed a presence of alcohol three times over the legal limit under French law; showed a presence ... of two fairly strong prescription drugs, and thirdly about a 23 per cent presence of carbon monoxide. Now that level of carbon monoxide alone would paralyze most people. He would certainly be completely dysfunctional. You'd have no balance; you'd be suffering from an extraordinary pounding headache in your temples. And if you compound that with the alleged alcohol and drug traces in the bloodstream, it is impossible to conceive of Henri Paul being able to even crawl, much less walk around the lobby at the Ritz Hotel, escort Diana and Dodi into the car, get behind the wheel and drive relatively safely according to eyewitnesses all the way up to the tunnel."

And further: "When Henri Paul arrived back at the Ritz Hotel - he'd been off duty for about two and a half hours - he ran into Trevor Rees-Jones and Kes Wingfield. They were having a light dinner in the bar in the lobby. Diana and Dodi were up in the Imperial Suite on the second floor, above the desk.

"Anyway ... it's acknowledged that [Paul] had one drink while they were sitting around. But both Rees-Jones and Wingfield said repeatedly that, had Henri Paul been drunk as a stoned cat, had he been dysfunctional because of carbon monoxide poisoning or prescription drugs, they would have detected it immediately. Also, when I was interviewed on British television in June '98, I was asked to comment on a one-hour documentary [*Diana: Secrets Of The Crash*]. They brought in experts in carbon monoxide poisoning, who explained that a 23 per cent dosage is near lethal. It would put most people in a coma, and they certainly would not be able to respond in any way/shape like a normal sober individual. So the whole thing is a great big question mark. And I think the best that can be said is that it raised serious doubts as to whether or not the blood test was accurately performed. Maybe it was an accurate test, but on somebody else's blood? There were half a dozen people brought into the morgue that night. It was the last weekend of the summer. I don't know, maybe some drunk fell asleep on one of the subway gratings and died of carbon monoxide poisoning, and that's the blood test that was taken. That's purely speculative. But the point is, the blood test does not conform to the eyewitness and videotape evidence of Henri Paul's state of being in the immediate period before the drive."

Indeed, it most certainly does not. So how *can* the concoction of alcohol, drugs and carbon monoxide alleged to have been swimming around in Henri Paul's blood be explained? The answer, of course, is straightforward. It can't be.

It is our contention, then, that the 'drink-drive' theory holds about as much water as a sieve might hold. Which is not very much at all.

CHAPTER 3

THE EVIDENCE (Part 2)
Inconsistencies And Incompetence

"...I can't see why they would drive past a competent hospital. I bet the doctors at the first hospital were furious. I mean, at the end of the day, they could easily have taken her to the first hospital and sent for the surgeon. He could have been there before she arrived. If there was a particular surgeon [required] he could have driven to the other hospital and treated her there ... they could have taken her straight to the nearest one and if they were short of qualified surgeons they could have sent for one."

Andy Palmer, Paramedic Superviser, November, 1998.

The Fiat Uno
And The Missing Tyre Marks

Despite initial efforts to convince us that Henri Paul was travelling at 121 mph at the time of the crash, it has since emerged that in fact he was travelling at no more than 63 mph - around 60 mph slower than claimed. In fact, Mercedes Benz's chief engineer said all along that the speedometer was not stuck at 121 mph following the crash, as reported by the tabloid press. In the event of an accident, he affirmed, it is designed always to revert to zero. Which it did. This statement, however, was overriden by the '121 mph' story - which, incidentally, was first concocted and published by one of the British Establishment's major media allies, The *Daily Telegraph*, before being blasted across the world as part of the Establishment's propaganda drive to discredit Henri Paul. The fabricated story was also supported by the French police. Indeed, Mercedes Benz's offer to send a team of highly qualified safety engineers to Paris in order to help in the analysis of the crashed Mercedes was rejected by the French authorities. Very strange. At the same time, Mercedes Benz was forbidden to make any statement regarding the crash and/or the subsequent investigation.

In any event, it has since been confirmed by the French investigation team that the speedometer did indeed revert to zero immediately following the crash. This leaves the true speed of the car at the moment of impact to be determined by crash experts.

Enter Professor Murray MacKay of Birmingham University - Britain's senior RTA (Road Traffic Accident) expert. Professor MacKay, who employed state-of-the-art computer-simulated reconstructions of the crash to enhance the accuracy of his findings, has been studying the causes and effects of car crashes for more than thirty years. When we interviewed him he made it clear that he did not wish to add to the speculation surrounding the crash. Given his position, of course, this was understandable. He was nonetheless very affable and helpful, indeed forthcoming, in particular with regard to the two most crucial factors concerning the crash itself - the speed of the Mercedes and the part played by the white Fiat Uno.

According to Professor MacKay, who has visited the Place de l'Alma underpass on several occasions, Diana's Mercedes was travelling at approximately 60 mph when it collided with the concrete pillar. This figure was calculated, he said, "without having to rely on any eyewitnesses".

He explained: "The speed on impact was about 60-63 miles an hour. That's based on the whole reconstruction process ... From the photographs you can compare the state of the car with that of an undamaged car, the amount of frontal crush, where it actually is ... so you get a pretty good idea as to the extent of the damage and the shape of the impact zone. From that there are crash reconstruction techniques; you can compare the crash with experimental crashes around the speed mentioned. You can use comparative techniques. When you crash any car it starts off relatively soft in terms of the structure, but then when you begin to hit the engine and destroy the engine mountings you get these heavy structures. The resistance builds up and then when you get even further into destroying the structure it starts to deform the transverse bulkhead and the actual body-shell of the passenger compartment. Then you get into some really stiff structure. I am saying this because you have to make assumptions about how the structure is deformed...

"...So there's some estimating to be done. That gives you what's called the 'Delta D', which is the 'change in velocity'. The change in velocity is something in the order of 50-54 miles an hour, based on the analysis. We know where the vehicle finished up in relationship to the point of impact - that's pretty well-defined from the police reports, and from the videos and photographs taken at the scene ... so the final position would be well-fixed. On impact [Diana's Mercedes] span out around 180-210 degrees ... anyway it spun round, and its distance from the pillar was something around 10 or 12 feet. We then do calculations in terms of the exit velocity of the car's impact with the pillar, which was around 5-8 miles an hour ... and that tells us that the over-the-road speed into the pillar was something in the order of 60-63 miles an hour."

Professor MacKay went on to say that, according to the reconstruction techniques employed by himself and his team, Diana's Mercedes would have been approaching "80 mph" when it entered the tunnel. It must then have collided with a "second vehicle inside the tunnel", he concluded, and in consequence would have spun out of control. When we questioned him on the somewhat suspicious presence of this "second vehicle", he commented: "It does make you wonder. But whether it [the Uno driver] was an innocent bystander who just wanted to maintain a low profile, [who] had his own reasons not to want to have contact with the police, well, you know. It may mean nothing more than that. The rest is speculation."

Indeed it is, to a certain extent. But the question has to be tabled: if the driver of the still-missing Fiat Uno was purely an innocent bystander, then is it not reasonable to assume that this person was/is a regular French citizen? And if this person was/is a regular French citizen then where is he now? Why has he not been traced? And moreover, given the fact that motor vehicles, their owners and their licence numbers are these days registered and logged on highly sophisticated central computing systems, how is it that the car has not been traced, either? True, it may have belonged to a foreign visitor who just happened to be driving around the centre of Paris at midnight. It may even have been an imported car that had escaped the French authorities. Perhaps an *illegally* imported car. But in reality, of course, this explanation seems no more substantive than all the other anomalous assumptions made with regard to this case. Less so. Indeed, is it not more likely that the Uno and its driver might have been part of an organized intelligence operation? Certainly if this were the case then one would not expect to trace either the vehicle *or* its driver. And that is precisely the situation as it stands. It should also be remembered that, despite several detailed eyewitness descriptions of the high-powered motorbike also involved in the incident, this vehicle and *its* driver and passenger remain unaccounted for, too. As does the Mercedes seen speeding away from the scene plus *its* crew. Remarkable. No less than three vehicles (together with Diana's Mercedes) involved in a major 'accident' in the centre of Paris. Two of these vehicles - the motorbike and the Uno - seen and described in some detail to the authorities by a number of eyewitnesses. And yet none have been traced. Not one. The fact that a silver 4x4 Jeep and a white Citroen AX also remain on the 'wanted' list only serves to demonstrate what a complete and utter hash the French investigators have made of this inquiry. Either that, or their efforts have perhaps been thwarted by an 'unseen hand' at play. This latter possibility, of course, throws into question the entire investigation. In particular when you consider, too, the fact that no video (outside CCTV - closed-circuit television) footage seems to exist, either of the chase from the Ritz to the ill-fated Place de l'Alma tunnel, of the crash itself, or of the Uno leaving the scene of the crash. Yet lining the entire route there are both outside CCTV cameras and radar-activated speed cameras (the latter being spontaneously activated to capture speeding vehilces). We can only surmise from this that all of these highly sophisticated pieces of technology were 'out of order' on the night in question - which to us seems an absurd notion. Indeed, if these cameras truly were idle on the night in question then it seems to us that either somebody switched them all off at the appropriate moment. Or somebody has watched a re-run of the entire tragic event and is refusing to share their information.

And either scenario implies a cover-up.

There is another factor to consider.

Professor MacKay confirmed to us that "tyre marks" (as distinct from 'skidmarks') had been found at the crash scene. It was estimated by the French investigators, as well as by Professor MacKay, that these tyre marks belonged to Diana's Mercedes - that they had been made as Henri Paul had swerved in order to try and avoid contact with the white Fiat Uno. However, what is interesting in this regard is that no tyre marks were made by the Fiat Uno. No skidmarks, no tyre marks. In other words, having been struck by a meaty Mercedes travelling at 80 mph; and further, having then witnessed that Mercedes slamming into a concrete pillar less than 2 seconds later and perhaps only metres away, the Uno driver did not slow dramatically, did not stop, but gaily went on his way, narrowly missing the crumpled wreckage of Diana's car as he did so. And thus - and only thus - there were no tyre marks made by the Fiat Uno. A most unlikely scenario, to be sure. After all, if you had been driving a smaller, flimsier car that was hit by a hefty Mercedes travelling at 80 mph, would you not have been forced to employ a correction manoeuvre that might have left tyre marks on the road? And further, if that Mercedes had then proceeded to slam into a concrete pillar just a few metres in front of you, would you have had the presence of mind to brake very gently in order to avoid leaving tyre marks on the road; casually change down a gear; change lanes in order to avoid colliding with the Mercedes' wreckage and simply drive past as if nothing had happened - all in the space of less than 2 seconds?

We put this most unlikely scenario to Professor MacKay, who was understandably reluctant to commit himself. Nevertheless he did infer that it seemed somewhat strange that the Uno driver had not braked rather more sharply - either on contact with the speeding Mercedes or when the Mercedes had slammed into the concrete pillar less than 2 seconds later, right in front of the Uno. Or indeed that the Uno driver had not performed some other manoeuvre in order to rectify the jolt of being clouted by over a ton of speeding metal. After all, a Fiat Uno is not the sturdiest of cars; the slightest graze at a speed of around 80 mph (estimated speed of Mercedes as it entered the tunnel) would surely have had its effect on the smaller, lighter vehicle. And unless this smaller, lighter vehicle (the Uno) was being driven by a very experienced driver who was expecting the collision - if it was being driven by, say, a regular French citizen going about his business in a routine manner - then surely that driver would, at the very least, have been forced into a reflex correction manoeuvre on contact with the considerably heavier, considerably faster Mercedes. And yet the evidence suggests otherwise - no Uno skidmarks; no Uno tyre marks, either on the road or against the kerb where it might have scraped its tyres or wheel rims on collision with the Mercedes. Apart from the smashed rear-light casing belonging to a Fiat Uno; the broken wing mirror belonging to a Fiat Uno; the traces of white paint belonging to a Fiat Uno (all found at the scene) - and of course the numerous eyewitness statements describing the Uno in some detail - it is as if the Uno was not there at all. But of course it *was* there. And the fact that it was suggests that it was being driven by someone who was not only expecting a collision (and was thereby able to brace himself *and* the car in advance of that collision). But by someone with intention to *cause* that collision in the first place. Though Professor MacKay confessed that, in his opinion, some rather "abnormal driving" had indeed occurred that night, the authority and status of his position prevented further speculation on his part. We nevertheless would like to thank Professor MacKay for being as frank and honest as he was.

In any event, we put this same scenario to our SAS source, from whom we were able to glean a somewhat different picture. Without hesitation he told us that the Uno driver would indeed have been highly experienced. And further, that in his experience the Uno would undoubtedly have been "custom-weighted" - "fitted up" for the job.

"It would have been weighed down low to the ground," he explained, "probably with bags of cement or concrete blocks, so that it held the road when it collided with the bigger vehicle ... so that it didn't roll on impact. That's basic ABC."

And further: "It would have had a very skilled driver who would've clipped the Mercedes just enough ... he would've dipped in front of the target vehicle at just the right moment so that the other [Diana's] driver was forced to swerve ... just enough to nudge it [Diana's Mercedes] off the road. When you're doing that kind of speed - 60-70 miles an hour - a nudge is usually enough."

So in his opinion was this scenario consistent with an intelligence operation?

"Oh, yeah. Look, I've already told you, but I'll tell you again. I've still got good contacts in the right places. Some are old mates. I keep my head low these days but I still keep an eye on what's going on, you know. I'm telling you straight, this was a hit. Everything about it - it just stinks of it. When you've done the things I've done and seen the things I've seen done in the name of queen and country - I'm telling you this was a hit. You'll never ever prove it because that's the way it works. But it was a classic deniable op. I've seen it and done it. If you can find anyone else like me they'll tell you the same."

One final question. If you were still in the SAS, would you have agreed to take part in such an operation, knowing the identity of the target?

"These boys weren't SAS, I'll tell you that now. There may've been one or two old boys, but the [SAS] wouldn't be used for something like this. Too f**king risky ... But yeah, there was a time I would've done. There's plenty of old boys around who would, that's for sure. You know, it's the ultimate, isn't it, Princess Di ... It's like a drug. It's the ultimate high. You're paid by the government so you know you probably won't get caught. You *can't* get caught, because if you do it leads right back to the government. You're a professional working for other professionals who know how to cover their tracks. At the end of the day, whether it's a princess or some African dictator, if you get your hands dirty then the government's in the shit. And if the government's in the shit then you're in even bigger shit ... When I say the government I don't mean the MPs or those idiots at MI5. I'm talking the real professionals, probably MI6, but they never say they are ... But that's who would've done it, one of MI6's D-op [deniable operations] units. It would've been organized by them but the actual hit would've been ordered from ... well let's just say from 'beyond the normal channels'. The hit itself would've been down to some private firm, mercenaries hired by the agency. There's always plenty of them looking for a few quid. And they don't mind how they earn it, either."

Evidently not.

The Rescue Operation

One further (and very pertinent) point to be considered is of course the rescue operation - the fact that the emergency services took so long to reach the scene of the crash. And then took even longer to ferry Diana to what turned out to be the wrong hospital. Many questions arise in this respect.

Why, for instance, did Dr Frederic Mailliez, the first doctor to examine Diana at the scene, initially describe her condition as "not catastrophic"? What prompted him to conclude that she "did not seem desperate" when some small time later she was dead? Why did paramedics take almost a quarter of an hour to reach the scene of the crash? According to official reports there was no traffic congestion in Paris that night.

And further: why was Diana treated by the paramedics for more than 90 minutes, both at the crash scene and in the back of the ambulance *en route* to hospital, when the cardinal rule states that it is crucial the injured party should receive hospital treatment within the first, so-called 'golden hour'? Why was she taken to Pitie Salpetriere hospital - the furthest from the scene - at a snail's pace, when no less than five closer hospitals could have dealt equally with the emergency? Surely if her condition was so delicate that the ambulance was forced to travel at a suspiciously slow pace then prudence would dictate she be taken to the nearest possible hospital for the swiftest possible medical attention. In this regard, Paris's most noted and, indeed, best-equipped VIP hospital, Val de Grace, is less than two miles from the scene of the crash. The ambulance drove straight past Val de Grace *and* Hotel Dieu (equally well-equipped) on its way to Pitie Salpetriere, which is a further two miles away from Place de l'Alma.

And there is a further question to be asked of the French emergency team in this regard.

Having for no apparent reason chosen the hospital furthest from the scene, why did the ambulance then stop for more than 10 minutes outside Paris's Natural History Museum, when Pitie Salpetriere's casualty department (and thereby the expert attention necessary to save Diana's life) was literally only seconds away? (Approximately 800 metres separates the hospital from the museum. An ambulance travelling at, say, 60 mph, would thus have taken around 30 seconds to reach the hospital from the museum. And yet Diana's ambulance, having already taken more than an hour and a half to get her that far, stopped for a further 10 minutes before completing the final 30-second leg of the journey. Why?)

Not for the first time in the course of this investigation, it seems, something here simply does not add up. Indeed, in light of these discrepancies one might be forgiven for suspecting that the so-called 'paramedics' who attended the crash were working for someone other than the French health authorities. Either that, or they were hijacked by someone who was. Indeed, in an article run by the German newspaper *Bild Zeitung* (intriguingly titled *Diana Died Because She Was So Famous* - 14th January, 1998) criminologist, lawyer and head of the European Commision on Crime, Dr Wolf Ullrich, charged that in his professional opinion "Diana could still be alive, had it not been for the incompetence of the doctors". And further: "They simply let her bleed to death."

Indeed, all the evidence suggests that this is precisely what they did.

In our endeavour to find out more about the rescue operation, we first put a few questions to *EIR* editor, Jeff Steinberg - who, remember, together with his internationally-based team of investigative journalists and their sources, has been investigating the crash since September 1997. We then referred Mr Steinberg's findings to Paramedic Superviser, Andy Palmer - compared the investigator's opinion with that of the expert, so to speak. The results were very intriguing indeed.

In the first instance, then, we spoke to Jeff Steinberg.

Q: Jeff, can you tell us what you have discovered with regard to the rescue operation on the night in question?

JS: My understanding is, going back to the basics that are known about the French emergency rescue team - who so horribly bungled the treatment of Princess Diana - that they really, by all rights, should be prosecuted for her death.

Q: Can you tell us what has led you to arrive at such a radical conclusion?

JS: First of all there's a whole big phoney argument that the French do things differently and they've got these super ambulances that are practically operating rooms on wheels. But the bottom line is that when there's been a crash of the seriousness of this one, the very first, automatic assumption has got to be that everybody who is still alive has internal injuries, probably has internal bleeding. So under those circumstances there is only one thing to do, whether you are in France or in the United States, or whether you are in Timbuctoo, and that is to get the person into the operating room as fast as possible; to cut them open to find out where the bleeding is and stop the bleeding. And then to provide various kinds of further treatment - obviously blood transfusions and things like that. One of the worst things you can do is pump the person up with IVs [intravenous solutions], because that tends to increase the blood pressure and accelerate the rate of bleeding internally, which is what the French did. Their excuse was that they wanted to stabilize her at the scene. But what they wound up doing made matters worse. They took over an hour before getting her into the ambulance, and then 43 minutes to drive only a few miles to the hospital.

Q: We have learned that the ambulance stopped for around 10 minutes when it was scarcely half a mile from the hospital?

JS: Correct. The ambulance stopped right outside the Emergency Room and sat parked on the side of the road for an additional 10 minutes. All of this is inexplicable behaviour. Now this is not just my opinion. In late May [1998] the magistrate in charge of the French investigation, Judge Stephan, ordered a federal review of the emergency medical response. My sources in Paris have said that the review consisted of lengthy interviews with the ambulance drivers, with all the medical personnel involved, and that the story that comes out of them is an absolute horror story - at best, murderous, bungling; at worst, some kind of action that had the effect of killing her [Diana].

Q: Do we know who these paramedics are?

JS: Not really. In early news coverage maybe one or two names came out, but this has been held really close to the chest. The names of the people who were on the hospital staff are really very well-known. They gave a press conference at about 4 in the morning, when they announced that she had died, to explain all that had happened. I had our Paris office interview a medical expert who basically gave us the interview on the condition that his name remain anonymous. But this is somebody who actually designed the French system, and therefore knows what the reality of the emergency medical capability in Paris is. What this person said is that:

a) under these kind of circumstances you do want to get the person to a hospital as soon as possible, even in France; the hospital she should have been brought to is the Val de Grace hospital, which is even closer - about a mile and a half from the crash. Plus Val de Grace is hooked up to the national military radio communication system, which means as soon as the first fire truck arrived at the tunnel, which is part of the emergency response, there was a kind of all-users message that went out by radio, alerting all the hospitals in the area to be ready for a VIP delivery. The fact is that standard procedure is that any VIP in any kind of traffic accident or emergency medical situation in Paris goes to Val de Grace. They have a medivac helicopter that could have been brought in and landed right outside the tunnel. The estimate of this person is that she could have been in surgery within 25-35 minutes after the first emergency response vehicles arrived. And this person believes, as do many medical experts, that if she had been in surgery within an hour even, that she would have stood an almost 100 per cent chance of surviving.

Q: There is some suggestion that the first doctor on the scene did not consider Diana's condition entirely critical?

JS: That's not certain. It's Dr Frederic Mailliez. What is certain is that he gave an initial interview with a French medical journal which was then first picked up and reported in *The Scotsman* in, I would say, some time during the month of September [1997]. Mailliez's initial response was that he felt that Diana was the one most likely to survive ["I thought her life could be saved", Dr Mailliez was quoted as saying] and he diagnosed from certain external signs that she had some kind of internal bleeding. There are standard signs. You don't have to cut somebody open under those circumstances to know that there is a likelihood that they are bleeding internally. There are external signs: sweating, puffiness in certain places, which tend to indicate that the person has internal problems. And that's the sign that they had better be off and running to get that person into surgery.

[Indeed, *The Scotsman*, which carried Dr Mailliez's interview, concluded: "What is puzzling about the treatment is that she was not hospitalized until her condition had deteriorated to a critical extent."]

Now the other thing that is very important here is who was in charge. If you know anything about France, it is probably the closest thing to a cloaked, benign police state that exists anywhere. It makes Britain look practically *laissez-faire* in comparison. The bureaucracy runs the country and especially in Paris, and especially when it comes to police matters. So the ambulance driver or even the medical emergency teams, and the firemen on the scene, the first thing they'd want to know is *who is in charge? Who do we report to? Who tells us what to do?* So that was the very important question we wanted to find out, and the answer is the Police Chief of Paris was there the whole time. His name is Philippe Massoni. He got there within 45 minutes after the crash. So he was on the scene supervising the rescue effort. The head of the criminal brigade, the investigative bureau of the Paris police, was also there in the tunnel. The Prosecutor from the Prosecutor's Office who wound up later being involved in the case, was at the tunnel. So you have a whole conclave of high-ranking, judicial police officials there running the show. The French Interior Minister, [Jean-Paul] Chevenement, had initially intended to go to the tunnel but was instead urged by Massoni to go to the hospital. Chevenement was at the hospital an hour before Diana got there. So you had, between the radio communication, Chevenement and Massoni, a very unambiguous chain of command supervising the rescue effort and the beginnings of putting the forensics together.

Q: Are you implying that some kind of high-level French cover-up was already at work?

JS: I don't know. I prefer to say that the issue is in their court to answer. I think we are still in the phase right now - fifteen months after the fact - where some of the key people who were there have a lot of explaining to do.

Quite.

In order to corroborate the claims made by Mr Steinberg (or to refute them), we spoke to Andy Palmer, Paramedic Superviser of some years and thus experienced in many emergency rescue operations. Mr Palmer kindly agreed to talk to us on the understanding that we showed him the manuscript before publication. Which we did. We met Mr Palmer at his home.

Q: In your experience, Andy, is it normal to treat someone at the scene of a crash for an hour or more, and then take a further half an hour or more to ferry them to hospital?

AP: Without being there it's hard to say. It's an Americanism really, as to whether people are 'big sick' or 'little sick'. The big sick you put in the back of the ambulance and do what you can and get them to hospital, because at the end of the day, somebody like Diana or anybody in an accident like that, they are not going to be saved by the side of the road. So there shouldn't be too much delay in getting them to hospital. We try to stick to what we call 'meaningful interventions' - that is procedures that are critical and have an immediate effect on the patient's condition. But it also depends on how easy it is to get access to the patient or to extricate them from the vehicle.

Q: According to all the reports, as well as photographs taken immediately after the crash, there was no suggestion that Diana was trapped in the vehicle for any length of time. Quite the opposite, she was treated on a stretcher by the roadside for almost an hour.

AP: I'd hope that I wouldn't treat someone on the scene for an hour if that was the case.

Q: What about the length of time it took to ferry her to hospital once they had finally got her in the ambulance?

AP: I don't know how far away they were from the hospital.

Q: Three miles, four at most.

AP: Yes, you shouldn't take that long - not unless you can't physically remove them.

Q: What about IVs? Is it normal to IV someone with suspected internal injuries?

AP: Yes, but setting up IVs takes time, so opinion is turning around now. It could be done en route to hospital to minimize delay.

Q: We were told that if you IV someone with internal bleeding at the scene of a crash, it makes the internal bleeding worse. It can be detrimental to the victim's chances of survival.

AP: It can be. You've got intravenous fluids, and we (in the UK) only replace fluids with plasma boosters - we don't routinely use blood or anything like that. But if you're chucking in fluid to try and keep their blood pressure up, yes, it can be detrimental to someone with, say, a small tear in the aorta. Obviously if you greatly increase the pressure in the vessel, this will exacerbate the split in the vessel wall. You can imagine a shirt that's too small, splitting at the seam ... the principle is the same. So we tend to steer away from putting in too much fluid.

Q: Is there anyway to tell at the scene whether or not someone has internal injuries or bleeding?

AP: No, not definitively, although the 'mechanism of injury' should raise suspicion. You would have to be monitoring blood pressure very accurately to spot that. You would only be certain when they were opened up in theatre and you could see it pouring out.

Q: But wouldn't it be an automatic assumption in a crash as horrific as this one that the victims might have internal bleeding?

AP: Well, regardless, the idea is to get them to hospital as soon as you can.

Q: But it took more than an hour and a half for the emergency services to get Diana to a hospital which was only four miles from the crash scene.

AP: Yes, that's not right. It wouldn't be normal. But again, it's so difficult without being there. Certainly there are emergency medical treatments - protocols - they are bound by. Obviously a mechanism of injury this extreme affects all of the body - it's what we call 'multi system trauma'. It affects your circulatory, respiratory, skeletal and nervous systems, so your standard priorities are the airway and the cervical spine - breathing and circulation. I don't know if she was collared at the time to protect her cervical spine - that's where all the vital nerves come from.

Q: Presumably you would expect her to have been collared up in an accident like that - a head-on collision at 60 miles an hour?

AP: Yes - and no seat belt. Yes, definitely.

Q: And if there *was* a problem with, say, Diana's neck - might this explain why the ambulance travelled so slowly to hospital?

AP: Possibly, yes. If there was a cervical spine injury ... and that was the only injury, then I would say that I would crawl possibly, because it can be really unstable. That's why it would take longer to get off the scene maybe, because you'd have to consider that. There's no point dragging someone out carelessly, laying them on the cot and rushing them to hospital because you suspect internal bleeding. If they've got a cervical fracture up here [in the region of the neck], and they can't maintain their airway, you know. But I'd be surprised if it took half an hour to travel four miles. It was in the middle of the night wasn't it, not much traffic about?

Q: That's right, there was no traffic. It was 2 in the morning.

AP: Well yes, that does seem odd. I'd be quite disappointed. I would have been banging on the dividing window to my mate in front, telling him to get a move on!

Q: Isn't there a rule in England to get someone to hospital within the so-called 'golden hour'?

AP: It's not a rule; it's a guideline. It's a principle that's come from the States. If you've got somebody that's critically ill then they've got to be under the surgeon's knife in an hour from the time that it actually happened. We try and do that but it's not always possible.

Q: Why is that?

AP: It's just because there are so many factors involved - response time, access to the patient, extrication time and the journey to the hospital all add up. On top of this it even takes some time to perform emergency procedures - the 'meaningful interventions' - in treating the patient.

Q: But the chances of survival are greater within that first hour?

AP: Yes. The principle really revolves around the fact that you are not going to save them on the roadside; no one is going to save them on the roadside. Bring everybody out of the hospital and they still wouldn't save them on the roadside. They need to be in the clinical environment, be opened up to see where it is bleeding, and then you can basically stitch up or clamp on or whatever to stop the bleeding. And then you can start putting it right. I'm not sure about the survival prognosis with time delay, but obviously it's just going to be worse and worse and worse the more time that goes by. If you can get them to hospital quickly, that's when their chances of survival increase.

Q: So would you say that the reason the paramedics treated Diana for so long at the scene was because they considered her condition too serious to move her straight away?

AP: I wasn't there; I can't really say. But that sounds plausible, yes.

Q: And that might account for why it took so long to get her back to hospital - why the ambulance travelled so slowly?

AP: I would still say 4 miles in half an hour is what - 8 miles an hour? I would still say that's unusual.

Q: What seems even more unusual to us is that, having taken so long to travel the 4 miles from the scene of the crash, the ambulance then stopped for a further 10 minutes when it was only 800 metres from the hospital.

AP: There are few things that would be worth doing that far away. I mean, if she had a massive airway problem, and she was completely blocked up, then they might have done a tracheotomy. I don't know if they can do that in France. We can't really do it here without authorization. But that's about the only reason, because I really think that even half a minute without oxygen is serious - bearing in mind they've got to unload the patient from the vehicle and wheel them into the relevant department; it's not going to get done in the corridor.

Q: Agreed. But they had already bypassed several hospitals. Would it not have been more prudent to take her to a nearer hospital rather than running the risk of having to stop and perform a tracheotomy?

AP: Yes, definitely. I'd go to the nearest one. On the other hand, if you can imagine - there's no point me driving to a hospital with a patient from a road traffic accident if it hasn't got a casualty department, because the nurse is going to come out and just scream. We would drive past if we had to ... Also, I have never had a member of the Royal Family in my ambulance. I mean, there may have been a consideration as regards security. The others may not have been very secure hospitals.

Q: There's a hospital which is a couple of miles closer to the crash scene, Val de Grace, which specializes in VIP deliveries. It's a military hospital, so one would assume that the security at this hospital is adequate.

AP: You'd think so, yes. But again, I don't know. I can't answer that one.

Q: But purely for medical reasons. Is there any reason why the ambulance should have bypassed one hospital for another?

AP: For medical reasons I can't see why. Even if they are only a few miles apart, the amount of time it was taking them anyway - at the end of the day they could have offloaded her earlier.

Q: They drove past a hospital called Hotel Dieu, which is about two miles from the scene. They literally went past the entrance to that hospital, and went on a further two miles to the hospital where she ended up. They also bypassed Val de Grace hospital. Given that they were having to travel at a snail's pace anyway, it seems strange that they decided to go an extra two miles. Like you say, if they had offloaded her at one of the other hospitals then the surgeon could perhaps have got to her in time to save her life.

AP: Right.

Q: Do you think the reason they went on to the furthest hospital - which is called Pitie Salpetriere - might have been because some form of specialist doctor or surgeon worked there, one better equipped to save Diana's life?

AP: Specialists are nice, but you don't need them straight away There are priorities, medically speaking, that any doctor - I mean a qualified doctor - would be able to take care of. They'd have an anaesthetist at any hospital to take care of the airway, put the tube down. Once that's in it's in; there's no question about there not being a patent airway. It's just a plastic tube; you can't go wrong. There will also be surgeons there. They might not be the top-notch surgeons, but they'll still be able to swab somebody up and cut them open without making anything worse. There's no medical reason to drive past. They actually stopped after they drove past that first hospital?

Q: Yes. In fact they drove past three hospitals, then drove a further mile and then stopped for 10 minutes to treat her in the ambulance.

AP: It depends what they did. But I don't know, it's difficult to know. Unless they had a brand new trauma department that had just been finished, purpose-built to treat patients like that, I can't see why they would drive past a competent hospital. I bet the doctors at the first hospital were furious. I mean, at the end of the day, they could easily have taken her to the first hospital and sent for the surgeon. He could have been there before she arrived.

If there was a particular surgeon he could have driven to the other hospital and treated her there. It was only a mile or two away?

Q: Yes, that's right. There were five other hospitals nearer to the crash scene than Pitie Salpetriere.

AP: Then they could have taken her straight to the nearest one and if they were short of qualified surgeons they could have sent for one.

Q: Quite. Thanks for your help, Andy.

AP: My pleasure. I hope it's of some use.

CHAPTER 4

THE SOURCES (Part 1)
The Avebury Meetings
by Jon King

"...[This information] came into my possession some short while ago, and it concerns a plot to eliminate one of the most prominent figures on the world stage ... I do not know precisely where or when the hit will take place. I do not know the precise schedule. But so far as I have been made aware it has been planned for a good many months and it will take place within days from now ... very soon ... I can tell you, Jon, this one will be bigger than Kennedy..."

'Stealth', US Special Forces veteran and CIA contract agent, 23rd August, 1997 - one week prior to Diana's death.

Raw Information

In the *Introduction* I explained that our investigation into Diana's death was the result of information received one week prior to the crash in Paris. I should stress that, while our investigation does not at all depend on this information, it was nevertheless the catalyst which initiated our interest. For this reason we have elected to include this chapter here.

As stated at the beginning of *Chapter Two*, this book was never intended as an investigation into the crash itself. But rather into the 'political and historical motives' which we believe lay behind Diana's death. In a sense this chapter is the start of that investigation. Indeed, our purpose in including it here is first and foremost to lay the foundation for Book Two: *Agencies Of Masonic Government*, in which we endeavour to present a comprehensive dossier on the agencies which stand accused of murder. And of course, those which stand accused of '*conspiracy* to murder' - the unseen financial and industrial oligarchs whose corporate empire, in effect, rules the Western world.

Also, of course, given that we are assuming the position of 'prosecuting counsels' in this case, we feel morally bound to present you, the jury, with all the evidence. Certainly to call our main sources to the witness-stand, so to speak. Of course, we could easily have omitted this chapter; it would have weakened our case not at all, perhaps even strengthened it. The fact that some unseen, anonymous 'source' elected to supply us with information, in secret - and the added fact that this information has been corroborated only by a second 'anonymous' source - simply would not stand up in a court of law. On its own it bears little credibility. We are acutely aware of this. Nevertheless the fact remains that it was this information which first prompted us to investigate this case. In our endeavour to be as open and frank as we possibly can - to tell you the whole story, as it unfolded, even though parts of that story might at first seem incredible, and indeed less relevant than the line of inquiry pursued in the previous chapters - even so we have elected to present this information here, in its raw state: *as it came to us*. Over the course of the proceedings we will of course endeavour to uphold and substantiate its credibility by presenting supporting evidence for all the major points raised. In so doing we hope that its relevance - indeed, its credibility - will in the end become evident enough.

In any event, what follows is a minimally edited account of how this information was received. And a detailed rendering - so far as I am permitted - of precisely the information gleaned from this source. It is not pretty. Indeed, in parts it is extremely ugly, unpalatable. In other parts it is seemingly bereft of all plausibility. But we must remember that it comes from a man who has spent perhaps too long in a world where fact and fiction merge to create a reality all their own - the wholly paranoid world of counter-espionage and above-top-secret deep-cover operations. Perhaps because of this, however, it does offer an insight into the mind of a man embittered by his long experience of serving corporate agendas which, according to him at any rate, eclipse those pursued by our elected governments. In this regard, of course, it also offers an overview of how and why assassinations such as that alleged to have killed Diana can be sanctioned from the highest level - without, necessarily, the knowledge or complicity of our elected representatives. Thus it constitutes a foundation for the line of inquiry pursued in Book Two. And thus - and only thus - we recommend this evidence to the jury.

The Contact

"Mr King?" It was copy deadline week, and accordingly I was to be found staring blankly at my computer screen, endeavouring with little enthusiasm to polish the final draft of a story which had been dumped on my desk a few moments earlier. But then, I guess that has always been the problem with copy deadline week: leave aside any current investigations, no matter how pressing, and attend to the mundane bread-and-butter task of editing - preparing this month's copy for public consumption. In this respect the telephone call I had just taken was a welcome distraction.

"Speaking." Hitting the button on my tape recorder I leaned back in my seat and checked my wristwatch, a habit. It was 11:45 am.

"I've just read your article on the US government's covert activities underground," the American accent calmly informed me. *"Project Noah's Ark.* Very interesting."

"Thank you."

"Sure."

"So how can I help you?"

"The article prompted me to call. I have some information."

"Go on."

A short pause, then: "It would be best if you left your office," I was told in a more critical tone. "We'll talk on another line. Go to a public call box and call this number, soon as you can." A mobile (cell) telephone number was given; I took it down.

"Can you tell me your name?" I said, probing, still jotting down the contact number, suspicious the man I was talking to would turn out to be yet another time-waster, one of a good many who had called in the past bearing similar promises, but who in the end had proved to be either hoaxers or people of unstable mind. At the same time, of course, I was hopeful he would turn out to be one of the very few who in the end prove genuine.

"Who should I ask for?" I ventured. "Can you ... hello?" But the line was already dead; the caller had hung up. In an instinctive attempt to trace the number I dialled *one-four-seven-one*, but to no avail -

We do not have the caller's number, a female voice told me.

- the number had been withheld.

Duly intrigued I reset the telephone in its cradle, turned off the tape recorder (which was wired to my telephone), waited a further minute or so, then got up from my desk and left the office, discreetly. So far as any of my colleagues knew I was off to purchase a sandwich for lunch.

As the caller remarked, I had recently been working on a case involving the investigation of government activities underground. Claims made by a number of independent witnesses (for a number of different reasons) pointed to the fact that a series of highly covert and extremely controversial military-industrial test programmes were in process, both in Britain and the United States. Or more precisely, several hundred feet *beneath* Britain and the United States. In short, many witness claims suggested that, deep inside some of the British and US governments' most top-secret deep-underground installations, some pretty nefarious activities were taking place. In the main these activities were said to involve secret-technology projects and highly illegal genetics, eugenics and cloning programmes (together with other biochemical and biotechnological programmes), the equal of which could only be imagined - and even then, only in one's most horrific nightmares. It was my report concerning the US programmes in this regard which had prompted the mystery caller to contact me. My hope now was that he would be able to pass some relevant information my way regarding Britain's endeavours in this same regard. I was not to be disappointed.

"...It's Jon King returning your call." A gusty November wind was whipping through the call box in which I now stood. I guessed it was probably a group of local kids with nothing much better to do who had smashed the glass panels on the call box door, both at face-height and again three panels further down. Indeed, I wondered if it was this same purposeless gang who had partially unhinged the door into the bargain - a gap tall enough for an ambitious limbo dancer to slither under now existed between the foot of the door and the concrete on which I stood. To make matters worse, the line was bad, the stranger's voice faint and breaking up. I pressed a thumb to my ear in an attempt to silence the drone of passing traffic.

"We should meet," I managed to decipher through the fizz of the mobile's poor-quality signal. "It would be easier that way."

"Well, with respect I'm a busy man," I said, fencing. "I really need to know..."

"It'll be worth your time," the voice calmly assured. "But the information I have for you is ... best not divulged over the telephone."

I paused for a brief moment at this point, quickly trying to measure the man - his tone, his character, his quiet, almost serene authority. Such cursory assessments are not always successful, of course. But more often than not they are. And in any case, in situations such as these there is scarcely the time to compile a casebook. He seemed sound enough. And until I could shake him by the hand and look him in the eye, that was all I had to go by. "Do you have anywhere particular in mind?" I said.

"Avebury," came the reply. "Avebury Stone Circles in Wiltshire. You know the place?"

"I do, yes." In fact I knew it very well. "When?"

"This Saturday, midday, in the car park opposite the Post Office."

I made a note. My pad was recording the conversation as we spoke it. "OK," I said, finally. "How will I recognize you?"

"You won't," the voice affirmed. "I'll recognize you. Saturday. Midday. Avebury. Opposite the Post Office. Are we agreed?"

"I'll be there."

That said, the line *clicked* dead. Not for the first time that day the man who for the next nine months was to be my most informative and penetrative contact within the paranoid world of British and US counter-intelligence hung up on me. Whereupon the call box ate my change.

I headed for the baker's shop.

At least next time there would be no windy call boxes, I thought to myself as I braved the chill, autumnal weather and made my way back across the street towards the smell of bread and cakes. At least next time we would talk face to face.

Stealth

Avebury was even colder than the call box had been. But at least it was good, clean country air, and aesthetically a good deal more pleasing to the eye than the high street in which the call box had stood. I consoled myself with these thoughts as I wrapped up against the bleak November day.

I had arrived at the Avebury car park about fifteen minutes earlier than our arranged meeting time. As usual it was more or less full, but from what I could make out my contact had not yet arrived. Having parked my car and gathered my attaché case I wandered over to the car park entrance and sat myself down on the ledge of a vacant wall, watching for the arrival of a single middle-aged male, which was the mental picture I had formulated on speaking to the mystery caller on the telephone. I did not have to wait long for his arrival. Moreover, as he drove into the car park I noted that the mental picture I had formulated was about right.

In fact he looked how you might imagine a mildly successful, late middle-aged businessman to look - around six feet, slightly overweight, thinning to grey on top and driving a silver Vauxhall Carlton. His handshake was firm.

Following a brief introduction we wandered out through the car park's rear entrance - a wooden field-gate that led into a grazing meadow famed for its sheep and megalithic standing stones. Despite the chill weather there were a good many other people strolling around the field, but none seemed too interested in anyone else. On the contrary, all seemed preoccupied with their own private business - milling round, chatting, taking photos of the stones (sometimes even the sheep): generally being tourists. In this respect it was a good place to talk about matters secret and classified.

My contact gave no name. For purposes of identification I have always referred to him (in my previous works) as 'Stealth'. On this particular occasion Stealth told me a little about his background and his reasons for wishing to pass information my way. He described these reasons as "personal", though this was said with some bitterness, as though by betraying his employers he was able to gain some amount of personal satisfaction. Possibly even revenge. I should stress, however, that this is my own interpretation.

He did imply, though, that he and a small faction within "the Agency" were keen to ensure that "certain information" made its way out into the public domain. On more than one occasion he voiced - in no uncertain terms - his disapproval of the high levels of political power wielded by the "corporate-funded intelligence community". He believed in democracy, he said. And he did not like what he had discovered with regard to the manipulation of democratically elected governments by extremely powerful cabals within the military-industrial complex. In particular, he said, he was unhappy with the way the intelligence community had, in effect, become the instrument by which much of this political manipulation was achieved. Indeed, in many respects, it had become little more than a "corporate watchdog", he said.

With regard to himself, Stealth told me that he was a US Special Forces veteran of several campaigns; that he had been involved in numerous covert operations run by the CIA, and that lately he had been assigned to a highly covert CIA/SIS cell stationed in Britain (SIS: Britain's *Secret Intelligence Service*, broadly known as MI6). He did not tell me exactly what this cell had been set up to achieve, though he did say that it operated at the bidding of a very powerful cabal within the British- and US-based military-industrial complex.

"SIS and CIA do the bidding of these people." he told me with some disdain. "We always do the bidding of these people."

According to Stealth, the higher echelons of British and US intelligence work hand-in-glove. Certainly he affirmed that this was the case with regard to MI6 and the CIA. In this regard, the joint British/US intelligence cell to which he had been assigned was so furtive, he said, its operations so covert, that its orders seldom - if ever - issued from the appropriate departments, from the offices of our elected representatives in Government. Rather they issued from some unseen and democratically unaccountable cabal made up of what Stealth referred to as "financial, industrial and political godfathers ... [who] operate quite independently of the law". Some very high-level military and intelligence chiefs also comprise part of this cabal, he said.

He also said that many of the highly covert, highly illegal operations carried out at the behest of these people are done so behind the smokescreen of National Security. He emphasized this point. The National Security screen was formulated to protect military secrets, he wanted me to understand - to ensure that top-secret military operations, experiments and programmes could be conducted behind closed doors, away from the prying eyes of Cold War Soviet spies and/or terrorists. But these days, he said, these same laws were being enforced illegally. The most dangerous secrets were no longer military, he explained; they were corporate. The most dangerous secrets were no longer being kept from Soviet spies, but from the public at large. The Cold War, he was keen to remind me, ended almost a decade ago.

"It's the kind of behaviour that flies in the face of democracy and the democratic freedoms on which our world is allegedly run," he said with some fervour. "And it is wholly unacceptable. These people are getting away with murder, sometimes literally."

He went on: "If I were to tell you all I know about the military-industrial complex, Jon - about the quasi-security and intelligence agencies and their underhand operations; about the *modus operandi* of some of the complex's most powerful chiefs - you would quickly become as old and embittered as I am." He let a half-smile lighten his face at this point.

A heartbeat later he banished it. "Not very far from here there are secret-technology programmes and experiments being carried out that would shock and astound you. But you cannot see them. You cannot see them because they're being conducted underground. And what is more they're being conducted in secret, concealed by what you have in this country - the Official Secrets Act. That is illegal. It is illegal because of the nature of the programmes involved. They are using the laws of National Security to further their own secret political ends. It riles me. It is fundamentally wrong."

Over the course of the following months Stealth was to underline precisely what those 'fundamental wrongs' were.

It was for these reasons that Stealth had decided to seek me out and talk to me, then. He had read my reports concerning my own investigations into these matters, he said, and he had decided to pass what relevant information he could my way, in particular with regard to the secret technological and biochemical programmes being carried out by the British- and US-based military-industrial complex, underground. And more specifically - so far as I was concerned at the time - those being carried out by the supersecret aerospace industry, both in Britain and the US, also underground. Much of that information forms the basis for my previous works.

But it is the information which is *not* contained in any of my previous works which is of paramount importance here. Indeed, it is this very information which, in effect, led to the publication of this book.

And once again, it came my way during a meeting with Stealth at Avebury.

Corporate Government

I met up with Stealth twice during the summer of 1997, and on both occasions he voiced his concerns about how long our meetings could and should continue. As it turned out, the second meeting that summer proved to be our last.

We had already met too many times for his own peace of mind, he said (we met four times in all). And in any case, he had by this time told me just about all he had intended to tell me regarding the aerospace industry's secret-technology projects. The same applied, he said, to the British and US governments' ongoing endeavours to construct and maintain deep-underground test facilities. And the dubious activities undertaken in them.

However, I should perhaps include here a few sentiments expressed by Stealth during a previous meeting. I feel that they are pertinent to understanding something of his reasons for divulging classified information to me, and thereby his reasons for choosing to tell me what he eventually did about the death of Princess Diana.

"What I'm about to give you is an overview of the situation as I have come to perceive it," he began. "It may not be absolutely correct, but it is close.

"For the past fifty years administrations in the West have become infected with a cancer called corporate government ... It all began immediately after the Second World War, when the corporate monopoly that ... funded the war effort really began to impose itself on peacetime administrations. The banks and the loan companies that had loaned money to the US, to Britain *and* to Hitler for the manufacture and supply of arms, suddenly began to call in their debts ... the entire operation was orchestrated from Switzerland ... It still is...

"...Around this time huge multinational corporations suddenly started springing up as a result of the rebuilding programmes ... [these programmes] spawned the new industries - the nuclear industry, the aerospace industry, pharmaceuticals, and other opportunist industries in science, defence and new technology. This is what I mean by the corporate government. It all kicked in immediately after the war, built on the proceeds of war ... on the misappropriated funds garnered as a result of the war's debtors paying back their loans to the world's banks and loan companies ... That was when the CIA was formed. And it wasn't long before it was running operations for the corporate government...

"...Slowly the CIA grew, or rather I should say pretty damn *quickly* the CIA grew into a ... well, in effect into a corporate giant itself ... It became the corporate world's own intelligence agency. It was funded by corporate money and so it was obliged to serve corporate agendas. It was never run by the White House - nor by any other democratically elected body - but by a joint British and American oligarchy ... basically the same oligarchy that was responsible for the founding of America and its Constitution under George

Washington ... [This oligarchy] still exists; it is extremely right-wing in its political orientation ... [and] it is run by some of the world's most powerful financial and industrial godfathers ... Its operations are run out of Virginia...

"...Well this [corporate government] soon became the authority to which the CIA answered. By the late 1950s the White House was crawling with CIA. By the time Kennedy took office, the 'intelligence coup' was complete...

"...That got Kennedy in all kinds of trouble. It was why he formed the DIA [US: *Defence Intelligence Agency*] in 1961 ... so that the White House, the President, would have at least one official agency working *for* him, and not *against* him ... The CIA and FBI were undermining everything he did, every major decision and democratic action he took ... By that time the CIA received over fifty per cent of its annual budget from corporate sources ... and the CIA and MI6 in Virginia were getting up to some pretty dirty tricks together...

"...It was the CIA and MI6 who finally took Kennedy out. The Mafia may have pulled the trigger, but it was the CIA who loaded the gun. It was MI6 who showed them how to do it...

"...Remember [the] CIA was formed by MI6. The same British and US corporate oligarchy that controls the CIA also controls MI6 ... The CIA was formed on MI6 blueprints. At the highest level the two agencies are still one and the same beast. That, Jon, is why I'm here. That is why I am stationed in Britain with the CIA. My agency and yours are run by the same godfathers...

"...I always refer to these people as 'godfathers' because that is what they are. They are the owners, directors and manipulators of the world's largest financial institutions and multinational arms, drugs, fuel and technology companies. Plus a few others I could mention. And they employ politicians and intelligence agencies just like they employ everybody else...

"...These people are rarely seen on a public stage. Their voices are seldom heard in a political arena. But you can be sure that their policies are the ones that will be implemented above all others, because their influence is what gives political power to the representatives you think you appoint to office...

"...The people you think you vote into office are ... in truth they are appointed by 'the sponsors'. And 'the sponsors' are the fat cats I have just told you about - the financial, industrial and political godfathers who preside over the actions and policies that govern the corporate world. By comparison, governing a country is chicken feed. Domestic politics is always a knock-on - the result of decisions already taken in the world of corporate politics. At best it's a by-product of the policies already sanctioned in the world of corporate government...

"...After all, who sets the exchange rates: the finance ministers or the governors of the world banks? Who sets policy: the president or the corporate executive that funds his campaign? I'm sure you can answer these questions for yourself...

"...Today I'm about to tell you, to show you just how powerful these people are ... just how far they are prepared to go to keep the world turning in the direction they want it to turn in. If that means the assassination of the President, or Martin Luther King, or John Lennon ... or anybody else for that matter, Jon ... [anybody else] with the ability, the charisma to reach the people ... [and] galvanize public opinion into actions against the status quo, well then so be it. Martin Luther King and John Lennon are simply the best-known examples of what I'm saying. I've already told you how James Earl Ray and Mark Chapman were CIA fall guys ... in the trade they are known as 'sleeper agents'...

"...I can tell you, Jon, I have seen things you would not believe. I have done things no man should ever do, and I'm tired because of it. But ... next to these people I guess I'm not so bad. Compared to economics human life means very little to these people."

Over the course of several further meetings Stealth went on to tell me some of what he knew about the British- and US-based military-industrial complex and its manipulation of world events. Much of this manipulation was achieved, he said, via what he referred to as the 'corporate wing' of the CIA and MI6. As we were to discover, and as presented in our chapters on *MI6* and *The CIA* in Book Two, there is far more substance to these claims than one might first imagine. Indeed, the claim that these two agencies might have combined to effect the assassination of Diana, Princess of Wales, became all the more plausible as our investigation progressed. As Stealth affirmed, and as we were to discover, at the top end of the chain MI6 and the CIA are indeed inseverable bed partners. If not interminable lovers.

In matters of international consequence, the one rarely acts without the other's express compliance.

One Last Pearl

Before parting company for what was almost certainly to be the final time (Saturday, 23rd August, 1997) Stealth told me that he wished to leave me with "one last pearl" of information, designed, for the most part, to substantiate his credential. He would tell me something that had not yet come to pass, he said. When it did come to pass I would at least know that he was indeed party to information unavailable in the public domain. Moreover, that he was party to information of the most highly sensitive and classified nature. In essence, this was the motive behind his decision to pass the following information my way.

Seating himself on a fallen 'standing stone', then, staring thoughtfully ahead, Stealth left me with the following, astonishing monologue - during which, I feel I should offer fair warning, *he did not mince his words*. I should add that the transcript has been minimally edited for publication.

"Remember I told you how certain people were taken out, people whose message was a threat because of their popularity, and because of their ability to mobilize public opinion - Kennedy, Martin Luther King, John Lennon, and others...?"

I do, yes.

"Well, Jon, I have in my possession some information. It might make an angle on which to build your story. It might not. But, well ... whatever you choose to do with it is fine by me...

"...[This information] came into my possession some short while ago, and it concerns a plot to eliminate one of the most prominent figures on the world stage, someone like Martin Luther King and John Lennon, someone with the ability to undermine the social and political control mechanisms currently in place...

"...I do not know precisely where or when the hit will take place. I do not know the precise schedule. But so far as I have been made aware it has been planned for a good many months and it will take place within days from now ... very soon ... I can tell you, Jon, this one will be bigger than Kennedy ... even my own sources are extremely nervous about this one. Provision for public reaction has already been considered. They have good experience of how to deal with public reaction ... it's being taken care of as we speak. The media is being primed, as we speak."

He went on: "I'm telling you this so that you can believe more readily what I have told you already, so that at least you'll know [that] the information I have given you is genuine ... so you can be assured that my sources are genuine. I really can't say what use this information will be to you other than that...

"...You must understand that I do not expect you to put your neck on the line with this. This is not evidence; you will never find the hard evidence necessary to prove a thing with this. I'm aware that you're unlikely to believe what I'm saying anyway, and I can't blame you for that." He turned and caught my eye at this point: "At least until it happens," he added. "At least until what I'm telling you actually happens. Then you'll believe it."

Just then a small party of tourists ambled by, some making

conversation, others seemingly prone to a world which existed only in their own thoughts. Momentarily Stealth fell silent. As the last of the tourists passed us by, I couldn't help but wonder how people might react should Stealth's information prove correct: should someone of global renown - "within days from now" - truly meet an untimely and horrific end, the result of political assassination. The prospect was chilling. So much so that, in a perverse kind of way, I was glad when Stealth resumed. It snapped me away from the growing sense of trepidation which was by now everywhere in me.

"...I was told that this person has to go for a good many reasons" he went on. "Not the least because they have become 'carcinogenic to the system'. That's a quote, which basically means they have become a threat to the stability of corporate government, just like John Lennon and the others before him, the others I've told you about. To the bastards who run things this person has become a cancer in the system; this is what I was told, verbatim. Listen carefully to what I'm saying here, Jon. This person has become a 'loose cannon on a world stage'. That's another quote. This person has upset an awful lot of very influential, very powerful people ... people of the calibre I have already told you about."

Can you tell me who this person is?

"I'll tell you what I know, Jon - you must read between the lines this time ... Someone big is going to get hit. That is all I can say for now."

He added a few moments later: "So far as I have been made aware ... well, you'll know soon enough who it is. And then you'll know that what I'm telling you is live intelligence. It's hot. So keep your lips sealed and your ear to the ground. Watch the news networks ... I can promise you one thing: it'll be bigger than Kennedy."

This information was imparted to me on Saturday, 23rd August, 1997, one week prior to Diana's tragic and mysterious death. Though Stealth never mentioned either Princess Diana or Dodi Fayed by name, I was nevertheless stunned as news of their tragic death became the day's sole headline one week later. I still cannot be certain that this information and Diana's death are linked, of course. On the other hand, I will never be convinced that they are not.

On leaving, Stealth made a point of reiterating that, in his opinion, the information that he had given me would make "a compelling read". He had already said that the information "might make an angle on which to build your story". And both times he'd said it in such a way that made me stop and think. It was as though he wished to affirm an ulterior reason for letting the information pass my way. He knew I was a journalist, of course, and that I could be trusted - that I would be more likely than most to follow up on the information and publish as much as I was able to corroborate. This much I had already done with the previous information he had given me. There was no reason for him to assume that I would not do the same again.

But I should also state that, in this instance, I sensed that *somebody other than Stealth* wanted this information in the public domain: that he was not alone in wanting this information published. Indeed, from what I learned of the man during our brief acquaintanceship, and from what I have since gleaned from other sources, I now suspect that Stealth was simply a 'go-between' or 'mouthpiece': that he was perhaps part of a more liberal faction within British and US intelligence who evidently opposed the assassination, but were powerless to prevent it. And who thus decided to spotlight it instead.

It is my belief that Stealth passed this information my way precisely for this reason. And it is precisely for this reason that we present it to you here in these pages.

BOOK TWO

AGENCIES OF MASONIC GOVERNMENT

"The Bilderberg Group was founded in 1954, an outgrowth of various right-wing and anti-communist organisations such as the American Committee for a United Europe ... It has connections with the CIA, OSS, Trilateral Commission, Council on Foreign Relations and other shadowy organisations ... To this day no one knows if this is its real name since it goes to any lengths to avoid publicity and membership is highly secret...

...The minutes of the group's first meeting recorded that one of its primary interests was in "evolving an international order" which would "look beyond the present crisis", and this goal of creating a one world government still seems to be its driving force. In 1989, it was alleged to have plotted the political assassination of Margaret Thatcher, because of "her refusal to yield British Sovereignty to the European Superstate...""

The Guardian, 1st October, 1993.

CHAPTER 5

MASONIC GOVERNMENT
Establishing The Corporate Initiative

"Give me control over a nation's currency, and I care not who makes its laws."

Mayer Amschel Rothschild (1743-1812)

Corporate Oligarchy

In view of the information received from Stealth (plus further information gleaned from our own research, and that from other sources - in particular see this chapter and *Sources Part 2*) throughout the course of this book the term 'corporate' and/or 'masonic government' will be employed. References to the various agencies associated with and utilized by masonic government will be made, and the agencies themselves cited with regard to the death of Diana, Princess of Wales. We felt it thus pertinent to include here a more in-depth description of what is meant by the term 'masonic government'.

As will be further explained in *The Sources (Part 2)*, the term 'masonic government' will be used here to describe the secretive, hierarchical structures and processes set up to orchestrate the machinations of corporate power. The claim is that, behind the Western world's democratically elected governments, there lurks a hidden, masonically structured body of financial, industrial and political oligarchs who, according to Stealth at any rate, "operate quite independently of the law". It is this 'corporate oligarchy' to which the title 'masonic government' has been given in this book, and at which the finger has been squarely pointed with regard to the death of Diana, Princess of Wales. This is a claim, of course, which is yet to be proven. But in any event, that this corporately funded, masonically structured oligarchy exists, that it does indeed operate above the law and that it influences to its own advantage the policies and economies of nation states worldwide, is in little doubt. As corporate power-broker and masonic-government architect, Mayer Amschel Rothschild, affirmed when formulating his plan of economic inductance as long ago as the eighteenth century: "Give me control over a nation's currency, and I care not who makes its laws."

Mayer Amschel Rothschild, of course, was right: his descendants -

and others like them - have been running the world ever since.

Or if not the entire world, then vast portions of it.

But perhaps the point so far as we are concerned is that it was this same corporate oligarchy - represented by such institutions as the Monarchy; the Church; Parliament; Congress; the so-called Democratic State - which came under threat from what it perceived as the "antics" of Princess Diana. Indeed, it was this very power structure that first christened her a "loose cannon". In the minds of the public, of course, those "antics" were seen in a different light entirely. Though it is little surprise that the princess was perceived as a "loose cannon" by those adversely affected by her humanitarian work, conversely, she was perceived by the public as a latter-day saint, in the truest sense of that term. And rightly so, we believe. While we do not wish to canonize Diana, it is nonetheless a sad day indeed when the exploits of someone - someone whose sole intent is to alleviate the sufferings of the forgotten majority - are perceived as a threat by what, in effect, is the ruling minority. And there can be little doubt that she was indeed perceived as a threat by this ruling minority. Equally, there can be little doubt that this ruling minority is a corporate one - that it is a plutocracy of the most brutal and insidious kind.

And that, when forced to the brink, it will retaliate in a swift and decisive manner. The fate of such luminaries as JFK and Martin Luther King bears ample testimony to this end.

But who or what, exactly, is this ruling minority? What exactly is corporate power? And perhaps equally pertinent: just how powerful is it? Just how did the corporate world come to gain such a monopoly on the economic and political structures endemic to the modern - so-called 'democratic' - world?

As stated above, the hypothesis here is that corporate power effectively governs the Western world, together with large portions of the rest of it. Whether or not this hypothesis proves ultimately correct, one thing is for sure: when push comes to shove, corporate power decisively eclipses the authority of Congress and Parliament alike. This is a bold statement, to be sure. But when the entire picture is presented and scrutinized it becomes perhaps less questionable, more evident. We should bear in mind here that corporate power is engendered and sustained by unlimited financial resources - resources upon which nation-state governments depend. It is a power that assures the preservation of such corporately governed institutions as the Monarchy, the Vatican and the Anglican Church (contrary to popular belief, the Anglican Church upholds and promotes the corporate banner in more than 150 countries worldwide). At the same time, it is corporate power - corporate funding - that subsidizes the Western world's nation-state budgets and underwrites its national debts to boot. And in so doing, of course, holds sway over just about every national government outside of Russia. And China.

Indeed, it is only the resistance of these two Communist superpowers that has thus far safeguarded the global economy from complete takeover by the West's financial institutions. One wonders how long this situation will prevail, however. In its endeavour to spin the volatile Russian economy into the international loop, for example, the 'corporate wing' of the CIA is reported to have forged links with the Russian Mafia. Indeed, the exploits of the Russian Mafia - for the most part made up of the former Soviet Union's most powerful financiers and industrialists, plus some of its most senior military and intelligence chiefs - have been largely responsible for the massive post-Cold War downturn in the Russian economy. (Some say this is a deliberate ploy on the part of the Russian Mafia and the CIA to force intervention, and thereby an effective degree of political and economic control, by America and the West - in whose relatively buoyant economies, of course, most of the Russian Mafia's illegal assets are invested.) A concerted effort to entice China into the fold is also under way. If one could but see it, the much-prophesied New World Order-One World Government scenario is being played out in front of our very eyes. At least in an economic sense. But then, as Mayer Amschel Rothschild declared when laying the foundation for his family-owned corporate empire, control of a nation's (the world's) economy equals control of its policy. And control of policy is absolute government. There are no two ways about that.

As explained by Stealth, though pursued for some three hundred years and more (since the establishment of the central banking system in the West, circa mid-to-late seventeenth century), in effect the corporate monopoly on national and international politics began to establish itself as an internationally structured body immediately following WWII. It was then that the vast, multinational financial and industrial corporations which today govern economic policy, and indeed, which exist on such a massive and unprecedented scale, emerged as an autonomous economic entity. It is known, for example, that, under directive from some of the world's most powerful families and institutions, the more successful independent post-war companies agreed to merge in order to gain monopolies on the new industries spawned as a result of the war. These mergers resulted in the formation of hugely powerful international cartels, and in some cases, conglomerate organizations, known today as 'multinational corporations'. The 'corporate initiative' had arrived. And before long it had resulted in a collaborative effort on the part of British and US intelligence to form corporations of their own - and moreover, to recruit the cream of the world's scientists and engineers necessary to make them successful. Many of these scientists and engineers were recruited from the ranks of the Third Reich, as we shall see. Many more learned their skills from teams of specially selected Nazi collaborators who, in exchange for post-war freedom, agreed to work hand-in-glove with British and US intelligence agencies in order to help establish this new 'corporate initiative'. It was an initiative that would serve well to advance ambitions for a masonically structured and corporately run United States of Europe. The fact that the CIA was formed, in part, to orchestrate this initiative, meant that its outcome was virtually assured from the outset.

Even today, high-ranking intelligence chiefs and deep-cover intelligence operatives populate the boards of many of the world's foremost oil, science, technology, arms and aerospace corporations - plus a host of others, including many of the world's most successful publishing and communications giants, and of course, most of the world's major-league financial institutions. Indeed, it would be true to say that many of these corporations comprise little more than 'front organizations' for British and US intelligence agencies. In many respects, this is the same as saying that they act as 'front organizations' for the CIA. Or at least that they work hand-in-glove with the world's *central* intelligence agency, continuing a tradition which has seen the CIA develop into the world's most powerful 'intelligence corporation'. In this regard, the CIA today is about as multinational as you can get, incorporating in its worldwide web any number of foreign intelligence agencies - Britain's MI6, Germany's BND and Israel's Mossad first among them. In terms of international policy-mongering in the so-called modern world, these agencies and others should be understood as little more than foreign-territory CIA outlets, as we shall see.

Since the formation of the CIA in 1947, then, these multinational cartels, corporations and other conglomerates have served the international agenda well, and indeed have grown to megalithic proportions in the process. Today they monopolize most every area of international commerce and industry (including, of course, the vastly profitable arms trade, which in turn includes the *anti-personnel landmines trade*). And they are known to utilize the well-established nexus of international intelligence channels in order to maintain this end. Indeed, it is our contention that this massively networked and masonically structured corporate body, in effect, runs the modern world. And the fact that it does means that some departments within the Western world's most powerful intelligence agencies are free to act without prior sanction from the democratically elected governments they - supposedly - represent (indeed, without regard for the laws by which those governments govern, and over which they are appointed to preside).

In the final analysis, and at the top end of the chain, these agencies are wholly unaccountable to the democratic system they are sworn to serve and preserve. Agencies like MI5, MI6 and the CIA, for example. And the global propaganda machine they largely own - a machine known more commonly as the media.

CHAPTER 6

MI5
And The Squidgygate Affair

"They [MI5] do it regularly. They have literally hundreds of hours of transcripts ... They are bugging all the Royals from the Queen downwards ... Even as I speak, Diana is being bugged ... They think she is unstable and could go off and do something - they want to know exactly what is in her mind."

James Whitaker, Royal Correspondent for the *Mirror*, (quote from the *People*, May 16th, 1993).

*

"Clandestine surveillance by the Security Services on the most intimate of situations was to culminate later in the assassination of Diana, Princess of Wales, of this I have no doubt."

Former Royal Personal Protection Officer, Mike Grey, October 1999.

Security Service

Before taking a more in-depth look at the structure and activities of MI6, we felt it pertinent here to include a brief outline of perhaps Britain's best-known intelligence agency, MI5. Officially known as the Security Service, MI5 (Military Intelligence Department 5) was established in 1909 as the domestic or internal arm of Britain's Secret Service Bureau. The 'Service' was set up, first and foremost, as a counter-intelligence agency under Sir Vernon Kell, a British Army Captain tasked with countering the efforts of German espionage agents in Britain. This remit effectively continued throughout World War I, and indeed, throughout the decade or so that followed.

However, in 1931, with the burgeoning threat of Soviet Communism looming menacingly on the Eastern horizon, and of course, of Fascist Germany even closer to home, MI5 began to assume new and broader responsibilities.

These included the assessment of threats to Britain's national security by a new breed of foreign spy - Russian and German espionage agents infiltrating British organizations and gaining access to sensitive information, and of course, infiltrating other groups and organizations for purposes of subversion. But these 'new responsibilities' did not end there. Still largely unsupervised by Government - indeed, for the most part supervised only by its own military commanders - MI5 began a major new crackdown on British subjects seen to sympathize with what are still considered 'fringe' or 'inappropriate' political movements and ideologies. A prime target for tracking down these so-called 'subversives' was, of course, the Trade Union movement, where members were frequently and wrongly accused of being both Communist spies and Fascist spies alike. Indeed, the wave of paranoia which seemed to overwhelm the Security Service at this time was quickly to become one of tidal proportions. The official Directive defined in 1952 regarding the parameters of activities undertaken by MI5, and the subsequent Security Service Act (1989) have achieved little - if anything at all - in terms of stemming this tide. On the contrary, to judge by more recent revelations, it has risen to even greater levels of paranoia.

The official line these days is that the role of the Security Service is to monitor and act against threats to the security of the British realm. In effect, it is Britain's domestic intelligence and counter-intelligence agency, although more recently it has begun to undertake tasks more usually associated with a 'secret police' bureau. Though the Service continues to counter foreign espionage and threats of mainland terrorism, the biggest controversy today surrounds the covert activities of the departments within MI5 known as 'A' branch and 'F' branch. Between them, these branches are responsible - among other abuses - for conducting surveillance operations and maintaining secret files on what they term 'internal subversives'. These so-called 'internal subversives' include 'radicals' such as political activists; animal and human rights activists; anti-nuclear campaigners and other 'troublesome minorities'; many left-wing politicians; editors/journalists; rock musicians, actors and other high-profile celebrities who dare to voice their 'inappropriate' opinions, etc. Plus, of course, members of the Royal Family who are considered to have 'overstepped the mark'. In this regard, it is now known that MI5 mounted a massive and vigorous surveillance operation against Diana, Princess of Wales, together with a parallel operation designed to discredit her in the British media. Though MI5's actions are officially accountable to Britain's Home Secretary, it is difficult to believe that even the Tory-run Home Office of the late 1980s/ early 1990s would have sanctioned such a directive as the one which saw the princess so viciously maligned by Britain's tabloids and broadsheets alike. Indeed, we know from MI5 whistleblowers such as David Shayler - an MI5 career officer for five years during the 1990s - that the Service continues to keep hundreds of thousands of records on so-called potential subversives, such as Labour MPs Harriet Harman, Peter Mandelson and Britain's current Home Secretary, Jack Straw - as well as Patricia Hewitt, former Legal Officer and General Secretary of the human rights organization, *Liberty.* Plus a host of others. And that many of the surveillance operations, phone tappings, property buggings and break-ins undertaken by MI5 agents today are still performed without the knowledge of the elected representatives to which they are - officially, supposedly - accountable. Even the downfall of prime ministers has been attributed to MI5 chicanery, the most famous and well-documented, of course, being that of former Prime Minister Harold Wilson. Another notable case involved the bugging of former Prime Minister Edward Heath - Conservative by name, though known to have advocated policies more left-wing than many of those advocated by proponents of New Labour. Including Tony Blair. When news of the Heath bugging broke, MI5 mumbled something about the former prime minister having met with too many Eastern European diplomats. And even though these meetings were all undertaken in an official capacity, the somewhat lame excuse offered by the Security Service was upheld. No action was filed against the Service. Indeed, the whole affair was officially denied. But then, with regard to the activities undertaken by such masonic agencies as MI5, denial, it would seem, is the name of the game.

Further contentious areas into which this secret policing agency has recently been entered include organized crime, illegal immigration, and even instances of welfare fraud. While these are certainly issues in need of address - indeed, which need to be tackled - Britain has a perfectly adequate, well-trained and well-resourced (and perhaps more importantly, a well-regulated) police force mandated to achieve this very end. Some of the more extreme powers invested in MI5, for example, do not - thankfully - apply with regard to the police. Phone tapping, property bugging, breaking-and-entering, covert surveillance - these are all operations for which the police must seek sanction from elected authority before they can implement them. MI5, on the other hand - certainly in this regard, and as recent revelations have shown - is a law unto itself. As the former Chief Constable of Devon and Cornwall Police, John Alderson, commented following revelations that MI5 was to broaden its remit even further to include investigations into organized crime: "It is fatal to let the Secret Service into the area of ordinary crime. MI5 is not under the same restraints as the police. They [MI5] infiltrate organizations, people's jobs and lives. They operate almost like a cancer." Former Chief Constable Alderson concluded that, in his opinion, MI5 should remain a domestic counter-intelligence organization or bust. He likened the expansion of MI5's remit to include the investigation of crime as a move towards the creation of a "Stasi" - a reference to former East Germany's ruthless 'secret police' bureau of that name.

And anyone who has ever suffered the indignity of coming under the MI5 microscope would surely agree with him.

Dirty Work

For the record, MI5 is officially divided into a number of departments, or 'branches', each with its own operational directive. Populating the sum of these branches is a staff of around 2000 (the current official figure is 1850). And they all work within an annual budget officially estimated at around £200 million.

As mentioned above, 'A' branch is allocated the task of breaking into private properties, planting bugs, intimidating 'targets' and generally snooping around. Officially, these kind of activities come under the heading of 'surveillance'. 'B' branch has the rather more laborious and bureaucratic task of dealing with personnel. Equally bureaucratic is the work undertaken by 'C' branch, which includes vetting civil servants and other government officials, and ensuring the security of Britain's state offices. Precisely what 'D' and 'E' branches get up to is anybody's guess (assuming they exist); they are not included in the official MI5 handout.

Surprisingly, though, the activities of 'F' branch are indeed elucidated, at least to some meagre degree. In effect, this department specializes in prying into the personal affairs of those it deems 'subversive', although it also conducts surveillance operations against the threat of mainland terrorist activities, including those of the IRA. And because it does, all other activities undertaken by this branch are deemed 'justifiable'.

There is another, even more mysterious and little-known department within the Security Service. Allegedly it is called MI9. This highly covert department is said to consist of six Signals Intelligence Officers (officially designated 'civil servants') whose specific task it is to monitor telephone calls made by the Royal Family. Though most members of the Royal Household are unaware that their every conversation is being eavesdropped, justification for the activities of MI9 falls under the heading of 'protective security'. In other words, the Security Service justifies the fact that it secretly listens to even the most intimate calls made by members of the Royal Family by claiming that this action is undertaken to ensure each individual member's safety - to ensure, for example, that they have not been kidnapped, or that they are not in any other kind of danger. While this justification may seem defensible to some, one can only trust that such powers - such privileges - are not being abused. After all, if MI5 agents can eavesdrop the Royal Family's most intimate moments, then what hope for us common 'subversives'?

Other MI5 departments include 'K' branch, which is tasked with gathering counter-intelligence against foreign espionage agents in mainland Britain, and 'T' branch, which leads the fight against international terrorism. 'T' branch - together with 'A' branch and 'F' branch - is said to work closely with other security forces, such as the SAS, in particular with regard to operations which require rather more 'heavy-handed' assistance. Instances of targets being physically intimidated, or even physically beaten, of course fall into this category. As do instances of targets being murdered.

In this regard, MI5 is known to contract the services of so-called 'private security firms' to carry out its dirty work (a similar policy is pursued by MI6). In the main these multimillion-dollar firms (or corporations) are run by and populated by former Special Forces and Intelligence personnel, and are contracted to carry out operations the Service would rather not be directly (or in any other way) associated with. In other words, operations which cannot be traced back to MI5, or to any other government department. One recalls the case of 78-year old Hilda Murrell, for example, an active anti-nuclear campaigner who disappeared from her home on 21st March, 1984. According to former RAF Police Special Investigator (Crime and Security), and former MI5 undercover agent, Gary Murray, who was himself hired by the Security Service to spy on anti-nuclear protestors, Miss Murrell had obtained information pertaining to the potential use of nuclear weapons during the Falklands War. Via her various contacts - which included a close friend whose father was a senior Signals Intelligence Officer at Britain's top-secret spy base, GCHQ (Government Communications Headquarters); and her nephew, Commander Robert Green, who at the time of the Falklands War was working for British Naval Intelligence - Miss Murrell had discovered that several ships in Margaret Thatcher's Task Force might indeed have been carrying nuclear weapons. She had also obtained incriminating information regarding the sinking of the Argentine battlecruiser, *General Belgrano*.

But what concerned the Security Service most of all was the possibility that Miss Murrell had obtained copies of official classified documents and raw signals relating to the *Belgrano* incident. And to the issue of nuclear weapons having been secretly deployed during the Falklands War. It was feared that this information, if leaked into the public domain, would have embarrassed and incriminated top nuclear chiefs. Moreover, it would have incriminated then-Prime Minister, Margaret Thatcher, too. Due to his highly sensitive post during the Falklands War, Miss Murrell's nephew, Commander Robert Green, had been privy to the documents and signals in question, and because he had expressed his concerns in this regard he had himself been the subject of investigation. It was feared that he might have made copies of the documents and signals before they were destroyed, and that he might subsequently have passed the information on to his aunt, Hilda Murrell, in support of her anti-nuclear campaign. For this reason MI5 was granted leave to break into Miss Murrell's home and search for the documents in question. Sadly, however, MI5 bungled the operation; Miss Murrell returned home early and confronted the intruders. It was the last time anybody ever saw her ... alive.

Three days later, 78-year old Hilda Murrell was found stabbed to death on a stretch of nearby wasteland.

In his book, *Enemies Of The State* (Simon & Schuster, 1993) Mr Murray also cites a second case, involving a Glasgow lawyer by the name of William McRae. Mr McRae had become frightened for his life after obtaining sensitive information which could have seriously damaged the nuclear industry. But what is most notable about this case is the specific nature of the information in Mr McRae's possession. The fact is that a stark similarity existed between the information obtained by Hilda Murrell and that obtained by Mr McRae. Certainly Mr McRae's investigation paralleled that of Hilda Murrell. If Mr McRae had caught wind of the same classified information (that Britain had secretly deployed nuclear weapons during the Falklands War; that the Navy had failed to retrieve nuclear depth-bombs from *HMS Sheffield* and *HMS Coventry,* both of which were sunk during the war; and further still, that the sinking of the *Belgrano* had been ordered for political rather than military reasons) then it would indeed have caused both nuclear and government chiefs a good deal of embarrassment, to put it mildly. In any event, a year after the murder of Hilda Murrell, Mr McRae was found slumped in his car in the Scottish Highlands. He had been shot in the head. The revolver, from which two bullets had been fired, was found on the ground some distance from the car, along with a pile of torn-up documents and McRae's watch, which had been smashed. Further investigation found that whoever had shot Mr McRae had been searching for documents; McRae's two brief cases were missing, for example (moreover, they were later returned by police officers to his brother, with no explanation of how they had obtained them or of where they had been found). The official investigation - which lasted only two days - found that Mr McRae had committed suicide: that he had shot himself in the head, and had then thrown the revolver out of the car window before sitting himself comfortably back in his seat and waiting to expire.

Several sources have since confirmed that both deaths were typical of MI5-sponsored operations. Dirty work indeed.

But perhaps the most revealing statement comes from a former MI5 officer whose quote adorns the back sleeve of Gary Murray's *Enemies Of*

The State - to wit: "MI5's operational role will, of course, change now that the Cold War is ended, but other than that it will be business as usual. Priority is now given to terrorists, especially the IRA, and quite rightly so, but you can take it from me the green brigade, along with all anti-nuclear protestors, will still be investigated. Nuclear energy is a major priority, and anyone upsetting the apple cart will be dealt with accordingly."

Indeed, when you consider that our own MI5 source told us that the Service had received information regarding Princess Diana's planned campaign on behalf of victims of nuclear-related cancers, one wonders if she too was "dealt with accordingly". After all, if Hilda Murrell was considered such a threat that MI5 deemed it necessary to murder her, then how big a threat would Princess Diana have posed in challenging the nuclear industry on the world stage?

Food for thought...

Incompetence

Back to the present...

Until recently, a little-known figure by the name of Stella Rimington filled the post of Director-General of MI5. However, in April 1996 Mrs Rimington left the Service and the £100,000+ per annum post was filled by counter-terrorist expert and former Director of MI5's Corporate Affairs department (before that, 'T' branch) Stephen Lander. Mr Lander is also experienced in counter-intelligence and counter-subversion, and it is widely accepted that his appointment above other candidates to the post of Director-General was largely due to MI5's newly expanded directive to tackle organized crime. And to assume the lead role from Britain's Special Branch in the ongoing struggle against terrorist activities in Northern Ireland (in particular those spilling over onto mainland Britain). During his 20+ year career with MI5, Mr Lander is known to have worked closely with MI6, whose counter-intelligence agents have also played a major role in the British Government's fight against Irish-based terrorism. Indeed, it is suspected that, following a series of accusations levelled at MI5's handling of the Northern Ireland situation - including accusations of "incompetence" (bungling operations and failing to prevent terrorist attacks), and perverting the course of justice (fabricating 'sting' operations in which MI5 agents staged mock weapons seizures in their efforts to repair the agency's failing reputation), Mr Lander and his impressive credentials were called in to help the reparation process. However, if this was indeed the case, then - perhaps not surprisingly to some - the plan failed. In June 1996, for example, scarcely two months after Mr Lander's appointment (and despite assurances from MI5's PR department that IRA terrorism in continental Europe had been successfully stamped out), a British Army barracks in Germany was promptly mortar-bombed. The IRA claimed responsibility for the bombing. At which point, Scotland Yard's anti-terrorist squad accused MI5 of "incompetence and bungling" (a view shared by the majority of British people, whose confidence in a Security Service more than capable of bumping off defenceless old ladies - such as Hilda Murrell - while at the same time failing miserably in the face of a real enemy, is waning). And despite Scotland Yard's persistent appeals to be left to its own devices with regard to anti-terrorist and organized-crime policing, MI5 has recently been granted further powers in this same regard - the Service is now to tackle the growing problem of narcotics being smuggled into Britain. By account, its agents are now bungling drugs-trafficking operations, too.

But then, given former MI5 officer David Shayler's revelations that a good many MI5 agents suffer low morale and alcohol abuse, is it any wonder?

Royal Bugging
Official Secrets

In January 1993 it emerged that MI5 had been busy listening in on private telephone conversations made by the Royal Family. Investigations confirmed that the Security Service - with a little help from its intelligence buddies down at GCHQ, based in Cheltenham, Gloucestershire - recorded the telephone conversations of members of the Royal Family on a regular basis. Further investigations revealed that MI5, utilizing the extremely sophisticated bugging technology housed at the top-secret GCHQ spy base, also listens in on telephone calls made by suspected 'trouble-makers' - i.e. 'subversives', in particular those of a high-profile nature. In this instance, subversives should be understood as anyone refusing to tow the party line. As former private investigator, Gary Murray, discovered when speaking to one of his several well-placed MI5 sources, the Service has simply lost its way. "It is now manifestly obvious that we have lost track of our true identity and role," the source was quoted as saying. "We waste a considerable amount of our time investigating people who are in no way associated with espionage or subversion. To make matters worse, we have our own subversive clique within the Service, who are a law unto themselves."

Indeed, this view is not an isolated one; it is shared by many similar sources, including Stealth (see *The Sources Part 1*), and former MI5 agent, David Shayler, who left the Service after five years for these very reasons. And he paid the penalty for stating those reasons publicly. At the time of writing, Mr Shayler has just been released from a Parisian jail, where he was awaiting trial, charged with breaking Britain's Official Secrets Act. This is a situation which has caused a great deal of concern. And no less reaction. Jonathan Holborow, for example, editor of Britain's *Mail On Sunday,* commented: "I am surprised that the might of the Establishment is ... trying to silence David Shayler in this new period of 'open government'. His revelations in last week's *Mail On Sunday* showed at the very least that there is a case for investigation into the Security Service, which seems on the face of it to have a disturbing flaw running through its management and methods of conduct. I would suggest that the Home Office, instead of asking Special Branch to investigate Mr Shayler, make attempts to assess the full extent of his evidence and institute an inquiry into the running of MI5."

To add to Mr Holborow's comments, Alan Beith, Liberal Democrat MP and member of the recently formed though largely ineffective House of Commons Intelligence and Security Committee, had this to say. "They [MI5] interpreted their work in dealing with what was called 'domestic subversion' far too widely, and accumulated information which was quite inappropriate and very undesirable in our kind of society." Despite these comments, however, a public - or even a behind-closed-doors Parliamentary - inquiry into the activities undertaken by MI5, and its accountability to elected Authority, is not expected. Britain's Official Secrets Act, it would seem, harbours far too many incriminating skeletons for it ever to be compromised in this way. Like a Swiss safe deposit box, its code must never be cracked. Its lid must remain forever sealed.

A further reaction was expressed by John Wadham, Director of *Liberty,* who offered to help Mr Shayler fight the charges brought against him. Mr Wadham told reporters: "These examples demonstrate that MI5 has not been under control ... I don't think they are really under any democratic or legal controls, and that means that we have to raise questions about their existence." He added: "It seems to us that [David Shayler's] revelations are in the public interest, and there should be no prosecution. He was acting in the best interests of our democratic society, and for society to prosecute him would be perverse."

Indeed it would.

But are the allegations made by David Shayler and other members of the intelligence community substantive?

It is certainly known that MI5 is indeed invested with the power to tap private telephone lines and intercept private mail. It is also known that the Service utilizes some very sophisticated technology in order to achieve the more sensitive bugging and phone-tapping operations. What is not so certain is to what extent this power and technology is being abused. Officially, agents require a Home Office warrant in order to undertake such furtive activities; official estimates reveal that around 1000 such warrants are issued each year. To counter this, however, GCHQ is said to arrange around 30,000 taps every year (35,000 in 1992 alone, a staggering 34,000 of which, it would seem, were unauthorized by the Home Office). This is a claim - in part - confirmed to us by a former MI5 officer, who told us that agents attached to GCHQ are able to listen in on the conversations of "who they like, when they like ... [and] they seldom bother to obtain the prior requisite authorization from either their own superiors or the Home Office".

This source added that telephone lines can be tapped "remotely", without ever having to plant a bug on the premises, and that, with the aid of an on-line transmitter, it is even possible to eavesdrop conversations taking place in the room where the telephone is housed - even when the telephone is not being used. He further revealed that, with the aid of sophisticated "encryption keys", agents are also able to eavesdrop mobile phone calls, "no matter where the caller is located". And by utilizing even more sophisticated laser technology, agents are able to penetrate windows and walls alike and listen to what is being said in any room, anywhere.

Moreover, this same source implied very strongly that these methods are being employed on a regular basis, and against a significant percentage of so-called 'internal subversives'. And what is more, they are being employed at will - without "prior requisite authorization". True, a so-called 'independent tribunal' (established under the Interception of Communications Act, 1985) is there to hear complaints from those who suspect they are being illegally tapped or bugged. But it would appear that the general public views this tribunal with suspicion. Certainly few have ever complained (around 30-40 per year). And of those who have, none has ever seen their complaint upheld. Not one.

Squidgygate

Perhaps the most perverse claim regarding this particular brand of MI5 behaviour came to light at the beginning of 1993. In effect, investigations revealed that MI5 agents had been illegally listening in on intimate telephone conversations held by both Prince Charles and Princess Diana. This much-publicized revelation - and the investigation which followed - became known as the 'Squidgygate Affair'.

Initially, it was claimed that radio hams - one in particular, retired bank manager, Cyril Reenan - had inadvertently tuned in to a private telephone conversation involving Princess Diana and a 'male friend', James Gilbey. It was reported that Mr Reenan had subsequently sold the tapes on to the tabloid newspapers. While this is ostensibly true, later investigations revealed that the conversation recorded by Mr Reenan had actually taken place four days prior to the day on which he recorded it. In consequence, it soon became apparent that MI5 officers at GCHQ (35 miles from Mr Reenan's home) had themselves recorded the "high-quality" tape, and had then rebroadcast it on a frequency known to be used by radio hams in order to ensure the leak. Mr Reenan himself is certainly convinced that he was used by the Security Service in this way. Though he refused to say whether or not he had been personally approached by MI5 officers, he confessed that the attitude shown him by police officers investigating the case was "lenient". He also said that, curiously, they had treated him "almost like a film star." The added fact that Mr Reenan was parked in a lay-by when he made the recording (and yet there is no sound of passing traffic on the tape); and further, that he was able to listen to the high-quality broadcast for an unusually long time without losing the signal, makes it almost certain that the signal was being broadcast from nearby GCHQ.

And that the broadcast was in fact a rebroadcast of the conversation originally eavesdropped and recorded by MI5, four days previously.

Following Mr Reenan's revelations, transcripts of the alleged telephone conversation between Princess Diana and James Gilbey, plus those of a further telephone conversation between Prince Charles and his years-long paramour, Camilla Parker Bowles, made front-page headlines across Britain. As did a taped conversation between Prince Charles and Princess Diana as the couple argued over Christmas arrangements regarding their children. In this instance, however, both Charles and Diana were in the same room, at the Prince of Wales's country residence, Highgrove (itself scarcely a whisper from GCHQ). It soon became evident, then, that the taped conversation was the result of a highly sophisticated remote bugging device, and not a telephone tap. Indeed, according to *the Mirror's* royal correspondent, James Whitaker, Charles and Diana are not the only Royals to have had their conversations bugged. The Queen, too, has suffered this same indignity, and on a regular basis. "The security services don't do it from time to time," he told *The People* (May 16th, 1993), "they do it regularly. They have literally hundreds of hours of transcripts ... They are bugging all the Royals from the Queen downwards." And further: "Even as I speak, Diana is being bugged ... They think she is unstable and could go off and do something - they want to know exactly what is in her mind."

Mr Whitaker said that his information had originated with a source inside GCHQ.

In one of the taped telephone conversations, Prince Charles and Camilla Parker Bowles - caught in the middle of a long-distance, bedtime tryst - are heard to declare their undying love for one another. In parts the conversation is extremely intimate, and sexually explicit. In the second of the taped telephone conversations, Princess Diana tells Mr Gilbey of her "torture" in being married to Prince Charles (a fact that would later become public knowledge via the BBC's now-famous *Panorama* interview, during which the princess openly stated, among other things, that there had always been "three people" in her marriage.) During the conversation between Diana and James Gilbey - in which Mr Gilbey refers to Diana as 'Squidgy' - the name of yet another of the princess's confidants is mentioned. His name is James Hewitt.

So far as we are concerned, the 3-year love affair between Princess Diana and former Guards officer, Major James Hewitt, is particularly revealing. Major Hewitt has repeatedly claimed, for example, that he received 'warnings' from Princess Diana's personal police protection officers - warnings to the effect that he should end the affair immediately. He also revealed that a member of the inner royal circle - indeed, a member of the Royal Family - warned him that his affair with the princess was dangerous, and that he should end it forthwith. "Be extremely careful," Major Hewitt was advised. "Your relationship is being investigated by MI5. Be on your utmost guard."

And the warnings did not end there. Major Hewitt received no less than six similar warnings in as many weeks, to the point that he began to fear for his life. In one such warning, for example, he was told that "it was not conducive to [his] health to continue the relationship".

During an interview conducted by ITN's royal correspondent, Nicholas Owen, Major Hewitt again claimed that he had received repeated warnings about the affair from Princess Diana's personal police protection officers. He further confirmed that he had received several more "threatening" warnings from an 'unknown source' in this same regard, plus a personal warning from a member of the Royal Family. "Your relationship is known about," he was plainly told. "It is not supported." And further: "We cannot be responsible for your safety or security. [We] suggest that you curtail [the relationship] forthwith." When asked if he thought there were those who would "wish ill" on the Princess of Wales herself, sufficient that they might "do something really terrible to her", he replied: "Yes, I do think there are people like that." Indeed, fearing for his life, and possibly for that of the princess herself, Major Hewitt took the advice he had received seriously; he curtailed the relationship "forthwith". He is reported to have told a close friend that, had he ignored the warnings, he feared that he might have ended up having an 'accident'. He already knew, of course, what had happened to a former confidant of the princess, Sgt Barry Mannakee - who, for a period during the 1980s, was Princess Diana's personal bodyguard. According to our main MI5 source,

Sgt Mannakee had not only become 'too well-acquainted' with the princess; he had also informed her that MI5 was actively monitoring her movements, that her private apartments were bugged, and that her telephones were tapped. In consequence, the princess started to show signs of concern, even mild paranoia. At which point her much-publicized eating disorders and emotional instabilities came to the fore, and they did so publicly. In short, being told that MI5 was actively monitoring her every move took its toll. From that day forth, the princess repeatedly voiced her anxieties about 'dying in an accident'. (Indeed, as this book was going to press we were fortunate enough to talk to one of Sgt Mannakee's professional peers, Royal Personal Protection Officer, Mike Grey, who told us: "Clandestine surveillance by the Security Services on the most intimate of situations was to culminate later in the assassination of Diana, Princess of Wales, of this I have no doubt." And further: "I have no doubts whatsoever, given my twenty years experience within various sections of the security industry, that Diana, Princess of Wales, was assassinated. The security service hallmarks are plain to see..." And again, speaking of the crash in Paris: "[The operation bore all the] classic hallmarks of a security service assassination - twenty years experience in the industry give me absolutely no doubt." Interestingly, we recall in this same regard the words of our former SAS source quoted in *Chapter Two*, who told us: "From the minute the decoy car left the Ritz to the moment the tail car closed in ... it was obvious what was going down. Anyone who knows what they're talking about'll tell you the same." Mr Grey, of course, does indeed know what he is talking about; he has worked as personal protection officer to some of the most important VIPs in the world, including royalty. And because he has, his observations - like those of our SAS source - should be considered in the highest regard.)

In any event, what is known for certain with regard to the princess and Sgt Barry Mannakee is this.

In September 1986, father-of-two Sgt Mannakee was relieved of his post as the princess's personal bodyguard, and was transferred to the Diplomatic Protection Corps. Evidently, members of the 'inner circle' had indeed stated their concern that the princess and the bodyguard had become 'too familiar'. But what is most chilling of all about this particular case is its tragic and untimely - some would say sinister - ending. Eight months after leaving his post as Diana's personal bodyguard, Sgt Mannakee was killed in a 'road traffic accident'. Several sources close to the princess have since voiced their concerns that Sgt Mannakee's death was in fact the result of an MI5 operation. Indeed, these suspicions have been confirmed by our own MI5 source, who told us quite unequivocally that Sgt Mannakee had been "taken out" because he had been "too willing" to impart information to the princess regarding MI5's surveillance of her. "Word got back that he had a loose tongue," our source said. And further: "People with loose tongues have accidents."

In other words, they are murdered.

But whatever the truth, it is clear that from this point on Diana became increasingly concerned for her own safety. And for the safety of others who might also be deemed to have 'overstepped the mark' - to have become 'too close' to her. "Any gentleman that's been past my door ... all hell's broken loose," she would later tell BBC's *Panorama.* And as her own tragic fate would later attest, of course, her concerns were not unfounded. And neither, it seems, were those of the man Diana openly confessed to have been in love with, Major James Hewitt. On the contrary, it is little wonder that Major Hewitt took so seriously the warnings he had received from his royal contact. To put it bluntly, it would appear that 'road traffic accidents' are flavour-of-the-month with regard to official assassinations, as affirmed by the death of Major Michael Marman (see *Chapter Two*).

Indeed, this would seem particularly evident when yet another, similar incident is entered into the equation - the attempted assassination of Camilla Parker Bowles.

Read on...

The Camilla Incident
And The Constitutional Crisis

According to our source, Camilla Parker Bowles has been the subject of a concerted MI5 surveillance operation for some years. Indeed, this information has since been confirmed by another source who until recently held a senior rank within a British Military Intelligence department. This source - who has now 'retired'; indeed, who has suffered in no small measure for the fact that he was party to the 'assassination scenario' from its inception - informed us that a "loose plan" to assassinate Diana, Princess of Wales, had "for some considerable time" been debated by both British and US intelligence agencies. And perhaps more surprisingly, that a parallel plot to assassinate Camilla Parker Bowles had also been tabled by MI5 chiefs. And more than this. That it had been attempted and bungled.

According to this source, then, an attempt on Mrs Parker Bowles's life had been made - and bungled - by MI5. And what is more, the operation had once again taken the form of a 'road traffic accident', as we shall see. The decision to assassinate Mrs Parker Bowles had been taken, we were told, as a measure to "clean up the constitutional mess" caused by the marital and extramarital predicament in which the Prince of Wales found himself. Indeed, we were told that the reason top executives within MI5 finally gave their support to the already existing MI6 plot to assassinate Diana was precisely because their attempt on Mrs Parker Bowles's life had failed. To add to this, at the time of the 'Camilla Incident' the existing MI6 plot had recently won the support of its American bed partner, the CIA. Evidently the CIA had finally given its blessing in this regard due to the unprecedented success of Diana's landmines campaign. In effect, Diana's ability not only to mobilize public opinion in her favour, but also to sway the opinion of the world's most powerful puppet, William Jefferson Clinton (who, we were assured, had privately agreed to back Diana's campaign by supporting a worldwide ban on landmines) had caused no small concern within the higher echelons of the US-based military-industrial complex. It emerged that arms-trade godfathers - who were still making a handsome buck out of arms sold to warring factions in Angola and other African states, as well as to Western-backed forces in Bosnia and the Balkans (arms which of course included anti-personnel landmines) - were furious that the President had acceded to the princess's wishes. This point will be more fully elucidated in chapters *Nine* and *Ten*. For now, a summary of the sequence of events which led to the assassination finally being approved and executed will at least suffice to illustrate the point at hand - which, in effect, is fourfold, as follows:

One: that so-called 'road traffic accidents' are indeed employed today by British and US Intelligence as their most 'deniable' means of assassination;

Two: that, seen in this light, the idea that Diana's death was the result of a 'drink-drive accident' becomes all the more untenable;

Three: that Diana was assassinated as a result of MI5's failed attempt to assassinate Camilla Parker Bowles;

Four: that, in the end, Diana's death was the result of a joint CIA/ MI6 'deniable operation'.

The sequence of events according to our sources, then.

Following Diana's much-publicized *Panorama* interview (BBC, screened November 1995) - during which she publicly attacked the House of Windsor; indeed, during which she expressed her opinion that Prince Charles was not fit to be King and at the same time invented herself as the 'People's Princess' - furious oligarchs within the British Royal Establishment initiated moves which eventuated in a plot to assassinate the princess. As British author, AN Wilson, commented in *The New York Times* (25th November, 1995) in response to the *Panorama* interview: "...When it comes to fighting a war, the Establishment can get very nasty indeed ... for all her undoubted popularity, if she continues to rock the boat in this way, the Establishment will simply get rid of her..."

Indeed, in the end, it seems, this is precisely what the Establishment did.

But at this early stage, and according to our sources, there were still those who opposed the proposed plot to assassinate the princess. Though MI5 had for some years prior to the interview conducted a massive and intrusive surveillance on Diana, even so it had always been considered by MI5 chiefs "too risky for the Princess of Wales to die in mysterious circumstances ... on home soil". (MI5, remember, is Britain's 'domestic' or 'home soil' intelligence agency.) And in any case - according our sources - MI5 chiefs were reluctant "from the beginning" that the princess should be the one to be assassinated. It was argued that a parallel plot to assassinate Mrs Parker Bowles should instead be initiated, and this for several reasons.

One: the death of Mrs Parker Bowles would serve "equally well to clean up the constitutional mess" resulting from Prince Charles's marital and extramarital predicament;

Two: the consequences of Mrs Parker Bowles's death "on home soil" would be "far easier to deal with";

Three: the sudden and mysterious death of Mrs Parker Bowles would be extremely unlikely to engender the same massive public protest feared by the authorities in the event of a similar misadventure befalling Diana, "no matter where in the world she died";

Four: the sudden and mysterious death of Mrs Parker Bowles would serve as a chilling and cautionary reminder to the princess - in effect it would serve as an adequate "deterrent", a means to dissuade Diana from her current posture in terms of her increasingly public 'humanitarian' role, and at the same time encourage her to desist from 'rocking the boat' - rather to "tow the line".

In short, MI5 argued that the sudden and mysterious death of Mrs Parker Bowles would be sufficient to resolve the immediate problem facing the Establishment ("the constitutional mess"); that it would cause far less fuss than the sudden and mysterious death of Princess Diana; and that at the same time it would terrify Diana to the extent that, henceforth, she would be more willing to conform to Establishment protocol.

Thus, at this stage, MI5 argued against the proposed plot to assassinate the princess. And instead to concentrate their efforts in this same regard on Mrs Parker Bowles.

However, the 'immediate problem' - "the constitutional mess" - was to be further compounded when in the summer of 1996 Diana's divorce from Prince Charles became absolute. In consequence, speculation regarding the future King's intentions to marry Mrs Parker Bowles, herself a divorcee, began to assume a new and more evident significance. In the event that

Charles *were* to marry Camilla, of course, on his accession to the Throne she would become Queen. However, in the summer of 1996 Diana was still alive. And that was the problem.

As everyone in Britain is - presumably - aware, while it would seem constitutionally acceptable for a king (or a queen, for that matter) to enjoy extramarital relations, it is wholly unacceptable for him to divorce and remarry. When a British monarch accedes to the Throne, by constitutional tradition he/she also assumes the office of Supreme Governor of the Church of England. And herein lies the problem. The Church of England forbids the remarriage of divorcees in church. And as the Church's Supreme Governor, Charles would be expected to 'honour and obey' this *Jurassic* edict and at the same time be seen to uphold the values of the very institution for which, once King, he would serve as supreme head. Of course, there is no requirement that Charles *should* remarry. But there is every chance that he might *want* to. Certainly to judge by comments allegedly made by Charles's closest friends - together with Camilla-friendly public relations exercises promulgated by royal spin doctors, and current moves in Parliament and the Church to reform the existing rules in this regard - at some time in the not-too-distant future it seems likely that Charles will indeed announce his intention to marry his longterm mistress. In fact, on 18th July 1997, just six weeks before Diana's "accident", the Parliamentary aide to Britain's Lord Chancellor, Tony Wright, stated in no uncertain terms that a constitutional crisis regarding the marriage of Prince Charles and Mrs Parker Bowles would result in the 'disestablishment of the Church'. In response, it was reported that frantic efforts had been initiated to relax the rules with regard to the remarriage of divorcees and/or to sever the centuries-long ties which still bind the Church to the State. Of note here is that, during the week leading up to Tony Wright's statement, Charles is known to have held meetings with many of Britain's highest-ranking Cabinet Ministers, including Britain's Foreign Secretary, Robin Cook (overall head of MI6), in an attempt to elicit Prime Minister Tony Blair's personal support for the marriage. To add to this, royal spin doctors were at the same time strategizing new ways to re-educate public opinion with regard to the British people's hostility towards Mrs Parker Bowles. Of equal note is that, on the very day Tony Wright's statement was made, Charles threw a 50th birthday party for Mrs Parker Bowles at his country residence, Highgrove. It was, of course, deemed imperative by royal spin doctors that, in order to gain political support for the marriage, it was first necessary to win the support of the British people. The media-hyped birthday bash was thus seen as part of Charles's spin-doctored offensive to soften public hostility towards his mistress. And to judge by current opinion polls, it has to be said that the attempt was a marginal success.

But in any event, it is evident that during the months and weeks prior to Diana's death all avenues possible were being pursued in an attempt to avert the constitutional crisis foreseen as a result of the proposed marriage of Charles and Camilla. *All avenues.* Staggeringly these avenues even included moves to disestablish the Church of England. And as we shall later see, any such move to disestablish the Church from the State would have amounted to the single biggest constitutional reform since the days of Henry VIII. Which only serves to demonstrate just how desperate the Establishment had become in its efforts to "clean up the constitutional mess" caused, in the first instance, by the Prince of Wales's philandering.

As stated, all the fuss in this regard stemmed from the fact that, in the event of Charles's marriage to Camilla Parker Bowles, the latter would become Queen. But the real problem at this time (following the divorce of Charles and Diana) arose in that, under constitutional law, the King's *new* wife and consort (in this instance Mrs Parker Bowles) could not become Queen so long as his former wife and consort remained alive. And Charles's *former* wife and consort, of course, was Diana, Princess of Wales.

Under the constraints imposed by the existing rules, then, Charles could not become King and Supreme Governor of the Church of England and marry Camilla as well. This, at any rate, remained the case so long as Diana remained alive. Were Diana to die, on the other hand, then this problem would simply no longer exist. There would be no question of the hugely powerful Church of England being disestablished, and no constitutional problems with regard to Camilla becoming Queen. Indeed, the Church of England's rules are quite specific in this regard - that, in the event that the divorcee should become a widow or widower, the rules governing the remarriage of the divorcee no longer apply. The "constitutional mess" would no longer exist. Immediately following the divorce, however, the "constitutional mess" certainly did exist. Thus MI5 came under increased pressure at this time to remove the cause of that "mess" - and in so doing free up Prince Charles to marry whomsoever he chose. The British Royal Establishment, of course, saw *Diana* as the cause of that "mess". MI5, on the other hand, saw *Camilla* as the cause of that "mess". The result: stalemate.

It should also be said that, at this time (July/August 1996), the problem remained more or less a British one. Pressure brought on MI5 to sort out the "mess" came solely from British Establishment oligarchs - the very same oligarchs who had for some time desired that Diana should be 'removed'. Though the divorce gave added impetus to their appeals, nevertheless MI5 chiefs remained reluctant to act on that impetus and give their support to the proposed plot to assassinate Diana, preferring still their alternative solution - to assassinate Mrs Parker Bowles. According to our sources, it was at this point (circa January/February 1997) that a new factor entered the equation. It was at this point that Establishment oligarchs were joined in their appeals by "American parties with vested interests". As we shall see in *Chapter Nine*, and as stated above, American support for Diana's 'removal' was the result of her meetings with Bill and Hillary Clinton, and the President's subsequent pledge to support a worldwide ban on landmines. Or as our sources put it: "Certain parties became very disenchanted with Clinton when they found out that he was prepared to - effectively - overturn US defence policy on the strength of what they considered the whim of a meddling British Royal. Especially as she was no longer officially royal ... The fact that she was an attractive young woman didn't help matters, of course. Apparently Clinton's partiality for attractive young women had been noted."

And further: "This was the reason the CIA got involved with MI6 to take care of the princess. MI6 had their own reasons for wanting rid of Diana. But from this point on it became a joint operation ... Diana's fate was effectively sealed then."

According to our sources, then, it was at this point that the CIA joined MI6 chiefs in adding their weight to the appeals of the British Establishment. "The word from then on was that, if MI5 wouldn't do it, then the CIA and MI6 would", we were told. The reason for CIA involvement was of course to repair relations between Clinton and the arms trade; once Diana was out of the way Clinton would be free to renege on his pledge and opt out of the proposed worldwide ban on landmines. Which, less then three weeks after the princess's mysterious death, is precisely what he did. Indeed, America was the only Western power to 'change its mind' in this regard and refuse to sign the Landmines Treaty, as we shall see.

With these new developments, then, the plot to assassinate Princess Diana - which until now had not substantially progressed beyond the fact that it had been tabled - began to assume new momentum. So much so, in fact, that MI5 stepped up its operation with regard, not to Diana, but to Mrs Parker Bowles. MI5 chiefs still held that the death of Mrs Parker Bowles would be less likely to engender public suspicion and backlash, would adequately resolve the constitutional problem and at the same time would terrify Diana into submission. However, at about this same time yet another factor entered the equation: one Dodi Fayed. Though American interest was scarcely affected by this development, British concerns overnight grew to even greater levels of paranoia. Dodi, of course, was the heir to a dynasty intermarried with the Ibn Saud Dynasty - in effect the Saudi Royal Family - a fact which engendered no small disquietude within the British Royal Establishment. As Andrew Golden commented in *the Sunday Mirror* (31st August, 1997) in an article written only hours before the fatal crash in Paris: "Diana has been told in no uncertain terms about the consequences should she continue the relationship with the Fayed boy ... *now the royal family may have decided it is time to settle up. "* [Italics in original copy.]

To add to this, Dodi - to whom Prince Philip himself publicly referred as an "oily bed-hopper" - was also the son of a major political and financial player, Mohamed al Fayed, whose petitions for British citizenship had for some years been thwarted by a well-publicized series of Establishment chicaneries. These chicaneries had largely been devised and spearheaded by the British Crown's favoured son and troubleshooter, Tiny Rowland - whose Lonrho corporation, interestingly enough, managed Crown assets in Angola and other African states (indeed, the name Lonrho was spawned from the nineteenth-century Crown asset, the London and Rhodesia Company - see *Chapter Ten*). In effect Mohamed al Fayed had been ostracized by the British Establishment; by the extended apparatus of bankers, businessmen and civil servants who form the royal circus, too - who band around the Monarchy and enjoy their own success on this basis. For the past decade and more Mohamed al Fayed had endeavoured without success to muscle his way in to this 'royal circus' and thus become part of the British Establishment himself. Long before Diana ever hooked up with the Fayeds they were loathed by both the Windsors and the Establishment. Thus all their attempts to 'muscle in' were blocked, and at every juncture. So far as the Establishment was concerned, of course, the Fayeds were now seen to be effecting a new manoeuvre. They were now seen to be luring the Princess of Wales into their fold, and thereby manoeuvring their way in to the very royal circle from which they had for so long been excluded. Indeed, Establishment oligarchs interpreted Dodi's relationship with Diana as purely a political manoeuvre on the part of Mohamed al Fayed - an attempt to manoeuvre his way not only in to the Establishment, but in to the heart of the Monarchy itself. In consequence, the excessive levels of pressure already brought on MI5 intensified even further. So much so that MI5 chiefs soon realized that failure to pursue their preferred course of action with regard to Mrs Parker Bowles would mean that MI6, together with the CIA, would swiftly seek to implement their own plan - a plan which, all along, MI6 chiefs together with Establishment oligarchs had endeavoured to foist on MI5. The very same plan which MI5 chiefs had feared "too risky" to implement "on home soil".

And in any event, according to our sources, at some point in or around May/June 1997 the situation reached fever pitch. Something had to give.

It was this sequence of events, then, which finally forced MI5 to act on its plan regarding Mrs Parker Bowles. At least this is the scenario according to our sources. What is of interest here is that, on the night of 11th June 1997, just two months prior to Diana's fatal 'road traffic accident' in Paris,

Mrs Parker Bowles was herself involved in a similar, though *non-fatal* 'accident'. The incident occurred as Mrs Parker Bowles was travelling to meet Prince Charles at his country residence, Highgrove - on a stretch of country road between the villages of Norton and Easton Grey in Wiltshire, about 8 miles from the prince's estate. According to police reports Mrs Parker Bowles was travelling at some speed when her car, a green Ford Mondeo belonging to Buckingham Palace, seemed to lose control and plough head-on into an oncoming vehicle - a Volvo estate driven by one Carolyn Melville-Smith of Easton Grey. As a result of the collision Ms Melville-Smith's car overturned in a ditch at the side of the road. She suffered chest injuries. Mrs Parker Bowles, on the other hand, was relatively unhurt; indeed, she immediately climbed out of her car and fled the scene in a self-confessed state of "sheer terror", leaving Ms Melville-Smith trapped and in pain in her overturned car.

For some days and weeks thereafter the incident became the focus of intense media interest, the details of the crash seeming to alter slightly with each passing day. Initial reports claimed that Mrs Parker Bowles had fled the scene of the crash in fear that she was being kidnapped by terrorists and/or that she was the intended victim of assassination. Certainly it is known that she fled the scene in fear for her life. "I panicked out of sheer terror", she told reporters. "I have constantly been warned that one day I might be attacked and I thought this is what might have happened." The question is, of course, attacked by whom - terrorists?

Or MI5?

Precise details of the crash are difficult to establish; there were no witnesses to the incident. But what is known for certain is that, following the 'accident', Prince Charles ordered that Mrs Parker Bowles's personal security be considerably stepped up - a curious response to an innocent 'road traffic accident', it has to be said. What is also known is that Mrs Parker Bowles did indeed leave the scene of the crash in something of a hurry - she did not attempt to discover to what extent the other driver (Ms Melville-Smith) might have been injured. And neither did she wait around to exchange names and addresses. A police investigation was thus launched into the incident, but no charges were brought against Mrs Parker Bowles, even though it is illegal in Britain (under the Road Traffic Act 1988) to evacuate the scene of a crash without first exchanging names and addresses with all parties involved. Failing to report an accident is also illegal. As Ms Melville-Smith commented in *The Independent* (14th June, 1997): "You should never leave the scene of an accident. If I had done it, I would be in a lot of trouble right now." Indeed she would.

The official explanation came in a statement from royal sources some days after the event, and contained few surprises. It was claimed that Mrs Parker Bowles had not evacuated the scene of the crash without good reason. She had climbed out of her car, the sources said, had checked to see that Ms Melville-Smith was alive and well (a claim refuted by Ms Melville-Smith) and had then returned to her car in order to salvage her mobile phone. She had then run away from the scene in order to call the emergency services from the brow of a nearby hill - from where she was able to obtain a clearer signal for her mobile phone. Having alerted the emergency services she had then called Prince Charles, who immediately dispatched his own police protection officer together with two royal valets and two other staff members to the scene of the crash.

It was also claimed that Mrs Parker Bowles had indeed left the scene so abruptly due to security reasons - evidently she had been under instruction to leave the scene of such an incident due to the risk of terrorist attack. Which in itself seems plausible enough. However, it has to be said that, if Charles and his personal security operation had been so concerned about the possibility of such an attack, then it seems curious to say the least that Mrs Parker Bowles should have been permitted to drive alone, at night, along deserted country roads, thus leaving herself entirely vulnerable to such an attack - to kidnap, or indeed, assassination. Also, of course - if the official explanation is correct and Mrs Parker Bowles did indeed check to see that Ms Melville-Smith was alive and well - then she would surely have realized that Ms Melville-Smith was alone and trapped in her car. And thus that she posed no threat - that there were no terrorists lurking in the back seat waiting to kidnap her or harm her in any way; that there were no other vehicles at the scene; thus that there was no immediate danger. Mrs Parker Bowles's reaction in fleeing the scene so abruptly, however, and in a state of such distress - "terror" - surely suggests otherwise: that perhaps an as yet unknown party was indeed present at the scene (or at least in the vicinity, close enough that they were detected by Mrs Parker Bowles). And that this is the reason she fled the scene in such a state of terror.

In any event, according to our sources this alternative scenario is closer to the truth than the later spin-story issued by Buckingham Palace. "She knew she was under some degree of surveillance, and that her position as Prince Charles's mistress was a precarious one," we were informed. And even more explicit: "She thought it was an MI5 job - that MI5 was trying to kill her. She was right, of course, but it all went stupidly wrong ... The reports had to make it look like an innocent accident."

Can you tell us if MI5 operatives were present at the scene of the crash?

A moment's pause, then: "If they were it was too late by then to effect the necessary outcome. The operation had already failed."

Yes but can you tell us if MI5 operatives were present at the scene of the crash?

A further pause, then: "Let us just say it was a bad day at the office for MI5."

Yes but...?

"A very bad day at the office".

Point taken.

It should be stated here that, in citing this incident as a bungled MI5 operation, we are in no way intending to implicate Ms Melville-Smith as an MI5 agent or accomplice. Indeed, Ms Melville-Smith would seem to have been entirely the innocent party. As we have seen with regard to the Diana crash (or indeed, the crash in which Major Michael Marman was killed - see *Chapter Two*) it is perfectly feasible that Mrs Parker Bowles's car could have been 'tampered with' at some stage prior to the incident. And that this could have caused Mrs Parker Bowles to lose control of the vehicle moments before it ploughed head-on into Ms Melville-Smith's Volvo estate. This is of course a speculative scenario. But similar thoughts would certainly seem to have troubled the mind of Prince Charles - who, remember, ordered that Mrs Parker Bowles's personal security be considerably tightened following the incident, even though the only other party involved was, allegedly, Ms Melville-Smith. To add to this, and for some as yet inexplicable reason, Mrs Parker Bowles herself believed that her life was in danger immediately following the collision. Even though the official spin-story maintains that she saw Ms Melville-Smith alone and trapped in her overturned car (and thus would have realized that she was not the victim of a terrorist attack) she nevertheless felt sufficiently threatened that she fled the scene in terror - in fear for her life. Curious, to say the least.

In any event, and despite its somewhat ambivalent message, the official explanation was in the end sufficient to save Mrs Parker Bowles any further embarrassment. The Crown Prosecution Service quickly concluded that, in the absence of any eyewitnesses, there was 'insufficient evidence' to prosecute. The incident was thus - somewhat conveniently - brought to a swift and undetermined close.

But whatever the truth in all of this, the fact remains that two months prior to the crash which killed Diana, Camilla Parker Bowles was herself involved in a similar 'road traffic accident', one that could just as easily have killed or seriously maimed her. Indeed, according to our sources, this was precisely the intention. Perhaps Mrs Parker Bowles should be thankful that it was an MI5 operation, then. Had it been the handiwork of MI6 and the CIA (or indeed, The Clinic - see *Chapter Two*) it is far more likely that she would indeed have lost her life.

And that, in consequence, Diana would almost certainly be alive today.

A Dress Rehearsal

Our sources also highlighted other events in the sequence which led to Diana's death. Perhaps most significant in this regard was the fact that a top BBC executive confided to one of our sources that, the day prior to Diana's death, a "dress rehearsal" had been conducted by the BBC with regard to "how to announce the death of a British Royal". Despite our own efforts to corroborate this claim - which involved several telephone conversations and a taped though clandestine meeting with a somewhat anxious spokesperson - the BBC flatly denied that such a "dress rehearsal" had taken place. Indeed, the officials we spoke to denied that any such "dress rehearsal" had *ever* taken place. Which, to us, seemed odd. After all, the British Broadcasting Corporation is effectively the British Establishment's public voice. In effect it is Britain's state-controlled television company, in any event the only one for which the British public is forced by law to pay an annual licence fee, and which is known to be sympathetic to the 'Establishment agenda'. The very idea that the BBC would not maintain a well-oiled contingency in this regard seemed to us preposterous. The announcement of, say, the Queen's death - or that of any other high-ranking royal - would by necessity require the utmost sensitive and strategic planning. Surely we were not expected to believe that the BBC would simply cast pearls to fortune in this regard and fumble its way through such an announcement without prior rehearsals. This, at least, remained the niggling suspicion at the forefront of our minds as we struggled to corroborate our sources' information. And it did prove a struggle, to be sure. In the end we were unable to confirm that a "dress rehearsal" had been conducted on the day prior to Diana's death. But we did discover that such a "dress rehearsal" had indeed been conducted some few weeks beforehand (Saturday, 5th July, 1997). And that the information contained in a BBC script for such a rehearsal (obtained by journalist, Chris Blackhurst) revealed clearly enough that, contrary to BBC denials, the Corporation does indeed maintain such a contingency. And what is more, that this same well-oiled contingency included a startling and strangely prognostic announcement to the effect that 'Princess Diana had been killed in road traffic accident'.

As Chris Blackhurst reported in one of Britain's most respected and reputable broadsheets, *The Independent on Sunday* (13th July 1997): "At 1.15 pm last Saturday ... transmission was interrupted by this announcement:

'This is BBC Television from London. A few moments ago, Buckingham Palace announced that Her Majesty Queen Elizabeth, the Queen Mother, has died. Normal programmes have been suspended.' Announcers on BBC 1 and BBC 2 had reached for their black ties, which they are required to keep close at hand, and the ritual began. It was a dress rehearsal, of course, but it says a lot about the relationship between the monarchy and the BBC."

Indeed it does. But what is even more revealing is that Chris Blackhurst's article also included the following, astonishing revelation:

"Previous rehearsals have been much more dramatic than the Queen Mother's last weekend. A BBC executive reveals that in the past the Corporation 'killed off' Diana in a car crash."

A staggeringly accurate prognosis, to say the least. Indeed, even more so when the words of the BBC's first and by far most influential Director-General, Lord Reith, are taken into account: "Perhaps if I had thought more, I would have tried to avoid the BBC becoming part of the Establishment, but perhaps not. Establishment has a good deal to say for it."

On the contrary, Lord Reith, it is the BBC who would seem to have a good deal to say for the Establishment.

Chris Blackhurst's article concluded: "Nowhere was that tradition of bowing and scraping to the great and the good more in evidence than in the BBC's treatment of royalty." And further: "...BBC executives ... have spent hours debating the wording of a Category One death announcement. It used to be 'It is with regret that the BBC has learned...' One casualty of the Andrew Morton book about the Prince of Wales' marriage and Diana's subsequent Panorama interview has been the deletion of the concept of 'regret'."

But whatever the truth behind the relationship between the BBC and the British Royal Establishment, and the Establishment's reluctance to announce Diana's death 'with regret', several salient factors have emerged from this line of inquiry:

One: that the BBC - together with other, independent broadcasting companies - does indeed maintain a contingency policy with regard to the announcements of royal deaths;

Two: that eight weeks prior to Diana's death the BBC did indeed effect a "dress rehearsal" with regard to announcing the death of the Queen Mother;

Three: that in the past the BBC had conducted a similar "dress rehearsal" with regard to announcing the death of Diana, Princess of Wales;

Four: that on this occasion the BBC announced that 'Diana had been killed in a road traffic accident';

Five: that, according to our sources, a top BBC executive revealed that a similar "dress rehearsal" had been conducted on Saturday 30th August, 1997, on the eve of Diana's fatal 'road traffic accident' in Paris.

It should be reiterated here that point *Five* has been flatly denied by BBC officials. But then, as we discovered, such a denial is nothing short of what should be expected. When, for example, we spoke to an ITV spokesperson we were told: "These arrangements are of necessity strictly confidential. I am surprised and saddened that Mr Blackhurst was able to obtain the script ... the secrecy is out of respect for the feelings of the Royal Family."

In any event, it was not long before the BBC was able to implement its "dress rehearsal" script for real. On 31st August, 1997, the black ties and the practised words informed us that Diana, Princess of Wales, had indeed died in an horrific 'road traffic accident'. And while the world mourned, the British Royal Establishment was heard to utter an enormous sigh of relief.

"The Media Is Being Primed, As We Speak."

Is it possible, then, we wondered, that the BBC had been manoeuvred by its Establishment overlords to prepare for the death of Princess Diana - even though the station's announcers (indeed, the entire BBC staff) would almost certainly have remained unaware that they were being manoeuvred in this way? Is it possible that a "dress rehearsal" for the announcement of Diana's death by 'road traffic accident' could have been part of an MI6 preparation schedule, and thus surreptitiously introduced into the BBC itinerary? It was our CIA/MI6 source, Stealth, of course, who told us one week prior to the princess's death: "Provision for public reaction has already been considered. They have good experience of how to deal with public reaction ... it's being taken care of as we speak. The media is being primed, as we speak."

If the BBC *was* being covertly primed in this way, of course, our sources' assertions that a "dress rehearsal" regarding the announcement of the death of Diana (that it had been conducted on the day before she died) might thus prove correct. But in any event, the question remains: might the BBC have been manoeuvred by the Establishment to prepare the British public for news of Diana's death? It is a question which should be posed in context with the sequence of events as detailed above, and reiterated here for clarity:

One: Diana's close relationship with her personal police protection officer, Sgt Barry Mannakee - who, having informed Diana that she was a target for MI5 surveillance, was removed from his post, transferred, and eight months later killed in a 'road traffic accident'.

Two: Diana's subsequent relationship with James Hewitt - who, we recall, was warned by a member of the Royal Family that his relationship with Diana was "not supported", and that in consequence he too had been placed under MI5 surveillance. We also recall that Major Hewitt was further warned by the Royal Family that "we cannot be responsible for your safety or security". In consequence Mr Hewitt ended the relationship "forthwith", and at the same time confided in a close friend that, had he ignored the warnings, he feared he might have ended up having an 'accident'.

Three: MI5's intensified surveillance of Princess Diana, in particular during the 1990s, the so-called 'Squidgygate Affair' being a primary case in point. "Clandestine surveillance by the Security Services on the most intimate of situations was to culminate later in the assassination of Diana, Princess of Wales," we were told by Royal Personal Protection Officer, Mike Grey, a man who for twenty years has worked in a similar capacity to that of Sgt Barry Mannakee.

Four: MI5's equally intensive surveillance of Mrs Parker Bowles, in particular following the divorce of Charles and Diana.

Five: MI5's directive to "clean up the constitutional mess" caused in the first instance by Prince Charles's philandering, and further compounded by his divorce from Princess Diana.

Six: MI5's decision to focus its attention on Mrs Parker Bowles with regard to cleaning up said "constitutional mess".

Seven: The increased pressure brought on MI5 by Establishment oligarchs following Diana's infamous *Panorama* interview, for which the BBC was severely chastized by the Establishment.

Eight: The intense interest shown in Diana by MI6 following her activities in Angola and Bosnia, where, as we shall see, MI6 and the CIA continue to carry out covert operations on behalf of the British and US governments - to supply arms and mercenaries to Angola's ruthless UNITA regime as well as to Western-backed forces in Bosnia and other Balkan territories, the Kosovo Liberation Army being a primary case in point

Nine: The emergence on the scene of the CIA at this time due to the success of Diana's landmines campaign and her meetings with Bill and Hillary Clinton. And the President's subsequent decision to support a worldwide ban on the manufacture, sale and deployment of anti-personnel landmines - the two primary regions where landmines are serving Western interests, of course, are Angola and the Balkans.

Ten: The subsequent emergence of Dodi Fayed - whose surprise arrival only served to compound even further the already severe constitutional crisis brought about by Charles's and Diana's divorce. This crisis was so severe, remember, that Establishment oligarchs even considered the disestablishment of the Church of England in their desperate attempts to find a resolution. Following Mr Fayed's arrival, however, such a constitutional move would have proved largely ineffectual. The crisis would not only have remained; it would have proved unresolvable no matter how drastic the constitutional reform(s) implemented, in particular if Diana had in the end elected to marry Mr Fayed - who, remember, was an Arab Muslim and heir to a dynasty intermarried with the Ibn Saud Royal Dynasty. Relations between the British and Saudi royal establishments are fraught, to say the least. In any event they are best preserved at a distance, and by diplomatic intervention. Relations between the British Royal Establishment and the Fayeds, of course, are notoriously hostile. They always have been.

Eleven: The eventual - and inevitable - attempt on Mrs Parker Bowles's life by MI5, the bungled and mystery-laden 'road traffic accident' which Mrs Parker Bowles survived. We should remember that, following the incident, Mrs Parker Bowles's personal security was considerably tightened by order of Prince Charles himself. We should perhaps also remember that former SAS officer, Sir Ranulph Fiennes, who revealed in his book *The Feather Men* that the death of Major Michael Marman by 'road traffic accident' was in fact a well-rehearsed assassination operation (see *Chapter Two*) is a personal friend of Prince Charles.

Twelve: The mysterious "dress rehearsal" for the announcement of a royal death, said by our sources to have been conducted by the BBC on the day prior to Diana's death, a fact disputed by BBC officials. In any event the "dress rehearsal" which did take place on Saturday 5th July, 1997, with regard to the announcement of the death of the Queen Mother. And the fact that during a previous "dress rehearsal" the BBC, in a strangely prognostic announcement, reported that Diana had been killed in a 'road traffic accident'.

Thirteen: The equally mysterious and tragic 'road traffic accident' in Paris during the early hours of Sunday, 31st August, 1997 - an 'accident' which Diana did not survive, despite the fact that, medically speaking, she should have. Indeed, the sheer volume of anomalies and still-unanswered questions regarding this case only serve to highlight even further the likely involvement of British and US intelligence agencies in the princess's death.

And the fact that 'road traffic accidents' are indeed employed by the intelligence services today as a well-practised and wholly deniable method of assassination.

As affirmed by former MI6 officer, Richard Tomlinson, then - who, we recall, testified to the French magistrate in charge of the official investigation, Judge Herve Stephan, that an existing MI6 plot to assassinate Serbian President, Slobodan Milosevic, was an effective replica of the operation which killed Princess Diana in Paris - 'road traffic accidents' would indeed seem to be flavour-of-the-month with regard to official assassinations. Indeed, our SAS source confirmed to us in no uncertain terms that "we used the blockbuster [in 'road traffic accident' operations] so many times in Northern Ireland, we got it down to a fine art". And further: "It wouldn't be the first time this method has been used in a deniable op."

Evidently not. But due to the massive publicity engendered with regard to Diana's own 'road traffic accident', let us hope it is the last time. Indeed, let us hope that this insidious and cowardly method of assassination has now been too widely exposed for it ever to be considered again.

And that sooner or later, one way or another, the perpetrators are brought to book.

CHAPTER 7

MI6
And The Priory Of Sion

"The paparazzi in London and Paris are crawling with British Intelligence. Some are freelancers on the MI6 payroll, others are our own deep-cover agents ... Even if only to monitor the movements of Princess Diana and Mr Fayed, the Paris paparazzi, on the night in question, would undoubtedly have accommodated a number of our intelligence agents. It would be foolish, quite naive for anyone to imagine otherwise."

British Intelligence source, 1997.

*

"I also learnt while in MI6 that one of the "paparazzi" photographers who routinely followed the Princess of Wales was a member of "UKN", a small corps of part-time MI6 agents who provide miscellaneous services to MI6, such as surveillance and photography expertise. I do not know the identity of this photographer, or whether he was one of the photographers present at the time of the fatal incident. However, I am confident that examination of UKN records would yield the identity of this photographer, and would enable the inquest to eliminate or further investigate that potential line of enquiry."

Richard Tomlinson, former MI6 Officer, 1999.

[Authors' note: Shortly after Mr Tomlinson's above statement was made public, one of the first photographers to arrive at the scene of the Paris crash, James Andanson, was found dead in a burnt-out car in the south of France. The cause of his death has never been satisfactorily established.]

———————

An Historical Motive

From this point on our investigation will be seen to take a new direction, to tackle hitherto unseen and - at first, seemingly - unrelated issues. In effect, this chapter marks the end of our straightforward 'cross-examination' of the facts surrounding the crash itself. And of the mysterious sequence of events which led to Diana's premature death. At the same time it marks the beginning of our inquiry into the 'bloodline secrets' and 'political intrigues' surrounding the princess's death - secrets and intrigues which, we discovered, pervade this case like an aggressive cancer. New areas of investigation will thus be opened up here - areas which may seem somewhat out of place to begin, but which in the end will form the basis for our later bloodline inquiry (in Book Three). For this reason we will not be focusing so much in this chapter on the present-day activities of MI6 - the agency's forays into the world of industrial espionage; its ongoing campaign to supply arms and mercenaries to selected Third World regimes; its so-called defence of the realm - although these issues alone would of course fill a book all by themselves. Plus some.

Rather we intend, in this chapter and the next, to lay the foundation for a broader understanding of how MI6 and the CIA operate worldwide. And more specifically, of how for the past fifty years and more their primary objective has been to ensure that a corporately based, masonically structured European Superstate, complete with its own central banking system, would eventuate from the ashes of World War Two. Also, of course, we intend to demonstrate how this very objective - in the end, and by necessity - extended to include the assassination of a princess. As we shall see, and as unlikely as it may seem, our research informed us that there was something extraordinary about Diana's blood - her heritage, her lineage, her ancestry. And that certain echelons within MI6 and the British Royal Establishment considered this somewhat unique lineage a threat, not only to Britain's current Royal Family, the House of Windsor. But also to the ongoing endeavour to unite Europe under a corporate banner. This theme will become more in evidence as we progress.

For now it is crucial we scrutinize the activities of MI6 and the CIA in this regard - in regard of their infiltration and hijacking of certain religio-royalist and other 'masonic' movements in continental Europe in order to suppress any designs on unification other than the corporate one. Why, for example, was it so important for these agencies to infiltrate and hijack the Priory of Sion? Indeed, who or what is the Priory of Sion and what is its significance in terms of present-day world politics? Why does it still pose the single biggest threat to the unification process? And what, in any case, is the common thread linking the Priory of Sion with the fate of Princess Diana?

And further: what could possibly be the significance of the Cathars in this regard - the medieval movement of Judaeo-Pagan ascetics who populated regions of southwestern France during the eleventh, twelfth and thirteenth centuries? Why were the Cathars deemed such a threat that the Church of Rome should order their massacre? What was the 'Secret' and the 'Treasure' said to have been possessed, first by the Cathars, and later by the Knights Templar? What did this 'Secret' and 'Treasure' signify and of what relevance would it prove in the death of a latter-day princess? And what of the earlier Merovingian kings in this same regard, who ruled large parts of France and Germany during the so-called Dark Ages? Why does history still refer to the Merovingians as the 'sorcerer kings'? What was it about these medieval monarchs that inspired such fear and perfidy in the major political powers of the day, in particular the Church of Rome?

Moreover, how are the Merovingians implicated in the death of Diana?

And further still: at what point did the Knights Templar and the Knights of Malta enter the fray? Why were the Knights Templar effectively eradicated by a joint Franco-Roman conspiracy at the turn of the fourteenth century? On the other hand, why did the Knights of Malta escape any such persecutions? Why is it that the Knights Templar were outlawed and suppressed while the Knights of Malta survived to become one of the best-organized, internationally structured intelligence agencies in the modern world? And again, what does this have to do with the death of Diana?

And finally: what significance would the discovery of ancient parchments in southern France in 1891 bring to bear on this investigation? Why were these parchments later 'procured' by a joint MI6/CIA operation? Why are they still locked away in MI6 archives, secreted in a box marked 'classified'?

And more to the point: what do these parchments reveal with regard to the assassination of Diana, Princess of Wales?

As unlikely as it all may seem, each one of these themes was to play a major role in, and bear a direct relevance to, our investigation into Diana's death. In short, the death of Diana, Princess of Wales, we discovered, was as much the result of an historical conspiracy as it was a current political and/or constitutional one. Indeed, it is our contention that the combination of these themes, when presented in context with Diana's role in the modern world, will expose the truly sinister historical secrets that lie behind the motives for her assassination. For this reason chapters Seven and Eight will focus largely on the hitherto unknown activities of MI6 and the CIA with regard to their ongoing endeavour to unite Europe. Or more specifically, their endeavour to centralize European power in the guise of a corporately based, masonically structured pseudo-democracy, complete with its own central bank and puppet monarchy - the House of Windsor. And to eradicate anyone and anything who might dare to challenge that endeavour.

Indeed, to eradicate the one person who, for reasons we will later discover, constituted its biggest and most dangerous threat.

Special Operations Executive

In a little under a century, MI6 has become one of the Western world's most notorious counter-intelligence organizations - comparable only, perhaps, to the CIA. It is certainly the most covert and compartmentalized agency in Britain. Probably the most unaccountable, too. With a staff said to number around 2000, and an annual budget estimated at £150 million (plus further subsidy from the corporate sector) MI6 boasts a record second only to James Bond. Indeed, author Ian Flemming's character 'M' was based on the fact that, by tradition, successive MI6 chiefs have signed themselves 'C'. It is a coveted designation. In 1994, for example, Sir David Spedding became the latest in an illustrious line of MI6 chiefs dating back to 1909, when the agency - in its present form - was established. It was in this year that MI6 was formally instituted as the foreign arm of Britain's Secret Service Bureau. The Secret Service itself, however, dates back centuries.

Officially, of course - unlike MI5 - MI6 does not exist. Access to MI6 operational records and archives is available only to an elite, covert few. And that 'few' do not necessarily include members of elected authority. Indeed, evidence that such archives even exist is based on the less-than-conclusive testimonies of a small number of former MI6 agents, plus those of one or two 'masonic' sources, including our own source in this regard (see *The Sources Part 2*). Some of these sources claim that the agency, by whatever name, and in effect, was founded during the latter part of the sixteenth century, under Sir Francis Walsingham, paymaster to Queen Elizabeth I. It is certainly known in this regard that successive monarchies down through the ages - in particular the Hanovers-Windsors - have relied heavily on the successes of in-house secret agents for their survival. It is also known, of course, that, even today, MI6 reports first and foremost to the Royal Establishment; though ostensibly accountable to the Foreign Secretary and the newly created House of Commons Intelligence and Security Committee, the higher, more covert echelons and departments within MI6 are run by, and liaise with, a select group of Establishment oligarchs who form the in-house masonic pillar upon which the institution of the British Monarchy is upheld. The extensive and internationally coordinated web of secret societies and masonic organizations utilized by MI6 - and its precursors - since Tudor times, still serves as a highly effective intelligence network via which the continued survival of the British Monarchy is assured.

But it was in 1909 that MI6 found its formal beginnings, certainly in terms of the agency we know today. It was in this year that, under Royal Navy Commander - later Captain - Sir Mansfield Cummings, the foreign arm of Britain's Secret Service Bureau was officially designated Military Intelligence (Department 6). To begin, this new department was tasked with infiltrating foreign-power military and industrial organizations, and gathering intelligence information overseas. In the main, this remit - foreign-power military and industrial espionage - remains number one priority back at MI6 HQ (Vauxhall Cross, South Bank, London). At least this is the case so far as the agency's legitimate operational directive is concerned. Beyond this official directive, however, what might be termed an 'international remit' is actively - though covertly - pursued, as we shall see.

In 1922, MI6 severed itself from the Secret Service Bureau and became an autonomous entity in its own right. Still under the command of Sir Mansfield Cummings - who developed the habit of signing himself 'C', a habit inherited by all of his successors, including the new incumbent (from September 1999), one Richard Billing Dearlove OBE - the agency was renamed SIS (Secret Intelligence Service). At this time SIS became divided and sub-divided into any number of compartmentalized departments. In 1940, for example, the Special Operations Executive (SOE) was formed largely out of SIS department 'D'. It, too, soon became an intelligence agency in its own right. Indeed, during the Second World War, SOE quickly evolved into a new species of intelligence agency entirely - a species more concerned with the 'international agenda' than the national one; more the 'corporate agenda' than the democratic one. Its highest ranking members, for example, were drawn not so much from the military as the corporate and financial world, in particular from the boards of well-known banking, shipping, publishing and insurance companies - most notably Guardian Assurance (later Guardian Royal Exchange Group, and more recently bought by the French insurance group, Axa) with specific connections to the First National Bank Of Chicago and its parent company, the First Chicago Corporation. Plus a host of other major-league companies and corporations, such as Cunard, P&O, Arthur Guinness, Dunlop, Hambros PLC and the National Westminster Bank. At the same time its ambitions included the formation of a corporately controlled United States of Europe. Its more clandestine activities thus included investigations into, and infiltration of, specific European royalist and masonic organizations seen to pose a threat in this regard, such as the mysterious - some might say infamous - Priory of Sion in France (known to support the European ideal, though for its own reasons), plus other neo-chivalric and

Freemasonic orders in Britain and Europe. To add to this, high-ranking SOE members would, together with other interested parties, in particular the CIA, coordinate the setting up of various pro-European lobby groups following the end of WWII. Via their personal connections in the world of banking and corporate finance, of course, untold funds would be generated in support of these groups.

In short, during its relatively short life span (1940-46) SOE developed into a masonically structured, international 'fix-it' organization with strong links to the corporate world, a host of secret societies and, of course, to America's OSS (Office of Strategic Services, precursor of the CIA). Indeed, the CIA would later be formed, in large part, on the SOE blueprint. Via the international web of Freemasonic and other secret societies constructed and coordinated by MI6, SOE's links to European and other foreign-power intelligence agencies should also be noted.

During WWII, of course, SOE worked hand-in-glove with OSS. Under the directorship of Sir Charles Hambro and the overall command of Britain's Minister for Economic Warfare, one Roundell Cecil Palmer, Earl of Selbourne, SOE, together with OSS, was responsible for many of the war's most daring and dangerous covert missions - missions more commonly associated today with, say, Britain's Special Forces elite unit, the SAS, or America's Delta Force. Many missions were undertaken behind enemy lines, for example. Operatives often liaised with local resistance groups, carried out acts of sabotage, and relayed crucial intelligence information back to Britain - such as the movements of enemy troops, enemy hardware, or the precise locations of enemy installations, which would later become targets for bombing raids. In this regard, the actions of SOE and OSS operatives should be commended in the highest degree.

However, there is another, more sinister side to this SIS division - SOE - the more covert activities of which (and their implications) obtain to this day.

Almost immediately following WWII, SOE was officially disbanded. While MI6 continued as Britain's official foreign-arm intelligence gathering agency, high-ranking members of SOE, together with those of the newly formed CIA, secretly pursued their ambitions for a corporately run United States of Europe. General Sir Colin Gubbins, for example, Executive Director of SOE at the end of the war, formed a Member's Association comprised solely of SOE veterans. At the same time, another former SOE operative, Roland Malreaux - together with his brother, Andre Malreaux, a high-ranking member of the Priory of Sion and former French Resistance coordinator - formed a similar organization in France. Together these organizations worked closely with the CIA, funnelling vast sums of money into the coffers of the burgeoning European Movement, creating and sponsoring 'front groups' for a united Europe, and sponsoring other leading protagonists of this same ideal - such as international power-broker and major-league player in the bid to unite Europe, Dr Josef Retinger. (Interestingly, and despite his Polish birth, Retinger was also an SOE operative during WWII - see *The Bilderberg Connection* in *Chapter Eight*.) Other than this shared ambition for the unification of Europe under a corporate banner - which, as we shall see, included moves to forestall the restoration of a certain royal dynasty to the Throne of France (perhaps even to the Throne of Britain), the formerly known Merovingian Dynasty - precisely the motivation for forming these organizations is little known. Precisely what they got up to is also little known. However, what *is* known is that, together with the CIA and high-ranking members of the Priory of Sion (including the Priory's then future Grand Master, Pierre Plantard de Saint-Clair) they played a crucial role in returning Charles de Gaulle to power in 1958, thus ensuring that the Communist movement in France at that time remained sidelined. And perhaps more significantly, it is also known that - again, together with MI6, the CIA and suborned members of the Priory of Sion - these organizations were responsible for the transfer of some rather intriguing documents, to Britain from France, some time during the mid-1950s.

It is these documents - or rather, parchments - that were to play a key role in our investigation.

The Parchments

No doubt due to the massive international success of *The Holy Blood And The Holy Grail* (Baigent, Leigh, Lincoln) plus a veritable welter of similar material published over recent decades, the story of the Rennes-le-Chateau mystery is today well-known. In brief, in the village of Rennes-le-Chateau in southern France, in 1891, a number of mysterious antique parchments were unearthed by the local parish priest, Berenger Sauniere. There are a number of significant factors surrounding this discovery which, in their synthesis, bear direct relevance to our own inquiry.

One: the region surrounding Rennes-le-Chateau is a former stronghold of both Cathars and Templars alike, and is the site of the so-called 'Albigensian Crusade' - the Church-sponsored massacre of thousands of Cathars (or Albigensians) at the beginning of the thirteenth century. This action would seem to have been prognostic of a similar action which would occur some seventy years later - the suppression and dissolution of the Knights Templar, in which many Templars also met their deaths at the hands of Church and government forces (AD 1307-1314). It would seem that, for some reason, both Pope Clement V and King Philippe IV (Le Bel) of France felt threatened by the continued existence of the Templars, as indeed their predecessors had felt threatened by the continued existence of the 'heretical' Cathars some seventy years earlier. While the Templars are known to have harboured some 'terrible secret' regarding Jesus and the Judaic royal bloodline, the Cathars - themselves of Judaic origin - are considered by some to have been the legitimate bloodline descendants of the above-mentioned Merovingians. Or at least that some of the Merovingians' descendants formed part of their number. In turn, of course, it is claimed that the Merovingians were the descendants of the Judaic Royal Dynasty of Kings David and Solomon - and purportedly, of Jesus, too. What is known for certain is that the Merovingians were indeed of Judaic origin, that they ruled over large parts of France and Germany from around AD 350-750, and that for some reason they were held in uniquely high regard by the relevant political and religious powers of the day - first among these, of course, the Church of Rome. What is also known is that, before being exterminated by the Church, the Cathars had been guardians of some as yet unidentified 'Secret' or 'Treasure', which they had inherited from the Visigoths, themselves historically related to the Merovingians by inter-dynastic alliances and marriages. Certainly it is known that the Cathars harboured an inestimable wealth, the origin of which has been associated with the Holy Grail, and with the lost Treasure of the Temple of Jerusalem, or the Ark of the Covenant.

Two: in AD 66-70, Jewish militants executed the latest in a series of failed uprisings against Rome. This particular uprising resulted in Jerusalem being sacked, hundreds of Jews being massacred, and the Temple's inner sanctum, the Holy of Holies, being plundered of its legendary 'Treasure'. The Treasure, said to have included the Ark of the Covenant and other gold artefacts, as well as certain 'scrolls', 'tablets', 'parchments' and other written 'texts', was subsequently ferried back to Rome, only to be plundered a second time in AD 410 - this time by marauding Visigoths who sacked Rome under Alaric the Great. Following the death of Alaric, in AD 412 the Visigoths invaded Gaul, and then Spain, establishing an empire which straddled the Pyrenees and included the mountain-top village we now know as Rennes-le-Chateau in southwestern France. Indeed, Rennes-le-Chateau was to become one of the most important bastions in the Visigoth empire, and according to some historians, was later established as the empire's northern capital. In consequence, the Treasure of the Temple of Jerusalem, plundered from Rome by the Visigoths, is said to have been deposited somewhere in the region of Rennes-le-Chateau, where it was later inherited by the Cathars and/or the Knights Templar, both of whom were to suffer unspeakable consequences as a result.

Three: in 1244, during the last days of the siege of Montsegur - the Pyrenean mountain fortress close to Rennes-le-Chateau, and the final Cathar stronghold against Pope Innocent III's forces - the Cathars' 'Treasure', in whatever form, is known to have been smuggled down the mountain and again deposited somewhere in the region of Rennes-le-Chateau, possibly even in the village itself. It is postulated that this Treasure, at least in part, took the form of the parchments discovered by Berenger Sauniere some six and a half centuries later, in 1891.

Four: two of the parchments are known to have contained genealogies, and that these genealogies prove the survival of the Merovingian bloodline. (Moreover, together with other recently unearthed genealogical records, they show that the House of Windsor is the product of a usurped - or 'politically cultivated' - strain of this same Judaic bloodline.) A third parchment contains what has been referred to as a 'secret of state' - the inference being that this so-called 'state secret' involves the restoration of the Merovingian bloodline to the Throne of France, possibly even the Throne of Britain - while the fourth contains biblical verses, cryptographically arranged. In effect, the significance of these parchments is that they bear witness to the still-existent, still-potent bloodline of Kings David and Solomon of Israel; moreover, to the legitimacy of this Judaic royal bloodline's claim on the French - possibly even the British - Throne. And what is more, together with other genealogical records known to be held by the Priory of Sion, they imply very strongly that this same Judaic royal bloodline can be traced back to Jesus - the insinuation being, of course, that Jesus too was a *de jure* King of Israel; and further, that he was married, that he sired children, that those children bore generations of their own, and that these descendants of Jesus and the Judaic royal bloodline today survive as a potential threat to both the institutions of the French Republic and the British Monarchy. Moreover, to Anglo-American ambitions for a corporately run United States of Europe. And in any event, that interested parties in the West remain acutely aware of the tremendous political implications involved in the discovery of the parchments is evident in their fastidious attempts to keep this information - these parchments - secret. Our own source in this regard, for example, claims that these and/or similar parchments and documents - plus others dating back to at least AD 200, which further confirm the survival of this same Judaic royal bloodline - are currently in the hands of MI6 (see *The Sources Part 2*). Certainly we know that British and US Intelligence obtained the 'Sauniere parchments', and that MI6 and SOE, together with the CIA, were largely instrumental in their transfer from France to Britain during the 1950s, as we shall see.

But whatever the truth of all this, one thing is clear. For some reason yet to be fully ascertained and understood, the discovery of these parchments made Berenger Sauniere a very wealthy man. Following the discovery, for example, and despite his relatively low-key standing as a parish priest, he is known to have spent vast sums of money, and to suddenly have become accepted into some very influential religious, political, social and Freemasonic circles indeed. Whether or not the parchments alone were the source of his sudden elevation to fame and fortune, of course, is not known. (Although this remains doubtful in the extreme.) What is known, though, is that British and US interest in the parchments was massive - at least sufficient that, during the 1940s and 1950s, MI6 and the CIA became deeply involved in the mystery. As did Mossad, French Intelligence, and before them, agents of Hitler's Third Reich. Indeed, Hitler himself. At the same time, of course, there is no doubt whatever that the existence of the parchments induced major solicitude in certain masonic echelons of the corporate world. And that, in consequence, agents of the corporate world sought to obtain them. And having obtained them, keep them secret.

That the 'genealogies' and the so-called 'state secret' contained in the parchments bear extreme relevance to the continuing bid to unite Europe under a corporate banner, then, would seem beyond question. That they are considered a threat to the continued ascendancy of the House of Windsor is equally evident. Indeed, that the 'common denominator' in all of these intrinsically interwoven themes is a mystery based on the preservation and restoration of a royal bloodline which is essentially Judaic in origin; and that - as we shall later explore - a 'bastardized', 'usurped' or 'politically cultivated' strain of this same Judaic bloodline underpins the House of Windsor and its ongoing endeavour to survive the unification of Europe, makes for a very interesting situation indeed. In particular when the relationship between Princess Diana and Dodi Fayed is brought into the equation. As we all know, in a political sense, Judaic and Arabic 'bloodlines' do not mix at all well. Indeed, genealogies such as those contained in the parchments - plus others we will come across later - show clearly enough the high-level intrigues and machinations which have conspired across centuries to keep this Judaic strain precisely that: Judaic. The inference being that, had the future Queen Mother of the House of Windsor ever married an Arab Muslim, then the House of Windsor's decades-long struggle to survive the unification of Europe as this bloodline's titular head would have been severely compromised. Indeed, the House of Windsor's position as this bloodline's titular head would have become untenable. End of story.

Of course, there is no concrete proof that Diana and Dodi ever did intend to tie the marital knot. But many factors conspire to suggest that indeed they might have done just that, given time. It was a real possibility. Could then the House of Windsor - and more importantly, those whose futures depend on the House of Windsor's post-European survival, say, the House of Windsor's corporate sponsors, the masonic oligarchy for which the House of Windsor stands as titular head - could they have taken the chance that the possibility of Diana's marriage to Dodi Fayed would never have become reality?

Or would they have been forced to *ensure* that it never became reality? Because if this is indeed the case, then there was only ever one way to achieve that.

MI6 Archives
The Priory Of Sion
And The Sovereign Military Order Of Malta

Certainly when we think of MI6, apparent 'myths' such as the survival of a royal bloodline which may or may not have included Jesus Christ seem less than credible, to say the least. That the agency might be actively pursuing a policy to conceal information regarding that bloodline - if for no more sinister reason than to prevent its influence from disrupting the unification of Europe - seems equally unlikely. It is almost as if two diametrically opposing worlds have become confused. On the one hand, the world of espionage and counter-espionage; on the other, the world of invention. The image of British spies infiltrating known terrorist organizations abroad, staving off the latest Communist threat or facilitating the rise to power of one or another Third World dictatorship of course seems more realistic; infiltrating foreign-power organizations and gaining access to military and industrial secrets perhaps even more so. But even this image is a romantic one; it is quixotic, if not flawed. As is the notion that Britain's Secret Intelligence Service was set up, first and foremost, to protect British interests abroad - military, industrial or otherwise. While designated departments within SIS are indeed there to ensure that this popular myth is actualized - that British interests abroad are indeed safeguarded against acts of terrorism, infiltration, subversion, etc. - the bulk of work undertaken by this agency is of an altogether different nature.

We have already asserted that MI6 utilizes an international web of secret societies and other masonic and Freemasonic organizations in its endeavour to keep abreast of world affairs. Indeed, to aid its foreign-territory operations, period. To some this may seem an unsubstantiated, purely speculative assertion. But it is not. On the contrary, it is an assertion based on already uncovered and substantiated evidence. And in any case, that agencies such as MI6 should utilize an already established, highly secretive and well-organized global network as a channel for sensitive communications is surely aught but logical. Many of these organizations, remember, are internationally structured, and thus are able to offer the perfect stage upon which to conduct secret international affairs. In this regard they offer a highly effective means by which to gather, exchange and disseminate intelligence information. Secret organizations, by their nature, are secretive. They hold secret meetings. They arrange secret functions, each exclusive to elected members. Among these members might be, say, the chiefs of various intelligence departments - Director of MI6 Operations meets CIA Head of Station in London, for example. Over a glass of wine names might be mentioned, introductions arranged, information exchanged. In any event, many high-ranking members of the intelligence community, be they British, American or otherwise, are known to be members of some of the world's most notorious secret and masonic organizations. Two examples in this regard are John McCone and William Casey, both former CIA Directors. And they were both members of perhaps the oldest and most formidable secret society-cum-intelligence agency in the Western world - the internationally networked Sovereign Military Order of Malta, (or the Knights of Malta).

The relevance of the Order of Malta in respect of our own investigation will become evident a little later.

Another example in this same regard - one more immediately pertinent to our investigation - is General Sir Colin Gubbins, Executive Director of SOE at the end of WWII. Gubbins is known to have forged suspiciously close ties with the Priory of Sion during his time in office (indeed, during WWII the Priory of Sion included many high-ranking members of the French Resistance, who in turn worked very closely with OSS, MI6 and, in particular, SOE). It is suspected that, during the 1950s, Gubbins became a member of the Priory of Sion himself - together with one or two very high-ranking US industrialists and CIA executives, as well as several other British dignitaries from the corporate and intelligence worlds. At any rate, this joint MI6/CIA infiltration programme, initiated soon after the war, and vigorously pursued throughout the decades which followed, was to prove an enormous success. In 1984, for example, it would prove responsible for the sudden and unexpected resignation of the Priory of Sion's then Grand Master, Pierre Plantard de Saint-Clair. (Indeed, some, including Pierre Plantard de Saint-Clair, would go so far as to refer to this programme as the 'Anglo-American' takeover - the hijacking of the Priory of Sion and its 'bloodline secrets' by British and US intelligence agencies, as indeed many other such masonic orders have been similarly hijacked for their usefulness in terms of international intelligence gathering. There is even reason to believe that this particular hijacking was a prime mover in forcing the Priory of Sion to 'go public' in 1956, after centuries of anonymity. Paradoxically, when push comes to shove, 'going public' is often deemed the most effective way to ensure the preservation of one's most valuable assets. In terms of international gamesmanship, of course, an 'open secret' can be as valuable to its keeper as a hidden one. Often more so. An 'open secret' can - and often does - elicit public support.)

Other suspected members of this infiltration programme included Lord Selbourne, Minister for Economic Warfare and overall head of SOE during WWII. Selbourne is known to have acquainted himself, somewhat intimately, with religio-royalist movements in continental Europe (in particular the Priory of Sion) and to have visited the region surrounding Rennes-le-Chateau, the site of the Sauniere discovery, on several occasions. Another suspected conspirator was Sir Thomas Frazer, described as a confidential agent of Buckingham Palace and Director of North British and Mercantile Insurance. Others included Sir William Stephenson and Sir Charles Hambro, director of SOE during WWII. Captain Ronald Stansmore Nutting, former director of Guardian Assurance, Governor of the Bank of Ireland and MI5 executive, was another. Also implicated - indeed, directly involved - was Viscount Frederick Leathers, who, like Nutting, also sat on the board of Guardian Assurance, as well as those of P&O shipping company and the National Westminster Bank. During WWII Leathers was a high-ranking minister on Winston Churchill's War Cabinet. His connections in the world of shipping and corporate finance made him a natural choice for his role as Minister of War Transport.

Of further interest is the fact that, following WWII, General Sir Colin Gubbins emerged as a major player in the joint MI6/CIA endeavour to buttress and galvanize the burgeoning European Movement - an operation which led to the inauguration of the Bilderberg conferences in 1954 (see *The Bilderberg Connection* in *Chapter Eight*). Indeed, one could safely assert that Gubbins was a founding member of the so-called Bilderberg Group. It is certainly known that this highly secretive international power group began life in the 'wilderness of mirrors' - in the scarcely definable, almost chimerical world of counter-intelligence, where corporate ambition, masonic edifice and the machinations of international espionage merge to form a very powerful international beast indeed. It is confederacies such as the Bilderberg Group - together with orders such as the Royal Institute of International Affairs and the Knights of Malta - which, to a very large degree, comprise this beast's framework. And in the files of this framework's membership the names of some of the Western world's most prominent intelligence personnel are to be found. Like the heads of MI6 and the CIA, for example.

In any event, according to certain notarized documents gleaned from the Priory of Sion by Michael Baigent, Richard Leigh and Henry Lincoln, the above-named Leathers and Nutting, together with one Major Hugh Murchison Clowes DSO, were responsible for the transfer of the 'Sauniere parchments' from France to Britain in 1955. In their book, *The Messianic Legacy*, Baigent, Leigh and Lincoln describe how these and a handful of other masonic luminaries - twenty-four in number, all from the corporate, political, military and intelligence worlds - secured the transfer of at least three of the four parchments to Britain from France for purposes of "historical research". The notarized documents made mention of the "demand for the recognition of Merovingian rights", and also stated that the three parchments, "whose value cannot be calculated", contained "proof of the direct descent" of the Merovingian bloodline "through the House of Plantard". Plantard, of course, was the name of the Priory of Sion's Grand Master from 1981-1984, Pierre Plantard de Saint-Clair, who indeed claimed that he and his family were direct lineal descendants of the Merovingian bloodline. He further claimed that the Priory of Sion was in possession of the lost Treasure of the Temple of Jerusalem (the same 'Treasure' allegedly possessed by the Cathars and/or the Knights Templar some 750 years earlier); that certain interested parties were concerned because of specific genealogical documents also possessed by the order (which proved both the origins and the survival of the Merovingian bloodline); and that, as mentioned above, the reason Pierre Plantard de Saint-Clair had resigned as the Priory's Grand Master in 1984 was due largely - if not entirely - to the influence of what he referred to as the "Anglo-American contingent". It would seem that, by 1984, the so-called "Anglo-American contingent" had infiltrated the order to the extent that it had indeed hijacked it. Certainly we know that, according to a disgruntled Priory of Sion, and as reported in *The Messianic Legacy*, the Sauniere parchments had been "obtained and brought to England 'by fraud'", and had subsequently "found their way into the Knights of Malta's archives". Given the Priory of Sion's somewhat radical standpoint with regard to the 'bloodline of Jesus', and conversely, the Knights of Malta's allegiance to an orthodox Vatican in this regard, it is easy to understand the Priory's concern. The added fact that the archives of the Knights of Malta and those of MI6 can, and these days often do, harbour the same data, would have served only to exacerbate the Priory's position.

For a period of some months following their transfer from France, the parchments were held by what appears to have been an MI6 'front company', the so-called International League of Antiquarian Booksellers (situated at that time in Great Russell Street, London, opposite the British Museum). A year later, however, at the personal request of Lord Selbourne, permission was granted by the French Consul-General in London for the parchments to be retained in Britain for at least a further 25 years. The document granting this permission contained the Consul-General's seal and signature, and was dated 29th August, 1956. (This in itself proved an enigma, however - the French Consul-General had no authority to grant such permission. On the contrary, permission of this nature could only have been obtained from the French Ministry of Culture in Paris. It would seem that, behind the scenes, an 'unseen party' had intervened in order to ensure that the parchments remained in British hands. Indeed, it is unlikely that any such permission was ever gained from the French authorities. Rather that the French Consul-General was either on the MI6 payroll, or that he was bypassed altogether - that the British Foreign Office had intervened, and that, as a result, the parchments remained the exclusive property of MI6.)

At any rate, according to this document the parchments were subsequently retrieved from their holding with the International League of Antiquarian Booksellers and deposited in a strongbox at Lloyds Bank Europe Ltd. Lord Selbourne's request included the provision that the existence of the parchments, and in particular the fact that they were to remain in British hands, should be classified. No one was to know about them. This is scarcely surprising. According to our own source, for example, the parchments *never were* deposited with Lloyds Bank Europe. Indeed, as Baigent, Leigh and Lincoln discovered, Lloyds Bank Europe did not exist in 1956. At that time all European branches of Lloyds were known as Lloyds Bank Foreign. It was not until 1964 that Lloyds Bank Foreign became Lloyds Bank Europe. (Once again, it appeared that MI6 and the British Foreign Office were manipulating events behind the scenes.) According to our own source in this regard (a former British Foreign Office historian) these parchments and others were in fact deposited not with Lloyds Bank, but with the British Museum - which, remember, is situated directly opposite the property which, in 1956, housed the so-called International League of Antiquarian Booksellers. More precisely, our source informed us that the parchments in question - and others like them - had been deposited in what he referred to as the "inner sanctum" of the British Museum, a claim which is further substantiated by former intelligence operative Dr John Coleman, who says that he once worked in the Museum in a highly classified capacity. And further, that the Museum's above-top-secret "inner sanctum" indeed houses some very interesting documents pertaining to the origins and legitimacy of the House of Windsor. But as we were to discover, what is of particular note here is the fact that the British Museum's so-called "inner sanctum" archives just happen to be one and the same with MI6 archives. They comprise the same 'strongbox', so to speak. The same 'vault'.

But what is even more revealing - and as stated above - is the fact that, in effect, MI6 archives and the archives of the Sovereign Military Order of Malta also comprise this same mysterious 'vault', metaphorically speaking. At least, according to our source, this is the case with regard to records and files of the nature described above. Circles within circles. It would seem that, in terms of the international agenda, the MI6 strongbox, the British Museum's "inner sanctum" and the archives of the Order of Malta (feasibly, the CIA's archives, too) in truth comprise the same box, the same vault, the same top-secret databank. As the Priory of Sion had claimed, then, the Sauniere parchments had indeed been "obtained and brought to England 'by fraud'", and had subsequently "found their way into the Knights of Malta's archives". The joint MI6/CIA operation - the "Anglo-American" bid to infiltrate the Priory of Sion in order to obtain the genealogical data contained in the Sauniere parchments - had been successful. The machinations of masonic government had seen to that.

The question is, of course, if the mystery surrounding Rennes-le-Chateau and the Merovingian bloodline - indeed, the threat posed by that bloodline's documented survival - is aught but invention, a lie, a myth (as the relevant authorities are all too eager to maintain), then why did MI6 and the CIA go to such inordinate lengths to procure the parchments in the first place - as evinced by the notarized documents gleaned by Baigent, Leigh and Lincoln and certified by one PJF Freeman, Notary by Royal Appointment? Why would documentary evidence of this kind - of this so-called 'medieval myth' - be deemed so important to the British and US authorities? Why were these parchments brought back to Britain and, together with previously acquired material in this same regard, locked away in a box marked 'classified'?

And moreover, why is this material still there? Might it conceal some deeper, more abstruse motive regarding the assassination of a Merovingian princess, for example?

Food for thought...

A Counter-Monarchy

The implications surrounding Princess Diana's death begin to assume major new proportions, then: global proportions; historical proportions. In particular when her name is linked, by blood, to the possible restoration of what can only be described as a 'counter-monarchy' to the Thrones of France and Britain. And as we shall see, Diana's name has indeed been associated with such a restoration.

The implication here, of course, is that, while the House of Windsor is known to represent a 'usurped', 'bastardized' or 'politically cultivated' strain of the Judaic-Merovingian royal bloodline (what today we might term a 'genetically modified' strain), Diana's lineage, like that of former Priory Grand Master, Pierre Plantard de Saint-Clair, can be traced directly back to the

Merovingian kings of Dark Ages Europe. She was thus recognized by the potentates of this politico-royal chess game to represent the legitimate strain of the Judaic-Merovingian royal bloodline. And because she was, her massive popularity became a very serious threat indeed. As we now know, the genealogies contained in the Sauniere parchments were procured by MI6 for the very reason that they referred to the "demand for the recognition of Merovingian rights". We also know that the parchments, "whose value cannot be calculated", and which contained "proof of the direct descent" of the Merovingian bloodline, ended up in "the Knights of Malta's archives". In other words, in MI6 archives. The reason they ended up in MI6 archives, of course, is that the information they contain fundamentally undermines the authority of the House of Windsor to reign. At the same time it recognizes "Merovingian rights" - the rights of the Judaic royal bloodline's legitimate heirs - to the Throne. (And as we shall see, moves to restore this 'legitimate' strain to the Throne of Britain, or at least to the Throne of an independent Scotland, are ongoing.) Indeed, for this very reason, and for purposes of political gain, this legitimate royal strain - its descendants and its heirs - has for centuries been suppressed, persecuted and eradicated by the sponsors of what has become, in effect, the genetically modified 'Windsor strain'.

The implications are thus momentous, and will be fully explored and elucidated in Book Three.

In any event, in regard of what might be termed the 'bloodline motive' behind the princess's death, the evidence suggests an historical link which seems inextricably bound up with British/US endeavours to unite Europe under a corporate banner. Or more precisely, under a Judaeo-Christian banner which is masonically structured and corporately funded, and which by necessity demands the continued suppression of the legitimate Judaic-Merovingian bloodline and its heirs. As we shall see, Britain and the United States have been steadily working towards the unification of Europe under a corporate banner for at least the past fifty years, while the British Monarchy in the meantime has asserted *its* authority on the process by virtue of its illegitimate claim on the Judaic royal bloodline - which, in one form or another, has ruled Europe for the past two thousand years. While MI6 and the CIA must remain prime suspects in our inquiry, then, nevertheless it is imperative we establish on whose behalf these agencies were working. And why Diana posed such a threat that they deemed her assassination necessary. True, Diana's landmines campaign impacted on international agendas at a deeper, more incisive level than many realize - in the minds of some people this in itself was reason enough for the assassination to be ordered. Our own investigation, on the other hand, has uncovered evidence which suggests that the landmines campaign was but the tip of the iceberg, so to speak. That while her landmines campaign undoubtedly made waves, it was the combination of Diana's newly found, highly effective and extremely high-profile ambassadorial role, plus the very fact of who she was (in an ancestral sense), and what she represented (in a political, constitutional and historical sense), that ultimately sealed her fate. Simply put, Diana was a modern woman ambushed by the requirements of a *Jurassic* though still powerful institution. Her mind was twentieth-century. But the fact that she had been selected as the mother of the future king meant that her destiny was bound by the constraints of institutions and traditions which root themselves in antiquity. For this reason we must scrutinize here the agencies which today represent that antiquity - those from which such modern-day agencies as MI6 and the CIA have evolved.

It is for these reasons that we have so rigorously pursued the 'bloodline conspiracy' in our effort to uncover the most likely - indeed, the most deep-rooted - motives behind Princess Diana's death. In Book Three we will outline the machinations of this conspiracy in more historical detail, and in far more depth. For now, however, we must go in search of the agencies which serve to maintain and sustain those machinations in the modern world - agencies which inspired the post-WWII creation of such a masonically structured, international intelligence network as exists today. Agencies which continue to provide the support and facility necessary to uphold such a secretive and well-organized global network. Agencies which continue to combat the restitution of an ancient and royal bloodline to the thrones of Europe - a bloodline represented in Kings David and Solomon, in Jesus, in the Merovingian kings of Dark Ages Europe. A bloodline also represented, as we shall see, in Princess Diana. At the same time, of course, these agencies continue to pursue the very goal they were set up to achieve: the unification of Europe under a pseudo-democratic system which is wholly masonic in its structure, wholly corporate in its ideology, and furtively totalitarian in its *modus operandi*. Agencies such as the Sovereign Military Order of Malta, for example.

The Knights Of Saint John

The Knights Hospitaller of Saint John - or as its major surviving offshoot is known today, the Sovereign Military Order of Malta, or the Knights of Malta - is perhaps one of the least-known, though best-organized and best-connected intelligence agencies in the Western world. It is known, for example, that this highly secretive masonic order, today based in Rome, constitutes the major conduit for intelligence information passing between the Vatican and the Western world's senior intelligence agencies - first among these, of course, MI6 and the CIA. Together with other neo-chivalric orders, secret societies and Freemasonic organizations, the Order of Malta has even been implicated in instances of assassination, as well as high-finance irregularities. By virtue of its association with the CIA-sponsored Masonic Lodge, P2, for example, and the Vatican's own dubious agencies, Opus Dei and Pro Deo, the Order has aligned itself with activities such as the assassination of Pope John Paul I in 1978, as well as those of international money laundering, and even the rigging of so-called 'democratic elections'. A case in point is the 'election' to power of the right-wing Christian Democratic Party in Italy in 1948. By the handiwork of agents such as Dr Josef Retinger and James Jesus Angleton - former CIA Head of Station in Rome - the Christian Democratic Party received millions of dollars in sponsorship funds. This plus a little counter-intelligence work on the part of MI6 and the CIA, together with agents of the Order of Malta, proved sufficient to ensure the party's success at the Italian 'elections'. Of added interest is the fact that, in 1946, James Jesus Angleton was decorated by the Order of Malta for his work in counter-intelligence.

Western powers would argue, of course, that the Christian Democratic Party was 'helped' to power in order to stave off the growing Communist threat in Italy immediately following WWII. But surely, a democratic system is a democratic system. Neither one side nor the other - neither Left nor Right - in an ideal society, should receive vast donations or any other kind of covert assistance from foreign governments in order to cheat its way into power. But then, we do not live in an ideal society. Indeed, to judge by these and other activities undertaken by MI6 - the covert supply of arms and mercenaries to Sierra Leone in 1997, for example, again ensuring the success of one political faction over another - we do not even live in a *democratic* society, much less an ideal one. The truth of the matter is, of course, that the operation which eventuated in the Christian Democrats gaining power in Italy, as long ago as 1948, was all part of the ongoing struggle to unite Europe under a corporate (or a Capitalist, non-Communist) government. For the record, this operation was also partly financed by Swiss-held Nazi funds. With a little help from CIA Head of Station in Bern, Allen Dulles, vast sums of Nazi 'black' money were channelled, via the Vatican - and the Order of Malta - into Christian Democrat accounts. Indeed, it is suspected that certain Nazi war chiefs and industrialists purchased their post-war freedom in this way. It is certainly known that P2, itself organized around neo-Nazi ideals, laundered millions of dollars of Nazi funds - 'black' funds - during its own rise to power in the late 1950s/early 1960s. The involvement of the Order of Malta in this regard is further implicated in that a number of P2 members were/are also Knights of Malta.

It should also be noted here that, although certain echelons of the Order of Malta are indeed deeply and directly involved in the world of international espionage, effectively it is still an hospitaller organization. The well-known 'St John's Ambulance' brigade in Britain (a Protestant offshoot of the original Knights Hospitaller of Saint John) is but one example of the original Order's ongoing work to minister medical care to communities worldwide. Indeed, the present-day 'Catholic' Order of Malta supports a similar service, and there can be little doubt that many of its members are motivated to join the Order purely for humanitarian reasons. In paradox, however, this makes the work carried out by its 'higher-ranking members' even more unspeakable. Though no less effective. Behind the facade - which includes an International Rescue-style operation which offers aid in instances of natural disaster, as well as leper camps, hospitals and other much-needed sanctuaries worldwide - international power games are planned and executed. The power game which most intrinsically affects our own investigation, of course, is the one which seeks to establish a united corporate front in Europe. And this requires precisely the kind of closely knit, well-organized, exclusively interconnected network provided by the Order of Malta. As well as by a number of other, similar international organizations. The reason we have elected to focus on the Order of Malta here is, firstly, to demonstrate how such organizations are indeed infiltrated and hijacked by the intelligence services, and subsequently turned to their own uses; and secondly, because - so far as can be ascertained - the Order's own in-house intelligence agency played a salient role, together with MI6 and the CIA, in procuring the Sauniere parchments from France. In so doing, of course, the Order clearly stated a commitment to British and US interests, in particular with regard to neutralizing existing threats to the unification of Europe - the unification of Europe, that is, according to the corporate ('Anglo-American') agenda. Given that the Order is traditionally allied to Vatican interests - and thus ostensibly opposed to British/US interests - it is equally clear that the information to be gleaned from the Sauniere parchments would have been of mutual benefit to both parties. And in any case, this would not have been the first time that the two sides had colluded. The above-cited 'election rigging' operation in 1948, for example, is a further case in point.

Factions

As we will explore in more detail later, there would appear to be two very distinct factions, each at odds with the other, with regard to the unification process. On the one hand, there is the so-called 'Anglo-American' faction, which would appear to be consolidated in, and directed by, a centralized policy-making group such as that which convenes, on an annual basis, at the Bilderberg conferences. This faction would appear to include German interests also. On the other hand, there is what might be termed the 'Franco-Vatican' faction, which presupposes a tacit alliance between the French administration and the Church of Rome (an alliance that dates back centuries, and to which, ordinarily, the Order of Malta is committed). Of course, nothing is ever so cut-and-dried in the world of international politics and power-brokering. The ground is often uncultivated, the boundaries demarcating one territory from the other ever shifting, and in many cases ill-defined. To add to this, of course, the sum of territories covered by both sides must at all costs be defended against infiltration by and/or threats from other, 'outside influences'. Russian influences might be a case in point. Those of oil-rich Arab power blocs might be considered another. Very often this situation forces an alliance between the two sides. Talks are held. Concessions are made. Deals are cut. Agreements are reached. By virtue of the fact that the two apparent disputants share a mutual interest, seek a mutual outcome, certain compromises are made by which both parties, to a large extent, are able to further their own interests and at the same time maintain their original postures. The two might collaborate, for example, in order to stave off the threat of Russian, or indeed Arab Muslim, excursions into the territories covered by either one or the other. Or in some cases both. Of course, one could argue that this is the very nature of politics anyway, be they local, national, or indeed - as in this case - international. The above definition regarding these two 'distinct factions' - Anglo-American, Franco-Vatican - offers a rudimentary overview, nonetheless.

A third faction should also be cited here. In terms of political power in the modern world, of course, this third faction should be understood as little more than a thorn in the sides of the aforementioned Anglo-American and Franco-Vatican factions. But its influence is nevertheless felt. Indeed, it is felt to the extent that the two senior feuding factions have, over the centuries - and no less concertedly and insidiously of late - conspired to neutralize this faction's stake in the game, so to speak. This has been achieved, in large part, by such operations as cited above: the joint MI6/CIA operation which succeeded in hijacking the Priory of Sion, and in consequence, obtaining - "by fraud" - the Sauniere parchments. At the same time similar operations designed to further incapacitate this faction's legitimacy - and thereby its influence - are ongoing. The faction in question, largely represented by the original, pre-hijacked Priory of Sion, together with other, lesser known bodies and certain suppressed royal houses, might be termed the 'Merovingian faction'.

We will of course explore this theme in greater detail in Book Three, *The Bloodline Conspiracy*. Suffice for now to say that, in terms of present-day international politics, the Merovingian faction has little to offer. It has been bled dry. And more than this. It has been systematically dismantled and disabled - and publicly discredited - by either one, or both, of the senior political factions vying for European supremacy. Indeed, this situation would explain the clandestine coalition between, on the one hand, MI6 and the CIA, and on the other, the Order of Malta and the Vatican. As we have seen, it is not uncommon for two seeming adversaries to pool their resources when both are threatened by a third, potentially dangerous force. It would seem that the Merovingian threat - represented by the Priory of Sion - was indeed seen in this light. And understandably so. As seen through the eyes of, say, MI6, for example, the Priory of Sion would have posed a threat of the highest order. Its assets, remember, included a 'Secret' (genealogical proof of the survival of the Merovingian bloodline) and a 'Treasure' (surviving legitimate heirs to that bloodline), the combined implications of which are so vast that they threaten the very existence of both the French Republic and the British Monarchy, as well as the Vatican. And perhaps even more alarming, this threat also extends to the Anglo-American assault on European unity. The Priory of Sion does not stand alone in representing this so-called 'third faction', of course. But it has, it seems, born the brunt of recriminations perpetrated against it, certainly during the latter half of the twentieth century. It is little wonder, then, that the Priory of Sion should have been set about by this intelligence 'pincer movement' - by MI6 and the CIA on the one flank, by the Order of Malta and the Vatican on the other.

Simply put, and in effect, the Priory of Sion - and by implication the third or Merovingian faction - has been successfully routed. Certainly with the hijacking of the Priory of Sion and its 'bloodline secrets' there would seem little if any hope of this faction ever regaining momentum.

Unless, of course, a certain Merovingian princess were to enter the fray. In particular a princess who was so popular that public opinion underwrote her every appeal. We noted the point.

Political Enemy Number One
And The Battle Of The Knights

Seen in this light, the Priory of Sion might be considered 'political enemy number one' by such organizations as the Order of Malta. And not only today. On the contrary, it would seem that this situation has obtained for some centuries. Both, for example, were born out of the religio-political situation which obtained throughout Middle Ages Europe, in particular as that situation pertained to geopolitical rights in Jerusalem. At this time there seems to have been two distinct European disputants with regard to who should control the Holy City. On the one hand, the Vatican, which had some centuries earlier constituted itself as the most powerful edifice in Christendom. And as such considered itself rightful heir to the Throne of Christendom's capital city,

Jerusalem. On the other hand, the vestigial Merovingian Dynasty, legitimate bloodline descendant of Kings David and Solomon, and purportedly Jesus, and which was by the turn of the second millennium AD represented by an organization known as the Order of Sion (precursor of the Priory of Sion). By virtue of the fact that the Order of Sion represented the House of Judah, it considered *its* claim on the Holy City the rightful one. The battle for Jerusalem had begun. And with it, of course, the battle for European supremacy, in both a political and an economic sense, as well as a religious sense. It is this same battle which, today, is culminating in the bid to unite Europe under a corporate banner.

At the turn of the twelfth century, however, the situation was somewhat different. Having effectively eradicated the Merovingian bloodline some four hundred years earlier, at least in terms of its sovereign and political power; and having subsequently established what were, in effect, usurper dynasties born of its own artifice on the thrones of many European countries, the Church of Rome, in seeking to further consolidate its already supreme power in Europe, sought to regain possession of the one asset which had eluded its grasp for more than half a millennium. It was the one asset which the Church sought above all others. Not only would it re-establish Rome's authority as absolute, as having been personally sanctioned by God, and thereby augment its secular power even further towards divine autonomy. It would also further legitimize the various usurper monarchies the Church had created and installed throughout Europe. In this regard, the Church saw possession of this asset as crucial to its political ambitions - the 'jewel in the crown' of its empire, so to speak. The 'jewel', of course - the asset - was Jerusalem.

As we know, however, there was a second European power, one that considered itself above the Church of Rome in respect of its claim on the Throne of Jerusalem. The best traditional history can offer with regard to this second power is to ascribe it the somewhat dubious honour of having been 'an anonymous cabal of political and religious potentates'. Further research has revealed, however, that this so-called 'anonymous cabal' was in fact the Order of Sion, and its 'potentates' were none other than the survivors of the Merovingian bloodline. In point of fact, not only did these 'potentates' claim direct lineal descent from King David and the succeeding Kings of Judah - and thus, some have argued, both a moral and a political right to Judah's throne. So far as they were concerned, they already possessed it: *they already sat upon that throne.* Indeed, the surviving Merovingians had occupied the Throne of Jerusalem since AD 1099, when Godfroi de Bouillon, heir apparent to the Judaic-Merovingian bloodline, had - at the head of an army of monks, knights and soldiers - captured Jerusalem from its Muslim occupiers. Despite the fact that, having conquered Jerusalem, Godfroi declined the title of King (preferring instead to be crowned 'Defender of the Holy Sepulchre'), in effect he became the first true king of the Judah bloodline to establish himself on Judaic soil for more than a thousand years. And because he did, he is still revered in France as a national hero, in much the same way as, say, Robert the Bruce is revered in Scotland, George Washington in America. Following his death a year later, Godfroi's younger brother, Baudouin, Count of Flanders, acceded to the throne. Indeed, to the title his brother had declined. In AD 1100, Baudouin became King Baudouin I of Jerusalem. And the House of Judah, if only for a brief moment in history, once again occupied what was considered its ancestral throne.

It was against this historical backdrop, then, abridged and simplified here for our own purposes, that both the Order of Sion and the Church of Rome emerged as political contenders. The Order of Sion represented the legitimate Judaic bloodline of the historical Jesus, who, according to genealogies in the Order's possession, had himself been a *de jure* King of Israel; the Church of Rome represented the rather more supernatural 'blood of Christ'. The Order of Sion pursued the restoration of the Judaic royal bloodline, Jesus's bloodline, on the Throne of Jerusalem; the Church of Rome, in making Jesus 'divine' rather than 'royal', sought to supplant that bloodline with dynasties of its own making, and for its own political ends. Simply put, the Order of Sion was effectively Judaic, and claimed the Throne of Jerusalem on the premise of dynastic succession. The Church of Rome, on the other hand, was explicitly Christian, and claimed the Throne of Jerusalem by divine right. And although in a cultural sense a kind of Judaeo-Christian mishmash has eventuated in the West over the centuries, in a political sense it remains either one or the other - Jew or Christian - as the current situation in Israel amply attests. Indeed, the one fundamentally contradicts the other. Though both parties have deigned to participate in moments of constructive dialogue over the years, at least since the advent of Merovingian rule in Europe (circa AD 350), the battle for Jerusalem - for the restoration of the Judaic royal bloodline on the one hand, to supplant that bloodline with a Vatican-created bloodline on the other - has raged on. And it is this battle which, at the turn of the twelfth century, gave rise to what would become two of the most powerful masonic agencies in history - the Church-sponsored Knights Hospitaller of Saint John, or the Knights of Malta; and the Merovingian-sponsored Poor Knights of Christ and the Temple of Solomon, more commonly known as the Knights Templar. While the Order of Malta continues to operate as one of the Vatican's most powerful allies (indeed, as an equally powerful collaborator with both MI6 and the CIA, as well as with French Intelligence and highly influential elements of organized crime) the Knights Templar have long been rendered effectively impotent.

But it was not always that way.

At the height of its ascendancy, for example, the Order of Knights Templar was a formidable power, not only in terms of its military proficiency, but also in terms of its economic and political influence. Indeed, during the thirteenth century, the Order wielded immense political power, owned vast amounts of land and property throughout Christendom, and by virtue of its presence in so many European countries, states and provinces, became what was, in effect, the first efficient banking system in the Western world. Initially created as the Order of Sion's paramilitary arm some time at the start of the twelfth century (history seems to disagree with itself over the precise date of the Templars' birth, though it can be safely asserted that, contrary to traditional wisdom, the Order existed at least as early as 1114, possibly even earlier) the Templars evolved into something of an autonomous order in their own right. Indeed, by the beginning of the fourteenth century, having broken away from its parent order, the Order of Sion, the Order of Knights Templar had become what has been referred to as a 'state within a state', and as such represented an irrevocable threat to King Philippe IV of France, as well as to other European monarchs, including England's effete Edward II Plantagenet. The added fact that the Templars claimed allegiance to the bloodline of Judah, of course (the Merovingian bloodline of Kings David and Solomon, and perhaps more significantly, of Jesus) meant that they were also seen as a threat by Philippe's major political ally and sponsor, the Church of Rome. In consequence, between 1307-1314 the Templars were systematically dismantled by a Franco-Roman conspiracy. Templar lands were seized. Templar properties were seized. Or razed. Or burned. Knights were summarily arrested, tortured and imprisoned. Many more were burned to death. Indeed, the Templars' Grand Master at that time, Jacques de Molay, together with another high-ranking Templar, one Geoffroi de Charnay, met an excruciating and horrific death. The two were arrested, convicted by show trial and roasted to death over a slow-burning fire, like pigs on a spit. Though small pockets of Templars survived in exile - in particular in Scotland, where the Order survives today - effectively this action proved terminal for the Knights Templar. It was the end, certainly in terms of influence wielded.

The Knights Hospitaller of Saint John, on the other hand, was an order still in its infancy.

Traditional history claims that the Knights Hospitaller of Saint John was first established as an official Order in or around the year 1100. Thirty years before, it is said, in 1070, a hospital had been erected in Jerusalem by members of the fledgling Order to cater for pilgrims, monks, knights, soldiers - those who, for one reason and another, had journeyed to the Holy Land and had found themselves in need of medical assistance. The operation had been inspired and organized by a group of Italian merchants from Amalfi. This, at least, is the official story. Given the political situation in Europe at this time, however, and in particular the strategic value of Jerusalem in this regard, one cannot help but wonder precisely who these 'Italian merchants from Amalfi' might have been. It is far more likely, of course, that they would have been acting on behalf of Rome rather than independently. Certainly Rome would have sought to establish itself in Jerusalem at this time, if for no other reason than to supplant the newly crowned Merovingian king, Baudouin. In many respects, of course, the Church had already vanquished its Judaic rival in Europe, the Merovingian Dynasty. Or so it thought. But in any event, the final coup would have been to establish its authority in Jerusalem.

Though to begin we are told that the Order did not include a military arm, instead concentrating solely on its hospitaller work, there is reason to believe that this assertion is not entirely correct. Historical records relating to this period are as unreliable with regard to the Order of Saint John as they are with regard to the Knights Templar. But sufficient information has survived that we can at least construct a loose outline of events. What is known for certain is that, in 1113 the Knights of Saint John resolved to defend the Holy Land by forceful means, suggesting that by this time the Order already had recourse to a military arm. It is also known that, by 1126, both the Knights of Saint John and the Knights Templar constituted a burgeoning military strength, one that would combine to face the might of the Muslim world in several campaigns over the coming decades. (As long ago as the twelfth century, then, a Judaeo-Christian alliance was happy to put aside its differences in order to stave off what was considered an even bigger threat - an Arab Muslim threat.) These campaigns - these bloody wars - would come to be known as the Crusades. The Knights Templar, of course, would engage the Muslim armies on behalf of the Merovingian claim on Jerusalem; the Knights of Saint John, on the other hand, would engage the Muslim armies on behalf of the papacy and its political aspirations. Of course, for the past six hundred years and more Rome had clung fast to the vestiges of its obsolescent empire, asserting its divine right to rule and eradicating - often by proxy, always by force - anyone who dared challenge this assertion. Removal of the Merovingian Dynasty in this regard - which it had achieved by the end of the eighth century - had proved Rome's finest hour. Until now. Now, it seemed, the Merovingians were fighting back. And to further compound the Church's instability, Rome was facing new problems closer to home.

As first Godfroi de Bouillon, then his brother, Baudouin, had asserted themselves as rulers of the new kingdom of Jerusalem, Rome was once again facing humiliation. Not only was the Church stricken with internecine strife; Rome itself was under siege. In 1084, for example, Rome had been sacked by a Norman army led by one Robert Guiscard. During the years that preceded the sacking, and those that followed, a series of popes and antipopes had come and gone, largely as a result of the political turmoil seemingly endemic to the Franconian-ruled Holy Roman Empire. But the Church would win the day. Though this period of instability more or less continued for the next three centuries, by the end of the fifteenth century the Merovingian threat, at least, had all but evaporated. Or at least it had disappeared 'underground'. Rome's new rival was the rising tide of Protestantism. But that, as they say, is another story.

In 1530, following their expulsion from Rhodes, the Knights of Saint John established themselves on the island of Malta, from which the name by which they are known today derived. There they would prove themselves one of Europe's most fiercely proficient military and naval powers. In 1571, for example, the Order's fleet won a decisive battle against the Turks, effectively annihilating Turkish supremacy in the Mediterranean. But such moments of glory were not to last. Across Europe the Protestant Reformation was gaining momentum, and its effect would soon rupture both the Order's Catholic-based membership and sponsorship alike. Protestant splinter-groups started to break away from the Order and form new, rival orders. Finally, in 1798, a depleted Order of Malta was expelled from the island by the advance of Napolean, and it was not until 1834 that the Order as it exists today finally established itself in Rome - which, in effect, had always been the Order's official headquarters. Over the course of the next century, the Order would regroup and rebuild, and in many respects re-establish itself as the power it once was. Links to the Vatican were consolidated and strengthened at this time, and by the outbreak of WWII the two agencies had once again cemented to become one of the Western world's most formidable intelligence organizations. At the same time the battle for Jerusalem still raged. Indeed, it was only international pressure brought by some of the world's most powerful corporate and political bodies which, at the end of WWII, prevented the Order of Malta from claiming the Holy City as its own sovereign principality - on behalf of the Vatican, of course. In the event, however, a new state of Israel was declared and handed over to survivors of the Holocaust (much to the disdain of the Vatican, it has to be said - even so, the papacy is finally making headway in its bid to control Jerusalem; a recent deal cut between America's Council on Foreign Relations, Britain's Royal Institute of International Affairs and the Vatican, means that moves by the Holy See to include political prerogative over the Old City of Jerusalem at some point early in the new millennium now seems ever more likely - we shall see). Following its failed bid to recapture Jerusalem, the Order of Malta remained in Rome, where today it enjoys the status of an independent sovereign principality with full diplomatic privileges. The Order's Grand Master - at present Prince et Grand Maitre, Son Altesse Eminentissme Fra' Andrew Bertie - is recognized as a head of state, bears the secular rank of prince and the ecclesiastical rank of cardinal. The fact that those immediately subordinate to him comprise some of the world's most influential corporate and political oligarchs, as well as some of the world's more notorious intelligence chiefs and Mafia godfathers, means that Prince Andrew Bertie is a very powerful head of state indeed.

And that the Order of Malta is today perhaps the most effective and powerful international 'fix-it' organization in the Western world.

MI6 In Paris

The very idea that MI6 is a group of stuffy, upper-class government spies housed in an office block in London, then, could not be further from the truth. This notion is in itself one of MI6's greatest propaganda triumphs. Indeed, given that MI6 commands the allegiance of such internationally-networked 'masonic' bodies as the Sovereign Military Order of Malta, it is easy to see how complex, international operations are arranged, coordinated and executed. With regard to the assassination of Princess Diana, for example, intricate planning and coordination of events would have been imperative to a successful operation. (Note: we do not in any way intend to implicate here the Sovereign Military Order of Malta in the operation responsible for Princess Diana's death.) As we know, following their flight from Sardinia, the couple were hounded by so-called paparazzi from the moment they touched down in Paris. Many of their movements were spontaneous and unplanned. Yet, as if by some gift of precognition, the paparazzi seemed to know in advance the couple's every move - even the fact that they would, on the spur of the moment, and as a direct consequence of being harassed by 'paparazzi' outside Dodi's apartment on the Champs Elysees, choose not to dine at their prearranged restaurant, Chez Benoit, but instead return to the Ritz. Indeed, it was reported that more than fifty paparazzi were their to greet the couple on their unscheduled return at around 10 pm. The question is, of course, how did they know that the couple would return to the Ritz when the word on the street was that they had already booked a table elsewhere? Who leaked this information? And moreover, who acted upon it?

What is known for certain is that an unusually high number of MI6 agents were stationed in Paris during the days that led up to the princess's death. A British Embassy leak reported that, on the night itself, there were at least six MI6 agents in Paris - more than comprise the entire (official) number of MI6 agents in Moscow. To add to this, former MI6 Officer Richard Tomlinson has told us that, not only was there an unusually high number of MI6 personnel in Paris on the night in question, but that those personnel included none other than MI6 Chief David Spedding's personal secretary. And what is more - in a statement released on 12th May 1999 - Mr Tomlinson revealed that, on the night Diana died, two senior MI6 Officers were in Paris on an "undeclared" basis, and that their directive was to liaise with MI6 informant, Henri Paul.

Mr Tomlinson stated: "In Paris at the time of M. Paul's death, there were two relatively experienced but undeclared MI6 officers. The first was Mr Nicholas John Andrew LANGMAN, born 1960. The second was Mr Richard David SPEARMAN, again born in 1960. I firmly believe that either one or both of these officers will be well acquainted with M. Paul, and most probably also met M. Paul shortly before his death. I believe that either or both of these officers will have knowledge that will be of crucial importance in establishing the sequence of events leading up to the deaths of M. Paul, Dodi Al Fayed and the Princess of Wales."

And further: "Mr Spearman in particular was an extremely well connected and influential officer because he had been, prior to his appointment in Paris, the personal secretary to the Chief of MI6, Mr David SPEDDING. As such, he would have been privy to even the most confidential of MI6 operations. I believe that there may well be significance in the fact that Mr Spearman was posted to Paris in the month immediately before the deaths."

Needless to say, neither Mr Spearman nor Mr Langman have ever been questioned with regard to their activities on the night in question. Nor indeed with regard to their alleged involvement in Princess Diana's death.

It is also known, of course, that both MI5 and MI6 agents regularly pose as freelance journalists and paparazzi. Indeed, it is regular policy for intelligence agents worldwide to gain employment with major newspapers and journals, if only to write stories designed to promote some or other agenda, to disseminate 'appropriate information' and, in many cases, disinformation. In 1977, for example, renowned *Washington Post* journalist, Carl Bernstein, famous for exposing the Watergate scandal which finally impeached President Nixon, revealed that more than 400 journalists in the US alone were either deep-cover CIA agents, or they were on the CIA payroll. There is no reason to believe that this situation is any different today. On the contrary, there is every reason to suspect that it still prevails. As much as anything else it provides the intelligence agency concerned with a public voice, as well as providing the agent concerned with an effective cover. And as we were told by our own intelligence source soon after the crash: "The paparazzi in London and Paris are crawling with British Intelligence. Some are freelancers on the MI6 payroll, others are our own deep-cover agents ... Even if only to monitor the movements of Princess Diana and Mr Fayed, the Paris paparazzi on the night in question would undoubtedly have accommodated a number of our intelligence agents. It would be foolish, quite naive for anyone to imagine otherwise."

That the paparazzi in Paris on the night in question included one or more MI6 agents, then, as well as one or two CIA agents, is not out of the question. Indeed, given that Diana and Dodi were in Paris it is nothing more than should be expected. Certainly when the meticulously organized, military-style operation which seemed to orchestrate the paparazzi's every move is considered, one can only surmise that intelligence information was being gathered on the couple's movements on a minute-by-minute basis. Moreover, once gathered, this information was then - *somehow* - being successfully disseminated throughout the paparazzi network (again, minute by minute), affording the paparazzi up-to-the-minute knowledge of where the couple were. And where they were headed. This would suggest, of course, that an informant, perhaps on the MI6 payroll, was working on the inside, close to either Diana or Dodi, or both, and was thus able to glean relevant information and transmit it back to the agents in charge of the operation. But if this is the case, who could that informant have been? Might it have been Henri Paul, for example? His position as Assistant Director of Security at the Ritz Hotel certainly meant that he would have been ideally placed for such a role. But what evidence is there in support of this allegation?

Well to begin, Henri Paul was himself a secret agent, of sorts. It is known that he was on the MI6 payroll (a fact confirmed by a number of sources, including Mohamed al Fayed's lawyers, former MI6 Officer Richard Tomlinson, and Henri Paul's closest friend, Claude Garrec), and almost certainly that of French Intelligence and other foreign intelligence agencies, too. It is also known that he was handsomely rewarded for his collusion. At the time of his death, more than Fr1,000,000 (around £100,000) was sitting in more than a dozen bank accounts and a safe deposit box, most of them in Paris, all in Henri Paul's name. And this despite the fact that he earned as little as Fr200,000 (around £20,000) a year. According to close friends, he spent at least that much on an annual basis. He spent large sums of money on personal pursuits, for example. Among those pursuits was his love of flying. Paul was an accomplished pilot. He flew regularly. And each time he took to the cockpit it cost him around £300. To add to this, it is known that a large percentage of the money paid into his various bank accounts was deposited in cash. Indeed, during the eight months prior to his death, Paul deposited Fr40,000 (about £4000) on five separate occasions. That amounts to Fr200,000, or around £20,000, an amount which would normally have taken him a year to earn. Once again these deposits were made in cash. But where did the money come from?

According to his best friend, Claude Garrec, Henri Paul had worked for both British and French Intelligence for at least eleven years - the length of time he had worked at the Ritz. Given the convenience of his position as Assistant Director of Security at an hotel such as the Ritz, where international businessmen, politicians and power-brokers alike often meet to discuss their secret affairs, the fact that he might have been recruited by intelligence agencies is far more likely than not. Indeed, a senior French Intelligence agent openly admitted as much to ITN's royal correspondent, Nicholas Owen, during the making of the programme, *Diana: Secrets Of The Crash*, screened in Britain to mark the first anniversary of Diana's death and presented by Owen himself. And there is further evidence to this same end. Former MI6 Officer Richard Tomlinson testified to the French magistrate in charge of the official investigation, Judge Herve Stephan, that Paul was indeed on the MI6 payroll. The British authorities are currently (at the time of writing) endeavouring to track Tomlinson down for the very reason that his participation in so many extremely covert operations afforded him access to some of MI6's most delicate and well-kept secrets. Among these secrets are the names of many MI6 agents, plus their 'freelance employees'. And among these 'freelance employees', according to Tomlinson, was a French informant who was paid large sums of cash for his compliance, and whose name was Henri Paul. Tomlinson also revealed to Judge Herve Stephan, remember, that the blueprint for an MI6 plot to assassinate the Serbian president, Slobodan Milosevic, mirrored the operation that killed Princess Diana.

With regard to Henri Paul's involvement with MI6, Mr Tomlinson stated: "In 1992, I was working in the Eastern European Controllerate of MI6 and I was peripherally involved in a large and complicated operation to smuggle advanced Soviet weaponry out of the then disintegrating and disorganized remnants of the Soviet Union. During 1992, I spent several days reading the substantial files on this operation. These files contain a wide miscellany of contact notes, telegrams, intelligence reports, photographs, etc., from which it was possible to build up a detailed understanding of the operation. The operation involved a large cast of officers and agents of MI6.

"On more than one occasion, meetings between various figures in the operation took place at the Ritz Hotel, Place de Vendome, Paris. There were in the file several intelligence reports on these meetings, which had been written by one of the MI6 officers based in Paris at the time (identified in the file only by a coded designation). The source of the information was an informant in the Ritz Hotel, who again was identified in the files only by a code number. The MI6 officer paid the informant in cash for his information."

Mr Tomlinson went on: "I became curious to learn more about the identity of this particular informant, because his number cropped up several times and he seemed to have extremely good access to the goings on in the Ritz Hotel. I therefore ordered this informant's personal file from MI6's central file registry. When I read this new file, I was not at all surprised to learn that the informant was a security officer of the Ritz Hotel. Intelligence services always target the security officers of important hotels because they have such good access to intelligence. I remember, however, being mildly surprised that the nationality of this informant was French, and this stuck in my memory because it is rare that MI6 succeeds in recruiting a French informer.

"I cannot claim that I remember from this reading of the file that the name of this person was Henri Paul, but I have no doubt with the benefit of hindsight that this was he. Although I did not subsequently come across Henri Paul again during my time in MI6, I am confident that the relationship between him and MI6 would have continued until his death, because MI6 would never willingly relinquish control over such a well-placed informant."

Mr Tomlinson concluded: "I am sure that the personal file of Henri Paul will therefore contain notes of meetings between him and his MI6 controlling officer, right up until the point of his death. I firmly believe that these files will contain evidence of crucial importance to the circumstances and causes of the incident that killed M. Paul together with the Princess of Wales and Dodi Al Fayed."

Despite Mr Tomlinson's sworn affidavit in this regard, however, this crucial evidence provided by him has never even been considered. Much less acted upon. On the contrary, it has been flagrantly ignored by both the British and French authorities.

To add to the above, there does seem to be a conspicuous dearth of information regarding Henri Paul's movements on the night in question. At best this information is sketchy, at worst contradictory, even non-existent. Having met the couple at Le Bourget airport earlier in the day, and having escorted them back to the Ritz, Henri Paul is said to have finished work at around 7 pm and retired for the night. Later that same evening, however - some say in response to a phone call from Dodi Fayed, others of his own volition - Paul returned to his place of work, and indeed was elected to drive the ill-fated Mercedes later that same night. But where *was* Henri Paul during his three-hour absence from the Ritz earlier that evening? Liaising with British intelligence operatives, perhaps? Collecting yet another pay packet from his MI6 benefactors, money in advance of the operation that would, ironically, cost him his life?

This possibility cannot be ruled out. Of course, Paul would not have known in advance the central role he was to play in the operation, much less that he would be placing himself at such personal risk. And even less would he have known that, like former CIA employee Lee Harvey Oswald before him, he was being set up as a patsy, a stooge whose blood tests would later tell the lie that he had been drunk at the wheel, as well as being further intoxicated with drugs (and suspiciously, carbon monoxide). Little would he have suspected that, twenty-four hours later, his name would be blazoned across newspapers worldwide, and that beside his name would be a photograph of a short portly man looking slightly worse for wear, drink in hand, and a headline that accused him of manslaughter. On the contrary, if indeed Paul was in any way involved in the operation, he more than likely would have thought that his part had been played in keeping his benefactors abreast of the couple's movements. And possibly helping them in other ways, too - like bugging the Imperial Suite, for example, the luxury Ritz apartment occupied by Diana and Dodi. Or furtively suggesting alternative plans of action to his boss, Dodi Fayed, cleverly manipulating events to ensure that, say, Dodi ordered *him* to drive the couple back to his apartment, and to take an unusual route in order to outwit the chasing pack of paparazzi. Still unaware of the enormity of the operation in which he was participating, perhaps even thinking that the entire operation had been devised simply to cause the couple further duress, in particular the princess, Paul would have taken to the wheel with dollar signs in his eyes, perhaps even planning to collect the remainder of his reward the following day. But, of course, there would be no following day for Henri Paul. The following day Henri Paul would be dead.

Equally alarming is the possibility that one or more of the people closest to the princess were also working for MI6. During his meeting with Judge Herve Stephan, former MI6 Officer Richard Tomlinson further revealed that one of the two bodyguards accompanying Diana and Dodi on the night in question, either Trevor Rees-Jones or Alexander 'Kes' Wingfield, was an SIS (MI6) contact. We have been unable either to confirm or refute this claim. To counter suspicions in this regard, however, Tomlinson emphasized that, so far as he knew, neither Rees-Jones nor Wingfield were involved in the conspiracy which killed Diana. But he clearly implied that Henri Paul was indeed involved in such a conspiracy, together with MI6. Indeed, when you think about it, what better plan than to hire the services of the man acting in charge of the princess's personal security on the night she is fated to die?

And in order to cover your tracks, kill him, too.

CHAPTER 8

THE CIA

And The Bid To Unite Europe

"In order to survive, nations need strong intelligence services. But the idea that the CIA is primarily an intelligence-gathering operation is itself one of the agency's greatest propaganda triumphs."

Mark Zepezauer, *The CIA's Greatest Hits*, 1994.

The Agency

Over the years the CIA has maintained a somewhat ambiguous profile, to say the least. Though its activities are officially accountable to the Director of Central Intelligence and the President of the United States, few are these days prepared to believe that this is the way it really works. Indeed, that the most covert departments within the CIA adhere to this mandate - that they heed it at all - is, according to many intelligence experts, little more than a propaganda exercise. Not unlike the 'Agency' itself.

The plain fact of the matter is that a very high percentage of the CIA's activities are shrouded, not so much in secrecy, but behind a deceptive and ever-shifting veil of obscurity. The agency's 'confirm or deny nothing' policy is testament enough to this end. Perhaps because of this policy, however, any number of reports associating the agency with extremely questionable activities and operations abound. It is reported, for example, that the CIA has been - and still is - associated with some very powerful neo-Nazi and other extremist movements; indeed, that many former Nazis were instrumental in helping to develop the CIA's *modus operandi* during the years following WWII. As remarkable as this may sound, there is ample evidence to support this claim, as we shall see.

But first, let us take a look at the official outfit and its official remit - acquaint ourselves with the devil's handshake, so to speak.

In effect, the agency's primary objective today is to ensure that US foreign policy prevails in as many nation states as can be photographed from orbit. In other words, where there is real estate, the CIA is there to ensure that, in one way or another, it will be governed by, and to the advantage of,

US interests. In this regard, the agency's official remit is to "provide the President and his senior advisers with accurate, comprehensive, and timely foreign intelligence relating to the national security; and to conduct counter-intelligence activities, special activities, and other functions relating to foreign intelligence and national security as the President and the National Security Council may direct." And further: "To fulfil its mission, the CIA must collect, process, exploit, analyze, and disseminate foreign intelligence by employing a highly skilled diverse workforce and state-of-the-art technical systems and devices; protect intelligence sources and methods; conduct research on, develop, and procure technical systems and devices; protect the security of its installations, activities, and people; and provide necessary administrative and logistical support, as well as services of common concern to the Intelligence Community."

In other words, in order to completely and successfully achieve its mission, as determined by the guidelines laid down in this *official* remit, the agency must of necessity employ an *unofficial* one which includes the provision that national-security interests always precede the law. Or how else might "special activities" and "other functions relating to foreign intelligence and national security" be interpreted? How else might these "special activities" be implemented, if not - when necessary - by unlawful means? An *unofficial* CIA remit might thus be summed up in that covert operations, economic and industrial warfare, election-rigging and sometimes even assassination, when requisite to the national security of the United States (or even that it can be argued thus) are justifiable. In this regard, the CIA's self-profile manual must read like a page out of Adolf Hitler's *One Hundred Ways To Rule The World.* Certainly over the years the agency has been accused of conducting activities which compare in every quarter with some of the more insupportable activities carried out by Third Reich-style dictatorships. Genocide, for one, as the CIA-sponsored murder of more than 600,000 Cambodians from 1969-1975 attests. Indeed, while working on a different investigation we happened to interview a former US Special Forces Command Sgt Major, one Robert O Dean, who told us that, like Stealth, he too had run operations for the CIA. One of those operations was in Cambodia. "When Nixon was telling people there were no US forces in Laos," Dean revealed, "I was there with about three thousand men. When he said there were no US forces in Cambodia, I was there with roughly *five* thousand men." And further, speaking of the increasing levels of power wielded by his former employers: "These bastards were never elected. You've been lied to. You've been manipulated. You're in the hands of, and being controlled by, an elite group of arrogant bureaucrats to whom the people have never given power. They have no authority." The problem is, of course, they *do* have authority, albeit undemocratic.

And there are other examples, including acts of international terrorism; international money-laundering; political scandals (the downfall of presidents and other high-profile politicians); the illegal rigging of elections; Watergate; Iran/Contra; drug-trafficking; the assassinations of popes, presidents and other high profiles; the supply of money, arms and mercenaries to ensure that the 'appropriate political faction' gains power in any one nation state (thus safeguarding US client real estate); the instigation of so-called 'civil unrest' - sometimes even 'civil wars' - in order to oust any one political regime and replace it with another (thus safeguarding US client real estate); infiltration of the media and other relevant organizations. Indeed, think of your worst nightmare, and even if only a small percentage of reports are to be believed, you will find that, at some time or another, the CIA has brought that nightmare to terrifying life. And then some.

In terms of the international agenda in the modern world, then ... well, the CIA created it.

Since its formation under President Harry S Truman, the CIA has grown to megalithic proportions. No doubt about that. In a little over fifty years it has become the Western world's most autonomous, most dubious, and probably its most democratically unaccountable intelligence agency. Certainly its most powerful. Formed on 18th September, 1947, out of the now defunct Office of Strategic Services (OSS), the CIA soon became a government in its own right. But it was with no small amount of help from its British counterpart, MI6, that the 'Agency' became the monster it is today. Like its predecessor, OSS, the CIA was modelled on the *modus operandi* of both MI6 and Britain's second wartime counter-intelligence agency, the Special Operations Executive (SOE). Indeed, one might say that MI6 and SOE are to the CIA what Charles Atlas is to Arnold Swarzenegger: role model and mentor supreme, with the added similarity that the protege has in the long run outstripped the achievements of his forerunner by a country mile. In this respect, the more covert echelons of MI6 these days comprise little more than a British CIA outlet, and vice versa. And there are many such outlets worldwide. Indeed, the CIA's role today is more that of an international policing agency, a kind of latter-day global *SchutzStaffel* (SS) with still-strong Third Reich connections to boot. And like its Nazi counterpart (as well as its British mentor), at the highest level the CIA is sponsored and directed by a consortium of the West's most powerful financial, industrial and political power groups. Most notably today these groups include the Council on Foreign Relations; the Royal Institute of International Affairs; the Trilateral Commission; the International Institute of Strategic Studies; The Davos Group (World Economic

Forum); The Business Round Table; The US Council of International Business; The European Round Table of Industrialists; the United Nations; NATO's ruling elite; the so-called Bilderberg Group. Plus a host of others (including, of course, the corporate wing of the CIA itself.) Within these highly elite financial and military-industrial circles, both national and international policy is drafted, debated and determined. And once again, like its Nazi counterpart (the SS), the CIA is there to ensure said policy is pursued. And implemented.

Perhaps not surprisingly, it is virtually impossible to calculate the number of foreign security agencies on the CIA payroll, much less the sum of its personnel. Officially the CIA staff numbers around 11,000, but this figure is of course a nonsense. Its foreign agents and contracted personnel alone number easily in excess of this figure. Plus some. The current Executive Director of the CIA is Distinguished Intelligence Medal winner, David W Carey, formerly director of the CIA's Crime And Narcotics Centre (crime and narcotics, of course, are two areas in which the CIA is particularly well-versed). The CIA's official budget is classified; its unofficial budget is incalculable, although an official statement released by Director of Central Intelligence, George Tenet, in March 1998, revealed that "the aggregate amount appropriated for intelligence and intelligence-related activities for fiscal year 1997 ... was $26.6 billion". The statement added: "The fiscal year 1998 figure is $26.7 billion." The sum of which, in these two years alone, amounts to $53.3 billion. While it is difficult to imagine precisely how much, in real terms, this amount of money actually is, in terms of human cost it amounts to around 100 million satisfied Third World bellies per annum. Add to this the equally grotesque amounts budgeted for, say, nuclear and other defence programmes, and one begins to understand what motivated Princess Diana to stand up and challenge the arms trade during her landmines campaign. One also begins to understand why that challenge would have been taken very seriously indeed.

But no matter how many taxpayers' dollars find their way into the CIA coffers each year, the figure, whatever it is, pales to insignificance when compared to the power invested in this faceless monster. More than faith in a pope. In this regard, the CIA is well-named; it is truly the Western world's *central* intelligence agency.

JFK

In terms of our own investigation into the death of Diana, Princess of Wales, it is of interest here to note some of the CIA's other excursions into the realm of political assassination. After all, if we are to cite the CIA with regard to the assassination of a princess, then a proven track record in this regard would go a long way towards substantiating this claim. Or at least that it is not beyond the bounds of probability. If the CIA's 'above-the-law' status is sufficient to sanction such actions as the assassinations of the brothers Kennedy, for example, plus the odd pope (Pope John Paul I) and the human rights activist, Dr Martin Luther King Jr, then who is to say that this same ungovernable agency, together with its Anglo-Saxon bed partner, MI6, would not stoop to levels which include the brutal murder of a princess? Or indeed, that it would not possess the wherewithal - the know-how from past experience - to achieve such a diabolical feat. And to get away with it.

According to the conclusion of many researchers, of course (including the New Orleans District Attorney at the time, Jim Garrison) it was the CIA who ordered and carried out the assassination of President John F Kennedy. This fact has today been largely substantiated; indeed, it is widely accepted. What is not so widely accepted, however, is the involvement of Britain's MI6 in this operation. But then, as we have seen, at the highest levels of secrecy and power, the CIA and MI6 are interminable lovers. At least this is the opinion of CIA operative 'Stealth', among many others, who told us that "it was the CIA and MI6 who ... took Kennedy out. The Mafia may have pulled the trigger, but it was the CIA who loaded the gun. It was MI6 who showed them how to do it."

Should this information turn out to be even only partially true, of course, it would certainly explain why such confusion, such controversy, such secrecy still surrounds this case, some thirty-five years on.

It is worth noting to begin (as Stealth confirmed) that the formation of the Defense Intelligence Agency (DIA), under President Kennedy in 1961, was met with no small amount of paranoia and hostility, in particular on the part of the CIA and FBI directorships. In 1961, the FBI, under the Directorship of John Edgar Hoover, and the CIA, under Nazi sympathizer Allen Dulles, enjoyed something of a monopoly on US security and intelligence policy. In this respect, the forming of the DIA was seen as a threat. Allen Dulles was not about to let his grasp on intelligence policy slip easily through his fingers, while FBI Director John Edgar Hoover was simply pissed at the fact that the young upstart Kennedy would even dare attempt to muscle in on matters which, according to Hoover, he had no business interfering in. Indeed, the power war that existed between Hoover and the Kennedys is no secret. Nor is the fact that, at least to some degree, Hoover held the President to ransom over 'acquired' photographs and 'private' correspondences disclosing Kennedy's infidelities. It is no secret either that Dulles also bore designs on Kennedy's downfall; indeed, that he too possessed compromising documents on Kennedy's not-so-private life. Part due to retaliation, perhaps, part due to the fact that Kennedy wished to regain at least some portion of control over the CIA/FBI monopoly on intelligence policy - thus re-establishing the President's direct authority in this regard - Kennedy pledged to "splinter the CIA into a thousand pieces and scatter it to the winds".

In 1961 the Kennedys and the intelligence community were at war, make no mistake.

In his fervour to sweep the intelligence carpet clean, President Kennedy, perhaps unwisely, set about making some pretty drastic changes. First he fired CIA Director Allen Dulles. But what was perhaps even more ill-advised, he also fired Deputy Director Charles Cabell (who just happened to be the brother of the Mayor of Dallas, where Kennedy was assassinated). Top names within the intelligence community began to seethe. As did Richard Nixon, Vice President under Eisenhower (Kennedy's predecessor) and longstanding CIA conspirator. For the record, Nixon was also a known Mafia associate and post-WWII Nazi sympathizer. Indeed, Nixon's political career began as it was destined to end: with a cover-up - the concealment and eventual disposal of highly sensitive Nazi documents in 1945, when he was working for US Naval Intelligence. According to Mark Aarons and John Loftus, the documents in question revealed links between former Wall Street lawyer and CIA Director Allen Dulles's primary wartime Nazi client, IG Farben, and a US/Nazi oil cartel, Kontinentale Ol AG (with further links to Aramco, the Arabian-American Oil Company). IG Farben and Kontinentale OI AG are known to have boasted an appalling record with regard to their treatment of Jews during WWII. IG Farben, for example, was responsible for tens of thousands of deaths at its chemical processing plant - otherwise known as the death camp, Auschwitz - where Jews were forced to work for a period, on average, of three months before being delivered into the gas chambers (see *The Nazi Connection*). Little wonder Dulles wished to cover his tracks, then; he had spent much of the war brokering deals between British/US-based financial and industrial companies and Nazi Germany, in particular IG Farben. Indeed, Dulles was well rewarded for this work, as we shall see.

Perhaps it will come as little surprise, then, that Nixon's co-conspirator in disposing of these documents was none other than Allen Dulles himself. In disposing of the documents, of course, Nixon helped Dulles destroy vital evidence implicating the US in wartime trade deals with IG Farben and Nazi Germany. In return for the 'favour', Dulles subsequently sponsored Nixon's early political career, underwriting his first congressional campaign and his subsequent presidential campaigns in 1947 and throughout the 1950s. And it did not end there. The Dulles/Nixon partnership was also instrumental in facilitating (and covering up) the steady influx of Nazis into the US during the late 1940s and 1950s. And their subsequent absorption into the extreme right-wing factions of the Republican Party and the intelligence community (in particular the CIA). In this regard, and perhaps not surprisingly, Watergate - responsible for Nixon's eventual downfall - concealed an awful lot more than has ever been made public. The CIA, together with Nixon's timely resignation in lieu of facing impeachment, made sure of that.

But Nixon was not the only politician to have opposed Kennedy in the formation of the DIA. Another was Kennedy's Vice President, Lyndon B Johnson, behind-the-scenes adversary and someone who would later be implicated in Kennedy's assassination. Indeed, by 1961 Kennedy had made some very powerful enemies. Looming darkly above the horizon, of course, was an even greater problem, a situation which Kennedy had inherited from Eisenhower, the Cuba situation and the Bay of Pigs. The Bay of Pigs fiasco, of course, and the subsequent Cuban missiles crisis (together with Kennedy's commitment to ending the Vietnam War) would ultimately be cited as the reason for his assassination. Indeed, Kennedy's pledge to end US involvement in Vietnam by the end of 1965 - and thus to deny untold billions in defence contracts to US arms and fuel corporations - was perhaps tantamount to signing his own death warrant. But it was the Cuba situation which first saw that death warrant tabled.

During the years leading up to Fidel Castro's victory over the CIA-sponsored Batista regime in 1959 (a victory which saw Castro claim power), a powerful CIA/Mafia-controlled cartel ran a string of casinos and brothels out of Cuba, the profits from which were enormous, and, of course, tax-free. However, when Castro established his Communist government in Cuba, he immediately closed down the casinos and the brothels and nationalized all Cuban-based businesses. Enraged, the cartel was forced to pull out. It was then that Vice President Nixon came to the fore.

Many of the world's leading corporates, of course, had fully expected Richard Nixon to succeed President Eisenhower in 1961. Indeed, so far as the right-wing oligarchy that sponsored him was concerned, this was the plan. Nixon had been working closely with the CIA and the Mafia since 1959 to conjure up ways of assassinating Castro and re-establishing the illegal 'free-enterprise' situation which they had enjoyed in pre-Castro Cuba. Needless to say, his sponsors fully supported him in this action; they had benefited greatly from the situation which had existed in pre-Castro Cuba, and they wanted it back. When, by no small twist of fate - and of course a little behind-the-scenes outmanoeuvring on the part of the corporate 'lefties' - Kennedy won power, the whole Cuba situation was cast in shadow. Naturally the CIA, the Mafia and a host of very influential crime barons still wanted rid of Castro. Under pressure, Kennedy agreed. But he was not prepared to use US forces to achieve this end. Rather, a force comprised of Cuban exiles who had opposed Castro's forces in 1959 was selected to spearhead an invasion planned for January 1961 - the now infamous Bay of Pigs invasion. The CIA was furious. In order to sabotage the invasion and make Kennedy look a fool, both politically and in the eyes of the American public, at the last minute a crucial supporting air strike was cancelled behind Kennedy's back. The invasion failed. Castro retained power. Kennedy's future looked grim.

To add to this, in 1963 Kennedy tabled a plan which pledged to withdraw all US personnel from Vietnam by the end of 1965. Indeed, he had already signed National Security Action Memorandum 263, which ordered the first 1000 American troops home by Christmas, 1963. At this point, of course, the situation in southeast Asia had not yet escalated to full-blown war. Even so, the promise of such a war meant the promise of lucrative defence contracts for US arms and fuel corporations - many of which, of course, were effectively run by the CIA. Every bullet, every bomb, every aircraft - all had to be purchased by the US government from these corporations. Every bullet fired, every bomb dropped, every aircraft lost - all had to be replaced. And that costs money. Lots of money. Thus the corporate czars who own the financial and industrial corporations which stood to make that money - the same corporate czars who had arranged the appointment of Lyndon Johnson as Vice President, against Kennedy's wishes - desired that the war in Vietnam should go ahead. At all costs. In consequence, corporate puppet Lyndon Johnson struck a deal with his military-industrial sponsors - in effect, he agreed to continue and increase US involvement in Vietnam in exchange for the presidency. In other words, he effectively sanctioned Kennedy's death warrant. It should be noted here that, on Tuesday, 26th November, 1963, the day after Kennedy's funeral, the newly sworn-in President Lyndon B Johnson signed National Security Action Memorandum 273, effectively reversing Kennedy's withdrawal policy and sanctioning a full commitment to the war in Vietnam. At the same time, of course, he secured the full support of the very corporate czars who, together with the CIA, had plotted Kennedy's demise.

It should also be noted that, in total, the Vietnam War cost the American government more than $220 billion (in today's terms more like $2 trillion), all of which was borrowed from the US Federal Reserve and handed over to the cartel of arms and fuel corporations which constitutes America's defence industry. The scam is, of course, that the czars who own the defence industry - such as the Rockefellers - also own the major shareholdings in the US Federal Reserve. In other words, the czars loan the money to the government, they charge interest on those loans, and then those loans are handed straight back to them in defence contract payments. Beautiful. In any event, the promise of war in Vietnam was a very lucrative promise indeed. And Kennedy's plan to end that war before it had even begun achieved little for his longevity. No doubt about that.

A combination of the above, then (the formation of the DIA, the failure to get rid of Castro, Kennedy's alleged deal with Russian Premier Kruschov to avert the subsequent Cuban missiles crisis, and his commitment to ending the Vietnam War - plus the Kennedy brothers' unforgiving, rigorous and public crackdown on Mafia-organized crime) is generally the reason given for JFK's assassination. But the question remains: who did it?

The official explanation for Kennedy's death, of course, is quite simply laughable. The Lee Harvey Oswald 'lone gunman' story is these days treated with the contempt it deserves by anyone who has seriously investigated the case. Indeed, the now famous 'Zapruder film footage' shot by eyewitness Abraham Zapruder (which recorded the assassination and which was used by District Attorney Jim Garrison in his case against CIA contract agent, Clay Shaw), clearly shows Kennedy being shot by at least three different bullets travelling in three different directions. As Garrison argued, this in itself proves a conspiracy. Three different bullets entering Kennedy from three different angles of course signifies three different gunmen stationed at three clearly different locations. And if three different gunmen shot Kennedy from three different locations, within seconds of each other, then there can be little doubt that all three were working according to a plan. A secret plan; a plot. Which in turn, of course - as argued by Garrison - signifies a conspiracy. Indeed, the *Concise Oxford Dictionary* (Ninth Edition) explains 'conspiracy' as "a secret plan to commit a crime or do harm, often for political ends; a plot". The point is, of course, that if a conspiracy to murder Kennedy existed then the conspirators either comprised the team of three or more gunmen, or far more likely, they comprised a much larger team for which the gunmen simply acted as hired assassins. And either way, a team was involved. The fact that neither the gunmen nor the 'team' were ever identified or brought to justice further suggests that this team was a highly organized and experienced outfit. (A similar question arises with regard to the death of Princess Diana, of course, in that the driver of the Fiat Uno - indeed, the Uno itself - and the two motorbike riders, have never been traced.) It is quite simply impossible to imagine that three wholly independent, 'wild bill' gunmen could have assassinated the President of the United States in broad daylight without being seen. (Or indeed, that Lee Harvey Oswald could have shot the president from three different angles all by himself.) Unless, of course, the gunmen in question - like the driver of the Fiat Uno and the motorbike riders - were working for an organization that knows how to cover its tracks. Someone like

MI6, for example, and/or the CIA, both of whom had every reason for wanting Kennedy out of the way and Johnson in the hot seat. As we have seen, British/US arms and fuel corporations, together with British/US banks and financial institutions, stood to make a veritable fortune out of the Vietnam War. Indeed, once Johnson was installed as President they made that fortune. 5000 helicopters were lost in Vietnam; they all had to be replaced. 6,500,000 tons of bombs were dropped on Vietnam; they all had to be replaced. More 50,000 American soldiers lost their lives in Vietnam, but who gives a damn about that. Certainly not, it would seem, the corporate godfathers who sent them to war in the first place - on the back of a propaganda sell they call the American Dream. Financially speaking, it is a very viable Dream indeed.

In any event, where District Attorney Jim Garrison's case succeeded was in proving beyond question that a team had indeed conspired to assassinate Kennedy. Where the case failed was in Garrison's attempt to prove that the 'team' in question was the CIA, and not some random, right-wing 'lynch mob'.

Of further interest is the existence of an 'unofficial' - allegedly uncut - version of the same Zapruder film footage. Indeed, this version is said to be the original version, and that the version subpoenaed by District Attorney Jim Garrison for his case against the CIA in 1969 had undergone something of a 'face-lift' during its five-year absence in the hands of the CIA (it had been kept in a secure vault for five years by the CIA following Kennedy's murder). In any event, this allegedly uncut version also shows Kennedy being shot from a variety of different angles. But staggeringly, it also shows him being shot by the driver of his own car, Special Agent William Greer. The film shows the cavalcade slowing down, Greer turning and shooting the president over his shoulder, and Jackie Kennedy screaming and scrambling out of the open-top car as a subsequent bullet - fired from an accomplice gunman - blows half of Kennedy's head off. Having viewed this footage ourselves, we have to say that it seems convincing. However, whether or not it is genuine remains neither here nor there; evidence sufficient to convict a murderer in a court of law exists without it. For those who operate above the law, however, it would seem that all the evidence in the world is worthless. In particular when much of that evidence relies on the testimonies of witnesses who mysteriously 'disappear'. In this regard it should be noted that all notable witnesses to the JFK assassination and/or those otherwise involved in the conspiracy - in other words, those who knew too much; and more to the point, those who were prepared to testify in court - died before District Attorney Jim Garrison's case against Clay Shaw was heard. In the absence of key witnesses, of course, the trial became little more than a show trial. It is also of note that around 200 material witnesses - or those otherwise involved in the conspiracy - died within two years of the assassination. The odds against this happening must surely be incalculable. In this same regard, one can only wonder at the fate of the Fiat Uno driver and the two motorbike riders, all three of whom are yet to be traced.

So much has already been penned regarding the Kennedy assassination that, given our space limitations, the above summary will have to suffice. There is of course a welter of further evidence and many more details involved in this affair which are not really relevant to our investigation. For this reason we have elected not to include them here. Nevertheless, when studied, they prove beyond all reasonable doubt that the assassination of President John F Kennedy was the result of a premeditated conspiracy coordinated by the CIA, perhaps in conjunction with MI6, and possibly even some other quasi-official agency too powerful to name. But the point so far as we are concerned is that, according to their own track records, these agencies are indeed capable of planning and executing operations which fall into the category of high-profile assassination. And in the final analysis, there were none more high-profile than JFK.

Except perhaps Diana, Princess of Wales.

The CIA
And Nazi Germany

To some, this may seem an inappropriate place for us to highlight the connection between the CIA and Nazi Germany. Or indeed, to delve the often paranoid world of international conspiracies, period. Some would no doubt prefer that Diana's memory be forever removed - or at least protected - from what would appear to be a rather unattractive association. This is of course understandable. Nevertheless, it should be remembered that this is not a book about 'fairy tales and princesses'; this is not a book about how photogenic Diana was, nor about her unrivalled status as the world's number one fashion icon. Rather this book is intended as a serious inquiry into the suspicious circumstances surrounding her death - or to be precise, into the 'bloodline secrets' and 'political intrigues' surrounding her death. Such an inquiry, of course, often demands that evidence of even the most disagreeable (in some cases downright shocking) nature should be explored, in particular when that evidence bears key relevance to the inquiry's outcome. In highlighting the various masonic agencies in this section - their history, their motive, their *modus operandi* - agencies which we believe were almost certainly behind the assassination of the princess, it is our hope that a more complete picture of the nature of these agencies will emerge. And that, as a result, people will be less reluctant to entertain the possibility that Diana was assassinated.

Though some of the evidence explored in this chapter will indeed seem alarming, then - to some, perhaps even bordering on the extreme - nevertheless it will serve to underline the fanatical and often brutal nature of the beast broadly known as masonic government: what its objectives are; how, where and why those objectives were born; the extreme measures often taken in order to ensure that those objectives are attained. And sustained. In the final analysis, and simply put, we believe on the evidence we have managed to obtain that Diana was assassinated by a joint MI6/CIA operation. But that assertion is itself incomplete without at least a cursory knowledge of who and what these two primary agencies really are. And who, in truth, governs them. As stated, we believe on the strength of our extensive research that MI6 and the CIA, at the top of the tree, are one and the same agency. Or at least that they are controlled by the same masonic oligarchy, that said masonic oligarchy has its latter-day roots in 1920s/30s Fascism, and that its primary objective is to oversee, orchestrate and implement the corporate agenda which is destined to culminate in a British/US/German-governed European Superstate. We also believe that the reason Diana was assassinated is that she had become a serious threat to the machinations of this corporate agenda, in more ways than one. And that this was the reason that she was branded a "loose cannon" by corporate and establishment oligarchs.

We also believe - again on the evidence obtained - that this same agenda is a political extension of the original Nazi ideal for a united Europe. In this regard - staggeringly - the evidence points to the very real possibility that Hitler himself was little more than a figurehead for a former generation of this same masonic oligarchy, and that Nazi aspirations for global dominion were sanctioned and sponsored, in large part, by both German and US corporate interests. British interests, too. Hitler's efforts were certainly funded, again in large part, by the same British- and US-based industrial and financial organizations which today continue to strive towards centralization (indeed, by those organizations which, as a direct result of WWII investments in Nazi Germany, today stand at the forefront of the centralization process). It is of interest to note in this regard that the British Monarchy and the British Establishment, together with British interests in the Virginia-based masonic oligarchy cited above, share a common Germanic - or Judaeo-Teuton - root. At the highest levels of corporate power, British, American and German blood is kindred. It shares the same political DNA. For these reasons we have elected to include the following brief history of the CIA/masonic government and its dealings with Nazi Germany.

Helped To Power

In our endeavour to outline the most notorious agencies employed by masonic government, then, and to highlight the fact that its major objective to centralize European political and economic power has obtained for at least the best part of a century and more, it is imperative we highlight what we might term here 'the Nazi connection'. A powerful body of evidence now exists to the effect that, following the Russian Revolution (1917), Hitler was selected, groomed and sponsored by a joint German/US masonic oligarchy to unite Europe against the increasing threat of Communist takeover. This claim is perhaps less absurd than it might at first seem. It was, after all, international pressure brought by Marxist power-brokers, together with Jewish financiers and industrialists, which effectively put an end to the First World War. Many high-ranking Germans felt both humiliated and betrayed by this turn of events; indeed, frontline German troops still occupied many enemy territories when hostilities were suddenly brought to an end in November, 1918. They did not know why the war had ended. Many of them were later convinced of a high-level conspiracy to undermine the German state in favour of financial and industrial takeover by a Communist-oriented Zionist elite (in this regard, Bolshevism and Judaism became confused in the minds of many German people at this time). Many more were equally convinced of British and US involvement in the conspiracy. Whether this be true or not, what is known for certain is that, for a decade and more following the end of WWI, Germany was plunged ever deeper into economic and political turmoil. Following the signing of the Treaty of Versaille in June 1919, for example - the terms of which, by design, were expressly biased towards the economic and social mortification of the new Weimar Republic - the Allies continued to blockade Germany. Sanctions were maintained on international trade and lucrative German export markets were effectively hijacked. As is so often the case when international sanctions take hold, however, it is the ordinary person who suffers, and not his political parents. Post-WWI Germany was no exception in this regard. Millions of Germans went hungry. Thousands more were made homeless. Equally vast numbers died of influenza, tuberculosis and other poverty-related diseases, while thousands more took to crime in order to fill their bellies. And those of their children. Between July 1921 and November 1923, the value of the mark fell from 76.7 to the US dollar, to a humiliating 4,200,000,000,000 to the same US dollar. Though the country enjoyed a brief respite between 1924-28, by 1929 unemployment was again sky-high. At the same time industrial production was at rock-bottom. In October 1929, when Wall Street finally crashed and the global economy followed suit, precipitating the withdrawal from Germany of massive US loans in 1931, the Weimar Republic fell into ruin. Its five major banks crashed. More than 20,000 German businesses folded. Politically, economically and socially, Germany collapsed.

Depending on how you look at it - the result of random consequences or international chess - the stage was now set for someone like Adolf Hitler to claim his place in history. And that is precisely what he did.

Out of the ashes of this collapse, then, it was foreseen that the Third Reich would rise and restore Germany to prosperity. In consequence, the growing Communist movement in Germany - which, up until the day Hitler became Chancellor, had threatened to win power - would be defeated and dismantled. Which it was. What had threatened to become another Marxist republic (in the wake of what had already happened in Russia), in the end reverted to nationalism - even racism - in the desperate hope that at least some semblance of national pride and self-worth would be restored. It is this sequence of events which has led conspiracy theorists - and an increasing number of economists and historians - to believe that the so-called Wall Street Crash of 1929 was no random event. But that it was deliberately engineered by 'interested parties' from the corporate sector - or to be more precise, by US-based financiers and industrialists who, above all else, required that the growing tide of Communism in Germany be subdued. If not extinguished. It is of course well-known that, during times of economic crisis, people tend to look to a strong, right-wing leadership as their best chance of recovery. As Johannes Zahn, influential economist and banker in Germany in 1931, commented during an interview conducted for BBC2's *The Nazis: A Warning From History* (in an episode curiously titled *Helped To Power*): "An unemployed man either joined the Communists, or he became a Storm Trooper [a member of the Nazi Party's elite - though brutal - paramilitary arm, later to become the SS]. And so business believed it was better if these people became Storm Troopers."

Indeed it did. And it went to some lengths in order to achieve this end - to ensure that the Nazi Party gained power ahead of the Communists. Funds channelled into Germany via Switzerland found their way into depleted Nazi coffers, for example, enabling Hitler to complete his vigorous 'Hitler Over Germany' election campaign in 1932. And having lost the election to then-Chancellor Paul von Hindenburg, it was pressure brought by so-called 'groups of powerful businessmen' which finally persuaded Hindenburg to relinquish the chancellorship (which he had won by democratic means) and hand it to Hitler. One such group included a former president of the *Reichstag,* who wrote to Hindenburg personally and demanded that Hitler be made Chancellor 'for the good of Germany'. To add to this, Hitler won the support of such powerful figures as industrialist Fritz von Thyssen, banker Hjalmar

Schacht and certain high-ranking members of the *Reichslandbund,* an organization with known foreign interests, specifically those of Prussian landowners. But it was largely via Thyssen's foreign connections - plus those of other high-ranking German industrialists - that Hitler was able to court such massive financial support from America, as we shall see. It seems that Hitler had amassed one or two very powerful allies, then, not all of whom were German.

But some were. As was further demonstrated in the so-called Munich *putsch* in 1923, in which 4 police and 16 Nazis were killed in street fighting. In consequence, Hitler was arrested and tried for attempted revolution, inciting murder and conspiring to rob a bank. The trial became a media sensation, a ticket-only extravaganza, as well as a judicial farce. Despite the severity of charges brought against him (and despite being sentenced to 5 years) Hitler served a mere 9 months in prison, during which time he drafted the manuscript for his book *Mein Kampf.* Curiously, the judge who sentenced him at Munich had also presided over another trial some two years earlier, in which Hitler had been convicted of disrupting a 'left-wing' meeting: his cronies had dragged the speaker off stage and beaten him up. Hitler had then claimed the vacant stage for himself, and had proceeded to preach revolution and the need for Germany to unite under a nationalist banner. For this action he received the minimum sentence possible, 3 months. And even then, the sentence was almost immediately commuted to 1 month, following - curiously - an appeal lodged by the judge himself.

As history tends to affirm, then, Hitler did not stand alone in his struggle to gain power. The only question is, was he helped to power purely by internal forces, or might external influences have played a role in preparing the ground for a Nazi dictatorship? Certainly there is a mounting body of evidence to this end. In the 1928 election, for example, the Nazis received a mere 2.3% of the national vote, entitling them to 12 seats in the *Reichstag*. By 1930, however, that percentage had risen to 18.3% (107 seats in the *Reichstag*). And two years later, at the 1932 general election, the Nazis claimed a massive 37.3% of the vote, the highest ever recorded in a free election. In the space of four years the Nazi Party had become the largest in the *Reichstag*, boasting a majority 230 seats. It was only Hitler's relentless pursuit of the chancellorship itself, and his subsequent refusal to participate at any other level of government, including president, which prevented the Nazis from claiming power there and then. Even in regions where there was no Nazi representation whatever, the populace was tending more and more to embrace Hitler and the Nazis as its hope of salvation. It is difficult for history to justify this seeming U-turn in popularity - although it has to be said, there is some evidence that US-backed 'irritants' were being deployed in these regions in order to foment nationalist support.

But whatever the reason, this sudden turnabout in Nazi popularity could never be put down to Hitler's natural charm, nor indeed his popular appeal. Despite historical myth, Hitler was not a charismatic statesmen - nor even a shrewd politician - though he was undoubtedly a master propagandist. But it is still unclear what caused the German people, virtually overnight, and in such substantial numbers, to shift their allegiance in favour of a Nazi dictatorship. Certainly in terms of 'winning votes' the Nazi campaign was flawed. Indeed, Nazi Party management centred not on winning elections, but on the salubrity and fettle of its membership. It was a members' party, never a people's party (much less a political party); more a cauldron of self-involved ideals than of political astuteness. The party was not at all well-organized, nor indeed well-funded, at least not by its German members and sponsors alone. As mentioned above, Hitler struggled to find the funds even to complete his now-famous campaign trail during the 1932 general election, which he narrowly lost to Hindenburg. Indeed, by the end of 1932, a matter of only weeks before Hitler finally took power, the Nazi Party was declared bankrupt. Yet during his first year in office (1933) Hitler was somehow able to appropriate more money for the German military than the German military was able to spend. The question is, of course, where did this money come from? Certainly it could not *all* have come from within Germany. As we know, German industry was at rock-bottom. The German economy was in serious difficulty, still reeling from the withdrawal of US loans and its subsequent, devastating effect on Germany's five major banks. To add to this, unemployment was at a record high, with more than 5.6 million out of work. The subsequent fall in tax receipts, together with increased welfare payments, meant that Germany's budget deficit was colossal. The idea that Hitler could suddenly conjure up sufficient funds to massively over-finance his military machine, then, is a curious one, to say the least. But that is precisely what he did.

So where *did* the money come from? Might it have originated, for example, with 'interested parties' outside of Germany? Western agencies, perhaps, willing to sidestep international embargos and enter into clandestine trade deals with the Nazis - say, via Switzerland? It is no secret that certain agencies in the West were keeping a sharpened eye on developments in Germany at this time. It is no secret, either, that these agencies wanted the Nazis in power ahead of Germany's Communist Party - which, together with the Nazis, commanded the majority of seats in the *Reichstag*. But what is also certain is that Germany was indeed doing business, via Switzerland, with certain British and US financial and industrial cartels at this time. Indeed, since the end of WWI, Germany had been effectively rebuilt, and Hitler's campaign financed, by covert British and US investments.

The bottom line is that, while British and US soldiers were dying at the hands of the Nazi war machine, and Jews were being exterminated in their thousands, British and US companies which had invested in post-WWI Germany continued to sympathize and trade with the Nazi regime. The bombs that levelled so many British cities, and killed so many women and children, may well have been manufactured in Germany. But it was largely British and US money that provided Hitler with the parts. The workforce to build them. And the fuel to dispatch them to Allied targets.

The Players

The Rockefeller-owned Standard Oil of New Jersey, together with Du Pont Chemical Corporation and General Motors (GM), is known to have been trading with Germany at this time. As was the US communications giant, ITT, as well as the Aluminum Company of America (or Alcoa) whose cartel-style arrangement with Nazi Germany fuelled a damning and unequivocal response from then-US Secretary of the Interior, Harold Ickes, who is reported to have said: "If America loses this war, it can thank the Aluminum Corporation of America." It was feared at the time, of course, that, by supplying the Nazis with much-needed aluminium for aircraft production, the requirements of the US Air Force in this regard would be compromised. If not undermined entirely. Indeed, similar fears were felt with regard to all of the US companies involved in backstairs deals with Germany. But the most telling deal of all in this regard was undoubtedly the Du Pont-controlled General Motors' collaboration with both the Nazi-controlled chemicals giant, IG Farben, and Germany's largest automobile company, Adam Opel AG. As a direct result of GM's collaboration with IG Farben, for example, a subsidiary company, Ethyl GmbH (now Ethyl Inc) was set up. Drawing on the expertise of its US partners, Ethyl GmbH was able to produce the antiknock agent known as tetraethyl lead - essentially a liquid gas added to petroleum in order to prevent premature combustion. Indeed, this collaboration and others - which also included Standard Oil (now Exxon, the biggest oil company in the world) - underwrote the Nazi war effort to the tune of billions of US dollars. Certainly it is accepted that, without this particular collaboration, Germany's own reserves in terms of synthetic fuels would not have been even remotely sufficient to satisfy the demands of war. As author Rodney Atkinson points out in his book, *Europe's Full Circle*, it was "Standard Oil's monopoly in synthetic rubber which greatly enhanced Nazi Germany's foreign exchange earnings and its capacity to manufacture war materials". And further:

"Iso-octane technology, essential for German aviation fuel, was provided exclusively by Rockefeller's Standard Oil of New Jersey."

But it was the investigations of researchers Morton Mintz and Jerry S Cohen that uncovered the Du Pont-controlled GM's collaboration with Adam Opel AG. In their book, *Power Inc.*, Mintz and Cohen state that:

"In 1929, GM acquired the largest automobile company in Germany, Adam Opel, A.G. This predestined the subsidiary to become important to the Nazi war effort. In a heavily documented study presented to the Senate Subcommittee on Antitrust and Monopoly in February 1974, Bradford C. Snell, an assistant subcommittee counsel, wrote: 'GM's participation in Germany's preparation for war began in 1935. That year its Opel subsidiary cooperated with the Reich in locating a new heavy truck facility at Brandenburg, which military officials advised would be less vulnerable to enemy air attacks. During the succeeding years, GM supplied the Wehrmact with Opel "Blitz" trucks from the Brandenburg complex. For these and other contributions to wartime preparations, GM's chief executive for overseas operations was awarded the Order of the German Eagle (first class) by Adolf Hitler.'"

Further evidence of this cartel-based conspiracy to undermine - indeed, *betray* - the Allied war effort, while at the same time tie up the world's industrial resources and markets, can be found in congressional records dating from the period, and in specific investigations undertaken by the FBI and the US Justice Department during the 1930s/40s. It can also be found in that, following the war, many of the US corporations involved in the supply of arms and other war materials to Nazi Germany had the audacity to sue the US government for war reparations - they claimed that Allied air raids had destroyed or otherwise damaged their factories and processing plants, which of course had been built on German soil. To add further salt in the wounds, some of the companies involved actually won their cases. As Asst Senate Subcommittee Counsel, Bradford C Snell, wrote in 1974:

"After the cessation of hostilities, GM and Ford demanded reparations from the US Government for wartime damages sustained by their Axis facilities as a result of Allied bombing. By 1967 GM had collected more than $33 million in reparations and Federal tax benefits for damages to its warplane and motor vehicle properties in formerly Axis territories ... Ford received a little less than $1 million, primarily as a result of damages sustained by its military truck complex at Cologne."

And further, in his book, *The Sovereign State of ITT,* Anthony Sampson writes: "... ITT now presents itself as the innocent victim of the Second World War, and has been handsomely recompensed for its injuries. In 1967, nearly thirty years after the events, ITT actually managed to obtain $27 million in compensation from the American government, for war damage to Focke-Wulf plants - on the basis that they were American property bombed by Allied bombers." The US Foreign Claims Settlement Commission was responsible for these and other reparations payments.

The US giant, ITT, is also implicated in the conspiracy, then - a conspiracy summed up in a statement made in 1937 by then-US Ambassador to Germany, William E Dodd.

"A clique of US industrialists is hell-bent to bring a Fascist state to supplant our democratic government, and is working closely with the Fascist regime in Germany and Italy. I have had plenty of opportunity in my post in Berlin to witness how close some of our American ruling families are to the Nazi regime." And further: "Certain American industrialists had a great deal to do with bringing Fascist regimes into being, in both Germany and Italy. They extended aid to help Fascism occupy the seat of power, and they are helping to keep it there."

It could not have been stated more clearly than that.

But, of course, none of these companies could have traded with the Nazis without help. Someone had to broker the deals.

Enter Allen Dulles, New York lawyer, OSS operative and future Director of the CIA. Together with his brother, John Foster Dulles, Allen Dulles was responsible for funnelling millions of dollars into Nazi Germany, both before and during the war. But then, the Dulles brothers were more than just lawyers: they were international finance-brokers supreme. Operating on behalf of the powerful Wall Street law firm, Sullivan & Cromwell, the two had even played a major role in finalizing the terms of the Treaty of Versaille in 1919, in particular the clause defining the currency in which Germany was ordered to pay war reparations to the Allies. According to the terms of the Treaty, the reparations were to be paid in gold. The problem was, of course, Germany had no gold, and so was forced to borrow the requisite amounts from Sullivan & Cromwell's clients in America. These so-called 'clients' included the huge US corporations named above - plus others, including the massive US publishing empire owned by William Randolph Hearst, and Henry Ford's equally massive automobile company. Plus other major-league financial and industrial concerns in the US, including the Rockefellers' Chase Paris Bank. And indeed, in Britain, including the Bank of England. The deals, of course, were for the most part brokered by Allen Dulles and/or his brother on behalf of Sullivan & Cromwell.

From that time on the Dulles brothers would represent their 'US clients' in Germany, negotiating massive contracts on their behalf, both prior to and during WWII. Towards the end of the war, of course, when it became evident that Germany would lose, priorities quickly shifted to thoughts of retrieval. *The investments had to be retrieved.* Over the course of the next few years - via a well-established network of money-laundering contacts in Liechtenstein, Belgium, and of course, Switzerland - the Dulles brothers managed to transfer millions of dollars out of Germany and channel them back to their various sources. Of interest is the fact that this operation was achieved with no small amount of help from certain agencies in Italy - most notably the Order of Malta and the Vatican. Indeed, the Vatican netted a tidy commission in this regard - in return for 'services rendered'. As authors Mark Aarons and John Loftus explain in their book: *The Secret War Against The Jews:*

"After the Nazis' 1943 defeat at Stalingrad, various Nazi businessmen realized they were on the losing side and made plans to evacuate their wealth. The Peron government in Argentina was receiving the Nazi flight capital with open arms, and Dulles helped it hide the money ... The Guinness Book of Records lists the missing Reichsbank treasure [estimated at $2.5 billion dollars] as the greatest unsolved bank robbery in history. Where did it go?

"...According to our source, the bulk of the treasure was simply shipped a very short distance across Austria and through the Brenner Pass into Italy. Dulles's contacts were waiting at the Vatican."

Indeed they were. James Jesus Angleton, future OSS (later CIA) Head of Station in Rome, via his contacts in the Order of Malta, had established a money-laundering operation there. His accomplice was none other than his father, Hugh Angleton. At this time the Angletons worked for the OSS counter-intelligence branch in Italy, X2, which in turn worked closely with the Order of Malta and the Vatican (indeed, James Angleton would later, in 1946, be decorated by the Order for his counter-intelligence work in Italy). With a little help from his contacts in Mussolini's Interior Ministry, Hugh Angleton had quickly risen to second-in-command of X2 under Colonel Clifton Carter, and it was from here that he had established substantial business interests, via Dulles, in Nazi-occupied territories. There was good reason, then, for the Angletons/Dulles-OSS/Vatican money-laundering operation. Hugh Angleton wanted his money back.

As Mark Aarons and John Loftus further state:

"...Another ardent Nazi propagandist and agent, Slovenian bishop Gregory Rozman, was sent to Bern with the help of Dulles's friends in US intelligence. Declassified US intelligence files confirm that Bishop Rozman was suspected of trying to arrange the transfer of huge quantities of Nazi-controlled gold and Western currency that had been discreetly secreted in Swiss banks during the war. For a few months the Allies prevented Rozman from gaining access to this treasure, but then the way was mysteriously cleared. In fact, the Dulles-Vatican connection had fixed it, and before too long the bishop obtained the loot for his Nazi friends, who were hiding in Argentina."

And further: "...Dulles and his colleagues exerted a great deal of influence to ensure that Western investments in Nazi Germany were not seized by the Allies as reparations for the Jews. After all, much of 'Hitler's Gold' had originally belonged to the bankers in London and New York. The ... captured Nazi loot went underground...

"...In the cause of anticommunism, and to retrieve its own investments in Germany, the Vatican agreed to become part of Dulles's smuggling window, through which the Nazis and their treasure could be moved to safety."

It would seem that the Rockefellers, then - along with other financial and industrial cartels in Britain and the US (it would seem Catholic ones in Italy, too) - had one or two rather substantial investments to protect. And prior to the 1932 general election in Germany, the survival of those interests was directly dependent on Hitler winning power. As economist and banker, Johannes Zahn, has already stated: "...business believed it was better if these people became Storm Troopers." Which, in effect, of course, is the same as saying that "business" wanted the Nazis in power, and not the Communists. After all, if Germany had indeed become a Communist republic, then massive investment potential would have been lost and international trade rather promptly curtailed. But perhaps even more significantly, masonic plans for a corporately controlled Europe - of which the Rockefeller empire is both a prime mover and a central cog - would have been severely compromised. As indeed they *were* severely compromised when, despite corporate efforts to the contrary, half of Germany finally did become a Communist republic following WWII. It took the West and its maze of Nazi-aided intelligence agencies a further forty-five years to dismantle that republic, along with the rest of the Eastern Bloc. As it is, Europe now stands on the verge not of Communist, but of Corporate centralization. And because it does, corporate sponsorship of Hitler's rise to power - and the subsequent loss of more than 55,000,000 lives during WWII - has been duly vindicated.

This, at least, would seem to be the considered opinion of those who stand to gain most from the newly emerging European Corporation. By account, it is a corporation which has been a very long time in the making.

The question most pertinent our own investigation is, of course: if masonic government is prepared to sacrifice 55,000,000 lives in the name of corporate freedom; and further, if it is prepared to sponsor and fund those deaths in order to safeguard its investments, then what price a princess? In particular a princess whose humanitarian work threatened to lift the lid on fifty years of corporate conspiracy, much less the centuries of masonic conspiracy which preceded it? As far-reaching as this allegation may seem, there is yet a vast body of documented and historical evidence to be presented in support of its veracity. The simple point being that, if Diana was indeed assassinated, then our democratically elected governments are not necessarily implicated in any way whatever. On the contrary, it is not the puppet but the puppeteer with whom the buck stops.

And in this instance the puppeteer is the corporately funded 'masonic government' as described in these pages.

Further Moves To Unite Europe

Since the National Socialist Party's rise to power in 1920s/30s Germany, the initiative to centralize European power has assumed various forms. Hitler's own attempt to unite Europe - and then the world - under the auspices of the reverse-swastika, of course, remains a case in point. Though Hitler's ideologies may well have failed due to the fact that he attempted to implement them by force, nevertheless they did not end with the cessation of hostilities in 1945. On the contrary, these same ideologies were both admired and adhered to by many of the world's most prominent oligarchs, and are still being pursued with some vigour by the various military-industrial power groups today in order to gain tighter and tighter control on international affairs. The only difference now, of course, is that these so-called 'Hitlerite ideologies' are being implemented surreptitiously, by means of covert socio-political control mechanisms and programmes. The powers-that-be have of course learned from experience that violent revolution is no longer the means by which to take control of nations or their assets; Hitler's failure to unite Europe by force demonstrates this point clearly enough. Faced with a clearly defined enemy, sooner or later people will revolt, resist, retaliate, as history attests. A faceless, insidious mechanism to conquer by surreptitious means, on the other hand, is rarely even perceived by its victims, much less challenged by them. It is a stealthy method, to be sure. But it is nonetheless an effective one. Covert infiltration of boardrooms, cabinet rooms, and the higher echelons of certain masonic agencies (such as the Priory of Sion, or indeed, the Order of Malta), it has to be reiterated, is far more effective than the 'old solution', which of course entailed mobilizing thousands of armed forces against doggedly resistant populations. (In the modern world, military coups are thus reserved for Third World nations and Hollywood.) With the people believing that they themselves 'voted' their government to power, they are of course left with little choice but to endure that government's term in office, and this notwithstanding the somewhat futile protests, petitions and pot-shots summarily aimed at bringing that government to book. It is a watertight strategy. And it is right out of

Hitler's personal collection of 'ways to rule the world'. It just so happens that he chose to employ the least effective one - force - and so, in the end, failed.

The connection between the CIA and Nazi Germany, then, is today more than ever becoming public knowledge. As is the fact that, as long ago as the 1920s, Third Reich overlords were acting on a US-backed policy 'to unite Europe against Communist takeover'. Owing to Hitler's chronic megalomania, of course, and that of his most trusted generals, this policy was pursued to the point that it exceeded even its sponsors' expectations. Simply put, the excesses of power invested in the Third Reich by ambitious British and US oligarchs, in the end, turned its leadership to acts of unprecedented sociopathy. The puppeteers entrusted too much; the puppets got out of hand. As a result, attempts to unite Europe under the banner of 1930s Fascism did not succeed.

But the desire for a United States of Europe clearly survived Hitler's 'suicide'. In the hallowed halls of corporate and masonic power, the dream lived on. It was not so much the *ideologies* which had failed, but the *methodologies* employed to implement them. In this regard, of course, Hitler should be understood as little more than a sacrificial cow - expendable in failure like any other hireling entrusted with such dangerous excesses of power. The elite circle of Hitler's most senior sponsors and advisers, on the other hand, formed in response to the masonic drive for a united Europe - indeed, as a vehicle for the emasculation and overthrow of European nation states, and their subsequent reconstruction into a corporate republic - was not and never could be deemed 'expendable'. Its generals were in dire need of a new approach, true enough. A new system. A new methodology wherein they might exchange their Nazi uniforms for charcoal suits and neckties, and their openly brutal methods for more subtle, more covert ways of achieving their goal. But the fundamental conspiracy to unite Europe under a corporate banner waged on, and the necessity for an international policing agency was thus born.

Enter the CIA. Under the guise of being a national intelligence gathering agency, the OSS (soon to become the CIA), together with MI6, set about formulating ways to organize the somewhat disparate factions of what by now had become known as the European Movement into a coherent whole. One of the first moves in this regard was the formation of a new and autonomous corporate body, a centralized intelligence agency with links to the world's major-league banks, industrial corporations, military agencies, governments, even the Vatican. Effectively this agency was to be a multinational corporation in its own right, an international policing agency with its headquarters in Virginia, USA (traditional home of the British/US masonic oligarchy in question), and with operational outlets in virtually every European nation state. It would be called the CIA. From this point on, all political and economic strategies regarding the centralization of European power would be coordinated and directed by the CIA.

Initial moves in this regard necessarily involved the regrouping of US resources. So far as America was concerned, the major reason for seeking to transform Europe into a single, autonomous body was to create a 'blockade against Communism'. Unlike the Pan-Europa movement, which had been formed in 1922 with the support of Winston Churchill, Albert Einstein and George Bernard Shaw, among others, and which sought a United States of Europe for perhaps more ideological reasons, the CIA was acting purely on behalf of US/corporate interests. And these interests, of course, demanded the creation of a centralized European power bloc which would act, first and foremost, as a blockade against the spread of Soviet Communism. It was an era in which the two superpowers sparred on a daily basis, each parrying and countering the other's blows with blows of its own - each seeking to establish itself as the world's leading superpower. Paranoia was rife. The Cold War was gaining a momentum all its own. The demand for military superiority - scientific superiority, technological superiority - was absolute. Both Russian and US intelligence agencies knew, of course, that, despite having lost the war, the Third Reich was in possession of some of the world's most advanced scientific and technological know-how. The Allies may gladly have disposed of Hitler, but his scientists and engineers were still in great demand.

The many scientific and technological advances achieved by Nazi scientists during the war were of course well-known to the West. Indeed, the West, in large part, had funded them. They had been made possible in the first instance by the vast amounts of corporate funding channelled into Third Reich banks, via Switzerland, by British and US intelligence agencies. But the question still remained: how could they be retrieved? How could the West's masonic oligarchy, having funded the war effort to the tune of billions of dollars, smuggle out of Nazi Germany the scientific and technological wisdom achieved by the Nazi scientists, and so reclaim its investment? And moreover, how could it accomplish this feat before the Soviets reached Berlin?

What is known for certain in this regard is this.

Towards the end of WWII, many high-ranking Nazis realized that plans to unite Europe by force, under Nazi auspices, was destined to fail. In short, they realized that Germany was about to lose the war. They saw America as their only hope - their only means of safeguarding both their own futures and that of the plan they had served so well: the plan to unite Europe. Negotiations in this regard began as early as 1943, when the corporate world's favourite prodigal, Allen Dulles, moved to Bern, Switzerland, in an official capacity as Head of Station for the OSS. In Switzerland, Dulles attended secret meetings with many Nazi top guns, some of whom, it should be said, rabidly opposed Hitler. Indeed, the now famous bomb plot to assassinate the increasingly megalomaniacal Fuhrer is said to have been orchestrated, at least in part, by Dulles and his band of Nazi apostates - which is said to have included the exiled German poet, Stefan George, and the conscientious Count Claus von Stauffenberg, accredited with masterminding the plot. Certainly it is believed that Dulles, in helping to coordinate the assassination attempt, was acting on a directive designed to have Hitler replaced by an altogether more affable 'Fuhrer' - one more sympathetic to corporate interests in the West. Indeed, one who would be prepared to negotiate peace terms with the Allies and at the same time maintain a corporately funded Nazi regime in Germany. And so salvage Western investments. As is of course known, however, the bomb plot failed to kill Hitler. If anything it made him even more paranoid. Following the attempt on his life, for example, Hitler ordered that the already brutal 'final solution' agenda - the mass extermination of European Jews - should be intensified even further. It was. A year later, this agenda had claimed the lives of more than 6,000,000 people of Jewish descent, most of whom died in what can only be described as barbaric and horrific circumstances. Whatever the real truth behind Hitler's hatred of Jews, it was surely more deep-rooted than the generally accepted understanding of the term 'racism'. Indeed, it was indelibly rooted in a past discoloured with the blood of biblical kings, as we shall see.

And as we shall also see, that same past leads directly to the present, and the masonically sponsored British Royal Family.

In any event, it would seem that Dulles was handpicked for the job of negotiating post-war freedom for those Nazis deemed of use to the ongoing corporate agenda. As we have seen, he had worked with many of the Nazi collaborators prior to the outbreak of hostilities, negotiating terms for contracts between the Third Reich and his US 'clients'. In consequence, Dulles had won favour with some very influential people, not least John D Rockefeller, Henry Ford and William Randolph Hearst. And there were others, including former President George Bush's father, Prescott Bush, together with Prescott Bush's father-in-law, George Herbert Walker, whose companies GH Walker & Co and Union Banking Corporation, in collaboration with a joint British/US banking and investment firm, Brown Brothers, Harriman, were investigated - and convicted - under the US Trading With The Enemy Act in 1942. According to Mark Aarons and John Loftus:

"Young George [Bush] was in flight school in October 1942, when the US government charged his father with running Nazi front groups in the

United States. Under the Trading With The Enemy Act, all the shares of the Union Banking Corporation were seized, including those held by Prescott Bush as being in effect held for enemy nationals. Union Banking, of course, was an affiliate of Brown Brothers, Harriman, and [Prescott] Bush handled the Harrimans' investments as well.

"Once the government had its hands on Bush's books, the whole story of the intricate web of Nazi front corporations began to unravel. A few days later, two of Union Banking's subsidiaries - the Holland American Trading Corporation and the Seamless Steel Equipment Corporation - also were seized. Then the government went after the Harriman Fifteen Holding Company, which [Prescott] Bush shared with his father-in-law, Bert Walker ... The US government found that huge sections of Prescott Bush's empire had been operated on behalf of Nazi Germany and had greatly assisted the German war effort."

Some decades later, of course, following his tour of duty as Director of the CIA, Prescott Bush's son became President of the United States. It would seem that, like Allen Dulles before him, the war with Nazi Germany served George Bush well enough (as indeed it might equally serve his son, George W Bush, at America's next presidential election).

And in any event it was a good investment for the Bush family.

But this, of course, is simply one example of how the corporate agenda works, and of how the British/US masonic oligarchy is able to control events worldwide. While the national governments of both Britain and America accrued vast debts as a result of WWII, the corporate oligarchy - headed up by the likes of the Fords, the Rothschilds and the Rockefellers - grew even fatter, even more powerful, even more influential in terms of national and international policy-brokering. After all, it had funded the war effort. It had supplied armaments and other resources to both the Axis and the Allied powers, and the end of hostilities in 1945 meant that it was time to call in its considerable loans. When you are indebted to someone - anyone - to the tune of billions of dollars, of course - as indeed both Britain and America were, and still are - well now...

But not all of Allen Dulles's 'clients' were American. His brother, John Foster Dulles, for example, sat on the board of the German multinational, IG Farben, and the brothers consequently forged acquaintances with many high-ranking German industrialists and bankers. Fritz Thyssen, for one, the high-powered German industrialist via whom the Bush empire's investments in Nazi Germany had, in large part, been secured. Another was German banker Hjalmar Schacht, who together with Thyssen had funded Hitler's rise to power during the 1920s. Yet another was General Reinhard Gehlen, Nazi intelligence chief for the Eastern Front and future CIA collaborator. Indeed, during his time as Director of the CIA (1953-61), Allen Dulles would work hand-in-glove with Gehlen, employing the former Nazi in the CIA's Cold War reconnaissance of Soviet Russia. But first there was the problem of Gehlen's post-war survival. A plan was needed. Together with Gehlen, Dulles devised one.

General Reinhard Gehlen was one of the most influential Nazis to escape war crimes charges following the end of WWII. With a little help from Dulles, Gehlen managed to convince the US authorities that the Soviets were planning to attack the Allies at the end of the war, and that he and his band of renegade SS officers could be of use as an intelligence window on Eastern Europe. In 1945, having surrendered to a US counter-intelligence unit, Gehlen was flown to Virginia, then to Washington, where he offered his services to the US government. With little ado, it would seem, an agreement was reached. In consequence, the US government sanctioned and funded the setting up of Gehlen's intelligence organization, which, before it evolved into the BND (Germany's present-day 'CIA') was known as the Gehlen Org. For a full decade following the war, Gehlen's intelligence machine was the CIA's Cold War window on Eastern Europe. Indeed, in 1948 Gehlen would receive the Order of Malta's most prestigious decoration, the Grand Cross of Merit, for his work as a CIA collaborator. (It would seem that the Order of Malta was less than circumspect in handing out decorations to both Allied and Axis war criminals. We recall, for example, that two years earlier, in 1946, the Order had decorated then-OSS Head of Station in Rome, James Jesus Angleton, for his so-called 'counter-intelligence work' in Italy. In truth, of course, this work involved aiding Dulles and the Vatican retrieve millions of dollars from Nazi Germany and channelling the money back to its corporate sources - as well as into the Vatican's own coffers and, over the course of the following two years, into the coffers of Italy's CIA-sponsored Christian Democratic Party.)

Once again, then, the facts tend to suggest that, at the top end of the chain, Germany's BND (the Gehlen Org) is - together with MI6 and the Vatican - little more than a European CIA outlet. The Order of Malta, of course, serves all four.

But Gehlen was not the only Nazi to curry favour with the Americans. The OSS (later the CIA) also contracted the likes of Holocaust mastermind, Otto von Bolschwing, and SS Colonel Otto Skorzeny, as well as the so-called 'Butcher of Lyons', Klaus Barbie. Barbie, of course, was head of the Gestapo in Lyons during the war, and won his now-famous nickname for atrocities perpetrated against captured French Resistance fighters. Other top Nazi scientists and aviation experts such as the infamous Von Braun were also poached by the CIA, and given their freedom - in exchange for 'services rendered'. One of the major reasons so many top Nazi scientists and aviation experts were included on the CIA payroll, of course, was that major scientific and technological advances had been made by them in terms of sophisticated flight-propulsion systems for aircraft, and equally sophisticated advanced-weapons technologies. Naturally the Americans sought to procure rather than destroy the new technologies on offer (particularly as US money had funded their development). It is no secret either that - with an unlimited number of 'human guinea pigs' available to them, mainly Jews and Gypsies interned in concentration camps - the Nazis had forged major breakthroughs in the field of genetics, even as early as 1943. As had the Japanese, who also figured prominently in the CIA's *Operation Paperclip* - the code name given to the operation responsible for coordinating the mass exodus of Nazi war criminals to the US, largely via Latin America, during the mid-to-late 1940s.

In this regard, the so-called Nuremberg War Trials should be understood as little more than sham - a political screen behind which *Operation Paperclip* became one of the most successful covert CIA (OSS) operations ever.

The Bilderberg Connection

To further the ambitions which had driven Hitler's Third Reich towards the establishment of a one world state (or at least a United States of Europe), in the late 1940s and early 1950s the CIA recruited many right-wing war veterans and sold them the idea of imminent Communist takeover. The self-professed anti-communists needed little convincing that a strong and united anti-Soviet European Superstate would be the only effective countermeasure to the threat of world domination by an increasingly hostile - and powerful - Soviet regime. In this regard, the CIA funded the campaign for 'European Unity' to the tune of £1.34 million, an awful lot of money in the 1950s. Behind the scenes, of course, this figure was surpassed countless times over.

As part of this move to establish a European Superstate, in 1948 the CIA procured the services of Polish emigre, Dr Josef Retinger. The former SOE operative and international power-broker, Retinger, flew to the US in July 1948 for talks with senior CIA officials and other pro-European protagonists - including, some say, President Truman. The result was the formation of what became known as the American Committee on a United Europe (ACUE). Of interest here is the fact that the man who had played such an active role in sponsoring the Nazis' failed attempt to unite Europe, future CIA Director Allen Dulles, was elected as ACUE's Vice-Chairman. ACUE's Chairman was one General William 'Wild Bill' Donovan, former OSS Director and active pro-European campaigner. Indeed, the movement attracted the services of some of the West's most esteemed military and intelligence chiefs. Former Director of Britain's SOE, General Sir Colin Gubbins, for example, and CIA Director General Walter Bedell Smith (1950-53), were both instrumental in the formation of ACUE's first major think tank. But it was not until former SS officer, IG Farben deal-broker and future World Wildlife Fund and 1001 Club President, Prince Bernhard of the Netherlands, added his support that this think tank took on major new proportions. And gained new momentum in the process. Between May 29th and 31st, 1954, the ACUE think tank convened at the now famous Bilderberg Hotel in Oosterbeek, a small town near Arnhem in Holland. And thus the CIA-funded Bilderberg Group was born.

Essentially, the Bilderberg Group is a *pot-pourri* of international financiers and industrialists; high-ranking military and intelligence chiefs; academics; economists; statesmen; politicians (both left and right); publishing magnates; editors on the CIA payroll; editors on the MI6 payroll; journalists. Common to each member (or conference attendee), of course, is the same collectivist ideal for a corporate-based European Superstate - complete with a European Bank, centralized administration and all the relevant trimmings, such as an electronic single currency and ID tagging, Big Brother-style. Indeed, if you are searching for evidence of the existence of Big Brother, search no more. The Bilderberg Group is as Big Brother as you can get. Affiliations with other members of the Big Brother family, other masonic organizations - the US-based Council on Foreign Relations, the British-based Royal Institute of International Affairs, the Trilateral Commission, NATO, the UN, the World Economic Forum, G7/8, the International Monetary Forum, the World Bank, P2, the overseeing Policy Committee, etc. - are incestuous, to say the least. Indeed, according to one inside source it is the consensus opinion of these power groups, debated and decided at their secret annual conferences, which effectively determines both national and international policy. But not before it has been approved and authorized by the so-called Policy Committee - the central Bilderberg control-body said to comprise 300 of "the most powerful men in ... the free world". In this regard, the Bilderberg Group should be understood as perhaps the most influential body of backstairs policy-makers in the Western world.

And the CIA, together with MI6, is its cat's paw.

Perhaps this is one reason why Bilderberg policies are always discussed behind closed doors, a policy adopted from its elder sibling, the Royal Institute of International Affairs, which convenes at Chatham House in London. The Institute's secrecy policy - the so-called 'Chatham House Rule' - is more or less well-known, and was devised to prohibit journalists from reporting on matters discussed at the Institute's conferences. Likewise, journalists attending Bilderberg meetings are ordered not to report the policies discussed and determined at the annual conferences. The journalists - some because they are deep-cover intelligence agents, others because they fear the consequences should they disregard the Rule - always comply. To counter this veil of mystery, however, the Bilderberg Group is not so secretive that it denies its own existence. On the contrary, a contact name and address is registered in the *Yearbook of International Organisations*, and included among its impressive list of conference attendees are some of the world's most distinguished luminaries. Global power-broker supreme, Henry Kissinger, for example, as well as President of the World Bank, James Wolfensohn. David Rockefeller, billionaire power-broker and Chairman of the Chase Manhattan Bank is another attendee; heir apparent to the House of Windsor, Prince Charles, is another. As is Giovanni Agnelli, Honorary Chairman of Fiat SpA; Jurgen Schrempp, Chairman of Daimler-Benz; Paul Allaire, Chairman of Xerox; Helmut Maucher, Chairman of Nestle Ltd; plus the chairmen of BP and Reuters, and the big guns from a welter of other major-league corporations and financial institutions. The list is seemingly endless.

Other known 'attendees' include Javier Solana, Secretary General of NATO; former CIA Director, John Deutch; Nancy Soderberg, Deputy Asst to the President for National Security; Canadian publishing tycoon, Conrad Black; Peter Jennings, ABC News; J Martin Taylor, CEO, Barclays Bank plc; Norman Lamont MP, former Chancellor of the Exchequer and Director of NM Rothschild; new British Tory Leader, William Hague; an assortment of other European prime ministers, foreign affairs ministers and opposition leaders; Leon Brittan; Kenneth Clarke; New Labour Defence Secretary, George Robertson. Plus, of course, the Bilderberg chairmen themselves, of which, over the years, there have been five.

Former SS officer and confidant of Buckingham Palace (indeed, comrade-in-arms to Prince Philip, the Duke of Edinburgh), HRH Prince Bernhard of the Netherlands (1954-75). It is of note here that Prince Philip's brother-in-law, Prince Christoph, was also an SS Colonel or *Standartenfuhrer*, on Heinrich Himmler's personal staff.

Former British Prime Minister, Lord Home (1976-79).

Former President of the Federal Republic of Germany, Walter Scheel (1979-85).

Then-President of SG Warburg Group plc, Lord Roll of Ipsden (1986-1989). It is of interest to note with regard to Lord Roll's appointment that, up until 1937, the Warburg family held controlling interests in the German chemicals giant, IG Farben. Circles within circles...

For the past ten years the Bilderberg Chairman has been Old Etonian, former Secretary of State for Foreign and Commonwealth Affairs and former Secretary General of NATO (among an impressive host of other prerogatives and designations) Lord Carrington. During his tenure as Secretary of State for Foreign and Commonwealth Affairs, of course, Lord Carrington would have been overall head of MI6.

A formidable confluence of mind, money and megalomania, then, to be sure. But that is not all. To add to this list are such passionate political bed partners as Bill Clinton and Tony Blair. To judge by Bill Clinton's recent 'sex at work' problems, it would seem that the wayward president may have upset one too many right-wing oligarchs over the years, and is today facing the consequences. In this regard, he will no doubt be thankful that the might of Bilderberg influence stands firmly behind him, and that it remains that way, certainly in terms of the impeachment proceedings currently under way (at the time of writing). Indeed, both he and Prime Minister Tony Blair should be understood as high-profile exponents of the same central agenda: to serve the Bilderberg directive and, at the same time, of course, to climb its political tree.

Or fall out of it.

In this regard, it is reputedly Bilderberg influence which makes or breaks politicians, decides which party ascends to power (and how long it remains in power), and dictates policy to US and European administrations as though orchestrating some global chess game. It was no surprise, for example, that so-called New Labour won the 1997 British general election under Tony Blair, who attended a Bilderberg conference prior to his appointment as Labour leader, some conspiracy theorists say for a 'final briefing'. Certainly we know that Bilderberg sister-organizations such as the so-called Davos Group (World Economic Forum), which convenes on an annual basis at the luxury ski resort of Davos, Switzerland, is divided into a number of 'inner clubs' or sub-groups, each masonically compartmented and titled according to its political or industrial sector - to wit: the 'Industry Governors Club'; the 'Global Leaders for Tomorrow Club'; the 'World Media Leaders Club'; the 'World Cultural Leaders Club'; the 'Forum Fellows Club', etc. Listed among the candidates in the 'Global Leaders for Tomorrow Club', for example, is Britain's current Chancellor of the Exchequer, Gordon Brown, as well as Director of Triodos Bank, Peter Blum, and high-ranking Bilderberger, Giovanni Agnelli, member of the International Advisory Board of the Council on Foreign Relations and Honorary Chairman of Fiat SpA. It is suspected that the Bilderberg Group is similarly compartmented, and that Tony Blair was perhaps sponsored by the Bilderberg Group's own version of 'Global Leaders for Tomorrow' during his meteoric rise to power. (Bill Clinton and Germany's newly elected centre-left Chancellor, Gerhard Schroeder, must also be considered in this same light.) What is certain is that Britain under a centre-left Socialist Government would have been considered far more malleable by the Bilderberg Policy Committee

- far more easily manipulated into a European Superstate than it would have been had the Conservative Party won power for the umpteenth time in succession. In this regard, it would seem that 'centre-left' is the agreed most effective pseudo-posture in terms of uniting Europe under a corporate banner. And a *pseudo-posture* it most certainly is. For the record, Margaret Thatcher's sudden and brutal demise is also attributed to Bilderberg chicanery, much the same as will be Tony Blair's, most theorists agree, just as soon as he has fulfilled his sponsors' requirement of him.

Official Response

It is quite simply extraordinary that, at the turn of this millennium, so many educated people claim never to have heard of the Bilderberg Group. It is equally alarming just how many refuse to believe that such organizations exist. Or that, if they do, they do so only in the paranoid and over-active imaginations of so-called 'conspiracy theorists'.

But perhaps what is most alarming of all is that so many seem happy to remain ignorant of the group's *modus operandi,* and indeed, its influence on global policy-making. And in turn, on their own personal lives. In this regard, we felt it pertinent to include here the following information, contained in a letter written by Linda Perham, MP for Ilford North, in response to a request for information from a member of the British public regarding the Bilderberg Group. Though the information derives from the International Affairs and Defence Section of the House of Commons Research Library, and is thus necessarily tainted by the official party line, it nonetheless provides conclusive evidence of the existence of the group, and insights into its functions and activities. By implication, of course, it also confirms the existence of other such international power groups, the closely guarded, secretive network which links them. And in turn, the masonic oligarchy which governs them.

The letter and information is reprinted here by kind permission of Ivan Fraser, Editor, *The Truth Campaign.*

```
5 August, 1997

Dear [name deleted],

Further to your visit to my surgery on 24 July, and
my letter of 31 July, the House of Commons Research
Library have prepared the enclosed briefing concerning
the Bilderberg Group...
```

Linda Perham MP.

*   *   *

Dear Ms Perham,

You have requested information on the Bilderberg Group.

I have found a contact name and address in the current edition of the Yearbook of International Organisations. I am afraid that there is no telephone number listed. The contact name and address is:

Ms Maja Banck-Polderman, Bilderberg Meetings, Herengracht 500, 1017 CB Amsterdam

The Bilderberg conference is a highly secretive, annual conference which was established in 1954 at the invitation of Prince Bernhard of the Netherlands at the Hotel de Bilderberg in Oosterbeek, the Netherlands. Its main founder was the Polish philanthropist Joseph Retinger and its members include political leaders, statesmen, academics, businessmen, bankers and union leaders from Western Europe and the NATO countries. They discuss the political, economic and military problems of Europe and the world.

Details of the group's membership are kept secret, although press reports have revealed that Kenneth Clarke attended the Conference in Athens in May 1995 and Mr Clarke and Tony Blair in 1993. Paddy Ashdown was at the conference in May 1989. There does not appear to be any evidence that this group formed an international conspiracy and "plotted the downfall of Mrs Thatcher". According to the Yearbook of International Organisations there is a Steering Committee and an Advisory Group with members from 19 countries. These are: Canada, USA, Austria, Belgium, Denmark, Finland, France, Germany, Greece, Iceland, Italy, Netherlands, Norway, Portugal, Spain, Sweden, Switzerland, Turkey, UK.

The following reports from The *Guardian*, 1 October 1993, and *The Times*, 25 April 1986, consider the Bilderberg Conference, shedding some light on its activities and membership.

1. *Guardian*, 1 Oct 1993.
Notes and Queries

The Bilderberg Group was founded in 1954, an outgrowth of various right-wing and anti-communist organisations, such as the American Committee for a United Europe. The main figure behind its formation was Joseph Retinger, an enigmatic Polish philanthropist and 'political philosopher'. It has connections with the CIA, OSS, Trilateral Commission, Council on Foreign Relations and other shadowy organisations.

It first met in the Hotel de Bilderberg in Oosterbeek, Netherlands, hence the name. To this day no one knows if this is its real name since it goes to any lengths to avoid publicity and membership is highly secret.

The minutes of the group's first meeting recorded that one of its primary interests was in "evolving an international order" which would "look beyond the present crisis", and this goal of creating a one world government still seems to be its driving force. In 1989, it was alleged to have plotted the political assassination of Margaret Thatcher, because of "her refusal to yield British Sovereignty to the European Superstate that is due to emerge in 1992".

The alleged list of attendees at the annual bash in 1991, held in Baden-Baden, included Queen Beatrix of the Netherlands, Kari Otto Pohl, then President of Deutsche Bundesbank, Katherine Graham, chairperson of the Washington Post, David Rockefeller, Lord Carrington and Governor Bill Clinton of Arkansas.

2. *Times,* 25 April 1986
Prince "in secret meeting"/Bilderberg Meeting
The Prince of Wales and Mrs Margaret Thatcher are thought to be among those taking part in a secret weekend conference of some of the most influential figures of the Western world.

The 'Bilderberg Meeting', named after the hotel in the Netherlands where it was first staged in 1954, is to begin tomorrow at the Gleneagles Hotel in Perthshire.

So secret is the meeting, at which East-West relations and world economic problems will be discussed, that its location was not officially admitted until yesterday.

Organisers would not say last night who would be attending, but participants at previous conferences have included Mrs Thatcher, Mr Denis Healey, Dr Henry Kissinger and senior financiers.

The organisers say that the 115 participants, from

Western Europe and the United States, would "exchange views on issues of common concern".

Subjects to be discussed are: The Soviet Union under Gorbachev - foreign policy implications; the Western global response to the Soviet challenge; the fragmentation of world economy - debt, currency disorder, protectionism, uneven growth; South Africa.

The annual meetings were founded by Prince Bernhard of the Netherlands in the hope of providing an off-the-record forum for talks. Government sources last night confirmed that Mrs Thatcher will be "looking in" on the conference but were unable to say whether she will address it.

Labour MPs are highly suspicious of the 'Bilderberg Meeting', and have criticised leading part figures for attending it in the past...

Bilderberg decisions are not debated in the British Parliament and there appears to have been very little parliamentary interest in the Conference over the last ten years. Below are some references to parliamentary questions on the Conference in 1986 and the only other parliamentary question since then:

```
1
TYPE :: WPQ
DISPLAY DATE :: 03.06.86
REFERENCE :: 98c397W
SESSION :: 85/86
CORPORATE AUTHOR :: Scottish Office
MEMBER :: Nellist/Dave; Mackay/John
DESCRIPTION :: (Pursuant to 19 May 1986 clW). What
```
were costs to public funds of policing of Bilderberg Conference.
```
2
TYPE :: WPQ
DISPLAY DATE :: 19.05.86
REFERENCE :: 98c1W
SESSION :: 85/86
CORPORATE AUTHOR :: Scottish Office
MEMBER :: Nellist/Dave; Mackay/John
DESCRIPTION :: What were costs to public funds of
```
policing Bilderberg Conference - Deferred

3
TYPE :: WPQ
DISPLAY DATE :: 19.05.86
REFERENCE :: 98c33-4W;98c33W
SESSION :: 85/86
CORPORATE AUTHOR :: Prime Minister
MEMBER :: Nellist/Dave; Thatcher/Margaret
DESCRIPTION :: What were the costs to public funds
of her attendance at the Bilderberg Conference

4
TYPE :: WPQ
DISPLAY DATE :: 01.05.86
REFERENCE :: 96c456W;96c454W
SESSION :: 85/86
CORPORATE AUTHOR :: Prime Minister
MEMBER :: BiggsDavison/John; Thatcher Margaret
DESCRIPTION :: For what purpose Prime Minister
attended the Bilderberg Conference

5
TYPE :: WPQ
DISPLAY DATE :: 19.03,96
REFERENCE :: 570c93WA
SESSION :: 95/96
CORPORATE AUTHOR :: Stoddart of Swindon/Lord; Chalker
of Wallasey/RtHonBaroness
MEMBER :: Nellist/Dave; Mackay/John
DESCRIPTION :: What was the purpose of the attendance
of Sir David Hannay at the Bilderberg Meeting in
Burgenstock, Switzerland, on 8th-11th June 1995, at whose
invitation did he attend and what report he filed to the
Foreign Secretary

I hope this is of use.

Yours sincerely,

Alison E Weston
International Affairs and Defence Section
[House of Commons Research Library]

The Elders Of Sion Of The 33rd Degree

That plans to unite Europe under a corporate banner are ongoing, then, is quite simply beyond question. That such plans have prevailed for at least half a century, and that a masonically structured, international network of political and economic power groups has been spawned as a result, is equally evident. But what is also evident is that parallel plans to unite Europe for perhaps more ideological reasons have obtained for even longer, maybe centuries. And that these plans have been systematically hijacked by succeeding political regimes and their intelligence agencies, and prostituted to their own advantage.

In this regard, masonic plans for a centralized European Superstate - and moreover, for a one world government - can be traced back at least as far as 1884, when a curious and controversial document purporting to outline the strategies necessary to achieve this end was unearthed. This document has been known by various names, the most widely employed today being *The Protocols of the Elders of Sion*. Establishment pillars, of course, claim that this document is spurious. But more recent research has led many scholars to conclude that in fact it is genuine. Or at least that the document as it survives today is based on an original document which was indeed genuine, and which meant something other to its author(s) than the surviving, bastardized version means to those who so radically altered it. Viciously racist, provocative in the extreme, the version of the *Protocols* in circulation today in effect propounds a blueprint for world domination by a covert "Super Government" composed of Jews. In his book, *Warrant For Genocide,* Norman Cohn describes the *Protocols* as "lectures or notes for lectures in which a member of the secret Jewish government - the Elders of Zion - expounds a plot to achieve world domination". Indeed, the document details in no uncertain terms the wholly machiavellian agenda which, even now, is being employed to achieve this very end - to wit: the surreptitious hijacking of the democratic process by finance and industry; the gradual creation of corporate monopolies; ownership of the world's most influential communications and media organizations in order to control the dissemination of information; replacing currency with credit; the creation of a worldwide web of masonic orders, international power groups and intelligence agencies. In short, the gradual and surreptitious centralization of political and economic power to the advantage of the privileged few; at the same time the subjugation and control of the masses by subliminal, insidious means. Thus the document boasts: "Who will ever suspect then that all these people were stage-managed by us according to a political plan which no one has so much as guessed at in the course of many centuries?"

Who indeed.

It should be noted that, curiously out of character with its political and economic master plan, the document also propounds the advent of a true 'bloodline Messiah' who will issue from "the dynastic roots of King David", and who will preside over the coming, Judaically controlled "Kingdom" with a fist of iron. It is this seeming discrepancy which has led some scholars to suspect a forgery. Or at least the superimposition of one author's work upon that of a different, original author. Even so, as it appears today, there can be little doubt that the document's main thrust is its detailed depiction of the socio-political and economic programme necessary to prepare the way for the emergence of some totalitarian, Jewish "Super Government".

But perhaps the most disturbing aspect with regard to this document is that, although compiled at least 115 years ago, its content - its stratagem, its programme for political and economic control - reads like an evaluation of late twentieth-century socio-political conditions. In other words, it describes in meticulous, almost uncanny detail the social, political and economic conditions prevalent today. And the elaborately unscrupulous methods by which those conditions have been achieved. Indeed, by which they are being maintained. Included, for example, is a plan "to establish a monopoly of industry and trade" in order to "give political force to those engaged in industry". And further: "Throughout all Europe, and ... in other continents also ... we have stretched into the cabinets of all States by means of politics, by economic treaties, or loan obligations." The document goes on to predict the decline in power wielded by the aristocracy (at least 115 years ago), and the subsequent creation of both working-class and middle-class hegemony, which did not properly establish in most European countries until well into the twentieth century. "...We must have everybody vote without distinction of classes and qualifications, in order to establish an absolute majority, which cannot be got from the educated, propertied classes." And again: "In order that our scheme may produce this result we shall arrange elections in favour of such presidents as have in their past some dark, undiscovered stain ... then they will be trustworthy agents for the accomplishment of our plans out of fear of revelations..." In this regard, one cannot help but view the United States of America as a case in point.

As stated, the document also speaks of supplanting currency with credit: "We shall replace the money markets by grandiose government credit institutions." Also on the agenda is a plan to control information so that the "goyim" (in this context the 'masses') can be unwittingly manipulated. "Not a single announcement will reach the public without our control ... Even now this is already being attained by us in as much as all news items are received by a few agencies ... These agencies will then be already entirely ours, and will give publicity only to what we dictate to them." And further: "Literature and journalism are two of the most important educative forces, and therefore our government will become proprietor of the majority of the journals. This will neutralize the injurious influence of the privately owned Press and will put us in possession of a tremendous influence upon the public mind..."

With particular regard to this section of the book, *Agencies Of Masonic Government*, the document is quite specific. "...We shall create and multiply free masonic lodges in all the countries of the world, absorb into them all who may become or who are prominent in public activity, for in these lodges we shall find our principal intelligence office and means of influence ... All these lodges we shall bring under one central administration, known to us alone and to all others absolutely unknown, which will be composed of our learned elders." And even more revealing: "Among the members of these lodges will be almost all the agents of international and national police..." Like MI6 and the CIA, for example.

In the final analysis, the *Protocols'* message is unequivocal. "God has granted to us, His Chosen People, the gift of the Dispersion ... which has now brought us to the threshold of sovereignty over all the world ... When the King of Israel sets upon his sacred head the crown offered him by Europe, he will become patriarch of the world."

The document concludes: "Signed by the representatives of Sion of the 33rd Degree."

Though the above extracts constitute but a fragment of the *Protocols* - which in their entirety comprise a substantial document of some twenty-four 'chapters' and more than 26,000 words - they serve nonetheless to convey the tenor of the programme contained in the document (which, remember, was composed at least as far back as the late nineteenth century). It is as though the document's author(s) had foreknowledge of precisely how conditions were destined to manifest at the turn of this third millennium AD. In this regard, the *Protocols* must either be considered an uncannily accurate fraud; a sort of socio-political prophecy penned by some late nineteenth-century soothsayer; or indeed, bone-chilling evidence of a cunningly devised and vigorously pursued blueprint for the centralization of US/European political and economic power. As conceded by at least a handful of leading scholars today, scrutiny of the document bears testimony to this latter conclusion clearly enough.

At first glance, the *Protocols* would seem to comprise little more than a vicious attempt at scaremongering. Certainly they purport a sort of 'manifesto for global takeover', a programme for world dominion penned by some covert Zionist elite or Jewish cabal (or at least by someone who wishes us to arrive at this conclusion). In short, and even though the programme contained in the *Protocols* seems eerily prognostic of present-day socio-political and economic conditions, on the face of it they would nevertheless seem to comprise little more than a malicious and elaborate hoax. Certainly it is easy to see why they have been dismissed as such by so-called 'intellectuals' and 'academicians'. Others, however, have not been so easily persuaded.

What is known for certain is that, since their emergence in the public domain, the *Protocols* have provoked a backlash of anti-Semitic feeling on a scale unprecedented in modern history. Their existence alone has precipitated the deaths of millions of innocent Jews. In 1919, for example, tens of thousands of Jews were summarily slaughtered by soldiers of the White Russian Army; as a result of anti-Semitic propaganda engendered by the *Protocols,* Jews were blamed for starting the Russian Revolution of 1917 (as indeed they were blamed for Germany's 'untimely surrender' to the Allies in 1918). Some two decades later, of course, millions of Jews would meet their death at the hands of Hitler's Third Reich. It is known, of course, that Hitler viewed the Protocols as a genuine document, and that he interpreted its content as plans for a global takeover by Zionist elites. In his book, *Mein Kampf,* the burgeoning Fuhrer used the *Protocols* to justify his own racist, genocidal tendencies. "On this first and greatest lie, that the Jews are not a race but a religion, more and more lies are based," wrote Hitler in 1924. And further: "To what an extent the entire existence of this people is based on a continuous lie is shown incomparably by *The Protocols Of The Wise Men Of Sion* ... What many Jews do unconsciously is here consciously exposed."

Hitler, then, was convinced of some imminent global assertion of power by an unknown Jewish or Zionist cabal - a cabal accredited with the document's authorship. Indeed, that he desired to emulate this Zionist elite - to achieve its aim sooner than *it* did, though by even more brutal and direct means - is evident enough. Even the most ghoulish of sociopaths must surely concede that the Holocaust constitutes the single most horrific and sickening atrocity ever committed. And there are any number to choose from.

But the point is that the *Protocols*, though dismissed by some scholars (often, it would seem, for reasons which condescend only to preserve intellectual autonomy), nevertheless boast a very interesting history. Though academia claims that the document originated in a French pamphlet in 1864 (that it was penned as a satire attacking Napolean III, and subsequently plagiarized and promulgated in a radically bastardized form for political purposes) more recent evidence suggests a different origin entirely. Certainly it is likely that the original *Protocols* predate the satire contained in the 1864 pamphlet; indeed, that the satire itself was based on an older, original document, as we shall see. The one point where academia and conspiracy theory tend to agree is that the original *Protocols* would seem to have been composed in

French.

The satire in question was written by one Maurice Joly, an eminent French lawyer who called the work *Dialogues aux Enfers entre Montesquieu et Machiavel* (Dialogue in Hell between Montesquieu and Machiavelli) and who was subsequently imprisoned for its publication. As stated, however, it is unlikely that Joly's satire was an entirely original work. On the contrary, the evidence suggests that the satire was based on original ideas prevalent in the secret societies of his time. Or perhaps on a document of the same origin, or even a 'blueprint policy' secretly promulgated by, and disseminated among, the burgeoning network of Parisian secret-society circles in which Joly is known to have participated. The *Protocols* conclude, for example: "Signed by the representatives of Sion of the 33rd Degree", explicitly inferring that the document boasts a masonic - or even a Freemasonic - origin. Joly's own interests in this regard are betrayed in that he wrote the satire in the first place, and in the added fact that he was himself almost certainly a member of a Rose-Croix order. Which is interesting. The idea that the *Protocols* originated with some or other 'Rosicrucian' order has certainly been mooted. As Baigent, Leigh and Lincoln comment in *The Holy Blood And The Holy Grail,* the "1884 copy of the *Protocols* surfaced in the hands of a member of a Masonic lodge - the same lodge ... [in which] the tradition of Ormus had first appeared - the legendary Egyptian sage who amalgamated pagan and Christian mysteries and founded the Rose-Croix". And what is even more revealing is that the Rosicrucian movement in Europe stemmed from - indeed, was created as a 'front' or a 'pseudomorph' for - our old friend the Priory of Sion. Once again, circles within circles...

There seems little doubt, then, that the earliest known copy of the *Protocols* emanated from Europe's nineteenth-century masonic underworld, in which Joly himself was known to have been active. At the level of the 33rd Degree, of course, one order would seem to interface with a host of other, similar orders, and we are faced with a matrix of labyrinthine twists and turns which tend, ultimately, to lead nowhere in particular. Such is the nature of masonic infrastructure. Nevertheless, the *Protocols* throw up their own unmistakable clues in this regard. Stark references to a true 'bloodline Messiah' who will issue from "the dynastic roots of King David", for example, tend not only to confirm the document's origin as being of a highly masonic nature. They also imply very strongly that the Priory of Sion was indeed the document's original architect. The fact that the document is signed by the "representatives of Sion of the 33rd Degree", of course, tends only to confirm this probability. And that Joly's satire - and later still the vitriolic and highly inflammatory version of the *Protocols* we know today - derived from this same original source. Given what is known about the Priory of Sion (that it has for centuries concerned itself with the restoration of the Judaic or Merovingian Royal Dynasty to certain European thrones, maybe even to *the* European Throne; and further, that said Merovingian Dynasty did indeed issue from "the dynastic roots of King David", and that its survivors still do) it is certainly reasonable to conclude that the original *Protocols* formed the basis of the Priory's 'creed', its 'articles of faith': its in-house memo, so to speak. The fact that certain agencies in the West - most notably MI6 and the CIA - have endeavoured for at least the past fifty years to compromise the Priory of Sion and its 'bloodline secrets' only serves to further confirm this probability. After all, what better way to compromise such an order than by obtaining what might well have been an in-house memo and, while retaining the salient ingredients of said memo, add to it a barrage of megalomaniacal rantings and turn it into the viciously racist, machiavellian article we know it to be today? And then disseminate it as propaganda.

Though this may seem an over-elaborate scheme, there is further evidence to support the fact that this is indeed the case. The version of the *Protocols* we know today, for example, first surfaced in Russia, at the court of Tsar Nicholas II. There were, of course, many Jews resident in Russia at the turn of the twentieth century, many of whom enjoyed prominent social positions. Though millions of Jews had fled Russia following severe repressive measures brought against them by Tsar Alexander III in 1881, and equally severe persecutions, nevertheless many remained. And many of these commanded positions of relative economic influence. In consequence, fears grew among certain elite Russian cliques that a Jewish takeover was imminent. Enter one Sergie Nilus, confidant to Tsar Nicholas II and spin-doctor extraordinaire. It is known that Nilus had become suspicious of certain powerful enclaves of occultists and other esoteric votaries who seem to have wielded some power at the Russian court. Rasputin, for example, is known to have wielded considerable influence at the court of Tsar Nicholas II. But there were others, too. And the evidence conclusively proves that their influence stemmed from their association with, and their allegiance to, some of the better known secret societies in France at this time - many of which were based on what might be termed 'esoteric Judaism'. The Priory of Sion, of course, is a case in point. Certainly we know that interest in occult ideas, and membership of occult and other masonic and secret orders, flourished in France during the nineteenth century. And that its effect subsequently spread across Europe and, indeed, as far afield as St Petersburg. In any event, Nilus seems to have procured a copy of the *Protocols*, and to have subsequently set about concocting his own vitriolic and thoroughly incendiary adaptation based on the original. He is then known to have presented the bastardized version to the Tsar in an attempt to convince him of a high-level Jewish conspiracy against the Russian Royal Establishment. The Tsar, however, was not to be fooled by Nilus's chicanery. Indeed, Nilus was banished from the court for his trouble, and the Tsar ordered all copies of the *Protocols* to be destroyed. But Nilus had a contingency plan.

Having failed to convince the Tsar that some faceless Zionist elite was about to overthrow Russia - and then the world - Nilus released the document for public consumption (still, of course, in its heavily doctored form). So far as can be ascertained, the document's initial publication occurred in 1903. Two years later it appeared as an appendix to a book by one Vladimir Soloviov, a renowned philosopher of his day. By the end of WWI it was known about and talked about in circles the world over. Hitler, for example, had obtained a copy. Or at least he had been persuaded by the argument of Nazi Party propagandist, Alfred Rosengberg, who was busy circulating copies of the document throughout 1920s Germany. Indeed, following their publication in the German newspaper, the *Frankfurter Zeitung*, Hitler would write: "They are based on a forgery, the *Frankfurter Zeitung* moans and screams once a week: the best proof that they are authentic." A sentiment shared by *The Times* in London, who published a critique on the document in 1921, only to later change its mind and proclaim the document a forgery. But then, in its present form the document most certainly *is* a forgery. There can be little doubt of that. The fact that one or two of the world's most outspoken and - it has to be said - thoroughly paranoid conspiracy theorists have of late used the *Protocols* to buttress their own fundamentalist prejudices and arguments, has only served to convince the academic world of their dubious origins. The added fact that Jews have - in our opinion quite wrongly - been singled out to bear the brunt of these prejudices is simply to miss the point entirely.

But the fact remains that, in their original form, the *Protocols* almost certainly emanated - or were leaked - from an organization whose secrets (like those of the *Protocols* themselves) bear immense political and economic implications today. And not only that. They also provide the 'missing link', as it were, between the CIA-sponsored drive to unite Europe under a corporate banner, and the so-called 'bloodline conspiracy' to which our attention will turn in Book Three. In the main the present-form *Protocols* purport a socio-political and economic programme for world dominion, true enough. But they nevertheless base their authority to perpetrate such a programme on the advent of a true 'bloodline Messiah' of the "dynastic roots of King David" - indeed, on the restoration of the "King of Israel" to the Throne of Europe.

In this regard, all the evidence points to the fact that the organization central to both themes - political and economic autonomy on the one hand, the restoration of a legitimate 'bloodline dynasty' on the other - is none other than the Priory of Sion. And that, in their original, pre-bastardized form, the

Protocols contained nothing more sinister than the Priory's intentions to restore the Judaic royal bloodline to the thrones of Europe.

Even so, it would seem that the Priory's most closely guarded secret, even today, remains the corporate world's most feared nemesis.

CHAPTER 9

THE MEDIA
And The Landmines Affair

"I'm a particularly conservative Conservative. I like to think the future King of England at least starts off the job without a blemish. And I don't think he could have done with Dodi as the stepfather."

Sir James Hill, Conservative Constitutional Committee, 1997.

A Corporate Oracle

In this twenty-first-century global village of ours, the media has become something of an oracle. It is to the media we turn for our daily fix of wisdom, so to speak. As in classical antiquity the ancients would address the oracle for advice, prophecy, guidance, so we in the so-called modern world turn to the media to inform us, to entertain us, to guide us. While most of us are these days aware that radio and television (together with the daily newspapers) are little more than socio-political tools, ever ready to feed us the preconceptions and prejudices of their owners and sponsors, nevertheless we tend largely to be persuaded by the opinions disseminated in the media. It thus becomes a truism that opinions are formed on the less than expedient counsel of this latter-day corporate oracle. Like some acquiescent pendulum, public opinion is swayed first this way and then that way in accordance with oligarchical agendas, as was amply demonstrated in the build-up to Britain's 1997 general election, when corporate publishing mogul Rupert Murdoch struck a deal with Tony Blair. In consequence, Murdoch's extreme right-wing British tabloid, *The Sun*, bamboozled its readership into switching its political allegiance from right to left - from the fiercely patriotic Tories to a Europe-bound New Labour. The shepherd changed his tack, and the flock followed suit.

Another - and perhaps more pertinent - example of how the media acts as a propaganda machine for its corporate owners is demonstrated in the way the British press elected to represent Princess Diana. Following her separation - and then her divorce - from Prince Charles, for example, left- and right-wing tabloids and broadsheets alike turned on the princess like a field of vipers on their prey. Indeed, during the last few years of Diana's life, the vipers' venom comprised an implacable and vicious tirade of personal abuse aimed squarely at demeaning the princess's public image. And undermining her self-esteem. Of course, no one is suggesting that Diana was entirely the innocent party. By her own admission she harboured personal agendas - agendas born of her endeavour to outshine the royal circles from which she had been excluded; agendas which the media served well enough. But the point is that the media harboured agendas, too. Seldom if ever did a story appear without clear propagandist design; clear political motive, one way or the other. While on the one hand editors clamoured after that as yet unseen photograph of Diana in order to sell their newspapers, on the other hand the stories that accompanied the photographs were more often than not laced with snide, often cruel attempts to hasten her fall from public - as well as from royal - grace. So far as the general public was concerned, of course, these attempts backfired. But the vipers hissed and spat, just the same.

Then came that fateful night in Paris. The princess was dead. It was time for the vipers to retract their fangs, adopt sympathetic postures and become squirming, sycophantic worms. Which is precisely what they did. Overnight the media's attitude towards the princess changed. Diana was now the tragic victim of circumstance, the caring humanitarian whose life and memory should of course be immortalized as a touchstone for all things abiding and decent and good. In accord with this new directive the headlines changed, too. The 'Queen Of Tarts' became the 'Queen of Hearts'; 'Demented Diana' became 'Saint Diana'. The so-called 'Loose Cannon' was overnight transformed into the 'People's Princess', as though all along the very media editors and press barons who had sold us the image of this 'misdirected meddler' had of course loved and respected Diana as much as anybody else. At the same time, though, we were cunningly fed the line that the Princess of Wales had been tragically killed in a 'road traffic accident', and were thus encouraged to grieve on a scale unprecedented in order to keep our minds from thinking the worst, the unthinkable: that in fact she had been assassinated. The ploy was so barbed it left scars. Following her funeral, of course, we were further encouraged to 'let Diana's memory rest in peace ... for the sake of the children', as if the very newspapers that had - only days and weeks earlier - promoted her as mentally unstable and unfit for royal office, really cared. They did not care, of course. They simply wanted us to think that way - in a way that turned our minds from mistrust, confusion, anger ... to all-consuming grief. And because by our nature we are sheep-minded, turn to grief we did.

The orchestra followed the baton; the flock followed the crook...

While expression of this sentiment is in no way meant as a slur on any individual's capacity to think and act of their own volition, and on personal convictions, nevertheless public opinion does tend to succumb to periodic - some would say irrational - mood-swings. And those mood-swings are in the main caused by collective reaction to opinions expressed in the media. It is not so much the printed word that sways minds, of course, as the way in which that word is presented - its slant, its bias, its capacity to arouse public emotion over and above individual discrimination. It is an insidious mechanism, to be sure. But it is nonetheless the way - the wisdom - of the corporate oracle. And it works. We are prevailed upon to respond - to think and act - in such a way as fosters least resistance to the agendas of this elite, plutocratic few (who themselves, of course, are wholly dependent on our compliance for their survival, their power, their facility to assert corporate policy on the democratic process). We are persuaded in our moral and political judgments by the brash tabloid headline on the one hand, by the intellectual argument of the broadsheet on the other. But both, of course, are instruments of the same corporate hand: the owner of the tabloid is the owner of the broadsheet; the owner of the left-wing radical is the owner of the right-wing reactionary. In the end we are like two bald men fighting over a comb, not knowing quite why we are fighting but knowing that we are, and, in the end, happy for someone else to come along and take away the comb. Tell us who to vote for. Tell us what to think. We make our choice, true enough. But it is a false choice based on at best partial, at worst extremely jaundiced information. It is an imposed choice based on a predisposed and politically weighted counsel. A machiavellian counsel. Thus we are inveigled into the pseudo-democratic web, into the system which serves insidiously to mould, manipulate, characterize and ultimately control public thought and opinion. And it does so by the power of the word - by the gleam of the salesman's smile and the information behind it. No bullets required. In this regard alone, the plan propounded in the *Protocols* would seem to be frighteningly authentic - to wit: "Not a single announcement will reach the public without our control ... Even now this is already being attained by us in as much as all news items are received by a few agencies ... These agencies will then be already entirely ours, and will give publicity only to what we dictate to them ... our government will become proprietor of the majority of the journals ... This will neutralize the injurious influence of the privately owned Press and will put us in possession of a tremendous influence upon the public mind...".

Indeed. As revered journalist and former Chief of Staff at the *New York Times*, John Swinton, commented as long ago as 1953, when asked to give a toast before the prestigious New York Press Club: "There is no such thing at this date of the world's history as an independent press. You know it and I know it. There is not one of you who dares to write your honest opinions, and if you did, you know beforehand that it would never appear in print. I am paid weekly for keeping my honest opinions out of the paper I am connected with. Others of you are paid similar salaries for similar things, and any of you who would be so foolish as to write honest opinions would be out on the streets looking for another job."

And further: "If I allowed my honest opinions to appear in one issue of my paper, before twenty-four hours my occupation would be gone. The business of the journalist is to destroy the truth; to lie outright; to pervert; to vilify; to fawn at the feet of mammon, and to sell the country for his daily bread. You know it and I know it, and what folly is this toasting an independent press. We are the tools and vassals of the rich men behind the scenes. We are the jumping jacks; they pull the strings and we dance. Our talents, our possibilities and our lives are all the property of other men. We are intellectual prostitutes."

And we - the impressionable public - are the clients who keep those prostitutes in work.

Loose Cannon

In January 1997, amidst a storm of international media attention, Diana, Princess of Wales, touched down in the Angolan capital, Luanda, armed with a mission. It was a mission that would change her life forever.

Over the course of the following six months, the Princess of Wales would campaign vigorously to highlight the massive and appalling cost to human life brought about by the deployment of anti-personnel landmines. Indeed, she would campaign for a total ban on the manufacture, sale and deployment of these insidious weapons worldwide. By her own admission the campaign was to become a "personal crusade" - a crusade in which she would invest so much of her own emotion; a crusade in which she would so passionately believe. Perhaps because of this, it was also a crusade that would win public and political support the equal of which has seldom before been witnessed on a global scale. Yet it was a crusade that would incense politicians and arms-trade barons the world over, as we shall see.

The princess already knew, of course, that Angola boasted the highest rate of landmine-related amputees anywhere in the world. This was due to the fact that untold numbers of landmines had been planted and abandoned during the country's so-called 'civil war'. Though ostensibly this war was an internal struggle - fought out between rival political factions following the collapse of Portuguese imperial rule in 1975 - in truth it was a vicious and bloody conflict perpetrated on behalf of US/European interests on the one hand, and Russian interests on the other. The reason? To gain control of the country's oil and raw-mineral reserves, first and foremost; also, of course, to gain strategic control of yet one more Third World nation in the ongoing game of international political chess. A familiar story. While the CIA and MI6 funded and armed Jonas Savimbi's merciless UNITA regime (and had indeed been responsible for the deployment of anti-personnel landmines in Angola since the late 1960s) the Soviets backed the rival MPLA faction, an equally ruthless though Communist regime which in the end won power. The irony is that, while the CIA and MI6 were busy funding Jonas Savimbi's war effort against the MPLA - and donating thousands of anti-personnel landmines to the cause - at the same time America and Europe were buying Angolan oil at a markedly reduced rate from the Soviet-backed MPLA. And they continued to do so throughout the eighteen-year war (which, in effect, rages on).

It was a war in which more than 500,000 Angolans were killed. A further 200,000 were maimed, widowed or orphaned, while an inestimable number remain unaccounted for. Due to the thousands of still-unexploded landmines summarily buried beneath Angolan soil, of course, these figures continue to rise, even today. But at least it was a war that provided the West with cheap oil.

This, then, was the country (indeed, the situation) into which Diana immersed herself - heart, soul and body - in January 1997. And it has to be said that she did so to great effect - a fact that upset a good deal of very prominent, very powerful people. Indeed, Diana's campaign spotlighted a major human rights problem which had been caused, on the one hand, by the US/European alliance's own political ambitions. And on the other, by the financial ambitions of the British Royal Establishment (see *Chapter Ten*). It was never simply the issue of landmines which prompted the British Establishment to publicly brand Diana a "loose cannon". It was never simply the issue of landmines which prompted such a knee-jerk reaction from both British and US oligarchs, though this in itself was indeed sufficient to ruffle a fair few military-industrial feathers. No doubt about that.

But rather it was the fact that, by highlighting the Angolan problem, inadvertently Diana had threatened to prise open a very unsavoury can of worms. British- and US-built landmines were still ripping life and limb from Angolan women and children. British- and US-based corporations were still seeking ways to gain control of Angola's oil and raw-mineral reserves. MI6 and CIA agents were - and are - still active on Angolan soil. Indeed, since the early 1970s, MI6 - acting on behalf of the British Crown and its neo-colonial cartel of corporations and NGOs (non-governmental organizations) - had been secretly financing and equipping teams of mercenaries to carry out its dirty work in Angola. Behind the scenes, much of this 'dirty work' was/is still going on - the covert supply of arms and other resources to in-house political factions within this and other Third World countries in order to ensure control of the Third World economy. And exploitation of its markets. Angola, of course, was one such country that 'profited' heavily from this strategy. Indeed, Angola should be understood here as one of the world's most prolific, most fecund Third World battlefields - fields cultivated by the West in order to feed its own political, economic and corporate ambitions. Its military ambitions, too. Like so many of the so-called 'civil wars' being fought out in the world today (Bosnia, Croatia, Kosovo) the war in Angola was designed, first and foremost, to prevent Communism from encroaching on corporate markets: to ensure that, when the film crews and news reporters descended on Luanda, the pictures beamed back to the West would contain not units of victorious Russian-backed forces. But billboards advertising the world's most popular colas, burgers, cigarettes. *Consumerism.* In turn, of course, this would assure the investments of such luminous corporate shareholders as the Queen and Prince Philip (see *Chapter Ten*). At the same time it would demonstrate Western superiority over the Communist world, both in a political sense and a psychological sense, as well as a strategic sense. In this regard, it is like a show of strength by two rival gorillas striving to gain control of their world - the West versus the Rest. The side seen to emerge from these pre-planned conflicts victorious, of course, receives the coveted title of 'Silver Back'. And the Silver Back rules the tribe.

He also wins the prize, which in this instance is multilayered and manifold. Firstly, of course, he wins the 'strategic prize', which means he gains control of yet another square mile of international real estate. Whether Capitalist or Communist, it makes little difference: real estate is a most valuable asset to either economy. Secondly, he wins the 'economic prize' - control of Angola's oil and raw-mineral reserves, which in effect means control of Angola's economic muscle; in turn, control of its policy. Thirdly, he wins the 'military prize', and is thus seen to be the biggest and the best and the strongest. In consequence, more and more investment in arms and technology programmes is secured. Which means multibillion-dollar contracts for the further development of weapons such as the anti-personnel landmine. Plus other, even more insidious and devastating weapons. Which further means that the masonic agencies involved in such covert deals as the CIA's 'Irangate' affair, and MI6's more recent arms-and-mercenaries trade-off with Sierra Leone, become even more powerful, even more independent of the democratically elected watchdogs employed to monitor their activities. And so the corporate agenda maintains its stranglehold on international affairs.

However, and as we all know, the development of new weapons demands that a market be created via which those weapons can be sold. This to balance the books. After all, if millions (in some cases billions) of dollars have been invested in the development of some or other new weapon, then those dollars and more must be recovered. And the only way that those dollars will ever be recovered is when the product that they paid for is put on the market and sold. But prospective buyers, of course, are not about to part with their money until they have seen the product in action. Which means that further 'civil wars' (on occasion 'international wars', or at least situations such as that which today obtains with regard to, say, Iraq) are necessary, both to maintain a stable world oil price (to the advantage of the West) and, of course, to demonstrate these new weapons in combat situations. Enter MI6 and the CIA. Mercenaries hired and equipped by these agencies provoke hostilities within the target nation (Angola, Kosovo, Bosnia,) and before you can *say political manoeuvre* a so-called 'war' results. The boundaries of Western real estate are thus pushed ever further Eastward; African and Balkan territories are clawed back from the grip of Communist Russia. And the West's (NATO's) so-called 'peace keeping' forces are on hand to ensure that said territories - the natural resources they yield, such as oil - remain the property of the Western world's corporate economy. (The Cold War continues, then, even today.) At the same time, of course, new weapons are demonstrated in these conflicts. Those that prove themselves in combat attract buyers. Profits are made. The books are balanced. And so the top-secret world of international real-estate-and-arms-trade-profiteering continues to spin on its own multibillion-dollar axis.

And God help anybody who dares stand in its way. Someone like Diana, for example.

The Falklands And The Gulf

This, then, was the true extent of the ugly reality spotlighted by Princess Diana's "personal crusade" against landmines. The world's most powerful military-industrial corporations - plus the British and US governments - had their noses pushed squarely out of joint. And they did not appreciate the fact. Indeed, they felt ominously threatened by Diana's unprecedented ability to mobilize public opinion against their activities, which were in danger of being exposed on a massive scale. People of this calibre, of course - the masonic potentates presiding over the highest echelons of military-industrial power - rarely sit back and count their blessings when their thrones are under siege, as affirmed in the highly suspicious deaths of Hilda Murrell and William McRae (*see MI5*). Ranks are closed. Countermeasures discussed. Contracts approved. And the corporate arm of MI6 and the CIA is of course at hand to ensure said contracts are discharged. Had Diana known the callous and ruthless nature of the beast she was confronting, of course, she may well have elected not to spearhead her landmines campaign. But she did. And because she did, the British Establishment branded her a "loose cannon" and cried "*off with her head!*". To judge by the tragic events which occurred in Paris on the night of August 30th/31st, 1997, one wonders now if this statement was meant in a purely metaphorical sense. Or in a rather more literal one.

Further evidence of this same policy being applied (included here to further highlight the extreme dangers involved in exposing the murky world of international arms-trade politics) can be seen with regard to Britain's Harrier jump jet. When first developed in the mid-1950s, the Harrier was met with much scepticism from prospective buyers. Indeed, work had begun to develop a vertical-take-off-and-landing aircraft immediately after WWII. But it was almost a quarter of a century later (1969) before the RAF felt sufficiently confident with the aircraft that it gave way to corporate pressure and formed its first Harrier squadron. And even then, it took a further decade and more for the Harrier to prove itself in combat (a feat necessary, of course, in order to entice foreign sales and so justify the vast amount of taxpayers' money that had been spent on the aircraft's development). Somewhat conveniently, some commentators have since remarked, in 1982 the opportunity for the Harrier to show itself off in a combat situation arose.

"For years and years we'd said what we really want is a small, local war where the Harrier can show itself to advantage - not many people killed, you know ... and we had one. And it was called the Falklands."

So said Harrier Chief Designer, Dr John Fozard, when commenting on the problem of convincing foreign powers of the Harrier's capability in combat. It is certainly interesting to note that, prior to the Falklands War, the Harrier was shunned by most of the world's air forces. It is of further interest to note that, as affirmed by the aircraft's chief designer, Dr John Fozard, the Falklands War was the perfect showcase for the Harrier. In point of fact, no other British aircraft could have fought such a war. The fact that the Falkland Islands are 8000 miles distant from Britain, and the added fact that Britain no longer possesses aircraft carriers large enough to accommodate the take-off runs of conventional fighter aircraft, meant that the Harrier, with its vertical-take-off-and-landing capability, was the only aircraft in the world that could have fought the Falklands War. And it did so to great effect. In total 24 Harriers (18 Sea Harriers and 6 RAF Harriers) took on more than 200 French-built Mirages, and won. 23 Argentine fighters were shot down in aerial combat, 9 more in ground attacks. Only 2 Harriers were lost, but not in combat. Sadly, they collided in atrocious weather conditions which included gale-force winds and thick fog. Whatever the real reason behind the Falklands War - a war that the Argentine government did not want to fight; a war initiated by Margaret Thatcher's own secret agenda, despite fierce opposition from many politicians, both left and right - one cannot deny that it was a war purpose-made to demonstrate the Harrier's capabilities in a combat situation.

And neither can one deny that someone made a tidy packet out of it. Since its unprecedented success in the South Atlantic, foreign sales of the Harrier have doubled and redoubled. Today it is the first-choice frontline attack aircraft in air forces the world over. And its huge commercial success is due solely to its performance in the Falklands War.

(As an added aside: it is of further interest to note that oil has recently been discovered off the Falklands' coastline (1997). Now there's a surprise! And what is more, owing to Britain's annihilation of the Argentine junta in 1982 - due largely to the success of the Harrier - these untapped oil reserves are now the exclusive property of Britain. One is left to wonder precisely what it was that Hilda Murrell and William McRae had discovered with regard to the Falklands War - what part the nuclear industry intended to play in it; why Margaret Thatcher so readily declined the option to resolve the conflict by diplomatic means, and instead gave the order to sink the *General Belgrano* when she was sailing back to port, away from the Task Force. And why MI5 deemed it necessary that Miss Murrell and Mr McRae should lose their lives in such a savage and undignified manner).

Which ever way you look at it, something mighty big went down in respect of the Falklands War. And it wasn't only the Argentine battlecruiser, the *General Belgrano*.

Speaking of oil ... a similar situation obtained with regard to America's Stealth aircraft, in particular the F117A Stealth fighter. Though development of the radar-invisible Stealth began as early as 1974, and the US Air Force took delivery of 42 of its 59 F117As in 1982, it was still not considered fully operational until 1988. And even then, it had still not been tested in combat (a feat necessary - in the case of the Stealth - to justify the billions spent on its development and so ensure further corporate investment in future research and development programmes). It should be born in mind in this regard that, by 1988, the Stealth programme had won any number of very powerful critics, both in Congress and the Pentagon, and indeed across the entire spectrum of military-industrial power. There was a very real possibility that the already foundering Stealth programme would be shelved. Which would have left the Bush administration to find ways of justifying the billions already spent on the aircraft's development.

Enter Saddam Hussein and the Iraq/Kuwait oil dispute. Enter American technology. Both corporate and congressional critics were about to be silenced.

Having sold to Kuwait the technologically advanced drilling equipment necessary to perform what is known as 'slant-drilling', the US government sat back and waited for the fireworks to begin. And they did not have to wait long. Kuwait, armed with this new US-built technology, promptly set about drilling for oil beneath Iraqi territory. Indeed, by the time Saddam Hussein responded to this provocation, Kuwait had extracted more than $14 billion worth of oil which, by rights, belonged to Iraq. This, of course, is a fact that never came to light via the mainstream, corporate-owned media. But it is a fact, nonetheless. As Mark Zepezauer points out: "Slant-drilling is enough to get you shot in Texas, and it's certainly enough to start a war in the Mideast."

Indeed. But what reason could the Americans possibly have had for wishing to provoke a Middle East conflict such as this one? And moreover, if it truly was to show off the Stealth in combat, then why select such a volatile region as the Middle East in which to carry out that test?

In an interview for BBC 2's *Decisive Weapons* programme, Lt Col Mike Mahar, Stealth test pilot from 1988 until 1992, hit the nail on its proverbial head.

"The training that we got in the Nevada area and the surrounding countryside was virtually identical to that which we would need in the Gulf War. So there was really no more perfect place we could go in the world than the Middle East."

42 F117A Stealth fighters flew more than 1200 missions during the Gulf War. There were no losses. The US - via the UN, UNSCOM and the CIA - continues to control Iraqi and Kuwaiti oil reserves (and thus continues to maintain the price of oil at a level which ensures vast profits for Western oil companies). And the giant aerospace corporations such as Lockheed-Martin and Northrop (who between them developed the F117A Stealth fighter and the B2 Stealth bomber) continue to win massive defence contracts from the US government. You scratch my back and I'll scratch yours. And thus, with scant regard for human life, the corporate agenda marches on.

The Balance Of Power
And The Third World Debt

The reason we elected to include the above examples of the Harrier and the Stealth is purely to highlight the backstairs political gamesmanship which obtains today in the world of masonic government. And the reason for wishing to highlight this situation is because Princess Diana, by spotlighting the landmines problem, and campaigning for a ban on the manufacture, sale and deployment of these weapons worldwide, came dangerously close to exposing the international power games played out by the West behind closed doors. With someone like Diana at the helm, of course, the resulting 'problem' could have amounted to 'Irangate' times ten. And then some. When we glibly remark: *"Oh, don't be so silly; they wouldn't have killed her just because she wanted landmines banned!"*, we do so with little awareness of the implications involved, and indeed, the sheer magnitude of backstairs policy under threat of being exposed. The issue of landmines was scarcely the tip of the iceberg. But it nevertheless constituted a threat sufficient to set alarm bells ringing in the corridors of unseen power. And they rang good and loud. According to our MI5 source, for example (and despite reports to the contrary), the authorities were concerned that Diana was on the verge of championing other, equally controversial causes - campaigning on behalf of victims of Gulf War Syndrome, for example, and victims of nuclear-related cancers. As many people would surely testify (those who are still alive to do so) taking on the nuclear industry is no mean feat; it forms the very pinnacle of the arms-trade industry and boasts its own police force and intelligence agency to boot - plus, of course, its own internal government which acts according to its own laws and mandates. In this regard, the nuclear industry should be understood as the nub of the military-industrial complex, the very heart of military-industrial power. And military-industrial power is a mighty power indeed. As President Dwight D Eisenhower affirmed in his Farewell Address to the Nation in 1961: "...This conjunction of an immense military establishment and a large arms industry ... is felt in every city, every state house, every office in the Federal Government. We must guard against the acquisition of unwarranted influence ... by the military-industrial complex." And further: "We must never let the weight of this combination endanger our liberties or democratic processes."

For almost forty years, it seems, former President Eisenhower's warning has gone unheeded.

It should also be remembered here that Diana was not some 'drop-out lefty' protesting from her soap box on Hyde Park Corner or Times Square. On the contrary, she was an aristocrat. She was a royal. And what is more, she was one of those very rare breed of royals who are actually able to relate to everybody else and so command their respect. She had tremendous charisma, to which many millions of people responded. And they did so on a global scale, and with an almost religious fervour. When Diana stood up and said, "*Hey, look at this problem*", people looked. When she said, "*We must do something about this problem*", everybody said, "*Yes, we must*". But what must be remembered here is that the problem highlighted by Diana (the manufacture, sale and deployment of landmines) was but a symptom of a far greater problem - the backstairs manipulation of Third World political and economic power, and the consequent control of half the world's wealth. In diagnosing the symptom, of course, there is always the danger that the greater problem will be exposed. This could never be allowed to happen. In particular when you consider just how vast that 'greater problem' is. As mentioned above, it cuts to the very heart of the backstairs international power games being played out by the West on a daily basis. The very fabric of covert international politics becomes threatened. In consequence, the balance of international power becomes threatened, too (at least the so-called 'balance of power' currently enjoyed by the West). As we all know, the reason the so-called Third World is so poor is because its governments owe their seats of power to foreign agencies - either the CIA together with MI6 elevated them to power, or the former KGB did. And either way, the Third World today is indebted (to the tune of trillions of dollars) to the US/European Superstate and/or Russia. This is what is called 'the balance of power'. Moreover, this is the situation which obtains in Angola today (indeed, it obtains in most every Third World nation bar none). Which is why the so-called 'Third World Debt' can never be forgiven. Not when it amounts to political and economic control (by the West) of such vast territories worldwide. Plus whatever resources those territories yield. Again, this is what we in the West are prone to call 'the balance of power'. In truth, of course, there is no balance at all. Only power.

In the final analysis, then, international politics is very like the board game *Monopoly*. The only difference is that, in the Third World, *Monopoly* money is worth more than real currency. And, of course, the West owns all the hotels.

Bosnia

By highlighting the landmines problem, then, Diana was in grave danger of exposing the international power games of which the manufacture, sale and deployment of landmines forms an integral part. A relatively minor part, true. But an integral part just the same. Exposing even the merest tip of an iceberg, of course, reveals the fact that an iceberg indeed exists - that lurking deep beneath that tip is a mass of jagged, frozen ice so vast that its true immensity remains unknown, unseen. According to Stealth (see *Chapter Four*), it is the fact that this iceberg was in danger of being revealed - if only by implication - which provoked such an instant and decisive reaction from those who wish to keep it concealed. And those who wish to keep it concealed, of course, are those with vested political and financial interests - not least among whom is the British Crown, headed up by the House of Windsor, as we shall see.

In short, then, Diana's landmines campaign in Angola threatened to become the *Titanic* of international arms trading. The 'unsinkable flagship' of corporate power was in danger of colliding with an iceberg which, until now, nobody had seen. The *Titanic* was in danger of sinking, and the ship's builders knew only too well that there were simply not enough lifeboats on board to save them all from drowning in the ice-flows of accountability. Fortunes would be lost. Heads would roll. Careers would be sacrificed. And thus drastic measures were required, in particular when you consider that, as we know, Angola was not the only *Titanic* on the ocean that day. The Angolan situation was not alone in forcing this iceberg's tip to the surface. A similar situation existed in Bosnia, where for decades East and West have battled for political and economic control of the Balkan territories. The battle for political and economic supremacy in the former Yugoslavia dates back at least as far as WWII, when the Serbs stood alone against the might of a Nazi regime befriended by the House of Windsor, largely funded by British and US financial and industrial corporations and supported in the Balkans by both Bosnians and Croats alike. (Before this, of course, Balkan unrest - brought about by Anglo-German royal frictions; in effect an in-house royal conflict waged between the British Crown and other royal houses in Europe for control of the Balkan territories - gave rise to the First World War, as we shall see.) Even today, the remnant of Nazi ideology as expressed in Western administrations remains hellbent on 'liberating' Bosnia, Croatia and Kosovo from Serbian rule. No matter the cost.

Diana, of course, would visit Bosnia some six months after her first trip to Angola. And she would take the world's media with her when she did. Which meant even more bad publicity for the arms-trade godfathers (as well as for the British and US governments). Even more information regarding illegal arms-trade activities (and possibly even the illegal presence of British and US irritant forces in the region) would be spotlighted and screened on the world's major news networks. Which in turn meant that public sympathy for Diana's landmines crusade would intensify. (Indeed, it did.) In their efforts to avert this situation, both British and US oligarchs endeavoured with no small amount of sniping and scheming to prevent the princess's visit to Bosnia from going ahead. Which, from their point of view, was understandable. There was good reason for the powers-that-be to try and avoid the spotlighting of any other Bosnia than the one depicted in the mainstream media - the Bosnia stricken by so-called 'civil unrest'. And more to the point, the Bosnia under threat of being overrun by Serbian leader and longstanding adversary of both Britain and the US, Slobodan Milosevic. (We recall here, for example, that former MI6 agent, Richard Tomlinson, recently divulged an MI6 plot to assassinate the Serbian leader, and he now finds himself in deep trouble for doing so. Far more pertinent to our own investigation, of course, is the fact that Tomlinson also revealed that *the planned assassination plot mirrored in every detail the operation which killed Princess Diana in Paris.* Once again, that 'road traffic accidents' are flavour-of-the-month with regard to political and other high-profile assassinations becomes conspicuously evident.)

But what was of paramount concern to the authorities, of course, was that Diana exercised an uncanny knack of bringing out the humanity in people - of being filmed in one-on-one situations with ordinary, everyday folk, no matter their nationality or their political bias. The last thing the authorities wanted was for us in the West to view the situation and the people in Bosnia - in particular Bosnian Serbs - through sympathetic or humanitarian eyes, any more than they would wish us to view the people of Iraq in a similar light. The situation in Bosnia was - and remains - too volatile: there were simply too many covert agendas being exercised via the Bosnian conflict, too many covert arms deals, too many covert policies being laundered with regard to the balance of European power. In short, the Balkan territories today - like Iraq - comprise little more than an economic and political laundry. A military laundry, too. And Diana was about to spotlight a mighty heap of hitherto unseen dirty washing. No doubt about that.

But it is also the effectiveness of Diana's "personal crusade" that must be considered here. Suddenly the world was alerted to the sickening atrocities being perpetrated on innocent Bosnians and Angolans by Western-backed guerrilla warfare. Suddenly the fact that innocent people and children were being maimed and killed on a daily basis was headline news. The perpetrators, of course, did not appreciate the fact. And neither were they happy that public opinion was being so massively influenced in support of a proposed worldwide ban on landmines. Not even the most powerful military-industrial potentates can afford to turn their backs on public opinion, of course (one reason why they go to such lengths to mould and manipulate that opinion via the media). The problem was that Diana was asserting a bigger influence on public opinion than their own propaganda machine was able to counter: the princess was outmanipulating the manipulators. According to our MI5 source, this was a situation which demanded a swift and decisive solution. After all, if Diana was capable of so affecting public opinion with regard to landmines, then what next? What 'Diana campaign' would the public support next? What cause would Diana so convincingly promote in the future? Once the world had rid itself of landmines, for example, would the public support Diana in her campaign against, say, nuclear weapons? Or at least in her endeavour to bring the nuclear industry to justice over the issue of nuclear-related cancers? For a moment at least, the entire corporate edifice was aquiver.

But not for long. Within six months of the campaign's start-date Diana would be dead. And the international concern engendered as a result of her campaign would, in large part, die with her. Though the name 'Angola' may remain etched on the minds of some, the fact that innocent Bosnians continue to face the threat of unexploded landmines has largely been forgotten. As has the fact that Angola is once again facing the threat of destabilization. The fact is that, since the princess's death, the spotlight of public opinion has dimmed. Accordingly, concern in the corporate world has abated. The illegal trade in landmines and other, even more deadly weapons is thus once again back on track. Whatever the truth behind the princess's premature death, the fact that she is no longer alive to spotlight these and other human rights issues means that those issues have quietly disappeared from public view - back behind the veil of corporate secrecy.

Simply put, when Diana was killed, the spotlight was extinguished. And the sleazy world of international arms-profiteering withdrew smugly back into its own sinister shadow - where to this day it remains. And prospers.

The Landmines Treaty

There are, of course, other examples which highlight just how effective Princess Diana's campaign was. At the time of her visit to Angola, for example, it was estimated that for every person living in this war-torn African nation there was at least one still-live anti-personnel landmine laying undetected - *unexploded* - beneath innocent feet. Many people living and working in Angola's open country fell victim to the mines on a daily basis (at the time of the princess's visit, more than 2000 Angolans per month were losing their limbs as a result of stepping on an unexploded landmine - that amounts to around 70 people a day). The Red Cross was simply unable to cope with such a vast influx of casualties. For one thing, it was grossly underfunded. It needed cash to build and maintain the specialist surgeries necessary to care for these kinds of injuries. Plus, of course, it needed specialized equipment and an equally specialist team to operate it. Needless to say this costs money. And it was money which the Red Cross simply did not have. Enter the Princess of Wales. During the year prior to the princess's visit, the Red Cross's landmines appeal failed to raise even £50,000 - scarcely sufficient even to build the necessary surgeries, much less man them. In the year following the princess's much-publicized visits to Angola and Bosnia, on the other hand, the appeal raised a staggering £1,200,000. And contributions are still pouring in.

But perhaps what made Diana's contribution even more telling is the fact that, almost single-handedly, she forced the issue of anti-personnel landmines into the forefront of the political arena. Until the princess's intervention, of course, the powers-that-be had been more than content to keep this issue locked safely away in the political closet. Or perhaps more accurately, beneath Angolan and Bosnian soil. Following her visits to America and her private talks with Bill and Hillary Clinton, however, the issue was suddenly top of the political agenda. Indeed, as a result of her meetings with the Clintons a plan was drawn up which would - and should - have amounted to a Landmines Treaty being signed by all the leading industrial and military powers. Clinton himself even agreed to the deal. In consequence, a conference was arranged for 19th September, 1997, to be held in Oslo, and to be attended by leaders of the world's most powerful nations. However, in the meantime it would seem that someone had taken it upon themselves to whisper a quiet word in Bill Clinton's ear. According to our MI5 source, Clinton was reminded in no uncertain terms that it was the very corporate czars he was about to betray whose complicity kept him in office. Enter the CIA and the President's 'sex-at-work' problems - should Clinton honour his pledge and sign the deal in Oslo, he was warned, then he would be facing serious problems, possibly even impeachment. In fact the wheels of what Hillary Clinton would later describe as a "right-wing conspiracy" against her husband were already in motion; the Paula Jones and Monica Lewinsky scandals were about to break, big time. Indeed, as a distraught Monica Lewinsky commented during an interview with Channel 4's Jon Snow (screened in Britain as a *Dispatches Special*, 4th March, 1999): "I think there's definitely a right-wing conspiracy to destroy the President. And I think I've been used as a pawn." In short, the threat had been issued. In consequence, the 42nd Presidency of the United States was in jeopardy of becoming only the second presidency in history to be brought to its knees. If Clinton wished to fulfil his term in office, we were told, then he would have to renege on his pledge to Princess Diana and refuse to sign the Landmines Treaty. And what is more, he would need to maintain his stance in this regard for the rest of his term in office.

"This was the reason the CIA got involved with MI6 to take care of the princess," our sources said. "MI6 had their own reasons for wanting rid of Diana. But from this point on it became a joint operation ... Diana's fate was effectively sealed then." And further: "The CIA assured Clinton that Diana would be out of the way by the time the deal was to be signed ... [by the time of] the conference in Oslo. With Diana gone, they knew that public focus on the [landmines] issue would diminish quickly - and that would leave the way clear for Clinton to opt out of the agreement without too much fuss."

What is clear in this regard is that, less than three weeks after the princess's death (on 19th September, 1997) when Britain and the rest of the Western world signed the Landmines Treaty in Oslo, America was the only Western power to renege on the agreement and refuse to sign the treaty.

And thus, as our sources rightly forecast, President Clinton duly survived the impeachment charges brought against him.

The Media
And The British Establishment

The effectiveness of the princess's work, then, simply cannot be ignored. Which, of course, it most certainly was not. On the contrary, it was noted at very high levels indeed. Senior Conservative politicians and right-wing civil servants, for example, plus a handful of other outspoken constitutional and establishment pillars in Britain, bitterly disagreed with her campaign. And they said so in no uncertain terms, publicly branding Diana a "loose cannon" among other, rather more derisory epithets. Evidently they felt that anyone representing the House of Windsor, either directly or otherwise, should smile sweetly for the camera while keeping their opinions quietly to themselves. Like obedient children, members of royalty - in particular those thus privileged purely by dint of marriage - should be 'seen and not heard'. This, at least, was the considered opinion of the empire-builders. And they were not afraid to voice that opinion publicly. Indeed, Diana was heavily and publicly criticized for bringing such an emotive - and politically explosive - issue to public attention.

Ex-Foreign Office Minister, Sir Nicholas Bonsor, for example, commented during an interview conducted for ITN's *The Trouble With Diana:* "For the princess to put herself so overtly at the head of a political campaign to abandon all landmines, and deprive our own soldiers of the use of such landmines, was in my view wrong of her." And further: "Princess Diana was potentially a threat to the Establishment and a threat to the Royal Family."

Well-known constitutional historian, David Starkey, added his support. "What is wrong, I suppose, is that she's called the Princess of Wales. She's quasi-royal. And we have had a Royal Family which, since the early nineteenth century, has steered very clear of politics. And a very good thing, too."

Possibly, if it were indeed true. Which it most certainly is not. While on the face of it - and in the public eye - members of the Royal Family may indeed steer clear of politics, their political opinions and personal views are heard loud and clear within the hallowed halls of Westminster and Whitehall alike. There can be few doubts about that. Indeed, the Royal Household's devoted circle of courtiers, equerries and other royal bondsmen (in particular the Privy Council) are there to ensure this very end. To some large extent, of course, it is this very band of reactionary bureaucrats, civil servants and government ministers (past and present) who form the highest echelons of the so-called British Establishment. And to claim that the British Establishment has no say in the so-called democratic process is, quite frankly, absurd. It is like saying the FBI has no say in matters of crime-prevention. Ludicrous.

In any event, Diana, along with the vast majority of ordinary British people, did not see her campaign as overtly political. At least not in a 'party political' context. Though the politics of landmines deployment was undoubtedly spotlighted - the politics of international arms-profiteering equally so - the idea that the campaign was Diana's way of making a stand on behalf of New Labour is quite simply absurd. Indeed, at a speech given by the princess at London's Royal Geographical Society (12th June, 1997), she stated her humanitarian motives in no uncertain terms. At the same time she declared her utter refusal to let the issue drop. What is more, she vowed to make it a "personal crusade". Aided by her friend, the former Minister of Information (1962-1964), columnist with *The Daily Telegraph* and fellow anti-landmines campaigner, Lord Deedes, she compiled a moving and powerful speech which stated in no uncertain terms her stance on the matter. She bravely attacked the arms trade for continuing to manufacture and sell these vicious and cowardly weapons. Moreover, she delivered a powerful and unambiguous broadside aimed squarely at the British Establishment, in particular at those she openly referred to as "those ghastly Conservatives" - who, she maintained, had wrongly interpreted her visit to Angola as a political statement in favour of Labour policy.

"It was not," she plainly told them. "I am not a political figure. And as I said at the time, and I'd like to reiterate now, my intentions are humanitarian."

And clearly they were.

Right-wing tabloids disagreed, however. Unashamedly siding with their Establishment supporters - and sponsors - they described the speech as "an unusual gesture of support for the Blair [Labour] administration". At the same time The *Daily Telegraph* accused her of having been caught "on the wrong side of the political fence". And Sir Nicholas Bonsor added: "There was a great difference of opinion between the Conservative Government and the successor Government about landmines. And for the princess to take a stance in favour of one and against the other [is] not ... a proper role for a member of the Royal Family."

Frank Cook MP, representing the All-Party Landmines Committee, however, strongly disagreed. "It's a cross-party issue," he told ITN's *The Trouble With Diana,* screened in Britain over the Christmas period, 1997. "[It's] nothing to do with individual parties. And it's quite wrong to make it so ... frankly I'm disappointed that any Member should be so short of media coverage that they've got to descend to this level."

Indeed.

But it wasn't only the issue of landmines that was getting the princess into trouble at this point; her private life was being severely criticized, too. A week and a half after her famous landmines speech, for example, Diana decided to take her sons to the cinema. It was Prince William's birthday, and quite on impulse she took the boys to see a film called *The Devil's Own*. What she did not know, however, was that the film was violent and pro-IRA. Needless to say, the media leapt at the opportunity. Once again they publicly crucified her.

Though genuinely upset that she had failed to check the film's content beforehand, and although she publicly apologized for her actions immediately following the incident, this latest *faux pas* - the so-called 'movie affair' - was of course further ammunition for her critics. And perhaps more to the point, it was to prove yet another severe setback for her landmines campaign. During this same week, for example, Diana was due to attend a Commons Committee meeting regarding the landmines issue. It was important that she attended this meeting as it could and would have gained her much-needed political support. Amidst all the brouhaha surrounding the 'movie affair', however, she was forced to cancel her attendance. The reason given for the cancellation was that Establishment protests over her public conduct and political interference had made her attendance at the meeting "untenable". Once again, it seemed, the Establishment had won the day. But not the war. Not yet, anyhow.

In response to the cancellation of the Commons Committee meeting, Diana released a statement expressing her sadness and extreme frustration. It is reported that the cancellation caused her much personal regret. However, she would not be deterred from continuing her battle against the manufacture, sale and deployment of anti-personnel landmines. Quite the opposite. On 8th August, 1997, just three weeks before she died, Diana flew with Lord Deedes to Bosnia in order to further comfort the victims of these abominable, cowardly weapons. And once again, the world's media, together with MI6, followed her every move.

What The Media And The Establishment Thought About Dodi And Diana

"You can't help regretting that this beautiful woman has chosen someone so trivial."

Sarah Bradford, the Queen's Biographer, 1997.

*

"I thought that the Fayeds were acting in a rather biased way - to try and get this young girl to become almost part of their inner circle. And I really didn't like it one little bit. And I don't think many people did."

Sir James Hill, Conservative Constitutional Committee, 1997.

*

"I thought at the time that she was allowing her position to be prostituted. She was being exploited for publicity purposes by the al Fayeds ... She seemed at her worst, at her most selfish."

Bruce Anderson, political columnist, *The Spectator, 1997.*

*

"I'm a particularly conservative Conservative. I like to think the future King of England at least starts off the job without a blemish. And I don't think he could have done with Dodi as the stepfather."

Sir James Hill, Conservative Constitutional Committee, 1997.

*

"There's no doubt that those who care about the Royal Family were very worried in those last few months as to what this girl would get up to. I mean, she seemed capable of anything. She seemed reckless, almost demented."

Bruce Anderson, Political Columnist, *The Spectator*, 1997.

*

"I think it was dangerous for the Royal Family to have a member of its clan, as it were, behaving in that kind of irresponsible fashion ... Princess Diana was potentially a threat to the Establishment and a threat to the Royal Family."

Sir Nicholas Bonsor, ex-Foreign Office Minister, 1997.

*

"If Lady Diana Spencer had known the record of this family [the Windsors] ... she might have learnt that the Princess of Wales is a title written in tears."

Germaine Greer, November, 1995.

*

"The important thing is that [Diana] should set limits to her ambitions. She has said she will not 'go quietly'. She must, however, not go too far ... The people know how much change in the system they desire. If the Princess exceeds their wishes, it is she who will become the casualty, not the monarchy."

John Keegan, military historian and former *Daily Telegraph* defence correspondent, November 1995.

*

"No one can deny that this was a skilfully organized attack on the institution of the monarchy itself. Not just on Prince Charles. Not just on the Queen, whom Diana obviously hates. But on the monarchy ... The example of Wallis Simpson and Edward VIII should be enough to tell Diana that when it comes to fighting a war, the Establishment can get very nasty indeed, and that for all her undoubted popularity, if she continues to rock the boat in this way, the Establishment will simply get rid of her."

British author, AN Wilson, commenting in *the New York Times* (25th November, 1995) in response to Diana's *Panorama* interview, screened by the BBC in Britain on 24th November, 1995.

MI6 Special Report On The Fayeds

The quote/article originally intended to occupy this space was written by Andrew Golden and appeared in the *Sunday Mirror*, Early Edition, 31st August, 1997 - the day Diana died. However, for reasons best known to Colin Myler, Editor of the *Sunday Mirror*, we were refused permission to reproduce the article in its original form. Having taken legal advice on this matter - and having further discussed the matter with our publisher - we were informed that in fact we *could* reproduce the article in abridged or paraphrased form on the grounds that; (a) it is in the public interest to do so; (b) it is legal in that, at the time of writing, the investigation into Diana's death is still deemed a 'current event'; and (c) it is legal under the clause of 'fair usage'. On moral grounds, of course, we feel that we are fully vindicated in reproducing at least the main points of the article as they convey the general mood or 'climate' in respect of the Royal Establishment's attitude towards Diana (in particular her relationship with Dodi Fayed) at the time of, and immediately prior to, her death. They also, we contend, constitute evidence of a Palace-sanctioned MI6 action against Diana and Dodi during the time-frame in which the couple mysteriously died.

For these reasons we have elected to reproduce a paraphrased form of the article here. It should be said that, in seeking permission from the *Sunday Mirror* to reproduce the article in full, we were not in any way concerned that the article was libellous or defamatory. Or indeed that there might have been any other good reason that the newspaper concerned - who was, after all, prepared to carry the article prior to Diana's death - would not have wanted it in the public domain *following* her death (particularly as it insinuates a rather unsavoury Palace/MI6 interest in Diana's relationship with Dodi, and thereby a strong suggestion that stern and covert measures were already being taken to curtail the relationship). In any event, our sole reason for taking proper and appropriate action (in seeking written permission in the first place) was born solely out of courtesy. Truth be told, though perhaps not entirely surprised, we were dismayed at the *Sunday Mirror*'s response in refusing our permission request.

The irony is, of course, in refusing us permission to reproduce the article in its original form, the *Sunday Mirror* has brought the spotlight of attention far more intensely on the article's content (or rather, on what it insinuates) than if we had been permitted to simply reproduce the article verbatim. Perhaps in the end, then, the *Sunday Mirror's* knee-jerk response backfired.

Queen 'To Strip Harrods Of Its Royal Crest'

The article concerned - entitled *Queen 'To Strip Harrods Of Its Royal Crest'* - began:

"The Royal Family may withdraw their seal of approval from Harrods ... as a result of Diana's affair with owner's son Dodi Fayed."

In other words, due to Diana's relationship with Dodi Fayed, the Queen had been advised by her senior Palace courtiers to withdraw the Prince of Wales royal crest from Harrods, the exclusive Knightsbridge store owned by Dodi's father, Mohamed al Fayed. So said Andrew Golden reporting in the *Sunday Mirror*. And Andrew Golden was not wrong. The prestigious royal warrant was indeed withdrawn when the matter came up for review the following February.

The article went on to reveal that the "Royal Family are furious about the frolics of Di, 36, and Dodi, 41, which they believe have further undermined the monarchy". Prince Philip "in particular", the article reported, was extremely unhappy about the relationship, even though Diana had for some time been ostracized from Royal circles and divorced from Prince Charles (who at the time, of course, had his own relationship problems to contend with). Indeed, the article reported that Prince Philip had "made no secret as to how he feels about his daughter-in-law's latest man, referring to Dodi as an 'oily bed-hopper'".

But what is even more intriguing is the fact that, according to this same article, "MI6 [had already] prepared a special report on the Egyptian-born Fayeds", which was to be presented to the Queen and The Way Ahead Group at Balmoral the following week. The Way Ahead Group is effectively the Queen's personal advisory board and spin-surgery. The Windsors were to "sit down with their senior advisers and discuss policy matters", the article confirmed. In view of what happened in Paris at this time, and the involvement of MI6 at the meeting, one wonders what those "policy matters" might have been.

The article also included quotes from an interview conducted with "a friend of the royals", who said:

"Prince Philip has let rip several times recently about the Fayeds ... He's been banging on about his contempt for Dodi and how he is undesirable as a future stepfather to William and Harry ... Diana has been told in no uncertain terms about the consequences should she continue the relationship with the Fayed boy..."

The article concluded: *"...Now the Royal Family may have decided it is time to settle up* [italics in original copy]."

It should be reiterated that this story appeared in the *early edition* of the *Sunday Mirror* on the day Diana died (31st August, 1997); it was already in print when news of Diana's death reached Britain. It was then withdrawn; it did not appear in subsequent editions. In consequence, most people in Britain (and elsewhere) did not get to read it - one reason we feel it imperative that at least its bones be included here.

It should also be said that we are not in any way seeking to impugn the *Sunday Mirror's* decision to publish this article, nor indeed to denigrate the *Sunday Mirror* itself - despite the unfortunate timing involved and the seeming hypocrisy in not being prepared to stand by its original story. As stated, we wish only to convey the mood of the Establishment and the Royal Family at the time of Diana's death - which, we contend (and as the tenor of this article suggests) was one of extreme displeasure with regard both to Diana and her relationship with Dodi Fayed. In so doing, of course, we are not accusing the Queen or any individual member of the Royal Family of collusion in an MI6 plot to assassinate Diana or Dodi. We are, however, endeavouring to present the evidence in full - *uncut, uncensored* - so that you the jury may make a fully informed decision in your deliberations on the final verdict.

If you would like to obtain a copy of the original article (as we did) then we suggest you contact **Historic Newspapers, PO Box 3, Newton Stewart, DG8 6TQ, Scotland** - and request a back-copy of the *Sunday Mirror*, Early Edition, 31st August, 1997. It should cost you somewhere in the region of £10 (or around $20 including postage and packing).

CHAPTER 10

AFRICA
A Covert Operation

**"...In the 18-month period just before her death, Princess Diana
was in correspondence with one of my staff people here at *EIR* ...
through that correspondence we had a sense that there was more
to Princess Diana than just the media profile ... Our sense was that
she was more involved in, and more aware of, important political
activities than most people thought, especially activities directed
against the power of the British Royal [Establishment], in particular
the Windsors. So when she died in this mysterious crash in Paris,
our immediate reaction was to have a lot of questions about
whether indeed this was simply an accident, or whether there was
something more to it."**

**Jeff Steinberg, investigative journalist and Senior Editor, *Executive
Intelligence Review*, 1998.**

Intelligence Review

I n chapters *Two* and *Three* we included the opinions and findings of
several interviewees, each of whom are experts in their own field. We
heard from Professor Murray MacKay of Birmingham University, for
example, who for the past 30+ years has investigated the causes and effects
of road traffic accidents. Indeed, Professor MacKay is recognized by his
peers as perhaps the world's leading expert in this regard. We also interviewed
Paramedic Supervisor, Andy Palmer - again, an expert in the field of emergency
rescue operations. We heard, too, from a former SAS sergeant who - for
reasons which are evident - requested that his identity remain secret.
Nevertheless we learned that he was a Special Air Service (SAS) veteran of
several campaigns, and that, over the course of some eleven or so years, he
had run numerous covert operations with Britain's elite Special Forces. And
thus that he too must be considered an expert in his own field.

However, it is rare that an expert in the field of intelligence and
counter-intelligence operations is willing to speak out. And what is more, that
he is willing to be named (in particular when speaking out about such a sensitive

and explosive allegation as the assassination of a princess). For this reason we are most grateful to yet another of our interviewees, Jeff Steinberg, to whom we referred on several matters in the course of chapters *Two* and *Three*. It should be said that it is Mr Steinberg's unflinching resolve in investigating often dangerous, often controversial issues - issues which certain echelons of corporate power would rather remained concealed from public view - that has made him a leading authority on the activities of the world's major-league financial, industrial and media corporations. And in particular their activities in connection with the British Royal Establishment and the British Secret Services. Indeed, this is the very reason we sought to interview him in the first place.

Jeffery Steinberg, then, is a renowned US investigative journalist, counter-intelligence expert and Senior Editor of the influential *Executive Intelligence Review* (*EIR*). For the past 25+ years, *EIR* (a weekly news journal run out of Washington DC) has investigated and reported on what might be termed 'the politics of the corporate initiative: its effect on the democratic process and its manipulation of the global economy'. Or to put it another way, 'the behind-the-scenes manipulation of democratically elected governments and Third World economies by vastly powerful financial and industrial corporations'. In this regard *EIR* might be compared to a rather more radical *Time* magazine - minus the sugar-coating.

In any event, a primary theme in *EIR* over the years has been its mistrust and subsequent investigation of the corporate activities of the House of Windsor. Indeed, it was largely *EIR*'s investigation of what Jeff Steinberg refers to as Prince Philip's "nefarious activities in Africa" (an investigation initiated in 1994) which led the journal's international team of investigators to probe the mysterious death of Princess Diana. Jeff Steinberg in particular has been at the forefront of that investigation from its inception. It is Mr Steinberg, for example, to whom British television networks have repeatedly turned with regard to the 'Diana crash'. And it is Mr Steinberg to whom we turn once again here. It should be said that some of the information contained in the following interview might at first seem shocking. But as our own subsequent investigation was to show, though shocking indeed, it nevertheless provided further clues with regard to the multiple motives which in the end seemed to lay behind the princess's death. For one thing, it proved extremely revealing with regard to the world of political subterfuge, guerrilla warfare and corporate genocide in Africa - the world in which Diana became enmeshed as a result of her anti-personnel landmines campaign in Angola.

And for another, it seemed to suggest that the conspiracy which - we maintain - ultimately claimed the princess's life, began far closer to home than even she must have believed possible.

The remaining points which came to light during our interview with Jeff Steinberg, then. The interview has been minimally edited for publication.

Jeff, can you tell us what prompted you and your organization to become involved in this investigation?

For one thing, in the 18-month period just before her death, Princess Diana was in correspondence with one of my staff people here at *EIR*. This was an outgrowth of some very controversial, historical research that we had done on the House of Windsor. And particularly on Prince Philip, the Royal Consort, in some very nefarious activities in Africa. We discovered that [these activities] were carried out under the cover of his position with [a well-known non-governmental organization, or NGO - name deleted due to legal reasons]. Basically we found out that [this NGO] was serving as a kind of cover for former SAS mercenaries to be shipped down to Africa to carry out political assassinations and other kinds of activities.

And Diana was made aware of this situation?

Correct. In November of 1994 we published a very extensive profile in *EIR* on this whole principle of dossier. It featured a lengthy lead article by one of our founding, senior contributing editors, Lyndon Larouche. We as a courtesy sent copies of that article to every member of the Royal Family, and the only response that we got was from Princess Diana in the form of a very kind letter, indicating that she had read the material and was quite interested and grateful for having received it. We sent her some further material on some subjects that were clearly of interest to her based on her own humanitarian activities in Bosnia and Africa [Angola]. We received a second letter from her in the Spring of 1997, less than six months before her death.

So through that correspondence we had a sense that there was more to Princess Diana than just the media profile - which sort of flip-flopped back and forth between, on the one side referring to her as a kind of jet-set vamp, and on the other side a kind of pre-version of Mother Theresa. Our sense was that she was more involved in, and more aware of, important political activities than most people thought, especially activities directed against the power of the British Royal [Establishment], in particular the Windsors. So when she died in this mysterious crash in Paris, our immediate reaction was to have a lot of questions about whether indeed this was simply an accident, or whether there was something more to it.

The initial reaction of most people we have spoken to was that Diana was murdered. Did you share this same reaction?

Well, we were familiar - from many years of historical research - with the capabilities and real power of the British Monarchy and the British Secret Services. And so naturally we did not rule out the possibility of murder. But neither did we jump immediately to the conclusion that it was automatically a murder. What we decided to do was begin gathering as much information as possible with an open eye. And so really, for a period now of 14-15 months, we've been tracking as much detail as possible as to what happened that day in Paris - what the background is to that Paris crash. And we've tried to keep our readership as well-informed as possible about the unanswered questions that frankly still remain.

We have discovered that several still-unidentified persons were caught on the Ritz security videos, and that they were observed outside the Ritz hotel during the afternoon and evening in question. Our own sources have suggested that they might have been intelligence operatives?

Yes, there were by best count seven people who were conducting surveillance in and around the Ritz Hotel in the evening, during that three-or-so-hour period when Diana and Dodi Fayed came back to the hotel for dinner. And just before they left on the fateful car ride. We published in December of 1997, both on the cover of *EIR* and several pictures inside, [photographs] from the surveillance cameras in front of the Ritz Hotel. They showed two men who were there for a considerable amount of time, practically the entire time that Dodi and Diana were in the hotel. These people are not to this day identified. They were not paparazzi; they were not chauffeurs; they were not guests in the hotel. And they were dressed to blend into the crowd. One guy was wearing a T-shirt and a jacket and a baseball cap. The other was wearing similar clothing. There were two other people parked inside the bar in the front lobby of the entrance of the hotel. There were a couple of other people who tried to give the appearance of being paparazzi, who walked in and out and around the hotel several times. And then there was at least one person - again, not one of the paparazzi - who was posted out the back of the hotel, and who made a cell [mobile] phone call seconds after the Mercedes drove off.

So this brings up all sorts of disturbing suggestions. For one thing, given who Princess Diana was, there was no way that British Intelligence would not have had some sort of surveillance in the environment. There were reports shortly after the crash that a five-person team from MI6 was in Paris at the time. There were reports that some of the paparazzi were actually informants for British Intelligence. And of course ... [Mohamed] al Fayed's lawyers have revealed they now have evidence that Henri Paul had been working on the payroll of the British Secret Services for more than a year before his death.

Jeff, as someone who has been in the system for some time - someone renowned for his knowledge of intelligence operations - would you say that the crash in Paris suggests the handiwork of, say, MI6?

Yes, I would say so. For one thing, the idea that Princess Diana was travelling about with Dodi Fayed, first in Sardinia and then in Paris, without there being very sophisticated continuous British Intelligence monitoring of her activities, is beyond belief. If you look at the *Sunday Mirror* that was published the day of the crash - in other words, the August 31st, 1997 *Sunday Mirror* [see *Chapter Nine*] - you will find there's an article in there which was obviously written before the crash, noting that there was deep distress among the Windsors over Diana's activities with Dodi; that there had been a full MI6 work-up order on Dodi; and that there was to be a meeting at Balmoral Castle of 'The Way Ahead Group' (the inner circle that advises Queen Elizabeth and Prince Philip) the very next week, to receive a briefing from MI6 on the Dodi investigation. So that was the story that came out. It was disconnected from the events in Paris because it was printed before the newspaper in question knew about the events in Paris. So it proves that a sophisticated degree of surveillance was already in operation at the time.

Surveillance is one thing. But an assassination operation mounted by British Intelligence?

Well, I've also been told by extremely reliable sources that British Intelligence has a relationship to a number of the paparazzi. They've got basically a structure in place in France, in Paris, through Embassy-based intelligence operatives, to have certain of the paparazzi on their payroll. Whether they know they're working for British Intelligence or not, the fact is that a bunch of these guys have a relationship. The point I'm making is, and of course you've got statements that have been made by [former MI5 officer, David] Shayler and [former MI6 officer, Richard] Tomlinson, which ... certainly suggest a standard surveillance on the Royals. Diana herself emphasized that she was basically terrified of British Intelligence.

Yes she did. And she certainly voiced her concerns, on more than one occasion, about 'dying in an accident'.

Exactly right. You've got - I forget if it was Tomlinson or Shayler - saying that British Intelligence had developed a skill for vehicular homicides. Northern Ireland was kind of a playground for testing out these skills in large situations also [a fact confirmed by own SAS source - see *Chapter Two*]. So you put all these elements together and the idea that there was no British Intelligence in the environment defies belief. We have the photographs that we published in December of last year on the cover of *EIR*, showing some people who were in the crowd in front of the Ritz Hotel in the evening who remain unidentified - who were not paparazzi; who were not limousine drivers; who were not guests in the hotel; who were not tourists. And who were there at the edge of the crowd for 2 or 3 hours while Diana and Dodi were in the hotel.

OK, Jeff, but what about motive? Do you think Diana's relationship with an Arab Muslim, for example, might have been significant in this regard?

Well, I think the normal view is to focus too much on the Islamic angle, and all of this stuff. The fact is that Mohamed al Fayed is an important political and financial player. He kind of typifies a lot of people who have money and a certain political clout, but who are completely ostracized by the circles around the Royal Family - by the extended apparatus of bankers and businessmen, and people who group around the power of the Monarchy and enjoy their own success on the basis of that.

Courtiers, equerries, nobles, top-flight civil servants...?

Exactly. Certain people are insiders and others are outsiders, and there's obviously a large racial element to that. But Diana, if you go back to 1991, from the point that she begins initially collaborating with the Andrew Morton book, all the way through to the BBC [*Panorama*] interview in November 1995, up to the interview which she gave to *Le Monde* that was published about 4 days before she died - she was directly challenging the viability of the House of Windsor. After 1995 she was on record as saying that she really didn't think Charles was qualified to be the successor to the Throne. The implication is that you might have a kind of Regency set-up around Prince William.

Right. We have evidence from a former British Foreign Office source to the effect that Diana might have been perceived as a counter-monarchy threat (see Chapter Eleven).

Exactly right. From her standpoint, being a member of the Spencer family, they have a history on the English Throne before the Windsors ever even learned to speak a word of English. They had three Stuart kings on the Throne who were blood relations of Princess Diana. So in a certain sense, because there's no formality for determining succession - except that you keep within a particular family dynasty; and I'm not saying that this was already something fully fleshed out - but you can't rule out that Diana was in a position to create a counter-monarchy, a counter-structure that could have become a rowing point for a lot of people who resented the way that Elizabeth and Philip do business.

So are you saying that Diana might have been involved in a challenge for the British Throne?

I'm saying that I think there was high politics involved in all of this. There's a power struggle that's being going on within the British elite for quite some time. It manifests in certain public issues like the transformation from Tory to Labour Government; whether to go it alone or go into the Euro; whether or not you are going to reform the Monarchy or dump it altogether.

Or just keep it as its stodgy old self. These issues have all been played out. It's been an ongoing, big political brawl within the British Establishment since 1992. Remember when the Andrew Morton book first came out in '92 - that was the year of the divorces; it was the year of the fire at Windsor Castle; it was the year Queen Elizabeth described as *annus horribilis*. So things have been ongoing for at least a half a dozen years. And during that time there's been, in a certain sense, both a succession fight and a fight over the structure of the future of the Monarchy.

> *Quite right. And it is still going on, of course.*

It is still going on but a major player has been taken out of action, a player who was increasingly becoming a serious impediment, particularly to Philip and Elizabeth. A *serious* impediment. But what you have is that the impediment has now been removed.

> *Indeed it has. Thank you for your time, Jeff.*

You're most welcome.

The House Of Windsor
And Neo-Colonial Africa

One of the most alarming assertions made by Jeff Steinberg and the *EIR* investigation is that Prince Philip - via his position with a well-known NGO which we are unable to name (due to legal reasons), and the Crown's almost incestuous relationship with MI6 - has been involved in some "very nefarious activities in Africa". The implication is, of course, that those "very nefarious activities" include the Crown's active though covert participation in the destabilization and overthrow of certain Third World governments, and the installation of other, more Anglo-American-friendly regimes in their place.

And perhaps more to the point: that one of the regimes actively supported by the Crown is UNITA - the British- and US-backed rebel army which is still fighting to gain control of Angola (aided somewhat, of course, by the many thousands of anti-personnel landmines deployed by British and US mercenary forces in Angola over the course of the past three decades).

In any event, the allegation is that the British Crown has used - abused - its patronage of a well-known NGO to further its interests in Africa and the Third World - in particular so far as we are concerned, in Angola.

Also claimed is that, by virtue of her secret correspondences with the *EIR* team, Princess Diana was acutely aware of this situation - and thus the political implications (indeed, the immense dangers) involved - at the time of her anti-personnel landmines campaign in Angola. For the record, Jeff Steinberg also claimed that Diana might have been involved in a "succession fight ... a fight over the structure of the future of the Monarchy". In other words, that the princess might have intended to use her unprecedented public support - which increased even further as a result of her landmines campaign - both to spotlight the House of Windsor's "nefarious activities" in Angola, and at the same time gain more of a say in how the Monarchy might proceed into the twenty-first century. We will of course be exploring this latter theme in some depth in Book Three.

However, in order to gain a better understanding of the subterranean and often dangerous world of imperial corporate politics (in which Diana became enmeshed as a result of her anti-personnel landmines campaign in Angola), an elucidation of the points raised by Jeff Steinberg, and their implications with regard to Diana's death, is included here. [Note: in its original form, this chapter included the results of our own research into the British Crown's dubious activities in Africa and the rest of the Third World. Plus, of course, their implications with regard to Diana's death. However, though many of the themes alluded to by Jeff Steinberg indeed emerged, quite independently, in the course of our own investigation, we were forced in the end to excise much of this information due to legal reasons. What we can say is this.]

The NGO alluded to by Jeff Steinberg - with which Prince Philip has been indelibly affiliated for almost 40 years - has certainly been implicated in some rather dubious activities on African soil. According to *EIR* at any rate (as well as our own very well placed source) the NGO in question has been used as a cover for covert operations in Africa and other Third World territories. In other words, it has been hijacked by British Intelligence and, unknown to the vast majority of its largely volunteer workforce, used as a cover for ferrying arms and mercenaries to Third World 'hot spots' - like Angola. A truly staggering claim. Perhaps when you consider that this same NGO also enjoys the affiliation of Prince Philip's lifelong comrade-in-arms, Prince Bernhard of the Netherlands, however, it is not altogether a surprising one. After all, we recall that it was Prince Bernhard who, following his days as an officer in Heinrich Himmler's psychopath-ridden SS, became an influential deal-broker with the Nazi chemicals giant, IG Farben, which in turn became directly responsible for the deaths of thousands of Jews interned at Auschwitz during WWII (see *Chapter Eight*). Prince Bernhard then went on to found the Bilderberg Group in 1954. And to found and co-found - with Prince Philip - two other very prominent NGOs which have indeed been implicated in "nefarious activities in Africa", but which we are not permitted to name due to the legal system which, true to its masonic roots, seems obliged to protect the questionable interests of the rich and the powerful at the expense of true justice - a travesty in the extreme, to be sure.

In any event, which ever way you look at it, Prince Bernhard and Prince Philip boast very chequered careers, to say the least.

It should be explained here that the NGOs in question (those founded, co-founded and patronized by Prince Bernhard and Prince Philip) fall into the category of what are officially known as 'non-governmental organizations' (NGOs). In other words, 'environmentalist', 'conservationist', 'humanitarian aid', 'human rights' organizations etc (a fact which makes the allegation that they are being used in covert operations all the more unpalatable). It should also be said that, unlike many other NGOs - which are of course funded, in the main, by the general public - the NGOs linked to Bernhard and Philip and named in the *EIR* investigation are funded largely by the corporate sector. And in particular by those banks and corporations which still harbour vested interests in Africa and other Third World territories. The vast majority of these banks and corporations, of course, are the spawn of Anglo-Dutch colonial rule in Africa and the Third World during the nineteenth and early twentieth centuries. In other words, they are Crown-allied (in some instances Crown-chartered) companies which have grown fat and powerful on the proceeds of Third World privation. Today they comprise what is considered by many to be the world's wealthiest and most powerful corporate body - the Anglo-Dutch financial oligarchy which effectively controls the City of London stock-and-bond markets. It should be noted here that, in a titular sense, this oligarchy is headed up by the House of Windsor. (We will explore in more depth the Anglo-Dutch takeover of London and the British Throne in Book Three.)

But what is even more pertinent to the point at hand is that, in a 'hands-on' sense, this same Anglo-Dutch oligarchy has for the past 40+ years been headed up by the Crown's arch representatives - to wit: Prince Philip (Anglo) and his Bilderberg buddy, Prince Bernhard of the Netherlands (Dutch). Due to legal reasons we are unable here to elaborate on the nature of the 'hands-on' work undertaken by these two latter-day Herods. But in any event, the NGO alluded to by Jeff Steinberg and implicated in "very nefarious activities in Africa" is largely funded and directed by this oligarchy, which in turn is served by MI6 and headed up by Philip and Bernhard.

Jeff Steinberg's allegation against Prince Philip, then, is not without some substance.

To add to this, it is known that the House of Windsor (or 'The Firm', as it is otherwise known) continues to invest heavily in corporations born out of British colonial rule in Africa. And that some of these corporations, in order to protect and advance their still-massive financial interests in the African 'colonies', have indeed been involved - together with MI6 - in some very dubious activities over the years. Suffice to say in this regard that the evidence we uncovered tended to support the fact that Diana was fully aware of this situation - indeed, that she was more politically aware than any of us might have imagined (although we remain convinced that any political motives harboured by the princess would have been driven by her obvious desire for a better world, and not for personal or party political gain). That Diana *was* aware of the Crown's covert activities in Africa, of course, and thus the extremely tenuous situation which exists in Angola - as well as in Bosnia - is born out by virtue of her secret correspondences with the *EIR* team. It is a fact which gives rise to enormous implications. It clearly suggests, for example, that Diana's campaign would have been undertaken in direct opposition to the Crown's covert activities in Africa and the Balkans. In other words, that she would have been acting in flagrant disregard of Palace and Establishment directives. This fact was demonstrated clearly enough by the Establishment's otherwise inexplicable hostile reaction to Diana's humanitarian campaign - the branding of Diana as a "loose cannon", for example. (The *Concise Oxford Dictionary, Ninth Edition* describes 'loose cannon' as "a person ... causing unintentional or misdirected damage". What possible "damage" might Diana have caused in seeking to help innocent victims of anti-personnel landmines, one wonders?). Also the Establishment's vigorous attempts to discredit Diana in the media, and thus undermine her campaign altogether (see *Chapter Nine*). The problem was, of course, the princess would not be bullied. "I shall not go quietly," she told BBC's *Panorama* in November 1995. "That's the problem, I shall fight." And fight she did. Indeed, focusing world attention on the plight of Third World countries such as Angola (and thus bringing to light the human rights crimes perpetrated by Crown-allied banks and corporations in those countries, as well as by Crown-sponsored NGOs and MI6), would seem to have been Diana's way of making a personal stand. Not only on behalf of victims of anti-personnel landmines (although her humanitarian motives must of course remain of primary significance here). But also *against* the illegal and often brutal activities perpetrated by Crown-allied banks and corporations in the Third World.

Or to put it more bluntly: against the House of Windsor's own "nefarious activities in Africa". And thus, as Jeff Steinberg affirmed, against the House of Windsor itself.

Clearly the two letters sent by Diana to *EIR* (dated 5th June 1996 and 6th March 1997 respectively) plus a further correspondence between *EIR*'s Scott Thompson and the princess's private secretary, imply that Diana was not only aware of the situation with regard to Crown-sponsored operations in the Third World. But that her campaign was, in part, her way of protesting against these activities, and was possibly even an attempt to expose - or at the least spotlight - the House of Windsor's secret involvement in this regard. Certainly the more we probed the princess's reasons for selecting Angola as a major focal point for her campaign, the more we realized that high politics must indeed have played its part. Moreover, that it would have been a prime mover in motivating her to focus world attention on the plight of war-ravaged Africa. After all, Diana's *raison d'etre* was surely to confront the world's major taboos and injustices (as evinced by, say, her work on behalf of HIV and AIDS victims, and indeed, victims of anti-personnel landmines). There was - is - of course, no greater injustice than that currently perpetrated on the Third World by the world's major-league banks and corporations, some of which, as stated, hold massive investments owned by the House of Windsor. Of course, if it had ever come to light that the British Crown, in order to protect its investments in neo-colonial Africa, was still vigorously pursuing a 'neo-colonialist' policy in African states (including Angola) - and thus could be implicated in acts of political subterfuge, guerrilla warfare, and even corporate genocides in those states - then the already foundering and desperately unpopular Windsor Dynasty might not have survived the public backlash. This, at any rate, would seem to have been one of the princess's major priorities in spotlighting the Angola situation - in making that situation known to a blinkered world. Also, of course, it would explain the Establishment's otherwise inexplicable knee-jerk reaction to Diana's 'humanitarian work'.

The allegation, then, is that, in her endeavour to remain part of the Royal Establishment (from which she had been so unceremoniously ostracized); and moreover, to gain an ever more influential position within that Establishment - perhaps even, as Jeff Steinberg put it, to "create a counter-monarchy", or at least "a counter-structure" within the Monarchy - Diana was attempting to expose the more covert and often brutal activities of corporations and other organizations allied to the House of Windsor. And thus, in effect, expose the House of Windsor itself - if not as a direct participant in, then as an active supporter of, the illegal activities carried out by Crown agents in the Third World.

Or again, to put it more bluntly: to expose the House of Windsor's own vested interests in the British- and US-backed atrocities being committed in countries like Angola.

And there is good reason for surmising that Diana would have wished to expose the House of Windsor in this way. As we know, she had already mounted a sustained attack on the Windsors over the course of the previous four to five years - not least by colluding with Andrew Morton on his book, *Diana: Her True Story*. Also, of course, by taking part in the subsequent and much-publicized *Panorama* interview (1995), in which she openly attacked the House of Windsor - and indeed, stated in no uncertain terms that, in her opinion, Prince Charles was not fit to be king. Her endeavour to expose the

Windsors' "very nefarious activities in Africa", then, should not be seen as an isolated event; rather as a continuation of her ongoing offensive against the Windsors as evinced by her collusion with Andrew Morton and her subsequent *Panorama* interview. It should be noted here that both of these events were unprecedented in British history. It should also be noted that a senior BBC official has since revealed that substantial portions of the original *Panorama* interview had to be cut due to the explicit nature of Diana's verbal attack on the family into which she had married. The family to which she had born two male heirs.

And perhaps more to the point: the family by which she had subsequently been ostracized.

According to the evidence compiled by *EIR*, then (together with our own evidence in this same regard, the bulk of which we are unable to include here) there would certainly seem to have been an ulterior motive behind Diana's landmines campaign in Angola - to wit: to turn public opinion even further against the already unpopular Windsor Monarchy and so further undermine the viability of the Windsor succession. At the same time, of course, to gain even more public support for herself and her 'own causes'. (Which she did.) As incredible as it may sound, and as Jeff Steinberg suggested, it is not out of the question that her 'own causes' might, at some point in the future, have included a direct challenge for the Throne. Or at least a serious attempt to modify the Monarchy to the extent that Prince Charles might be bypassed in the line of succession in favour of Prince William (a mood already prevalent in Britain at the time of Diana's death; and moreover, a theme to which the princess herself alluded during her *Panorama* interview in 1995). Indeed, in the eyes of many Windsor supporters and Establishment oligarchs, Diana's impressive Stuart heritage (see Book Three), together with her unprecedented public appeal, constituted a very serious threat to the continued succession of the House of Windsor. And thus to the very fabric and stability of the British Royal Establishment itself. We will of course pursue this theme in greater depth - and present our own evidence in its favour - in Book Three.

As for our sizeable and compelling body of evidence regarding Crown-sponsored covert operations in Africa and the Balkans - sadly, we are simply not permitted to include it here. In short, it involves naming major Crown-allied corporations and organizations (plus those who run them - all names on file) which are simply too powerful for our publisher - indeed, ourselves - to take on, blow for blow. Indeed, we have been warned in no uncertain terms of the consequences should we dare to name names with regard to the Crown's dubious business dealings in the Third World. Without wishing to blow our own trumpet here, the fact that we have gone to such meticulous lengths to authenticate our information, it seems, means that the evidence we have uncovered - and which we have endeavoured to present in the course of this book - has been taken rather more seriously than is ever likely to be admitted. In short, we have been warned off. In consequence, we are unable to present to the jury the full extent of evidence which, in a truly democratic inquiry, the jury, by rights, is entitled to hear.

And thus by threat and intimidation the meat of the story is concealed. The cover-up is maintained.

In any event, the fact remains that Diana's secret correspondences with *EIR* (on file) clearly imply that the princess was fully aware of the House of Windsor's vested interests in Africa - including Angola. And that, moreover, she was also aware of the lengths to which the British Royal Establishment is prepared to go in order to protect and advance those interests (indeed, she is perhaps more aware of this now than ever). It should be remembered that Diana was made aware of this information immediately prior to her anti-personnel landmines campaign in Angola.

And that, in consequence, her landmines campaign would have born far greater political implications (would have posed a far greater threat to the Crown and the Establishment) than any one of us might imagine.

The Queen's £3 Billion Portfolio

The idea that the House of Windsor is little more than a cultural or constitutional figurehead, then - that the Queen exercises little or no power over the democratic process, and that the Royal Family is little more than a tourist attraction maintained in order to buoy up the British economy - is quite simply a flagrant propaganda sell. The fact is that the House of Windsor is effectively a multinational corporation in its own right. Or at least a figurehead (Chairman of the Board) for the neo-colonial cartel of banks and corporations (the so-called Anglo-Dutch financial oligarchy) which today exercises a brutal and thoroughly inhuman control over much of Africa and the rest of the Third World. And this despite so-called 'declarations of independence' pursued by numerous African nations over the past few decades. Indeed, in cases where nations have seemingly won independence from imperial rule, all that has happened in truth is that direct rule has been replaced by covert rule. Nothing more. The colonial conquerors have pulled out and, in their place, Western-backed (in some cases Russian-backed) compradors have been elevated to power. But the song remains the same: while the puppets may have changed, the puppeteers have not. In this regard it is quite evident that neo-colonialism remains the most vigorously pursued policy on the African continent today (and neo-colonialism, of course, includes the deployment of anti-personnel landmines in countries where the struggle for covert control has not yet been fully achieved - countries like Angola, for example, where British/US- and Russian-backed regimes continue to struggle for control of Angola's natural wealth). With the handover of Hong Kong to China in 1997, then, the sun may finally have set on the geopolitical British Empire. But in the corridors of corporate and masonic power, the British Empire still reigns supreme. Make no mistake about that. It simply goes by a different name these days: the US/European Alliance.

(And contrary to popular belief the US/European Alliance is still headed up by the House of Windsor, as we shall see.)

This certainly remains the case in Africa, a continent on whose soil British agents and mercenaries are still fighting to maintain neo-colonial supremacy. Angola, of course, is one such country. And there are others, many of whom still play host to the furthest outreaches of colonial power. In other words, even though they may seem to have won independence, they continue to play host to the same corporations and agencies whose wealth and influence facilitated their present 'quasi-independent' state. The same corporations and agencies whose brutal practices have effectively raped their lands, destroyed their economies and subjugated their peoples. And in the process, of course, provided a succession of Windsor Monarchs with diamonds and castles. Little wonder Africa weeps.

It should be reiterated here that, in the main, these multimillion-dollar corporations (names on file) subsist largely on the vast profits made from Africa's untapped oil and raw-material reserves. And what is more, that their major shareholders include, among others, the British Crown - in particular the private investments of the Queen and the Duke of Edinburgh, both of whom have made vast private fortunes out of the unethical and often brutal methods employed by these corporations in Africa and other Third World territories. The fact that the financial-and-industrial-espionage wing of MI6 is on hand to safeguard these investments, of course (by means fair or foul); and the added fact that the world's leading financiers are ever on hand to 'advise' Her Majesty in her investment-and-trader dealings, means that Queen Elizabeth II is today the wealthiest woman in the world (with a penchant, it is said, for buying up blue chip stocks and bonds to supplement her already vast holdings in real estate, raw minerals and oil). The added fact that, for the past half-century (until recent changes were forced on the royal income) the Queen has been free to amass as much wealth as the royal purse would bear, *tax-free*, means that her portfolio is now reported to have increased from a mere £50 million (estimated in 1953) to a staggering £3 billion (estimated today).

Or to put it another way: the scope of the Queen's private investments has increased from an estimated 1 million starving Africans per annum to an estimated 60,000,000 starving Africans per annum.

A portfolio worth protecting, then.

Indeed, had Diana's activities in Angola uncovered the source of this wealth - and more to the point, the way in which it had been amassed - then the money-making Merry Windsor monopoly machine might just have come under serious scrutiny, not least from those Diana represented above and beyond the Queen herself: the British people. When you consider also that the House of Windsor's viability to reign relies entirely on its position as titular head to the world's most powerful financial oligarchy, the implications regarding exposure of its "nefarious activities in Africa" (and the consequent damage to Prince Philip's and the Queen's personal wealth which such an exposure might have engendered) begin to assume new proportions. After all, what financial oligarchy in its right mind would want a mendicant monarchy as its figurehead?

The Rape And The Pillage

To clarify: as much of our evidence had to be excised from this chapter, we have elected to include here a brief itinerary of British colonial rule in Africa, from its inception under Queen Victoria to its fruition under Queen Elizabeth II. Four generations, no more, and the largest, most fecund, most mineral-rich continent on the planet has been bled dry. And on the proceeds of this blood the House of Windsor rules supreme.

What the Western world has achieved, then, in order to build its empires, maintain its castles, and line the pockets of its corporate and royal masters. And moreover (according to the evidence we were not permitted to include in this chapter) what Princess Diana threatened to expose as a result of her anti-personnel landmines campaign in Angola:

1) the rape and pillage of African natural resources - mainly oil, uranium, precious metals, raw minerals - as well as the subjugation of African peoples and the acquisition of African real estate;

2) the supply of arms and mercenaries to specific African states (including Angola) in order to facilitate *Point 1*;

3) the supply of arms and mercenaries to specific African states in order to ensure the rise to power of favoured political factions following the so-called 'collapse' of colonial rule, and the subsequent withdrawal of imperial administrations - examples: Zimbabwe, Burundi, Rwanda, Uganda, Sudan, the Congo, Tanzania, Kenya, South Africa ... and of course, Angola, among a host of others;

4) the continued manipulation and control of Third World economies

to the advantage of British (Crown) and US corporate investment;

5) the creation of the so-called Third World Debt as a result of *Point 4*; and in consequence, the creation of poverty, squalor, disease, famine and mass extinctions of human life - in short, a Crown-instigated corporate holocaust;

6) the instigation of internal conflicts - civil wars, corporate genocides - in specifically targeted regions in order to destabilize those regions, oust their governments, install others, and so maintain covert, neo-colonialist supremacy in Africa and other Third World territories;

7) the hijacking and utilization of certain Crown-allied NGOs by MI6 (in particular those NGOs substantially represented in African countries) in order to help achieve *Points 1, 2, 3* and *6*;

8) the creation of so-called 'protected areas' - game reserves, national parks, conservation areas - by UN- and Crown-allied NGOs; the locating of these areas (some of which are the size of small countries) on strategic borders; the expulsion of native populations from these areas (thus making them, in effect, Western enclaves); and the subsequent utilization of these areas by US- and Crown-sponsored mercenary forces and rebel armies in covert operations;

9) the continued control of Africa - her natural resources, her economies, her policies - even today, by British- and US-led Western governments.

10) the assassination of Diana, Princess of Wales, in large part due to her anti-personnel landmines campaign in Angola - in particular, of course, the fact that the princess's actions in Angola threatened to expose, on a scale equal to her unprecedented popularity, *Points 1-9*; and that, in consequence, the British Crown, together with its US colonial and corporate bed partners, might just have been exposed for continuing to support the summary rape and pillage of Africa to its own financial advantage.

Indeed, that the House of Windsor might just have been exposed for the neo-colonial rapist which, by proxy, it undoubtedly seems to be. And that, in consequence, it might finally have lost what little public sympathy it is still able to educe.

The Joshua-Jericho Syndrome

In the final analysis, then, the fact that many NGOs are both run by and supported by well-intentioned environmentalist, conservationist, humanitarian aid and/or human rights groups, we conclude, should not cloud our perception on a number of other counts:

1) that British and US intelligence agencies maintain an international network of their own self-created, self-regulated NGOs (there are more than 500,000 registered NGOs in Britain alone); and that this network was created on the blueprint for the original network set up for humanitarian purposes;

2) that this network is used as a cover for covert operations in mainly Third World countries;

3) that British and US intelligence agents have indeed infiltrated, on occasion, and to some greater or lesser degree, certain of the best-known and already established NGOs; and thus that, unbeknown to the vast majority of their workers and supporters, these organizations are also being used as a cover for covert operations on foreign soil;

4) that, to further consolidate their foreign-territory *modus operandi*, British and US intelligence agencies also utilize an international network of what might be termed 'masonic' organizations - such as Freemasonry and other secret-society networks, the Sovereign Military Order of Malta (or the Knights of Malta) being a primary case in point - see *Chapter Seven/Eight*;

5) that these NGO and 'masonic' networks together comprise an international web of foreign-territory outlets via which numerous MI6/CIA operations are orchestrated and implemented;

6) that the British Crown (the House of Windsor), via its shareholding in some of the world's largest, most powerful - and indeed, most unethical - fuel and raw-mineral corporations, plus its almost incestuous relationship with MI6, exercises an often brutal control over many Third World countries;

7) that many of those countries are in Africa; and more to the point, that one of the countries currently being exploited in this regard is Angola;

8) that, according to *EIR*, the mechanism employed to facilitate control in this regard is broadly known as the Club of the Isles, a masonic-style royalist body named after King Edward VII (the first Prince of the Isles); presided over today by Her Majesty, Queen Elizabeth in conjunction with the current Prince of the Isles, Prince Charles; and established in the first instance to protect the corporate and neo-colonial interests of Europe's extended Royal Family (which is headed up, of course, by the House of Windsor);

9) that a sub-body in this same regard is known as [name deleted], and is described by *EIR* as a quasi-conservationist body allied to [name deleted] and the Bilderberg Group (see *Chapter Eight*). [Name deleted] was established in 1971 by ... you guessed it: Prince Bernhard of the Netherlands. According to *EIR*, it was set up largely to fund operations covertly facilitated via the NGO structure, and thus to protect and advance neo-colonial interests in Africa and other Third World territories. It is actively supported by Prince Philip, the Duke of Edinburgh. In particular, *EIR* claims, this elite body was set up to protect and advance the interests of the so-called Anglo-Dutch

financial oligarchy which today controls the City of London, the financial centre of the world. This oligarchy was responsible for setting up the Bank of England in 1694, for colonizing vast portions of Africa in the nineteenth century, and is today responsible for maintaining neo-colonial control on the African continent. And perhaps more pertinent: it is also responsible for maintaining the House of Windsor as its titular head. Which in turn, of course, means that the House of Windsor is the most powerful and influential corporate dynasty in the modern world - thanks largely to its massive investment in neo-colonial Africa and the Third World;

        10) that, due to her correspondences with *EIR*, Diana, Princess of Wales was fully aware of these facts: thus that she was aware of Crown-orchestrated operations in Angola and Bosnia at the time of her landmines campaign; that her landmines campaign would thus have been conducted in direct opposition to the policies pursued in this regard; and moreover, that her landmines campaign would almost certainly have been designed, in part, to spotlight (possibly even expose) MI6's - and by association, the Crown's - "nefarious activities in Africa" and the Third World.

        In short, it is our contention that Diana's landmines campaign threatened to expose the Crown's vested interests in the outcome of Angola's 'civil war'. And in consequence, of course, the Crown's vested interests in the continued deployment of anti-personnel landmines in Angola (landmines are and have for the past three decades been an integral part of the British/ US war machine in Angola, as well as in Bosnia). As ex-British Foreign Office Minister, Sir Nicholas Bonsor, commented shortly after Diana's death: "For the princess to put herself so overtly at the head of a ... campaign to abandon all landmines, and deprive our own soldiers of the use of such landmines, was in my view wrong of her." And further: "Princess Diana was potentially a threat to the Establishment and a threat to the Royal Family."

        Indeed she was. In fact, which ever way you look at it, the irony is that while Diana was campaigning to *stop* the continued deployment of landmines in Angola and Bosnia, Crown agents were all the while working behind the scenes to undermine the princess's campaign and so protect the vested interests of the British Establishment and the House of Windsor. It is an irony in the most double-edged extreme.

        And what is more: it is an irony which we believe cost the princess her life.

        In light of the above information, then, it is our conclusion that Diana's anti-personnel landmines campaign posed a far greater problem to the British Royal Establishment than anyone might have imagined. Indeed, extrapolated to their most likely, most predictable outcome, it is our contention that the repercussions of Diana's landmines campaign might just have precipitated the Joshua-Jericho syndrome all over again. In other words, the trumpets of truth which accompanied the princess during her humanitarian campaign might just have brought the walls of Windsor Castle to rubble. And in consequence, of course, exposed its occupants and their "nefarious activities" to the full glare of public scrutiny. In our opinion this is something the House of Windsor simply could not have afforded. Nor indeed, survived.

With the premature death of Diana, however, the House of Windsor has not only survived the promise of its own twentieth-century Jericho. To judge by recent opinion polls it has witnessed its own spin-doctored rebirth to boot. Which surely suggests that Diana's death was, *at best*, the result of a tragic though extremely convenient 'road traffic accident'. And *at worst*, the result of a clinically contrived conspiracy perpetrated by the British Establishment to protect the Windsor power-base. It is our opinion that the *at worst* scenario remains the most likely.

In other words, that Diana was assassinated to protect Crown interests in the very country which served as the major focal point for her campaign. This, at least, is the conclusion we put to you, the jury.

And we do so with unmitigated conviction.

BOOK THREE

THE BLOODLINE CONSPIRACY

"...The point is that these secretive - and some not so secretive - power blocs all want to possess the Grail. In other words they seek control of the bloodline, the bloodline of the House of Judah, and of course its heirs, like Prince Charles and Prince William."

Former Foreign Office (MI6) Historian, 1998.

CHAPTER 11

THE SOURCES (Part 2)
The Foreign Office, MI6
And The Secret Of The Bloodlines

"Off the record, I would say that her removal, in one form or another, would have become almost a necessity the minute her divorce from Prince Charles was made final, never mind her subsequent relationship with a Muslim ... an Arab Muslim of all people. That would most certainly have been the final nail in her coffin, I have to say."

Former Foreign Office (MI6) Historian, 1998.

Political Bloodlines

Some way into our investigations we were made aware that someone of high social standing might be willing to talk to us. The source who brokered our meeting told us that this person had first-hand knowledge of high-degree corporate and masonic government; that he was "very well connected" with "ears and eyes" inside Britain's Secret Intelligence Service (MI6); and indeed, that his former position as a British Foreign Office (MI6) historian had afforded him access to both MI6 and Royal archives which would prove of substantial significance so far as our own investigation was concerned.

So far as we are permitted to say, this source once worked in a highly classified Foreign Office (MI6) department, where his task was to sift through historical and genealogical data due for classification review. The material still considered too sensitive for public release, we were told, was further classified and vaulted, while still other material was considered too sensitive even for review. This material, he said, consisted in part of records and documents dating back to the first and second centuries AD. And beyond. He added that some of the records contained genealogical information pertaining to what he somewhat curiously referred to as "political bloodlines", and that some of the more highly placed members of Europe's aristocracy - the social class into which he himself had been born - were indeed aware that their own ancestries could be traced back, via the Merovingian Kings of Dark Ages

Europe, to the Judaic Royal Dynasty of ancient Israel. Staggeringly, they could also be traced back to the historical Jesus, he said.

This source was unable to offer us information pertaining directly to the death of Diana, Princess of Wales. Even so, he claimed to have gained access to a highly classified historical, genealogical and constitutional database, the import of which, he said, suggested very strongly that Diana's "removal ... would have become almost a necessity the minute her divorce from Prince Charles was made final". Her subsequent relationship with "an Arab Muslim of all people", he said, would have been "the final nail in her coffin".

On a surprisingly mild, sunny day in the depths of winter we made the journey to London, to our arranged meeting place, an hotel overlooking (precise location deleted). With our informant's permission we set a tape recorder inconspicuously on the table next to him, at which point he set about telling us what he knew.

[**Note:** As stated in the *Introduction*, it should be reiterated here that what this source told us may at first seem shocking, unbelievable even. But we ask that you bear with it. As with our interview with Stealth (*The Sources, Part 1*) we have elected to present this information raw, *as we received it*, and in the ensuing chapters present evidence in support of its veracity. Indeed, as incredible as it may sound in its raw state, the bulk of this information was ultimately to prove chillingly verifiable, and in the end led us to uncover perhaps *the* primary underlying motive behind Princess Diana's death. And more than this: it led us to uncover perhaps the most scandalous and far-reaching conspiracy of our time.]

The Political Holy Grail

In response to initial questioning this man of apparent high standing began by alluding to the existence of what he referred to as "historical grapevines" - genealogies, bloodlines, ancestries. He spoke of royal family trees that he said were "self-evident" of both "religious and political intrigues". In this respect his finger pointed directly at the European nobility - a dark mass of roots and branches appended to the same arcane tree, we were to discover. He suggested we investigate that tree.

He also alluded to some tacit "Judaeo-Christian agency" or "strain", which he spoke of in terms of a "political bloodline". This "bloodline", he said, was the "political Holy Grail ... in more senses than one". Indeed, he claimed that it was fairly responsible for maintaining the ascendancy of the European noble lineage, and in particular the sovereignty of Europe's several latter-day ruling dynasties (the House of Windsor, of course, first among them). And thus, in some backstairs, masonic sense, he said, it was also responsible for maintaining the very political edifice underpinning Western democracy.

"The entire Western infrastructure, economic and political, has been built on this Judaeo-Christian theme," he said. "We all share this same cultural ancestry." He paused at this point, as though to emphasize what he would say next. Then: "Our god is Jehova," he said with some meaning. "Theirs is Allah." The look on our faces at this point must have told him that we were uncomfortable with this remark.

He explained: "I say this in a purely political context, of course. But even in this context, 'Jehova' is a very jealous God. He is not at all enamoured with the idea of sharing his secular domain with some upstart Arab deity who, after all, is a good deal younger than he is, and so might be seen as a sort of young pretender to his throne. In other words, 'Jehova' - who in this context represents European and American power blocs, *political* power blocs - ahh ... 'Jehova' is not at all pleased at the prospect that his power blocs might be, shall we say, supplanted by 'Allah', who in this same context represents the Arab nation and *its* power blocs - which of course have become ... relatively *recently* become really very potent indeed."

He went on: "For centuries now Europe has been ruled by the authority of the Judaeo-Christian blood strain ... of which I have already told you. This authority is held by certain families of noble descent who, by the process of political and masonic viticulture [the grafting of bloodlines - the management of political alliances and marriages within the European nobility] can all claim descent from the Royal House of Judah. But this claim is upheld purely in a political sense, and by the process of its later, shall we say ... its later Christianization, again in a purely political sense. I'll come back to that point in a moment. Ahh ... but these families, you see, they comprise a sort of legitimate noble mafia ... effectively this mafia rules Europe and has some fair amount of leverage in America, also. Of course, these days collusion with extremely powerful corporate and economic bodies - and I suppose, ultimately, political bodies, also - goes without saying. But to a large extent it is still the nobility that holds power, ostensibly at least, in a titular sense ... in a purely political sense, a *masonic* sense." He emphasized the word 'masonic'.

Can you explain what you mean by 'masonic' in this context?

"Oh, yes. I mean the secretive structures or ... or the sort of quango-style governmental bodies who comprise the financial and industrial power blocs that control Western policy ... the unseen masonic and hierarchical structures by which this is achieved ... The point being that the control is achieved, quite literally, by masonic or secretive structures and processes."

When you refer to 'secretive structures and processes', are you referring to those structures and processes represented in such bodies as, say, the Bilderberg Group?

"Yes, precisely, quite right. And there are others, too. But ... the Bilderberg objective has become perhaps the most powerful and influential of them all. The centralization of economic and political power in Europe is very largely due to the influence of the Bilderberg conferences and their attendees, who of course occupy, or at least go on to occupy very powerful positions indeed ... once they have been taken into the fold, as it were. Their given mandates thereafter, of course, are to actively promote the centralization process."

Have you ever attended a Bilderberg conference?

A wry smile. Then: "No."

Can you name anyone you know who has attended a Bilderberg conference?

This time a shrug. Then: "Charles, for one."

Prince Charles?

"Yes, Prince Charles. But that's pretty common knowledge. Tony Blair's another. Margaret Thatcher, Bill Clinton. But, you know, this is all well documented. There are fewer restrictions on the identities of those who attend the conferences than there are on the mandates for policies discussed [at the conferences] ... But you can be sure that the policies enforced by the Bilderberg-controlled governments in Europe, of which today there are a good many - and that includes Britain under New Labour, as well as America under Bill Clinton - ahh ... their policies will be in direct concurrence with Bilderberg policies. Or rather with those of the financial and industrial groups who, shall we say, launder their policies through such masonic organizations as the Bilderberg Group...

"...So, yes, the Bilderberg Group is indeed fundamental to the mechanism of masonic government. Most certainly so."

Is what you refer to as the 'masonic government' the same as what others refer to as the 'secret government' or the 'New World Order'?

"Well, I have to say that I dislike both of those terms. I dislike them immensely. It makes it all sound as if the entire scheme has been dreamed up by conspiracy theorists, when in fact these structures are there for anyone and everyone to see. But yes, I suppose it is that sort of thing, although to call it a *new* world order I think is a mistake. The masonic structures I am talking about have been in place now for at least three hundred years - those that bear relevance today at any rate. In their own way they have been in place for much longer than that. The European nobility and its secret societies, its chivalric orders and such, plus of course the Catholic and Anglican Churches - they have simply been supplanted by, or rather have become the public faces of the corporate power blocs that wield influence today. The power *they* usurped from the true bloodline dynasty has itself been usurped by the corporate bodies I have already mentioned. But it is still run along masonic lines. It's all masonic in its structure."

Can you say something about how this power was usurped?

"Yes. By political manipulation and assassination, to come straight to the point."

And can you say who was responsible for the manipulation and assassination?

"Oh, well, in the first instance, of course, it was Rome. Depends how far back you wish to take it."

As far back as remains relevant to Diana's death.

"Well, yes - then let's start with Rome. Ahh ... when I say Rome, of course, I mean the relevant power structures of the day, structures represented in Rome and Constantinople. Oh, I suppose we're talking somewhere in the region of 200, 300 AD. Perhaps a little later. Around this time the House of Judah had become mostly prominent in what has become known as the Merovingian Dynasty - the Merovingians were Frankish rulers descended from the Royal House of Judah, which of course meant that, while Judea may still have been a Roman province, the power inherent in the Judah bloodline was beginning to take hold in Europe, in the persons of the exiled Merovingian kings, who for the next two or three hundred years would rule large parts of France and Germany and so on."

And that bears relevance today?

"...Yes, of course. Today's European nobility has been modelled on the Judaic structure, you see. Rome saw the Merovingians, realized the immense potential for power inherent in the House of Judah, and thought, ahh! The result is the House of Windsor, among others...

"...But there was a problem. Unlike royal houses today, Merovingian kings ... were openly recognized as the true bloodline descendants of Judah. They wore the traditional long hair of the Judah kings and were reportedly blessed with certain powers of healing and such forth. Archetypally speaking they were considered very wise kings. They were priest-kings. They possessed some sort of special, almost divine quality, a genetically distinct quality that, well ... to which their subjects responded. It gave them absolute authority. And this is what the secular powers of the day feared most of all...

"...Ahh ... so their authority was never questioned and, so far as we know, it was never abused either. As I say, this of course gave concern to certain parties, in particular the most powerful governments of the day, in Europe that is. And the most powerful government of the day was of course Rome...

"...Now Rome had been at war with Judea (or more precisely Judah) for centuries, but conquest of the Holy Land was no longer sufficient to maintain ascendancy over the Judah kings - who, remember, possessed a sort of 'mystical' or genetically inherited power that was seen by Rome to be inherent in the Judah blood. Now as I have said, by this time the Judah bloodline was becoming ... very prominent throughout Europe, in particular in France and Germany, both of which were of course bastions of both the old and new [Roman] empires. So, in a nutshell, rather than continue to use bows and arrows to defeat the House of Judah - which it ultimately feared more than any other power - ahh ... rather than continue to perpetrate war against Judah, Rome simply killed off the more illustrious Merovingian kings, married a few of their own contenders into the Judah household as part of the plan and, well, the Church of Rome took control of the bloodline in this way...

"...That's the situation as it stands today. To this day European monarchs are still crowned by the Pope, or by the Archbishop of Canterbury. It's all still carefully managed and cloaked in masonic ritual. But the point is that present-day royal houses are the product of this misappropriation of Judaic royal authority. They are usurpers whose dynasties are sponsored by political agendas and run by a form of ... of corporately funded masonic government."

We are still a little unclear about what you mean by the terms 'corporate government' and 'masonic government'.

"Well, as I've already said, ahh ... by corporate government I mean the sponsorship of democratically elected governments by the world's most powerful financial and industrial corporations, and thereby, of course, the influence of these non-elected bodies on policy-making. By masonic government I mean the secretive hierarchical structures by which this influence is administered. In this, of course, you are quite right to employ the term 'secret government', but I would still refrain from employing that term myself. As much as anything else it implies a cohesive secretive body of behind-the-scenes government, when in fact there are several behind-the-scenes bodies ... several power blocs, each with its own political aspiration...

"...But, ahh ... well, yes, it certainly is a sort of behind-the-scenes administration, formally structured ... modelled on a form of masonic hierarchy. And the several discrete lodges of this hierarchy represent the several discrete power blocs - corporate power blocs, masonically structured - that sponsor and control elected governments in the West and the Middle East, and many Third World governments, also. Ahh ... that's about the best I can do, I'm afraid."

No, no. You explained the point very well, thank you. But perhaps we could get back to the question of the bloodline.

" ... Well, the point is that these secretive - and some not so secretive

- power blocs all want to possess the Grail. In other words they seek control of the bloodline, the bloodline of the House of Judah, and of course its heirs, like Prince Charles and Prince William. And this is where the idea of a masonic government bears relevance, you see. This is how they are able to manipulate Western policy, at least the religious and economic institutions by which that policy is seen to be formulated and imposed. By being seen to represent the bloodline and its, shall we say, ahh ... its 'mystical powers', the European nobility, its ruling dynasties, become the Grand Master Masons of masonic government. They give that government structure and tenability. They give it hierarchy. In so doing, of course, they constitute a viable titular head for what appears to be a legitimate and democratic form of constitutional government. But of course it is *not* a legitimate *or* a democratic government. It is not a legitimate or democratic *anything*. Quite the opposite. It is more a political *coup d'etat*...

"...They are usurpers, you see, as I have already said. They are interlopers who have been manipulated into positions of ostensible power by the ruling economic and political bodies of the day. The Windsors and the House of Hanover; now there's a perfect example. The House of Windsor today, which is merely an extension of the usurper House of Hanover ... [the House of Windsor] is the titular head to one of the most influential power blocs in the Western world, if not *the* most influential power bloc in the Western world. Again, this power bloc is corporately funded and masonically structured - it depends on the House of Windsor to give it that structure. Do you see? And other members of the European nobility, other royal dynasties ... have in the past represented this same masonic scheme...

"...However, with regard to your investigation into the Diana affair, and in particular the involvement of Dodi Fayed ... the point I was making ... what I was saying was that, with the discovery of oil in the Middle East, and the vast amounts of wealth and power generated as a consequence ... well now there are new families and, shall we say, newly engendered Arab dynasties ... Muslim power blocs that wield some sizeable amount of influence of their own. [Name deleted] for example, now there's an almighty thorn in terms of European masonic government. [Name deleted] and *their* masonic sponsors comprise yet another. No wonder the establishment is more than reluctant to grant Mohamed Fayed British citizenship; they fear the power bloc he might represent, you see. And there are others, too ... the point [being] that they all represent a threat to the masonic structures central to British - and indeed, European - ahh ... as well as American government. And this is precisely because the American and European structures are founded on Judaic blood...

"...So of course Diana's involvement with Dodi Fayed - which I must say I think was rather foolish on her part - but, ahh ... of course it would have concerned certain parties, in particular those parties with a vested interest in the Judah bloodline, again in a political sense. But to what extent it may have provoked a reaction I am not in a position to comment. Not officially, at any rate. Off the record, I would say that her removal, in one form or another, would have become almost a necessity the minute her divorce from Prince Charles was made final, never mind her subsequent relationship with a Muslim ... an Arab Muslim of all people. That would most certainly have been the final nail in her coffin, I have to say."

So the reason for British and American paranoia in this regard would have been due to the emergence of oil-rich Arab-Muslim power blocs and their apparent designs on European policy-making?

"Precisely, yes. After all, you see, the masonic structures intrinsic to European policy-making, and more to the point, the centralization of European policy-making - or rather the plans to centralize European policy-making - they are not new. As I have already told you, they have been in place now for ... well, for more than a thousand years, in fact. But, ahh ...well, most certainly for the past three or four hundred years these structures have been carefully formulated to accommodate the determining political agendas of masonic government. And as we've just been saying, those agendas reflect an underlying policy to centralize European and American masonic government purely on the strength that it is to be founded on this Christianized Judah bloodline, politically speaking. That, of course, is the ultimate plan. I mean ... well, the centralization process ... one can see it for oneself; no one seems to be making any secret of the fact these days...

"...This plan has been pursued for a very long time. What you are seeing in terms of the centralization of European political and economic government is the product of centuries of very thorough planning, not to mention political ambition. No one is prepared to stand by and watch, ahh ... shall we say, the outsider power blocs - no one is prepared to stand by and watch these outsider power blocs make their move on the existing power blocs. It's a question of territory, political and economic territory, and of course the power and influence that territory affords. Do you see? I cannot put it more clearly than that."

Are you saying that a conspiracy to centralize political and economic power in the West is currently being pursued, that this conspiracy goes back centuries, and that this same conspiracy is at least in part responsible for the death of the Princess of Wales?

"I don't know that I'd use the word *conspiracy*. But that's the nub of it, yes."

That's an extravagant claim, and probably difficult for many

people to accept. Can you say what has led you to this conclusion?
"...Well, yes, as I have already told you ... the documents stored in [file and place names deleted] ... the archives I told you about, they show quite clearly how the Catholic Church ... how the Church of Rome became an enormously powerful political force that literally usurped the power inherent in the true bloodline dynasty of Middle Ages Europe - which, according to the records ... the true bloodline dynasty had descended from Kings David and Yeshua [Jesus] of Judah. What do you think the Crusades were all about? Why would the medieval knights and their armies have gone all the way to Jerusalem to fight Muslims if not to protect this ... this truly historic political secret? Why does this same conflict continue today ... in the form of the Middle East crisis? What, in a political context, is so important about Israel? Think carefully before you give an answer...
"...They [the documents] also show how that same political force, that same political bloodline ... how it was won and lost countless times over by various nation states and governments, most notably, of course, France and Britain. But it belonged to Rome initially ... to the Royal House of Judah before that...
"...But they [the documents] even describe the political games played by the old Roman Empire, the appointment of the Herods as puppet or usurper monarchies, for example. I realize this sounds a bit extreme. But I can assure you it was no coincidence that the Roman authorities installed Idumean Arabs [the Herods] on the throne of Israel back in ... ahh ... in the days before Jesus. It was all part of the plan to weaken the genetic ascendancy of the House of Judah over its political rivals ... so that its political power could be tapped and controlled, and eventually usurped. That same plan is still effective today."

King Yeshua Of Judah

Can you explain what you mean by the "true bloodline dynasty" and its "genetic ascendancy"?
"Well, as I began to explain just now, it has always been assumed in masonic circles that the bloodline of the Royal House of Judah is genetically distinct from other bloodlines, that it has some 'extra quality' or other - hence the 'mystical' quality attributed to David and Solomon, and of course to Jesus and the later Merovingian kings. They are all kings of the House of Judah ... Some believe that this quality is purely metaphysical. But I have seen documents that lead me to believe it is genetic; this is certainly the belief of those who struggle to control it. And anyway, that is why the House of Judah, indeed, that is why *all Jews* have been persecuted throughout history - the

bloodline has always been confused with, or rather attributed to the Jews as a people, when in fact it is a purely political strain, at least it is these days. It never used to be, of course. But, ahh ... it is also why so much emphasis is placed on, shall we say, navigating that bloodline towards political ends. An example can be seen in the public crucifixion of Jesus, or King Yeshua; it was a political *coup de grace* on the part of the Roman authorities in first-century Judea. By ridding Judea of its *de jure* king..."

You mean Jesus Christ?

"...Jesus, yes, the 'Son of David', the descendant of King David of Judah. His name is Yeshua. He was Israel's *de jure* king, as I'm sure many people now realize, and as such he would have been referred to as the messiah by the Judean people, which translates through the Greek to Christos, or Christ. But all it means is that he was Israel's *de jure* king, Israel's rightful heir apparent to the throne, which as you know was occupied by the Herodian dynasty of Idumea. It's all in the records ... and if you care to look closely it's in the Bible as well ... Oh, yes, Yeshua - or Jesus if you prefer, Jesus Christ that is - was far from the humble Galilean carpenter we have been led to believe of him. Which is not to say that he wasn't a religious man; quite the opposite. As messiah in Judaic law and custom he would have been seen as a sort of high priest to the people, as well as being their king - their religious as well as their political leader. Remember, the Judah kings are more than just constitutional figureheads. They are priest-kings ... incumbent upon whom is the responsibility to serve their people in both a political and a religious context. Politics and religion are inseparable in Judaism, always have been...

"...But Jesus was of noble stock, and he was *known* to have been of noble stock. Naturally the same can be said of his wife, Mary Magdalene, whose name translates to something like Queen Mary of Magdalene, or Magdala, in the documents I've seen. And of course the same can also be said of many other of the characters depicted in the New Testament, especially those numbered among the 'disciples'. The story of Jesus and his so-called 'disciples' - according to the documents at any rate - is a codified depiction of the political struggle undertaken by Israel's ruling dynasty at that time, the Royal House of Judah. It is a coded message in many respects ... a cryptographic record of their struggle to oust the Roman occupiers and win back the throne from the Herods, whom we know were little more than puppet kings installed by the Romans for very specific political reasons. And in any case, if Jesus was anything other than what I am telling you he was, well ... well how else do you suppose he would have been able to galvanize public support to the degree that he undoubtedly did? Look at Palm Sunday ... There's more to Palm Sunday than meets the eye."

Palm Sunday? Could you elaborate?

"Well, I should be careful how I pitch this one ..."

At this point our man took a moment to himself, seemingly to consider his position. He ordered a cognac; we each ordered a coffee. Perhaps the cognac helped to ease his mind, because a short while later he resumed. "There is still some evidence in existence, in the records I've seen, that tells of entire periods in history having been ... well, having been erased, or at least dramatically altered. The period from 6 or 7 BC to around 36 AD is a worthy example. As you know, this is the approximate life-span given to Jesus in history, and this period has simply been erased from the records, even from the records that I know are still being held in confidence by ... well, let us just say by the authorities."

Can you say why this should be?

"I can only surmise - I have to say it in this way - I can only surmise that it is to conceal the fact that, like several others before him, Yeshua led an uprising against Rome, and indeed defeated Rome, if only temporarily. That is when he marched into Jerusalem, or rather he rode into Jerusalem on his donkey to the acclaim of thousands of Jews. He was at the head of a victorious revolutionary army, the Zealots. He had just re-taken Jerusalem from Rome and been crowned King, and this was his *tic-a-tape* parade in celebration of his victory and his coronation ... it also meant, of course, that he had reclaimed the throne from Rome's puppet kings, the Herods ... I mean, it's a ludicrous notion to think that the Roman authorities would have allowed him to perform such an action under any other circumstance. The fact is Rome did *not* allow him to ride into Jerusalem; he did so with flagrant disregard for the authority he had just defeated. A short while later ... Rome retaliated and crushed the Zealot army in occupation of Jerusalem. Within a day or two Jesus was crucified, and soon after that Pontius Pilate was recalled to Rome, no doubt for a severe ticking off, perhaps something worse than that...

"...But in any event he [Jesus] was king. That is stated very clearly in the records, and of course in the Bible as well. The Roman authorities were certainly aware of this fact; well, that is why they put him to death. But, ahh ... well the fact that the Bible has been, shall we say, *encrypted,* makes it difficult for people to realize. But like Diana, Yeshua or Jesus, or whatever you wish to call him, ahh ... like Diana, Yeshua was a people's king, as well as being the *de jure* heir apparent to the House of Judah, which was Israel's ruling royal dynasty at that time, and had been for centuries, since David..."

"...And in any event, that is why Rome put him to death. By ridding Israel of its true bloodline king, and some centuries later re-writing the historical records to make it seem as though he was purely a spiritual messiah sent from God - and also, of course, to make it seem as if the Jews themselves had demanded his death - ahh ... in this way Rome was able to create a myth of the man and sell that myth to the people as political propaganda. Do you see? In creating the 'Son of God' story Rome in effect created an enormous political edifice, which eventually became known as the Vatican State ... [it became an edifice] from which to gain immense secular power throughout Europe...

"...Now, the records I have seen tend to suggest that, while it is perhaps a bit naive to think of Yeshua as the Son of God ... there does seem to be a recognition of something rather special about the Judah bloodline, the blood itself. And in any event that 'special something' has become the source of immense political power today. And of course it remains *of Judah.* Arab families are still seen in the same light as the Herods. Which is precisely the point I began to make with regard to Diana and her affair with Dodi Fayed."

We would like you to clarify this point. Are you saying that, in your opinion, there is a direct connection between the special quality attributed to the Judaic royal bloodline and the death of the Princess of Wales? And if so, what would you say that connection is?

"I would say it's self-evident, although I must say I cannot be certain there *is* a connection. What I mean is, I cannot be certain that the Princess of Wales was assassinated. I have no hard evidence of that."

But if she was then do you think the motives behind her death are directly related to the bloodline conspiracy, as depicted in the documents you've seen?

"Most certainly, yes, of course. But whether or not it is ... I have to say that will have to remain your own conclusion. You will need to discover the legitimate origins of the Windsor bloodline for yourselves and make up your own minds about that. But, ahh ... yes, if she *was* assassinated then you need look no further than this for your prime motive ... [no further than] the political intrigues that have shaped the current situation by, ahh ... well, by creating the usurper monarchies, royal *and* political, who today rule Europe as a centralized power bloc."

Can you say something more about the "legitimate origins of the Windsor bloodline" in this regard?

"Not at this present time, I'm afraid. That is something you will have to discover for yourselves, given what I have already told you, of course. That should at least guide you in the right direction. Indeed, I have told you too much already. But, ahh ... well, what I will say ... the important thing to bear in mind in all of this is that we are talking about something of tremendous political significance. The Windsor bloodline today is a *political* bloodline, do you see? We are talking about ... in effect we are talking about the political Holy Grail. Quite conceivably the *literal* Holy Grail, also. The Judah bloodline is effectively the Holy Grail, the Blood Royal."

The Holy Grail?

"Yes, the Holy Grail."

But we have always been told that the Holy Grail is a mystical artifact or quality that belongs solely to legend.

"Quite, so, yes, precisely the point. It suits all manner of agendas to keep this information secret ... to keep the hoi polloi of the mind that the Holy Grail belongs only to the world of myth and legend, as you rightly say. But in fact the Holy Grail is the most sought-after political artifact in the Western world. It has become the masonic watchword for the royal bloodline, the messianic bloodline of David and Yeshua ... [and] that is precisely what it is...

"...As I'm sure you realize, it [Holy Grail] comes from the Old French, 'Sangraal', meaning 'Blood Royal', though it has been deliberately mistranslated as 'Holy Grail' for centuries. It has been deliberately mistranslated and packaged as myth and legend, as romance, purely to deflect attention away from its true meaning. [This is because] it is a *political bloodline.* In other words the mystique it has generated by being transformed into a legend - and, let us not forget, into the world's most politically influential religion, also - this mystique now serves a purely political agenda. And it serves that agenda very well indeed, as I have already explained to you. And as I have also explained to you, I fear I have said too much. We must leave it there. I have told you as much as I am able."

That said, our source suddenly downed the last of his cognac and made moves to leave. "I fear I have said too much already," he said again, pushing himself up from his seat. "I wish you well in your endeavours."

Before you leave, would you please clarify the significance of the Judaic royal bloodline with regard to the death of the Princess of Wales?

Rearranging his white silk scarf around his neck, tying it as though it was a cravat, this enigmatic aristocrat paused for a final moment, during which he peered long and hard across the table one last time. Then: "The Judaic royal bloodline ... the Blood Royal is the political Holy Grail," he wanted us to appreciate. "Do you realize what I am saying to you? An ostensibly legitimate claim to the bloodline is an ostensibly legitimate claim to the Grail. And whoever possesses the Grail possesses power. In this day and age the Grail Dynasty - in our case the House of Windsor - stands as titular head to a very powerful corporate and masonic elite indeed. It really is very simple. Whoever possesses the Grail rules the Western world. Or at least holds sway in large parts of it." A moment's pause. Then: "Do you see?"

We said we thought we did. At which point our conversation came to rather an abrupt end. Our contact did not speak again. Instead he simply nodded, as if to say: "Well, then, the rest is up to you." Having put on his overcoat and picked up his attache case he then dipped a hand in his pocket and headed for the exit. We have not heard from him since.

The Man Who Would Be King

Though the above transcript contains the largest part of what this source was able to tell us, at our meeting we were made aware of further information also - some of which we will come to in a moment, though a small part of which he requested we keep in the strictest confidence. He said that, although we might wish to exploit this 'further information' during the course of our investigation - that it might serve as a "pointer" to lead us in "the appropriate direction" - publication of specific names, dates and processes would almost certainly place him in explicit danger. However, with regard to the masonic agencies involved in what he referred to as the 'centralization process' (the centralization of European political and economic power), this source cited further organizations, some of which, he said, formed a sort of 'oligarchical consensus' with the Bilderberg Group. Most of these organizations are named in *Book Two* - to wit: the International Monetary Fund; the World Economic Forum; the World Bank and the European Bank; the International Institute of Strategic Studies (which, this source claimed, is an MI6-run foreign-policy operation set up to monitor and - where possible - orchestrate a "strategic balance" in terms of political/military power abroad); the United Nations; the British-based International Institute of Foreign Affairs; the US-based Council on Foreign Relations, etc.

Interestingly, though, he also cited an organization called the European Council of Princes (ECP), to which he professed his own allegiance. Or at least his sympathy with regard to ECP's current president. To what degree, if any, his sympathy was active, he would not say. But he did infer that investigation of ECP might, in some indirect way, throw up clues with regard to the royal bloodline of Judah, and in consequence, could prove helpful in our efforts to establish possible motives behind Diana's death. (He emphasized, however, that ECP would not in any way have been involved in the princess's alleged assassination.)

Duly, we contacted one Sir Laurence Gardner, Kt St Gm KCD KT St A, whom, we discovered, is currently Presidential Attaché to ECP. He also boasts the impressive credential of appointed historian and sovereign genealogist to thirty-three royal families. Perhaps understandably, Sir Laurence voiced his reservations with regard to our source's claim that he was in some way affiliated with ECP. "Please be wary of citing people who claim affiliation or connection to the European Council of Princes," he wrote. "If your man resides in this country, then he cannot possibly be so attached. The only Council member living in Britain is its current president, HRH Prince Michael of Albany, and the only authorized attaché is myself."

Despite Sir Laurence's understandable caution, however, what *is* of interest is that ECP's current president, HRH Prince Michael of Albany, boasts a very intriguing pedigree indeed. He is the current head of Britain's estranged Stuart Dynasty, for example, which ruled Britain for most of the seventeenth century and which claims direct lineal descent from the Merovingian Dynasty of Dark Ages Europe - and thus from the Royal House of Judah. Moreover, while the House of Windsor is reputedly the descendant of a 'usurped' or 'politically cultivated' strain of this Judaic royal bloodline, the House of Stuart claims that *its* descent is legitimate. Had they not been deposed at the beginning of the eighteenth century, of course, and the Throne effectively usurped by the German House of Hanover (alias the House of Windsor), the Stuarts would still be occupying Buckingham Palace. And what is more, HRH Prince Michael of Albany would be King of Great Britain today.

But what is of even greater significance is this. Ever since the usurpation of the Stuarts in 1688/9, and again in 1714, our source said, Stuart supporters - or at least supporters of the legitimate strain of the Judaic royal bloodline - had been struggling desperately behind the scenes to re-establish and reclaim the Throne of an independent Scotland. Perhaps even, ultimately, to reclaim the Throne of Britain. He said that he was particularly aware of this situation as it had been specifically his department which had dealt with "the counter-monarchy problem" during his time at the Foreign Office. He also said that, in his capacity as a 'special remit' Foreign Office (MI6) historian, he had been party to certain genealogical records and documents which not only severely compromised the legitimacy of the House of Windsor in this regard. But which - should the information they contain ever be leaked into the public domain - could even engender a situation tantamount to civil war. Indeed, he stated quite unequivocally that this was the very reason MI6 had gone to such lengths to obtain the documents in question. And having obtained them, lock them away in a vault marked classified (*see Chapter Seven*).

Moreover, this source also implied very strongly that, in the event that Diana *was* assassinated - which, he emphasized, he had "no hard evidence of" - then her death would almost certainly have been linked to this theme. In fact he said: "I have heard whispers, rumours, nothing more ... that the late Princess of Wales had been courted by certain agencies ... who seek to restore the Merovingian line to the Throne." When we questioned him as to the ambiguity of this statement, he said: "Look to Scotland. And to Diana's popularity."

Despite further attempts on our part to press for a more lucid explanation, he refused to elaborate, seeming instead to revel in the cryptic nature of the riddle he had posed. Even so, this riddle - its implications - though ambiguous at the time, became clear enough as our investigation progressed.

This same source had already stated, remember, that in his opinion Diana's relationship with an "Arab Muslim of all people ... would most certainly have been the final nail in her coffin". He was referring, of course, to the issue of 'bloodlines' in this regard. And more specifically, to the fact that the bloodline in question was essentially Judaic, at least in a political sense, and thus that Diana's involvement with an "Arab Muslim of all people" would have been tantamount to 'political treason'. But now he was implying that there was a parallel issue to be considered - in effect, the issue of the "bloodline monarchies" versus the "usurper monarchies". Or to put it in a less cryptic context, the Merovingian-Stuarts versus the Hanover-Windsors. Indeed, as we were to discover, the enmity which still exists between the House of Stuart and the House of Hanover-Windsor dates back several centuries. And as we further discovered, Princess Diana, who married into the House of Hanover-Windsor, was herself a bloodline descendant of the Royal House of Stuart. Indeed, her Merovingian-Stuart heritage, we discovered, was extremely impressive. While we were still uncertain at this point as to the significance of these discoveries and their relationship to the information we had obtained (or indeed, whether they bore any real significance at all), we nevertheless resolved to investigate them further. In essence, *Book Three* details this investigation in some depth.

As our source rightly pointed out, then, the issue of bloodlines was indeed to play a major role in our investigation. At the time of the interview, of course, we were unable either to verify or refute the information imparted to us by this source. Until now our endeavours had been largely focused on investigating, collating and sifting the evidence presented in the preceding chapters. So far as we were concerned, of course, this in itself was sufficient to warrant serious examination, even if only within the form of a book such as this one. But now we were faced with a new line of inquiry altogether. Suddenly we were faced with the distinct possibility that, at least to some immeasurable, indefinable degree, Diana's death was the result of a two-thousand-year-old political conspiracy which stemmed from the life of no less a figure than Jesus Christ (or King Yeshua, as our source had referred to him). And that this same conspiracy also involved what we understood to be a private war between the present-day House of Windsor and supporters of the House of Stuart (or if not the House of Stuart, then some other legitimate 'bloodline' dynasty which laid equal claim to the Throne). A truly staggering hypothesis in itself; indeed, one worthy of its own controversy, equal in every measure to the possibility that the Princess of Wales had been assassinated. On this basis alone we felt compelled to at least make attempts to either verify or refute this information. In particular, of course, as that information seemed to suggest that Diana may or may not have allied herself to the Merovingian-Stuart cause.

"I have heard whispers, rumours, nothing more ... that the late Princess of Wales had been courted by certain agencies ... who seek to restore the Merovingian line to the Throne." So said our Foreign Office source.

Indeed, had this statement been made by someone of lesser credential we would almost certainly have left it to simmer. In the event, however, it had not been made by someone of lesser credential. On the contrary, it had been made by someone of noble stock; and moreover, by someone who claimed he had once been a 'special remit' Foreign Office (MI6) historian whose security clearance had afforded him access to genealogical documentation specific to our investigation. Or at least specific to information which promised to shed new light on our investigation. Nevertheless the question remained: what had he meant by this statement? That Diana had been courted to support a Stuart restoration? Or even more unbelievable: to figurehead that restoration?

Needless to say we came away from our meeting slightly perplexed, and equally uncertain as to where our investigation might lead next. Even so, we remained intent on piecing together the somewhat cryptic clues this source had proffered. After all, if only a grain of what he had told us proved of any substance at all:

If the House of Windsor could indeed be traced back by lineal descent to the Royal House of Judah;

If it could be shown that the Judaic royal bloodline had included among its heirs the historical Jesus;

If it could be shown that the authority of the Judaic royal bloodline had been "usurped" by the Church of Rome during the Middle Ages and turned to its own political end - in other words, that the Church had effectively hijacked the authority of the Judaic royal bloodline, and by that authority had subsequently created royal dynasties of its own (the dynasties of the Holy Roman Empire, for example);

If this same 'bastardized strain' of the Judaic royal bloodline could also be shown to underpin the structures and edifices intrinsic to present-day masonic government; and further, that for the past 300 years (since 1714) it had been headed up by the House of Hanover-Windsor;

And further still: if it could be shown that Diana's unique Merovingian-Stuart heritage, her Stuart blood, together with her unprecedented popularity, threatened the viability of the House of Windsor sufficiently to warrant her "removal" (as alluded to by Jeff Steinberg in *Chapter Ten*);

And that, moreover, Diana had indeed been "courted by certain agencies ... who seek to restore the Merovingian line to the Throne";

Then this Judaic-Merovingian-Stuart bloodline warranted very serious examination indeed.

CHAPTER 12

THE BLOODLINE DYNASTIES
Genealogies Of The Windsors And The Spencers

"In terms of bloodline inheritance, Diana's family line is very
impressive - stemming from the Lusignan Kings of Jerusalem and
from the Royal House of Stewart. In comparison, the Saxe-Coburg-
Gotha-Windsor line is only tenuously linked to the original Grail
stock."

Sir Laurence Gardner, Kt St Gm KCD KT St A, appointed historian
and sovereign genealogist to thirty-three royal families and the
Jacobite Histriographer Royal, 1998.

Blue Blood

If there is one quality above all others which determines the condition of
royalty, it is of course the colour of its blood. Or more precisely, the stemma
of its bloodline - its distinction from other bloodlines. In short, royal
ascendancy is both assured by and dependent upon the pedigree inherent in
its blood.

We have all heard the term 'blue blood' applied to the Royal Family,
as though coursing the veins of Charles, William, Harry *et al* is a substance
unlike that found in us mere mortals. This is of course nonsense. Even so,
there is a fundamental truism concealed here. And it is a truism we are
invited to explore. For one thing it reaches to the very heart of the mystery
we are endeavouring to penetrate. And for another, it unmasks the counterfeit
currency upon which the authority of the Windsor bloodline is both created
and sustained.

But what, precisely, is this 'blue blood'? What entitles its heirs above
others? What are its qualities - its root, its culture, its racial strain: its religious
and political bias? What makes this blood royal? And why?

And perhaps more pertinent so far as we are concerned: is it worth
killing for, this blood? Is it so distinct from common-or-garden red blood that
fear of its contamination (and thus dilution of its political potency) might provoke
desperate, pre-emptive measures on the part of its political sponsors - the
assassination of its own finest example, for instance, its own high princess?

This is one question we do not need to answer for ourselves, of course; history answers it adequately enough on our behalf. *Yes, to keep the strain free from unwanted influences, it is certainly worth the head of the odd noble here and there, or that of the odd political opponent. Yes, the occasional assassination does indeed serve - always has served - to isolate the requisite blue from the common-or-garden red, the politically viable from the politically impotent, the puppet from the household rebel.* Indeed, the past millennium alone has proved this convention many times over.

But does it still apply, this same convention, at the turn of this third millennium AD? Does it still apply at this time of so-called social and cultural enlightenment?

Yes, of course it does. No matter the time, no matter the age, no matter the technological and scientific achievements heaped upon us in the name of evolution, this same rule must of necessity still apply. The intrinsic brutality of human ambition has, after all, softened not one jot behind the facade of intellectual civilization. And neither is it ever likely to. Indeed, a cursory study of the Windsor family tree will suffice to betray the game clearly enough. It will show that, in effect, the so-called royal pedigree (the Windsor family tree) is little more than a monument to a centuries-long series of religious and political manipulations. Also, of course, it will show the preferred bias of those manipulations as that bias has evolved down through the ages. It will show how the shrewd grafting of one bloodline onto another by the process of selective, in-house interbreeding is the very means by which the succession of one or other royal dynasty to the British Throne has been assured. What it will not show, of course, is the complexity of masonic treacheries and intrigues underpinning those means. It will not show how the ascendancy of one royal house over another has always been the result of some or other backstairs political agenda, political ambition, and that this same situation obtains today. It will not show how the almost 'mystical' power ascribed to the Judaic royal bloodline was usurped during the so-called Dark Ages by the Church of Rome, and subsequently applied to the royal dynasty of Rome's favour in its bid to build and maintain empires. Nor will it show that, for at least the past millennium and a half, the desire to possess this 'mystical power' (and so gain control over those empires) has been the cause of constant political and economic warfare; indeed, often literal warfare. It will not spell out the fact that the Windsor family tree - like its blood - conceals a lie. But it will point the finger squarely in that direction.

Simply put, it will expose the British Throne as little more than a socio-political seat for global dominion. And those who sit upon it as impostors.

Ever since the days of perhaps the most famous Saxon Britain has known, King Alfred the Great - who, according to legend, burnt his cakes some time between AD 871-899 - no less than *eleven* different royal dynasties have fought and won possession of the British Throne. And the power and privilege attendant upon it. What this says, of course, is that succession to the British Throne is not some God-given birthright, to the Windsors or anybody else. Rather it is up for grabs. Like the chair on a board of directors. Like a seat in the House of Commons. Or the presidency in some throneless republic. Like in America. The difference being, of course, that, in a republic, the lie is at least open to scrutiny.

The successive ascendancy of any royal dynasty, then, is and always has been the product of much behind-the-scenes political artifice - cloaks and daggers and lies and spies. And cover-ups. Indeed, this royal chess game has so often inflamed the various factions vying for its power that acts of betrayal, murder, political assassination, even out-and-out warfare, have become almost a tradition. The in-house political bickerings scudding back and forth between the various feudal factions endemic to the ruling classes (in particular to the European nobility and its political sponsors) are notorious for their regularity. The Windsors, of course, are simply the latest in a long line of said feudal factions to win possession of the British Throne. In truth, it is no more Prince Charles's birthright to become king than it is yours or ours. He just happens to head up the right faction, figurehead the right sponsor. And herein lies the key to our investigation.

What is of interest so far as we are concerned is the identity of the feudal faction to which the House of Windsor belongs - for which in-house noble and political 'clique' it acts as figurehead. In order to discover this we must first break down the nobility into its existing cliques and factions, and identify by lineal descent the bloodline to which the Windsor allegiance is pledged. The reason for achieving this is as follows.

Information received from our Foreign Office source (see *The Sources Part 2*) led us to believe that the assassination of Princess Diana, at least in part, was linked to the issue of royal bloodlines and their successive claims on the British Throne. More specifically this source informed us that what we should be looking for, among other things, were the "legitimate origins of the Windsor bloodline". We told him that we were not sure what he meant by the term "legitimate origins". He declined to elaborate. What he did say, however, was that discovery of said "legitimate origins" would almost certainly help us to understand in far greater depth why Diana's relationship with Dodi Fayed was doomed from the outset - why it could simply never have been tolerated by the British Establishment. Having told us one or two other things in this regard, and having hinted at several more, he then left us to our own devices - to investigate the clues, piece together the evidence, draw our own conclusions. This, to the best of our ability, we have now done. We believe we have now managed to string together the few pearls this source placed in our hands. Plus a few more we discovered independently along the way. Though it was a long and somewhat convoluted investigation, at its end we believe we uncovered the very reason why the House of Windsor simply could not have survived Diana's threatened marriage to Dodi Fayed, nor even a lengthy and involved relationship with him. Like any political party, a royal house needs its sponsors. The Windsors are no exception in this regard. The only difference, of course, is that sponsors of political parties sponsor policy, while sponsors of royal houses sponsor blood. The Windsor bloodline, we discovered, is the result of an ancient alliance of Germanic and Judaic royal bloodlines which is and always has been predominantly Judaic. And therein lies the clue. Dodi Fayed, of course, was an Arab Muslim. Judaeo-Christians and Arab Muslims, like cats and dogs - like Israelis and Palestinians - do not mix at all well. In particular when the Arab Muslim concerned happens also to have been an Egyptian. The Judaeo-Christian/Egypt conflict is of course well-documented: from the days of Moses and the Jewish enslavement in Egypt (circa 1300 BC) to the Six Day War in 1967, Egyptian and Judaeo-Christian cultures have been at variance, if not at daggers drawn. Indeed, this situation has achieved little but shed blood for at least three millennia, and to this day continues to dominate the religio-political landscape of the Middle East. As is widely known, this landscape is today largely the result of British and US political endeavour. What is not so widely known is that this political endeavour is itself the result of an ongoing masonic struggle to maintain control over the destiny of the Judaic royal bloodline, as we shall see. Indeed, our research indicates quite implacably that this same Judaic royal bloodline is the very authority upon which the most powerful right-wing US/European faction of masonic government was - and remains - founded. And moreover, that the House of Windsor remains this faction's titular head.

Within such a powerful oligarchical coalition as this, of course, intimate relations with Arab Muslims are simply not permitted.

The Dynasties

Before introducing the theme of the Blood Royal - and thereby the involvement of biblical kings, bloodline messiahs, medieval knights and their quest for the Holy Grail (and, of course, their relevance to the death of Diana); plus the very real, first-hand involvement of masonic and Vatican agencies in this sordid affair - we felt that we should first explore in brief the ancestries of the two dynasties in question: the Windsors and the Spencers. Trace them back to their roots.

In the following chapters, we will indeed pursue our in-depth exploration of the secret history and intrigue traced by the Judaic royal bloodline. In so doing, of course, we will endeavour to highlight its participation in - and its commitment to - what we believe to have been the assassination of Diana, Princess of Wales. Before we do that, however, we felt it pertinent that we study at least the skeleton of both the Spencer and Windsor ancestries - descended as they both are, we discovered, from the Judaic Royal Dynasty which first came to prominence under King David of Israel (circa 1000 BC). We are, after all, looking for clues as to the motive behind such a callous and brutal deed as the assassination of a royal heretic, as Diana herself may be affectionately described. Family trees tend naturally to provide insights into the selective processes undertaken in the forging of a noble or royal bloodline - the arranged marriages; the political marriages; the forbidden marriages: the grafting together of selected bloodlines for purposes of dynastic and political ascendancy. As we shall see, neither the Windsors nor the Spencers are exceptions to this rule. (Indeed, Diana was herself the unwitting victim of this centuries-old convention, prised as she was from relative obscurity and thrust into the royal spotlight, a vacant and suitable womb for bearing royal heirs. She never was the choice of Prince Charles, of course. Rather of convention, of necessity. Handpicked for the task, she nonetheless performed her duty with aplomb. And because she did, the ascendancy of the royal line of Judah today remains intact.)

And in any event, in the final analysis noble families, royal dynasties, royal bloodlines - they are scarcely what they seem.

The House Of Windsor

To speak of a bloodline, royal or otherwise, running untainted through successive generations is of course quixotic, unrealistic. Four generations at most and already the genes have become a little frayed at the edges. Five and they are positively ragged.

This is as true for the Windsors as it is for any one of us. After all, even the least royal among us can boast claims to some or other familial past, some or other interconnected root or vine. The difference is, of course, that, as if by some divine alchemical right, the more socially elevated families and houses lay claim not to roots, but to entire family trees. Not to vines, but to entire vineyards. In this regard it would be fair to say that a bloodline of sorts can be traced back, through virtually every noble - royal, aristocratic - family in Europe, at least as far as the seventh and eighth centuries AD. Beyond that, any such bloodline as might be accorded a royal pedigree assumes a new significance entirely.

The royal dynasty we today refer to as the House of Windsor, of course, began life as the House of Saxe-Coburg-Gotha, itself a bastard amalgam of the Teutonic/Judaic Houses of Ansbuch, Mecklenburg-Strelitz, Wettins and Hanover. But then, every so-called royal house or aristocratic family is today a bastard amalgam or offshoot of some or other equally diluted ancestry which stretches back into the murky mists of Dark Ages Europe. By the process of politically shrewd interbreeding, the European nobility has survived its own stranglehold on international power for centuries without end, and in this regard the House of Windsor is no exception. On the contrary, it is this same incestuous amalgam of quasi-elite blood which today traverses the veins of Sandringham and Balmoral, Buckingham Palace and Windsor Castle alike - albeit under a pseudo-guise. Albeit under the guise that the Royal Family is what it claims to be, and is thus entitled to enjoy the sheer obscenity of privileges accorded it. Albeit under the guise that the royals are blue-blood British. They are not.

It was Sophia, granddaughter of King James 1 of England (King James VI of Scots) and Queen Anne of Denmark, who effectively married the British Throne into the Hanoverian Dynasty. Herself the daughter of King Frederick of Bohemia, Sophia married Ernst August, Elector of Hanover, and so introduced to the British people probably the most debauched of all the royal dynasties Britain has thus far endured (although this, of course, remains marginal). Between them Sophia and Ernst produced seven children, among whom was George (born 1660) later to succeed the last of the Stuart monarchs, Queen Anne, and become King George I of Great Britain. Though traditional history justifies this 'changing of the guard' - from the Stuarts to the Hanovers - by playing up the fact that George was the great-grandson of King James I of England and Scots (and thereby claimed at least some right to the vacant throne), in truth it was an entirely political manoeuvre on the part of Britain's landed elite. Under *de facto* law it was a quasi-legitimate manoeuvre, true. But in reality it was little short of political usurpation. The ascendant Whig Party and their ever more powerful sponsors (the newly allied Anglo-Dutch oligarchy comprised of Britain's landed elite and Holland's most powerful financiers), much to the consternation of the less dominant Tories, offered the throne to George in the knowledge that he spoke no English whatever. And that he would spend most of his time in his native Germany. Which he did. In the process, King James II's son and heir, James Francis Edward Stuart (*de jure* James III England), following an unsuccessful attempt to gain the throne in 1715, was sent packing - by the Whigs - back to his seat in exile, at St Germain-en-Laye, near Paris, France. With the *de jure* Stuarts successfully deposed, and the *de facto* Hanovers firmly installed (though largely absent, and wholly ineffectual), the royal coup was complete. Indeed, it left a financier-controlled Parliament free to run Britain however it saw fit. (And an unsupervised, inaccessible and wholly undemocratic parliamentary oligarchy free to become the fat and overfed cow it is today.) From this point on, Britain would be ruled by a financier-controlled Prime Minister and an entirely undemocratic 'inner circle' of so-called Cabinet Ministers, who would - and still do - decide policy behind locked doors and in accord with their sponsors' directives. Thus the British people - indeed, the majority of elected MPs - would from this time on have no say whatever in the decisions taken by their elected representatives. Of course, a quasi-legitimate monarchy was still needed (as it is today) as this parliamentary oligarchy's titular head - to give tenability to the new, financier-controlled, masonically governed Parliament. The Parliamentarian oligarchs had of course learned from past experience (under landowner, Oliver Cromwell, some half a century earlier) that the British people would not readily succumb to a forceful takeover. Nor even to the overt establishment of a parliamentary republic. Such a clandestine and insidious takeover as this one, however - whereby a parliamentary republic was installed behind the facade of a parliamentary monarchy - was scarcely even detected, much less opposed. It was an ingenious move.

Thus Britain became the pseudo-democratic state it is today. Thus the religiously and politically tolerant Stuart Dynasty was deposed and ousted. Thus the British Monarchy became emasculated of its own inherent power, and simultaneously transformed into little more than a convenient figurehead for masonic government.

And thus George, Elector of Hanover, favoured son of the then Habsburg-controlled Holy Roman Empire under Charles VI, acceded to the Throne of Britain. The Judaeo-Teutons - the politically illegitimate descendants of the Judaic Royal Dynasty - had arrived. And despite a little mixing and grafting of selected bloodlines down through the generations, the Judaeo-Teutons are still here. No Muslims allowed.

But that was just the start of it. On the death of George I came George II, and several more Georges followed - plus a William (the Fourth of Hanover), the notorious Queen Victoria of Hanover, an Edward (the Seventh of Saxe-Coburg) another George, then another Edward (the Eighth). It was Edward VIII, of course, whose reign was infamously cut short due to his abdication in 1936. Of interest here is the fact that, though traditionally blamed on his decision to choose love over royal obligation, the real reason behind Edward VIII's enforced abdication was his unashamed, intimate and surprisingly public relationship with Adolf Hitler and the burgeoning Third Reich in 1930s Germany. In essence, King Edward VIII was a fascist who admired Hitler's policies and methodologies to the extent that he supported the establishment of a similar system in Britain. Indeed, his many trips to

Germany during Hitler's tyrannous rise to power were perceived as an affirmation to this end. But then, Edward was a Saxe-Coburg-Gotha; he was a Hanover. And the Hanovers, of course, were traditionally fascist. Little has changed.

In any event it is the Hanovers who, in effect, still occupy the Throne. Queen Elizabeth II, for example, is the great-great-granddaughter of the German Prince Albert of Saxe-Coburg-Gotha and Queen Victoria (the last of the crowned Hanoverians). Her great-grandfather, the notorious King Edward VII, is effectively billed as the first - and last - of Britain's Saxe-Coburg monarchs. Although giving the lie to this is the fact that his son - King George V, the present Queen's grandfather - succeeded him, albeit the result of his brother's abdication. For reasons that will become all too apparent in just one moment, however, George V did not end his reign as a Saxe-Coburg, but as the first of the Windsor monarchs. The reason? The German name Saxe-Coburg had become something of an embarrassment - if not a downright affront to the British people - as British and German troops had fought bayonet-to-bayonet on the killing fields of World War I. Thus, on July 17, 1917, with the prospect of public outrage looming darkly over peace-time Britain, the German family name was duly (and somewhat conveniently, it has to be said) dropped. On that same day the House of Windsor was born.

But then, a thorn by any other name...

It should be said that such in-house royal politics as ignited hostilities across Europe - and then the world - in 1914, is not uncommon among the ruling classes, although World War I must surely be considered *the* prime example of this highborn dysfunction. The so-called Great War, in effect, was the result of several royal houses (or perhaps more accurately, several apartments within Europe's royal household, several royal cousins one-too-many times removed) unable to reconcile familial differences. Ultimately this resulted in the Habsburg Dynasty's heir apparent, Archduke Ferdinand of Austria, being assassinated, allegedly by a Bosnian Serb. (By whom in reality, of course, who knows?) But what is of interest is the fact that the Habsburgs and the Hanovers (the Saxe-Coburgs/Windsors), who went to war following the assassination, represent fingers on the same genealogical glove. As does the House of Hohenzollern, the ruling dynasty in Germany during WWI, at that time headed up by Kaiser Wilhelm II (1888-1918). Germany's Wilhelm II, of course, was Queen Victoria's great-nephew, King Edward VII's nephew and cousin to King George V, who ruled Britain during WWI. The millions of soldiers maimed and killed as a result of this war, on the other hand, bore no relation at all to the feuding cousins. But they were forced to give their lives for king and kaiser, just the same.

What began life as an in-house royal dispute, then, in the end turned rather more pernicious. Austria, so suddenly bereft of its Archduke Ferdinand, retaliated by declaring war on Serbia; and Germany, having declared war on Russia and France in response to Austria's lead, invaded neutral Belgium. In the face of global opinion, Britain (whose secret agents had lent a covert hand in the assassination of Ferdinand in the first place) was thus left with little choice but to declare war on Germany. So it did.

And so it is that the so-called Great War now adorns the annals of history.

It should be said at this point that, in terms of human life, World War I must surely be recognized as the most costly domestic struggle on record. At the now-famous Battle of the Somme alone, for example (1916) more than 420,000 British soldiers lost their lives in a futile attempt to heal the royal rift. Then again at the Battle of Passchendale (1917) 400,000. A year later (1918) the newly christened House of Windsor emerged unscathed. The deposed Habsburgs would live to fight another day.

From a brief but attentive study of history, then, it would certainly appear that dynastic warfare is almost a normality - if not a formality - within the ranks of the European nobility, the one house supplanting the next with regular aplomb. The House of Windsor, for example, is the ninth royal dynasty to rule over Britain since William the Conqueror and his Norman invaders supplanted the Saxons in 1066. One wonders if there might be a tenth. And if so, which of the current crop of surviving noble dynasties might attempt the coup. The reconstituted Habsburgs, perhaps? Or the still-powerful Stuarts?

This latter possibility is perhaps more feasible than it might at first seem, as we shall see.

The House Of Spencer

In many respects the House of Spencer lays a more legitimate claim to the British Throne than does the House of Windsor, though both can be traced back to the first Stuart monarch, King James I of England (1603-1625 - James VI of Scots from 1567). Beyond this the Stuart Dynasty can be traced back at least as far as Robert II of Scots, who reigned from 1371-1390. Indeed, via the Celtic High Kings of Scots and Ireland, certain noble families in what is today France, and the Merovingian Kings of Dark Ages Europe, the Stuart bloodline can be traced back both to Jesus, and to Jesus's brother, James. In turn Jesus and James are known to have been the bloodline descendants of Kings Solomon and David of Israel (circa 1000 BC). While the Windsors are largely descended from a politically cultivated strain of this Judaic royal bloodline - a strain created by the Church of Rome on the one hand (circa 754 AD), and by the marriages of Jewish exiles and German noble families on the other (circa 800 BC) - the Spencers are said to be the direct lineal descendants of the conjoined bloodlines of the brothers Jesus and James. Of course, this is a highly contentious claim which has provoked no small reaction from the Church of Rome and the Church of England alike, both of whom flatly refuse to acknowledge - at least publicly - the genealogical documentation recently unearthed from the vaults of the Celtic Church. It is also an argument into which we need not enter in the course of our investigation. The point so far as we are concerned is not which of the two houses - that of Windsor or Spencer - is most closely related to Jesus. Rather the point is that *both* are descended from this Judaic royal bloodline. And that the perpetuation of that bloodline today in the House of Windsor, and its influence on present-day masonic politics, is in some way related to the motive behind Princess Diana's death. This is the sole reason we are obliged to include the fiercely contested 'bloodline of Jesus' theory in our investigation.

In any event, the only link that the Windsors can claim with regard to the legitimate, Merovingian strain of this bloodline, is that King James I's daughter Elizabeth married Frederick of Bohemia, and their daughter Sophia in turn married the German Elector, Ernst August of Hanover. It was the son of Sophia and Ernst August, George, who in 1714 was installed on the Throne of Britain by the Anglo-Dutch financial oligarchy responsible for establishing the Bank of England (see *Chapter Fifteen*). It is from this extremely tenuous and politically based link that the Windsors have descended, and by which they lay claim to the British Throne today. They are nonetheless of ancient Judaeo-Teuton stock.

The Spencers, on the other hand, are the direct lineal descendants of King Charles (Stuart) I of England (1625-1649), and their English heritage dates back even further than that. Indeed, so far as can be traced, the less-tainted, less-tangled Spencer family roots bury themselves in the Norman conquest of ancient Britain, which of course dates back to the eleventh century AD - to the year 1066, the days of Kings Harold II and William I, best known as William the Conqueror. It was during this darkly emergent period that the first of the truly English Spencers began to acquire their fabulous wealth. And their equally notable station. This they achieved by the acquisition of land, property and vast numbers of sheep, together with carefully manoeuvred marriages to some of the most eligible heiresses in Britain and Europe. With the acquisition of such wealth and station, of course, came titular endowment and authority.

By 1506 the Spencers' fortune was increasing still, and considerably so. It was in this year, for example, that Sir John Spencer acquired the impressive country estate which had been leased by his uncle from the Abbot of Evesham twenty years earlier, in 1486. Today this acquisition is recognized the world over as the Spencer family estate at Althorp, Northamptonshire - where Diana was finally laid to rest. Over successive generations the estate was improved upon and even further enlarged; so much so that by 1603 it could finally be said to have arrived on the map of royal association. For it was during this year that Baron Spencer of Wormleighton played host to Queen Anne of Denmark, consort to King James Stuart I. Queen Anne was reportedly *en route* from Scotland to join the King in London, when she interrupted her journey to attend a masque written by the acclaimed British playwright, Ben Johnson, in honour of her visit. The Queen was accompanied by her eldest son, Henry, soon-to-be invested as the 10th Prince of Wales, though never to be crowned king. He would die at the age of nineteen while his father still occupied the throne.

Some years later another Henry, the eldest son of the 2nd Baron Spencer, was to claim an unique place in British history. Though his life was to be cut cruelly short, it was nevertheless to prove quite remarkable. At sixteen years of age, for example, Henry inherited the title of 3rd Baron Spencer. Three years later he married the renowned Lady Dorothy Sidney and, soon thereafter, became the Lord Lieutenant of Northamptonshire. But even more notable was the fact that, when King Charles I raised his standard in Nottingham in August 1642, at the start of the English Civil War, it was the newly invested Lord Henry Spencer who financed the Stuart king's campaign against the Parliamentarian forces to the tune of £10,000 - a princely sum in 1642. He did not go unrewarded. In June 1643 he was made Earl of Sunderland. A few months after that, however, at the age of twenty-three, Henry the first Earl Spencer was killed in battle - at the Battle of Newbury - fighting for a heritage and an institution in which he fervently believed: the survival of the Stuart bloodline and its ascendancy on the British Throne.

But if Henry Spencer lived an extraordinary life - albeit a fast, a furious and an all-too-brief one - his eldest son Robert, the 2nd Earl Spencer of Sunderland, was to emerge even more noteworthy.

It was undoubtedly Robert who, quite irrevocably, sealed the ancestral alliance which still exists between the Spencers and the royal succession. Known as a man of his time, Robert, 2nd Earl of Sunderland, it is said, bore few airs. Even fewer scruples. He was reputedly an adept strategist, availing his talents in the service of three successive kings, two of the House of Stuart - King Charles II and King James II - and the third King William III of Orange. Notably, in 1677 the Dutch Stadtholder William had conveniently married Queen Mary II Stuart in preparation to usurp the English Throne from the Stuarts. In consequence - again in conspiracy with the Whigs (Britain's landed elite) and the Dutch Staats-General - in 1689 William successfully ousted James II and claimed the Throne for himself. From 1689-1702, William

III of Orange and Mary II Stuart thus occupied the throne jointly, James II having escaped to France - to St Germain-en-Laye, near Paris - where he lived out his life in exile.

During this time the Whigs (to whom William owed his seat of power) beavered away behind the scenes preparing the ground for the completion of their royal *coup d'etat* - which gained further momentum in 1702 with the death of William and the succession of Mary's sister, Anne. Although of Stuart descent, Queen Anne herself had conspired both with William and the Whig oligarchs in their endeavour to supplant the Stuart Dynasty with the German House of Hanover. Whether Anne's collusion had been self-determined - or not - is debatable: the inquirer is left to read between the lines. What is of note is that, having conceived no less than eighteen times, but having given birth to only five still-living children, all of whom died in infancy or childhood (some say suspiciously); and having thus produced no surviving heirs to the throne, Queen Anne was left with little choice but to comply with Whig demands. She thus duly nominated Sophia, Electress of Hanover, as her successor. The fact that Anne survived Sophia, however, meant that Sophia's son, George, succeeded to the throne in 1714.

In the meantime, in 1705 the Whig Parliament had passed what it termed the *Alien Act*, which in effect forced the Scots to accept Anne's nominated successor in place of Britain's *de jure* successor, James III Stuart. Simply put, the *Alien Act* decreed that the Scots either accept the Hanovers as their future monarchy or face economic sanctions, trade embargos and, ultimately, military invasion. The Scots, who wanted James Stuart as their king, had little choice but to agree. In consequence, in May 1707 the Whigs dissolved the Scottish Parliament and the United Kingdom was born (albeit by Caesarean section). On the death of Queen Anne in 1714 the Whig oligarchy completed its royal *coup d'etat* by installing the puppet Hanovers on the newly formed Throne of Britain. And despite Jacobite efforts to the contrary, thus it has remained to this day.

Of further note is the fact that, in 1693, the Dutch William III of Orange, having gained possession of the throne in conspiracy with the Whig/Dutch-financier alliance, established what would come to be known as the central banking system. This he achieved by chartering the Bank of England and initiating what is today known as the National Debt - a sort of mythical collective overdraft manipulated by corporate godfathers to the glee of successive governments and the utter bewilderment of everybody else. By borrowing £1,000,000 (from the Anglo-Dutch financial oligarchy which had put him on the Throne, and which from this point on would control Parliament via its controlling share in the Bank of England) at an interest rate of 10%, the deed was done. And in relative terms, so it remains. And what is more, it was rumoured to have been, at least in part, the brainchild of Robert Spencer, 2nd Earl of Sunderland.

But it wasn't only the world of high finance in which Robert Spencer's talents came to the fore. He also achieved considerable notoriety in the field of politics, achieving no less status than Secretary of State, Foreign Ambassador (to Paris, Cologne and Madrid), Lord Chamberlain, Lord President of the Council and - his *piece de resistance* - Knight of the Most Noble Order of the Garter. He was the first of the Spencers to attain this eminent title.

As perhaps befitting a man of such elevated social and political station, however, Robert Spencer is said to have enjoyed a somewhat exuberant lifestyle. His love of the arts, French landscape and Italian architecture in particular have been elaborately recorded (perhaps understandably, his excessive taste for rather more carnal pursuits has not). Indeed, a famous Italian architect was hired by the earl to redesign both the interior *and* the exterior of the house at Althorp, while the landscape artist who designed the famous gardens at Versailles, *Le Notre*, was brought to England to renovate the estate's eight and a half thousand acres of parkland. The estate's most famous acquisition in this regard were the several avenues of Dutch elm (later destroyed by the plague of Dutch elm disease which ravaged Britain's tree population during the 1970s). The cost of the renovations were said to be enormous, and were thus seen as a symbol of the family's ever-increasing accumulation of wealth. And it did not end there.

Robert Spencer was succeeded by several further generations of equally successful heirs - heirs to a bloodline quickened by such good fortune as he himself had enjoyed. And thus the Spencer family continued to prosper. The 3rd Earl Spencer of Sunderland, for example, entered politics at an early age, becoming a Whig politician who, like his father before him, ascended to the rank of Lord President of the Council. He later became First Lord of the Treasury - which in today's terms might be compared to, say, the Chancellor of the Exchequer, or even the Prime Minister - and so took control of the so-called National Debt. Circles within circles. Some two generations later the 5th Earl, Charles, inherited by special patent the fabulous Blenheim Palace (later the birthplace of Sir Winston Churchill) the title of 3rd Duke of Marlborough to boot. At the same time his younger brother, the Hon. John Spencer, as well as inheriting Althorp Park, received an enormous legacy in money, property, paintings and horses on the death of his affluent - and no less *puissant* - grandmother, Sarah Jennings, Dowager Duchess of Marlborough. Indeed, it was Sarah Jennings who would, prior to her death, first introduce to the world the name of Lady Diana Spencer.

As we know, in 1735 the House of Stuart no longer sat upon the

Throne of Britain; some twenty-one years earlier the Throne had been usurped by a joint Whig/Dutch-financier/Hanover plot. Thus, in place of the deposed Stuarts sat the German (Judaeo-Teuton) House of Hanover, direct bloodline antecedent to the present royal dynasty, the House of Windsor. At that time the Prince of Wales was one Frederick of Hanover, eldest son of George II. Like his titlesake down the ages (in particular those produced by the debauched Hanoverian dynasty), this particular Prince of Wales was not averse to excessive merrymaking and the spending of substantial royal funds (provided, of course, then as now, and as always, by the British taxpayer). This latter pastime, in fact, Frederick had achieved with some aplomb. Indeed, by 1735 he had accumulated debts rather more considerable than the British taxpayer could readily underwrite. He needed help.

Enter the Dowager Duchess, Sarah Jennings, grandmother of the Hon. John Spencer and of John's younger sister, Lady Diana Spencer. Seizing the moment - and the opportunity - the Dowager Duchess secretly arranged for the betrothal of her granddaughter to the positively errant Prince of Wales. This she achieved by providing a dowry of some £100,000, a fortune to be sure; indeed, one vastly sufficient even to service the Prince of Wales's somewhat compromising financial predicament. Frederick had little choice but to accept the offer. Secretly, the deal was agreed. Lady Diana Spencer would become Diana, Princess of Wales. And on Frederick's accession to the throne, of course, she would become Queen Diana I of England.

But it was not to be. At the last minute politics stepped in and rearranged the wedding plans. Government agents caught wind of the plan; the secret had leaked out. And before long it had made its way back to Britain's Lord of the Treasury and Whig oligarch, Sir Robert Walpole (recognized as Britain's first effective Prime Minister). Fearing some royal *coup d'etat*, Walpole immediately informed the king, who for reasons best known to backstairs political requirement agreed that the wedding should not go ahead. Indeed, he *decreed* that the wedding should not go ahead. In its stead the two co-conspirators - King George II of Hanover and Sir Robert Walpole, leader of the landowner-controlled Whig Party to whom the Hanovers owed the British Throne - arranged for Lady Diana Spencer to marry the Duke of Bedford, thus preventing her from becoming the first Spencer to acquire the title of Princess of Wales. At the same time, of course, this manoeuvre ensured that the British royal bloodline - by now well-steeped in the Germanic/Judaic heritage of Hanover - would become further vitiated towards this end. Thus in April 1736, at the express behest of Robert Walpole and his Anglo/Dutch-controlled Whig Parliament, Frederick, Prince of Wales, duly married the German Princess Augusta of Saxe-Gotha, Queen Victoria's great-grandmother. And thus the way was paved for the coming of the Windsor

Dynasty.

Which in truth, it has to be said, is no more British than the Mercedes in which Diana was killed.

The Cultivation Of Grapevines

As can be deduced from the above, then, the European nobility - from which the House of Windsor descends - is something of a mixed cauldron, to say the least. But it is essentially Judaeo-Teuton.

Not that this in itself is crucial, of course, at least not in any cultural, racial or, indeed, literal sense. (Indeed, we should emphasize here that any references to Germanic and/or Judaic bloodlines are meant only in a political sense.) What does matter, though, is the manner in which these bloodlines have, over many centuries, been both politically and artificially cultured, grafted together in order that the ostensible power thereby engendered - the misappropriated power and authority invested in, and enjoyed by, said nobility - may be used to political ends. This generation of 'power as currency', achieved by the manipulation of so-called royal bloodlines, is known in the higher, secretive echelons of masonic government as the science of viticulture (literally: *the cultivation of grapevines*). For centuries this science has been employed from behind the scenes to ensure the perpetuation of a false, symbolic or politically cultivated bloodline. The reason?

Because today that false bloodline provides an ostensibly secure power base upon whose authority British and US political supremacy is founded. It is thus perceived as an agent for political and economic ascendancy in the so-called modern world. It is a political bloodline, or as our Foreign Office (MI6) source phrased it: "...in effect we are talking about the political Holy Grail."

(The significance of the Holy Grail with regard to this bloodline will become more evident as our 'bloodline inquiry' progresses. Indeed, it will be seen to make the difference between the so-called "bloodline monarchies" and "usurper monarchies" alluded to by our Foreign Office source. And what is more, it will also play a major role in defining the motives behind the alleged assassination of Diana, Princess of Wales, as we shall see.)

Created as long ago as the eighth and ninth centuries AD, then, this false bloodline has for more than a millennium served to uphold usurper monarchies and governments in both Europe and the US. It was created when the once-great Merovingian Royal Dynasty in France was deposed and supplanted (by papal decree): first by the upstart Pepin III, heir to the Church-sponsored dynasty known as the Carolingians; then by the Holy Roman Empire itself, headed up by Charlemagne. Indeed, ever since AD 754, when the Church of Rome suddenly conferred power upon itself sufficient to create monarchs, this false or symbolic bloodline has been nurtured and cultivated, like some terrible secret, and perpetuated by a very long series of papal and other quasi-religious manoeuvres and behind-the-scenes political chicaneries. The result is a masonic power cabal sufficiently influential that, in effect, it governs the Western world. And the so-called House of Windsor, of course, is this power cabal's titular head.

As we have seen, and in effect, the Western world today is governed not by a federation of democratically elected nation-state governments. But by a backstairs British/US oligarchy which is corporately based, and whose political power depends on masonic structure, ritual and symbol. And on the fruits of a political conspiracy which has its roots in Dark Ages Europe. Hugely powerful institutions such as the Holy Roman Church, the Anglican Church, the Monarchy, plus the highest, most secretive echelons of Royal Arch Masonry and the British Establishment (and any number of other highly secretive political and corporate agencies operating within the web of religio-masonic influence) - all are structured on the edifice of masonic government. Moreover, all have played their part in the perpetration of this centuries-old royal and political conspiracy. It is a conspiracy which has, in effect, dictated the course of political and monarchical ascendancy for so long that today it has become an institution in its own right. Yet it has been so ingeniously crafted, so masterfully concealed, so stealthily established, that very few are even aware of its existence, much less its influence upon the course of their lives. Their minds. And therein lies its greatest, most insidious efficacy.

The simple fact that we are dealing with something which has become so insidiously ingrained on our personal and collective psyche - what Carl Jung described as our subconscious - means that the conspiracy can now be played out in front of our eyes and not be seen, only its shadow, which of course bears the same semblance, the same effect. The symbol and the manifestation, the dream and the reality - both have come to mean the same lie. The so-called 'royals', like other figures of authority, represent such powerful archetypes to our collective and personal subconscious that we automatically respond to the hierarchy they represent. They embody such evocative symbols in the various realms of our personal psychology that, in the end, the characters - Philip, Elizabeth, Charles, Diana - they become almost interchangeable, certainly disposable. It is not Charles or Diana we are mesmerized by; it is the Prince and the Princess of Wales. It is not the reality of monarchy which so compels us; it is the fairy tale, the mystique. It is not John Paul, but the Pope; not Bill Clinton, but the President. In short, it is not the individuals playing the roles but the roles themselves which effect such deep psychological responses within us. And those appointing the characters to office - those grafting the vines and mixing the blood - are well aware of this fact. Thus they are able to maintain control over the socio-political structures endemic to the so-called free world.

However, it should also be said that, every now and then, something (or someone) comes along who gives the lie to this seeming truism, someone like Diana perhaps, a genetic anomaly, a genetic throwback to the politically untainted, messianic bloodline from which the House of Spencer descends. After all, the science of viticulture states that, every now and then, and for no apparent reason, a genetic anomaly is indeed produced - a vintage wine is indeed crafted from the seeds of previous generations. It is the same principle at work. Every now and then something moves beneath the surface of the water, causing ripples. As if from nowhere it simply arrives, this something (this someone), this beautiful virus, and threatens to expose the game: threatens to challenge the wisdom of the unholy blood and overturn the balance of power. Worse: it threatens to capsize the very status quo. Shockwaves are felt in the corridors of power and measures are therein taken to prevent this virus from spreading its influence. Quite often those measures are extreme, as history attests. Indeed, quite often they result in assassination, as we shall see.

But first we must turn our attention to the ancient root of this vine, and to perhaps the most famous, the most renowned, the most revered of all genetic anomalies. The most vintage of all vintage wines. The claim, after all, is that this Judaic royal bloodline has its roots in no less a figure than Jesus Christ. Or at least that Jesus was a genetic model spawned from this same royal bloodline, this same messianic vine. If this claim above others can be substantiated, of course, then the implications regarding the so-called 'bloodline conspiracy' begin to assume new proportions entirely. Regardless of religious bias, one cannot deny that Jesus fulfilled all the above criteria. Unlike, say, the monarchs of the Hanoverian bloodline, Jesus did indeed threaten to 'expose the game'. He did indeed challenge the wisdom of those in authority. He did indeed threaten to capsize the status quo, and in consequence was executed for his trouble. Not that we are endeavouring to pigeonhole Diana in the same category as Jesus Christ the myth. But in an historical context the similarities are evident enough. Though the assassination of Diana is yet to be proven, nevertheless that she threatened the establishment in much the same way as others of her own ancestry - the Stuart Kings, the Merovingian Kings, Jesus - is clearly evident. And in any event, that Jesus was a bloodline king of the Royal House of Judah remains a case to be proven.

CHAPTER 13

JESUS
And The Royal House Of Judah

"A table of the descent of Jesus Christ, son of David, son of
Abraham.
Abraham was the father of Isaac, Isaac of Jacob, Jacob of Judah and
his brothers, Judah of ... Obed (his mother was Ruth), Obed of
Jesse; and Jesse was the father of King David.
"David was the father of Solomon ... Solomon of Rehoboam,
Rehoboam of Abijah, Abijah of ... Manasseh, Manasseh of Amon,
Amon of Josiah; and Josiah was the father of Jeconiah and his
brothers at the time of the deportation to Babylon.
"After the deportation Jeconiah was the father of Shealtiel,
Shealtiel of Zerubbabel, Zerubbabel of ... Eleazar, Eleazar of
Matthan, Matthan of Jacob, Jacob of Joseph, the husband of Mary,
who gave birth to Jesus called Messiah.
"There were thus fourteen generations in all from Abraham to
David, fourteen from David until the deportation to Babylon, and
fourteen from the deportation until the Messiah."

Matthew 1:1-17.

Bloodline Of Judah

Over the past couple of decades, a plethora of material has emerged in support of the probability that the historical Jesus was a true blood line king of Israel. It is not a new idea. Because so much has already been penned in this regard, we will keep what we have to say here to an absolute minimum, and refer the reader to the many available works by other authors for further information. The reason that we have elected to include even this much here is simply to remind the reader of the vast body of evidence which is now available. After all, if it can indeed be shown that Jesus was the rightful bloodline heir to the Royal House of Judah - and thereby the *de jure* heir apparent to the Throne of Israel - then the implications with regard to our own 'bloodline investigation' assume even greater proportion than that already attained. That said, it should be remembered that our own investigation does not at all depend on the verification of claims that Jesus was a king. Neither does it depend on the authenticity or otherwise of his alleged divine status.

However, in terms of present-day masonic government and its seeming dependence on the authority of the Judah bloodline, what *is* of significance is the very real possibility that said bloodline might even now carry Jesus's genes - either literally or symbolically. Or both. And either way, the inference is that Jesus was married, and that he sired children who themselves became heirs to the same royal bloodline which included Kings David and Solomon before them. Further, that the descendants of these heirs emerged during the so-called Dark Ages as the most prolific ruling dynasty in Western Europe, the Merovingian Dynasty; that, via the Celtic Royal Houses of Dunkeld and Stewart (later Stuart), the messianic strain of this same royal bloodline not only survived, but prospered - first in Ireland, then Scotland, and finally in England; that a politically engineered strain of this same royal bloodline was created, cultivated and employed by Rome for purposes of political and economic ascendancy (later procured by the corporate and masonic bodies currently striving for the centralization of political and economic power in the West); and that the House of Windsor is today the most influential product of this 'usurper strain' - indeed, that it is its titular head.

And that, because it is, the Princess of Wales is no longer alive.

If our hypothesis is to stand on its own in this regard, then it must at least be shown that the bloodline still exists, and that it still possesses the same potential for achieving political power today as it did at the height of its legitimate ascendancy - say, during the reigns of Kings David and Solomon. In order to achieve this, of course, then so far as is possible said bloodline must be traced back to its roots, and then back again to the present day. If Jesus was indeed at some time heir apparent to this messianic bloodline then he too must be included in our investigation. Indeed, he above all others. After all, though the bloodline itself must remain the prize (with or without Jesus) what greater prize to possess than that born of the seed of Jesus? What greater tool for tilling political favour? What greater asset for gaining political power? And moreover, what greater motive for seeking to keep that bloodline 'pure' - free from outside influences? Arab-Muslim influences?

That Jesus was a legitimate bloodline king of the Royal House of Judah, that he was married and that he sired children is today considered a very plausible historical fact. That this fact may bear direct relevance to the death of Diana, Princess of Wales, cannot be sidestepped. Nor can it be swept under the carpet in one's endeavour to cause the least possible backlash. And neither can it simply be ignored. On the contrary, if our investigation is to be seen as a vigorous and a thorough one, then it must be explored in full.

This, then, is the sole reason behind our decision to include this chapter here.

The Son Of God
And The P2 Scandal

Whatever one's own religious convictions, it would surely be remiss of any one of us to simply ignore the evidence. That the story of Jesus as depicted in the four Gospels included in the New Testament is largely a fiction, for example - or at best a dramatically revised version of original accounts - is today supported by a vast body of historical documentation, as well as by an equally vast body of thoroughly researched and wholly credible evidence. This fact is now widely accepted. More than this: it is proven history. Though it may well be difficult for many committed Christians to accept that the very belief system in which they have invested so much was formulated, first and foremost, for its political usefulness, the plain fact of the matter is that the evidence now outweighs the myth. Of course, social conditioning in this regard will always make it difficult to break free of the accepted creeds and dogmas which conspire to shape any one person's reality. But the evidence is there just the same.

In the Gospel of Matthew, for example (1: 1-17) "a table of the descent of Jesus Christ, son of David, son of Abraham" is clearly presented. It states quite unequivocally that Jesus was indeed the patrilineal descendant of Kings David and Solomon - of Abraham, Jacob and Judah before that. In consequence, Jesus is identified in the Gospel of Matthew as "Jesus called Messiah". In other words, he is identified as Israel's true bloodline king of the House of Judah, and not - as the later Church of Rome would insist - the "Son of God". On the contrary, this appellation did not obtain until some centuries later, and was largely the product of a series of Church councils convened during the third and fourth centuries AD (culminating with the Council of Nicaea, AD 325). These councils were convened in order to formulate the creeds and dogmas which would come to be known as Roman Catholicism. It was during these councils, for example, that many of the original texts depicting the life of Jesus were either modified (some rather drastically), re-written or simply discarded. Which was odd. Unlike the four Gospels included in the Bible, many of these so-called 'apocryphal' texts had been penned by those who had actually lived and worked with Jesus. Many others contained the teachings and philosophies to which Jesus himself had adhered. Indeed, those he had espoused. Even so, the Church in its wisdom elected to draw from the largely Pauline texts in its possession - texts which had been compiled many decades after Jesus's death; texts which deviated greatly from the original Nazarene teachings adhered to by Jesus; texts which proclaimed Jesus the "Son of God" and taught salvation through him and through him only. In short, the Essene/Nazarene philosophy adhered to and espoused by Jesus and his closest followers was, quite simply, dispensed with. In its place the Church elected to adopt its own largely unrelated canon based on the fanatical and wholly distorted interpretations of St Paul. In our opinion, there can be only one motive for such a manoeuvre. And it is this.

By turning this first-century Jewish folk hero into a Son of God - by claiming he was born of the Church-invented 'Holy Spirit' and attributing him with miracles which included raising people from the dead (indeed, being raised from the dead himself); and further, by proclaiming itself the legitimate guardian of this folk hero's 'divine' legacy on Earth - Rome was thus able to preserve (some would say salvage) its increasingly floundering empire. By establishing a new religio-political administration the Church Fathers were able to replace the obsolescent military-controlled empire with a Church-controlled one. It was a ploy that worked. For the next millennium and more the so-called Holy Roman Church would become the most powerful political seat in Europe and the Americas, sponsoring and creating as many 'democratic' governments and 'usurper' monarchies as was necessary to maintain political dominion. And so it remains today. Though cloaked in the pseudo-pious attire of pomp and pelf, as flaunted by bishops and cardinals alike (indeed, by the Pope himself), the Vatican continues to maintain its political posture in terms of latter-day masonic government. It is no secret, for example, that the venerated Church of Rome has latterly entered itself into the world of illegal finance, corporate power-mongering and organized crime (as alluded to in *Chapter Eight: The CIA And The Bid To Unite Europe*). And, of course, the covert manipulation of politics and politicians worldwide.

Indeed, this much - and more - was brought to light in what became known as the 'P2 Scandal', which involved the murder of a Pope (John Paul I, found dead in the early hours of September 29th, 1978) and investigations into gross irregularities at the Vatican Bank. Also highlighted at this time was the Vatican's involvement with P2, a highly illegal, CIA/Mafia-controlled 'masonic lodge' which included among its members more than 100 Vatican-based cardinals and priests. It should be remembered here that Canon Law forbids any practising Catholic to be a Freemason; indeed, to be a Freemason is to evoke immediate and automatic excommunication from the Church. Yet the Vatican was (in 1978) crawling with Freemasons, from the lowliest priest to the highest echelons of papal power. It still is. And what makes this situation even more sinister is the fact that the so-called 'masonic lodge' to which these Vatican hierarchs belonged, P2 (*Propaganda Due*), had little to do with orthodox Freemasonry. Rather it was, and still is, an illegally run and highly secretive international 'fix-it' organization comprising more than 2000 members worldwide. Of these, 300 have been described as "the most powerful men in ... the free world", and include among their number high-level politicians, military and intelligence chiefs, financiers, industrialists, academics, media owners and their editors, corporate and Mafia godfathers - plus, of course, some of the highest ranking cardinals in Rome. According to former intelligence agent, Dr John Coleman, these 300 P2 members comprise what is known as the "Committee of 300". Others know this same elite body as the Policy Committee, the overseeing body of policy-makers central to the Bilderberg Group (to be distinguished from the Bilderberg Group's so-called Steering Committee). But by whatever name, it is reported that, in effect, this 'Committee' controls just about every political and economic laundry in the Western world. As well as in the Third World and in many Second World countries also. At the Vatican, it seems (the official state-entity representing Jesus on Earth) God has become big business. Dirty business.

It should be said here that, considering the true motives and agendas which conspired to bring about the formation of the Church in the first place, this situation is perhaps nothing less than should be expected. Such had the Vatican's secular power been eroded by the turn of the twentieth century, for example, that, of political necessity, some pretty drastic measures had to be taken. And in light of the fact that papal power seems once again to be prospering, said drastic measures would appear to have worked. Since the ratification of the Lateran Treaty in 1929, for example, which officially established Vatican City as a Sovereign State (and thereby the Pope as a recognized Head of State), the Holy Roman Church has chosen to sleep with bed partners its faithful would rather it had not slept with. As well as receiving vast amounts of funding from German and Swiss Nazis, both during and after WWII, and involving itself in the world of masonic politics - crime, corruption, murder - the Vatican has reinvested vast sums of money in companies which produce, among other things, condoms and birth-control pills. And this despite the fact that all forms of contraception are forbidden to the Catholic masses. One rule for the shepherd, another for the flock. Hypocrisy, it would seem, breeds swiftly among the pious.

The point so far as we are concerned, then, is the wholly unquestionable fact that the Vatican is, quite simply, corrupt. It is dishonest, fraudulent and unprincipled. It tells lies and it is involved in high-level conspiracies and cover-ups. It boasts close ties with MI6, the CIA and the godfathers of organized crime. Some of its highest ranking officials are known Freemasons. Most of these are members of P2. It murders its own when its own refuses to tow the party line, and has done for centuries (and like the European nobility, it is not deterred by rank in this regard - in September

1978, remember, Pope John Paul I was murdered only 33 days after his election to office, and all because he dared to challenge those responsible for the Vatican's highly irregular financial affairs and the Church's direct involvement with the deadly P2 cabal). Moreover, it has for centuries promulgated a false history and a manufactured religion in order to gain political influence.

In the final analysis, the official Vatican version of Jesus - the Galilean carpenter; the miracle worker; the Son of God - must be perceived as highly questionable, to say the least. Certainly it should be perceived against the agendas and sub-agendas which conspired to create the Vatican in the first place. For it is those same agendas which conspired not to create a seat of learning, wisdom, justice, compassion (in accord with the Nazarene tradition as taught by Jesus). But to create the most powerful religio-political seat in the Western world. For this reason alone the Vatican version of Jesus must surely be seen for what it is: a politically inspired myth. Or at best a gross revision of Jesus's life and status for purposes of political gain.

And either way, this version is flawed. To our mind it carries about as much weight as a sack of plucked feathers.

King Of The Jews

If, then, Jesus was *not* the infallible, heaven-sent miracle worker we have always been led to believe - who was he? What was his social status and why does half the world still venerate him? Moreover, in stark contrast with Jesus himself, why does his 'chosen' body of representatives on Earth enjoy power and privilege to the point of obscenity when so many of his flock can scarcely afford to eat? Something somewhere simply does not add up.

According to our Foreign Office (MI6) source, of course, Jesus was the rightful bloodline King of Israel who, in or around the year AD 36, led his people in a military campaign against Rome. Our source reached this conclusion, he said, as a result of being privy to certain records and documents currently in the hands of MI6. He also said that the "uprising", for reasons which are self-evident, had subsequently been erased from the annals of traditional history. From the documents he had seen our source surmised that Jesus - or King Yeshua, as he referred to him - had been an integral part of some revolutionary force or army which had taken control of Jerusalem on Palm Sunday, approximately one week prior to the most famous execution in history: the Crucifixion. He surmised that Jesus himself had led this army to victory, and that this was the reason that Rome had ordered his execution.

But what evidence is there to support such a seemingly outrageous claim? After all, though many people are now aware of these relatively new perspectives on the life and status of Jesus, he is nevertheless still venerated by countless millions worldwide. He is still perceived by the vast majority of Christians as God's only son, the miracle-working saviour promulgated by the Church of Rome. Are we then not playing with fire here? Are we not guilty of transgressing some immutable divine law by questioning the Church's copyright on the image and status of Jesus? On the other hand, do we not have the right to question this dogma? Did Jesus himself not question the established creed of his time, and those who sought to defend it?

Accordingly, do we not have the right to suspect the motives of such a politically motivated and morally corrupt organization as the Vatican?

In view of the vast body of highly credible evidence now available, in particular its implications regarding the usurpation and manipulation of the Judaic royal bloodline for political purposes today, it has to be said that, *yes,* we believe we do have the right to question. After all, we are not only concerned with the salvation of souls here; we are concerned with the issue of socio-political control. And for those thus inclined, with spiritual control, too. We are concerned with the manipulation and oppression of countless millions worldwide who are simply too frightened to question the creeds and dogmas which uphold their private belief systems. This is of course understandable. So many have invested so much in the official story it is little wonder they are reluctant to listen to a new one, even though this new one might just bring them a little closer to the historical truth. That the powers-that-be do not want the historical truth published, of course, is evident in their - so far successful -attempts to conceal it. But whatever one's predilection in this regard, in the final analysis the evidence is there to be had. And it tends to reveal a very different Jesus to the one promulgated by Rome.

Certainly if we are to take the Gospels at face value - if we are to view them in terms of their historical and cultural significance, and without religious bias - there can be little doubt as to Jesus's royal ancestry. Indeed, the Gospels make no bones about the fact that Jesus was both recognized and treated as heir apparent by his contemporaries, both Roman and Jew alike. He was often referred to directly and specifically as the "Son of David", for example, which, in first-century Judean-speak, of course, meant that he was recognized as the *de jure* King of Israel, or 'Messiah'. Or at least as the *de jure* heir to Israel's deposed House of Judah, and thus to Israel's occupied throne. In this regard, Jesus would have occupied much the same position as, say, Britain's *de jure* King Charles III Stuart, best known as Bonnie Prince Charlie (1720-1788). Though it may well be difficult for some to accept such a comparison, nevertheless in an historical context, and despite Jesus's alleged divine status, it is justified in that both were *de jure* kings whose thrones had been usurped - the one by political conspiracy, the other by military occupation.

Britain, remember, had been hijacked by a joint Whig/Hanover alliance, in much the same way as Israel, at the time of Jesus, had been conquered by a joint Rome/Herod alliance. In consequence of the Whig/Hanover alliance, Charles Stuart had been forced to live much of *his* life in exile, in France, as indeed Jesus had been forced to live much of his life in effective exile, in the hills, in the desert, in secret. And there are other similarities. As Charles had been forced to take up arms in his endeavour to recapture the British Throne from the puppet Hanovers, for example (the Jacobite uprising of 1745), Jesus would have been forced to strike a similar posture in his endeavour to recapture the Jewish Throne from the puppet Herods. It is inconceivable to imagine that the historical Jews would have supported Jesus in any other light. Moreover, as Charles had been forced to face the might of the Hanovers' sponsors (the formidable military forces of Britain's landowner class) in his quest to regain the throne, so Jesus would have been forced to face the might of the Herods' sponsors, the even more formidable military forces of Rome, as we shall see. Indeed, according to our source (and many leading historians and scholars today) this is precisely the situation in which Jesus would have found himself in his position as *de jure* king. It is worth noting here that the Jewish populace at this time was suffering from what can only be described as a major epidemic - an epidemic which might be termed 'messianic fever'. Unlike the Church's interpretation of this term, however - that the Jews were waiting for God to send his only son - history tends to compare this 'epidemic' to the Jacobite movement of early eighteenth-century Britain. In other words, as many English and Scots desired the return of their *de jure* monarchy (the Stuarts) on the Throne of Britain, so many Jews likewise desired the return of their *de jure* monarchy (the House of Judah) on the Throne of Israel. Having emerged from the Celtic High Kings of Ireland and Scots, the Stuarts were seen by the British people as rightful heirs to the throne 'by divine right'. Similarities with Israel's House of Judah in this regard are thus self-evident. Indeed, the growing army of Jewish militants, the so-called Zealots - many of whom were numbered among Jesus's closest followers, as we shall see - had organized themselves for the very purpose of ousting the Roman occupiers and supplanting the puppet Herods with the *de jure* "Son of David" - or Jesus, heir apparent to the deposed House of Judah. And at any rate, this historically founded depiction of events is surely far more realistic than the intellectually impotent myth promulgated by Rome. It is an honest depiction consistent with both anthropological and geopolitical history. And of course, unlike the biblical account - penned by the Church of Rome some three centuries after the event - it is bereft of political agenda.

Further evidence of Jesus's royal status can be found in the account of his confrontation with the Roman Procurator, Pontius Pilate, which occurred immediately prior to his crucifixion (circa AD 33-36). Here we find quite unequivocally that Jesus is to be crucified for the crime of sedition, and not blasphemy (indeed, crucifixion was reserved for crimes against Rome, not God). In the Gospel of John, for example (19: 19-22), Jesus is clearly and quite unmistakably addressed, not as 'rabbi', but as "King of the Jews". Again, in an historical context, this can only be understood as an official title, much the same as that still worn by, say, Albert, King of Belgium, whose official title, even today, is 'King of the Belgians'. In ancient Europe, of course, such appellations were common - 'King of the Picts', for example, 'King of the Britons', 'King of the Franks', 'King of the Gaels'. Or, indeed, 'King of the Jews'. Indeed, a more modern translation of this same title would read, quite simply, 'King of Judah'. Or 'King of Judea'. In much the same way as the title 'Messiah' has been mistranslated down the ages due to its origins in antiquity, so the title 'King of the Jews' has likewise been misunderstood. In this regard, there is absolutely no plausible reason why Pilate would have referred to Jesus as "King of the Jews" - unless, of course, Jesus *was* King of the Jews. And neither was there reason sufficient for Pilate to have condemned Jesus to death by crucifixion - unless, of course, Jesus had become a considerable threat to the socio-political stability of the Roman province of Judea. Indeed, if Jesus truly had been found guilty of blasphemy (as claimed in the Bible) then at worst he would have faced the punishment of stoning to death. And this punishment, in accord with Roman Law, would have been determined and administered by the Jewish Sanhedrin, not the Roman Prefecture. In the event, of course, it was the Roman Procurator of Judea, Pontius Pilate, who determined Jesus's fate. (The story of Pilate offering licence to the Jews to determine Jesus's fate is now known to have been a later, spurious addition to the original texts, and is seen by modern scholars as Roman propaganda. By making it appear as though the Jews themselves had determined Jesus's fate, Rome was able to extricate itself from all blame in this regard - a necessary move, of course, in order to establish itself as the centre of Christendom.) In any event, it would seem that Pilate so wanted it known that it was the King of Israel he was putting to death - and not some mild-mannered spiritual teacher - that he had the slogan "King of the Jews" inscribed in Hebrew, Latin *and* Greek before decreeing that it be displayed on the cross along with Jesus himself. (Again, a curious action - unless, of course, it the King of the Jews he *was* putting to death.) It was as if the revolt-fearful Procurator wished to send a fear-inspiring, bone-chilling message to Jewish militants - a message that told them in no uncertain terms that the Throne of Israel belonged not to the House of Judah, but to Rome. And anyone who dared challenge this assertion could expect to suffer a similar fate to the king.

Posthumously, of course, Jesus has been proclaimed 'Messiah' and

'Son of God' by countless generations, even though said generations have acted purely according to Church doctrine, and thus with little real understanding of either the cultural or historical significance attached to these terms. Or indeed, the cultural and historical background against which their 'saviour' lived. Taken in this light, and as most if not all biblical scholars and historians now agree, 'Messiah' (even as applied to Jesus) means simply 'the anointed one' - one who has undergone the ceremony of 'the anointing' in readiness for their accession to the throne (see *The Coronation Of Jesus* in *Chapter Sixteen*). It was a title that dated back centuries, even from Jesus's time, and was reserved specifically for invested monarchs of the Royal House of Judah (in Judaic tradition, of course, even today, King David - who reigned 1000 years before Jesus - is recognized as Israel's first 'Messiah'). In ancient Israel the rightful heir to the throne by dynastic succession was thus understood as a 'divine representative on Earth'.

But this rule does not apply uniquely to Israel; it can even be traced back to the Pharaohs of ancient Egypt, from whom it is thought that this messianic system of monarchy was adopted by the Jews - a consequence of their time in captivity in Egypt. Here too the rightful bloodline monarch, or Pharaoh, was perceived as something of a divine incarnation, a "Son of God". Or at the very least a divine representative on Earth - someone bestowed with divine sanction to reign as *de jure* monarch by virtue of dynastic right. It should be remembered that, like ancient Egypt, Israel was (and in many respects still is) a theocracy - a form of government in which politics and religion are indelibly interwoven. Thus Jesus, seen as Israel's *de jure* king, would indeed have been proclaimed 'Messiah'. Like 'Pharaoh', 'Messiah' is and always has been interpreted, in a symbolic sense, to mean 'God's representative on Earth'.

Quite simply, there is no more divine interpretation to be made of this purely secular title.

Bloodline Messiah And Warrior King

But if Jesus truly was a bloodline king of the Royal House of Judah, what evidence is there to suggest that he was a king like any other king - a military commander, for example, intent on ridding his country of some oppressive occupying power, in this instance Rome?

Certainly we know that Jesus numbered several so-called 'Zealots' among his closest followers, and that the Zealots themselves constituted the militant arm of the Essene/Nazarene culture prevalent in Israel at this time.

A fiercely patriotic movement comprised of militant nationalists, the Zealots sought to oust Roman rule from Israel, and at the same time reclaim the throne from the Herods (and, according to biblical account, they were prepared to take up arms in order to achieve this ambition). With Rome and the Herods ousted, their subsequent aim was to reinstate Israel's true bloodline king on the vacant throne. So far as the Zealots were concerned, of course, Jesus was undoubtedly that king.

The characters of Simon Zealotes (Simon the Zealot) and Judas Iscariot (Judas the Sicarus, named after the *sica*, a curved dagger used by the Zealots) certainly provide an insight into the way in which some of Jesus's followers were prone to think and act. The fact that Simon Peter (almost certainly one and the same with Simon Zealotes) was reported to have struck off the ear of the High Priest's servant at the time of Jesus's arrest in Gethsemane, for example, only adds weight to the probability that Jesus's so-called 'disciples' were in fact high-ranking militants in command of Zealot armies. And that Jesus himself, in his position as bloodline Messiah, would indeed have been seen as 'commander-in-chief' of this revolutionary outfit. (Or if Jesus truly was aught but a mild-mannered spiritual teacher sent from God, then what on earth was his most senior disciple doing in possession of a sword, much less that he was more than prepared to use it? This point alone has been the cause of fierce debate - and no less embarrassment - among Christian hierarchs for centuries.)

The often-told story of Jesus upending market stalls and expelling the moneychangers from the Temple on Palm Sunday begins to take on a new significance in this light. Evidence now suggests that it is far more likely, for example, that this action was part of the military offensive waged by Jesus and his 'Zealot' liberation army than that of a mild-mannered spiritual teacher who suddenly lost his temper, and decided to take it out on those who in his opinion were most worthy of God's wrath. This action occurred, remember, shortly after Jesus's triumphal entry into Jerusalem. The Bible tells us that he rode into the Roman-occupied city to the acclaim of his several thousand supporters and followers, many of whom waved palm branches and exclaimed "Hosanna to the King" (equivalent in first-century Judean-speak to "God save the King"). Indeed, the New English Bible is even more explicit in this regard. In John 12: 13 it states quite unequivocally that the crowds lining the streets of Jerusalem "took palm branches and went out to meet him, shouting ... 'God bless the king of Israel!'" There is nothing ambiguous about that.

According to our source, of course, the biblical account of Palm Sunday, like many other New Testament stories, is necessarily a "codified" depiction of events (necessary in order to disguise the true nature of historical events, and thus cunningly transform the secular 'Son of David' into the divine 'Son of God'). In this respect the biblical version of Jesus upending market stalls and expelling the moneychangers from the Temple would indeed stand out as one such "codified" depiction. It would certainly appear that this passage is a carefully reworked allusion to the battle which would surely have accompanied Jesus's 'triumphal' entry into Jerusalem. Or at least the battle which would surely have preceded it, or followed it. The very idea that a 'man of peace' such as the Jesus promulgated by Rome would have been allowed to get away with such an action by a team of burly, street-wise market traders - much less that Pilate and his garrisons would have stood idly by while Jesus rode through the streets of Jerusalem proclaiming himself "King" - is in itself a ludicrous one. Little wonder that the uprising was put down within the week and that Jesus was arrested and charged with sedition. The fact that some centuries later this charge was transmuted to one of 'blasphemy' - and thus the blame for Jesus's death cunningly shifted onto the Jews themselves - only serves to highlight the extent to which the original biblical texts were indeed modified to better serve Rome's political ambitions.

With regard to our source's assertion that a Jesus-led Zealot army took control of Jerusalem - surprisingly there is some very cogent biblical evidence to support this theory. And it is very intriguing indeed. It should be said that it is a theory which is not entirely new; it has been alluded to by other authors and, indeed, exploited in Jon King's 1997 novel, *The Ascension Conspiracy: 2013*. It is, however, the first time it has come to light by way of official documentation allegedly held by MI6. For this reason alone it is worthy of our most rigorous interrogation, as follows.

Certainly we know that several major uprisings, involving well-trained, well-organized units of Jewish militants, did indeed occur during the first two centuries AD. And that an ongoing guerrilla-like series of skirmishes obtained throughout the life span of Jesus. In AD 6, for example, following the annexation of Judea by Rome, a man known to history as Judas of Galilee emerged at the head of a new and fervently nationalist movement which would later become known as the Zealots. By all accounts, Judas was a fire-and-brimstone prophet and freedom-fighter whose descendant Eleazar would later command the Zealot garrison which captured Masada from Rome (circa AD 66). The Zealot occupation of Masada was to last some seven years, and was the culmination of subversive activities waged against Rome throughout the decades immediately proceeding and succeeding Jesus's crucifixion. In the final act, it led to the sacking of Jerusalem and the complete annihilation of the Temple by Roman garrisons in AD 70. And the massacre of hundreds of Jews. Indeed, a similar massacre had occurred in neighbouring

Samaria around the time of Jesus's crucifixion - the result of a Samaritan uprising against Rome. Interestingly, this uprising was led by a Samaritan 'messiah' who had gained the support of his countrymen at the same time that Jesus would have been engaged in a similar exercise in Judea. A further revolt in AD 132-135 was the last uprising by Jewish militants known to traditional history.

But what evidence is there that a similar uprising could have occurred around the year AD 36 in Judea? And moreover, that it could have been led by Jesus?

First and foremost, of course, we must take into account the cultural and historical backdrop against which Jesus lived. It is one thing for us today to think of Jesus as some humble, miracle-working saviour figure who died on the cross for our sins. But where did this image originate? Not with those who lived and worked alongside him. This much is certain. On the contrary, this false image of Jesus did not obtain until some years after his death, largely the brainchild of the religious fanatic, Paul (who never knew Jesus, and who, of course, even after his so-called 'Road to Damascus' conversion, was a Roman citizen). It was an image which was vigorously and consistently refuted by the Nazarene Church in Jerusalem. It was also bitterly contested by Jesus's own brother, James.

But perhaps the most crucial point in this regard is that first-century Israel was an occupied territory. Its people were fighting for their independence. In consequence, any would-be messiah emerging from the wings would, first and foremost, and of necessity, have been a military figure - someone with the strength, charisma and resources necessary to rally the various factions of Zealot militants to war. Jesus would have been no exception in this regard. Indeed, as early as AD 6 Judas of Galilee had been proclaimed 'Messiah' by enthusiastic Jewish militants (there is evidence to suggest that Judas of Galilee was of the same bloodline stock as Jesus). There had been others before him. And there were others that followed. Around the year AD 57, for example, yet another 'messiah', said to have come from a Nazarene community in Egypt, and who was possibly a first- or second-generation descendant of Jesus, rallied the Zealots against Rome. But once again, the revolt was crushed (though not the Jewish spirit). Further guerrilla activities were undertaken by Zealot militants until finally the new 'commander-in-chief' - the head of the Nazarene community in Jerusalem - was executed, circa AD 65. His name was Jacob, best known today as James, Jesus's brother. Other claimants to the title of 'Messiah' had come and gone like bishops come and go: without note. And without the spiritual and cultural - or indeed, the ancestral - qualification representative of their office.

This is something that cannot be said of Jesus, of course. On the contrary, not only did Jesus demonstrate his qualification, clearly enough. But if our source is to be believed (together with evidence presented by other scholars and authors in this regard) then Jesus's status as *de jure* heir apparent to the Royal House of Judah meant that his claim was a legitimate one. Jesus was perhaps one of several legitimate contenders, perhaps one of several legitimate 'messiahs' to whom the various factions of Jewish militants had looked for leadership. But it was Jesus's legitimate royal status according to the Judah bloodline that would have made him stand out above all others. In his position as *de jure* king one would assume that he would have been endowed with the authority (and, of course, the charisma which comes with being king) to lead and galvanize his people into consolidated actions against the Roman occupiers. In this light, of course, he would also have been seen by Rome as 'public enemy number one' - which, according to the Gospels at any rate, he most certainly was. Indeed, he would be crucified for this very reason.

That Jesus was steeped in Essene/Nazarene tradition, then, and that he numbered among his associates members of the nationalist Zealot movement, is now beyond question. That he was *de jure* king of the Royal House of Judah is equally incontestable. And from the evidence we have managed to glean, both from our Foreign Office source and other, more accessible sources (including the New Testament) it would seem that he could indeed have led a revolt against Rome around the year AD 35-36, during the weeks and days leading up to his crucifixion.

In the Gospel of John (18: 3), for example, we are told that a "detachment of soldiers and police ... equipped with lanterns, torches and weapons" was sent to arrest Jesus on the eve of his crucifixion. We are also told that Jesus was in a place called the Garden of Gethsemane at the time of his arrest, along with his twelve disciples. Curiously, however, the Gospel of Luke (22:36) tells us that, some short while before the arrest took place, Jesus had instructed his so-called 'disciples' to arm themselves with swords. And what is more, he had justified this instruction by openly declaring that he too was one of the "outlaws" (a modern - and disguised - translation of "zealots"). Thus, by his own declaration, Jesus was indeed a Zealot. And more than this: it would seem that he was perceived as the Zealots' 'commander-in-chief'. The fact that his followers addressed him as 'Lord', and that by his command they had armed themselves for battle, surely substantiates this assumption clearly enough.

What is incontestable, of course, is that at least one among their number was indeed equipped with a sword at the time of Jesus's arrest: Simon Peter, or Simon the Zealot. Moreover, we know that Simon used that sword. We also know that there were at least two others present at Jesus's arrest who were armed with swords. The passage in Luke which refers to the Zealots equipping themselves with arms concludes: "Look, Lord ... we have two swords here." And although the title 'Lord' may well be applied to someone sent from God, it is also a title which has been applied to kings since time immemorial. Thus the Zealots' reference to Jesus as 'Lord' does not in any way presume his divine status. On the contrary, if anything the use of this form of address, together with the verse from John (18:3), which speaks of "a detachment of soldiers and police ... equipped with ... weapons" being sent to arrest Jesus, presumes his status as a military commander - in particular when the original translation of this verse is entered into the equation.

There are, of course, many different translations of the biblical texts, which were originally written in Hebrew, Aramaic and Greek. The most commonly employed today, of course, certainly in Western Europe and America, is the *King James Authorized Version* (published 1611). Plus the many subsequent, more modern variations thereof (including the *American Standard Version* of 1901). However, the Catholic Church possesses a far older translation which dates back to the fourth century AD, and which is included in a book called the *Vulgate* (meaning, according to *The Concise Oxford Dictionary*: "the traditionally accepted text"). In this translation, the above verse (John 18:3) makes for very different reading indeed.

While we are told in the later, modern-day translations that a "detachment of soldiers and police ... equipped with lanterns, torches and weapons" was sent to arrest Jesus (or variations thereof, depending on which version one is reading) the Vulgate is far more specific. Instead of a "*detachment* of soldiers and police" being sent to arrest Jesus, the Vulgate states quite unequivocally that a "*cohort*" of soldiers was sent to arrest Jesus. This throws an entirely new light on the matter. In the first-century Roman army, of course, a cohort was a division of soldiers numbering anywhere between 600 and 2000 men. But even more revealing is the fact that, in first-century Palestine a cohort was generally taken to mean a division of men which included 760 foot soldiers and 1240 on horseback: 2000 men. Yet this "cohort", we are told (these 2000 fully trained, fully armed soldiers, more than 1000 of them on horseback) was sent together with a number of police equipped with "weapons" to arrest a peace-loving guru and his twelve disciples as they prayed together in an olive grove. This is an absurd notion, to say the least. Absurd, that is, unless Jesus was indeed something other than a lamb-like spiritual teacher, and his disciples were likewise something other than spiritual devotees - if Jesus was King, for example, and his so-called 'disciples' the King's defeated army. Indeed, many scholars now concur that the so-called 'arrest' of Jesus at Gethsemane was in fact a full-scale battle - a vicious and bloody battle waged between a sizeable Roman army and an equally well-organized Zealot army commanded by Jesus himself.

"I have not come to bring peace, but a sword," Jesus tells us in Matthew (10:34-35). Indeed, according to Luke (22: 36-38), his so-called disciples bore the same unequivocal message.

[Note: As mentioned at the top of this chapter, there is simply not the time or space here to include all the historical evidence with regard to Jesus's royal status and/or the genealogical evidence with regard to the survival of Jesus's family. In this regard, we would refer you to such formidable works as *The Holy Blood* And *The Holy Grail* and *The Messianic Legacy* by Michael Baigent, Richard Leigh and Henry Lincoln, together with *Bloodline Of The Holy Grail* by Sir Laurence Gardner. In them you will find the evidence of which we speak, and an added bibliography for further reading.]

CHAPTER 14

THE MEROVINGIANS
Sorcerer Kings Of Dark Ages Europe

"According to tradition, Merovingian monarchs were occult adepts, initiates in arcane sciences, practitioners of esoteric arts ... They were often called 'the sorcerer kings' or 'thaumaturge kings'. By virtue of some miraculous property in their blood they could allegedly heal by laying on of hands; and according to one account the tassels at the fringes of their robes were deemed to possess miraculous curative powers."

Michael Baigent, Richard Leigh and Henry Lincoln, *The Holy Blood And The Holy Grail*, 1982.

Origins

Accoring to our Foreign Office source, documents held in secret by the British government depict a somewhat different version of Western history than that taught in our schools, in particular with regard to the period we call the Dark Ages. Perhaps this is because the documents in question contain a record not of *social* evolution, but of *political* evolution - of the agendas and sub-agendas pursued by the ascendant political powers of the day. Perhaps also it is because someone does not wish us to know what those agendas are.

In this regard, our source said, it was during the early part of the seventh century AD that Europe became subdivided into two main political power blocs - the first sponsored and controlled by Rome, a usurper regime which, in effect, evolved into the power bloc we today call France; the second bloc was comprised of a well-established Judaeo-Teuton alliance forged by the intermarriages of exiled Judaic nobles with the resident Germanic royal families of the era. This power bloc, loosely speaking, we today refer to as Germany. (It is of interest to note in this respect that France and Germany, together with Britain, today comprise the major political forces within the European Union. It is of further note that the nation state we today refer to as Britain resulted from the commingling of Franco-German blood and its designs on an independent British Throne. Indeed, until at least the fourteenth century

AD, French was the national language of England - it was not until the eighteenth century and the politically manoeuvred usurpation of the British Throne by the House of Hanover that German interests in Britain were finally consolidated.) However, our source also wanted us to appreciate that both of these power blocs - France and Germany - should be understood not merely in terms of their status as nation states. But in terms of their political and economic ascendancy within the Western-world web of masonic government. In this regard, and in effect, the Europe we know today was forged by the political and economic struggles played out between these two formidable centres of political power.

But there was also a third political force, our source said, of which little has been recorded by traditional history, but which, in its day, represented the true bloodline dynasty of Judah. In this respect, the third so-called power bloc gained its authority from the fact that its heirs were both recognized and acknowledged as the legitimate bloodline descendants of Kings David and Solomon. Indeed, even Jesus. By this time (the seventh century AD) this third or 'bloodline' power bloc had for two centuries and more been known as the Merovingian Dynasty. It was a dynasty whose influence ranged far and wide. It would later emerge, for example, as the consolidating force which would unite Britain's true Celtic heritage of old, unifying as it ultimately did the several royal dynasties of ancient Ireland and Scotland in the Houses of Dunkeld and Stewart (later Stuart). But in the seventh century AD it was known as the House of Meroveus: the Merovingian Dynasty.

According to our source - and equally to traditional history - the Merovingian kings descended from the Sicambrian Franks, a Judaeo-Teuton people who by this time had settled large parts of France and Germany. However, far from the blood-and-thunder, patriarchal bias epitomized by some of the other Teutonic/Judaic tribes prevalent in Europe at this time, the Merovingians were recognized for their political and religious tolerance, as well as for their cultural liberalism (qualities which would also be attributed to their bloodline descendants, the Stuart kings of Scots and England, some one thousand years later). Also of note was their apparent mystical quality and seemingly inherent judicious nature. Though certainly capable of conquering the odd territory here and there (as well as defending their own, and with some zeal), the Merovingian kings were nonetheless of peaceful disposition, preferring diplomacy over war, education and learning above political and military supremacy. Perhaps in the end this somewhat 'politically naive' inherence would be a major factor in their ultimate downfall. Certainly in terms of their political relations with the Church of Rome, the Merovingians would prove easy prey - like lambs to the slaughter they would succumb to Roman propaganda and, ultimately, to the Church's designs on European supremacy. In short, though politically dominant in Europe for several centuries, and fabulously wealthy, they nonetheless seemed to belong to a world in which the quest for cultural and spiritual nourishment outweighed that for political and economic advantage. Not unlike, say, the Native American Indians of the eighteenth and nineteenth centuries, it would seem that the Merovingians understood little of 'white man's' obsession for territorial gain and political predominance. And equally little of his 'fork-tongued promises'. This much is evident in the pact agreed between King Clovis I and Rome in AD 496 - which assured the succession of the Merovingian bloodline on the thrones of Christendom, but which was broken by the Church in two major, subsequent events: firstly, the Church-sponsored assassination of King Dagobert II in AD 679, effectively bringing an end to Merovingian ascendancy; and secondly, the usurpation of the Merovingian Throne in AD 754 by the Church-created Carolingian Dynasty. And the subsequent establishment in AD 800 of the Holy Roman Empire. In effect, the Holy Roman Empire was simply the old Merovingian kingdom hijacked and rechristened.

In terms of political chicanery and international power-brokering, then, the Merovingians, though a proud and noble people, were simply no match for the Church of Rome. Indeed, employing today's terminology, and to judge by their famous long hair, acclaimed supernatural prowess, their propensity for star-gazing and a self-chronicled affinity with nature (their reputed ability to communicate with trees and animals, for example, and to heal by the laying on of hands), the Merovingians had more in common with the Druids of ancient Britain and Ireland than with the strictly Pauline regime of Dark Ages Rome. By their own account they were 'sons of the Mother Goddess'. They were unashamed pagans. If not hippies. And what is more, their mysterious esoteric and psychic powers were taken very seriously by Rome.

Indeed, Rome envied them and feared them, both at once. And so wiped them out.

What traditional history does not stipulate (at least not with the same fervour with which it defends and promotes the Pauline creed) is where precisely the Merovingians might have originated. And with whom they might have mixed their blood. Indeed, it seems somewhat conveniently to sidestep this issue, and at every possible juncture. It speaks of an ongoing struggle for political and military supremacy, clearly enough, one which seemed to be centred on the ability to manipulate papal power: indeed, that the political powers of the day were intent on little else but warring for control of Rome, the Church, and thereby for political ascendancy in Europe. Nothing new there. But clearly what traditional history tends to evade, among other issues, is with whom the Merovingians may already have commingled. Also, of course, from which racial and cultural background they may have derived. According to our source they were the descendants of the exiled Royal House of Judah. They derived from Israel, some say from the deposed Royal Family which found exile in southern France following the crucifixion of Jesus - among whom was Jesus's wife, Mary Magdalene, and of course their children, who generations later would intermarry with the Sicambrian Franks and become known as the Merovingians. Other accounts, though, say that the Merovingians originated in what is today Germany, and before that, Arcadia in ancient Greece - that exiled Jewish nobles had fled to Greece from Israel and intermarried with Arcadian royal blood, and had subsequently migrated east as far as present-day Germany and intermarried with Teutonic royal blood, thus engendering the Sicambrian Franks. But if this claim is correct, then their must surely be a record of at least one mass exodus out of Israel which predates the Merovingians' rise to power. After all, if the Merovingians were descended from the House of Judah (some say from the House/Tribe of Benjamin, too - that in the Merovingian kings the blood of *both* Israel's two ruling dynasties, Judah and Benjamin, was conjoined) then at some point in history their forbears must have migrated north and west from Israel. And if such a migration indeed took place then it must surely be documented in history.

The Diaspora

Historical records certainly do refer to such an exodus having occurred. Indeed, more than one. But you have to look closely. And even then the inquirer is left to piece together the many elusive and fragmentary bits of available historical data before anything like a coherent picture emerges. But it can be done. Following the two major Jewish revolts against Rome, for example (at least those recorded by history - AD 66-74 and AD 132-135) large numbers of Jewish partisans and refugees are reported to have settled in Alexandria and other parts of Egypt. Which in itself is interesting. Considering the theme of this book, and the fact that Dodi Fayed was of Egyptian heritage, it is to say the least ironic that the first real stronghold of Judaeo-Christian culture outside of first-century Palestine was to be found in Egypt. The Gnostic (Essene/Nazarene/Zealot) school of thought to which Jesus himself adhered quickly took root in Egypt during the first two centuries AD, a fact to which the discovery of Gnostic texts such as the Nag Hammadi Scrolls attest. Indeed, by the fifth century AD, Rome was still endeavouring to crush the Egyptian Church and its 'heretical' teachings (which in fact were far more closely aligned with the original Nazarene teachings adhered to by Jesus than were those promulgated by Rome). The destruction of the Library of Alexandria and its wealth of historical data in AD 411 - again, ordered from Rome - bears ample testimony to this end.

It is of interest to note here that, while Rome was busy building empires, and establishing itself as a potent political force in Europe - and doing so on the authority of a strictly Pauline-based regime which clearly and drastically deviated from the teachings of Jesus - the vestiges of the original Nazarene-based church in Egypt remained politically innocent. In many ways the Egyptian Church resembled the Celtic Church of ancient Britain; certainly both were founded on teachings strangely reminiscent of the Nazarene teachings of first-century Israel. Indeed, there exists a powerful body of evidence to the effect that Nazarene and Celtic philosophy, like that of the early Egyptian Church and, indeed, of the Cathars a millennium later, derived from a similar - if not the same - 'Druidic' school of thought. Like the Druids of Celtic Britain, for example, and indeed the Essenes/Nazarenes of Qumran, Egyptian Christians were ascetics whose lifestyles betrayed an inherent understanding of, and veneration for, the wisdom/pagan tradition to which Jesus - as a Nazarene - would himself have adhered. Roman Christians, on the other hand, were adherents of an hierarchical regime which clearly demonstrated less regard for the teachings of its founder than for political predominance. Today, it would seem, the song remains the same.

It should also be noted that, in some historical accounts (and certainly according to our source) allusion is made to a further Jewish exodus having occurred some time during the seventh and eighth centuries AD. Evidently this resulted in large numbers of Jewish emigrants settling in Germany and Bavaria. It is further considered that, in terms of social status, these emigrants derived for the most part from apostate factions of the Judaic nobility together with political and religious conspirators from what was formerly known as the 'Sadducee' caste - in modern terms a sort of upper middle-class administrative caste not dissimilar to that produced by, say, Britain's present-day public school system. In turn, certain of these emigrants are said to have intermarried with nobles from the resident Teutonic tribes, thus engendering a new ruling class. At some stage this new ruling class gained recognition as a new strain of royal blood - a strain recognized at least in terms of its political sovereignty, if not for its bloodline legitimacy. It was this strain which, according to our source, gave authority to the second European power bloc cited above - the power bloc which, in masonic terms at least, we today refer to as Germany. Indeed, it was this same Judaeo-Teuton strain which, according to our source, would some centuries later consolidate itself in the German Royal House of Hanover: alias the House of Windsor.

But what is even more evident is that this latest migration, though perhaps notable in itself, and certainly of consequence so far as we are concerned, was nonetheless merely the latest in a long line of similar migrations into Europe from Israel. And that the blending of Judaic and European blood reaches back even further than this. Indeed, as far back as Old Testament times.

The migrations known to history as the Diaspora (literally: the dispersion of the Jews among the Gentiles) traditionally occurred around 800-600 BC. By this time the Throne of Judah and the Throne of Israel had become separate entities. While the descendants of David continued to occupy the Throne of Judah at Jerusalem, claimants to a parallel succession established by King Jeroboam in 922 BC occupied an independent Throne of Israel at a place known as the Hill of Samaria. It was a time of much internal, internecine warfare, as well as prolonged struggles to defend home territories against the invading Syrians, Assyrians and Chaldeans, among others. When in 722 BC the Israelites' Hill of Samaria fell to Assyrian forces, and in consequence 27,000 Israelite prisoners were abducted by the Assyrian King Sargon II, the kingdom of Israel effectively ceased to exist. Indeed, it was the fact that these 27,000 Israelites were never seen again which spawned the legend of the 'lost tribes of Israel'. And although the Kings of Judah would successfully defend Jerusalem for a further century and more, in 597 BC the Babylonian King Nebuchadnezzar II would add vast numbers to the Diaspora by carrying off captured Jews into exile. For the next half a century thousands of Jews would live in captivity in Babylon, while many more would flee Judea and settle the northern and western territories - what is today Eastern Europe. According to traditional history it was these migrations which marked the beginning of the Diaspora - the 'dispersion of the Jews among the Gentiles'. But as we know, traditional history is not always as accurate as the authorities would have us believe. Quite the opposite. It is more often than not suspiciously reluctant to reveal those facts which do not support and uphold the system it has been designed to serve. Thus we are forced to seek out other sources of information to fill in the mysterious 'black holes'.

It was Michael Baigent, Richard Leigh and Henry Lincoln, of course, who, in their ground-breaking and internationally bestselling book, *The Holy Blood And The Holy Grail,* first brought to light the exodus of large numbers of Jewish emigrants from Israel some half a millennium earlier than the so-called Diaspora. Indeed, this exodus occurred around 1100 BC. Though deemed of some moment in the Old Testament, it would seem once again that traditional history would rather ignore - or at the very least make scarce allusion to - its impact on succeeding generations. And to its political significance today.

The Baigent/Leigh/Lincoln team also highlighted the fact that these earlier emigrants almost certainly belonged to the Tribe of Benjamin. This is of particular consequence to our own investigation. By meticulous study of certain secret documents in their possession - documents gleaned from perhaps the most substantive secret society of our time, the Priory of Sion - Messrs

Baigent, Leigh and Lincoln discovered that, having been forced to flee their homeland as a result of hostilities between themselves and the rest of the Israelite tribes, many of the most influential members of the Tribe/House of Benjamin had indeed taken up exile in Arcadia, Greece. This is of particular note for the fact that the later Merovingians - now thought to have been part-descendants of the exiled Benjamites, as well as of the later-exiled House of Judah - themselves claimed to have issued from Troy and Arcadia. Historical texts and archives tend to support the fact that indeed they did.

Of historical note here is the fact that the hostilities which forced the Benjamites out of Israel had been sparked by a typically savage biblical incident. According to the bible account (Judges 19-21), a posse of frenzied Benjamites raped and killed the concubine of a Levite who had sought refuge for the night in Benjamite territory. Though the Levite's host had offered his own daughter, a virgin, to be ravaged in place of his female guest, for some inexplicable reason the Benjamites were not interested. They wanted the Levite's concubine. Presumably fearing for his own life, the Levite finally "took hold of his concubine and thrust her outside for them"; whereupon they "assaulted her and abused her all night till the morning". At dawn she was found dead. On his return home, having transported the body of his concubine on the back of his donkey, the Levite proceeded to "cut her up limb by limb into twelve pieces". He then sent her, piece by piece, "through the length and breadth of Israel" in order that every Israelite should know of the gruesome deed perpetrated by the Benjamites. It turned out most every Israelite did indeed find out about the atrocity. And according to the *Book of Judges,* most of *them* attended the ensuing council.

> All the Israelites, the whole community from Dan to Beersheba and out of Gilead also, left their homes as one man and assembled before the Lord at Mizpah. The leaders of the people and all the tribes of Israel presented themselves in the general assembly of the people of God, four hundred thousand foot-soldiers armed with swords...

Needless to say the Benjamites were under some pressure to explain themselves. The tribe was ordered to deliver those among its number responsible for the deed, but for some reason (one which remains curiously unexplained by the Old Testament scribes) the Benjamites refused. Instead they elected to take up arms and engage the rest of Israel in civil war. Well-documented in the *Book of Judges*, the war was vicious and bloody, and resulted in large numbers of Benjamites being forced to flee Israel, almost certainly for Arcadia in Greece. Indeed, in the documents unearthed by Baigent,

Leigh and Lincoln, it clearly told how the Benjamites took up exile in Arcadia, "where they supposedly became aligned with the Arcadian royal line". The documents went on to reveal the following:

> Towards the advent of the Christian era, they [the Tribe of Benjamin] are then said to have migrated up the Danube and the Rhine, intermarrying with certain Teutonic tribes and eventu ally engendering the Sicambrian Franks - the immediate fore bears of the Merovingians.

By the seventh century AD, of course, the Merovingians had become the undisputed ruling dynasty in Western Europe.

The Bloodline And The Holy Grail

That Teutonic and Judaic nobles did indeed intermarry, then - and so in time produce a new Judaeo-Teuton bloodline, that of the Sicambrian Franks - is in little if any doubt (and this despite the conspicuous dearth of information provided by traditional history in this regard). By the time the immediate descendants of this Judaeo-Teuton alliance, the Merovingians, migrated west in the fifth and sixth centuries AD, for example, it is known that they did so as the ruling Sicambrian class - perhaps the most prolific of the Frankish royal houses. But what is most significant about the Merovingians so far as we are concerned is the cloak of mystery which still surrounds them, even to this day. And perhaps even more of note is the fact that latter-day royal houses and power-brokers alike - the House of Windsor and the Vatican first among them - acknowledge this mystery with some awe.

But what exactly is it, this mystery? What is it about the Merovingian bloodline, the Judaeo-Teuton bloodline, which still has the Windsors and the Vatican foaming at the mouth for possession of it? According to some commentators, of course (including our Foreign Office source) it is nothing less than the legendary Holy Grail.

Aside from rumours of secret documents hidden away in the vaults of some of Europe's most clandestine masonic and chivalric orders, information pertaining to the Holy Grail has, to say the least, been elusive - sparse, vague, cloaked in mystery. And up until recently, even that much (at least so far as 'non-members' are concerned) has been flavoured by romance. Indeed, it has been cloaked largely in medieval epic, chivalric poems and stories which have come to be known as the Grail romances, such as Wolfram von Eschenbach's *Parzival* and Sir Thomas Malory's later *Le Morte d'Arthur*. Though many modern writers on the subject of Judaic lineages have waxed well and lyrical, both on the meaning of, and their connection to, the Holy Grail, once again it was the team of Baigent, Leigh and Lincoln who first put two and two together and came up with the right answer. Or at least what certainly appears to have been the right answer.

In the first instance, their years-long research led them to discover a very potent and intriguing connection between the medieval Grail romances and what they termed "matters of lineage and genealogy". It seemed the more they studied the medieval manuscripts the more plausible they appeared to be. Indeed, after some scrutiny they started to realize that the so-called romances contained more than just romance: they seemed to contain, if not clear historical facts, then allusions to historical facts - facts which suggested an irrefutable connection between the Holy Grail and the royal bloodline of Judah. And the royal bloodline of Judah, they discovered, reached all the way back to Kings Solomon and David, almost certainly via Jesus himself. A truly explosive discovery.

But there was more. Something of even greater moment was yet to emerge, something of more diabolical consequence even than the fact that Jesus and the Holy Grail were indelibly rooted. They were to discover what the Holy Grail actually was. *What it actually is.*

In legend, of course, the Grail is often depicted as little more than a relic, albeit of inconceivable value, both spiritual and secular. A relic, nonetheless. To some this relic is a precious stone, a crystal or jewel - the so-called Philosopher's Stone perhaps, by which spiritual enlightenment is achieved. To others it is represented by a blood-filled chalice, said to be the cup which conveyed the blood of the crucified Christ to Europe, and later, to Britain. To others still it is a silver dish or platter, denoting the ideal of *service*, the one true quality said to be prerequisite to discovering the Grail and acquiring its attendant magical powers. *Whom does the Grail serve?* the questing knight is instructed to ask on discovery of the mysterious object. The answer is fundamental. The Grail, of course, serves the land, its rightful king and its people in equal and just measure. Thus the knight's quest is fulfilled in his own subsequent service to his king and his king's people, in equal and just measure. And thus the 'Grail Code' is enlivened by true wisdom; the land becomes fertile once again, its people prosperous. To employ the Grail's powers in service to oneself, on the other hand, is to lose sight of the very mystery which has all along been the object of one's quest. The king remains impotent and the land infertile. And the people become the unwitting subjects of some usurper royal dynasty cloaked in pomp and pelf.

Thus the successful quest for, and employment of, the Holy Grail and its attendant powers is wholly dependent on the ideal of *service*, an ideal which, over the years, has become known as the Grail Code. It was an ideal made manifest, of course, in the life of the 'People's Princess', Diana. Indeed, no other royal has yet come close to manifesting the so-called 'Grail Code' in anything like the manner demonstrated by the late Princess of Wales. But then again, as we shall see, in Diana a somewhat unique genetic signature recurred - a signature found only in the most noted heirs to the Judaic royal bloodline. And as Baigent, Leigh and Lincoln were about to discover, the Judaic royal bloodline was synonymous with the Holy Grail itself.

As is so often the case when legend is undone by scientific inquiry, it turned out that the Holy Grail was somewhat less a mystery than its fabulous cloak all along had us believe. Though it was no less explosive for that. In studying the early manuscripts, the Baigent/Leigh/Lincoln team found that the Holy Grail had originally been called, as our source had rightly pointed out, the 'Sangraal' or 'Sangrael', and that in translation from Old French into modern English the word had been broken in the wrong place. They set about putting it right. Instead of making it read 'San Graal' or 'San Grael' (hence Saint Graal or Saint Grael: Holy Grail) the team divided the word into two equal halves, making 'Sang Raal' or 'Sang Rael'. In this new form, of course, a straight translation from Old French meant something else entirely: Blood Royal or Holy Blood. It seemed that, as our source had rightly claimed, 'Holy Grail' had all along been a misnomer, the result of a simple mistranslation (or more likely - again as our source had claimed - a *deliberate* mistranslation). Indeed, in light of this new translation the so-called 'mystical power' attributed to the Merovingians began to take on an entirely new significance. Like Solomon and Jesus before them, the Merovingians *themselves* could now be identified as the 'chalice' in which the Blood Royal - the Holy Grail, the Judaic royal bloodline - was contained. In them it survived. And thrived.

Armed with this new information, it soon became apparent that the Judaic royal blood coursing the veins of some of Europe's most powerful masonic and chivalric orders was none other than that of Jesus himself. At least in a symbolic sense, an arcane sense - even a political sense - if not a literal one. This, of course, began to make sense of certain legends pertaining to Jesus, too - legends which, in their former context, seemed more aligned with fantasy than fact, more myth than history. For example: did Jesus travel to Europe? To Britain? Did he marry? And if so, *whom* did he marry? Mary Magdalene? Was Jesus a bloodline king of the Royal House of Judah? Was Mary Magdalene a bloodline queen of the Royal House of Benjamin? Did they produce children? And if so, where were they now? Could the Merovingian kings have been descendants of Jesus and Mary Magdalene?

And moreover: was the survival of Jesus's royal bloodline synonymous with the secret of the Holy Grail?

Incredibly the evidence tended to say *yes* to all of the above questions. It said that Mary Magdalene was almost certainly of noble stock, for example, that she was almost certainly of the Tribe/Royal House of Benjamin. And that her marriage to Jesus (heir apparent to the Royal House of Judah) would, therefore, almost certainly have been a marriage of dynastic alliance. In this regard it would have represented a political reconciliation between the two ruling tribes of Israel, the Tribe of Judah on the one hand (whence had come Kings David and Solomon), and on the other the Tribe of Benjamin - large numbers of whom, remember, had been exiled some centuries before (circa 1100 BC). It was the Tribe of Benjamin, of course, which had furnished Israel with its first effective messiah, King Saul of Hebron, whom David had succeeded upon marrying King Saul's daughter, Michol. To add to this, recently unearthed genealogical records show beyond question that the Judaic and Benjamite bloodlines were later conjoined in the Merovingian Dynasty of Dark Ages Europe, and subsequently in the Celtic Royal Houses of Dunkeld and Stewart (later Stuart). Which in turn, of course, means that the royal bloodlines of Jesus (Judah) and Mary Magdalene (Benjamin) were indeed conjoined in Diana, Princess of Wales, descended as she was from King Charles I (Stuart) of England and Scots. And the fact that by her charismatic appeal and humanitarian tendencies she was seen to demonstrate the qualities traditionally associated with the most noted heirs to these bloodlines - that, in effect, she was seen as a 'genetic throwback' to these heirs - meant that she was a very dangerous threat indeed. Her unprecedented popularity and ability to mobilize public opinion against the status quo bears ample testimony to this end.

In any event, that the patrilineal and matrilineal strains of Israel's primary royal bloodline had been conjoined in the marriage of Jesus to Mary Magdalene now seemed more likely than not. This, of course, bore immense implications. The conjoining of these two ruling dynasties, for example, would have added much political weight to the so-called 'mystical power' attributed to the Judaic royal bloodline. Its descendants would, from this point on, be seen to carry the genes of both Jesus and Mary Magdalene, of both the Royal House of Judah and the Royal House of Benjamin, and would thus be seen to represent such consummate levels of political power as were so vigorously pursued by Rome.

Little wonder the Merovingians were possessed of such awe and mystery, then, especially in the eyes of other ruling dynasties of the period (in particular, of course, the Church of Rome). Little wonder they were possessed of such mystique. Little wonder the Church deemed them of such significance that it should conspire to eradicate them from the pages of history (which it did, very successfully, along with the entire period of their ascendancy, the so-called Dark Ages - which, contrary to popular belief, represented a time of cultural and spiritual enlightenment). Little wonder we know virtually nothing about them today.

Indeed, little wonder the Church saw fit to usurp the very power which had elevated them to the status of legend.

In this regard, we should interject here a word or two from Sir Laurence Gardner, Kt St Gm, KCD, appointed historian and sovereign genealogist to thirty-three royal houses, and author of *Bloodline Of The Holy Grail*. For many years Sir Laurence has researched and documented evidence regarding the lineage of royal bloodlines. Being at the same time Britain's Grand Prior of the Sacred Kindred of Saint Columba, he has also been afforded unlimited access to Celtic Church records dating back to AD 37 (records suppressed by the Churches of Rome and Canterbury alike). His office has also afforded him access to Knights Templar documents dating back to 1128.

According to Sir Laurence, many royal archives secreted away from public scrutiny document the fact that, at least up until the seventh and eighth centuries AD, Jesus had indeed been recognized by the Church and the nobility as Israel's *de jure* bloodline king. Also, of course, that he had been married and that he had sired children. According to Sir Laurence, these same documents also record the bloodline descendants of Jesus, collectively known as the Grail Dynasty, the Grail Family or the Messianic Royal Family. Among its members are to be found such illustrious historical figures as Bron (Bran The Blessed); Meroveus (after whom the Merovingian Dynasty was named); the great Welsh Bard, Taliesin; Perceval, Lancelot, Galahad: even King Arthur himself. Most of these figures and more, we are told, belong only to legend - the legend of the medieval Grail romances. Not so, say the documents. On the contrary, they all lived: they were all historical figures and they were all descended from Jesus. Indeed, other research shows that many royal families are well aware of this fact; some even consider themselves to be the direct lineal descendants of Jesus and the Judaic royal (Grail) bloodline today. Shocking as it may seem, this line of thought is not new. As Sir Laurence rightly explains in his ground-breaking book, up until medieval times (a period in history which officially began around AD 400, and reigned until the fall of Constantinople in 1453) the fact that the European nobility was in some way descended from Jesus was fairly common knowledge. And not only was this knowledge common in Britain. Nor only to the privileged few. It was common throughout Europe and to every rank and file of European society - which (as stated above) was far more cultured and enlightened than the history books would have us believe. A subsequent Middle Ages purge sanctioned and sponsored by Rome, however (known loosely to history as the *Inquisition*) meant that most if not all of this information went underground. Or more precisely, into the vaults of the most highly secret Catholic and religio-royalist archives of the period - both of which, of course, are but branches of the same masonic tree. The same masonic oligarchy. In consequence, Rome - and later the Judaeo-Teuton dynasties of northern Europe, from which descended the House of Windsor - were able to assert their own political and sovereign authority over and above the rightful bloodline authority inherent in the Merovingians (and later the Stuarts). Europe's most incisive and far-reaching political *coup d'etat* ever had been accomplished in this way.

And so it obtains today. For within those secreted vaults the power to manipulate history and to create usurper monarchies still remains. (In this regard, the records and documents alluded to by our Foreign Office source take on new significance. And indeed, added credibility.)

This, then, would certainly explain why bodies such as the Church and certain factions of the European nobility have been more than content for the so-called Grail legends (legends which perhaps are not legends) to remain in the realms of fantasy for so long. It would explain why the powers-that-be remain content for the populace to believe in the dark and wholly falsified history which has been perpetrated by the establishment for centuries. Indeed, it would explain why the British Establishment - whose very power rests on the secret of a bloodline which has its roots in Judaism - could not possibly tolerate the close proximity of an Arab Muslim to the British Throne. This would be particularly so, of course, if said Arab Muslim were to gain close proximity by virtue of marrying a true bloodline Grail Queen - a descendant 'queen' of the Judaic royal bloodline. Which Diana undoubtedly was. The House of Spencer, remember, can indeed be traced back to the Celtic Royal Houses of Dunkeld and Stewart (later Stuart), the first truly messianic royal dynasties of the Scots and the direct lineal descendants of the Merovingians.

Indeed, according to Sir Laurence Gardner, the Stuarts were the last ruling dynasty in Britain in which both primary strains of the messianic bloodline were conjoined. And it was the Stuarts, of course, who were deposed by the German House of Hanover.

The Power Of Symbol

The bloodline conspiracy allegedly responsible for the death of Diana, Princess of Wales, then, begins here, with the Merovingians. The mysterious bloodline descendants of Judah and Benjamin are central to the plot, both in an historical and a political context. A metaphysical context, too. Or perhaps more accurately, a *symbolic* context. The continual struggle for control of masonic power is, in effect, the struggle for control of the mystical, symbolic power ascribed to Jesus and the Merovingians. By controlling the symbol, the ability to control governments and to create usurper monarchies is achieved. It is in this regard, and as our source rightly claimed, that the struggle for political power is to be seen as a struggle for possession of the Holy Grail.

And it is certainly a struggle that continues to this day. It is the reason for all the ceremony and pomp surrounding the coronation of present-day monarchs, for one thing - or rather the *creation* of present-day monarchs. (Of note here is the fact that the Merovingian kings were never *created* - they underwent no such coronation ceremonies, or if they did, the ceremonies were in recognition of their inherent sovereign status rather then being a political attempt to falsely create that status. As stated, in many respects Merovingian society can be likened to Native American society. Certainly the Merovingian kings - in particular the fact that they represented rather than governed their people - had more in common with Native American chiefs than with latter-day parliamentary monarchs.) The present-day masonic pomp and pageantry, then, can only be understood as a conniving though convincing attempt on the part of an inherently impotent establishment to recreate the true 'bloodline power' possessed by the Merovingians (or a counterfeit variant thereof). In purely symbolic terms, it is an attempt to recreate the Holy Grail by ritualistic and ceremonial means; a way to appease the collective psyche and at the same time justify the continuation of a politically manufactured aristocracy (which in literal terms means "government by the nobility or a privileged group"). In stark political and historical terms, of course, it is the means by which to generate - and regenerate - the power necessary to support this kind of elitist government: a power usurped from the Merovingians by the Church of Rome, remember, on the assassination of King Dagobert II, AD 679 (an assassination sanctioned and orchestrated by the Church in the first place). The death of the Merovingian King Dagobert II effectively brought to an end the Merovingian Dynasty - at least in terms of its political and sovereign ascendancy - and thus finally enabled the Church to establish quasi-dynasties of its own: first the Carolingians, then the Holy Roman Empire (which, contrary to popular belief, reigned until the nineteenth century). For some time the Church wallowed in its own success; after all, it had finally acquired the Holy Grail. It had finally acquired the power to create kings. And thereby, kingdoms. Perhaps not surprisingly, however, the very fact that Rome had acquired this pseudo-mystical power meant that it also gained some very powerful enemies. Bloody wars ensued, and political intrigues, as the Judaeo-Catholics and the Judaeo-Teutons battled throughout the centuries for possession of this most prized of masonic symbols, the political Holy Grail - a fact which is scarcely surprising. It is a symbol, after all, whose influence can manipulate the wills and the minds of elected governments worldwide. In the absence of legitimate prerogative, of course, symbol is crucial. And the Holy Grail must surely be perceived as the aristocracy of all symbol. It is lineage. It is heritage.

And heritage - legitimate or otherwise - is power. No question of that.

The connection between Princess Diana and the Merovingian Dynasty becomes all the more evident when we turn our attention to the power of symbol, then. Whatever one's own propensity in this regard, it is nevertheless of consequence so far as our investigation is concerned. It is the power of symbol, remember, upon which the entire masonic empire has been built. It is this same power of symbol which sustains that empire, even today: the power of masonic ritual and ceremony, for example, perhaps the root of all symbol, and exemplified in the many ceremonies performed by succeeding monarchs - the state opening of Parliament, or even the Coronation itself. In terms of its effect on the archetypal, subconscious mind, of course, this kind of masonic ceremony evokes a wholly reflex response in us all. We are bombarded with the power of visual impact, for example - inviolable castles, fantasial palaces, virgin princesses in tailing white gowns, their weddings enacted on the world stage, captured on film and projected on screens for all the world to see. Their funerals, too. These symbols not only profoundly affect us; they effectively control us. Not in some paranoid, conspiratorial sense, of course. But rather in a subtle, subliminal, subjective sense, a psychological sense - in the sense propounded by Carl Jung and other great psychologists and philosophers of our time (and amply demonstrated by the vast millions who tuned in to the marriage of Prince Charles and Princess Diana in July 1981, and indeed, to Princess Diana's funeral in September 1997).

In short, the effect on our subconscious is both evocative and indelible. We simply cannot help but respond to the signals these archetypal images trigger in our minds. In this regard, it is the power of symbol which gives might to the structure and influence of masonic government today. Though the power is unquestionably sham, manufactured, usurped: the symbol is as real as thunder. It is an echo of the inner hierarchy which forms the very edifice of our subconscious world. And because it is, we are slaves to its command - and in turn to the pseudo-democratic culture it enlivens and maintains. One reason we might wish to learn from the egalitarian structure of more ancient cultures than our own, then. The Merovingian culture, for example, in which the power of perhaps the most compelling and deep-rooted symbol of all, the Holy Grail, was employed *on behalf* of its people. And not against them.

The Huntress And The Moon Goddess

On a more subjective note, perhaps one of the most powerful symbols connecting Princess Diana to the Merovingians is that of the Huntress, or the Moon Goddess - an allegory employed by Diana's brother, Charles Spencer, in his moving and provocative eulogy given in memory of Diana and heard by the millions worldwide who attended her funeral. Indeed, in some instances both of these ancient representations - the Huntress and the Moon Goddess - have been equated with Gaia, the Mother Goddess, a form of Deity revered by the Merovingians themselves. The Merovingians, of course, first issued from Arcadia in ancient Greece, and the cult of the Mother Goddess was the established religion of the Arcadians, as well as of many Jewish tribes. The Tribe of Benjamin, for example, many of whom we know escaped to Arcadia around 1100 BC, worshipped the goddess Belial (known also as Ishtar and Astarte). It should be remembered here that worship of the female aspect of Deity in ancient Israel was far more prevalent than is generally thought. It is certainly known that the early Israelites (1100-600 BC) worshipped the Mother Goddess in the form of Asherah, Ashtoreth and Anath, Queen of Heaven. Despite the efforts of the proselytizer Moses in delivering the Ten Commandments (circa 1300 BC), it was not until after the Jews' enforced exile in Babylon (circa 536 BC) that the male-female character of Yahweh, or YHWH (represented by the four aspects of Deity: El-Asherah, He-Anath, corresponding to father-mother, son-daughter) suddenly translated to the angry male dictator he is today: Jehova. And even then, it was only when the later Pauline-Christian version of God emerged from Dark Ages Europe that Jehova fully assumed the principle of fear for which he is best-known today. By purposeful promulgation of this fear principle, of course, the Church became the most powerful political edifice in Europe and the Americas. Even today, millions are held to ransom in the name of this Vatican-invented, fire-and-brimstone version of God. In return for their strict devotion, the millions-strong congregation can expect a safe and uninterrupted passage to Heaven in the afterlife, true enough. In the present life, however, the Pope and his pompous prelature enjoy the fruits of Heaven on Earth. Perhaps Machiavelli is the true God of the Christians, then.

In any event, as the tribes migrated westward towards the advent of the Christian era, so did the Mother Goddess. By the time the old Roman Empire had put down the last of the Jewish uprisings in Palestine during the first and second centuries AD, the Arcadians had become the Sicambrian Franks, and the Mother Goddess had become the Moon Goddess, Diana. Later still, when the Sicambrian Franks had settled regions of what is now Belgium and northern France, and their kings had become known as the

Merovingians, Diana had evolved into the tutelary goddess of the Ardennes. Her new name was Arduina. It was from the Ardennes in northern France, of course, that the Merovingians later issued southward and westward across France. And they took Diana with them when they went.

A further interesting connection in this respect can be seen in that the Sicambrians, forebears of the Merovingians, worshipped Diana in the form of the bear. Or more precisely, in the form of the female bear, or she-bear. This deity, called by the Arcadians Kallisto, was the ancient totem of the Moon Goddess, Artemis (Diana). According to Greek myth, Kallisto was also the son of Arkas, which, translated into modern English, means 'bear'. Indeed, Arcadia actually means 'people of the bear', and it is thus no coincidence that both fables and histories relating to the later Merovingians, descendants of Arcadia, tell of the legendary Prince Ursus or King Arthur as 'Grail King' or 'Keeper of the Grail' (the former, Prince Ursus, an historical Merovingian King, circa AD 877-879; the latter, King Arthur, an historical Celtic High King of the Britons, circa AD 575-603). Of further interest is the fact that 'Ursus' is Latin for 'bear', while 'Arthur' or 'Arth' is Welsh for 'bear', though the name 'Arthur' in fact derives from the ancient Celtic (Irish) 'Art' or 'Artur'. And in any event, the 'people of the bear' translates to the 'people of Arthur', giving sense to the Grail romances and their seeming preoccupation with the legendary King Arthur. Equally, of course (and perhaps a more appropriate translation so far as we are concerned) the 'people of the bear' also means the 'people of Diana', the female bear deity and Moon Goddess worshipped by the Merovingians from their inception.

And neither do the correlations end there. Far from it. According to some commentators, for example, Pont de l'Alma, the Parisian underpass in which Diana's Mercedes mysteriously crashed, is a site where sacrifices were once made to propitiate cosmic forces. Pagan in origin, this site conveyed a special significance to the Merovingians. Certainly the French capital (founded and named 'Paris' by the Merovingians in the sixth century AD) is littered with such sites. Some, like this one, predate Christianity by many centuries. Most, if not all, were recognized and further utilized by the Merovingian kings and their people, who, as we have seen, were known to have been sensitive to the various highways and crossroads of interlocking telluric energies. (In other words, they knew a sacred site when they saw one!). Pont de l'Alma is no exception in this regard.

Indeed, during the age of Merovingian ascendancy, Pont de l'Alma is said to have been a place where invocations were made to the Moon Goddess, Diana, and to other goddesses, in particular those representative of wars and disputes. Some legends say that if two Merovingian nobles were found to be in dispute, usually due to an argument over land or property, they would settle their differences in combat at Pont de l'Alma. Though the winner of the duel would claim the land or property over which the argument had arisen, in effect he would be deemed to have lost the battle. The mortally wounded 'loser', on the other hand, would in fact be deemed the true victor. This is due to the fact that, so legend tells, anyone killed at Pont de l'Alma goes directly to Heaven, where they reside in the presence of the Godhead until their death has been avenged. For in the presence of the Godhead, it is said, they are empowered to direct events back on Earth to their own advantage, utilizing the light of the full moon (the favour of the Moon Goddess, Diana) by which to see. In this regard, one is left to wonder at the curious nature of life, and death: its ironies.

It is most interesting to note also that the death of the most famous Moon Goddess of her time, Diana, Princess of Wales, occurred on a particularly auspicious day - the day of the month known as the Dark of the Moon (31st August, 1997). Coming to pass on the night prior to a new moon, this is the only night in any month when there is no moon at all in the sky, not even a sliver. How strange the fact that, so legend tells, on some subsequent full moon vengeance will have its way. Or if not vengeance, then justice. And that Diana, Goddess of the Moon, will preside.

A Common Enemy

We began this chapter by asserting that, in effect, and according to our source, the early part of the seventh century saw Europe become subdivided into two main political power blocs. We identified these power blocs - in a masonic context - with modern-day France and Germany. Or more precisely, with a Franco-Roman alliance which, in effect, evolved into the masonic power bloc we today refer to as France; and a Judaeo-Teuton alliance forged by the intermarriages of exiled Jewish nobles and Teutonic royals. This power bloc - again, in a masonic context - we identified with modern-day Germany. We also asserted that Britain as constituted today evolved out of the commingling of Franco-German blood and its designs on an independent British Throne. Though some pedants will no doubt find fault with this simplified overview of European history, we nevertheless stand by our initial assertion in this regard. Certainly history tends to confirm that present-day Europe is largely the result of the political, economic and military warfare waged between these Judaeo-Roman and Judaeo-Teuton power blocs. And that caught in the middle of this warfare was a third, politically naive power bloc: the Merovingians.

But there was another power bloc, too, perceived since time immemorial as *the* major threat to Western ascendancy, giving rise to nationalistic phobias more malign even than those engendered by, say, the Communist regimes of

Russia and China. It continues to do so today. Even though a political wedge has been well and truly driven between the two primary warring factions - Judaeo-Roman and Judaeo-Teuton - there remains one enemy common to both. And its potency is sufficient that, in moments of crisis, it has proved the only force capable of uniting these warring factions - indeed, uniting Europe - against its perceived threat. Even Communism did not achieve this; on the contrary, it achieved the opposite, slicing Europe in half and pushing back the boundaries of Western supremacy for almost half a century. This other power bloc, on the other hand, is perceived by the potentates of masonic government as an even more insidious threat. Indeed, as 'enemy number one'. Europe and the United States; Judaeo-Roman and Judaeo-Teuton; the Vatican and the House of Windsor. Any and every one of these powers would rather give up the Holy Grail to their bitterest political rival than to an enemy such as this one.

The enemy?

Why, the Moors, of course. The Saracen (Arab Muslim) hordes who, in the eyes of the masonic West, symbolize an age when an Idumean Arab, Herod, occupied the throne of David. It cut deep.

Thus today we look back on a history fairly stained with the blood shed between these two bitterest of political enemies: Judaeo-Christian and Arab Muslim. The barbarous and savage nature of the so-called Holy Crusades is a case in point. The political chess game being played out in modern-day Israel and the Middle East - Iraq, Iran, Libya, Kuwait - is another. Our contention in this regard, of course, is that - at least to some substantial degree - the motives behind the assassinations of Dodi Fayed and Diana, Princess of Wales, were born of this same, seemingly irrational political posture. For reasons unrelated to rhyme or reason, it would seem, this situation remains as critical today as it has done for two thousand years. Indeed, the division of the so-called Holy Land (and in particular, of course, of Jerusalem itself) is a stark reminder of this centuries-old struggle for political and economic supremacy. It is a struggle which continues to be fought out today. Not only by the Judaeo-Roman and Judaeo-Teuton factions (headed up by the Vatican and the House of Windsor respectively). But by new factions as well. New kids on the block, so to speak. Oil-rich dynasties with designs on purchasing a share of the political Holy Grail for themselves. Indeed, our source quoted several of these new factions, most of which, by his wishes, we are unable to name here. But one of the most prominent new factions in this regard - if not *the* most prominent, and one that we *are* able to name - is the House of Ibn Saud, in effect the Saudi Royal Family, intermarried with whom is of course the al Fayed family. Circles within circles. Certainly when the British Establishment's knee-jerk reaction to Mohamed al Fayed's petition for British citizenship is entered into the equation, the picture comes a little clearer. The motives behind Diana's death become ever more plausible. In the final analysis, and in terms of the ongoing struggle for political and economic ascendancy at the turn of this new millennium, it would seem that the game has engendered new pretenders to the Grail Throne. And so far as the Western world's masonic potentates are concerned, of course, these pretenders must be kept at bay. At all costs. Not even a princess is priced out of the equation (certainly not a Merovingian one).

The point of this line of investigation, then, becomes all the more evident in this light. By taking what is essentially a twentieth-century assassination plot and placing it against its own true historical and political backdrop, the motives become all the more evident. And no less admissible. After all, we are investigating both an historical and a political assassination - if indeed Diana's death *was* the result of assassination, which we firmly believe it was. Political assassination, of course, in whatever guise, is not new. It has happened before, many times, across many centuries: the crucifixion of Jesus; the murder of the Merovingian King Dagobert II; the execution of King Charles I Stuart; the assassinations of the brothers Kennedy, Martin Luther King, Pope John Paul I - to name but the prominent few. It would be foolish and naive to believe it might never happen again, in particular when you consider the motives behind each of the 'assassinations' above-cited:

That each of the victims, in their own way, had become a very serious threat to the agendas of a corrupt status quo;

That each of the victims, in their own way, had become a "loose cannon on a world stage", capable of causing irreparable damage to an establishment with much to hide, and even more to lose;

That each of the victims, in their own way, had refused to balk in the face of social and political injustices. Indeed, not only had they publicly opposed those injustices, they had elicited massive public support in the process. Much like Diana. Add to this the issue of political bloodlines and the motives for the princess's 'removal' become doubly evident.

What is most strikingly similar regarding the above-named 'assassination' victims, then, is that they all possessed a charisma sufficiently magnetic, and a persona sufficiently attractive, that they could - and did - elicit instant and massive public support against the status quo. Diana, too, demonstrated this ability. The added fact that her relationship with Dodi Fayed effectively opened the door to the British Establishment's 'enemy number one' would almost certainly, we believe, have evoked a swift and decisive response from those threatened by this action. Indeed, according to our Foreign Office source, this action "would most certainly have been the final nail in her coffin". And to judge by the evidence thus far presented, we have to say we agree.

In short, Diana's relationship with an Arab Muslim, though perhaps not the sole motive for her death, was nevertheless, we believe, the 'final straw that broke the camel's back'. And in this instance, of course, the camel was the masonic oligarchy headed up by the House of Windsor.

CHAPTER 15

THE STUARTS
And The Judaic Genetic Signature

"Jewish Line Traced Back To Moses."

The Independent, 9th July, 1998.

The Bid To Unite Britain

According to Sir Laurence Gardner - who, we recall, is appointed historian and sovereign genealogist to thirty-three royal houses, Grand Prior of the Celtic Church's Sacred Kindred of St Columba and Jacobite Historiographer Royal - the Stuarts were the direct lineal descendants of the Merovingians. Or, as Sir Laurence himself writes in his book, *Bloodline Of The Holy Grail*:

"Scotland's Royal House of Stewart arose from a marital union of the hereditary lines of Jesus and his brother James - springing from the Merovingians' own source on the one hand, and from the Celtic Kings of Britain on the other. The Stewarts emerged, therefore, as a truly unique Grail dynasty and have long been known as the 'House of Unicorns'."

Indeed, according to Grail lore, this appellation - the *House of Unicorns* - arose by virtue of the fact that the Stuarts represent the Messianic bloodline of Judah.

It was in 1603 (by which time the House of *Stewart* had become the House of *Stuart*) that King James VI Stuart of Scots was invited to succeed to the Throne of England - and thereby effectively unite the Crowns of England and Scotland. James VI of Scots thus became James I of England. But he did so under somewhat dubious circumstances, it has to be said. The Tudors, who in Henry VII had usurped the throne in 1485 from the House of Lancaster (and who had thus immediately preceded the Stuart succession) felt that they themselves had a suitable heir in Edward Seymour, Lord Beauchamp. Though Queen Elizabeth I had not married, and thus had died heirless, nevertheless Edward Seymour, by descent from Henry VII and thereby of legitimate Tudor stock, became the natural-choice successor to the 'Virgin Queen' on her death in 1603. Parliament, on the other hand, harboured ideas of its own. It wanted the Throne of Scotland. It had done for centuries. And in the death of the childless Elizabeth it recognized a prime opportunity to finally accomplish this end.

Ever since the days of Simon de Montfort, Earl of Leicester (despite his title, a French baron who in 1265 effectively formed what would later become Parliament), a Franco-English endeavour to unite the Crowns of England and Scotland had obtained. It was an endeavour which would assume obsessive proportions under Edward I, who reigned from 1272 until his death in 1307. But in 1265 a different problem faced the English Monarchy. A year earlier, in 1264, Simon de Montfort and his proposed baronial Council of Nine (later to become Parliament) had plunged England into civil war, whereupon the celebrated Frenchman had overthrown the Monarchy (Henry III Plantagenet) and assumed control of England. It is important to remember here that, at this early time, England and France were still effectively Siamese twins - still joined at the hip by dint of interdynastic marriages and a political legacy which dated back centuries. The national language of England was still French. The ruling English dynasty, the House of Plantagenet (like its predecessor, the House of Normandy) was also of French origin. And the same can be said of many of England's ruling families at this time. Thus the Crowns of France and England, in effect, were little more than provincial crowns, and as such the politics of the one was inextricably linked with that of the other. Indeed, for a good part of the preceding century, Henry II Plantagenet (reigned 1154-1189), described as "one of the most remarkable characters in English history", had ruled an empire which included the French provinces of Anjou, Normandy, Aquitaine and Brittany - as well as England, Wales and Ireland. Under King John some two decades later, however, the empire began to crumble. John's refusal to accept the Pope's candidate for Archbishop of Canterbury prompted a joint Franco-Roman conspiracy against the English Throne, and in consequence England was subjected to Papal interdict. In turn this led to the signing of the Magna Carta in 1215 - which, in effect, took power from the English Throne and placed it in the hands of a fledgling Parliament. Which may sound all well and good, on the face of it. But what would later become Parliament, of course, was at this time little more than a plutocratic conclave of French and English aristocrats, many of whom were sponsored by Rome - all of whom were equal in power and ruthless ambition to the Monarchy itself (and thus, though the aristocrats have since been joined by less noble oligarchs, the model for future Parliament was defined).

By the time Henry III succeeded King John (1216), pressure brought by French and English nobles was already forcing the Monarchy to cede many of the privileges and powers it had previously enjoyed. To add to this, by 1259 Gascony was the only remaining French province in English hands.

A year earlier, in 1258, Henry III had been forced to accept a settlement known to history as the *Provisions of Oxford*. This settlement's main protagonist was none other than the French baron, Simon de Montfort, who in consequence was elected head of the baronial Council of Nine formally established by the settlement to regulate the Monarchy. The Council and the King did not see eye to eye, however. Indeed, the fact that England was being forced to cede its French territories by this increasingly powerful, largely French conclave, was the very situation which led to civil war in 1264 - the first round of which saw de Montfort and his nobles triumph. A year later, though, Henry III's son Edward (later King Edward I) defeated de Montfort at the Battle of Evesham. The Monarchy was reinstated. And Simon de Montfort - whose father had led the Pope's army to ignominious victory over the peaceable Cathars some half a century earlier - was killed and dismembered.

A reconstituted Parliament would live to fight another day.

Following the death of Henry III in 1272, Edward acceded to the Throne. It was at this point in history that Franco-English designs on the Scottish and Welsh Thrones assumed new proportions. Four years after his accession, for example, in 1276, Edward I Plantagenet embarked on what was to become a life-long quest (or obsession): to expand the English empire to include the indigenous (Celtic) territories of Wales and Scotland. His first endeavour in this regard was to engage the Prince of North Wales, Llewellyn ap Gruffyd, in war - an endeavour, by any standards, which was to prove very successful indeed. By the following year Edward had invaded North Wales and had forced Lllewellyn's surrender. When in 1282 Llewellyn mustered his troops in further resistance against the English, he was humiliated, defeated and killed. But the biggest humiliation was yet to come.

Because two years later, in 1284, the Kingdom of Wales was finally annexed to the English Crown. In consequence, Edward's son (later Edward II) was not only born at Caernarvon Castle: to add insult to injury he was also invested at this ancient seat of Celtic-Welsh heritage as the first English Prince of Wales. And despite Welsh protests to the contrary, it is a tradition which has endured ever since.

But that was not the end of it. The power-thirsty Edward did not fulfil his expansionist quest with the annexation of Wales alone. On the contrary, like so many of his breed Edward was an empire builder; his thirst would not be quenched until a unified Kingdom of Britain was established and ruled from London. And in order to achieve that, he first had to lay his hands on the one prize which had thus far eluded his grasp - the jewel in the crown of the English empire, so to speak. Thus Edward set his sights on the Throne of Scotland.

Two years after Edward's success in Wales, in March 1286, Alexander III of Scots fell from his horse and died while travelling to meet his new queen. He was succeeded by his three-year-old granddaughter, Margaret, daughter of Eric II of Norway and thus known to history as the 'Maid of Norway'. Some four years later, Edward, tormented by his obsession to unite the English and Scottish Crowns, arranged for the seven-year-old Margaret to marry his six-year-old son, Edward of Caernarvon, Prince of Wales. Perhaps not surprisingly, many Scots opposed the marriage, and in consequence Margaret was killed while on her way to Caernarvon to marry the child prince. The marriage never took place; Edward's plan was thwarted. And thus the Crowns of England and Scotland remained independent of one another - for a time, at least.

However, the death of the child Queen Margaret precipitated what is known to history as the first *Scottish Interregnum* (an interval between the successive reigns of monarchs or governments). This left Scotland bereft of a monarch. And indeed, a government. At which point Edward seized his opportunity. Bullying his way into Scottish affairs he selected the Scottish aristocrat, John Balliol, out of three primary contenders and appointed him King of Scots. But only after John had sworn fealty to Edward - a move, it would seem, which served only to appease the English king while at the same time affording John time to consolidate his position in Scotland. Had Edward the resources at his disposal, of course, he would have invaded Scotland and claimed the throne himself at this point. But while Edward had been so obsessively focused on uniting the kingdoms of England, Wales and Scotland, King Philippe IV of France had been busy reclaiming French territories behind Edward's back. By the time Edward had installed his vassal on the Scottish Throne, Philippe had confiscated England's last remaining French territory, Gascony, and had subsequently summoned Edward to his court. The English king was furious, the French king no less intransigent. Thus in 1293 the seemingly congenital dysfunction of Anglo-French fisticuffs was resumed. Not for the first time, nor indeed the last, England and France went to war.

In the meantime, John Balliol ignored Edward's summons to attend him in battle against the French and instead formed an alliance with Philippe against the English Crown. In consequence, Balliol was forced to abdicate the Scottish Throne for contumacy (refusal to comply with Edward's wishes), and was subsequently imprisoned. Balliol's abdication, of course, precipitated the second *Scottish Interregnum*, during which Edward took control of Scottish affairs from London. He also ordered what was seen as the single most treacherous act against the Scots any Englishman had ever dared perpetrate: the removal of the fabled Stone of Destiny from Scone Abbey in Scotland, and its subsequent transfer to Westminster, England. It was a deed which would engender Scottish hatred of the English for centuries to come.

According to tradition, the Stone of Destiny originated in Judea, and is said to have been the stone pillow on which Jacob slept as he dreamt of 'Jacob's Ladder' (Genesis 28: 10-22). In any event, the Stone is said to have been transported to Ireland around 586 BC, the year Nebuchadnezzar II of Babylon destroyed the Great Temple of Jerusalem. At that time King Zedekiah of Judah was captured by Nebuchadnezzar's forces and taken to Babylon, where, according to Jeremiah (39: 6-7/52: 10-11), "all the princes of Judah", including Zedekiah's sons, were put to death. And Zedekiah himself was blinded.

His daughter, Tamar, on the other hand, is said to have escaped to Ireland, and to have given her name to Tara, the legendary seat of the Celtic-Irish High Kings. Some one thousand years later, during the fifth century AD, the Stone is then said to have followed the Kings of Dalriada (of whom the most famous is King Arthur) to Scotland, where in the ninth century it was finally installed at the famous Scone Abbey by King Kenneth I MacAlpin. According to Sir Laurence Gardner, by the early thirteenth century "the Stone of Destiny bore witness to nearly a hundred coronations in sovereign descent from King Zedekiah". Sir Laurence also asserts that the stone stolen from Scone by Edward I in 1296 was in fact nothing more than a lump of sandstone culled from a monastery doorway, and that the real Stone of Destiny was, on word of Edward's intentions, secreted away by the Abbot of Scone, and thus it has remained ever since. The irony is, of course, that, if this claim is true, then the subsequent coronation of English monarchs from the thirteenth century onwards has been witnessed not by the mystical Judaic artifact so jealously sought after by the English. But by a bogus lump of cumbersome sandstone gladly given up by the Scots to the English in 1296.

Little wonder, then, the Scots have never tried to recapture the Stone from England. Little wonder Robert I (the Bruce) declined an offer for its return at the Treaty of Northampton in 1328. Little wonder its more recent return to Scotland (November, 1996) was met with minimal enthusiasm. After all, of what use is a lump of bogus sandstone to a nation already possessed of the genuine article?

Birth Of The Stuarts

By the time James VI Stuart of Scots acceded to the Throne of England in 1603, then, plans to unite the Crowns of England and Scotland were old news. But they were no less ambitious for that.

By 1603 Parliament had evolved into something of a new and powerful administrative body. It was by this time comprised of a new and burgeoning landowner class which had, since the dissolution of the monasteries (1536-39) under Henry VIII, and the subsequent establishment of a new State Church, assumed a strategically Protestant posture. Together with the newly invested Anglican prelature (the Church of England hierarchy) the English Parliament had become of more consequence in terms of power and influence wielded than the Monarchy had ever been. Certainly with the death of Elizabeth I Tudor this situation increased in dramatic measure. But the jigsaw was still incomplete. The Monarchy was still an effective, substantive power which stood between the parliamentary oligarchs and their ultimate ambition - to unite the Crowns of what would soon become Great Britain: to have only one British Monarchy to contend with; to base that Monarchy in London; to discredit and defame that Monarchy, to constrain its power sufficiently that it would become ineffectual, manoeuvrable, controllable. And ultimately, of course, to depose that Monarchy, and if necessary, supplant it with a less dominant, more compliant one. A puppet monarchy. Which is precisely what happened.

And what is more, the Stuarts were to prove the ultimate fall guys in this political *coup d'etat*.

Having proclaimed himself Lord Paramount of Scotland in 1290, Edward I's struggle to unite the two nations under English rule continued. It would prove a savage and bloody struggle, to be sure. By virtue of installing John Balliol on the Scottish Throne in 1292, Edward made new enemies, not the least of whom were Robert the Bruce (later Robert I of Scots) and 'Braveheart' Sir William Wallace, stalwart supporter of Robert the Bruce and champion of Scottish independence. Indeed, Scottish forces under Wallace would deliver a hefty defeat to the English at Stirling in 1297. A year later, however, Edward's army would deploy the longbow and arrow for the first time in British warfare, and rout Wallace at Falkirk. Seven years later, in 1305, Wallace was captured and executed: surprised in his sleep by one Sir John Menteith, Wallace was taken to London, granted a show trial and found guilty of treason. Though the Scotsman protested his innocence in that he had never been a subject of the English Crown, his conviction was upheld. On 23rd August, 1305, Sir William Wallace was hung, drawn and quartered. His body parts were distributed to cities in the north of England and Scotland as a warning to those who might also wish to challenge English sovereignty. His head was impaled on London Bridge.

But far from dissuading the Scots in their struggle for independence, the execution of William Wallace only served to strengthen Scottish resolve. A year later, in 1306, while England and France were busy persecuting and expelling Jews and Knights Templar (England alone seized the property of more than 100,000 Jews in this year, and then expelled them), Robert the

Bruce was crowned King of Scots. Three years later, in 1309, the new king convened his first Scottish Parliament, and five years after that he defeated Edward II's army at the now famous Battle of Bannockburn, aided by a force of exiled Knights Templar. Scotland's independence was thus finally assured.

It was Robert the Bruce's grandson, however, King Robert II of Scots, who became the first true Stewart monarch, descended as he was from the Scottish High Stewards from which the Stewarts took their name. In turn the family of High Stewards (according to Leo van de Pas, *Ancestors Of Diana, Princess Of Wales*, published by *Heraldry Today*) had descended on the one hand from King Alpin of Scots (780-834) and King Kenneth I MacAlpin of Scots and Picts (800-859), who themselves had descended from the Dalriadic Kings of Scots and Ireland. On the other hand (again, according to Leo van de Pas), the High Stewards had also descended from the Sicambrian Franks, from whom in turn had descended Clodion of Tournai and Queen Basina, whose son Meroveus founded the Merovingian Dynasty. And thus the Stuarts, as Sir Laurence Gardner affirms, were indeed of impressive Judaic royal heritage - a heritage according to Sir Laurence and others, which includes the brothers Jesus and James, as well as Kings Solomon and David before them. For the record, Diana, Princess of Wales, was the direct bloodline descendant of perhaps the most remarkable of all the Stuart monarchs, King Charles II of Great Britain, by his mistress Barbara Villiers.

But it was Walter Stewart, Third High Steward of Scotland to Alexander II of Scots, who in 1204 became the first of the High Stewards to take the name Stewart. By 1371 the Stewarts had succeeded to the Scottish Throne, and it was Walter Stewart's great-great-grandson, Robert, Seventh High Steward and grandson of Robert the Bruce, who was crowned King Robert II Stewart of Scots. And thus the Stuart Dynasty was born.

Civil War

Though of Celtic-pagan origin, and later of Presbyterian (and later still Catholic) persuasion, the Stuarts were known for their religious tolerance. Not unlike their Merovingian forbears, the Stuarts' 'divine right' to monarchy rested on the constitutional tradition of *service*: they were sworn to *represent* rather than *govern* their people; to use their position to serve the people, rather than using the people to serve their position. In direct opposition to the religious dogmas of the day, they were active patrons of the arts, as well as of many arcane sciences, and as such were given to the principle of free thought - to liberty, to both religious and political tolerance, to social justice, to equity. In short, they were Grail Kings in the tradition of Jesus himself; their sovereign power was founded on the very principles intrinsic to the Grail Code, the very same principles demonstrated by their most noted forbears. Indeed, this was one reason why the English Parliament decided to invite James VI of Scots to ascend the English Throne in 1603. Not because the Puritan and/or the Anglican hierarchs at Westminster bore illusions of a religiously tolerant government. Quite the opposite. They saw the Stuarts (like the Merovingians) as politically naive, certainly in terms of the machiavellian procedures seemingly endemic to oligarchical democracy. As we have seen, their sole intentions in bypassing the Tudor claim in Edward Seymour and inviting the Stuart succession in its stead was simply so that Scotland and England (together with Wales and Ireland) could at last be ruled from Westminster. Once this centuries-long ambition was fulfilled, they would then rid England of its Scottish monarchy at the first possible opportunity and replace it with a far less effectual dynasty than either the Stuarts *or* the Tudors. And so gain control of the newly created United Kingdom of Great Britain themselves. As history attests, this is precisely what they did. Firstly by force under Oliver Cromwell in 1642; secondly by threat of force under William of Orange in 1688; and finally by installing the usurper Hanovers-Windsors on the newly created Parliamentary Throne of Great Britain in 1714. This final manoeuvre, of course, would prove both successful and abiding.

But their first move in this regard was to ensure that the Tudor succession did not prevail following the death of Elizabeth I. Thus the Stuarts were duly installed and the religio-political chicanery which would later see them deposed in favour of a more manipulable parliamentary monarchy was instituted. The Westminster oligarchs knew, for example, that the king of the newly formed Throne of Scotland and England, James I Stuart, would be expected by tradition to become Supreme Governor of the Church of England. They also knew, of course, that, in turn, this would - and did - effectively leave the Scottish Presbyterians, as well as the Irish Catholics, bereft of sovereign representation. Both the Anglicans and the Puritans were only too aware of the very serious implications this situation was bound to engender. To compound matters further, the Stuarts had introduced a new Scottish Episcopal Church into the equation, and King James himself would later be responsible for producing the new *Authorized Version* of the Bible - a fact which would displease both the Anglicans and the Puritans in no small measure. By the time James's son, King Charles I, acceded to the Throne in 1625, the situation had become impossible. And it was not helped any by the fact that, on 1st May of that same year, Charles married the sixteen-year-old sister of Louis XIII of France, Henrietta Maria, who just happened to be a Catholic. In consequence, the religious warfare engendered by the succession of the

Stuarts in the first place at this point erupted into the sectarian battlezone foreseen by the Westminster oligarchs some two decades earlier. And what is more, it was a battlezone which left Britain effectively bereft of political leadership. In 1629 Charles was thus forced to dissolve the English Parliament and form his own administration in its stead. Which he did. Though popular for a time, it was a move Charles would live to regret.

By 1640 the situation had become even more critical. In this year Charles was forced to reinstitute Parliament, which by now had been well and truly hijacked by the sanctimonious Puritans, soon to be headed up by one Oliver Cromwell. To add to this, the Scots were in protest over the Archbishop of Canterbury's attempts to impose Anglican doctrines in Scotland. At the same time, Irish Catholics were up in arms against the flood of Protestant immigrants - English Protestants who were being encouraged by the Church of England hierarchy to migrate to Ireland and establish a strong Anglican base in that country, too. (Thus began the troubles which continue to this day in Northern Ireland.) In the meantime, Parliament's dominant Whig party - together with their landowner sponsors - had been secretly negotiating with bankers from one of Britain's long-term enemies, the Netherlands. These negotiations would later lead to the establishment of the so-called Bank of England (despite its name, a privately owned - or at best quasi-public - multinational financial corporation) under the Dutch usurper William III Orange in 1694, as we shall see. Suffice here to say that, at this time, Britain's economy was in a state of ruin. Parliament desperately needed funds. Negotiations for loans deals - and for how those loans might be repaid - were thus initiated with the Dutch central bank (the Bank of Amsterdam - established 1609). In effect, the deal was pretty straightforward: in return for the massive loans necessary to buoy up the flagging economy - and so finance the Parliamentary *coup d'etat* under Oliver Cromwell - the Stuarts would be unceremoniously deposed and the Dutch House of Orange would be offered the British Throne. In 1688, this is precisely what happened.

Back in 1641, however, moves to this end had already begun. In May of that year King Charles's chief adviser, Thomas Wentworth, Earl of Strafford, was beheaded at the Tower of London. And two months later Parliament was reshaped in favour of Puritanical autonomy - the King's Council (known as the Star Chamber) was abolished and an official list of complaints known as the Grand Remonstrance was drawn up against Charles himself. In 1642 the Puritans finally locked the gates of London against the beleaguered king, and Charles was left with little choice but to raise his standard in civil war. Which - with the financial support of Princess Diana's forbears, the Spencer family - he did.

Having been forced to install the legitimate Messianic bloodline on the Throne of Britain in order to achieve this political *coup d'etat*, the first serious attempt to remove it again had begun. And before long, attempts to replace it with a bogus, 'politically cultivated' Judaeo-Teuton strain - the House of Hanover-Windsor - would prove of equal success.

Behind The Scenes

It is important we take a brief look here at what was, both in the lead up to and during the Stuart succession, transpiring behind the scenes.

As the Scots - headed up by the Merovingian-Stuart cause - had been openly fighting for their independence, in France and Germany (and to some extent in England) a similar struggle had obtained behind the scenes. It was a struggle which would culminate in the establishment of Freemasonry and other 'masonic' bodies following the suppression and dissolution of the Knights Templar in 1314. It was also a struggle which would, in the end, assure the succession of the Judaic royal bloodline to at least one of Europe's thrones.

As stated, the start of the fourteenth century saw both the English Parliament and the English Crown endeavouring with some force to prevent the continued succession of an independent Scottish monarchy. Though the motives behind Parliament's aspirations in this regard are self-evident, the Crowns of England and France bore their own reasons for wishing to prevent Scottish independence. Both knew that in Scotland, of course, the bloodline of Judah survived in the Stewarts. Both also knew that, though not yet crowned, the Stewarts were thus recognized by certain powerful cliques of Scottish and English nobles, as well as by underground chivalric and royalist movements in France - notably the Order of Sion and the Knights Templar. Though by this time the Templars had broken away from the Order of Sion (more likely for strategic reasons than for reasons of in-house politics), they were nonetheless still recognized as defenders of the Judaic royal bloodline, and at the same time champions of the cause to restore that bloodline's heirs to the thrones of Europe. Scotland was the one European throne which neither the English nor the French (nor even the Church of Rome) could yet lay claim to. It is perhaps understandable, then, that the French and English Crowns viewed the situation in Scotland with some trepidation. And why both were prepared to implement such extreme measures in their efforts to secure the Scottish Throne ahead of the Merovingian-Stewarts.

In 1305, remember, Sir William Wallace had been executed and quartered for his part in supporting the Scottish cause. Extreme measures indeed. A year later, however, as Robert the Bruce had assumed the mantle King of Scots, even more drastic measures were taken. For in this year

(1306) a persecution which had begun some fifteen years earlier culminated in both England and France expelling thousands of Jews (more than 100,000 from England alone). Though a seemingly unrelated event, and contrary to historical tradition, there is in fact good reason to surmise that these actions were in direct consequence of Scotland's defiance. It would seem that, in fear of some Jewish uprising in support of a Judaic-Merovingian restoration in Scotland, the English and French Crowns, in persecuting - and subsequently expelling - the Jews, had signalled a timely and brutal warning to both the Order of Sion and the Knights Templar: a warning which demanded in no uncertain terms that they desist from their efforts to restore the Merovingian bloodline to the Scottish - or any other European - Throne. But it seems the warning went unheeded; the Order of Sion and the Knights Templar did not desist. In consequence, many more Jews would face persecution, expulsion and even death at the hands of the Inquisition - the same Inquisition which would, some eight years later, be responsible for the ultimate demise of the Templars themselves.

We recall in this regard that in 1307, just one year after the persecution and expulsion of Jews from France and England, King Philippe IV of France (in conspiracy with Pope Clement V) began a seven-year persecution of the Templars. In 1308, Pope Clement's approval was given to torture captured Knights, to seize their property, to expel them from France (where the Papal Court was in temporary exile, at Avignon). And ultimately to execute those found guilty at the hands of the Inquisition. In this same year the Templars were also suppressed in England, Wales and Ireland. By 1312 the Order had been officially abolished in France. And in 1314 its seventy-one-year-old Grand Master, Jacques de Molay, was arrested, tried before the Inquisition in Paris, found guilty of heresy and roasted to death over a slow-burning fire.

But what is of particular note here is that, two months after Molay's death, a sizeable contingent of exiled Templars fought alongside Robert the Bruce in his defeat of Edward II (who, despite his predilection for male company, was married to the French king's daughter, Isabella). Robert's victory at the Battle of Bannockburn not only established Scottish independence. It also paved the way for the restoration of the Merovingian-Stewart Dynasty, in Scotland at least. Indeed, there is every reason to believe that a deal was struck between the Templars and the Scots at this time - one which would, at some given point in the future, assure the succession of the Merovingian-Stewarts to the Scottish Throne. Following the Battle of Bannockburn Robert would remain king, true enough. But in return for their help in precipitating this outcome, the Templars would demand that Robert's daughter be given in marriage to the heir of the Stewart line - Walter, Sixth High Steward of Scots. And in so doing unite the two primary strains of Judaic royal heritage

- of Jesus and James, of Judah and Benjamin: of the Merovingians on the one hand, and the Celtic High Kings of Scots and Ireland on the other. And this is precisely what happened. In 1315 - just one year after the Battle of Bannockburn - the Merovingian-descended Walter Stewart married Marjorie Bruce, herself a direct bloodline descendant of the Celtic High Kings of Dalriada. Thus the succession of the reconjoined Judaic royal bloodline was assured. In 1371 Robert Stewart, son of Walter Stewart and Marjorie Bruce, became Robert II of Scots.

And in Robert's descendants (included among whom was Diana, Princess of Wales) the conjoined bloodlines of Judah and Benjamin would survive. And prosper.

A Merovingian-Stuart Restoration

If, then, the persecution and expulsion of Jews from England and France in 1306 could indeed be linked to the fate of the Templars a year later (as well as to the struggle for Scottish independence at this time), we wondered: what else might be learned from a brief study of history's 'persecution of Jews'?

It was our Foreign Office source who first inferred to us that Jews had been persecuted "throughout history" on behalf of the Judaic royal bloodline and it heirs. In view of what occurred in England and France in 1306, this claim seemed plausible enough. But, we wondered, could this claim be equally substantiated with regard to the persecution of Jews "throughout history"?

In response to a question regarding the "true bloodline dynasty", our source told us: "...It has always been assumed in masonic circles that the bloodline of the Royal House of Judah is genetically distinct from other bloodlines, that it has some 'extra quality' or other - hence the 'mystical' quality attributed to David and Solomon, and of course to Jesus and the later Merovingian kings. They are all kings of the House of Judah ... Some believe that this quality is purely metaphysical. But I have seen documents that lead me to believe it is genetic; this is certainly the belief of those who struggle to control it. And anyway, that is why the House of Judah, indeed, that is why *all Jews* have been persecuted throughout history - the bloodline has always been confused with, or rather attributed to the Jews as a people, when in fact it is a purely political strain, at least it is these days."

For the record, this source also stated that the Royal House of Judah, in its present form, was in some way connected to the European Council of Princes. And as we discovered, the President of the European Council of Princes is none other than HRH Prince Michael of Albany, the current head of the deposed House of Stuart. Or to put it another way, the current heir apparent to the legitimate Messianic strain of the Royal House of Judah. (This is not meant to imply, in any way, that the European Council of Princes - ECP - is affiliated to the Stuart Dynasty or its cause. Rather that our source offered us a lead in this regard, and that, in pursuing that lead, we discovered the identity and status of Prince Michael of Albany. And thus also the survival of the Merovingian bloodline today. This is the only reason for citing ECP in this book.)

In effect, then, HRH Prince Michael of Albany is the present-day 'King of the Jews'. Of note in this regard is that, according to our source at any rate, the 'Jews' (the Judaic royal bloodline and its heirs) are currently planning something of a comeback. Indeed, the restoration of the Merovingian-Stuart Dynasty, either to the Throne of an independent Scotland, or indeed to the Throne of Britain and/or France, has been top priority to a number of chivalric-masonic bodies for at least the best part of the twentieth century, as we have seen.

But, astonishingly - and as we also discovered - what is of particular note so far as we are concerned is that this planned Merovingian-Stuart restoration might of late have involved the promotion of a certain Merovingian princess, a certain beloved Grail Queen: Diana, Princess of Wales. This at any rate would seem to have been what our Foreign Office source had implied when he said (see *Chapter Eleven*):

"I have heard whispers, rumours, nothing more ... that the late Princess of Wales had been courted by certain agencies ... who seek to restore the Merovingian line to the Throne." And further: "Look to Scotland. And to Diana's popularity."

As startling as this may seem, there is good evidence in its favour. Anglo-American endeavours to unite Europe under a corporate banner, remember, depend absolutely on the absence of a legitimate bloodline monarchy in Europe and the perpetuation of oligarchical democracy in its stead - the form of quasi-democracy for which the puppet House of Hanover-Windsor stands as titular head. A legitimate 'People's Monarch' such as Diana, of course, as popular and influential as she had undoubtedly become, *worldwide*, would have proved an insurmountable obstacle in this regard (as indeed the Stuarts had proved a similar obstacle to Anglo-Dutch attempts to unite Britain in the seventeenth century, again under the banner of corporate - or oligarchical - democracy). The reason for this is simple: the Stuarts - the bloodline, its sponsors and its heirs - oppose a united Europe ruled by the central banks and their major stockholders, in effect the international financiers and industrialists who so desperately seek to establish a corporately run European Superstate. In short, a Stuart or 'bloodline' restoration to the British Throne would mean a return to 'constitutional monarchy' - the egalitarian system of monarchy by which the Stuarts once reigned and by which the people are protected by a Written Constitution. That constitution, moreover - should the people want it - would include the right to a disinvestment from corporate autonomy.

The 'parliamentary monarchy' currently headed up by the House of Windsor, on the other hand, and as we have seen, is in effect a corporation in its own right. It thus fully supports the corporate agenda by which it has become so powerful, and by which it is contriving to survive the unification of Europe as that corporate agenda's titular head. The same corporate agenda which has succeeded in transforming Europe into a playground for plutocrats.

To add to this, Diana was unquestionably of legitimate Merovingian-Stuart stock; she could by right have claimed the support of any group or body which might have stood behind any such attempted Merovingian-Stuart restoration. Moreover, our research revealed that certain masonic echelons of the British Establishment were more than a little concerned that Diana displayed symptoms of being a 'genetic throwback' to the purest strain of Judaic royal blood - that in Diana the 'genetic signature' of Kings David and Solomon (indeed, of Jesus) and of the most notable Merovingian and Stuart kings had recurred (see *Discovery Of Judaic Genetic Signature* below).

And that this might have accounted for her unprecedented popularity and her ability to mobilize public opinion in favour of her own chosen cause.

Which gives rise to the question: what if that cause, at some point in the future, had indeed embraced the idea of a Merovingian-Stuart restoration? And further: what if Diana herself, by popular request, had agreed not only to champion that cause, but to publicly assume her rightful bloodline station and figurehead that cause, too? Might the British people have supported their 'People's Princess' in such a contest? Might they, in full knowledge that they were subjects of a usurper monarchy (in the House of Windsor) have elected to support the restoration of the legitimate Judaic-Merovingian-Stuart royal bloodline at the expense of the Windsors? In particular if that bloodline had been headed up by the most popular royal of the twentieth century: Diana, Princess of Wales? Or at least if it had been publicly supported by her? It is of consequence to remember here that Prince William, future heir to the Windsor Dynasty, by descent from Diana might also carry this same genetic signature. It is also worth noting that the Windsors had become increasingly concerned about William's close relationship with his mother. Might this concern have arisen from fear of Diana's vision for William's future? Indeed, might Diana have been grooming William, if not for a Merovingian-Stuart restoration, then at least for a return to the values and protocols associated with such a restoration? The values and protocols intrinsic to 'constitutional monarchy' by which the Stuarts once reigned, as opposed to those of the present-form 'parliamentary monarchy' by which democracy has become prostituted to the requirements of an insidious and wholly corrupt corporate agenda?

It is certainly food for thought. And it is a possibility we will explore in greater depth later.

Of course, what *is* evident in all of this is that, should it turn out that even the remotest shred of truth be found to underpin this hypothesis, then in the hallowed halls of royal-masonic oligarchy, Diana's death would have been considered with the same urgency as that of perhaps her most belaboured Stuart forbear, King Charles I of Great Britain. Like the execution of King Charles in 1649, Diana's assassination in 1997 would thus have become imperative. According to our CIA/MI6 source, Stealth, of course, as well as our MI5 source, Diana's assassination was indeed considered imperative.

And more than this. According to both of these sources it was considered of such consequence that it had been planned "several months" in advance.

Discovery Of Judaic Genetic Signature

Before moving on, and in light of the enormous implications engendered by propounding the above hypothesis (and the fact that said hypothesis rests, in part, on the basis of an alleged 'genetic signature') we felt it pertinent here to include the following brief information. If nothing else, it shows beyond question that a genetic signature can indeed be identified with certain Judaic bloodlines, and moreover, that it can indeed be traced back to the very roots of our cultural history. It also demonstrates, of course, that the scientifically studied 'genetic throwback' theory is more than mere speculation.

In an article published by one of Britain's most respected broadsheets, *The Independent* (9th July, 1998), Science Editor Steve Connor reported the findings of an Oxford University study in genetics. The article boasted the headline: *Jewish Line Traced Back To Moses*.

The article went on to say that an analysis of the male 'Y' chromosome in more than 300 Jewish men had resulted in the discovery of a specific genetic signature. This genetic signature, the report concluded, indicated a "common male ancestry" which originated "about 3,000 years before present". Indeed, according to Professor David Goldstein, lecturer in evolutionary biology at Oxford University, the genetic signature in question was shown to belong to a "homogenous" group of Y chromosomes which could be traced back to Aaron, brother of Moses. The findings were also supported by no less a figure than human geneticist, Professor Peter Goodfellow, of Smith K-line Beecham.

As stated, it was our Foreign Office source who first inferred to us that Jews had been persecuted "throughout history" on behalf of the Judaic royal bloodline and it heirs. And further, that documents currently held by MI6 revealed that the Judaic royal bloodline is "genetically distinct" from other bloodlines - that it has "some 'extra quality' or other", and that, moreover, this fact is recognized by the highest, most powerful echelons of masonic government. And that this is the reason the bloodline has been pursued and persecuted "throughout history".

Certainly we know that Oxford University is one of several primary recruiting grounds for both MI5 and MI6, and that top-secret scientific studies are carried out at such institutions on behalf of the military-industrial complex and the government. It is scarcely surprising, then, that the above-cited study in genetics was undertaken at Oxford University. Equally, it would be of little surprise to discover that the published findings of this study constitute the merest tip of an iceberg which includes knowledge of other genetic signatures, all of which have also been traced back to their racial and cultural roots. We have been reliably informed in this regard that the results of biological, technological, biochemical, biotechnological and other scientific studies are, by rule of thumb, kept secret from the public, sometimes for many years. And that the information which *is* released generally forms only a small part of a much larger picture. Might then this be the case with regard to the 'Moses' and 'Aaron' genetic signature cited above? Certainly if it is, then information regarding the signature(s) of other bloodlines - in particular such a 'politically sensitive' bloodline as the Judaic-Merovingian-Stuart bloodline, a bloodline which might, after all, challenge the right of the Windsors to reign - would surely be classified and vaulted away. According to our Foreign Office source, of course, this information has indeed been classified and vaulted away - it had at one time, remember, been our source's very task to sift and reclassify much of this information. Indeed, it was on the basis of this information, he said, that he had been able to furnish us with the grounds for our bloodline investigation. We were by now beginning to take the assertions made by this source with a little more sobriety, then. We were beginning to consider what he had told us a little more seriously.

The Persecution Of Jews

Ostensibly, then, our source's claim with regard to the persecution of Jews seemed plausible enough. Indeed, in light of the evidence at our disposal, more so. That Jews had indeed been persecuted "throughout history" (and to an even greater extent than we had first realized); and that the timing of said persecutions seemed strangely to parallel salient events in the history of the Judaic royal bloodline, became all the more evident as our research intensified. In 1306, for example, as we have seen, thousands of Jews were robbed, persecuted and expelled from France and England for reasons which - according to traditional history - remain unclear. Or at best dubious. About this same time the Knights Templar, champions of the Judaic royal bloodline, its mysteries and its heirs, were also persecuted. Indeed, they were suppressed and effectively eradicated.

And there are other examples, other correlations.

More than a century earlier, we discovered, at the height of the Crusades, attacks on European Jews had become commonplace. In 1190, for example, 500 Jews were massacred at York Castle in England, evidently blamed for engendering the situation in Jerusalem which in turn had led to the Crusades. In truth, of course, responsibility in this regard lay squarely with the Order of Sion and its endeavour - successful for a time - to restore the Judaic royal bloodline to the Throne of Jerusalem. Might the seemingly unrelated attacks on 'Jews' at this time in fact have been a consequence of the Order's actions? Unable to root out and suppress the Order's mysteriously veiled leaders, might this have been the only effective means of retribution? In any event, it would seem that 'Jews' bore the brunt of recriminations in this regard.

Also of note is the fact that, at about this same time, Jerusalem fell into Muslim hands and the Order of Sion (ostensibly at least) severed itself from its military arm, the Knights Templar. The Order itself disappeared into the mists and thus out of reach of persecutions. In consequence, a decade or so later the so-called Albigensian Crusade was initiated and thousands of Cathars were subsequently massacred. The Cathars, of course, were themselves of Jewish origin; they espoused Judaeo-pagan doctrines and even numbered among their movement descendants of the Judaic royal bloodline. Within the span of a century both the Cathars and the Templars would be eradicated - along with thousands of 'Jews'. And Wolfram von Eschenbach, having accompanied a contingent of Knights Templar to the Holy Land during this time, would begin work on his seminal romance, *Parzival*. As we have seen, in fear of impending persecutions the Templars fed Eschenbach secret information related to the bloodline - which he in turn proceeded to incorporate into his work in order to preserve its mystery for future generations. It would seem that the lives of countless more 'Jews' would be the price paid for this action - at the hands of the Inquisition.

Towards the end of the fourteenth century, thousands more Jews were persecuted and killed in Spain, blamed - again, according to traditional history - for the spread of the Black Death. From this time on, of course, thousands of Jews would face death and persecution at the hands of the Inquisition - which in truth, there now seems little doubt, was perpetrated not only to establish Catholic autonomy in Europe. But also to eradicate the surviving bloodline of Jesus - its genetic signature - a fact history tends to neglect. Or at best conceal behind the facade of religious warfare. The reason for initiating the Inquisition in the first place, of course, was that - according to the Church of Rome - the beliefs, customs and practices of the Jews were heretical (as were those of anyone and everyone other than Roman Catholics). But history leaves us in little doubt that the Jews were the intended target. After all - again, according to the Church of Rome - the Jews were responsible for crucifying Jesus Christ. It was the perfect excuse for genocide. As we now know, however, Jesus did not die as a consequence of Jewish decree, but of Roman law. The erroneous idea that Jews decided Jesus's fate is now known to have been the result of Roman propaganda - a deliberate misconstruction of historical facts by which Rome was able to gain political supremacy in Dark and Middle Ages Europe. It is a lie which obtains to this day. And because it does, Rome continues to enjoy the political and financial privilege for which it has become best known.

But if the Jews did not precipitate Jesus's death, then what might the real reason have been for implementing such a barbaric and desperate measure as the Inquisition? Barring some highly irrational and inexplicable phobia on the part of Rome, it could only have been that the survival of the Judaic royal bloodline - Jesus's bloodline, its genetic code, its genetic signature - posed an irrevocable threat to the ascendancy of Papal power in Europe. It is a threat which has obtained through centuries, even to this day. As has the Church's racist attitude toward 'Jews'. Certainly it is interesting to note that, contrary to popular belief, the Inquisition was not officially abolished until well into the nineteenth century. And even then it continued a pace - if not by name, then by deed - in the form of Royalist persecutions in Revolutionary Russia. And of course, in the form of Fascist persecutions in Nazi Germany (and as we have seen, those persecutions were funded, at least in part, by Vatican money).

Indeed, by the close of the Second World War, the Inquisition - by whatever name - had claimed the lives of more Jews than were living in Judea at the time of Jesus.

In any event, according to traditional accounts, in 1492 more than 150,000 Jews were ordered by the Spanish Inquisition to leave the country 'for the honour and glory of God' (those that were not killed, that is). In 1496 thousands more Jews were summarily slaughtered in Portugal. In 1555, Pope Paul IV decreed that Rome's Jewish quarter should be walled off from the rest of the city, thus creating the infamous Ghetto of Rome. In 1563, Ivan IV (the Terrible) of Russia ordered the drowning of hundreds of Jews in the River Dvina. Thousands more met their death in the Ukraine in 1648, reportedly the result of a Greek Orthodox pogrom and an attempt by Cossack leader, Bogdan Chmielnicki, to establish Ukrainian independence from Poland. Perhaps it is not surprising that the noted seventeenth-century artist, Rabbi Jacob van Ruisdael, produced in 1655 his widely acclaimed work, *The Jewish Graveyard*. But sadly, there were many more deaths yet to come. The Judaic royal bloodline still survived; the graveyard was not yet full.

In 1743, Russia stepped up the seemingly wholesale slaughter by initiating the massacres of thousands of Jews. At this time, of course, Russia was ruled by the Romanov Dynasty, blood cousin to the usurper Hanover Dynasty, which by now was firmly entrenched on the British Throne. The following year (1744), a purge sanctioned from Rome drove many more Jews from their homes in Moravia and Bohemia. 1881 marked the start of yet another wholesale Jewish persecution, whereby millions of Jews were victimized (many murdered) and hounded out of Russia by Tsar Alexander III; in this instance, Jews were blamed for the assassination of Alexander's father, Alexander II. Evidently the Romanovs feared that the Judaic royal bloodline, having been ousted from its European base, might subsequently endeavour to establish itself in Russia. Certainly this was the fear of Sergie Nilus, confidant to Tsar Nicholas II and the man responsible for presenting the Tsar with his own bastardized version of *The Protocols Of The Elders Sion* - an attempt, by all accounts, to convince the Tsar of a high-level Jewish conspiracy against the Romanovs. Though Nilus was banished from the court for his trouble, his fear of a Jewish takeover was shared by many others. Indeed, it was a fear which pervaded the Russian Royal Establishment to its ignominious end in 1917. And it did not end there. Two years later 'Jews' were blamed for the Russian Revolution itself, and in consequence thousands more were killed - this time by soldiers of the White Russian Army. Also in 1919, of course, a so-called high-level Jewish conspiracy was held by German nationalists to have been responsible for bringing World War One to a premature end. Thus 'Jews' were blamed for the fact that Germany lost the war. As a result, a young corporal by the name of Adolf Hitler would bear a lifelong antipathy towards Jews. There is little need here to detail the fate of the 6,000,000+ Jews who met their deaths at the hands of the Third Reich in 1930s/40s Germany.

What is of consequence in this regard, however - and as we have seen - is the fact that the late nineteenth and early twentieth centuries witnessed a concerted endeavour on the part of the Priory of Sion to restore the Judaic-Merovingian bloodline to the thrones of Europe. Indeed, this was precisely the situation which led to the Priory of Sion being hijacked by British and US intelligence agencies. And its subsequent and very public emergence on the world scene in 1956 after centuries of anonymity. The added fact that World War Two was precipitated and largely financed by Anglo-American financial and industrial interests only tends to cast suspicion on the true motives behind Hitler's perpetration of the Holocaust. Might this latest in a very long line of similar - though lesser - holocausts, for example, have been *the* final warning to the Priory of Sion, to the Priory's co-conspirators, to the heirs and the champions of the Judaic royal bloodline?

Indeed, when we look back on history at the plight of the 'Jews', might we not also be looking back at a parallel plight? That of the Judaic royal bloodline?

A critical study of history certainly suggests that this might indeed be the case. In any event, it remains a possibility that should not be ignored.

The Birth Of Masonic Government

Following the death of Oliver Cromwell in 1658, Britain was a nation in reform. Which is scarcely surprising. The Church had suffered greatly under Cromwell's regime, and was eager to restore its state authority. Likewise, the parliamentary oligarchy responsible for Cromwell's rise to power in the first place had been effectively cashiered, and thus it too was keen to reinvent its former position as Britain's ruling administrative body. The situation was not unlike that of Hitler some three hundred years later; once in power, the puppet dictator had loosed himself from the strings held by his puppeteer sponsors, and had instituted a regime over which he had ruled supreme. Indeed, within a few years of his victory over Charles I, Cromwell had abolished Parliament, and in its stead had established a fierce - if not brutal - military regime. Free thought was outlawed. Free speech was outlawed. All effective forms of education and learning were suppressed. At the same time many religious practices were forbidden and the celebration of religious festivals tabooed; Christmas, together with Easter, was effectively erased from the British itinerary. To add to this, theatres were closed, entertainment prohibited, private and public meetings strictly forbidden. And while single mothers faced imprisonment without trial, anyone suspected of adultery faced death by the hangman's noose. Needless to say, Cromwell's death was greeted with an enormous sense of relief in just about every quarter of British society - not least, of course, in the corridors of oligarchical power. Indeed, though Cromwell's son, Richard, succeeded him as Lord Protector in 1658, by May of the following year Parliament was effectively re-established at Westminster and Richard Cromwell was forced to resign. When in 1660 the Stuarts were invited back to Britain and Charles II officially restored to the Throne, there was dancing in the streets. A new dawn beckoned, and with it, hope.

In Parliament, however, minds were already devising new ways to replace the Stuarts with a monarchy it could control. But it would have to bide its time. The increasingly powerful Parliament had by now learned that a military coup was no longer the most effective way to depose the monarchy and seize control of the nation's affairs. But it had other plans. Negotiations with Dutch financiers were already under way for the institution of a British central bank; the Dutch, who had already founded their own central bank in Amsterdam in 1609, would largely underwrite what became known as the Whig Revolution - the effective usurpation of sovereign power by Parliament, which of course was controlled by the landowner Whigs. In return for their complicity the Dutch would gain the British Throne under William of Orange in 1688 - a move which would at least engender a lasting peace between Britain and the Netherlands. In effect, however, it would also mark the beginning of what is today referred to as corporate government - or masonic government - as we shall see.

While King Charles II was endeavouring to negotiate a peace treaty with France and the Netherlands, then, supporters of the Parliamentary Whig Party were secretly negotiating terms for the institution of a Dutch-sponsored British plutocracy. In other words, the creation of a privately owned central banking system which would take away the power of government to control the nation's economy (and thereby its policy) and place it in the hands of independent bankers and financiers. It is a system which has endured ever since. Neither King Charles II nor his successor, James II, would sanction such a system, of course. But with the effective removal of the Stuarts in 1688, and the subsequent exile of James II in France, the way was made clear for the Dutch usurper, William III of Orange, to ascend the Throne. And for Parliament to make its move. Which it did. In return for a loan of some £1,000,000 to the Treasury, in 1694 the Anglo-Dutch consortium of bankers and financiers which would henceforth be known as the Bank of England was chartered by the government. And thus the National Debt - and with it the insidious and corrupt system known as 'fractional reserve banking' - was born. It was a system which would both cripple and corrupt governments for centuries to come. Moreover, it was a system by which usurper monarchies such as the House of Hanover-Windsor could be bought and sold on the open market - like second-hand cars.

In 1714, of course, a mere twenty years after the birth of the so-called Bank of England, this is precisely what would happen - Britain would buy itself a second-hand monarchy. And it would do so as a direct result of the government having been hijacked by this new and all-powerful plutocratic oligarchy - otherwise known as masonic government.

Fractional Reserve Banking
The Coming Of The House Of Windsor

"In our hands is the greatest power of our day - *gold*." So say *The Protocols Of The Elders Of Sion*. When the wholly disreputable practice of 'fractional reserve banking' is set against this and other claims propounded in the *Protocols*, it is easy to see why many scholars now consider them with some awe.

As we have seen, it was the Knights Templar who established the first effective modern-day banking system. This they achieved by lending gold and silver coin at interest (a practice known as 'usury'). But although they were the first to employ this system in Europe, they were not the first to corrupt it. On the contrary, like most else undertaken by the Templars, the system of banking employed by them was perhaps the most 'straight-down-the-line' system ever to have been successful. But then, it was never intended as anything other. It was never intended simply as a means to profit from others. But rather to serve the nations in which the Order found itself by way of holding, brokering, transferring and - above all - protecting those nations' assets. The interest paid in return for this service was minimal and fair. It did not take long, however, for others to realize that vast profits could be made by employing this same system - albeit by 'modifying' the rules somewhat.

In an excellent book and video on this subject, boldly titled *The Money Masters: How International Bankers Gained Control Of America* (Patrick SJ Carmack BBA, JD, corporate law expert, former Administrative Law Judge and member of the bar of the US Supreme Court) perhaps one of the 'easiest-to-understand' explanations of 'fractional reserve banking' is presented. Anyone wishing to understand the full extent to which the British and US governments (along with most every other government) are today held to ransom by the so-called Money Masters, should acquire a copy. It will elucidate far more extensively the system we are only able to explain here - space limiting - in summary form. We have nonetheless elected to include this brief explanation because, as we shall see, 'fractional reserve banking' was - and remains - ultimately responsible for the overthrow of democracy in the modern world. Indeed, it was this wholly corrupt and insidious mechanism which finally paved the way for the coming of the House of Windsor.

In brief then, it was the goldsmiths of medieval Britain and Europe, by emulating - and criminally modifying - the methods employed by the Templars, who effectively initiated the banking system which today controls monarchies and governments alike. At this early time, of course, currency *per se* was not in circulation. It did not exist. Wealth was largely assessed by possession of land, property and livestock, and weighed against the market value of gold. Which is where the goldsmiths entered the frame. By accepting gold deposits from the landed and the moneyed (gold deposited with goldsmiths for safekeeping) and by issuing paper receipts in exchange for the gold, the goldsmiths became the first effective bankers - at least as we understand that term today. Before long the paper receipts issued by the goldsmiths bore the signatures of the depositors, and so became accepted as currency between one depositor and another. But as Patrick Carmack points out in *The Money Masters*: "Over time, to simplify the process, the receipts were made out to the bearer, rather than to the individual depositor, making them readily transferable without the need for a signature." And thus what must surely be seen as the biggest and most far-reaching fraud ever perpetrated was duly initiated. And this is how it worked.

By replacing the paper receipts with the first effective bank notes - i.e. receipts made out to 'the bearer' rather than to the individual depositor - the gold deposits could no longer be identified with the individuals who had deposited them. Thus from this time on the goldsmiths were free to lend money - the newly created 'bank notes' - to individuals who had made no such deposit. These loans, of course, were made with interest. And what is more, the goldsmiths found that they were able to lend up to ten times the amount they held in reserve, with interest, and with little chance of being found out. In other words, a goldsmith holding, say, £5000 in gold reserves (deposits), discovered that he could lend out up to £50,000 (all with interest) by printing more receipts (bank notes) than he had gold in reserve. This was possible, the goldsmiths learned, because - then as now - only a small number of depositors ever wished to withdraw their gold at any one time. And even then, it was unlikely that they would wish to withdraw all of it.

Even today, should everyone, say, in Britain and the US, suddenly decide to withdraw all their money from the banks where that money is deposited, there would be nothing like sufficient funds to cover those withdrawals in cash. This is because your bank and ours, even today, persist in the corrupt methods first employed by the goldsmiths of medieval Europe. As stated, this system is known by the self-descriptive term, 'fractional reserve banking', or 'fractional reserve lending' - i.e. the 'lending' out of money, with interest, of which only a 'fraction' of the 'reserve' is actually held on deposit. Anyone reading this who might have, say, £5000 or $5000 deposited with any one bank can thus rest assured that said bank has loaned out up to ten times that amount to other clients - all off the back of *your personal deposit*. Said bank has also collected the interest on those loans, of course, which - even at the modest rate of 10% - is sufficient to cover the amount originally deposited by you. The remaining £50,000 (or $50,000) is sheer profit, even though it is money which does not actually exist. It has never even been printed, much less deposited. It certainly does not exist as hard currency. In this way the pennies we earn are translated into literally billions of counterfeit dollars on the open market. And it is the national central banks such as the Bank of England and the US Federal Reserve Bank - owned not by the people, of course, nor even by national governments, but by their majority shareholders, the so-called independent banks such as Barclays, the National Westminster, Chase Manhattan, Citibank, etc - who launder this 'non-existent' money and enjoy the sheer obscenity of privilege it affords. Indeed, this is why stock markets fluctuate, and sometimes crash. It is how economic 'booms' and 'depressions' can so easily be - and are - deliberately created (as, for example, the Great Depression of the 1930s, which in turn led to the emergence of Nazi Germany, a regime funded, as we now know, by shareholders of both the Bank of England and the US Federal Reserve Bank). If the amount of money floating around on the world markets truly was 'real money', of course, such booms and depressions simply could not happen, much less could they be created for personal gain. That most of this so-called money is in fact 'non-existent money', on the other hand, means that its circulation can indeed be manipulated and controlled by the world's most powerful financial institutions. Indeed, this is precisely the case.

And it all began with the goldsmiths of medieval Europe.

By the time Elizabeth I Tudor ascended the English Throne in 1558, then, the so-called Money Masters (one and the same with 'masonic government') had become very powerful indeed. It is no secret, for example, that throughout her reign Elizabeth fought a running battle with this increasingly powerful masonic oligarchy for control of England's economy. And that, as a result, by her death in 1603 England's economy was in effective ruin. Apart from a brief recovery during King Charles I Stuart's reign - between 1629-1640, when the king dissolved Parliament and took charge of the economy himself - it was a condition which would obtain throughout the seventeenth century. Indeed, it was a condition which would lead to the overthrow of the monarchy in 1688 and the subsequent emergence of plutocratic government.

As we have seen, by installing the Stuarts on the newly created Throne of England and Scots in 1603, the still-formative landowner class had instituted new and unprecedented moves to gain control of Britain's political and financial affairs. With the death of Charles II Stuart in 1685, and the subsequent overthrow of his brother and successor, James II, in 1688, the seeds sown more than a century beforehand began to take root. More than this: they began to blossom. By manipulating the marriage of James II's daughter, Mary Stuart, to Prince William III Orange, the latter was able with some legitimacy to invade England and depose James II. In consequence, the accession of the Dutch Stadtholder William to the British Throne initiated the final move in the establishment of oligarchical democracy - or masonic government - in Britain. Indeed, Britain was the first powerful nation in the world to be hijacked in this way. In 1694, just five years after William's coronation, the Bank of England was chartered, and within a very short period it was dictating financial policy and underwriting the activities of Parliament. And of course, lending out far more money than it had in reserve. Though initial shares in this new, privately owned financial corporation amounted to around £750,000, for example, it nevertheless began trading by lending the British government £1,000,000 - the result of 'fractional reserve banking'. In effect, the deal was that the Bank of England would lend the government as much as the government could spend by printing money beyond the value of its shareholding (indeed, within four years the initial £1,000,000 loan had risen to £16,000,000 - a debt secured, of course, then as now, by the British taxpayer). In return the Bank was granted permission to print money, to effectively set national interest rates, and to sell stocks and shares on the open market. Which it proceeded to do. The upshot being that Britain's currency - owned, by right, by the British people - fell into the hands of international financiers and bankers who in turn speculated that currency on the open market for their own personal gain. The British taxpayer would not share in the profits. On the contrary, from this time on said taxpayer would be forced to tithe a percentage of his/her income to the Treasury in order that the government could keep up its payments on the interest accrued on the loans. (The loans themselves, of course, were/are never meant to be repaid. For one thing, it is a business arrangement by which many top-flight politicians benefit, in particular those who occupy seats on the boards of the independent or so-called 'High Street' banks, which in turn are the Bank of England's major shareholders. Also, of course, should the loans ever be repaid then the Bank of England would become effectively impotent; the government would regain control of the economy, the bankers and financiers would be out of business, and - perhaps more to the point - the politicians out of pocket. Needless to say, this could never be allowed to happen.)

   Thus only the interest on the loans is ever met. However, this in turn means that whenever the government loans money from the Bank - which it of course continues to do, and on a regular basis - more and more taxes are required to meet the amount of interest accumulated on those loans. Which is why industry is so desperately needed (to keep the plebs in work to pay their taxes) and why everything bar fresh air - which there is increasingly little of - also carries exorbitant tax rates. Certainly this is the case in Britain. (In point of fact, fresh air, together with light, *was* taxed during William III's reign. And it continued to be taxed well into the nineteenth century. One year after the establishment of the Bank of England, in order to meet the loan repayments, the government introduced the taxing of each individual window above six in every house - which is why in England one is still able to see the bricked-up windows of houses dating from this period.) Today, everything we earn, purchase and own is still taxed by an effectively bankrupt government. And the revenue collected of course finds its way directly into the coffers of those responsible for the government's state of bankruptcy - the Money Masters who own the Bank of England.

Loans for taxes, taxes for loans. It is a self-perpetuating circle which is never destined to be broken.

With the 'non-existent' money created by the fraudulent system of 'fractional reserve banking', then, the Bank of England effectively bought the rights to the British Treasury. Or more precisely, to Britain itself. It also bought the square mile in the centre of London commonly known as 'the City'. Here it was that the Bank's masonic sponsors erected a monument to their success - the grimly opulent baroque edifice which houses the Bank of England - and set up their own law enforcement agency to boot - the City of London Police. Of note is the fact that this force of more than 2000 officers is autonomous from the nation's primary police force - the Metropolitan Police based at Scotland Yard - as well as from all other police forces across Britain. It continues to protect the gold-plated square mile - otherwise known as 'Fort Knox' - even today. And it is easy to see why. Though ownership of certain other areas in London remains desirable to the super-rich, it is the City of London, together with the neighbouring City of Westminster, which houses both the puppets and the potentates of masonic government - its Monarch, its Parliament; its Prime Minister and its Chancellor of the Exchequer. In short, the aristocracy and the British Establishment. As Patrick Carmack rightly points out: "The symbiotic relationship between the Money Changers and the higher British aristocracy continues to this day. The monarch has no real power, but serves as a useful shield for the Money Changers who rule the City - dominated by the banking House of Rothschild."

Indeed, this is why so great a deal is made of the Rothschilds and the Rockefellers today in terms of their role in masonic government. For while the Rothschilds continue to dominate the City of London, it is the Rockefellers' Chase Manhattan Bank (major stockholder in 1930s/40s Nazi Germany and now merged with Chemical Bank), together with Citibank NA, which boasts the majority shareholding in America's own central bank - the US Federal Reserve Bank. In other words, the US government today subsists largely on the spilt blood of six million slaughtered Jews and their still-unaccounted-for gold reserves. (Perhaps, then, the US central bank should thus be renamed, more aptly: The Murdered Jews' Stolen Gold Reserve Bank.) In any event, it is certainly of interest to note that, in truth, the so-called Federal Reserve is neither 'federal' nor possessed of the massive 'reserves' insinuated by its name. On the contrary, like its British counterpart, the equally misnamed Bank of England, the 'Fed' is a privately owned (or at best a quasi-public) multinational financial corporation chartered to print - or 'create' - new money whenever the US government is short of a few bucks. Which, it would seem, is reasonably often. Indeed, the Fed hands over around $1,000,000,000 (one billion) a day to the ailing US economy. This money is simply created out of thin air; it is conjured up against reserves which largely do not exist and subsequently loaned to the government (with interest, of course). And it is paid for by the American taxpayer. It is both an ingenious and a scurrilous design, to be sure - one that serves the Money Masters well enough.

Also of note is that the US government currently owes upwards of $5,000,000,000,000 (five trillion) to the 'Fed'. Not bad. Five trillion in debt and still the wealthiest, most powerful nation on Earth. One cannot help but notice, however, that this money, together with that owed by Britain, is owed to private individuals: to the Rockefellers, to the Rothschilds, to the world's other top-flight banks and ruling families - most of whom are the leading lights of the Bilderberg Group and other such masonically structured international power groups. In consequence, one cannot help but notice who in truth holds the purse strings of the Western world. And thus who governs its policy.

The Electors Of Germany

By 1702, then, the Bank of England and its newly purchased Parliament was in firm control of Britain. It was in this year that, on the death of William of Orange, Queen Anne Stuart ascended the British Throne. But her reign - indeed, her choice as successor to the Dutch usurper - was a complete and utter sham. While history tells us that Anne had turned traitor to both the Scots and the Stuart cause, in truth the British Throne was by this time little more than a totem, a notch on the armament of Westminster. As it is today. In consequence, Anne - as head of an increasingly powerless Stuart Dynasty - was left with little choice but to conform to the dictates of this (by now) wholly autonomous and plutocratic conclave: Parliament. Thus in 1706, at the behest of the Westminster oligarchy, Anne was forced to dissolve the Scottish Parliament for which her forbears had so diligently fought. Though the Scots of course protested this decree, and with some vigour, in the end they too were compelled - by threat of sanctions and military invasion - to capitulate.

In consequence, one year later, in 1707, the Crowns of England and Scotland once again came under the rule of Westminster - this time, it would seem, for good. (As our Foreign Office source claimed, then, the centralization process instituted by masonic government indeed began, in earnest, some three hundred years ago.)

But there still remained the question of who should succeed Queen Anne. The Scots, of course, had already made their choice; they wanted the man who, by right, should have succeeded James II to the Throne of Britain. But as we know, James had been deposed by Westminster some two decades earlier, and thus his son and heir, also James, did not figure at all in their reckonings. Though the Scottish Covenanters, in defiance of Westminster, went ahead and proclaimed James Francis Edward Stuart *de jure* King James VIII of Scots, his reign, in effect, was never recognized in England. Nevertheless his bloodline continued, and it is by this ancestral line that James's patrilineal descendant, HRH Prince Michael of Albany, President of the European Council of Princes, claims his right to the Scottish Throne today. Indeed, had James II elected to sell his soul to Parliament in the manner of the Hanovers-Windsors, he would doubtless have been considered a more viable investment by the burgeoning Bank of England - and thus might have remained king. A king without integrity. A king, nonetheless. And in any event, HRH Prince Michael of Albany would thus have been recognized as King of Great Britain today.

But it was not to be. King James II did not sell his soul, to Parliament or anybody else. In consequence, the true bloodline monarchy of Britain - or at least Scotland - remains sidelined. And this is the reason why.

Back in 1707 the Westminster oligarchs forced Queen Anne to nominate her own successor from the German Electors of Hanover - a family no more royal in Germany, of course, than it would prove to be in Britain. But the point was that it was a family whom the joint Bank-of-England-and-Westminster oligarchs felt confident they could control - for a price. And they were not wrong. As an added security, many have since commented, they also made absolutely certain that a legitimate Stuart heir did not survive Anne herself. Certainly it is a curious fact that, although during her reign she conceived no less than *eighteen* times, and indeed gave birth to five children, none survived their formative years. Much less their mother. In consequence, Anne was once again forced to acquiesce to the Westminster dictate and nominate her own successor. Or rather, the successor she was told to nominate. She thus chose the German Electress, Sophia. By the time Anne died in 1714, however, Sophia herself was dead. And it was thus Sophia's son, George Guelph, Elector of Hanover, who acceded to the Throne of Britain in 1714.

The Hanovers, described by many historians as the most debauched of all royal dynasties ever to have occupied the English Throne, had arrived. What irony, then, that the present-day heir to this corrupt Judaeo-Teuton dynasty would marry a Merovingian princess. And thus that their son, Prince William, heir to the Windsor Dynasty and future King of Great Britain, might also carry the same Messianic gene as his mother - the Judaic genetic signature of the Grail Kings. Indeed, let us pray that he does.

CHAPTER 16

THE CORONATION
A Masonic Legacy

"And as Solomon was anointed king by Zadok the priest and Nathan the prophet, so be thou anointed, blessed and consecrated Queen over the People."

Extract from the Coronation Ceremony of Queen Elizabeth II, 1953.

The Antimonarchy

In many respects the arrival of the Hanovers-Windsors was the arrival of the Antimonarchy. In other words, the arrival of a royal dynasty established in direct opposition to what was once regarded by many as the true bloodline dynasty of Judah. Like an antichrist, an antimonarchy describes a dynasty sponsored by those with vested interests in its institution. And its subsequent preservation. Its continued succession. The Windsors are one such monarchy. Unlike the Stuarts in Scotland, for example, or indeed the Merovingians in Dark Ages Europe or the Davidic Kings in pre-Roman Palestine, the Windsors were installed on the British Throne purely for reasons of political gain. The establishment of plutocratic government in Britain towards the end of the seventeenth century, evinced by the founding of the Bank of England in 1694, demanded a new breed of parliamentary monarchy, one that would not undermine - or at least would endorse rather than challenge - the autonomy of Parliament. And the Windsors - then the Hanovers - were seen as the perfect candidates for the job. For one thing they were German; they were foreign. They spoke little or no English and displayed no interest whatever in the affairs of Great Britain. To add to this they were indeed of Judaic stock (albeit of the usurped Teuton strain first cultivated by the Church of Rome, a strain which prospered through the lines of the Black Guelphs and other lines of what is still known as Europe's Black Nobility). They nevertheless carried the requisite 'blue blood' in their veins, the quasi-Judaic blood which, still today, gives authority and meaning to the otherwise impotent prerogative of masonic infrastructure. And being of this politically cultivated Judaeo-Teuton strain of course meant that the question of royal intervention simply would not arise - a prerequisite condition underpinning their contract with the British

Parliament, a condition with which the Hanovers were more than happy to comply. But then, like others of this same bogus strain they were well-versed in the art of feudal warfare, of political artifice - the very craft which had seen them so prosper in their native Germany that they had risen to the status of Electors (nobles of the Holy Roman Empire whose task it was to elect the Emperor). Thus they knew the ropes, so to speak. They were fully conversant with the rules of masonic government, of oligarchical imperialism, and as such were a 'safe bet' for a parliamentary oligarchy seeking to consolidate its own position in this regard. (Indeed, the British Empire would fairly burgeon under the Hanovers, its tendrils of imperial tyranny gaining a stranglehold on virtually every point of latitude, reaching so far and wide that, until the surrender of Hong Kong in 1997, the sun had not set on British sovereign territory for centuries. An impressive investment in real estate, to be sure. And real estate, of course, is prime collateral to an empire with its own central bank.)

Parliament would not be disappointed with its new acquisition, then.

Also, of course, Parliament knew that the first Hanover king, George I, would spend almost his entire reign abroad - in his native Germany and in other, more appealing European countries. It was known that, rather than become embroiled in the somewhat tedious task of upholding the rights of his people against the whim of a self-elected government (the *de facto* duty of a constitutional monarch), he would choose instead to neglect those over which he had been crowned king as though neglecting an unwanted toy. In this regard George would prove the model puppet-king, the dream figurehead for a government still endeavouring to firmly establish itself as *the* sovereign and political power. In return the Hanovers would enjoy obscene privilege and untold wealth. They would also be promoted as the model monarchy. In the years to come they would be presented to the British public as the finest, the noblest, the most exemplary monarchy ever to have graced the British Throne - when in truth they are quite the reverse, as their own sordid track record attests. Yet, even today, this 300-year-old stratagem remains a propaganda triumph of untold proportions. The Bank of England continues to govern Parliament. Parliament continues to govern the Monarchy. And the Monarchy continues to govern the masonic structures and edifices which uphold the now well-established system of oligarchical democracy, in a titular sense at least. It also, of course, continues to enjoy the obscene levels of wealth and privilege first pledged in the terms of its initial contract with Parliament. It is the ultimate foolproof sting. And it has served the perpetrators well enough.

Meanwhile, at the lower end of the chain, an apathetic British public continue to accept whatever imposture is perpetrated upon them. And there are many to choose from. The coronation ceremony, for example, is one such imposture. For one thing, it is a latter-day - though bastardized - version of the coronation ceremony of King Solomon himself, as we shall see. It is thus a testimony to the power still vested in the usurped strain of the Judaic royal bloodline of old - the bloodline of David, of Solomon, of Zedekiah. Of Jesus and the Merovingian kings. Of the Stuarts. In this way the messianic legacy of Judah continues to uphold the political and sovereign power wielded by masonic government today. And it does so by virtue of the inglorious House of Windsor.

The Power To Create Monarchs

That the Judaic royal bloodline is today of utmost importance, then, most specifically in terms of its symbolic representation, both in a masonic and a political sense, is beyond question. One need look no further than the most important ceremony in the land, the coronation ceremony, to discover the wholly masonic and magical ritual involved in the creation of a latter-day British (or European) monarch. That, and the added fact that its power, its true investment, remains rooted in the quasi-magical lustre of biblical rite: Judaic rite.

What this reaffirms, of course, is that the aristocracy, and in particular the monarchy, is indeed today little more than a public figurehead for some hidden masonic government - a government whose authority rests upon (and is made tenable by) the usurped power vested in the Judaic royal bloodline. As such, by its nature, it deals not in the welfare and prosperity of its people (the very qualities ascribed to the legitimate bloodline and its heirs), but rather in its own continued succession. Indeed, that such a feudal institution as the present-form parliamentary monarchy has managed to survive its own historical and political caricature - with so little resistance from its realm, and for so long - is evidence enough to this end. That it intends to survive a good deal longer, no matter the cost, is equally evident.

In short, what historical research and documentation tend to reveal is that the 'mystical' power embodied by the European nobility stems from some alchemical (and historical) infusion of Judaic blood - a fact supported by a sizeable body of evidence, as hitherto presented. Indeed, it is supported in the first instance by the very pomp and ceremony ascribed to our own traditions, our very own national rites and functions - all of which are Judaic/masonic in origin. And in fibre. The ceremonies performed in our churches, for one, unlike those of, say, pagan and other less hierarchical religions, are based purely and solely on Judaic/masonic legacy. They are Christian, of Jewish origin; Jesus was first and foremost a Jew, and the ceremonies performed in his name are essentially Judaic. Indeed, the entire Christian ceremony is based on a *pot-pourri* of Judaic/masonic hierarchical pomp and paraphernalia.

When one kneels at the feet of a cleric, for example, and receives the 'blood and the flesh of Christ' - albeit in good faith, albeit as an act of atonement, and of pure intention, in particular on the part of the devoutly religious - one is nevertheless enacting a role. That of the neophyte receiving mystical licence from the Grand Master Mason. Or of the wandering Jew receiving the blessings of Yahweh from the Jewish high priest or rabbi. The point being that the apparent differences between these seemingly discrepant ceremonies are purely cosmetic, and are due purely to the passage of time and the cultural species in which they have subsequently emerged. The fact that the participant's intention is sincere only serves to legitimize - give weight to - the imposture being perpetrated.

But it is surely the coronation ceremony itself which constitutes the greatest imposture of all. For it is by way of the coronation ceremony that the monarch is seen to emerge a divine incarnation, imbued with divine sanction like some out-of-time Pharaoh or Messiah. Indeed, it is this cunningly devised ceremony which, above all else, serves to perpetuate the quasi-messianic system of monarchy adopted - or rather usurped - from the Royal House of Judah in the first place. Within the precincts of masonic ceremony, the Grand Master Mason (or in the case of the coronation, the Archbishop of Canterbury) is presumed to possess magic sufficient to effect a 'transfiguration' of the candidate's blood. Thus the mortal heir is transformed into a divine monarch.

In short, the Archbishop is invested with the 'power to create monarchs'.

Of note, however, is the fact that the Archbishop of Canterbury inherited this power not from God, but from Henry VIII, who in turn usurped it from the Bishop of Rome (the Pope) in 1534. It was then that the ageing Tudor king established the Church of England in order that he might divorce and marry whomsoever he chose (a privilege no longer afforded princes or kings - or, indeed, it would seem, princesses). Of further interest - and as we now know - is the fact that the Pope himself first usurped this same mystical power (though for different reasons, for *political* reasons) from a dynastic bloodline which was also Judaic in origin, the dynasty of remarkable warrior/priest-kings known as the Merovingians. It was this mysterious royal dynasty, of course, which claimed direct lineal descent from one King Yeshua of Judah, best known the world over as Jesus the Christ.

However, it is important that we focus our attention here on the present-day coronation ceremony itself. It is important that we demonstrate the fact that underpinning the European monarchical infrastructure is a secret and a tradition - symbolized in the form of a bogus bloodline - which is wholly Judaic in origin. And that it is a secret and a tradition which bears immense political power, even today. Indeed, over many centuries this secret - this bogus bloodline - has established an extraordinary stranglehold on Western society: on its politics, its economic structures, its very psyche. Naturally it does not wish to see that stranglehold weakened, undermined, or in any way compromised - infiltration by what might be considered a 'virus', for example, a foreign power capable of manipulating that stranglehold and turning it to its own vested interest, its own political end. An Arab Muslim too close to the throne would certainly be considered such a virus. Especially an Arab Muslim as rich and powerful as an al Fayed. Especially an Arab Muslim who also happened to be Egyptian. From the days of Moses and the biblical Exodus to the establishment of the modern state of Israel in 1948; from the Six Day War in 1967 up to and including the present-day Middle East crisis and its ever-floundering peace process, Egypt and Israel have been at war. Make no mistake. Even at the time of Jesus, the bitterest pill for any self-esteeming Jew to swallow was not merely the fact that Rome had invaded the Holy Land - though this of course engendered its own hatreds and reprisals, in particular giving rise to the nationalist movement of Zealots to which Jesus himself belonged (indeed, which Jesus would have spearheaded as Israel's *de jure* king.) But it was the fact that Rome in her worldly wisdom had installed an Arab dynasty, the Herods, on the Throne of Israel that roused the various Judaic factions to war. This same situation, of course, or another one built upon it, obtains today. It is this same worldly wisdom which is of equal effect in the corporate and masonic diplomacies currently being applied to the Middle East situation. The destiny of that relatively small though politically enormous parcel of Middle East territory is today, as always, in the hands of a small number of political and economic potentates who play off Jew and Arab against one another as though presiding over some machiavellian chess game. Indeed, in many respects successful manipulation of this chess game is their passport to continued financial and political ascendancy. It is their political Holy Grail, so to speak. Control of Arab oil reserves by the enforcement of political and economic sanctions and the threat of military action is evidence enough to this end - the Iraq-Kuwait oil dispute being a primary case in point.

The final approbation, though, the final seal (indeed, the final insult) is attained by the fact that all of the above chicanery is played out in the public arena for the entire world to see, like some terrible secret concealing itself in the full glare of public ignorance. For the world, quite frankly, has not a clue what is being achieved, at whose expense, or why. If we could but see it, the biggest imposture perpetrated upon us is achieved in front of our very eyes.

And paradoxically, this is precisely the reason it works.

The Coronation Of Elizabeth II

In his book, *Defender Of The Faith: The Church And The Crisis In The Monarchy*, Ted Harrison conscientiously outlines the coronation ceremony of Queen Elizabeth II. It was of course the last ceremony of its kind to be performed in Britain (1953), and will remain so until such times as Prince Charles (or Prince William, depending on the national climate) steps forward to be 'anointed' and infused with the same sacerdotal powers.

Mr Harrison, who also seeks to highlight the Judaic character inherent in the ceremony (although for his own reasons) and the fact that it has become a tradition which originated with the coronation of King Solomon, comments:

> After the Creed the Archbishop begins the ancient hymn, '*Veni Creator Spiritus*,' invoking the inspiration of the Holy Spirit. At this point, while the Queen kneels at a faldstool, she is stripped of her crimson robe and sits unadorned and expectant, awaiting her hallowing. After a prayer beginning 'O Lord, Holy Father, Who by anointing with oil didst of old make and consecrate Kings, Priests and Prophets to teach and govern Thy people Israel,' there follows the central act of the whole religious ceremony, the Unction, whereby the Queen is 'anointed, blessed and consecrated' to her high office. Four Knights of the Garter hold over her a canopy of cloth-of-gold, almost concealing her from sight. The Dean of Westminster brings from the Altar the Ampulla filled with oil, some of which he pours into the Spoon (probably the most ancient of all the Regalia). The Archbishop, dipping his finger in the oil, goes beneath the canopy and anoints the Queen in the form of a cross, thus signing her with the Sign of the Cross, as in baptism, 'in token that hereafter she shall not be ashamed to confess the faith of Christ crucified, and manfully to fight under his banner against sin, the world and the devil, and to continue Christ's faithful soldier and servant unto her life's end.'Indeed, in mediaeval times, as the Canonist Lindwood expresses it, an anointed King or Queen was regarded as 'mixta persona,' half-ecclesiastic and half-laic, possessed of an inalienable and ineffaceable 'character,' so that 'Not all the water in the rough rude sea can wash the balm off from an anointed King'.

At this point in the ceremony the heir apparent receives what is known as the Unction, the 'anointing of the head with oil'. This is accompanied by the following words:

"Zadok the priest, and Nathan the prophet, anointed Solomon the King. And all the people rejoiced and said: *God save the King; Long live the King; May the King live for ever. Amen. Hallelujah.*"

Until the moment of the Unction the succeeding monarch is neither qualified nor entitled to receive the emblems of his/her royal estate. In other words, a monarch is not a monarch until he or she has been anointed with the sacred oil, and has subsequently sworn allegiance to the masonic body of which he/she is about to become the official and abiding public figurehead.

As evidence that this ceremony indeed dates back to the anointing of Kings David and Solomon - and thereby signifies the symbolic though tell-tale dependence of present-day monarchies on the Judaic royal bloodline, its assumed sacerdotal power and its expression in masonic government - included here is the passage from the Old Testament which recounts Solomon's own coronation. Particular attention should be paid to the fact that, as in the coronation of Queen Elizabeth, it is the anointing of Solomon with oil that marks the moment when he becomes king. And that the names of the high priest and the prophet summoned by King David and appointed to preside over his son's coronation are the same high priest and prophet summoned in the present-day coronation ceremony of British monarchs.

The extract is taken from the New English Bible, 1 Kings, 1:32-40.

> Then king David said, 'Call Zadok the priest, Nathan the prophet, and Benaiah the son of Jehoiada.' They came into the king's presence and he gave them these orders: 'Take the officers of the household with you; mount my son Solomon on the king's mule and escort him down to Gihon. There Zadok the priest and Nathan the prophet shall anoint him king over Israel. Sound the trumpet and shout, "Long live King Solomon!" Then escort him home again, and he shall come and sit on my throne and reign in my place; for he is the man that I have appointed prince over Israel and Judah.'
>
> Benaiah son of Jehoiada answered the king, 'It shall be done. And may the Lord, the God of my lord the king, confirm it! As the Lord hath been with your majesty, so may he be with Solomon; may he make his throne even greater than the throne of my lord King David.' So Zadok the priest, Nathan the prophet, and Benaiah the son of Jehoiada, together with the Kerethite and Pelethite guards, went down and mounted Solomon on King David's mule and escorted him to Gihon.

Zadok the priest took the horn of oil from the Tent of the
Lord and anointed Solomon; they sounded the trumpet and all
the people shouted, "Long live King Solomon!" Then all the
people escorted him home in procession, with great rejoicing
and playing of pipes, so that the very earth split with the noise.

In reading the following extract taken from the script of the Queen's
coronation ceremony, once again attention should be paid to the names of the
high priest and the prophet referred to by the Archbishop of Canterbury.

Archbishop of Canterbury says: "Be thy Head anointed
with holy Oil: as kings, priests and prophets were anointed.
And as Solomon was anointed king by Zadok the priest and
Nathan the prophet, so be thou anointed, blessed and
consecrated Queen over the People, whom the Lord thy
God hath given thee to rule and govern, In the Name of the
Father, and of the Son, and of the Holy Ghost. Amen."

Amen indeed. From that day forth, all British nationals - resident in
both Britain and the Commonwealth alike - became the Queen's property,
literally, as indeed those same British nationals had been the property of King
George VI before her. We are thus officially dubbed the Queen's 'subjects',
her captive liegemen and liegewomen (in Britain we do not bear the status of
'free citizens', as is the situation in, say, the United States; but rather we bear
the status of 'subjects of the Crown', and are thus literally subject to the
whim of Her Majesty's Pleasure).

And more than this. Every child born within the precincts of the royal
estate during the Queen's reign - in Britain, the Commonwealth, as far as her
empire may reach - rightfully, legally and properly belongs to the anointed
representative of God: the Queen. In this regard we should perhaps consider
ourselves fortunate that, following her coronation, Queen Elizabeth II did not
share the same ambitions as King Herod the Great!

That aside, the point of including this ceremony is to highlight the fact
that the British monarchy is not what it seems. It is not what it would like us
to think it is. It is not a *de jure* constitutional figurehead representative of its
people. Rather it is a *de facto* parliamentary figurehead representative of the
corrupt and wholly masonic system which employs it. It is a *political*
figurehead, a *masonic* figurehead, and in this context it is the twentieth-
century product - the *politically cultivated* or *usurper* product - of the Judaic
Royal Dynasty and its messianic heirs. Likewise Queen Elizabeth II is the
twentieth-century version - the *politically cultivated* or *usurper* version - of

the Messiah. Thus she is seen to embody the perpetuation of Judaic royal blood in the context of twentieth-century masonic government. The implications regarding Diana and Dodi in this regard, of course, become flagrantly apparent. Sadly, in the world of corporate and masonic government, Judaeo-Christians and Arab Muslims go together like two north poles.

Because Britain was at war with Germany in 1917, remember, the British monarchy did not want its subjects to think of it as German. So it changed its name from Saxe-Coburg to Windsor. Similarly, and in light of Diana's death, there are extremely profound, extremely pertinent reasons why the British monarchy does not want us to think of it as Judaic (or at least that its sovereign power rests on a bloodline which is quintessentially Judaic). The future Queen Mother, Princess Diana, was - possibly - about to marry an Arab Muslim. In purely constitutional terms this situation is explosive enough. When the machinations of masonic government are entered into the equation, however - and the fact that this government's titular head embodies a heritage and a tradition which buries its roots in the ancient Royal House of Judah - this same situation becomes quite simply untenable. The bloodline (*the empire*) must at all costs be preserved - protected from contamination.

(We would like to reiterate at this point that this and any other such references to the Judaic royal bloodline are not in any way intended to implicate the Jewish people in any conspiracy of any kind whatever. The point highlighted here is not to do with racial status, nor indeed cultural identity. On the contrary, the point is purely and only a political one. It is representative of the fact that the authority of the Western world's behind-the-scenes government depends on the continuation of this illusion by blood. The future of centralized government in the so-called free world is upheld purely by the power possessed by the Church to create monarchs and sponsor governments alike. In turn, that power depends on the continuation of this bastardized, usurped strain of the Judaic royal bloodline, together with the continued suppression of the legitimate Messianic bloodline of David and Solomon and Jesus. And the Merovingian-Stuarts. This is the only context in which the term 'Judaic' should be understood in these pages.)

The Coronation Of Jesus

This term, then, 'Messiah', 'Pharaoh', or 'God's representative on Earth' (and other variations thereof) is a term and an office reserved for monarchs everywhere, even today. In 1953, as we have seen, Queen Elizabeth II was crowned 'Defender of the Faith'. She thus assumed the office of both Queen of Great Britain and Supreme Governor of the Church of England. Together these offices comprise the latter-day equivalent of the original office of Messiah - the 'anointed one' sanctioned to preside in both a religious and a political context. Thus the newly crowned Queen Elizabeth II became 'God's personal emissary' - God's 'anointed one' divinely sanctioned to preside over her subjects in Britain and the Commonwealth alike. Unlike the true bloodline Messiahs of old, of course, the present-day parliamentary messiah should be understood in a purely titular sense, a decaffeinated sense which, in effect, leaves her subjects entirely bereft of sovereign representation, both spiritually and politically. But Elizabeth is effectively 'messiah' just the same. Prince Charles, should tradition endure, will also wear this same sanctimonious privilege - one day. As will Prince William. It thus becomes patently clear that the 'priest-kings' of modern-day Europe are in fact politically created replicas of the true Judaic Messiahs of old.

There can be little doubt, then, that the coronation of British and European monarchs today is an attempt on the part of an inherently impotent establishment to perpetuate the messianic system of monarchy intrinsic to the Judah Kings of old. In consequence, the very fabric of masonic government is seen to be upheld by, steeped in and based upon Judaic/masonic tradition and ritual - a tradition and a ritual which find their roots in the ancient biblical ceremony known as 'the anointing'. This ceremony dates back at least as far as 961 BC and the coronation of King Solomon. Which in itself is of some interest so far as we are concerned. The legend of King Solomon and his famed Temple, of course, and of the equally famed Treasure housed in that Temple, is at the very heart of modern-day Freemasonry (and thereby at the heart of masonic government and the institution of the Monarchy as well). Of note is that this same legend was also central to the Knights Templar (or to call them by their unabridged name, the Order of the Poor Knights of Christ and the Temple of Solomon). In any event, it is indeed the very mystery upon which European Freemasonry was founded.

To add to this, and as stated above, Solomon's coronation, his 'anointing' (1 Kings, 1:32-40) depicts a very ancient and mystical ceremony from which critical parts of Britain's present-day coronation ceremony derive. Whatever the truth concerning the survival of the Judaic royal bloodline and its influence on latter-day democracies, the mystery begins with the anointing of Israel's bloodline messiahs, in particular with King Solomon himself.

But it does not end there. This same ritual is also alluded to in the New Testament (and if our source's assertion that the Bible has been "codified" is correct, of course - and there is little doubt that this is indeed the case - then *allusions* to real events are about the best we can expect). But what is of particular note in this regard is that the New Testament passage to which we refer alludes to the coronation of no less a figure than Jesus himself.

According to the Gospel of John (12: 1-8), Mary Magdalene -

sometimes referred to as Mary of Bethany - anoints Jesus with "pure oil of nard", though for what reason is not made entirely clear. But whatever the reason, it is evidently deemed of some significance by Jesus. In Matthew (26: 6-13), Jesus tells us: "Wherever in all the world this gospel is proclaimed, what she [Mary] has done will be told as her memorial." Indeed, a closer inspection of the New Testament texts reveals precisely why Jesus considered his anointing so significant. It also reveals the precise reason for his anointing. As John in fact tells us, and as the passage from Matthew states even more clearly, it is in preparation for his "burial".

As chronologically detailed in the Gospel of Matthew, and clearly cited in the Gospel of Luke, Jesus is to be understood in this context as the direct lineal descendant of King David. And as such the heir apparent to the Royal House of Judah. In other words, he is to be understood as the *de jure* heir apparent to the Throne of Judea. To add to this, study of the less sullied Judaic texts - texts mysteriously excluded from the Bible; the Apocrypha, the Dead Sea Scrolls, the Nag Hammadi Scrolls, among others - reveals that this so-called "burial" was in fact a ritual central to the Essene/Nazarene/Zealot movement to which Jesus himself belonged. Indeed, it was central to the Judaic way of life. Moreover, it was by tradition a ritual performed on the heir apparent in preparation for his accession to the throne. The heir apparent symbolically 'dies', is 'buried' and 'anointed', and the 'resurrected' king emerges from the ritual a fully-fledged Messiah. Of note is that this precise same sequence of events is mirrored in the present-day British coronation ceremony - as we have seen, the heir apparent is covered over (or buried) with cloth-of-gold, is anointed with oil, and subsequently emerges from this symbolic death a fully-fledged monarch. The added fact that the present-day coronation ceremony is largely a plagiarization of Solomon's own coronation ceremony demonstrates clearly enough that this 'burial' and 'anointing' ritual was one and the same with ancient Israel's traditional coronation ceremony. And that Jesus's own 'anointing with oil' in preparation for his 'burial', as told in the Gospels of Matthew and John, was therefore an allusion to - in the original, unadulterated texts - his coronation as King of Israel.

Also of note is the fact that Jesus's 'anointing' immediately preceded his triumphal entry into Jerusalem, and his subsequent procession through its streets on the back of an ass. This ceremonial act, it seems, depicts yet another tradition followed by a succession of Judaic messiah-kings, as alluded to in the so-called 'prophecy of Zechariah' (Zechariah 9:9), which speaks of Israel's king being "humble and mounted on an ass". This same 'prophecy' is further quoted in the New Testament (John 12: 15) where it states: "Fear no more, daughter of Zion; see, your king is coming, mounted on an ass's colt."

However, there is no evidence whatever that this so-called 'prophecy' is indeed a prophecy. On the contrary, when taken in context there is more reason to believe that it is simply a line from the ancient Judaic coronation or anointing ceremony (or that it alludes to same) and that the newly crowned king's entry into Jerusalem on the back of an ass or a donkey was an integral part of that ceremony. In this same manner, for example, a newly crowned monarch of Great Britain would, even today, parade through the streets of London, albeit in a horse-drawn carriage. No one would assume from this action that they were fulfilling some ancient prophecy. Rather that they were simply following tradition. And in any event, this would indeed explain why Jesus took it upon himself to follow this so-called 'prophecy's' instruction so precisely. And why the crowds lining the streets of Jerusalem greeted him with the words: "Hosanna to the King" (equivalent in first-century Judean-speak to "God save the King"). Indeed, as stated in our chapter on Jesus, the New English Bible is even more explicit in this regard. In John (12: 13) it states quite unequivocally that the crowds "took palm branches and went out to meet him, shouting ... 'God bless the King of Israel!' The situation is surely no different from the day Queen Elizabeth II paraded herself through the streets of London following her own coronation in 1953. On that day, too, the crowds waved and cheered, and cried: "God save the Queen!" The fact that Jesus rode on an ass and the Queen in a solid-gold carriage, of course, only serves to emphasize the stark contrast between a true bloodline monarch and a politically created one. Indeed, these two images side-by-side serve to illustrate in one fell swoop what a thousand words might fail to achieve, no matter how often they are reiterated.

The story of Jesus riding an ass through the streets of Jerusalem on Palm Sunday, then - the adulterated version contained in the Bible - would indeed appear to be an allusion to the culmination of the ancient Judaic coronation ceremony. Certainly this rather than the fulfilment of some or other Old Testament prophecy, as claimed by some, including the Church. Indeed, as we have seen, Solomon's own coronation culminated in a similar way: "They sounded the trumpet and all the people shouted, 'Long live King Solomon!' Then all the people escorted him home in procession, with great rejoicing and playing of pipes, so that the very earth split with the noise." According to the Gospels, remember, on the day before Palm Sunday Jesus had been 'anointed' in preparation for his 'burial' (his accession to the throne). He too, like Solomon before him, had just been installed as King of Israel, at least by his own supporters (in much the same way as, say, James VIII of Scots - *de jure* James III of Great Britain - was proclaimed king by his supporters in 1707, in defiance of Parliament's *Treaty of Union* - the official establishment of the United Kingdom of Great Britain). Having been thus crowned, Jesus would of course have been expected to follow the coronation ceremony to the letter, to have completed the ceremony with the traditional 'walkabout' among the crowds, so to speak. Which, it seems, is precisely what he did. And the fact that he did would certainly explain Rome's enthusiasm for his death, as indeed Westminster had demonstrated a similar enthusiasm for the death of James Stuart (or any other such 'pretender' exercising a legitimate claim to the Throne). Similarly, there can be little doubt that Jesus exercised a legitimate claim to the Throne of Israel. And that the people of Judea recognized him thus - as evinced by his almost fanatical reception when he entered Jerusalem on Palm Sunday, the day after his 'anointing'. In this regard the Judean 'pretender', Jesus, would indeed have been considered a serious threat to the socio-political stability of the Roman province of Judea.

And this, of course, would explain why he was charged with the crime of sedition, and sentenced to death by the Roman penalty of crucifixion.

Jesus As Grail King
Diana As Grail Queen

Before wrapping up this chapter on *The Coronation*, we felt that it would serve us well to include here further evidence of Jesus's royal status - the fact that he was indeed crowned King of Israel, that Rome was fully aware of his royal status, that he indeed sired children who later became known as Grail Kings. And thus that Jesus himself, in effect, and seen as the father of the Grail Dynasty, was the most influential Grail Monarch of all time.

Until today, that is...

The appellation 'Grail King', of course, is both a curious and a deliberate one. Curious for the fact that it tends to establish what is otherwise a relatively straightforward historical inquiry into the life and status of Jesus in the wholly dubious realm which exists somewhere between fact and romance. Deliberate for what it conceals.

If we are to take our source's assertion seriously - that the Bible has been "codified" in order to conceal certain facts with regard to the true identity and status of Jesus - then we must learn to read between the lines in order to discover what it is that is being concealed. This is a line of inquiry pursued by many modern scholars and historians. And it is a necessary one. The Bible in its present form is fraught with contradictions and discrepancies which simply cannot be reconciled in scientific inquiry. Only religious fanaticism is able to harmonize what is undoubtedly a work of extreme disparity.

To add to this, whether codified or not, it is certainly known that the Bible as read today is based on texts which have been drastically altered. Allusions to Jesus's royal status, and to the fact that he undoubtedly married and sired heirs, thus remain concealed in the part-factual, part-fictional vestiges of the original texts which constitute the New Testament today.

But there are other sources to whom we can refer. We know from the Jewish chronicler, Flavius Josephus, for example (from whose work much of what we know about first-century Palestine has been gleaned) that the Jewish uprising against Rome in AD 66 was a desperate and a bloody one, and that it resulted in the complete annihilation of Jerusalem and its Temple in AD 70. And the subsequent massacre of hundreds of Jews. This is now accepted as historical fact, in much the same way as, say, William the Conqueror's victory at the Battle of Hastings in 1066, or Horatio Nelson's victory at the Battle of Trafalgar in 1805, are also thus accepted. Or indeed, George Washington's victory in the American War of Independence. We accept these facts as historically correct because they were witnessed, chronicled and subsequently related through the centuries by historians like Josephus.

As well as chronicling the Judaeo-Roman war (AD 66-74), then, what Josephus also tells us is that Jesus was a Zealot in the tradition of others of his status and heritage. In other words, and as Josephus affirms, Jesus was a political revolutionary and, moreover, a "king who did not reign". As stated, unlike other texts and chronicles depicting Palestine at the time of Jesus, Josephus's account is not flavoured by religious fanaticism (as is, say, the New Testament book, *Acts Of The Apostles*). And neither has it been doctored by a Church seeking political power. On the contrary, so far as can be ascertained it is a straightforward historical account penned by someone who lived at that time and who was, therefore, steeped in the cultural and political nuances of the period. Indeed, had Josephus been present at Yorktown in October, 1781; and further, had he chronicled events at that time, it is most unlikely that anyone would have questioned his account of how General Cornwallis surrendered his army to the forces of George Washington, thus ending the American Revolution and War of Independence. But because Josephus's account of first-century Palestine has been told against Rome's own biased and bastardized account of this same period, not only has he been discredited by the various Church hierarchies. By virtue of the fact that his account disagrees with that of Christianity he has also been branded a liar. As most if not all historians now concur, however, Josephus's account of this period should be accepted as the most authoritative account we have.

Born Joseph Ben Matthais in AD 37, Josephus was himself a Jewish aristocrat (like Jesus) who at the start of the uprising in AD 66 became

Governor of Galilee. As such, he assumed command of the Galilean Zealots and led them in battle against Rome. His part in the uprising, however, was short-lived; early on in the conflict he was captured by the Roman Emperor Vespasian - whereupon he turned traitor, assumed Roman citizenship, married a Roman heiress and lived out the remainder of his life in luxury by favour of the Roman Emperor. Thereafter known by the Romanized name, Flavius Josephus, he subsequently accompanied the Roman army to Palestine where he chronicled events which led to the sacking of Jerusalem, the summary massacre of hundreds of Jews, the razing of the Temple of Solomon. And the subsequent mass suicide of 960 Zealots, Essenes and Nazarenes (including women and children) at Masada, April 15th, AD 74. Archaeological research has since substantiated Josephus's account of the siege of Masada, contained in his work, *The Jewish War*.

According to Josephus, then, the image of Jesus as a humble carpenter is a false one (though one that serves the Church's political agenda well enough.) While the Church continues to sell us this false image for purposes of political gain, history - Josephus - tells us that Jesus was in fact a political revolutionary and *de jure* claimant to the Throne of Israel who failed in his bid to oust the Romans from Palestine. And likewise, the Herods from the Throne of Israel. He was thus chronicled by Josephus as a "king who did not reign".

(Of significance here is the use of the term 'carpenter' in the New Testament, a term applied to Jesus's father, Joseph, and by insinuation to Jesus himself. Once again we find that this term was mistranslated, almost certainly with deliberate intent, by the founding Church fathers. It was subsequently applied - or misapplied - to Jesus in order to transform him from the wealthy, aristocratic and revolutionary king he is now known to have been into the poor working-class, lamb-like guru promulgated by the Church of Rome. For the record, translated directly from the original Greek *ho tekton*, 'carpenter' means in this context 'master craftsman', or 'master of the craft' - a degree still employed by modern-day Freemasonry and a rank of the highest order in the first-century 'mystery-school' sects of Essenes and Nazarenes. Thus there is no contradiction in Jesus as both 'king' and 'carpenter'. On the contrary, a bloodline messiah who also happened to be a Nazarene would have been expected to hold the highest Nazarene rank, just as Queen Elizabeth holds the rank of Supreme Governor of the Church of England today. 'Carpenter' - or 'master of the craft' - then, was an ecclesiastical rank, an office held by Jesus and by his father before him. Thus there is every reason to believe it was an office held by the succeeding Kings of Judah.)

In any event, there are other sources, even more specific regarding the royal status of Jesus, of Jesus's family, and the fact that genealogical records pertaining to the Royal House of Judah were summarily burned or otherwise destroyed, both by the Herods and by Rome. Around the year AD 200, for example, the historian Julius Africanus, wrote: "Herod, who had no drop of Israelitish blood in his veins and was stung by the consciousness of his base origins, burnt the registers of their [the House of Judah's] families." And further: "A few careful people had private records of their own, having either remembered the names or recovered them from copies, and took pride in preserving the memory of their aristocratic origin." Africanus goes on to describe the descendants of the Judaic royal bloodline as the *Desposyni*, or Descendants of the Master. It is these descendants who, according to a further source - one Eusebius, Bishop of Caesarea during the fourth century AD - survived Roman persecution and in so doing threatened the legitimacy of the burgeoning Church of Rome. In later tradition these descendants, the so-called *Desposyni*, would become known as the Grail Family, or the Grail Dynasty - heirs to the legendary Sangraal.

It is unclear precisely where or when the term Sangraal (or Sangrael) originated. The earliest known use of this term is to be found in the many Grail romances which adorn the pages of medieval literature. As we have seen, however, the so-called 'legends' contained in the Grail romances in fact depict the story of the survival of the Judaic royal bloodline, albeit - of necessity - in codified form. Like the *Protocols Of The Elders Of Sion*, derived from the religio-royalist movements of seventeenth- and eighteenth-century France, the stories contained in the Grail romances were drawn largely from Templar origins. Wolfram von Eschenbach, for example, author of perhaps the most significant of Grail romances, *Parzival*, was himself a Knight of the Holy Roman Empire who is known to have forged close ties with the Templars. Indeed, Wolfram states quite unequivocally that his rendering of the Grail story was based on privileged information. Which, it turns out, it was. His main source of information was none other than one Guiot de Provins, a prominent Templar spokesperson during the twelfth and early thirteenth centuries. And the Templars, of course, self-confessed 'guardians of the Grail', had been established as a military force by the Order of Sion for the very purpose of restoring the Merovingian (Judaic) Dynasty to the thrones of France and Jerusalem. And feasibly to the thrones of other European nations, too. The 'terrible secret' said to have been harboured by the Templars is now known to have been that Jesus was a *de jure* King of Israel, that he was married, that he sired children and that those children bore generations of their own who eventually came to power in Europe in the guise of the Merovingian kings. Further, that the Church of Rome effectively eradicated the Merovingian succession and duly supplanted it with dynasties of its own making. Following the establishment of the Holy Roman Empire in AD 800, though the Merovingian bloodline was forced underground and existing records of its somewhat unique origin subsequently destroyed, surviving genealogical documentation regarding the descendants of Jesus and the Judaic royal bloodline was kept and maintained by the Order (later the Priory) of Sion. And defended by the Knights Templar. As we have seen, between the years 1307 and 1314 the Knights Templar, like the Merovingian kings before them, were persecuted and eradicated by the Church of Rome. Knowledge of the survival of the Judaic royal bloodline was thus suppressed and, in effect, excised from the pages of history.

However, in order to preserve this knowledge, it would seem that certain authors and poets sympathetic to the Templar cause, in particular Wolfram von Eschenbach, were commissioned to record the genealogical information in the form of epic stories. These stories were based on the lineage of the Sangraal - the Blood Royal - but in mistranslation became known as the Grail romances: stories of the Holy Grail. Thus the descendants of the Judaic royal bloodline became known as the Grail Family - a code name employed both to protect and preserve the bloodline and its surviving heirs. And thus the protagonists in these stories - the heirs apparent to the bloodline - became known as Grail Kings, or Grail Queens. In retrospective context, of course, Jesus too becomes a Grail King. Indeed, in many respects the first, the most famous, the most significant. Certainly in terms of the threat this bloodline has posed to the Church of Rome, the most dangerous. Indeed, in terms of the numberless crimes and atrocities perpetrated by the Church in its attempt to suppress this bloodline and its heirs, Jesus's status as primary protagonist is surely without challenge. In terms of present-day corporate and masonic politics, however, one cannot help but identify the emergence of a more contemporary threat, equally significant for its ability to arouse public support, equally dangerous for its audacity to challenge the status quo.

And equally legitimate for the fact that she too was a provable lineal descendant of this same bloodline of Judah, the Sangraal. She too was a Grail Queen. And what is more, we believe the evidence suggests very strongly that this is precisely the reason she is no longer alive.

EPILOGUE

We set out to present evidence of an assassination plot against Diana, Princess of Wales. And further, that this plot was implemented and that it was subsequently covered up by its perpetrators. We also endeavoured to present evidence of motive - reasons behind the plot to kill the princess. This, we feel, we have achieved to the best of our ability. We can do no more. Though we believe the evidence presented is compelling, we certainly do not believe that it will be considered thus by the relevant authorities, nor that it will prove successful in bringing the perpetrators to justice. That was never our realistic aim, though it remains our most fervent hope.

In the course of our investigation we also sought to present evidence of a 'bloodline conspiracy' - a conspiracy which has its roots in biblical Palestine and which, according to our Foreign Office source, constituted the primary motivation behind the British Establishment's phobia concerning Diana. Thus that it constituted a primary motive - if not *the* primary motive - in her assassination. As we have seen, this line of inquiry led us on a veritable odyssey which resulted in our investigation of the Judaic royal bloodline - the bloodline of Jesus, the Merovingians, the Stuarts. And of course, the House of Windsor. In tracing this bloodline back to its earliest roots we endeavoured to uncover one or two critical though hitherto secreted facts which we feel were crucial to presenting a complete picture. To some these somewhat unorthodox claims may well have seemed inadmissible, unpalatable, extraordinary - perhaps all of these things. But we believe we have been vindicated in our endeavour to establish them in historical and political fact, just the same. Or at least in our quest to present an alternative historical and political landscape to that upheld by orthodoxy. And that this alternative landscape is closer to the historical and political truth than its traditional counterpart.

To recap, then, and to clarify, below is a summary containing a list of the points we have endeavoured to establish in fact:

(1): that the Judaic Royal Dynasty of David and Solomon, the Royal House of Judah, the Davidic or Messianic bloodline, is still in existence;

(2) that its most famous heir is no less a figure than Jesus;

(3): that its heirs today, by means fair or foul, by legitimate or illegitimate descent, comprise the larger part of the European nobility;

(4): that the ceremonial power vested in the usurped strain of this Judaic royal bloodline is the counterfeit authority upon which US and European government is founded;

(5): that said US/European government is entirely masonic; that it is an unelected, undemocratic oligarchical plutocracy, a corporate plutocracy comprised of two major financial and industrial factions, one extreme right-wing, the other a tad more liberal, and that at any given time one or other of these masonic factions controls to a very large degree the policies pursued by the so-called democratically elected governments in both Europe and the US;

(6): that the right-wing faction of masonic government is made up of the British Royal Establishment together with certain British/US financial and military-industrial interests traditionally based in Virginia;

(7): that, by virtue of the British Crown's reign in colonial America - the Thirteen Colonies, in particular the state of Virginia - until 1776, Crown interests in Virginia obtain to this day; and thus that the House of Windsor still stands as titular head to the Virginia-based right-wing faction of British/US masonic government;

(8): that the authority wielded by both factions of masonic government eclipses that of Parliament and Congress, and that, effectively, it also funds and controls the most highly covert departments within MI6 and the CIA (it is of note in this regard that the CIA is headquartered in Langley, Virginia);

(9): that the power wielded by masonic government is wholly dependent upon, and sustained by, the covert perpetuation of the usurped, illegitimate or politically cultivated strain of the Judaic royal bloodline; on keeping that strain free from 'contamination' by 'outsider blood' (in this instance, Arab Muslim blood); and on the continued suppression of the legitimate, Messianic strain of this same Judaic royal bloodline;

(10): that the succession of this bloodline's illegitimate strain and its heirs is thus ensured by secret masonic policy;

(11): that, at certain times in history, the succession of this bloodline's legitimate strain and its heirs was achieved by non-political means; indeed, that the bloodline in question was a purely 'royal' or 'messianic' strain, in the truest sense of those words; that its heirs were - and are - compelled by the values and protocols described by the Grail Code; and thus that they were completely untainted by political ambition;

(12): that the Judaic royal bloodline, in its purest strain, is both spiritually and genetically distinct from other bloodlines; that this distinction is described by an unique genetic signature; and thus that the bloodline has produced heirs spiritually and genetically distinct from what might be termed the 'normal human condition' - Kings David and Solomon, for example; Jesus; the Merovingian Kings Clovis and Dagobert; King Arthur of Dalriada; King Charles I; King Charles II; and, of course, Diana, Princess of Wales;

(13): that knowledge of this bloodline's spiritual and genetic qualities, as described by its unique genetic signature, is the most jealously guarded -

and feared - political secret in known history;

(14): that this secret has always been known, but that it has been concealed by various conclaves of initiated priests and royal sponsors down through the ages - the Essenes of Qumran to name but one such conclave, the Knights Templar to name another; the inner sanctums of the Catholic Church to name a more politically-biased conclave in this regard, the Priory of Sion to name a more contemporary one;

(15): that, at various points in history, this secret and its attendant power has been discovered and misappropriated by contemporary political powers (such as by Rome during the period known as the Dark Ages, for example, and of course by the House of Hanover-Windsor and its masonic sponsors in 1714);

(16): that the secret of the Judaic royal bloodline has thus been usurped - 'hijacked' - and turned to political use;

(17): that the usurpation of this secret and its attendant power was most successfully (and completely) accomplished by the Church of Rome and its political sponsors - firstly, during the Councils of Carthage, Hippo and Nicaea (circa AD 200-325), at which time the 'Son of God' story was formulated and the Christian religion formerly established as a tool for social and political control; secondly, in AD 750-800 (circa) when the Church-sponsored Pepin III was crowned King of the new Frankish 'Carolingian' Dynasty (the old Merovingian Dynasty) under the aegis of the Holy Roman Empire; in this way Rome finally gained its most prized political possession - control over the Judaic royal bloodline - and thus the process of hijacking the Judaic royal succession and transforming it into what is now the European nobility (and thus into a useful political tool) was, in effect, begun;

(18): that a second major usurpation of this secret and its attendant power was accomplished by Rome's imperial successor, the US/European Alliance - the US/European masonic government as described in point *Five*;

(19): that the secret pertaining to the succession of the Davidic heirs is best depicted in the symbolic language of viticulture (literally: *the cultivation of grapevines*), and that royal and political alliances and marriages are thus seen in this regard - the grafting of vines to produce the desired grape; the grafting of political agendas and royal bloodlines to produce the desired power base;

(20): that every so many years, for no predictable reason, a grape is produced which yields what is known as a 'vintage wine'; that every so many generations, for no predictable reason, an heir is born who is seen in this same regard - someone who, like David, Solomon, Jesus, Arthur, *like Diana*, displays a behaviour and a charisma 'beyond the normal human condition';

(21): that, within the ranks of masonic government - in particular the masonic oligarchy which stands behind the British Monarchy, as well as the more legitimate masonic agencies such as the Priory of Sion - the Judaic Royal Dynasty is known as the Grail Family, or the Grail Dynasty (from Old French: *Sangrael* or *Sangraal*, meaning Blood Royal), and that its rightful heirs - in particular those who display the tendencies described in point *Twenty* - are thus known as Grail Kings, or Grail Queens;

(22): that Diana, Princess of Wales, was one such Grail Queen - a 'genetic throwback' to the legitimate bloodline dynasty of old; that she was publicly recognized and regarded as such, even though subconsciously, and that this was the reason for her otherwise inexplicable and wholly unprecedented public appeal;

(23): that the enormous public support Diana was thus able to generate - with regard to her landmines campaign, for example, as well as other, future campaigns with which she had been identified (Gulf War Syndrome, nuclear-related cancers), and which might also have included her allegiance to a Merovingian-Stuart restoration - posed a massive and irrevocable threat to masonic government, to its political and economic stability, and in particular to its bid to unite Europe under a corporate banner (an eventuality which, as we have seen, demands that Europe remains bereft of a legitimate or 'messianic' bloodline monarchy, in particular a monarchy headed up, or even supported, by Diana, Princess of Wales);

(24): that the world was suddenly exposed to a true matrilineal messianic figure; that, in effect, a latter-day Magdalene was let loose on the world stage, and that, in constitutional terms alone, this posed an enormous threat to the politically sponsored Windsor Dynasty, to its continued succession (its ability to survive the unification of Europe), and thereby to the masonic oligarchy for which the Windsors stand as titular head;

(25): that Diana's relationship with, and proposed marriage to, an Arab Muslim would have further destabilized the covert machinations of masonic government, founded as it is on the power created by the usurped, illegitimate, politically cultivated strain of the Judaic royal bloodline, and on keeping that bloodline (at least in a political sense) free from contamination by 'outsider blood' - in particular, of course, Arab Muslim blood;

(26): that a combination of the above points is the reason Diana is no longer alive.

There is one further point to consider, one which we have only briefly and obliquely touched upon in the course of this book. And it is this.

In our chapter on *The Stuarts,* we highlighted the fate of literally millions of Jews at the hands of successive governments and authorities throughout the world and "throughout history". We linked these persecutions with the parallel fate of the Judaic royal bloodline, and made mention, too, of the similar fate met by such bodies as the Cathars and the Knights Templar. That the bloodline's heirs suffered in this same manner is also evident. Certainly we know that Jesus and his followers met with similar persecutions. As did some of the more prominent Merovingian kings and their supporters, and of course the Stuarts and *their* supporters, too. King Charles I, for example, was deposed and beheaded. James II was deposed and supplanted while *de jure* James III and Charles III were defeated in battle and sentenced, on pain of death, to life in exile. Indeed, the Stuart Dynasty in general - with the possible exception of Charles II - has been defamed and discredited out of hand by traditional history (the version of history taught in our schools). An example in this regard is the deliberate historical misrepresentation of the Stuarts' 'messianic' or 'divine right to rule' system of monarchy, in particular the branding of King James I as a mad autocrat who believed he was God's personally chosen emissary (James I was known as the 'British Solomon' by his subjects, but history renamed him the 'wisest fool in Christendom'). This is pure character assassination. As is the claim made by the Whigs and the Hanovers that King James II's wife, Queen Mary d'Este, was the illegitimate daughter of the pope. She was not, of course; she was the daughter of the Duke of Modena, and her descendants by James II (via their son and heir, *de jure* James III Stuart) still constitute Britain's legitimate royal bloodline. Perhaps this is one reason why James III's son and heir, Charles Edward Stuart (Bonnie Prince Charlie) is known to students of history today as a 'traitor', 'warmonger' and 'usurper' - erroneous claims made by the real usurpers (the Hanovers) and their political sponsors (the 'Anglo-Dutch' Whigs) in order to influence public opinion against the attempted Stuart restoration of 1745. It was a propaganda sell that worked. And it continues to work to this day. Though the Whigs have become New Labour, and the Hanovers the House of Windsor, the song remains the same. And it remains the same because in 1807 the Stuart line was officially declared 'extinct in exile' by a jubilant Parliament. (Of course, this declaration - though written in stone in the annals of British history - is a lie. The Bonnie Prince's direct bloodline descendant and present-day heir is alive and well. He is known as HRH Prince Michael of Albany. And he is recognized by many Stuart supporters as Britain's legitimate bloodline king, even today.)

To add to this, of course, supporters of the Stuart cause have, over the past millennium, been hounded down and in many cases killed. Sir William Wallace is a case in point. And there have been many others, including a man known to history as Charles Radclyffe, an influential Stuart supporter who was beheaded in 1746 for this very reason. Indeed, Radclyffe was Charles II's grandson, his mother having been the illegitimate daughter of the Stuart king by his mistress Moll Davis. Together with such historical luminaries as Sir Isaac Newton and Robert Boyle, Radclyffe espoused the seventeenth-century Rosicrucian movement which in turn had been spawned by the Priory of Sion and which, in effect, engendered the basis for European Freemasonry during the eighteenth century. Indeed, the entire web of British Freemasonic and other-style secret orders was initially established by - or with the sanction and support of - the Stuarts. And more specifically by the diligence of Radclyffe himself. These earliest orders, of course, were established in order to protect and preserve, not only the Judaic royal bloodline, its heirs and its secrets. But also the Gnostic principles and philosophies propounded by the Priory of Sion and the original seventeenth-century Rosicrucians - the same principles and philosophies earlier espoused by the Cathars, the Essenes, the Nazarenes, the Druids, the Gnostics of the early Egyptian Church and others. And of course, by Jesus himself. By their nature these principles and philosophies were in stark contrast with the dictates of institutionalized religions such as Roman or Anglican Christianity, and as such posed a serious threat to Parliament, which of course relied heavily on the support of the Anglican Church for its survival. It still does. And in any event, and contrary to the claims of some 'conspiracy theorists', the earliest Freemasonic Lodges were founded for the sole specific purpose of preserving the Gnostic principles and philosophies espoused by the heirs to the Judaic royal bloodline for millennia. The fact that Freemasonry has since been hijacked and counterfeited is another matter entirely.

Quite naturally, then, these principles and philosophies posed a solemn threat to the institutions of the Church and Parliament. Indeed, they were not only frowned upon by these institutions; they were also feared by them. And it is easy to see why. For one thing, they held more in common with the arcane wisdom tradition of, say, Cabalistic Judaism, as well as Esoteric Buddhism and its Western expression in Theosophy, than with the established - authorized - religions of the day. And for another, they advocated the dawn of a New Age in which mankind would awaken to new levels of understanding, and thus would no longer capitulate to the obsolescent values of greed, hatred and oppression. They also served, of course, to encourage rather than suppress the age-old disciplines of self-exploration and self-knowledge (or 'gnosis'). By their nature they served to empower rather than disempower the individual explorer, urging discovery of one's own inherent divinity against the exclusive divinity of the Church-created 'Son of God'. Thus they tended to free rather than shackle minds, to encourage rather than suppress individual thought, experience and expression. In consequence, Freemasonry (and its sister orders) attracted some of the most pre-eminent minds and personages of the era. Not least of whom was Sir Isaac Newton, reputedly the nineteenth Grand

Master of the Priory of Sion and President of the most noted Masonic institution in England at this time, the Royal Society - otherwise known as the 'Invisible College'. Of note is the fact that, with the restoration of the Stuarts in 1660, the 'Invisible College' gained a new patron and sponsor - none other than Charles II himself.

For these same reasons, however, the movement also elicited the censure of the Church and Parliament - neither of whom desired the advent of a New Age nor the self-empowerment of thousands of people. Thus measures were taken - often extreme - to suppress the movement. And to eliminate its main protagonists. Of note in this regard is that Charles Radclyffe, founder of the esoteric 'Scottish Rite' Freemasonry and Grand Master of all French Freemasonic Lodges during the 1720s/30s (and who succeeded Isaac Newton as the Priory of Sion's Grand Master in 1727) would himself fall victim to these extreme measures. True, for the next eighteen years Radclyffe would covertly facilitate the dissemination of 'gnosis' and the secrets of the Judaic royal bloodline via the establishment of Freemasonic Lodges across Britain and France. And more than this. According to our sources (as well as other authors, including Baigent, Leigh and Lincoln) he would also seek to establish an even more esoteric brand of Freemasonry than Scottish Rite - one which included initiation into what his protege, Karl Gottlieb von Hund, referred to as 'Strict Observance'. By Hund's account, 'Strict Observance' - which he claimed had originated with a secret conclave of 'unknown superiors', for whom it is presumed Radclyffe acted as mouthpiece - would have shed new light on the most ancient of ancient mysteries. According to our own sources, it would also have outlined in more specific detail preparations for what the Rosicrucians had already referred to as the 'new era', the so-called New Age. And moreover, that this New Age would witness the restoration of the Judaic royal bloodline to the thrones of Europe.

But it would not come to pass under the tutelage of Radclyffe. Hund was initiated by Radclyffe in 1742. By 1745, sooner than Hund had received full instruction from either Radclyffe or his 'unknown superiors', Radclyffe's fate had been effectively sealed. In this year he was captured and imprisoned, and a year later, beheaded. In consequence, Hund's 'Strict Observance' remained sidelined. Though not altogether suppressed. As we shall see, it would emerge in a new guise around a century and a half later. And its secrets would emerge with it.

Together with so many other Priory/Stuart supporters, then, Radclyffe was hounded down and murdered by the corporate oligarchs who were seeking to establish their new form of democracy at this time. As we have seen, however, this new form of democracy was anything but democratic. On the contrary, it was entirely plutocratic and machiavellian. In other words, it was established by the rich for the rich, and was achieved by surreptitious and cunningly fraudulent means. Those means of course included - and still include - the forcible imposition of Anglican Christianity on the British people, in a socio-political sense at least. Anglican Christianity is not supported by the tenets of Gnosticism. Nor vice versa. This, at least, remains the dogmatically held belief of the Anglican hierarchs. Thus the Gnostic philosophies of Freemasonry and the Judaic royal bloodline were outlawed, along with the bloodline itself.

It should be noted here that, as our research intensified, strains of a new and hitherto undetected scenario seemed to be emerging. A hitherto unseen plan or design - one which had crossed centuries - seemed to be formulating into an identifiable pattern, a recognizable sequence of events. Or intended events. It began to seem for all the world as if the 'terrible secret' at the very core of this mysterious 'bloodline' bore even more far-reaching implications than we had thus far imagined. Indeed, we began to suspect that the Gnostic principles and philosophies central to the bloodline and the movement which supported it, though depicting the beliefs of its supporters and protagonists clearly enough, and of undoubted profundity and wisdom, were nonetheless subordinate to an even greater mystery. An even greater secret. And what is even more intriguing so far as we are concerned is that - according to our Foreign Office source at any rate - this 'greater secret' had more recently been manipulated to unfold in the person of Diana, Princess of Wales - as we shall see.

As part of the scheme to sustain this new breed of corporate democracy, then, Freemasonry - along with many if not all other original forms of secret and masonic order - was and has continued to be systematically infiltrated and hijacked by agents of masonic government. We have seen, for example, how even the Priory of Sion itself was finally hijacked by MI6 and the CIA - the so-called 'Anglo-American contingent' - during the 1940s/50s. By this time many of its offshoot orders had already fallen victim to this same fate. In consequence, and in order that they might survive at all, the Gnostic 'secrets' central to the Priory of Sion - to original Freemasonry, the Rosicrucians, Scottish Rite, Strict Observance - were, via various sister-agencies, filtered out into the public domain. As we know, the Priory of Sion was itself forced to 'go public' in 1956 for this very reason, and in consequence the secret of the Judaic royal bloodline became public knowledge for the first time, largely through the work of the *Holy Blood, Holy Grail* team, Baigent, Leigh and Lincoln. The movement known as Theosophy has also played a major role in this regard. As have many others. But it was the work of one

Madame HP Blavatsky via the Theosophical Society, together with that of Alice A Bailey via a body known as the Lucis Trust, who would take the lead in finally establishing this ancient knowledge in the public arena. Via Blavatsky and Bailey the mystery - and the 'secret' central to it - would finally be unveiled, and presented for public consumption.

According to our sources, the Theosophical Society and the Lucis Trust were, in effect, later representations of Hund's 'Strict Observance'. Or at least the product of the same secret conclave of 'unknown superiors'. Like Hund before her, in or around 1875 Blavatsky claimed that she too had been initiated by a secret order of adepts, from whom she had obtained the 'ancient wisdom' teachings which subsequently formed the basis for her works *Isis Unveiled* and *The Secret Doctrine*. Though somewhat archaic and involved, wordy, the sum of Blavatsky's work was nonetheless a seminal masterpiece. As was that of her successor, Alice A Bailey, who in 1919 published the first of numerous works extrapolating and systematizing the information contained in Blavatsky's original works. As well as providing a treatise on the esoteric nature of life and the cosmic laws which govern it, Bailey, like Blavatsky before her, posited the dawn of a New Age towards the end of the twentieth century. She also posited the existence of an ancient 'brotherhood' of adepts, an ancient 'bloodline' of 'occult masters' who had once reigned over large parts of the Earth, who had since been forced into 'exile' by their persecutors, and who included among their number none other than Jesus himself. All of which seems entirely consistent with the secret harboured by the Priory of Sion, the Knights Templar, the Rosicrucians. Indeed, the secret spawned by the bloodline itself.

But what is of real significance here is that, according to Bailey, this ancient order of adepts, this 'exiled bloodline', has since the fifteenth century been planning something of a comeback - a *restoration* which, according to a secret schedule revealed by Bailey, is now imminent. Indeed, like Radclyffe's 'Scottish Rite', Hund's 'Strict Observance', and information contained in the so-called Rosicrucian Manifestos before that (published 1614), Bailey claimed that this 'restoration' had all along been planned to coincide with the advent of what the Rosicrucian Manifestos referred to as the 'new era'. And what Bailey herself termed the New Age. As we know, Bailey's 'New Age' was scheduled to emerge some time towards the end of the twentieth century, and would continue to establish itself - again, according to the schedule revealed by Bailey - well into the new millennium. Bailey's final work in this regard appeared in 1949.

Since that time, this knowledge - this secret history, this arcane wisdom, its 'terrible secret' - though still demonized by the authorities, as well as by

Christian hierarchs and fundamentalists, has played a major role in freeing many from the maw of Church dogma and authoritarianism. Moreover, it has played a major role in establishing what has indeed become known (in the course of more or less the past two decades, and as foretold by Bailey's secret schedule) as the New Age - a movement very similar in many respects to that of the Druids, the Cathars, the Nazarenes and other Gnostic sects now lost to history. Indeed, like all others associated with these arcane philosophies through the centuries, the New Age, together with those associated with it, has been duly ridiculed and discredited - even satanized - by the relevant authorities, in particular by the Church and the media. But not only them. It has also been misunderstood by a handful of fundamentalist 'conspiracy theorists', who have confused Blavatsky's and Bailey's 'secret order of adepts' with the authors of the bastardized version of *The Protocols Of The Elders Of Sion*. Thus the writings of Blavatsky and Bailey - in particular the contents of Bailey's secret schedule - have been confused with some Zionist masterplan for global takeover. (This confusion has arisen largely because Blavatsky's work, *The Secret Doctrine*, is based on a translation of ancient Tibetan texts known as *The Stanzas Of Dzyan* - though 'Dzyan' is in fact pronounced 'Djian', a typically English pronunciation perverts the sound to 'Zion', and in consequence the parallels are drawn. However, we should remember here that - at least according to our sources, as well as our own conclusions based on the evidence presented - the *Protocols*, in their original, 'pre-bastardized' form, contained a schedule for the intended restoration of a royal bloodline to the thrones of Europe. And *not* a schedule for a proposed global takeover by some unknown Zionist elite, as contained in the later, bastardized version. We should also remember that the royal bloodline in question - its sponsors and its heirs - has been purposely misrepresented down the ages by those it threatens most. And those it threatens most, of course, are the high priests and potentates of masonic government - the very high priests and potentates responsible for disseminating the bastardized version of the *Protocols* in the first place.)

In any event, it is this misrepresentation - or mispronunciation - which has caused many to believe, erroneously in our opinion, that the New Age is synonymous with the idea of a New World Order-One World Government, a term adopted (or rather hijacked) from Bailey and promptly twisted to suit corporate agendas. Today it has come to mean something altogether different - the imposition of a One World Government headed up by the United States of America jointly with a European Superstate. In effect, the world's political and economic power centralized in Washington, London and Brussels. But this interpretation could not be further from what was originally intended - the re-emergence (or restoration) of a true New World Order headed up by the bloodline and its heirs. And according to the evidence at our disposal, this 'restoration', it seemed, was to coincide with the dawn of a New Age which had been planned and prepared for over the course of centuries.

Our research tended to suggest, then, that the so-called New Age is no flight of whimsy. Nor even a random event. But that it is largely the result of a concerted endeavour on the part of the bloodline, its heirs and its sponsors, down through the ages. Indeed, that it is the result of a meticulously adhered-to schedule rather than some astrological or prophetic design. Also, of course, that its coming - its advent - should be understood in terms of an *earthly* event, a *secular* event, a *political* event - the restoration of a secular kingdom as opposed to the Church-invented 'heavenly' one. This would certainly seem to be the expectation of those who have sponsored the bloodline for the past two millennia - those who have harboured and nurtured this 'secret', this plan, for so long. And it has indeed been a very long time in process. We know, for example, that, according to Bailey, this 'restoration' has been planned and prepared for since at least the fifteenth century. And that the Order of Sion was pursuing this same plan some four centuries before that. But it is also evident that this same plan, this same objective - the struggle to restore the bloodline to the thrones of Europe (in particular the Throne of Israel), and in so doing inaugurate what the Rosicrucians referred to as the 'new era', Bailey as the 'New Age' - dates back even further: indeed, to the time of Jesus. It is directly related, at least, to Jesus's own attempts to wrest the Throne of Israel from Rome, the Herods, and so reclaim it on behalf of Judah. It was Jesus, after all, who first proclaimed the advent of such an age - the coming of the 'kingdom of God on Earth', or the 'second coming'. Despite the way this idea has been presented by the Church, there is no real evidence that Jesus was referring here to the advent of a 'spiritual' or 'heavenly' kingdom. On the contrary, given that the historical Jesus was the *de jure* King of Israel, that his throne had been usurped jointly by Rome and the Herods, and that, in consequence, he and his Zealot followers had spent much of their adult lives endeavouring to reclaim that throne, might not Jesus's proclamation of the 'second coming' have referred to his own 'restoration'? Or at least to the restoration of his bloodline to the Throne of Israel at some future date? Might not his proclamation of the coming of the 'kingdom of God on Earth' have referred to a liberated State of Israel ruled by the divinely sanctioned (and thereby the *de jure*) bloodline monarchs, the 'messiahs' of the Royal House of Judah? Certainly in first-century Palestine such a restoration would indeed have been equated with the advent of the 'kingdom of God on Earth'. As we know, politics and religion are synonymous in Judaic culture; they are inseparable, even more so 2000 years ago than today. And in any event, that Jesus was referring to a rather more secular than spiritual event becomes all the more evident when his words are considered in this context.

"Take care that no one misleads you," Jesus tells us in Matthew (24: 4-5). "For many will come saying ... 'I am the Messiah'; and many will be misled by them." He then goes on to warn of someone he refers to as the 'abomination of desolation'. And moreover, that this particular 'false messiah' will, at the time immediately prior to the 'second coming', be identified as a usurper. "...When you see the 'abomination of desolation' usurping a place which is not his ... [and] if anyone says to you, 'Look, here is the Messiah' ... do not believe it." And further: "Impostors will come claiming to be messiahs..." (Mark: 13:14-22).

Given that the heirs to the bloodline - Jesus's own 'messianic bloodline' - are themselves recognized as the true 'messiahs', the *de jure* bloodline monarchs (like Jesus himself; indeed, like David and Solomon before him, and later the Merovingians and the Stuarts) might not Jesus have been making a purely political statement here? Instead of understanding the 'restoration' (the 'second coming') as a spiritual, or even an apocalyptic event as invented and promulgated by the Church, might it not rather be a reference to the very struggle to which Jesus gave his life as the *de jure* King of Israel? To wit: the restoration of the messianic bloodline to the Throne of Judah. Certainly in our opinion this alternative understanding is a more realistic one. And if this hypothesis is correct, then Jesus's warning with regard to 'false messiahs' would have meant something altogether different to the 'false prophet' scenario promulgated by the Church. An alternative translation might thus be: "Beware of those who claim to be legitimate bloodline monarchs ('messiahs'), when in fact they are 'wolves in sheep's clothing' - 'impostors', 'usurpers', 'false messiahs': false monarchies created and sponsored for political gain." In this same context, of course, the so-called 'abomination of desolation' could only be interpreted to mean the 'usurped strain of the Judaic royal bloodline', together with those who represent it and the impostures and injustices perpetrated in its name. In this regard the House of Windsor must surely stand alone as the foremost contemporary example.

To add to this, Jesus also alluded to the *time* of this 'restoration' - the time of the 'second coming' - and described the conditions which he foresaw would obtain at this time. Like the Priory of Sion, the Rosicrucians - like Bailey - Jesus too referred to this time as the 'new age'. "...Nation will make war upon nation, kingdom upon kingdom; there will be famines and earthquakes in many places. With all these things the birthpangs of the new age begin." (Matthew 24: 8.) As stated, Bailey too affirmed that the restoration (to which, on occasion, she also referred as the 'second coming') would coincide with the arrival of the New Age. And what is more, that the bloodline's heirs would be seen at this time to emerge on the world stage, championing the causes of those less privileged, exposing injustices, upholding human and civil rights, propounding alternative ways to achieve social, political and spiritual freedoms. Campaigning on behalf of victims of anti-personnel landmines, for example. Or victims of nuclear-related cancers - HIV, AIDS, Gulf War Syndrome. Someone like Diana, perhaps - who, as we now know, was indeed seen as a genetic throwback to the most noted of the bloodline's heirs. And thus as an heir to the bloodline herself.

But what is of particular note here is that, according to Bailey, at this same time the bloodline's heirs would also be manoeuvred into positions of power and influence - positions which would help facilitate the restoration of the bloodline to its former glory. Thus the question once again confronts us: is it possible that Diana was being sponsored and groomed to represent - perhaps even figurehead - the bloodline at this time of its proposed restoration? Might Diana's unprecedented public appeal - her ability to win public support - have been noted by the bloodline's latter-day sponsors? And given the plan to which their movement had adhered for so long - a plan which foretold the emergence of the bloodline's heirs on the world stage at the dawn of the New Age, the time of the 'restoration' - might those sponsors have seen in Diana the potential to finally fulfil this plan?

"I have heard whispers, rumours, nothing more ... that the late Princess of Wales had been courted by certain agencies ... who seek to restore the Merovingian line to the Throne." So said our Foreign Office source.

As fantastic as this may seem, there is yet further evidence which suggests that this could indeed have been the case, as we shall see.

It should be pointed out here that it is not our intention to promote Diana in context with the 'second coming', at least as that idea is understood in a Christian sense. On the contrary, we fear that this idea, like so many others incorporated in the Christian creed, has been deliberately distorted from its original meaning for purposes of political gain. For as long as Jesus and his kingdom remain purely 'spiritual' or 'heavenly' - and thereby, of course, destined never to return in reality - the Church will continue to retain its monopoly on his divinity. Thus it will continue to enjoy the financial and political advantage it has enjoyed for centuries as a result.

It should also be said that, in promoting Diana's name in conjunction with the 'second coming', we do not in any way wish to imbue her with a false sense of exclusive divinity. In other words, we do not wish to canonize Diana. We do not wish to make of Diana what the Church has made of Jesus. Neither do we wish to compare Diana with the Church-created 'Son of God'. So far as we are concerned, though we have endeavoured to present the historical Jesus in a sympathetic light, we do not subscribe to the politically inspired design which has transformed the historical man into a god. We do not believe that Jesus Christ is or ever was the sole exclusive 'Son of God', but that the Church invented him as such to the benefit of its own financial and political advantage. In this regard we have endeavoured to present Jesus as the historical king he undoubtedly was - Jesus the human being. In this context - and this context alone - do we speak of Diana in the same breath as Jesus.

And neither do we wish to confuse the proposed bloodline restoration - the so-called New Age - with the Church-invented 'second coming'. Nor with the fulfilment of any other 'biblical prophecy'. Rather our intention is simply to highlight the fact that the so-called 'second coming' has been deliberately imbued with false meaning for purposes of political gain. And that it is thus more likely a Church-distorted propaganda triumph than a real event - that the 'second coming' referred to by Jesus bore a different meaning entirely to that promulgated by the Church today. In light of the evidence thus far presented, we contend that this 'different meaning' referred to the 'restoration of the Judaic royal bloodline' to the Throne of Israel (as pursued by the bloodline's sponsors and supporters down through the ages). And that later this same ambition was expanded to include the thrones of other European states. We also contend that Diana, like Jesus before her, was a legitimate descendant of this bloodline, and so claimed a legitimate right to stand as its representative in any proposed restoration bid - or at the very least that others recognized her as such. And moreover, that behind the very public media war which raged between Diana and the Windsors - a war which raged for at least the last decade of the princess's life, and which saw Diana reinventing and reasserting her public persona in no ambiguous terms - a battle royal was being fought for possession of the Throne itself, if not in reality, then in effect. What is equally apparent, of course, is that Diana was winning that war, hands down. While the Windsors remained many levels removed from the common people, Diana chose instead to identify with those same common people. To all intents and purposes she became the people's monarch - the 'People's Princess', the 'Queen of Hearts'. It is our contention that Diana alone could not have been responsible for reinventing herself in this way. But that certain bloodline supporters were responsible for engineering this media war. And that their ultimate motive in this regard was to further damage the image of the Windsor Dynasty in the eyes of the public, and at the same time sponsor and present Diana as a legitimate contender in their challenge for the British Throne. Or at least to use her public appeal to further their own ambitions in this regard. As we shall see, this notion is not so absurd as it might at first seem. And should it bear any truth, of course, it would have proved ample grounds for murder. No doubt about that.

So what was it about Diana which might have prompted some bloodline supporters to stand behind her in this way?

Firstly, of course, the bloodline has been successfully suppressed for at least the past 300 years (since the succession of William III Orange in 1689 and the subsequent succession of the House of Hanover in 1714). And one of the major reasons that the bloodline *has* remained sidelined for so long is that its heirs have been forced to live in relative obscurity. As we have seen, in 1807 Parliament finally sealed the bloodline's fate by declaring the Stuarts - and thereby, in effect, the bloodline itself - 'extinct in exile'. Even today, the vast majority of British people have never even heard of the current head of the Stuart Dynasty, HRH Prince Michael of Albany, much less would they be likely to support him in any attempted restoration bid. Diana, on the other hand, was the most famous, most admired, most sought-after person in the world. Her ability to sway public opinion was second to none. Indeed, had it been put to the people - had there been a referendum in Britain regarding the future of the Monarchy while Diana was still alive - then it is inconceivable that Diana would have gained anything but a landslide victory. Or at the very least the support of the British people to the extent that she might then have commanded a major say in how the Monarchy should proceed into the twenty-first century. At her petition, of course, the majority of British people would unquestionably have demanded that Prince Charles be bypassed in the line of succession and Prince William made king before him. Following Diana's death public opinion polls confirmed the national mood in this regard clearly enough. And unlike Charles, of course, Prince William is Diana's son. He too - at least on his mother's side - is a legitimate heir to the bloodline, and as such possibly carries the genetic signature common to the bloodline's most noted heirs - the very signature said to have recurred in Diana herself. Even had Diana been unwilling to stand personally against the Windsors, she was nevertheless in prime position to help William recognize his true heritage - to foster, cultivate and encourage the qualities inherent in that heritage. The qualities inherent in the bloodline itself. Like her forbears - the Merovingians, the Stuarts - Diana is known to have supported the form of monarchy known as 'constitutional monarchy' (as opposed to those displayed by Britain's current 'parliamentary monarchy', the Windsors). The difference is quite diametric. A parliamentary monarch is bound by the dictates of Parliament and its corporate overlords, and possesses no constitutional right to defend the civil rights and liberties of the people against the impostures and improprieties of Parliament. In other words, a parliamentary monarch is little more than a figurehead for, and an enforcer of, the absolute authority of Parliament. A constitutional monarch, on the other hand, is installed not by Parliament, but by the people, and is sworn by Written Constitution to uphold the rights of those people against any injustices perpetrated by Parliament (it should be noted that Britain is the only European nation that does not have a Written Constitution).

In any event, the evidence suggests clearly enough that Diana's influence on Prince William in this regard - that she wished to instill in him the qualities inherent in the bloodline, the qualities of a constitutional monarch: wisdom, compassion, justice - was almost certainly the cause of the Establishment's foremost concerns regarding her 'close relationship' with her sons.

To add to this, of course, there can be little doubt that Diana was possessed of a similar charisma to others of her *Sangraal* heritage, including Jesus. And thus that she displayed an uncanny ability to win public support and to galvanize that support into consolidated actions in favour of her own causes. She was also extremely aware of the significance of the New Age - which, remember, at least in terms of a proposed restoration on the part of the bloodline, had been planned and prepared for by supporters of the bloodline since at least the fifteenth century. Indeed, according to the evidence on offer, the New Age is largely - if not entirely - the result of the bloodline's 'secret teachings' (its Gnostic principles and philosophies) being forced out into the public arena. And in consequence, being adopted by a growing number of people worldwide. (And this despite official attempts to ridicule and suppress those teachings, along with the New Age itself.) Certainly it is known that Diana herself espoused these same principles and philosophies - the principles and philosophies which have hallmarked the bloodline for centuries; the principles and philosophies which, until their enforced release into the public domain, had been suppressed and supplanted by the Church's own politically-biased doctrines; the principles and philosophies which have duly become the backbone of the Rosicrucians' 'new era', of Bailey's 'New Age'. Indeed, it could even be argued in this regard that Diana was the most famous and influential 'New Ager' of her day. She is known to have visited psychics, astrologers and alternative therapists, for example, and indeed to have included other New Age adherents among her closest friends. She is also known to have adopted so-called 'New Age thought' as her own personal creed. Certainly her public demeanour, together with her much-publicized humanitarian works - often performed in defiance of both Church and Royal protocol, her open and public support for the gay rights movement being a primary case in point - betrayed a character fairly imbued with the values and qualities associated with the New Age, as well as with others of her *Sangraal* heritage. Indeed, the very same values and qualities demonstrated by Jesus, the Merovingians, the Stuarts; advocated in the works of Blavatsky and Bailey; adopted by a growing number of people today and central to original

Freemasonry and the Grail Code itself - to wit: to serve the greater humanity (symbolized by the Holy Grail, the bloodline, its genetic signature) regardless of class, creed or culture - or indeed, sexual preference - and without seeking reward in return. And again: to use one's position to serve the people, rather than to use the people to serve one's position. That Diana displayed these values and qualities is surely beyond debate. What is also beyond debate is that, like Jesus before her, and due to her massive popular effect, she upset a good deal of very prominent, very powerful people in the process.

But what is also evident is that - again, like Jesus before her - she *inspired* a great many people, too. We know, for example, how the sheer presence of Jesus - as the rightful bloodline King of Israel, the 'messiah'- galvanized the various factions of Jewish militants into consolidated actions against Rome. We also know that, like Diana, the most famous Grail King of all time rejected the established protocols and institutions of his day - the puppet Herods (equivalent in many respects to the present-day House of Windsor); imperial Rome (the United States of America); the Sanhedrin (the British Parliament); the high priests and Temple authorities (the Church). In fact he referred to these institutions and those who governed them as 'vipers', 'liars' and 'hypocrites', and no doubt employed other, less righteous expletives as well. In this same way Diana referred to the British Establishment as "those ghastly Conservatives", and so influenced others to express their own, similar views in this regard (of note here is that, shortly after this comment was made public, the Conservative Party was voted out of office for the first time in almost two decades.) Jesus, too, wielded a similar influence. He is still noted today for his ability to read the lie behind the smile - to expose the impostures and injustices lurking behind the facade of apparent democracy. Though undoubtedly a man of high spiritual values and irrefutable wisdom, nevertheless in many respects Jesus might be equated with the first documented 'conspiracy theorist' - the first to see through the lies and deceptions perpetrated by those in positions of false power. Indeed, those driven by the need to exercise that power over others. Certainly he was not afraid to stand up and be counted in this regard. Nor indeed was Diana, as affirmed by her willingness to expose the evils perpetrated by Western governments in Angola and Bosnia, for one, despite the obvious dangers to herself. Jesus's many violent outbursts against the authorities of his day must surely constitute a parallel example. The manner in which he drove out the money-changers from the Temple precincts is a further case in point. Indeed, it would appear that Jesus was fairly pissed at the fact that these first-century Money Masters were ripping off the Jewish people. They were no different in relative terms to, say, the Bank of England today. Or the US Federal Reserve. Or the European Central Bank. Or the World Bank. All of whom make vast fortunes out of the tax revenues forced on ordinary people, as we have seen. And so did the money-changers of Jesus's day. By limiting the circulation of the half-shekel to ordinary Jews, and by setting the market value of that half-shekel to serve their own greed, the Temple money-changers were able to pull off a similar sting. In short (as explained by Patrick SJ Carmack) by gaining a monopoly on the value and distribution of the half-shekel - the only coin acceptable to the Jews; the only coin which did not bear the face of Caesar - the money-changers were able to demand extortionate rates of tax from their own countrymen. And Jesus was having none of it. As Mark tells us (11: 15): "...he went into the temple and began driving out those who bought and sold in the temple ... he upset the tables of the money-changers." Indeed, were he alive today, Jesus would doubtless upset a few more corporate tables. As indeed did Diana. And with the same far-reaching effect. In so doing, of course, she was branded a 'loose cannon on a world stage', as no doubt Jesus would himself have been branded an 'insurgent', a 'subversive', a 'lefty', an 'activist', had he lived in Diana's time. He would undoubtedly have faced ridicule and defamation - possibly even assassination - at the hands of those who continue to prosper in his name: those who use and abuse his name for political and financial gain. He would surely, at any rate, have been seen to speak out against the impostures and injustices perpetrated on ordinary people by the latter-day money-changers - the high priests and potentates of corporate and masonic government. Just as he did back then.

Indeed, just as every noted heir to the Judaic royal bloodline has done since time immemorial. Including Diana. Which surely suggests that a genetic catalyst - an unique genetic signature - might indeed be responsible for this seemingly heroic behaviour. This is neither the time nor the place to start hypothesizing about where and when the somewhat unique genetic signature inherent in the bloodline may have originated - with whom, or why. But the evidence certainly suggests that it indeed exists, that it has existed for a very long time. And moreover, that it was noted as having recurred in Princess Diana. As we have seen, studies undertaken by some of the world's most eminent geneticists, at one of the world's most eminent academic institutions, Oxford University, show beyond question that such a genetic signature could indeed have originated many thousands of years ago. And that, almost certainly, it would still exist today. We have also seen that a special, almost 'mystical' quality has always been ascribed to those noted by history to have carried this gene, this genetic signature, in their blood. The Merovingians, for example, are a case in point, described by history as the 'sorcerer kings', or the 'thaumaturge kings'. And by Baigent, Leigh and Lincoln thus: "By virtue of some miraculous property in their blood they [the Merovingians] could allegedly heal by laying on of hands; and according to one account the tassels at the fringes of their robes were deemed to possess miraculous curative powers."

That Jesus was also attributed with these same "miraculous curative powers", of course, and that he was possessed of a knowledge and a wisdom 'beyond the normal human condition' is in little need of elucidation here. That the Merovingians were the documented descendants of Jesus, and thus were likely to have possessed a similar DNA patterning, ditto. And despite the often vicious claims made by traditional history, the most prominent Stuart kings too were said to be possessed of a knowledge and a wisdom 'beyond the normal human condition'. Certainly that 'condition', though perhaps not miraculous in the religious sense, nevertheless engendered a system of monarchy which embodied and promoted the principles of liberty, justice and freedom. And religious tolerance. Thus it was considered a threat by the architects of 'corporate democracy' and so was disposed of accordingly. It has remained sidelined ever since.

Until today, perhaps...

What is of significance to us in this regard is that, according to a very well-placed member of the British aristocracy and former Foreign Office (MI6) historian - whom we interviewed - moves are under way in Britain to restore the Stuarts - the bloodline - to the British Throne. Or at least to the Throne of an independent Scotland. "I have heard whispers, rumours, nothing more ... that the late Princess of Wales had been courted by certain agencies ... who seek to restore the Merovingian line to the Throne." Indeed, such moves have been under way for some time, and thus the threat to 'corporate democracy' has once again been seen to rear its head, in particular with regard to British and US moves to unite Europe under a corporate banner (the Stuarts - or at least the bloodline, its heirs and sponsors - oppose a united Europe ruled by international financiers and industrialists). As we know, the Stuart Dynasty is currently headed up by HRH Prince Michael of Albany, who would naturally succeed as Scotland's king should this eventuality transpire. Prince Michael, however, is not widely known, even in Britain, and the limited publicity he has thus far attracted has been largely derisory. In short, true to the mechanism of the corporately-owned media, and like his forbears - the Merovingians and the Stuarts - Prince Michael has been defamed and discredited by the mainstream media; his claims to the Stuart heritage have been made to seem laughable. Thus, as our source explained, certain conclaves of bloodline supporters have been forced to look elsewhere.

They did not have to look far.

With the unprecedented rise to fame of Diana, our source revealed, certain agencies (Stuart supporters, or at least supporters of the 'bloodline') had of late initiated moves to promote Diana herself as a figurehead for a counter-monarchy. Diana too, remember, was a bloodline Stuart. And her incomparable public persona was seen as something which could have been used to sway public opinion against the puppet Windsors and in favour of an alternative monarchy (a mood which was already prevalent by the time of her death). Although it is extremely doubtful (though not out of the question) that Diana would personally have stood against Queen Elizabeth in this regard, nevertheless the Windsors' concerns over her close relationship with Prince William - and thereby her ability to influence the opinion of Britain's future king, this way or that - is no secret. That she might have been grooming him in this regard cannot be ruled out. As we know, in 1995 Diana publicly stated that, in her opinion, Prince Charles was not fit to be king. At the same time she reinvented herself as the 'People's Princess', and in so doing won the support of a vast percentage of the British people. In short, if plans for a Judaic-Merovingian-Stuart restoration *are* on the table - and we have evidence that this is indeed the case, or at least that it *was* the case until Diana's 'accident' - then so far as the Windsors and their supporters are concerned, Diana must surely have been seen as a prime contender. Indeed, in realistic terms she would have been the only contender capable of carrying off such a coup - the only one capable of winning the support of the majority of British people. For this reason alone she would have been greatly feared. With Diana out of the picture, of course, any realistic 'counter-monarchy' threat has been duly abated. If not eradicated altogether. Indeed, the Windsors are currently enjoying something of a spin-doctored rebirth as a result.

And Prince William, of course, having been saved from the 'crazy notions' espoused by his mother, has been duly returned to the fold. Rehabilitated.

To conclude, then...

Based on the information we have managed to glean - both from our named and our anonymous sources, together with that gleaned from hitherto secreted historical records, and that unearthed by other researchers - it is our contention that the 'secret' at the very heart of the Judaic-Merovingian-Stuart bloodline refers to the restoration of that bloodline to the thrones of Europe. And the inevitable dismantling of masonic government and its corporate breed of democracy as a result. We also contend that Diana was emerging as a prime contender to figurehead this restoration - either as Queen or, more likely, as Queen Mother and adviser to the future king (King William). And that, by virtue of this position, she would thus have been able to instil the future king with the values and qualities inherent in the bloodline - and so direct him towards adopting a system of monarchy which has been outlawed in Britain since the end of the seventeenth century: the just and egalitarian system of monarchy by which the Stuarts - and before them the Merovingians - once reigned. With these things in mind we conclude that a combination of the following is the reason the princess is no longer alive.

One: Diana's unprecedented ability to mobilize public opinion in favour of her own causes - her anti-personnel landmines campaign being a primary case in point. According to our MI5 source, Establishment oligarchs were concerned that she was about to initiate and personally champion further politically sensitive campaigns - on behalf of victims of Gulf War Syndrome, for example. And moreover, victims of nuclear-related cancers. (These two causes alone bear far greater implications than one might first imagine.) Certainly the more this "loose cannon" was allowed to roam free, becoming ever more popular and drumming up public support worldwide in the process, the more dangerous she became to an already foundering and desperately unpopular Windsor Monarchy. Based on the evidence compiled, and the information received, it is our contention that this "loose cannon" simply had to be dealt with. And in a swift and decisive manner.

Indeed, it is our contention that this is precisely what happened.

Two: Diana's relationship with Dodi Fayed, and this for several reasons. Firstly, of course, Mohamed al Fayed is an extremely powerful political and financial player. He has been ostracized by the British Establishment - in particular by the masonic oligarchy which stands behind the House of Windsor. But also by the extended apparatus of bankers, businessmen and civil servants who form the royal circus, who band around the Monarchy and who enjoy their own success on this basis. For the past decade and more Mohamed al Fayed has endeavoured without success to gain British citizenship - to muscle his way in to this 'royal circus' and thus become part of the British Establishment himself. Long before Diana ever hooked up with the Fayeds they were loathed by both the Windsors and the Establishment. Thus all their attempts to 'muscle in' were blocked, and at every juncture. But Mohamed al Fayed was one step ahead of the game; he was now seen to be luring Diana into his fold, and thereby manoeuvring his way in to the very royal circle from which he had for so long been excluded. The fact that he had now begun to manoeuvre his way not only into the heart of the Establishment, but into the heart of the Monarchy itself, caused outrage among many Establishment oligarchs. Indeed, according to these oligarchs this latest manoeuvre was one manoeuvre too far.

As the Chairman of the Conservative Constitutional Committee, Sir James Hill, commented shortly after Diana's death: "I thought that the Fayeds were acting in a rather biased way - to try and get this young girl to become almost part of their inner circle. And I really didn't like it one little bit." And further: "I'm a particularly conservative Conservative. I like to think the future

King of England at least starts off the job without a blemish. And I don't think he could have done with Dodi as the stepfather."

It is our contention, then, that Diana's relationship with - and proposed marriage to - Dodi Fayed was interpreted by the Establishment as a political manoeuvre on the part of Mohamed al Fayed. This plus the problems thrown up as a result of both the constitutional and bloodline issues, together with those described in point *One*, was sufficient ammunition, we conclude, for the Establishment oligarchs to finally have Diana and Dodi 'removed'. We also conclude that the method chosen to most effectively execute this 'removal' was the notorious 'road traffic accident'.

As detailed elsewhere in this book, the so-called 'road traffic accident' in Paris does not stand alone in terms of government-backed assassinations. Several other instances of 'assassination by road traffic accident' have been cited, in particular with regard to Northern Ireland. But in other places, too. Including England and other European states. A further example is the alleged assassination of former Hollywood star, Grace Kelly - later Princess Grace of Monaco. Princess Grace died in 1983 when her car inexplicably plunged over a cliff. But what is of particular interest to us here is that, only a short while before her death, Princess Grace had been initiated as High Priestess of the Order of the Solar Temple, a highly secretive neo-Templar order known to harbour political as well as spiritual ambitions. Indeed, some commentators have even associated the order with the Priory of Sion itself. Or at least have suggested a common thread with regard to political aspirations. Certainly it is known that, at the time of Princess Grace's induction and initiation (early 1980s) the Priory of Sion was undergoing severe internal difficulties. Indeed, it was at this time (1984) that the joint CIA/MI6 infiltration programme, initiated in the 1940s/50s (see *Chapter Seven*), finally forced then Grand Master Pierre Plantard de Saint-Clair to resign. Faced with similar difficulties in the past, the Priory has always disappeared 'underground', away from public scrutiny (as indeed was the case following the premature resignation of Pierre Plantard de Saint-Clair). What is also evident is that, during such periods of anonymity, the Priory has always tended to re-emerge in the guise of some or other seemingly disconnected order - the Knights Templar during the Priory's early wars with the Vatican, for example, the Rosicrucians during the Inquisition. And later still, faced with the forcible imposition of Anglican (or Corporate) Christianity in Europe, Freemasonry. It is not out of the question, then, that the Order of the Solar Temple might have been established as a latter-day pseudomorph or 'front' for the hijacked - and thereby incapacitated - Priory of Sion. And that, as such, British and US intelligence agencies would have visited the same close attention upon the Order of the Solar Temple as they had already visited upon the Priory itself. Certainly if they feared for one moment that a number of the Priory's (or the 'bloodline's') most loyal supporters were continuing their struggle under cover of a seemingly independent, neo-Templar order - in particular an order which now included Princess Grace as its High Priestess - then they would have sought to emasculate that order, too. In this regard the question arises: Might Princess Grace - who, like Diana, is known to have become disenchanted with corporate corruption and royal protocol, as well as Roman Catholocism; indeed to have embraced the Gnostic principles and philosophies central to Bailey's New Age - might Princess Grace have been selected to figurehead a neo-Templar or 'bloodline' restoration bid in France? Is this why she was initiated as the order's High Priestess? Indeed, might she have been a precursor of Princess Diana in this regard? We should remember here that, at the time of Princess Grace's involvement with the Templars - the late 1970s/early 80s - Princess Diana was still very young and would certainly not yet have been considered a serious contender for any such restoration bid. Princess Grace, on the other hand, was beautiful, mature, adored by her subjects and every bit as popular in France as Diana would later become worldwide. What is also of note is that, since the highly suspicious death of Princess Grace some sixteen years ago, more than 50 other members of this neo-Templar order have also been found murdered. And what is more, not one of these murders has ever been solved. Not one. Indeed, the death of Princess Grace - her 'road traffic accident' - is still under investigation.

Add to this the fate of Princess Diana's personal police protection officer, Sgt Barry Mannakee, who was killed in a 'road traffic accident' following revelations that he had informed Diana of MI5's surveillance on her (see *Chapter Six*); the alleged attempt on the life of Camilla Parker Bowles, also a 'road traffic accident' (see *Chapter Six*); the assassination by 'road traffic accident' of Major Michael Marman, as revealed by former Equerry to the Queen, Air Marshall Sir Peter Horsley and former SAS officer, personal friend of Prince Charles and world famous explorer, Sir Ranulph Fiennes (see *Chapter Two*); the fact that former MI6 officer Richard Tomlinson testified that a current MI6 plot to assassinate Serbian President Slobodan Milosevic mirrored the 'road traffic accident' which killed Diana; the testimony of our own SAS source in this regard (see *Chapters Two and Three*); plus, of course, the fate of Diana herself - and the 'road traffic accident' is surely seen to emerge as leading nominee for the most unprovable and deniable method of assassination employed by the intelligence services today. Indeed, it wins the Oscar, hands down.

We thus contend that the so-called 'road traffic accident' in which Diana died was no accident. But that it was a pre-planned, calculated and well-practised assassination operation perpetrated by MI6, together with the

CIA, and executed by a highly trained, mercenary-style special-forces unit hired specifically for the task.

And there is yet another motive to add to the list.

Three: the very real and very serious threat posed by Diana's popularity in terms of a suspected 'monarchical coup' staged by Stuart (or 'bloodline') supporters. Or at least that she might have influenced Prince William in this regard - that she might have influenced Prince William to espouse (indeed, implement) the principles of 'constitutional monarchy' once he was king. The Windsors are not a constitutional monarchy; they are what is known as a parliamentary monarchy. They owe their seat of power not to hereditary right, but to Parliament. Which means that they are constrained by the dictates of Parliament and are thus unable to exercise their constitutional duty: to uphold the rights of their subjects against the impostures and injustices perpetrated by Parliament. The Stuarts, on the other hand (like all other legitimate bloodline dynasties) are sworn to the system of constitutional monarchy by which they once ruled. Contrary to traditional history, the Stuarts - like the Merovingians before them; indeed, like Diana - are sworn to represent rather than govern their subjects: to use their position to serve the people, rather than to use the people to serve their position. Indeed, should they regain power, they are sworn to reinstitute this very system. And to ensure that this system is upheld in a written constitution. Under this system Parliament would remain but would not be ruled, as it is today, by the Bank of England (and thus by international financiers and industrialists). Rather it would be subject to those it is supposed to represent - those who elect its officers to power: the British people. And the monarch, instead of being a parliamentary puppet, would be the people's constitutional voice, the people's champion. Much like Diana. Indeed, this is the very reason the Stuarts were deposed in the first place.

In any event, it is our contention that a combination of the above is the reason Diana is no longer alive. Like the Stuarts before her, she simply posed too great a threat to the current and wholly corrupt system of corporate democracy headed up by the equally corrupt House of Windsor. Let us not forget that she was perceived by the highest echelons of masonic government as a Grail Queen - a direct bloodline descendant of, and a genetic throwback to, the signature of David and Solomon and Jesus, as well as the Merovingians and the Stuarts. Thus she was seen as a latter-day embodiment of the 'secret' at the very heart of the bloodline itself - which, as we have seen, refers to the restoration of that bloodline to the thrones of Europe. Monumental issues are at stake here, not least the bid to create a European Superstate ruled by the central banks and their major stockholders - the international financiers and industrialists who constitute masonic government. Britain under a constitutional

Stuart Monarchy - or any other 'bloodline' monarchy, a monarchy founded on the principles central to the Judaic-Merovingian-Stuart bloodline - would pose an irrevocable threat to a corporately-governed, plutocratic Europe. In particular if that monarchy was headed up, or at least supported, by someone like Diana - whose proven ability to win public support could, in the extreme, have even engendered a situation tantamount to civil war. For this reason alone Diana surely constituted the single biggest threat to the House of Windsor since the Jacobite (Stuart) uprisings of the seventeenth and early eighteenth centuries. Indeed, for this same reason she threatened the very fabric and stability of the British Establishment itself.

As *EIR* Senior Editor, Jeff Steinberg, observed: "...You can't rule out that Diana was in a position to create a counter-monarchy, a counter-structure that could have become a rowing point for a lot of people who resented the way that Elizabeth and Philip do business." And further: "There's a power struggle that's been going on within the British elite for quite some time ... It is still going on, but a major player has been taken out of action, a player who was increasingly becoming a serious impediment, particularly to Philip and Elizabeth."

Indeed, as our CIA/MI6 source, Stealth, affirmed one week prior to the crash in Paris, Diana simply "has to go".

A week later, of course, she was gone; the impediment had been removed for good.

But above and beyond this, Diana's ability to convince people of ideas and philosophies alien to established modes of thought - that it was right and proper (indeed, that it was spiritually profitable) to serve the welfare of others before that of oneself, for example; to stand up to the arms-trade godfathers in the face of almost certain personal danger; to stand up to the entire British Royal Establishment while so many fawn at its feet; and moreover, to form a relationship (an alliance?) with an Arab Muslim and heir to a bloodline diametrically opposed to that which upholds the House of Windsor - perhaps constituted, in sum, the greatest threat of all. In particular when this threat is coupled with the very real possibility that she might, at any given time, have agreed to figurehead - or at least publicly support - a bloodline which not only undermines the authority of the House of Windsor. But which threatens the very establishment of a European Superstate controlled by the central banks - by the high priests and potentates (the international financiers, industrialists and power-brokers) who constitute masonic government.

Indeed, when the many other qualities Diana displayed are considered in this same context, each of which, in their own way, added to the clear and present danger posed by the entire person - the uncut, the unabridged, the inviolate and consummate Grail Queen: Diana, Princess of Wales - the motives for her assassination become evident enough. For this reason, together with those cited above, we conclude that the 'road traffic accident' which killed Princess Diana was no accident. But that, consistent with the many glaring anomalies and still-unanswered questions surrounding the crash itself - plus the fact that so-called 'road traffic accidents' have been shown to constitute the favoured and most deniable method of assassination employed by the intelligence services today - the so-called 'road traffic accident' which killed Diana and Dodi Fayed was in fact a premeditated, well-rehearsed assassination operation orchestrated by MI6 and the CIA. And carried out by a 'private security firm' hired specifically for the task.

We thus conclude that Princess Diana was indeed assassinated.

In any event, we duly submit the evidence to you, the jury. And we do so in the fervent hope that pressure brought by public opinion will in the end be sufficient to force an open and public inquiry into the princess's mysterious death. Perhaps even bring the perpetrators to justice. As unlikely as this eventuality must remain in reality, even so, it must never remain beyond the bounds of possibility. For where fervent belief and serious inquiry concur, together with a brave heart, there is hope. And our most ardent hope remains that one day the perpetrators will indeed be brought to book for the murder of Diana, Princess of Wales. Indeed, for their malefactions, period.

In the meantime, we can only pray that Diana may now find the peace which so eluded her while she was with us.

ADDENDUM (i)

A PERSONAL INTERVIEW WITH

HRH Prince Michael James Alexander Stewart

7th Count of Albany
Prince *de jure* of Scotland
Titular Prince of France and Poland
Head of the Royal House of Stewart
26th Lord High Steward *de jure* of Scotland
Count Stuarton
Duke of Kendal and Kintyre
Duke of Normandy and Aquitaine
President of the European Council of Princes
Knight Grand Commander,
The Chivalric Military Order of the Temple of Jerusalem

Rare Fortune

As this book was quite literally on its way to the printers we met with the rarest of fortune - we managed to track down and gain an audience with HRH Prince Michael of Albany (at the same time Prince Michael also agreed to write the *Foreword* for this book).

You may recall from chapters 11 and 15 that Prince Michael is the present-day Head of the Royal House of Stewart (we have been reliably informed by Prince Michael that the family name has again reverted to its original spelling). Indeed, had the House of Stewart (then 'Stuart') not been deposed by a joint Parliament-Church conspiracy in 1688/9 (in favour of the Dutch usurper, William of Orange), and again by a joint Parliament-Church-Bank of England conspiracy in 1714 (this time in favour of the House of Hanover-Windsor), Prince Michael would be King of Great Britain today. And what is more, the people of Great Britain would enjoy the status of free citizens under a Written Constitution upheld by a Constitutional Monarchy. As it is, of course, the people of Great Britain do not enjoy this status. On the contrary, we remain subjects of a remote and inaccessible Parliamentary Monarchy, with no stated civil rights or liberties - a situation which Prince Michael is, even today, endeavouring to remedy. Indeed, Prince Michael now lives and works in Edinburgh, Scotland, his adopted home since 1976, from where he actively promotes Scottish independence, the reinstatement of Scotland's Written Constitution and the restoration of what he refers to as Scotland's "forgotten Monarchy". Prince Michael returned to Scotland at the age of 17, from exile in Belgium, precisely to take up these somewhat lofty - and laudable - causes.

"...I'm the first one since 1887 to again raise the issue of the Stewart claim," he told us.

Prince Michael is now 42; he has been actively campaigning in this regard for almost a quarter of a century. And yet, due largely to British media manipulation - the result of the British Royal Establishment's active and ongoing campaign to suppress the Stewart claim - his case is still to be heard by the majority. Indeed, even by those who persist in bleating banefully on about how we all live in a fair and just democracy. So far as we are concerned, Prince Michael's case gives the lie to this mechanical 'tritism' all by itself.

In any event, our primary reason for wishing to include this rather rushed though provocative and highly pertinent interview was simply to substantiate our own claims regarding Prince Michael's existence, status and *raison d'etre*. Also, of course, to corroborate many of the points we made in *Book Three* regarding the history and fate of Prince Michael's family (see *Chapter Fifteen*). When we interviewed him, however, we discovered that Prince Michael himself had some very interesting things to say regarding Diana's death; indeed that, in his opinion - based on his own and his family's first-hand experience at the hands of the British Royal Establishment - Diana's death was not an accident. More specifically he told us that Diana's Stewart heritage, coupled with her unprecedented popularity, would have posed a very serious threat to the British Royal Establishment, as well as to the continued succession of the Windsors - and thus that this would almost certainly have proved a primary factor in her death. Like our Foreign Office source before him, Prince Michael also cited Diana's relationship with Dodi Fayed as a major factor in this same regard, and went on to confirm the existence of the highly top-secret MI6 department our Foreign Office source had claimed to work for - the department specifically tasked to deal with what this source had referred to as "the counter-monarchy problem". Moreover, Prince Michael confirmed that this so-called "counter-monarchy problem", at least in large part, specifically referred to the British Royal Establishment's ongoing attempts to suppress knowledge of the Stewarts' - and thus his own - legitimate claim to the Throne. In this regard he told us of the time his home was broken into and his personal files searched by agents of the British Crown.

With regard to Diana's Stewart heritage, Prince Michael told us: "It is all to do with the question of the blood ... Diana was a Stewart by descent, and the Windsors ... felt threatened by this." And further: "The Windsors saw her as a threat. They have always seen the Stewarts as a threat. They still do."

All the more reason that we should include this interview here, then - present you, the jury, with the testimony of a man who not only understands from the inside the often brutal and treacherous measures employed in the lust for royal ascendancy. But whose family has suffered the consequences of those measures for generations.

Her Britannic Majesty's Government

It was an unusually cloudless day in August 1999 when we finally made the long haul to Scotland in order to meet Prince Michael. Our pre-arranged meeting place was an hotel lounge in Edinburgh. We would like to state from the outset that we found Prince Michael extremely convivial and equally approachable - something we could not say of the Windsors, who refused to comment on Prince Michael's existence and status. Indeed, when we spoke to the Press Office at Buckingham Palace regarding Prince Michael we were met with a barrage of confusion and silence. Firstly confusion: the general flap caused by our enquiry saw us passed around from one person to the next like an unwanted disease. Then: silence. Finally we were told that neither the Royal Family nor Buckingham Palace could officially comment about a person or a family they had never heard of. Which was strange. The Windsors' claim that they had never heard of the very family they supplanted surely beggars belief. It leaves one wondering precisely what it is they fear in this regard - what it is they are trying to hide.

In any event, we can confirm that Prince Michael is indeed who he says he is, and that both his claim and status are authentic. We obtained a copy of his 1994/95 British Visitor's Passport, for example (on file), which clearly bears the title "HRH Prince Michael James Alexander Stewart of Albany". The passport also bears the official stamp: "Her Britannic Majesty's Government". The reason Prince Michael was forced to apply for a *Visitor's Passport*, we discovered, was because the British authorities, together with those of his native Belgium, have refused him a full passport since 1978. Which means he is unable to travel - except to "those countries with which Her Majesty's Government have reached agreement". In particular this passport is marked: "...*Not* valid for any visits to the United States of America". The relevance of this restriction will become evident during the interview below.

We also obtained a copy of a letter addressed to Prince Michael from the British Home Office. Despite Parliament's still-extant declaration of 1807 - which, Prince Michael confirmed, officially declared the Stewarts and their royal succession 'extinct in exile' - this letter also bore the title 'HRH Prince Michael of Albany'. In other words, even though the British Government maintains that Prince Michael's family and royal status have been 'extinct in exile' for almost 200 years, the Home Office nevertheless presumed to write to Prince Michael at his British residence and address him 'HRH' (His Royal Highness). We wondered how Home Secretary Jack Straw might explain this anomaly, so we asked him. Or at least we endeavoured to. Like all true ivory-tower politicians, however, Jack was unavailable for comment. So we asked his spokesperson instead. In fact we asked the Home Office *and* Number Ten Downing Street why the British Government might wish to correspond with someone who, it maintains, does not exist. And further, why the Home Office might elect to address this non-existent person 'HRH' when his status as Head of the Royal House of Stewart is no longer recognized by Parliament. Needless to say our efforts were fruitless.

"We remain unconcerned with this person unless he makes a direct and formal challenge for the British Throne," the Home Office spokesperson said.

"Fine, but that wasn't our question," we pressed.

"We have no further comment."

"Can you tell us, then, why you refuse to grant Prince Michael a full British Passport?"

"No further comment."

"Well can you at least tell us why...?"

"Thank you for your enquiry."

"Don't mention it."

We turned our attention to Number Ten. "Can you please confirm the existence and status of His Royal Highness Prince Michael James Alexander Stewart of Albany?"

"Who?"

"We understand that the Home Office has been in correspondence with His Royal Highness Prince Michael James Alexander Stewart of Albany. We also understand that, according to an official parliamentary declaration dated 1807, Prince Michael does not exist. Can you please confirm this, and explain why the Home Office should write to Prince Michael at his British residence and address him as 'His Royal Highness' when he and his family succession is officially 'extinct in exile'?"

"Who says that his family succession is 'extinct in exile'?"

"Parliament. But we think Parliament is lying."

A short silence, then: "Are you saying that this person is laying claim to the British Throne?"

"No."

"The Scottish Throne?"

"Yes."

"The Scottish Monarchy is extinct. There is no Scottish Monarchy."

"So what about His Royal Highness Prince Michael James Alexander Stewart of Albany?"

"There is no Scottish Monarchy."

"But we have spoken to Prince Michael. He is the senior hereditary descendant of King James II Stuart of Great Britain and he is very much alive and well."

"But the Stuarts are extinct."

"Precisely our point."

A further pause: a long, slow, agitated breath. Number Ten was discernibly pissed. Finally: "So your question is: if the Stuarts are 'extinct in exile', how is it that the Home Office wrote to Prince Michael at his British residence and addressed him as 'His Royal Highness'?"

"Correct."

"We remain unconcerned with this person unless he makes a direct and formal challenge for the British Throne." Or words to that effect. At which point our call was terminated.

Despite these official fob-offs, of course, neither department was able to deny Prince Michael's status or existence. On the contrary, like Buckingham Palace, both seemed conspicuously uncomfortable at the mention of his name - as though some troublesome ghost from the past had come back to haunt them. To us this seemed confirmation enough that Prince Michael is indeed who he says he is. And moreover, that the British authorities are fully aware of this fact. Indeed, the Home Office's letter to Prince Michael is irrefutable evidence in this regard.

And there is yet further evidence to support the authenticity of Prince Michael's claim and status. During our interview, for example, Prince Michael produced two of his credit cards, each of which bore the title 'HRH Prince Michael of Albany'. It should be noted that the title 'HRH' (His/Her Royal Highness) is bestowed only on those born of legitimate royal stock and, on occasion, on those who marry into royalty (HRH Princess Diana of Wales, for example). It should also be noted that Prince Michael is recognized by thirty-three of Europe's most senior royal houses - included among whom is the Royal House of Bourbon, whose current head is none other than King Juan Carlos of Spain. The Royal House of Bourbon, along with all thirty-two of Europe's other senior royal houses (excluding the Windsors), is represented in the European Council of Princes (ECP). Prince Michael, we recall, is the current President of ECP. And what is more, Prince Michael is eligible to serve as President of ECP precisely because he is recognized by Europe's royalty as Scotland's Prince *de jure*. In other words, as Scotland's rightful Prince and Heir. Parliament on the other hand - Number Ten Downing Street, the British Home Office, Buckingham Palace - maintains that Prince Michael does not exist (that his family line 'died out' in 1807). And thus that Scotland's royal family is extinct and therefore that the Stewart claim to the Throne is impotent. Not for the first time in this inquiry, it seemed, someone somewhere was telling less than the whole truth.

One final - and incontrovertible - piece of evidence should also be noted. And it is this.

Eminent genealogist Leo van de Pas, and appointed historian, sovereign genealogist to thirty-three of Europe's senior royal houses and the Jacobite Historiographer Royal, Sir Laurence Gardner, were both able to confirm Prince Michael's claim and status by virtue of genealogical records in their possession. These records, which date back more than a thousand years, include the official family tree of the Stewarts. And what is more, they clearly show the hereditary descent from Robert the Bruce - via some twenty-one generations, including Charles I Stuart, James II Stuart and Charles III Stuart *de jure* - to Prince Michael himself. Of note is that these records also confirm the Stewarts' descent from the Merovingian Kings of Dark Ages Europe and Princess Diana's descent from Charles II Stuart. That Prince Michael is also officially recognized in International Law (ratified by the International Parliament and endorsed by the United Nations) as Titular Claimant to the Throne of Scotland and Legal Pretender to the Throne of Britain; that he bears the title 'Count Stuarton' (inherited from his ancestor Prince Edward James Stuart, son of Bonnie Prince Charlie); and that he is recognized by the Jacobite community, even today, as King Alexander IV *de jure* of Scots, only serves to substantiate his hereditary entitlement even further. Prince Michael's claim and status simply cannot be called into question, then.

Indeed, so far as we have been able to ascertain, Parliament is the only administrative body in Europe, and the Windsors are the only royal family in Europe, who refuse to recognize the status and claim - even the *existence* - of HRH Prince Michael James Alexander Stewart of Albany (a somewhat expedient denial, it has to be said). We, of course, now know that he *does* exist. And that his claim to the Throne of an independent Scotland - indeed, to the Throne of Great Britain, from which his family was unceremoniously and unconstitutionally deposed in favour of the Hanovers-Windsors - is both legitimate and authentic.

We thus present you, the jury, with the following testimony from Prince Michael himself, and urge that you read his words in light of the evidence already presented - throughout the course of this book.

HRH Prince Michael Of Albany
And The Royal House Of Stewart

Prince Michael, for the benefit of our readers would you please introduce yourself and state your raison d'etre?

I am HRH Prince Michael James Alexander Stewart of Albany. I am the Heir to the Honours of Scotland and Head of the Royal House of Stewart. My *raison d'etre* is very much that the monarchy in Scotland should be reintroduced - although I could quite happily live as a citizen in a republic of the Scots. I would rather live as a free citizen in a republic of the Scots than as a subject of the Windsors, let us put it that way...

...So far as I am concerned, my first priority is Scottish independence. Scotland was a kingdom once, and it was very successful in Europe. When one talks in terms of the Scots, there are forty-two million people worldwide. For example, twenty-seven million Scots live in America and Canada combined. You know, there is such a thing as a *Diaspora* of the Scots worldwide. It's not just the Jews - it's the Italians; it's the Irish. And it's the Scots. My point of view is that Scots working and living abroad should be given the opportunity to retain their cultural identity, to work for this country and lobby in favour of Scottish independence, cultural independence, political independence - independence fullstop. So basically that's what I am all about.

Could you tell us more about who the Stewarts are, and why in your opinion the British people seem to know very little about your family?

Well it's very much to do with the fact that history, particularly British history - whether it's Scottish or English or Irish or Welsh - is not really taught at school. What you have is Victorian history onwards. You may skim over 1066 and all that, or if you're in Scotland you may skim over the wars of independence with Robert the Bruce and so forth, perhaps Mary Queen of Scots or even Bonnie Prince Charlie. But as a whole the Stewarts have been totally sidelined in favour of Victoria and her ilks up to the present day. The Stewarts, in fact, were the longest lasting dynasty in Europe. Scotland's royal family - and I do mean Scotland's, not Britain's - Scotland's royal family is the oldest royal family in Europe. We are older than Christianity itself. In fact I can trace my family tree back to, say, the Kings of Judah, and even as far back as the eighteenth Egyptian Dynasty - without a break in the family. We are talking 1500 BC. So we are the oldest royal family, possibly in the world, still surviving...

...We were also great achievers. Think in terms of James IV, for example, who introduced the first Navy in Britain, which was the Scottish Navy. He also introduced the first education bill, so that by the year 1500 the whole of Scotland was literate. Now compare that to the rest of Europe - or compare that to England, whose people were still illiterate, except for the aristocracy, and even they were not that literate! Also, think in terms of James VII of Scots - James II of England - who decided in 1686 and 1687 and 1688 to try to introduce a bill whereby all people, across the board, from John O'Groats to Dover, would have the right to worship according to their conscience. Let's remember that, even in those days, Britain included many Jews, and also the Quakers. We had Catholics without any rights whatsoever, and Anglicans and Presbyterians as well. So this was a man who was prepared to stand up and be identified with his people. I mean, we would take this for granted nowadays - that everyone would have the right to worship according to their conscience - but not so in 1688. Basically we lost the Crown for that particular reason. The Church of England kicked us out.

Do you think that was the ultimate reason?

Yes, we were too tolerant in the eyes of Parliament; they [Parliament] could not control us and so therefore they could not control the people. But yes, the ultimate reason was that the Church of England - which was basically created for two sole purposes, firstly to give Henry VIII a divorce, and secondly to allow the Protestant Church, or the Anglicans, to steal the land from the Catholic Church, the monasteries and so forth - and the Church of England was of course married to the state. So what the Church wanted Parliament wanted as well. I mean, it's nothing new; it's happened numerous times throughout history. But the point is, when you introduce a concept whereby Catholics, Quakers and Jews are granted the same civil rights and liberties, it becomes a threat to the status quo. You must remember in Britain, even today, people don't have any civil rights and liberties - there is no such thing as a Written Constitution in Britain, the only country in Europe not to have one, incidentally. One of the very few in the *world* not to have one, incidentally. And this is the country that calls itself the Mother of all democracies - big joke. And we have to remember that. Indeed, take that into account and compare it to the achievements of the Stewarts, and you will see that something is not quite right...

...Take the Declaration of Arbroath, for example, whereby in 1320 you had the first Written Constitution in Europe, actually written down on a piece of paper, giving people civil rights and liberties - *and* the concept that sovereignty does not rest with the King or Parliament, but with the people. Now that is of paramount importance because the Declaration of Arbroath contains these civil rights and liberties, *written down*. Because they *are* written down, of course, if politicians or the monarch ignores them, they can be brought to task. It gives the people the right to do this. We must remember that all other decent countries worldwide have adopted these civil rights and liberties - the civil rights and liberties first written down in the Declaration of Arbroath...

...The Declaration of Arbroath 1320 is the one upon which all subsequent written declarations or constitutions, including the American Constitution, were based. In fact, my ancestor, King Charles III *de jure*, or Bonnie Prince Charlie, was offered the Crown of America in 1782. He was invited to become King Charles I of America by George Washington following the American War of Independence. This was before the American Constitution was drawn up. He respectfully declined the offer, however, because he was old and he feared that the Hanovers would gain the American Throne on his death. At that time he was separated from his wife, and the prospects of him being able to obtain a divorce, remarry and produce a male heir were uncertain. I mean, the last thing he wanted was to open the door to the Hanovers - to inflict the Hanovers on the American people - so he felt obliged to decline the offer...

...But yes, the Declaration of Arbroath was the first Written Constitution in Europe, and the one upon which the American Constitution was based.

Another declaration, issued by Parliament in 1807, states that the Stewart succession is 'extinct in exile'.

That's right, yes. But as you see, I am here and very much alive!

Indeed you are. But why do you think Parliament would have perpetrated such a fabrication?

Well you have to perpetrate such a lie when your aim is to dispossess a royal family who is the real thing - [when your aim is] to dispossess the real royal family in favour of ... well, I think you know what I mean. Think of the accession of George I Hanover, for example - there were fifty claimants with a better claim to the Crown of Great Britain than George I. Five-O: *fifty*. So you have to perpetuate the lie that, a) we [the Stewarts] were no good; and b) we were dispossessed because of our Catholicism, which is a load of rubbish. We acted on behalf of the Quakers and the Jews just as much as the Catholics. And anyway, if what you want is a parliamentary royal family - it is a parliamentary royal family you have today; the Queen is not a constitutional monarch, she is a parliamentary monarch - and you need to get rid of the constitutional monarch in order to achieve this, then you need to perpetrate a lie, which is precisely what they [Parliament and the Church] did. And once you have established a parliamentary royal family, of course - which has really nothing to say; they represent Parliament, not the people - then of course you have to perpetuate that lie: the lie that brought about the situation in the first place. You have to perpetuate it. And what better way to perpetuate that lie than to declare my family extinct. But we are not extinct. We have always been around, even though we have been forced to live in exile.

So would you agree that the Hanovers-Windsors were deliberately installed by Parliament as a puppet-monarchy - to head up the new breed of 'corporate democracy' sought by Parliament at that time?

Definitely. And the biggest joke is that they couldn't even speak English! They couldn't possibly function as Britain's monarchy; they didn't even *try* to function within British society. It was not until George III, remembered first and foremost for his insanity, that the first Hanover monarch was born in Britain. And even *his* son, George IV, spoke with a German accent. Indeed, this is a royal family who spoke German with one another right up to World War One, and in fact even up to World War Two. And then, of course, there was Edward VIII - I bet you he conversed well enough in German with his friend Adolf Hitler!

Absolutely. But would you say that the reason the Hanovers-Windsors were offered the Throne was because of the way so-called democracy was heading at that time, particularly in terms of establishing the central banking system - the Bank of England?

Well, let's face it, there's no such thing as democracy in Britain. Certainly the reason James II was deposed in favour of William of Orange had nothing to do with democracy. Not true democracy. As for banking, yes, the Bank of England was established at this time, but again it was William of Orange who did that, not us, not the Stewarts. We were largely opposed to that idea - to the idea that the Dutch should rule Britain through the Bank of England and the Monarchy. Well let's face it, that's really why Parliament and the Dutch - who already had their own [central] bank - that's why they wanted William of Orange - or Wee Billie Windmills, as he was known - as King. And *that's* why James VII [James II of England] was forced to give up the Throne and leave Britain. They concocted this idea that he favoured Catholics over Protestants, but this is rubbish. The truth of the matter is that he was simply not prepared to play their game...

...But you must also remember that Scotland had gained two banks as well - the Bank of Scotland and the Royal Bank. So England certainly did not have a banking monopoly in Great Britain. In fact, today, most people throughout the world would rather deal with a Scottish bank, which is much more liberal than the Bank of England - which is, or at least was at that time, very restrained. Well let's face it, it was run by Westminster, and you can't get much more restrained than that! But, ahh ... certainly in Scotland we don't have this problem. We don't have a banking history, for example, where our bank is under the yoke of Westminster, you know, a kind of Westminsterian autocracy.

So why do you think this happened in England? Why do you think the English people supported such a 'Westminsterian autocracy', as you put it?

Well they really didn't have a choice, not in those days. They had no say in the way their country was run, in the way Parliament governed, because they didn't have a Written Constitution. They still don't have a Written Constitution. You must remember that England only has Magna Carta, and I think that the crux of the matter - particularly the English concept of politics, and certainly the English concept of democracy, which of course does not exist - [the crux of the matter] is that the English people have been told since medieval days, 'well you do have Magna Carta'. And yet very few people have ever read Magna Carta. But they should read it, simply because, if they were really to read it, they would quickly realize, 'wait a minute, that's not for us, it's for them'...

...Ahh, but of course they are not told this. They have never been told this, so they had this great belief in so-called democracy. They still do. They still have this great belief that England offered so much to the world in terms of democracy. And looking at the history of England and its Empire - you know, the so-called British Empire, it was really the *English* Empire ... democracy has never been part of it. They [the English] only got out of countries when there was nothing left to pillage and steal. You know, once a country under British rule became bare of all its assets, then they decided, 'well yes, now you can have your independence'. But of course, it's not really independence; there's no real democratic process in those countries. In truth they are still ruled from Westminster. And anyway, the Bank of England played a big part in all of this, which is why they needed a monarchy like the Hanovers, the Windsors - which brings us back to the point about why we lost the Crown. The Church of England kicked us out because of our so-called Catholicism. But that is a load of rubbish. The Church was part of the same system; it was all ruled from Westminster, and the Hanovers, who are really the Windsors, played their role to perfection. And this is why Scottish independence is so important today - to have a Scottish parliament and monarchy based here, in Edinburgh, free from the yoke of Westminster.

Genealogies

According to genealogist Leo van de Pas, the Stewarts descended from the Merovingian Kings of Dark Ages Europe. Could you please confirm this claim, and tell us what is so significant about the

Merovingians?

Well I don't think it's so significant nowadays - you know, we're only a branch of the Merovingian family. There are quite a few branches - it's quite an extensive family. It is true that, in the days of the Merovingian Kings, they were considered semi-divine, and it is true that there is a Judaic descent to which we belong ... So yes, we are descendants of the Merovingian Kings.

This is a fact confirmed by royal genealogist, Sir Laurence Gardner. In fact he says that the Merovingians were descended from the family of Jesus, and that Jesus was himself a rightful King of Judea.

Well yes, this is common knowledge in our family, but this does not make us divine. We look upon Jesus as a man like anybody else. But ahh ... if you look at the Islamic records, for example, records dating from the 9th and 10th centuries in Spain, you will see that it was known, even in Islam, that descendants of Jesus and of his brothers survived, and that some of these descendants later became known as the Merovingians ... We have a name for these descendants, the *Desposyni*, who later became known as the Grail Family. Basically, when one talks about the Desposyni or the Grail Family, one is talking in terms of the descendants of Jesus Christ, and of his brothers and sisters, because he had two sisters also. So it's significant in the sense that we don't consider - within my family - the divinity of Jesus. We know perfectly well that he was a man just like anybody else, that he died just like anybody else, and that he was buried just like anybody else. And yes, that he was a King, and that his descendants were Kings after him. The rest is all part of the dogma created by the Roman Catholic Church...

...It is also significant, I suppose, in that the Merovingians were declared extinct, just like the Stewarts were also declared extinct: we posed a similar threat to the authorities of the time ... But this is extremely difficult to prove for such an extensive family. You know, if you take, for example, the fact that my ancestor Robert III had twenty-three children, to actually state that the Royal House of Stewart is extinct today is rather nonsensical.

If we might just dwell on the 'Jesus bloodline' theme for a moment...

Yes, OK.

...Even though you and your family tend to play down your descent from Jesus, your political opponents - Parliament, the British Monarchy, the Church of Rome - tend nonetheless to take it very seriously. Indeed, would you agree that your heritage in this regard has been hijacked for political gain?

Oh yes, but that is what politics is all about. It always has been, and particularly during the Dark Ages in Europe. It was then that the Catholic Church was able to make a political move and take prominence in European politics, largely by doing away with the Merovingians, with our bloodline, so that it could be hijacked as you say, or at least intermarried into the royal houses created by the Church. But then, you know, you do have several popes - if you look at Sylvester II, for example, who was also a Merovingian Prince...

Sylvester II?

...Yes. He was the only Merovingian ever to make it there - that's why they killed him! He only lasted four years - from 999 until 1003 - and then he was poisoned. But Sylvester II realized that, what he really needed to do was to bring the power of the Papacy down, and that of the Bishops as well, in order to bring Europe in line with the industrial and scientific equivalent to [that of] Spain and the rest of the Eastern [Islamic] world. Sylvester had studied at the University of Cordova, which was a Muslim university, and he realized that Europe, under the yoke of the Papacy, was lagging behind in terms of industrial and scientific education. He realized that this had to be changed, but in order to do this he had to curtail the power of the Papacy. He was the only one who tried to do this, and as I say, he lost his life for doing it...

...And anyway, he [Sylvester II] certainly knew who he was and where he came from - you know, who one of his particular ancestors happened to be. Of course, the Church knew this as well; it was no big deal to Sylvester, but to the Church it was reason enough to kill him ... So anyway, the rise of the Roman Catholic Church - or rather, 'Churchianity' - is what has curtailed the political liberation of Europe. Even to this day, the fact that we still have the Archbishop of Canterbury or the Pope, or any of those patriarchs being able to lord it over everybody else, telling them that you can't use condoms, for example, even though AIDS is still a huge problem; or that women have no choice to decide for themselves over the issue of abortion - to me these attitudes and these people are so medieval they should be put against a wall and shot, for God's sake! I don't mean that literally, of course. But you know, they are nothing more than hypocrites and bigots.

Quite right, Especially as the Vatican invests vast amounts of money in companies which actually make condoms and birth-control pills.

Yes, and machine guns! It's totally unacceptable.

So the Merovingians, including Pope Sylvester II, would have known that they were the descendants of Jesus?

Oh yes, for sure. Look, you must remember one thing - it may be news to people today, in 1999, because these days this information has been suppressed and a new, false history has been written. But let me tell you that in the 5th century AD, in the 8th century AD, in the 12th century AD, even in the 16th century AD, this was not news. No one denied this fact then -

except perhaps the fathers of the Church. But as a whole no one challenged this historical fact. Even the leaders of nations - Popes, Kings, Princes, whatever - didn't deny the fact that, yes, Jesus Christ had descendants. It was certainly something that was known well up to the 4th century AD, that there were people around who were descended from Mary Magdalene and Jesus Christ. It's simply the fact that you have had the ascendancy of the Church of Rome, and of Constantinople, that all of these records and this knowledge has been destroyed. It is also the fact that you had a descendant of Jesus Christ in the Emperor Constantine the Great, who declared the Christian Church the State Church. And from then on, because he had done that, the descendants of Christ had to be sidelined, and the Papacy had to take over. It was a political *coup d'etat*. And it was a *coup d'etat* which was formulated by a man who was part of the Desposyni family - Constantine the Great - through his mother. Whether this was what he had in mind, I have no idea. But certainly it has made life difficult for most of us because the Church, being then in charge, decided that these people could not go on saying what they were saying, even though it was true. So you had a genocide organized by the Church - a genocide in Europe and the Middle East - which is why the Crusades took place. You know, we talk of a false history, or a secret history ... well I can tell you there was a Papal plot to send people to the Middle East in order to kill the descendants of the Desposyni family over there.

Are you aware of any genealogical records still in existence which might corroborate what you are saying?

Well you would be hard pressed to find records dating back that far; they have all been destroyed. But you might find gravestones - of Jesus's son, for example, Jesus Justus, probably in France. Also Mary Magdalene's grave has been found - centuries ago, during the 16th century. The Cathars knew about this as well, which is why they were massacred. Muslim Spain during the 9th and 10th centuries talked openly about it, about Jesus's family tree. Celtic monks - be they in Ireland or Scotland or Wales or wherever - knew about this as well. This is why they made the concept of Abbots hereditary, from father to son, or cousin to cousin or whatever. But they kept it within the family. And the concept came from the fact that most of them were descended from Judaic stock - either going back to Jesus or previous to him. But certainly from within that family...

...So even if there aren't any papers, certainly there is a tradition - an oral tradition - there was an oral tradition that was passed down from generation to generation. And people don't carry on a tradition for nothing; they do it for a particular reason. So far as we are concerned, of course, whether we are the descendants of Jesus Christ or not - it is simply not important. We know that we are but it is not important. We live today and we have a legitimate royal heritage - with or without Jesus. It is the Church that has made such a big deal out of Jesus, not us. It is the Church that has gained such political power out of Jesus, not us.

Her Majestyís...
...Some Or Other Department

What little information we have been able to glean about you and your family - in particular information presented by the British media, the British media's treatment of the Stewarts - has been of a derogatory nature. Do you think this is because you still pose a threat to the British Establishment?

Well the British media is not particularly informative at the best of times! But yes, of course, I still do pose a threat. I still cannot travel, for example; I am a prisoner in Scotland - which is the greatest country to be a prisoner in - but it is still the case that I cannot travel.

Can you tell us why?

Yes, It's quite simple - I can't get a passport! I was made stateless in 1991, and the reason is because the Queen was travelling to Washington to address the Senate that year, while I had been invited to open the Costa Mesa Highland Games in Los Angeles, in front of 50,000 people. Well, according to those who tread the corridors of Whitehall, the fact that both myself and the Queen were to be in America at the same time meant that the American press would have been drawn in two - one side would go on about the Queen and the other side would go on about me. Which would of course have meant that I would have achieved a lot of publicity. However, the Queen being who she is - being the ruling, reigning monarch - well she was allowed obviously to go to the States and address the Senate, but they decided that I should stay in Britain. So they refused me a British passport - they have the right to do that...

...So I took my outdated passport to the Belgian Embassy to have it renewed there. I was very naive in those days! So anyway, I took my outdated passport - which had been outdated since 1978 - and when I got to the Embassy they let me fill in the application form and asked for my old passport, which I gave them, and my ID card, which I also gave them. Well they took a pair of scissors and cut up both my passport and my ID card - which meant that in the European concept of things I no longer existed. I was suddenly stateless - it only took about 30 seconds. And then I was informed that there would not be a passport issued to me. And that remains the case to date...

...So that's how easily two states can actually do this, without actually breaking the law. Because if you look at your passport, it's not your property; it is the property of the state. So they can take that away from you anytime they wish to, for no reason - they don't need to give you a reason at all. They just take your passport and say 'thank you very much', and that's it.

At about this same time, we understand that you were visited by British agents, government agents.

Yes, that's right. It was about eight o'clock in the morning, and these two gentlemen from Her Majesty's ahh ... well, some or other department, visited me and said to me: "We wish to talk to you about your passport." So I said: "Well I wasn't issued a passport, so there is nothing to discuss." And they said: "Nevertheless we wish to talk to you about your passport." So anyway, I made tea for them, so that at least they would not think I was inhospitable. And, you know, the funny thing was that they made statements. They didn't actually ask questions; they just made statements, such as: "We believe you tried to acquire a British passport under false pretences. This is against the law." So I said: "Well actually, I know something about the law; my ancestors wrote the law in this country!" And then I said: "I was not acting under false pretences. On the contrary, it is the people for whom *you* are working who are acting under false pretences..."

...They then informed me that I had tried to acquire a British passport for terrorist purposes, to which I simply replied: "Don't be ridiculous!" You know, I might pose some sort of threat, but I am not a terrorist. In fact I have always said that the pen is mightier than the sword, or even the machine gun. So I told them: "No, you certainly can't drop that one on me." And then eventually the truth came out. They said: "We believe you tried to acquire a British passport in order to further your claim for the Scottish Crown." *Ah*, I thought, *now we're getting to the crux of the matter...*

...Well I could have said yes, but I didn't know where I would stand. So I just said that I was applying for a British passport as a free citizen, because of my wish to travel. They then asked me where I kept my family file. Which was strange, because I do have a file - I call it the 'Albany File' - and it contains several of my family papers, my birth certificate, various letters from MPs, the Prime Minister and so forth. And so I said: "I'm afraid it's in the bank; it's in a vault in the bank." They quickly said: "No it isn't; we know where it is." And one of them looked at the very drawer where I kept this file at home. The only way they could have known this, of course, was that they had been in my home behind my back, searched my premises and found my personal file. They were not even terribly subtle about it. Anyway, that's when you realize, of course, that you're still being monitored. Which means you are still a threat - you are still thought of as a threat, which is fine by me. From my point of view, I must be getting somewhere if the state still considers me a threat - if the state decides that its secret departments should keep an eye on me. I must be worth the bother, so I must be doing something right.

The House Of Windsor

Would you say that the House of Windsor fulfils its moral and constitutional duty as Britain's present-day monarchy?

Oh my God, certainly not! As I said before, the House of Windsor is not a constitutional monarchy. They don't represent the people; they have no constitutional right to stand against the improprieties of Parliament. The state is today very much rowing against the wish of the people, so the state is overreaching itself. Number Ten is overreaching itself. But even when told by the people that it is overreaching itself, it really doesn't care. And this is a monarchy which has no right to stand up and be counted along with the people. So, certainly from a constitutional point of view, it's not working...

...From a moral point of view - I think we should really leave morality out of the picture, because at the end of the day, you can make what you want of morality. And I don't believe in being overly moralistic in any case.

Yes, but we mean 'moral' in terms of the hidden political agenda which seems to be responsible for upholding this parliamentary monarchy. For example, does this agenda serve the people, or does it serve those in power, those who benefit from it, those who have a vested interest in the continued succession of the Windsors? We also mean 'moral' in terms of where they are really coming from, the Windsors - who they really are in terms of their relationship with Parliament and their so-called subjects.

Well I don't think they know that themselves, to tell you the truth. I think that's the problem. They have had to reinvent themselves so often that, every time they wake up in the morning, the question they must ask themselves is 'well, who exactly am I supposed to be today?'.

But that's precisely our point. They don't seem to care who they are, just so long as the ploy keeps working...

That's right, so long as it suits the purposes of both themselves and the state. Yes, I suppose you have a point there, viewing the morality of the situation in that sense. But when you're part of a system - remember, [the Stewarts] got out of this system because we didn't believe in it; or rather we were kicked out of this system because we didn't support it - and basically we just don't think like the Windsors. In fact very few other monarchies in Europe today think like the Windsors. If you look at King Juan Carlos of Spain, for example, who rides his motorbike in public. Or Queen Margaret of Denmark, who goes shopping by herself and meets people and does things that other people do. The same goes for the King of Sweden and the King of

Norway. And then there is the Belgian Royal Family, which is a constitutional monarchy, and the Dutch monarchy, which has always been what I call a 'bicycle monarchy' - Holland being a flat country! In fact I have tried this in Edinburgh, but you know this is a city built on seven hills, and so you very quickly exchange your bicycle for a car...!

...But, you know, these are populist monarchies - it is not a populist monarchy in Britain. The monarchy or the state, they are just not interested in the views of the people. There is too much at stake.

Even though your claim is at present for the Throne of an independent Scotland, you were in fact deposed from the Throne of Britain. With this in mind, if you were invited by the British people to once again succeed the Throne of Britain - say, as the result of a plebiscite - how would the way in which you would conduct yourself as King differ from that of Queen Elizabeth II?

Well, first of all, the people of Britain need to learn about me and hear what I have to say. Otherwise there is no chance of a plebiscite...

And, of course, they have to hear what you have to say directly, as it were, without the British media getting hold of it and twisting it to suit their own agenda.

Exactly.

But assuming for the moment that you were King, how would your reign differ from that of the Windsors?

Well as a Stewart, you know, the thing about my family is that we love politics. I don't mean that I would want to be a politician - I don't. But we love politics, and the Stewarts were the most successful royal family in Europe. If you look at the traditional historical records people may not think so. But in actual fact, if you look at the true record of the Stewarts, we were the most successful royal family in Europe. And the reason is quite simply that we cared about people. We still do - I do. Plus, of course, we had the constitution, and we upheld that constitution - the Declaration of Arbroath, 1320. So first of all I would insist upon a Written Constitution for England, a Written Constitution for Scotland, and a Written Constitution for Wales. And they would have to be different because the psyche of each nation is different. What Britain needs today is at least two monarchies - and if the Welsh could trace their own royal family as well then that would be very good. But what I'm saying is - let's go back to our roots. Let all nations within Britain be independent, represented equally and constitutionally, but separately, with a monarchy in Scotland, a monarchy in England, and a monarchy in Wales.

But that would mean that the English - which is us - would still be lumbered with the Windsors and the style of 'corporate democracy' they represent.

No, no, that's not what I'm saying. Things *would* be different because you would have a Written Constitution, and the Windsors or whoever would have to uphold that Constitution, or they would be out. The power would rest with the people. Sovereignty would rest with the people; that's what a Written Constitution is all about...

...From my point of view, you see, what is needed is a monarch who when things are not right, when Number Ten Downing Street is not getting it right, what is needed is a monarch who is prepared to stand up and say: "Right, back to your drawing board and give us something better." This is what I would do. Being a Stewart I believe in the concept of 'Guardian of the Realm'. And basically this is what I would do - I would uphold, verbally and actually, a Written Constitution which declares the civil rights and liberties of the people. I would tell politicians: "Well, the people are grumbling, you're not listening, now I'*m* telling you." This is what a constitutional monarchy is all about - to represent the people. It is not there to represent big business or politics. It is not there to represent politicians either; it's above party politics, or it should be. But it *is* there to represent *common-sense* politics. And that's the people.

When you're as far removed from the people as the present monarchy is, of course, it's simply not possible to represent them.

Well right, the biggest problem for the Windsors is that they're on a pedestal, and they've got to come off that pedestal. They were put there such a long time ago that - well, you know yourself, it's easy to get on it, but getting off it is extremely difficult. But that's the problem with Britain generally, it's stagnant. You know, people and nations have moved on, but Britain really hasn't. It is a country that once upon a time, industrially, led the way - but it no longer does. I mean, it is still today the fifth richest country in the world. But Scotland is the seventh richest. Scotland is the seventh richest nation with only five and a half million people; Britain, with sixty million, is only fifth. And it's simply because, industrially and in business, Britain is stagnant. And it's all very well to adhere to tradition, if these traditions are productive. But if they impede your industrial, financial and social evolution, then I'm afraid you have to put those traditions aside and create new ones...

...Certainly this applies to England. You know, I have to be honest with you, the biggest problem that my family, the Stewarts, and myself have is that we do not comprehend the English temperament. You are the most - *perhaps not you two!* - but the nation of England as a whole, collectively, has the most unfathomable psyche ever devised on planet earth. I mean, eccentricity, yes, by all means, because that makes life much more interesting. But you are so damned obtuse and stubborn, to the point of idiocy. And it's not just me; the majority of Europe thinks this too. You know, it's not just

Parliament or the Monarchy - it's the people. It's the people themselves who bugger it all up. If you want change then you must stand up and say so, for God's sake!

But the problem we have as English people is that we don't have a true racial or cultural identity - say, like the Scots or other Celtic peoples. We've had to invent one. We've had to invent an identity because we've never had one. That's what the Empire was all about. It's a bit like being a school bully - he invents himself as a bully because he's insecure about his own identity. He needs to prove himself, so he invents himself in this way.

Which is what the Hanovers did, of course. The Empire was built under the Hanovers.

Right. It was all about inventing a cultural and political identity. Once the Stewarts were deposed in favour of the German Hanovers and the Dutch Bank of England etc - you know, we no longer knew who we were. We still don't. Which is why we don't know how to change. We don't know how to rebel against the deep flaws in our democracy.

Why not?

Because like the school bully we don't know who we really are. You can see the same thing happening in America today. We're a racial and cultural cocktail, like America. And because we are we feel safe in this system of 'corporate democracy', this 'Empire democracy' - that's our identity. We call it Great Britain but really it's England. Great Britain is really just an extension of England, so we can't fight for independence like the Scots.

But of course you can. I do hear what you're saying, but you *can* change it. You *must* change it. If it is good enough for the Scots to liberate themselves then the English can do it too. If the Scots can liberate themselves from the yoke of Westminster then the English can do it too.

Yes, but within the psyche of English people, Westminster represents the system which has become our identity. Effectively Westminster is England.

No, Westminster is *not* England. This is what the English people must come to terms with. Westminster is not England; the *people* are England. The *Scots* are Scotland. The *Irish* are Ireland. You know, my grandfather always said that what we need is a damned good revolution. It needn't be one with guns, but it certainly can be a cultural one; it certainly can be a socio-political one. You know, forget the politics; forget the politicians. It's about the people standing up for themselves. It's about time that people drew strength from the Sixties, and learned from the Sixties. People knew how to demonstrate then, how to stand up for their civil rights and liberties. I mean, I was born in

1958, so I do remember the Sixties. In fact my mother took me to a demonstration - you know, she hit people with her umbrella, even policemen if they came too near! But you know, I remember that. I remember the atmosphere or the spirit that was in people then. It sounds strange, but at the end of the day, at least people were active within the socio-political scene. If they didn't like what was going on they made the politicians know about it. Nowadays, I mean look at us, we demonstrate *silently*. Now what's the point of demonstrating *silently*? Nothing is achieved by demonstrating *silently...*

...Look at the Poll Tax, for example, which good old *'oh dear, so dear'* Margaret Thatcher introduced. It was introduced in Scotland a year before it was introduced in England. Now in Scotland we demonstrated silently, and people were even sent to prison for refusing to pay their Poll Tax. You know, we're talking the latter days of the twentieth century, for God's sake - it's shocking! But in Scotland we demonstrated *silently*, and nothing was done about it; nothing was achieved...

...But then it was introduced in England, and overnight London erupted into flames. Shops were looted; cars were overturned and burned; and you had riots on the streets of London. And because of this, good old *'oh dear, so dear'* Margaret Thatcher was forced into a position where she had to scrap the Poll Tax altogether, and replace it with something else. And it proves one thing - and I hate to say it, because I don't believe in violence - but it does prove that if you overturn cars, and if you loot shops, and if you have riots in the streets, sometimes it's the only way to make those blasted politicians listen. I mean, they should be listening anyway. But they're *not* listening. And sometimes you have to stand up and make yourself heard. Those politicians - they're not there for Tony Blair or Margaret Thatcher or to enforce party policies. They're there for you and me, and even for the people who did not vote for them. That's democracy. And until they realize this they will be no good to any of us...

...And I'll tell you something else. The best thing we could do at the next general election is this: no one but *no one* should turn up at the polling stations and vote. Then what would happen? Well I'll tell you. They'll come up with a great big zero and guess what - no more Westminster...!

...So you see, it can be done. But the English people must take it into their own hands. No one else is going to do it for them.

The European Council Of Princes And The Power Of The Media

While researching our book we learned that you are the current

President of an organization called the European Council of Princes. Could you tell us something about this organization?

Well basically it was founded in 1946 by the Kings of Eastern Europe [the Habsburgs] who had been deposed, so that they would still have some kind of podium in their war on Communism. But today it has a different purpose. Over the years it lost its momentum, until in 1992, with the advent of the EEC, it sort of regrouped and changed its name to the European Council of Princes. It then took in royal houses from Western Europe as well, so now it is represented by a number of royal families - Denmark, Sweden, Norway, Spain, Portugal, Holland, Belgium, Luxembourg, Austria, Germany, Bavaria, Romania: all the little states that once were independent states within Germany are represented as well. Altogether there are thirty-three of us. I represent Scotland, not Britain. The Windsors decided not to be represented; every time they were asked to join they said 'not interested', which is fine by me. We are currently hoping that Russia will join as well, because we still consider Russia as part of continental Europe...

...So basically, with the advent of the EEC and the EU - the problem is that even the EU does not have a Written Constitution. So that's item one. Item two is that the EU promulgates legislation which infringes on various nations' Written Constitutions in Europe. So we tend to point out to Brussels or Strasbourg what is going on and request that they put it right ... Basically what we are trying to do is ensure that the Written Constitutions of European nation states are not infringed on or otherwise compromised by EU legislation. Now as I have said, Britain does not have a Written Constitution, so again, before we can properly represent Britain in Europe, Britain needs a Written Constitution - a constitution which is not the result of political expediency, or something based on various treaties like the Treaty of Union of 1707, or Magna Carta, which really does not relate to the rights of the people, only to [those of] the barons who concocted it. So a Written Constitution is what is desperately needed in Britain. And the quicker this is done, the better it will be for Britain in Europe - for Britain under EU legislation. You have to remember that none of those EU Commissioners were elected. Someone has to keep an eye on what they are getting up to!

Right.

Anyway, that's basically the purpose of the European Council of Princes.

So it's not a secretive organization like, say, the Bilderberg Group or G7/8 or the Davos Group?

Absolutely not! The very concept of these organizations is to me frightening. The very idea that a minority 2% of the world owns the assets of the world - that to me is frightening. And it's frightening because none of us know these people. They meet once a year to discuss the industrial climate, the financial climate, how many people are going to be made unemployed etc. We don't know where they meet or what their agenda is. They're not elected, and they are the ones who, in effect, tell governments what to do. Yet it is you and I who vote those governments into power. And it simply proves one thing: that whether we have the vote or not, it comes down to the same thing - for as long as these people remain unchallenged, for as long as they remain unaccountable, we do not have the power to choose for ourselves, to decide for ourselves what we want. At the end of their meetings there is no report available to the public. These people are not accountable, and they should be. What we need is a people's forum ... to demand that these meetings are made more accountable to the public ... to tell these financiers and industrialists, *and* the politicians, that they are there to represent and to be accountable to the people, not just to themselves.

How do you think we could ever make these people more accountable?

Well, I've always said that the pen is mightier than the sword. But the problem is that these politicians, even Downing Street, have a pen which is bigger than ours - than the three of us put together. That's the unfortunate thing about it. And we have to agree with this. We have to recognize that, at the moment, their pen is bigger than ours. It is bigger than all the people - than the entire English, Scottish and Welsh nations put together. That's the problem. They own the media - be it television, radio or newspapers - and so they have tremendous influence on the way people think. I mean, had it not been for the fact that Tony Blair went to Australia to meet Rupert Murdoch prior to the last general election, you may be sure that he would not have been voted Prime Minister of Great Britain. It's the power of the media, which is largely owned by these people - that's how simple it is...

...I mean, let's face it, if I had the *Sun* and whatever other newspapers that are owned by Rupert Murdoch deciding tomorrow, 'OK, we'll make Michael James Alexander Stewart, King Alexander IV of Scots', you may be sure that within a year I would have been crowned.

Exactly right - that's the power the media has over people. But it's so hypocritical. Take Princess Diana, for example. When she was alive she was constantly attacked by the media, but the minute she died she was suddenly transformed into a kind of latter-day saint.

Yes, you are quite right. But I'm afraid that is how it always is, the royals or anybody. People are always treated better when they are dead. When they are alive - especially Princess Diana, especially if they pose some sort of threat to the Establishment or the Monarchy or Westminster or whatever - they are always ridiculed when they are alive. But they are always so great when they are dead. And people believe it, that's the worrying thing. But again, that's the power of the media today...

...Take the Queen Mother, for example. Now, we are told that the Queen Mother was the first real outsider to enter the Royal Family, but she wasn't an outsider at all. Because of what we are told by the media, people have the concept that she was an outsider, but she was not. She was always part of 'The Firm' - her family has been part of 'The Firm' from a long, long time back. But then, you know, royal marriages within the Windsor family are generally arranged according to blood, and political expediency.

Could you elaborate on this point?

Well ... Sarah Ferguson and Diana Spencer were the first true outsiders - the first true ones to come in from the outside. In fact the first one was Marie Christine von Reibnitz [Princess Michael] of Kent, and she was given a hard time as well - not just because she was a Catholic. But because, if you look at her roots and her genealogy, she is much better connected than all of the Windsors put together.

As was Princess Diana.

Yes, Princess Diana was extremely well connected within the British aristocracy. In fact she was far better connected than any of the family into which she married. You know, out of the whole damn lot, the Queen Mother is British, Diana Spencer and Sarah Ferguson were also British. But anything beyond that is all German. If you look at old Queen Mary, clad in black and always with a stick and looking very regal - she was known as Princess Mary of Teck, but her full name was Maria Victoria Wurtenburg von Hohenstein, Princess in von Teck! And the 'Teck' title became so Britishized that people today still believe that Teck is a place in Britain, in England. But it isn't; it's in Germany. But there you are; that's how it's done. Also, if you look at Prince Philip of Mountbatten [the Duke of Edinburgh] named after his mother, Alice of Battenburg, who was the daughter of Victoria of Hesse. Philip was not named after his father for obvious reasons - it is never good to have it known that your father was declared a traitor by the Greek parliament. You know, if they could have got their hands on him he would have been put against a wall and shot. So of course you change your name to that of your mother, especially if you are to marry the Queen of England! Then, of course, you Britishize it by changing it even further, from Battenburg to Mountbatten.

Perhaps the biggest imposture of all was when the Windsors, who were then Saxe-Coburg-Gothas, changed their name during World War One.

That's right, in 1917. They named themselves after a castle in England. It's ridiculous. Although I must say, they were offered the name of Stewart as well, which of course they rejected. They said: "Oh no, we couldn't possibly do that!" And of course they couldn't, because there is a copyright on that name - we own it!

Diana And Dodi

As you know, we have just finished our book - an investigation into the death of Diana, Princess of Wales. It's interesting because we have covered much of what we've been talking about today in terms of genealogies - the Stewarts and the Windsors etc.

Right.

So with regard to Diana, can we ask your opinion about her death? For example, do you think her death was suspicious?

Doesn't anyone? Don't you find it rather strange that she died so soon after she got together with Dodi Fayed? I mean, I believe that there are times when coincidences do take place. However, do you think honestly that the British aristocracy, never mind the present British Royal Family, would have been happy with the idea of the former wife of the Prince of Wales marrying a Muslim? Especially as she was still of the age to bear at least two children, who would have been able to call the future King of England their brother. Do you think honestly that they would have been happy to let that happen? Well, I'll tell you that the answer to that is a resounding *'no'*, I can assure you. No, no - *anything* to stop this from happening...

...Now, I do believe that the Windsors were not at all happy with this situation. And you can see why. When you see photographs of Diana with Charles Windsor, she is never happy. At best it's a slight smile. But it's never beaming, it's never warm, not even in the beginning, not really. However, with Dodi Fayed you can see that she was happy, that she was at ease, that *he* was at ease - you know, the body language said it all. The body language with Charles was always so remote, but with Dodi Fayed it was much more relaxed. So as they say, the picture tells the whole story...

...So, from my point of view she certainly was set on this relationship with Dodi Fayed, possibly even on marrying him. Now the only definite way to prevent such a marriage was by, shall we say, the rather drastic measure of removing lives.

You mean by murdering Diana and Dodi?

Well you have to look at the facts. I mean, look, Diana had an accident, yes, OK. However, when you look at the circumstances, and listen to what the eyewitnesses say - that this white car was also involved in the crash, it was seen going into the tunnel; Diana's car was being pursued by another car, and then suddenly the white car which was also involved disappeared, never to be found. I mean, please. And in any case, you don't drive that quickly in the middle of the night in Paris unless you have very good reason - unless you are running for your life. So there is something very strange about the whole incident. I mean, I am quite sure that even William has enough sense to realize, one day, that something is not quite right.

One thing that seems strange to us is the fact that both the Windsors and the Government have acted as though it was a clear-cut accident from the very beginning, even though the evidence suggests otherwise. What we're saying is, if it had been your daughter-in-law, your ex-wife, your mother, surely you would want to find out what really happened?

Yes, but it is easier to perpetuate the concept of an accident than it is to accept the concept of murder. You know, the British people would have a huge problem with that. The reaction of the nation, for example, coming out and mourning like they've never mourned for anybody else before - certainly not for any other member of the Royal Family - spoke volumes.

But such an attitude on the part of the Windsors and the Establishment surely suggests a cover-up. To so actively promulgate the concept of an accident rather than to try and find out what really happened - surely this standpoint suggests a cover-up. And a cover-up, of course, in turn suggests foul play.

Oh yes, no question. But you see, if you are going to murder someone as famous as Diana, then you need to make sure you cover your tracks. And this brings us back to the point we made earlier about the media. We have already spoken about how the media is able to make people think in a certain way, and about who really owns the media, who is really behind it. You know, these people are not stupid; they know exactly what they are doing and how to do it. They have used the media to perpetuate the concept of an accident, and so people have started to believe that it was an accident. But actually I think that many people, deep down, still believe that there is something very strange about the whole affair - that something is not quite right. For sure very few people speak in terms of an accident. Almost everyone I have spoken to - and I'm talking normal, everyday people - they say: "I'm sorry, I don't believe it was an accident; something is not right here; something simply does not feel right about this." You know, people I have spoken to - colleagues of mine, friends, the conversations I might have overheard in the streets, at the bus stops, in the restaurants, wherever - most people simply do not believe in the theory of 'accident'. And I must admit I agree - I don't accept the theory that it was an accident.

Diana The Grail Queen
Her Stewart Heritage
And The Counter-Monarchy Problem

We would like to ask you about the Stewart bloodline - to determine if any political motives in this regard might have been behind Diana's death.

Yes, all right.

Firstly, in our book we refer to Diana as a 'Grail Queen' - in other words, as a legitimate descendant of what you referred to earlier as the Desposyni, or the Grail Family. Could you confirm that we are correct in referring to Diana in this way? Only some of our readers might think we were somewhat 'off the wall' in claiming that Diana had descended from what is generally perceived as a myth!

Certainly I can say that the Grail Family is not a myth, even though it has been presented as a myth in Victorian history - which is what you are taught at school. And yes, you are quite right, Diana was a member [descendant] of this family, so the title 'Grail Queen' is not out of place. In fact I think I also referred to her as a 'Grail Queen' in my own book, which came out last year in Scotland and went to Number Two on Scotland's bestsellers' list. It reached Number Seven in the UK.

Yes, we bought a copy about a week ago ['The Forgotten Monarchy of Scotland' - see Bibliography]. We thought it was excellent. Presumably more people now know about you and your cause.*

A few more, yes. But there is still a lot of work to be done.

Well hopefully this interview will help bring even more attention to your endeavour.

Oh, that would be very good. I hope so, yes...

...To return to Diana's Stewart heritage. While researching our book, we were fortunate enough to talk to a former Foreign Office historian - in actual fact it was this person who informed us about you, and it's taken us this long to track you down.

Well yes, where I am is not so widely known.

Now this source told us an awful lot about the whole business of the Merovingian-Stewart bloodline. He specifically told us that MI6 - or some or other Foreign Office department therein - holds genealogical records which prove the Merovingian-Stewart claim, and that the reason the government keeps these records under wraps is to suppress knowledge of the Stewarts' legitimate claim to the Throne. He also made us aware of

Diana's Stewart heritage, and inferred that this might have been one of the factors in her death.

Well first let us talk about Diana's Stewart heritage. The idea in bringing Diana into the Windsor fold was first and foremost to reintroduce the Stewart strain into the Royal Family. It was a political marriage, I can assure you.

Right, but our Foreign Office source told us that Diana then became too popular, and that the combination of her popularity and her Stewart heritage became a threat.

Well yes, it would have done; it's a typical Stewart thing, you see! Ahh ... but we are a popular monarchy - look at Charles II, for example. Even James VII [James II of England] was popular in his own right. He was more austere and sober than Charles II, but he was still popular. I mean, Charles II knew how to enjoy himself, whereas James VII always felt slightly guilty at enjoying himself. But that's just the difference between one and the other. Ahh ... but yes, as a whole the Stewarts have always been popular with the people, and so yes, we still are considered a threat. Like Diana, we have our human frailties and we're not afraid to talk about them and show them. We are happy to identify with the people.

This, of course, was one reason why so many people related to Diana.

Well yes, quite right. There was a lot of Charles II in Diana, particularly in the sense that she talked to people - she would talk to anyone. Now, if you asked the Queen to do this, she wouldn't know where to start. I mean, this is not a criticism; it simply is not taught. You know, talking to unemployed people, or people with AIDS or whatever, Diana was very natural at this. And that is what the Windsors saw as her Stewart heritage. You see, the Stewarts have always tried to be like that. We have always been like that; we still are. We have always tried to be a popular - or populist - monarchy. We represent the people and so we need to know about people...

...I'll give you an example. A very good journalist friend of mine had just interviewed me over dinner; it was for *The Herald.* And we had a tremendous meal - we finished at about ten or ten-thirty at night, and he went his way and I went mine. And on my way home I happened to pass this homeless chap on the street - he was sleeping rough on the street, in a doorway. And I said to myself, *why is he unemployed and homeless; here am I, quite lucky in that I have what this chap obviously does not have.* And so I thought I'd better go and find out about him...

...So I went over to him, and I said: "I hope you don't mind, but I'd like to ask you a question." He said: "Anything mate, anything." So I asked what had happened to him and why he was in that position. And he said: "Well, circumstances. I was married, I got divorced, and I really sunk to the depths because of it." He also told me that he was a trained chef, but that he couldn't find work because he was homeless. If you have no fixed address employers won't employ you - it's a *Catch 22* situation...

...Now all I'm saying is that I can in some way relate to this chap's problems, his predicament. I would be no use as King if I can't relate to the problems people have. And you know, quite often people are unemployed or homeless through no fault of their own. Certainly if you become homeless you have no right to work because you don't have a fixed address, and you also have no right to vote. So suddenly you see how important it is to have a Written Constitution, to protect the civil rights and liberties of people who are, for example, homeless. I mean, you don't even have the right to beg; you will be arrested because it's against the concept of a 'clean' and 'civilized' Britain. And so we must remain aware of people who are in need of help. We must, in a sense, forget about the circumstances which led to their present situation and remember to give, to help. And I think this is what Diana was very much aware of - the homeless, the unemployed, the sick, the needs of various charity organizations etc. But people saw that her sympathy was genuine ... I'm not surprised that the Windsors saw her as a threat. They have always seen the Stewarts as a threat. They still do.

In this same regard, our Foreign Office source told us that he had once worked in a department which dealt with what he referred to as "the counter-monarchy problem". I now realize, of course, that he was probably referring to the Stewarts.

Oh yes, because we've been here all the time; we have never really gone away. You know, it wasn't just in 1715 or 1745, or 1759, or 1798 in Ireland, or 1820, or 1887 - we crop up every so often. But I'm the first one since 1887 to again raise the issue of the Stewart claim.

Yes, presumably that's why our Foreign Office source pointed us in your direction - we think he was trying to insinuate a hidden connection between your claim and that of Diana, perhaps even that Diana herself had become involved in a 'succession fight'. He certainly inferred that Diana's Stewart genes, coupled with her growing popularity, would have constituted a tremendous threat to the Windsors.

Certainly, it is all to do with the question of the blood, you see. Now, with regard to this question of the blood, there are two factors to be considered. Firstly, Diana was a Stewart by descent, and the Windsors, on the one hand, felt threatened by this, and on the other, wanted very much to reintroduce the Stewart strain into their family. Well, let's face it, if we are to believe the workings of genetics and DNA, then Queen Victoria was illegitimate. It has all been covered up, of course ... but there is even a book that has been written by two [genetic] scientists, a husband and wife team [*Victoria's Genes*, PM Potts and WTW Potts] showing that Queen Victoria was illegitimate. In the book is also the fact that Queen Victoria introduced the gene of haemophilia; the genetic disorder of porphyria came from George III, but Queen Victoria introduced the gene of haemophilia into the Royal Family...

...So anyway, Queen Victoria may have been the daughter of Victoria of Saxe-Coburg, the Duchess of Kent, but definitely not the daughter of Edward Hanover, Duke of Kent, who died before she was born. There are even papers which were written by the Prime Ministers of the time, referring to Edward, Duke of Kent, who was supposedly the father of Queen Victoria. In these letters it states, 'Thank God that the Duchess had some help from somewhere else', you know, in producing this posthumous daughter who later became Queen Victoria. In fact there is a belief that Edward, Duke of Kent was actually barren - I mean, he could not produce children. It is widely known that he had several mistresses, for example, and that none of them produced children by him. So of course, even the Stewart strain which came from James VI [James I of England] down to Edward, Duke of Kent, totally disappeared at this time, because Victoria was not his daughter ... the strain that came through Charles I and his daughter, Henrietta Anne and the Orleans family, or through Princess Elizabeth who married Frederick V of Bohemia, also disappeared at this time. That was the line that George I came from. But the Stewart strain totally disappeared from the Royal Family at this time, because none of the other [Stewarts] ever married into the Hanoverian family. Nobody wanted to. So the Stewart strain which came from James VI and Charles I became more diluted, to the point of non-existence, which meant in a political sense that the Windsors no longer had Stewart blood in them. None at all...

...So the problem they [the Windsors] had, was that the Stewart strain which made George I a legitimate claimant to the Throne in the first place had now disappeared. Another problem was that Queen Victoria, this illegitimate girl, became Queen of Great Britain. And she was married to her cousin, who had no Stewart blood either. So from that time on they were on the look out for it, and it was only achieved when the Queen Mother married George VI. But with Sarah Ferguson and Diana Spencer they found two girls who were both descendants of Charles II. Diana, of course, was extremely well situated, genealogically speaking, which means that William and Harry are also well situated - they carry the Stewart DNA as well. So Charles Windsor's marriage to Diana Spencer was something the Windsors had been on the look out for - I mean, you know, in terms of whatever it is that you gain through a political marriage...

...So anyway, in Diana, certainly they succeeded in reintroducing the

Stewart strain, but of course when she became so popular she became a threat precisely because of this.

So you can confirm that our Foreign Office source knew what he was talking about in this regard?

I would say so, yes. Certainly there is a department within Her Majesty's, shall we say, Civil Service, or Secret Service, dedicated to - what did you call it...?

Our Foreign Office source called it "the counter-monarchy problem".

...Yes, certainly there is a department that deals with this. Of course there is. But rather than get myself into too much trouble(!), I will instead tell you to watch a film called *A Very British Coup*. Watch this film. *A Very British Coup* will tell you precisely how the state can organize a silent, very clever, very subtle conspiracy. And of course it works. It is only a film, but it will illustrate my point: which is that within the Civil Service, or the Secret Service, there is a little man, not unlike your Foreign Office man, who is assigned to monitor the situation - in this instance the 'counter-monarchy problem'.

And in order to resolve this 'problem', do you think the British Establishment would resort to murder?

Well I sincerely hope they don't resort to murder in my particular case! Ahh ... but yes, of course they would, undoubtedly. I have already said that I don't believe Diana's death was an accident. But whether or not she died because of her Stewart heritage, or because of her relationship with a Muslim, well we can't be certain of course. Perhaps it was a combination of these two things...

...But [the Windsors] were certainly very aware of her Stewart blood. It is why she was chosen as a wife for Charles Windsor in the first place.

Prince Michael, thank you very much for taking the time to talk to us.

No, no - my pleasure.

[Note: we would highly recommend that you read Prince Michael of Albany's own book, *The Forgotten Monarchy of Scotland* - Element Books Ltd, 1998, ISBN: 1-86204-234-9 - in which the true history of the Stewarts, together with the story of Prince Michael's struggle for recognition, can be found. We would also like to extend our sincere thanks to Prince Michael for granting us permission to include this interview in our book.]

ADDENDUM (ii)

THE FRENCH REPORT

Official Verdict

Shortly after we had prepared Prince Michael of Albany's interview for publication, the French magistrates finally published the results of their own, *official* investigation into Diana's death. Though these results were far from substantive, much less conclusive, nevertheless we felt it pertinent to include them here - if for no other reason than to offer you the opportunity to compare the official verdict with your own.

In short, then, Judges Herve Stephan and Marie-Christine Devidal decided that all charges against the paparazzi (nine photographers in all), plus one photo-agency motorbike driver, should be dropped. The report concluded that the death of Diana, Princess of Wales, was entirely the result of a 'drink-drive' accident. And thus that Henri Paul was entirely to blame.

However, the many questions and anomalies highlighted in the earlier chapters of this book still remain. Some, it would seem, were not even addressed by the French investigators. And of those that were, none has been satisfactorily resolved. The mystery surrounding the White Fiat Uno and the high-powered motorbike, for example - described in detail by at least seven eyewitnesses - will not be investigated further. Both vehicles plus their occupants have disappeared without trace, the French team concluded, and that's the end of it.

No surprises there, then.

More questions were asked of the French investigation team with regard to the appalling and thoroughly inadequate medical treatment administered to Diana immediately following the crash. Why the emergency services took such an absurdly long time to treat Diana at the scene of the crash; why they took her to Pitie Salpetriere hospital - the furthest from the scene; why she was taken there by an ambulance travelling on average less than 7 miles an hour; why she was not taken to hospital by helicopter; and moreover, why she was not taken to Val de Grace hospital, which is fully equipped for VIP deliveries and less than two miles from the scene of the crash. These points, it would seem, have scarcely been investigated, much less resolved. Indeed, they all remain a rather expedient mystery.

We recall the testimony of US investigative journalist, Jeff Steinberg, for example - someone who, together with his team of internationally placed investigators, has been investigating Diana's death since September 1997. Jeff told us: "...Val de Grace [hospital] is hooked up to the national military radio communication system, which means as soon as the first fire truck arrived at the tunnel, which is part of the emergency response, there was a kind of all-users message that went out by radio, alerting all the hospitals in the area to be ready for a VIP delivery. The fact is that standard procedure is that any VIP in any kind of traffic accident or emergency medical situation in Paris goes to Val de Grace. They have a medivac helicopter that could have been brought in and landed right outside the tunnel. The estimate ... is that she could have been in surgery within 25-35 minutes after the first emergency response vehicles arrived ... If she had been in surgery within an hour even ... she would have stood an almost 100 per cent chance of surviving."

There is no response to any of these points in the official report.

To add to this, the extremely suspicious circumstances surrounding Henri Paul's forensic blood test, together with the mystery of the unusually high-level carbon monoxide trace found in Henri Paul's blood, seem to have been brushed over by the French investigators purely to make the verdict stick. We have learned from the official report, for example, that two blood samples were taken from Henri Paul's body - the first immediately following the crash. This sample was taken from the chest cavity, and because it was, the likelihood is that it would have been contaminated with bits of gore and tissue from other parts of the body. Indeed, during the making of *Diana: The Paris Crash - A Special Inquiry* (a documentary investigating the results of the French report, screened on British television on Friday 3rd September 1999) eminent forensic pathologist and assistant coroner Dr Robert Forrest confirmed to senior British barrister and former Chairman of the Bar Council, Anthony Scrivener QC, that Henri Paul's aorta had been ruptured as a result of the crash impact. In consequence, blood had spilled into Henri Paul's chest, and the French forensic team had assumed that this blood was "heart blood". But it was *not* heart blood. Rather it was an *ad hoc* cocktail of aortic blood, lung blood, lung tissue, plus of course various other bits of blood and gore which had found their way into Henri Paul's chest as a result of the violent impact. And in any case, as Dr Forrest explained, blood for a forensic test following death should, when at all possible, be taken from the femoral vein, not the heart or the chest. This first test thus proved inconclusive - a fact reluctantly acknowledged by the French investigators following complaints from Henri Paul's family that the tests had not been properly conducted.

In an attempt to resolve this problem, the French forensic team extracted a second sample from Henri Paul's body. This sample was indeed taken from the femoral vein - in accordance with proper procedure - but was not taken until four days after Henri Paul's death. The 23% carbon monoxide trace contained in the original blood sample had by this time decreased to 13%. Even so, this level of carbon monoxide is still regarded by the experts as excessively high. According to Dr Robert Forrest, for example, a person who smokes twenty cigarettes a day would expect to have somewhere between 5% and 8% carbon monoxide in their blood. 10% is very high, he said. Given that Henri Paul was not a heavy smoker, the question of the carbon monoxide poisoning remains a mystery.

But what constitutes an even bigger mystery is the seemingly slipshod and unprofessional manner in which the French investigators dealt with this problem. Firstly, until a British television documentary, *Diana: Secrets Of The Crash,* highlighted this mystery in August 1998 (a full year after the crash), the French investigation team had not even addressed it. Much less investigated it. Following the screening of this documentary, of course (watched by some 20 million viewers) they were forced to try and come up with an answer.

Duly they instructed their own forensic man, one Dr Pepin, to re-examine the results of Henri Paul's blood test. In particular Dr Pepin's task was to determine the true level of carbon monoxide in Henri Paul's blood at the time of death - to set the record straight, so to speak. However, his methods in achieving this end were, to say the least, highly irregular. If not bizarre in the extreme.

Staggeringly, Dr Pepin took the results of the two tests and calculated the mean average of carbon monoxide found in both of them. In other words, he took the 23% reading from the original blood sample, and then the 13% reading from the subsequent blood sample, and came up with a mean average figure which then became the official amount of carbon monoxide found in Henri Paul's blood at the time of death! *Bizarre.* The second blood sample, remember, was not taken from Henri Paul's body until four days after his death. Moreover, there is no record of how Henri Paul's body was stored for these four crucial days. *Help!* In any event, and as forensic pathologist Dr Robert Forrest agreed, after four days the amount of carbon monoxide in Henri Paul's blood would of course have dissipated. In consequence, the carbon monoxide reading would have decreased. Which, of course, it had. Thus Dr Forrest agreed that Dr Pepin's method in determining the level of carbon monoxide in Henri Paul's blood at the time of his death was wholly unsatisfactory - a word we would readily employ to describe the entire French investigation and its so-called forensic evidence, it has to be said.

Despite this travesty, however, the results of these tests still confirmed that an inexplicable and unusually high level of carbon monoxide was swimming around in Henri Paul's blood on the night he died. Indeed, Dr Robert Forrest testified that, in his many years as a forensic pathologist and assistant coroner, he had never before come across such high levels of carbon monoxide as those found in Henri Paul's blood. So the question still remained: where did it come from, this massive carbon monoxide trace? And moreover, how did it get there?

Well the French forensic team revealed clearly enough how they believed such a vast amount of carbon monoxide had found its way into Henri Paul's blood. It was the combined result of *'heavy smoking'* and *'carbon monoxide which had leaked from a tear in the Mercedes's air bag'*, the French report concluded. However, though ostensibly plausible, both of these explanations are in fact groundless. According to Dr Robert Forrest, for example - among other, equally eminent experts - smoking does not cause excessively high levels of carbon monoxide in the blood. As we have already seen, even the heaviest of smokers (and despite claims to the contrary, Henri Paul was *not* a heavy smoker - according to friends he smoked only a few cigars a day) would expect to find no more than about 10% carbon monoxide trace in their blood. An average smoker, Dr Forrest confirmed - say, a person who smokes twenty cigarettes a day - would expect to find between 5% and 8% carbon monoxide trace. These figures simply do not compare with the near-lethal 23% trace found in Henri Paul's original blood sample. Nor indeed with carbon monoxide expert Dr Alastair Hay's findings that, an hour or two prior to the crash, Henri Paul's blood would have contained something in the order of 30% carbon monoxide trace - a conclusion based on the fact that carbon monoxide contamination decreases by roughly half every four to five hours. This means that, if the carbon monoxide level in Henri Paul's blood was around 23% soon after the crash, then two hours prior to the crash it would have been somewhere in the region of 30%, or even 35%. According to the experts, these kinds of levels cause severe difficulties - pounding headaches, nausea, dizziness, loss of consciousness - and in some cases can be lethal. And yet the Ritz security footage shows Henri Paul calm, congenial and coherent throughout the two hours prior to the crash. Curious, to say the least. Indeed, even the French investigation team concluded that Henri Paul could not have had such high-level carbon monoxide poisoning while at the Ritz. Which, of course, means that he must have been poisoned at some point during the four minutes it took to drive from the Ritz to the 'crash tunnel'. As neither Diana nor Dodi Fayed - nor indeed Trevor Rees-Jones - were found to have been contaminated with carbon monoxide, we can safely assume that there were no carbon monoxide fumes inside the car (say, fumes which might have leaked from a faulty exhaust). Indeed, the French report concurs with this conclusion.

So how *did* such a vast amount of carbon monoxide (and alcohol) find its way into Henri Paul's bloodstream in such a short amount of time? There are, of course, only three possibilities, as detailed below. We should point out that it is the third of these possibilities - the 'air bag theory' - which is favoured in the French report.

The three possibilities, then.

One: the 'injection theory'.

As we proposed in *Chapter One*, operatives at the scene of the crash (perhaps the Fiat Uno driver) injected Henri Paul with a cocktail-concentrate of alcohol and drugs. Or at least with sufficient alcohol concentrate that his blood tests would later confirm that he was 'drunk at the wheel'. Though this explanation might sound farfetched, it cannot be ruled out. After all, if Diana's death *was* the result of an intelligence operation (an operation designed from the outset to lay the blame squarely at Henri Paul's feet) then surely every detail would have been thoroughly thought through beforehand. Injecting Henri Paul with sufficient alcohol concentrate to ensure that he was 'drunk at the wheel' - and thus that he was entirely to blame for the 'accident' - would, after all, have been the simplest part of the operation. The 'injection theory' thus becomes entirely plausible. On the other hand, of course, it still does not explain how such high levels of carbon monoxide also found their way into Henri Paul's blood.

Two: the 'wrong sample theory'.

This theory maintains that the blood sample on which the forensic tests were carried out did not belong to Henri Paul. As Jeff Steinberg suggested in *Chapter Two*: "Maybe it was an accurate test, but on somebody else's blood? There were half a dozen people brought into the morgue that night. It was the last weekend of the summer ... maybe some drunk fell asleep on one of the subway gratings and died of carbon monoxide poisoning, and that's the blood test that was taken." On first hearing, of course, this explanation might seem, if not quite so farfetched as the 'injection theory', nevertheless fairly unbelievable. When one considers the series of associated blunders, however - blunders which occurred at the hospital and in the pathology lab, and which in themselves reveal the negligence and incompetence of the French medical and forensic teams - the 'wrong sample theory' becomes (sadly) all the more admissible.

We have already noted, for example, that there is no proper record of how Henri Paul's body was stored - and this despite the fact that Paul's blood test would of course have proved crucial in determining the cause of the crash. *Incredible*. We have also noted that the original blood sample was taken from the wrong part of the body, the chest cavity, and so was likely to have been contaminated with blood from other parts of the body. *Incredible*. But what is even more incredible is this: despite the high-profile nature of this case, the French report has revealed that Henri Paul's original blood sample was 'not properly labelled or documented'. In other words, no one could even be certain that the blood sample in question had been taken from Henri Paul's body, much less that it had been taken from his chest cavity, as originally claimed. This is quite simply scandalous (indeed, little wonder Henri Paul's family has continued to deeply distrust the findings of these forensic tests). Of course, despite these howling indiscretions, we must nonetheless assume that the subsequent blood sample was indeed 'properly labelled and documented' (although this too would seem in some doubt). We must also assume that, on this occasion, it was taken from Henri Paul's body - rather than, say, from the "drunk [who] fell asleep on one of the subway gratings and died of carbon monoxide poisoning", as suggested by Jeff Steinberg. Though seemingly improbable, this possibility is certainly not out of the question either - as we shall see.

But even assuming that this subsequent blood sample *was* taken from Henri Paul's body - his femoral vein - we must remember that it was not taken until four days after his death. We must also remember that there is no proper record of how Henri Paul's body had been stored during this time. The list of irregularities is endless. Indeed, one recalls to mind a similar list of irregularities regarding President Kennedy's autopsy in 1963 - which, of course, conspired to substantiate the so-called 'lone gunman theory'. In other words - as more recent investigations have shown - they were all part of the cover-up which deflected attention away from the real assassins and at the same time focused attention on Lee Harvey Oswald, the 'patsy', the 'stooge': the so-called 'lone gunman'. One wonders, then, if that might be the case here, too - that the highly dubious irregularities regarding Henri Paul's autopsy also conspire to substantiate the 'lone gunman theory'. Or in our case, of course, the 'lone driver theory': the 'drink-drive theory'. Indeed, one cannot help but wonder if the autopsy itself - its dubious results, the dubious manner in which those results were obtained - was designed from the outset to deflect attention away from the real assassins and at the same time focus attention on the 'patsy', the 'stooge', the 'lone driver': Henri Paul. Whether this be the case or not - whether these irregularities are purely the result of negligence, incompetence, or indeed, something altogether more sinister - remains open to debate. But what is not open to debate is that these irregularities exist, and in significant number. Which in turn means that no substantive conclusion can be drawn.

Indeed, the only conclusion to be drawn from this highly irregular forensic investigation is that Henri Paul's blood test engendered more questions than answers. And that none of these questions has been satisfactorily resolved.

So ... might the forensic tests which found that Henri Paul was 'drunk at the wheel' have been carried out on someone else's blood? In other words, might Henri Paul's 'unlabelled' blood sample have become confused with another, similarly 'unlabelled' blood sample? And further, as Jeff Steinberg suggested, might it have been this other 'anonymous' blood sample which contained the high levels of alcohol and carbon monoxide later attributed to Henri Paul? Given that Henri Paul's blood sample was 'not properly labelled or documented'; and further, that the excessively high-level carbon monoxide trace, together with Henri Paul's perfectly sober appearance minutes before the crash, is still to be explained, the answer to these questions would appear to be 'yes'.

Which leaves us with one further, rather more controversial question to consider. And it is this.

Assuming that the blood tests *were* carried out on the 'wrong sample', was that action purely the result of negligence? Incompetence? Or was it the result of something altogether more sinister, something planned and contrived from the outset? Was it, for example, the result of a deliberate 'switch' - a premeditated action on the part of those responsible for Diana's 'accident'? After all, as we have already considered, if Diana's death *was* the result of an intelligence operation (designed from the outset to lay the blame squarely at Henri Paul's feet) then presumably that operation would have included provision for substantiating Henri Paul's inebriated condition. In other words, *someone* would have had to ensure that the tests proved alcohol-positive. Given that Henri Paul's alleged inebriated condition is still to be explained, a 'switch', therefore, cannot be ruled out. Certainly it would not have been beyond the capability of a highly trained covert-operations unit hired from, say, one of the various 'international security firms' which form the backbone of the British Royal Establishment's own private security forces, and which are known to service agencies such as MI6 and the CIA. The fact that the assassins might have made this switch with blood from a "drunk [who] ... died of carbon monoxide poisoning", of course, is entirely plausible.

In any event, whether genuine mistake or premeditated action, either way, the forensic evidence which found that Henri Paul was 'drunk at the wheel' becomes inadmissible in light of these irregularities. Indeed, it is fundamentally flawed, if not entirely null and void. If the inexplicably high-level carbon monoxide trace still cannot be accounted for after more than two years then it is highly likely that the contaminated blood did not belong to Henri Paul in the first place. Certainly the fact that Paul's blood sample was 'not properly labelled or documented' throws up serious doubts in this regard.

And so long as even the least doubt exists regarding the origin of the blood tested by the French forensic team, of course - any doubt at all - then the forensic evidence which convicted Henri Paul must be discounted altogether (as it would be in a court of law). There is simply no other conclusion to be drawn.

Three: the 'air bag theory'.

On close scrutiny, then, the 'wrong sample theory' becomes far more plausible, far more likely in light of the above facts. Certainly in our opinion it is a scenario which should not be ruled out. Because the fact remains that if neither of these two theories is correct - the 'injection theory' or the 'wrong sample theory' - then the high-level carbon monoxide trace found in Henri Paul's blood on the night he died simply cannot be accounted for.

Or can it? There is still possibility number *Three* to consider, of course: the 'air bag theory' proposed in the French report. As we shall see, however, this theory is even less plausible - even more contrived - than either of the two already presented. In fact it is quite simply impossible to substantiate.

According to the report, Henri Paul's blood became contaminated with carbon monoxide not only as a result of smoking. The Mercedes's safety air bag is also cited as a major contributor. Indeed, *the* major contributor. When the bag activated on impact, the report said, it must have ripped and released carbon monoxide, which Henri Paul must then have breathed into his lungs. This is the official explanation of how such high levels of carbon monoxide found their way into Henri Paul's blood. However, there are one or two rather painfully obvious problems with this theory - problems the French team seem to have, quite astonishingly, overlooked.

Problem number one, of course, is that all reports confirm that Henri Paul was 'very dead, very quickly' following the crash. In fact, medical reports confirm that he died 'instantly'. We can safely assume, then, that he did not have sufficient time to inhale vast amounts of carbon monoxide while he sat in his driver's seat waiting to die. The only way carbon monoxide or any other gas could have found its way into Henri Paul's bloodstream is of course by inhalation. And he would indeed have had to inhale vast amounts in order to have been contaminated by anything like a 23% trace. The moment he ceased to live, of course, he ceased to breathe. And the moment that happened - which, according to the medical report, was 'instantly' - there was no possible way that Henri Paul's blood could have become contaminated. For the record, this opinion is shared by no less eminent figures than Anthony Scrivener QC and world-renowned crash expert, Professor Murray MacKay, who dismissed the 'air bag theory' as "complete rubbish". Indeed, both of these highly regarded and equally eminent observers concluded that Henri Paul could not possibly have been contaminated with carbon monoxide in this way - an opinion endorsed, of course, by the fundamental laws of physics.

However, for those who remain less convinced than either Anthony Scrivener QC or Professor Murray MacKay (or indeed, Sir Isaac Newton and the rest of us thinking apes), there is an even bigger problem to be considered, as follows.

Problem number two - and by far the most glaring oversight on the part of the French investigators - is that Mercedes Benz (Daimler Benz) have always made it very clear that they *do not* use any carbon monoxide whatever in any of the air bags fitted to their cars. Which of course means that, even if the air bag *did* tear on impact, the gasses released could not possibly have included carbon monoxide - a simple though somewhat crucial and well-known fact. Had the French team bothered to ask Mercedes Benz about the design of their air bags, of course, then we can safely assume that they would have been informed of this rather crucial detail. And had they been informed of this rather crucial detail, then - presumably - the official report would not have maintained, *unbelievably*, that the carbon monoxide trace found in Henri Paul's blood was the result of the air bag splitting on impact! Remember, the French team has had two years to come up with this specious twaddle - two years and unlimited resources. Scary.

In any event, that the French investigators failed to ascertain the full facts before boldly announcing their verdict is quite simply beyond words. That they seem not even to have explored the 'injection theory', or in particular the 'wrong sample theory', equally so. Indeed, were we dealing with a more trivial, less serious case, this *Inspector Clouseau*-style investigation might be deemed laughable. In the event it must surely be deemed, at the very least, outrageously incompetent, its findings indefensible, its published report ill-founded and invalid. Meaningless.

This, at any rate, is our recommendation to you, the jury, based on the report's deficient, inept and wholly inadmissible content.

Manslaughter Or Murder?
A Provocative Conclusion

There is one other point worth mentioning.

A rather intriguing conclusion emerged from the documentary screened on prime-time British television on Friday 3rd September, 1999 (*Diana: The Paris Crash - A Special Inquiry*). Like its forerunner (*Diana: Secrets Of The Crash*, screened in August 1998) this documentary was presented by ITN's royal correspondent, Nicholas Owen. However, the investigation itself was handled by one of Britain's leading barristers and former Chairman of the Bar Council, Anthony Scrivener QC, himself a forensic expert in criminal crash investigations. Though predictably dismissive of a conspiracy with regard to Diana's death - predictable given his status and position - Mr Scrivener nevertheless concluded the programme with a very provocative statement.

In *Chapter Two* we presented evidence of an assassination technique currently employed by the intelligence services of both East and West - a technique referred to by former SAS officer Sir Ranulph Fiennes as the "Boston brakes method". We suggested - based on the testimonies of several eyewitnesses and security sources - that the high-powered motorbike and the White Fiat Uno might have been involved in an operation of this nature. In other words, that these two vehicles, plus their drivers and passenger(s), may well have been hired by the intelligence services to assassinate Princess Diana. And in particular that the high-powered motorbike, its driver and pillion rider, would thus have played a major role in the operation. To add weight to our own conclusions in this regard, this same theory was also proposed by no less an Establishment figure than ITN's royal correspondent, Nicholas Owen. It was also confirmed by our own security source (*Chapter Two*), and further corroborated by former MI6 Officer Richard Tomlinson as well as by other security sources we have interviewed.

In light of the above, then, what we found particularly intriguing were the words of Anthony Scrivener QC - who, in his summing up, concluded this investigative documentary with the following statement:

"We have to ask ourselves whether enough was done to identify that motorcyclist. Because in my judgment - in French law, or British law for that matter - there's enough evidence to charge him with manslaughter."

This was the conclusion of prominent British barrister, former Chairman of the Bar Council and forensic expert in major criminal crash investigations, Anthony Scrivener QC. And other than the fact that we would recommend the charge of manslaughter be commuted to first degree murder - and brought not only against the elusive motorcyclist, but against everyone involved, from the highest echelons of corporate power and the British Royal Establishment to the thugs on the streets of Paris who carried out the assassination - we have to say we agree with him.

ADDENDUM (iii)

AFFIDAVIT

The Sworn Affidavit
Of Former MI6 Officer, Richard Tomlinson

A t various points throughout this book we referred to claims allegedly made by former MI6 officer, Richard Tomlinson, and in particular the claim that the operation which caused Diana's death mirrored an existing MI6 plot to assassinate Serbian leader, Slobodan Milosevic. In order to substantiate this claim, and to offer further information provided by Mr Tomlinson, we elected to present you, the jury, with this sworn affidavit penned by Mr Tomlinson himself (reproduced here, in its entirety, by kind permission of *Nexus* magazine). It should be remembered that, at the time of writing, Mr Tomlinson is still 'on the run', so to speak - he has been exiled from his native Britain; hounded from country to country; refused entry to several countries, including the United States of America (where he was due to be interviewed by NBC); arrested and beaten by the French Secret Service, DST (in order to deter him from giving evidence to Judge Herve Stephan, the French magistrate in charge of the official inquiry into Diana's death); and prevented from speaking publicly about his knowledge of MI6's involvement in the operation which killed Princess Diana, Dodi Fayed and Henri Paul.

In short, Mr Tomlinson has been illegally and violently gagged by the British, US and French intelligence services, and as a result of his courageous efforts to speak out regardless of this predicament, he now lives not only in enforced exile, but in constant fear of reprisals. Possibly even in fear for his life. In support of Mr Tomlinson's struggle to be heard, then, and vindicated, we have elected to include his sworn affidavit here, so that you, the jury, may at least decide for yourselves with regard to the veracity or otherwise of his personal testimony. Once again we would ask that you read Mr Tomlinson's testimony in light of the evidence already presented in the course of this book.

Below is a sworn and testified statement that I have made on 12 May 1999 to the enquiry into the deaths of the Princess of Wales, Dodi Al Fayed and Henri Paul.

I firmly believe that MI6 have information in their files that would assist Judge Stephan's enquiry. Why don't they yield up this information? They should not be entitled to use the Official Secrets Act to protect themselves from investigation into the deaths of three people, particularly in the case of an incident of this magnitude and historical importance.

I, Richard John Charles Tomlinson, former MI6 officer, of Geneva, Switzerland, hereby declare:

1.

I firmly believe that there exist documents held by the British Secret Intelligence Service (MI6) that would yield important new evidence into the cause and circumstances leading to the deaths of the Princess of Wales, Mr Dodi Al Fayed, and M. Henri Paul in Paris in August 1997.

2.

I was employed by MI6 between September 1991 and April 1995. During that time, I saw various documents that I believe would provide new evidence and new leads into the investigation into these deaths. I also heard various rumours which - though I was not able to see supporting documents - I am confident were based on solid fact.

3.

In 1992, I was working in the Eastern European Controllerate of MI6 and I was peripherally involved in a large and complicated operation to smuggle advanced Soviet weaponry out of the then disintegrating and disorganised remnants of the Soviet Union. During 1992, I spent several days reading the substantial files on this operation. These files contain a wide miscellany of contact notes, telegrams, intelligence reports, photographs, etc., from which it was possible to build up a detailed understanding of the operation. The operation involved a large cast of officers and agents of MI6.

On more than one occasion, meetings between various figures in the operation took place at the Ritz Hotel, Place de Vendome, Paris. There were in the file several intelligence reports on these meetings, which had been written by one of the MI6 officers based in Paris at the

time (identified in the file only by a coded designation).
The source of the information was an informant in the
Ritz Hotel, who again was identified in the files only by
a code number. The MI6 officer paid the informant in cash
for his information.

I became curious to learn more about the identity of
this particular informant, because his number cropped up
several times and he seemed to have extremely good access
to the goings on in the Ritz Hotel. I therefore ordered
this informant's personal file from MI6's central file
registry. When I read this new file, I was not at all
surprised to learn that the informant was a security
officer of the Ritz Hotel. Intelligence services always
target the security officers of important hotels because
they have such good access to intelligence. I remember,
however, being mildly surprised that the nationality of
this informant was French, and this stuck in my memory
because it is rare that MI6 succeeds in recruiting a
French informer.

I cannot claim that I remember from this reading of
the file that the name of this person was Henri Paul, but
I have no doubt with the benefit of hindsight that this
was he. Although I did not subsequently come across Henri
Paul again during my time in MI6, I am confident that the
relationship between him and MI6 would have continued
until his death, because MI6 would never willingly
relinquish control over such a well-placed informant.

I am sure that the personal file of Henri Paul will
therefore contain notes of meetings between him and his
MI6 controlling officer, right up until the point of his
death. I firmly believe that these files will contain
evidence of crucial importance to the circumstances and
causes of the incident that killed M. Paul together with
the Princess of Wales and Dodi Al Fayed.

4.

The most senior undeclared officer in the local MI6
station would normally control an informant of M. Paul's
usefulness and seniority. Officers declared to the local
counterintelligence service (in this case, the Directorate
de Surveillance Territoire, or DST) would not be used to
control such an informant, because it might lead to the
identity of the informant becoming known to the local
intelligence services.

In Paris at the time of M. Paul's death, there were

two relatively experienced but undeclared MI6 officers. The first was Mr Nicholas John Andrew LANGMAN, born 1960. The second was Mr Richard David SPEARMAN, again born in 1960. I firmly believe that either one or both of these officers will be well acquainted with M. Paul, and most probably also met M. Paul shortly before his death. I believe that either or both of these officers will have knowledge that will be of crucial importance in establishing the sequence of events leading up to the deaths of M. Paul, Dodi Al Fayed and the Princess of Wales.

Mr Spearman in particular was an extremely well connected and influential officer because he had been, prior to his appointment in Paris, the personal secretary to the Chief of MI6, Mr David SPEDDING. As such, he would have been privy to even the most confidential of MI6 operations. I believe that there may well be significance in the fact that Mr Spearman was posted to Paris in the month immediately before the deaths.

5.

Later in 1992, as the civil war in the former Yugoslavia became increasingly topical, I started to work primarily on operations in Serbia. During this time, I became acquainted with Dr Nicholas Bernard Frank FISHWICK, born 1958, the MI6 officer who at the time was in charge of planning Balkan operations.

During one meeting with Dr Fishwick, he casually showed to me a three-page document that on closer inspection turned out to be an outline plan to assassinate the Serbian leader, President Slobodan Milosevic. The plan was fully typed and attached to a yellow "minute board", signifying that this was a formal and accountable document. It will therefore still be in existence. Fishwick had annotated that the document be circulated to the following senior MI6 officers: Maurice KENDWRICK-PIERCEY, then head of Balkan operations; John RIDDE, then the security officer for Balkan operations; the SAS liaison officer to MI6 (desination MOD/SO, but I have forgotten his name); the head of the Eastern European Controllerate (then Richard FLETCHER); and finally Alan PETTY, the personal secretary to the then Chief of MI6, Colin McCOLL.

The plan contained a political justification for the assassination of Milosevic, followed by three outline proposals on how to achieve this objective. I firmly believe that the third of these scenarios contained information that could be useful in establishing the causes of death of Henri Paul, the Princess of Wales and Dodi Al Fayed.

This third scenario suggested that Milosevic could be assassinated by causing his personal limousine to crash. Dr Fishwick proposed to arrange the crash in a tunnel, because the proximity of concrete close to the road would ensure that the crash would be sufficiently violent to cause death or serious injury, and would also reduce the possibility that there might be independent, casual witnesses. Dr Fishwick suggested that one way to cause the crash might be to disorientate the chauffeur using a strobe flash gun, a device which is occasionally deployed by special forces to, for example, disorientate helicopter pilots or terrorists, and about which MI6 officers are briefed during their training.

In short, this scenario bore remarkable similarities to the circumstances and witness accounts of the crash that killed the Princess of Wales, Dodi Al Fayed and Henri Paul. I firmly believe that this document should be yielded up by MI6 to the Judge investigating these deaths, and would provide further leads that he could follow.

6.

During my service in MI6, I also learnt unofficially and second-hand something of the links between MI6 and the Royal Household. MI6 are frequently and routinely asked by the Royal Household (usually via the Foreign Office) to provide intelligence on potential threats to members of the Royal Family whilst on overseas trips. This service would frequently extend to asking friendly intelligence services (such as the CIA) to place members of the Royal Family under discrete [sic] surveillance, ostensibly for their own protection. This was particularly the case for the Princess of Wales, who often insisted on doing without overt personal protection, even on overseas trips.

Although contact between MI6 and the Royal Household was officially only via the Foreign Office, I learnt while in MI6 that there was unofficial direct contact between certain senior and influential MI6 officers and senior members of the Royal Household. I did not see any official papers on this subject, but I am confident that the information is correct. I firmly believe that MI6 documents would yield substantial leads on the nature of their links with the Royal Household, and would yield vital information about MI6 surveillance on the Princess of Wales in the days leading to her death.

7.

I also learnt while in MI6 that one of the "paparazzi" photographers who routinely followed the Princess of Wales was a member of "UKN", a small corps of part-time MI6 agents who provide miscellaneous services to MI6, such as surveillance and photography expertise. I do not know the identity of this photographer, or whether he was one of the photographers present at the time of the fatal incident. However, I am confident that examination of UKN records would yield the identity of this photographer, and would enable the inquest to eliminate or further investigate that potential line of enquiry.

[Authors' note: Shortly after the release of Mr Tomlinson's affidavit, one of the first photographers to arrive at the scene of the crash, James Andanson, was found dead in a burnt-out car in the south of France. The cause of his death has never been satisfactorily established.]

8.

On Friday 28 August, 1998, I gave much of this information to Judge Herve Stephan, the French investigative Judge in charge of the inquest into the accident. The lengths which MI6, the CIA and the DST have taken to deter me [from] giving this evidence, and subsequently to stop me talking about it, suggests that they have something to hide.

9.

On Friday 31 July, 1998, shortly before my appointment with Judge Herve Stephan, the DST arrested me in my Paris hotel room. Although I have no record of violent conduct, I was arrested with such ferocity, and at gunpoint, that I received a broken rib. I was taken to the headquarters of the DST and interrogated for 38 hours. Despite my repeated requests, I was never given any justification for the arrest and was not shown the arrest warrant. Even though I was released without charge, the DST confiscated from me my laptop computer and Psion organiser. They illegally gave these to MI6, who took them back to the UK. They were not returned for six months, which is

illegal and caused me great inconvenience and financial
cost.

10.

On Friday 7 August, 1998, I boarded a Qantas flight
at Auckland International Airport, New Zealand, for a
flight to Sydney, Australia, where I was due to give a
television interview to the Australian Channel Nine
television company. I was in my seat, awaiting take-off,
when an official boarded the plane and told me to get
off. At the airbridge, he told me that the airline had
received a fax "from Canberra" saying that there was a
problem with my travel papers. I immediately asked to see
the fax, but I was told that it was "not possible". I
believe that this is because it didn't exist.

This action was a ploy to keep me in New Zealand so
that the New Zealand police could take further action
against me. I had been back in my Auckland hotel room for
about half an hour when the New Zealand police and NZSIS,
the New Zealand Secret Intelligence Service, raided me.
After being detained and searched for about three hours,
they eventually confiscated from me all my remaining
computer equipment that the French DST had not succeeded
in taking from me. Again, I didn't get some of these
items back until six months later.

11.

Moreover, shortly after I had given this evidence
to Judge Stephan, I was invited to talk about this evidence
in a live television interview on America's NBC television
channel. I flew from Geneva to JFK Airport on Sunday 30
August [1998] to give the interview in New York on the
following Monday morning.

Shortly after arrival at John F. Kennedy Airport,
the captain of the Swissair flight told all passengers to
return to their seats. Four US immigration authority
officers entered the plane, came straight to my seat,
asked for my passport as identity and then frogmarched me
off the plane. I was taken to the immigration detention
centre, photographed, fingerprinted, manacled by my ankle
to a chair for seven hours, served with deportation papers
... and then returned on the next available plane to
Geneva. I was not allowed to make any telephone calls to
the representatives of NBC awaiting me in the airport.
The US immigration officers - who were all openly

sympathetic to my situation and apologised for treating me so badly - openly admitted that they were acting under instructions from the CIA.

12.

In January of this year [1999], I booked a chalet in the village of Samoens in the French Alps for a ten-day snowboarding holiday with my parents. I picked up my parents from Geneva airport in a hire car on the evening of 8 January and set off for the French border.

At the French customs post, our car was stopped and I was detained. Four officers from the DST held me for four hours. At the end of this interview, I was served with the deportation papers below ... [not included here] ... and ordered to return to Switzerland. Note that in the papers, my supposed destination has been changed from "Chamonix" to 'Samoens". This is because when first questioned by a junior DST officer, I told him that my destination was "Chamonix". When a senior officer arrived an hour or so later, he crossed out the word and changed it to "Samoens" without ever even asking or confirming this with me. I believe this is because MI6 had told them of my true destination, having learnt the information through surveillance on my parents' telephone in the UK.

13.

Whatever MI6's role in the events leading to the deaths of the Princess of Wales, Dodi Al Fayed and Henri Paul, I am absolutely certain that there is substantial evidence in their files that would provide crucial evidence in establishing the exact cause of this tragedy. I believe that they have gone to considerable lengths to obstruct the course of justice by interfering with my freedom of speech and travel, and this in my view confirms my belief that they have something to hide. I believe that the protection given to MI6 files under the Official Secrets Act should be set aside in the public interest in uncovering, once and for all, the truth behind these dramatic and historically momentous events.

BIBLIOGRAPHY

Ancestors Of Diana, Princess Of Wales, Leo FM van de Pas, 1998, Heraldry Today.

Bloodline Of The Holy Grail, Sir Laurence Gardner, Kt St Gm, KCD, KT St A, and Jacobite Histriographer Royal, 1996 - ISBN 1852308702 Element Books Ltd, Shaftesbury.

The CIA's Greatest Hits, Mark Zepezauer, 1994. Odonian Press, Box 32375, Tucson, AZ 85751, USA. Tel: 520 296 4056 or 800 REAL STORY. Fax: 520 296 0936. E-mail: odonian@realstory.com

Defender Of The Faith: The Church And The Crisis In The Monarchy, Ted Harrison, 1996 - ISBN 000627983x Fount, London.

Enemies Of The State, Gary Murray, 1993 - ISBN 0671711946 Simon & Schuster, London.

Europe's Full Circle: Corporate Elites And The New Fascism, Rodney Atkinson, 1996 - ISBN 0952511002 Compuprint.

Executive Intelligence Review (ISSN: 0273-6314). Senior Editor, Jeffery Steinberg, 317, Pennsylvania Avenue, SE, 2nd Floor, Washington DC, 20003, USA. Tel: (202) 544-7010. E-mail: eirns@larouchepub.com Website: http://www.larouchepub.com

The Feather Men, Sir Ranulph Fiennes, 1991 - ISBN 0747510490 Bloomsbury, London.

The Forgotten Monarchy of Scotland, HRH Prince Michael of Albany, 1998. ISBN - 1-86204-234-9. Element Books Ltd.

The Holy Blood And The Holy Grail, Michael Baigent, Richard Leigh and Henry Lincoln, 1982 - ISBN 0224017357 Jonathan Cape, London. Also: 055212138X Corgi Books.

The Messianic Legacy, Michael Baigent, Richard Leigh and Henry Lincoln, 1986 - ISBN 0224021850 Jonathan Cape, London. Also: 0099664216 Arrow Books.

The *Money Masters: How International Bankers Gained Control Of America*, Patrick SJ Carmack. Book and Video available from Royalty Production Company, 5149 Picket Drive, Colorado Springs, CO 80907, USA. Tel: 719 520 7264. Fax: 719 599 4587. Website: <www.themoneymasters.com>

NEXUS New Times - ISSN 1039-0170. www.nexusmagazine.com

Power Inc., Morton Mintz and Jerry Cohen, 1976 - ASIN: 067057032X Pub?

The Secret War Against The Jews, Mark Aarons and John Loftus, 1997 - ISBN 0340171952 St Martins, New York.

Sounds From Another Room, Sir Peter Horsley, 1997 - ISBN 085052810 Leo Cooper, London.

The Sovereign State Of ITT, Anthony Sampson, 1973 - ISBN 0340171952 Hodder & Stoughton, London.

Warrant For Genocide, Norman Cohn, 1970 - ISBN 0140211748 Penguin.

World History: A Chronological Dictionary of Dates, Rodney Castleden, 1994. ISBN 1-85813-423-4. Parragon Book Service Ltd.

Warrant For Genocide, Norman Cohn, 1970 - ISBN 0140211748 Penguin.

World History: A Chronological Dictionary of Dates, Rodney Castleden, 1994. ISBN 1-85813-423-4. Parragon Book Service Ltd.

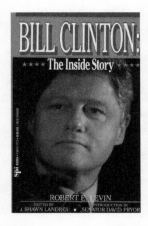

Bill Clinton: The Inside Story

by Robert Levin

Down deep, what are Clinton's core convictions and values? What forces have shaped his character? The answers are in this bestselling Presidential biography with over 250,000 copies in print and translations in seven languages. This is the first and only authorized biography of president Clinton. Author Robert Levin has secured exclusive access to sources close to Bill Clinton and his campaign, as well as vocal opponents of the man who was President of the United States Of America.

Paper, Retail $5.50

Compromised: Clinton, Bush and the CIA

by Terry Reed and John Cummings

Reed, a CIA asset turned into a fugitive for opposing government drug trafficking, presents damning evidence placing Bill Clinton and George Bush (Senior) directly in the Iran-Contra loop, complete with a trail of Contra training, money laundering, dealings with Oliver North, the involvement of the U.S. Attorney General, and more.

Hardcover, Retail $23.95/ Special Price $19.95

The Mafia, CIA and George Bush

by Pete Brewton

If you thought the S&L scandal rocked the Bush administration, you've got to read what this investigative journalist has uncovered about the former president, a circle of Texas cronies and billionaires, the Mafia and covert CIA assistance. The U.S. taxpayers lose out to the tune of half a trillion dollars, while the criminals go free and get richer!

Hardcover, Retail $22.95

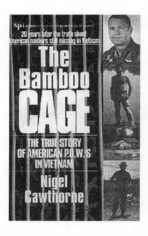

The Bamboo Cage: The True Story of American P.O.W.s In Vietnam

by Nigel Cawthorne

The government claims that over 2,000 American soldiers missing-in-action in the Vietnam War are dead. The author, a respected British researcher and published writer of dozens of books, fought for crucial information and documentation from the CIA, the Pentagon and even the authorities in Hanoi to prove otherwise. Revealed here are the cruel and illegal secrets that the U.S. government doesn't want you to ever know.

Paper, Retail $5.95

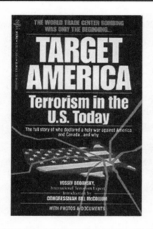

Target America:
Terrorism in the World Today

by Yossef Bodansky

Can we breathe easier now that the World Trade Center terrorists are behind bars? Not according to the Director of the U.S. Congress's Republican Task Force on Terrorism & Unconventional Warfare.

Terrorist groups from Islamic and Balkan countries are primed to strike both in Europe and in the U.S. This book reveals much previously unknown information on these dangerous criminals.

Paper, Retail $5.99

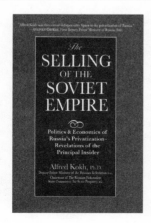

The Selling of The Soviet Empire:
Politics and Economics of Russia's Privatization--Revelations of the Principal

by Alfred Kokh

Here, for the first time, are the revelations from a central figure in the creation of the "New Russia". Alfred Kokh was one of Boris Yeltsin's Deputy Prime Ministers and privatization chiefs before he was forced out by the opposition in the intense media war that erupted in the wake of the privatizations.
This is the exclusive story of how Kokh and his privatization team worked to divide the wealth of the most vast empire ever.

Hardcover, Retail $25.00/ Special Price $21.95

Evil Money: The Inside Story of Money Laundering and Corruption in Government, Banks and Business

by Dr. Rachel Ehrenfeld

A chilling and fascinatin exposé of how one trillion dollars in annual drug revenues is laundered through banks in the U.S. and abroad. *Evil Money* exposes readers to the existence of a sophisticated worldwide underground economy that links drug cartels, terrorists, and even legitimate governments and businesses in illegal enterprises. The results are the growing numbers of multi-billionaire drug lords, crooked lawyers and bankers, and corrupt political regimes--with no solutions in sight if present trends continue.

Dr. Rachel Ehrenfeld is an investigator, scholar, and political commentator and one of the leading authorities on the topic of banking and drug money laundering. Her writing has appeared in *The Wall Street Journal, The New York Times, The Los Angeles Times, The New Republic, and National Review.*

Paper, Retail $5.99

U.F.O.s Are Real: Extraterrestrial Encounters Documented by the U.S. Govt.

by Sergeant Clifford E. Stone (ret.)

The U.S. official position is that there are no flying saucers, landings by or encounters with extraterrestrial beings. Government sources like the U.S. Air Force, on the other hand, do have extensive records of unexplained sightings of UFOs. For too many years none of these classified records were available for release to the public. Now, however, U.S. Army Sergeant Stone has finally obtained declassified documents going back to the 1940s that will shake up any UFO skeptics. Using the Freedom of Information act to patiently outduel bureaucrats at Air Force and Navy Intelligence, the CIA and the State Department, Stone obtained documents with minimally excised portions and with significant testimony still intact.

Sergeant Stone, U.S. Army (ret.) served for more than 20 yrs as a Nuclear/Biological/Chemical Retrieval specialist. He has been studying the Roswell, NM incident and the government's mysterious relationship to UFOs for decades and serves as Director of Research at the Roswell U.F.O. Enigma Museum.

Paper, Retail $20.95/ Special Price $18.95

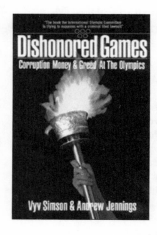

Dishonored Games: Corruption, Money & Greed At The Olympics

by Vyv Simson & Andrew Jennings

Every four years, the Olympics are celebrated with a flood of congratulatory coverage. In all the books, articles and documentaries extolling the beauty and purity of the Olympic Ideal, only cursory notice is given to the Lausanne-based International Olympic Committee (I.O.C.) and its little-known President, Juan Antonio Samaranch.

These British journalists/authors explode the carefully cultivated image and idealistic hype behind the I.O.C. and its self-perpetuating leadership. The book also reveals influence peddling, lavish gifts and bribes, and abuse of power in today's Olympic movement.

Hardcover, Retail $19.95/ Special Price $16.95
